An Introduction to Policing

Second Edition

An Introduction to Policing

Second Edition

John S. Dempsey
Suffolk County Community College

West/Wadsworth Publishing Company
I⓪P® **An International Thompson Publishing Company**

Belmont, CA • Albany, NY • Boston • Cincinnati • Johannesburg
London • Madrid • Melbourne • Mexico City • New York
Pacific Grove, CA • Scottsdale, AZ • Singapore • Tokyo • Toronto

Criminal Justice Editor: Sabra Horne
Assistant Editor: Claire Masson
Marketing Manager: Mike Dew
Development Editor: Dan Alpert
Editorial Assistant: Cheri Hackelberg
Project Editor: Jennie Redwitz
Permissions Editor: Yanna Walters
Print Buyer: Karen Hunt
Production: Professional Book Center

Photo Research: Professional Book Center
Cover Design: Joan Greenfield
Interior Design: Harry Voigt
Compositor: Professional Book Center
Copy Editor: Susan Brown
Cover Images: Clockwise starting from top: © Tony Stone Images/Mitch Kezar; © Tony Stone Images/Jonathan Nourok; © Michael Heller/911 Pictures; © Terry Qing/FPG International; © Tony Stone Images/Robert E. Daemmrich
Printer: R.R. Donnelley

COPYRIGHT © 1999 by Wadsworth Publishing Company
A Division of International Thomson Publishing Inc.
The ITP logo is a registered trademark under license.

 This book is printed on acid-free recycled paper.

Printed in the United States of America
    5 6 7 8 9 10

For more information, contact Wadsworth Publishing Company, 10 Davis Drive, Belmont, CA 94002, or electronically at http://www.thomson.com/wadsworth.html

International Thomson Publishing Europe
Berkshire House
168-173 High Holborn
London, WC1V 7AA, United Kingdom

Nelson ITP, Australia
102 Dodds Street
South Melbourne
Victoria 3205 Australia

Nelson Canada
1120 Birchmount Road
Scarborough, Ontario
Canada M1K 5G4

International Thomson Publishing Southern Africa
Building 18, Constantia Square
138 Sixteenth Road, P.O. Box 2459
Halfway House, 1685 South Africa

International Thomson Editores
Seneca, 53
Colonia Polanco
11560 México D.F. México

International Thomson Publishing Asia
60 Albert Street #15-01
Albert Complex
Singapore 189969

International Thomson Publishing Japan
Hirakawa-cho Kyowa Building, 3F
2-2-1 Hirakawa-cho, Chiyoda-ku
Tokyo 102, Japan

All rights reserved. No part of this work covered by the copyright hereon may be reproduced or used in any form or by any means—graphic, electronic, or mechanical, including photocopying, recording, taping, or information storage and retrieval systems—without the written permission of the publisher.

Library of Congress Cataloging-in-Publication Data

Dempsey, John S.
    An introduction to policing / John S. Dempsey. — 2nd ed.
       p.   cm.
    Rev. ed. of: Policing. c1994.
    Includes bibliographical references and index.
    ISBN 0-534-54675-7 (alk. paper)
    1. Law enforcement—United States.   2. Police—United States.
I. Dempsey, John S. Policing. II. Title
HV8138.D37   1998
363.2'0973—dc21   98-28391
                                                                          CIP

*This book is dedicated to my late father, Daniel Joseph Dempsey.
I hope I made you proud.*

About the Author

John S. Dempsey was a member of the New York City Police Department (NYPD) from 1964 to 1988. He served in the ranks of police officer, detective, sergeant, lieutenant, and captain. His primary assignments were patrol and investigations. He received seven citations from the department for meritorious and excellent police duty. Since retirement from the NYPD, Mr. Dempsey has served as a professor at Suffolk Community College on eastern Long Island, New York. In 1994, Mr Dempsey won the college's prestigious "Who Made A Difference Award" for his teaching and work with students. He also teaches at Long Island University in its graduate and undergraduate program. Mr. Dempsey is the author of *An Introduction to Public and Private Investigations,* published by West in 1996.

Mr. Dempsey holds A.A. and B.A. degrees in behavioral science from the City University of New York, John Jay College of Criminal Justice; a master's degree in criminal justice from Long Island University, C.W. Post College; and a master's of public administration degree from Harvard University, the John F. Kennedy School of Government.

Mr. Dempsey is married and has four children and two grandchildren.

Contents

Preface xv

Part I
POLICE HISTORY AND ORGANIZATION

Chapter 1
Police History 1

Introduction 2
Early Police 2

English Policing: Our English Heritage 3
Early History 3
Seventeenth Century and Thief-Takers 4
Henry Fielding 4
Peel's Police 5

American Policing: The Colonial Experience 6

American Policing: Eighteenth and Nineteenth Centuries 7
The Urban Experience 8
The Frontier Experience 11

American Policing: Twentieth Century 13
Policing from 1900 to 1960 13
Policing in the 1960s and 1970s 17
Policing in the 1980s and 1990s 23

Chapter Summary 27

Chapter 2
Organizing Public and Private Security in the United States 31

Introduction 32

The U.S. Public and Private Safety Industry 32

Local Law Enforcement 34
Metropolitan Law Enforcement 35
County Law Enforcement 35
Rural and Small Town Law Enforcement 36

State Law Enforcement 37

Federal Law Enforcement 38
Department of Justice 39
Treasury Department 41
Department of the Interior 43
Department of Defense 43
General Services Administration 44
U.S. Postal Service 44
Department of Transportation 44
Other Federal Enforcement Agencies 44
Task Force Approach to Enforcement 44

International Police 45

Private Security 45
What Is Private Security? 46
History of Private Security 47
Operations of Private Security Today 47
Private Security and the Courts 48
Current Problems of Private Security 48

Licensing of Private Security 48
Professionalization of Private Security 49
Forecasts Regarding the Need for Private Security 49

Private Employment of Public Police 50

Community Self-Protection 52
Target Hardening 53
Neighborhood Watch Programs 53

Impact of Recession on Police Agencies and Police Consolidation 53

Chapter Summary 54

Chapter 3
Organizing the Police Department 57

Introduction 58

Organizing the Department: Managerial Concepts 58
Division of Labor 58
Chain of Command (Hierarchy of Authority) 58
Span of Control 58
Delegation of Responsibility and Authority 59
Unity of Command 59
Rules, Regulations, and Discipline 59

Organizing by Personnel 60
The Civil Service System 60
Quasi-Military Model of Police 61
Sworn and Nonsworn (Civilian) Personnel 61
Rank Structure 62
Other Personnel 65
Some Personnel Issues 68

Organizing by Area 69
Beats/Posts 69
Sectors/Zones 71
Precincts 71

Organizing by Time 71
The Three-Tour System 71
Tour Conditions 73
Steady (Fixed) Tours 73

Organizing by Function or Purpose 74
Line and Staff (Support) Functions 74
Police Department Units 74

Chapter Summary 78

PART II
THE PERSONAL SIDE OF POLICING

Chapter 4
Becoming a Police Officer 81

Introduction 82

Finding Information on Jobs in Policing 82

The Recruitment Process 83

The Job Analysis 86

The Selection Process 87
Characteristics of Good Police Officers 88
Guidelines for the Selection Process 90
Written Entrance Examination 91
Oral Interview 92
Psychological Appraisal 93
Polygraph Examination 93
Medical Examination 95
Physical Agility Test 95
Background Investigation 95

Standards in Police Selection 96
Physical Requirements 96
Age Requirements 97
Education Requirements 98
Prior Drug Use 100
Criminal Record Restrictions 100
Residency Requirements 100
Sexual Orientation 101

The Police Training Process 101
Recruit Training 101
In-Service, Management, and Specialized Training 105
Training for the Police Corps 105

Community Policing Training 106
Probationary Period 106

Chapter Summary 106

Chapter 5
The Police Role and Police Discretion 111

Introduction 112

The Police Role 112
Crime-Fighting Role 112
Order Maintenance Role 113
Ambiguity of the Police Role 114

Goals and Objectives of Policing 116
Primary Goals and Objectives 116
Secondary Goals and Objectives 116

Police Operational Styles 117
Broderick's Police Operational Styles 117
Wilson's Police Operational Styles 118

Police Discretion 119
What Is Discretion? 119
How Is Discretion Exercised? 121
Why Is Discretion Exercised? 121
What Factors Influence Discretion? 121
How Can Discretion Be Controlled? 123

Chapter Summary 123

Chapter 6
The Police Culture: Personality and Stress 127

Introduction 128

The Police Culture or Subculture 128

The Police Personality 129
What Is the Police Personality? 129
Are They Born Like That, or Is It the Job? 131

Police Cynicism 133

The Dirty Harry Problem 133

Police Stress 135
What Is Stress? 135
Nature of Stress in Policing 135
Factors Causing Stress in Policing 136
Effects of Stress on Police Officers 137
Stress and Police Families 138
Police Departments Dealing with Stress 139
Testing for Ability to Handle Stress 140

Police Suicide 141

Chapter Summary 142

PART III
POLICE OPERATIONS

Chapter 7
Police Operations: The Traditional Approach 147

Introduction 148

Traditional Methods of Police Work 148

Evaluating the Effectiveness of Police Work 148

Random Routine Patrol: The Kansas City Study 149
The Kansas City Study in Brief 149
Results of the Kansas City Study 150
Critiques of the Kansas City Study 150
Value of the Kansas City Study 151

Rapid Response to Citizens' 911 Calls 151
Early Studies of Rapid Response 152
Later Studies of Rapid Response 152

Retroactive Investigation of Past Crimes by Detectives 153

Police Patrol Operations 154
Activities of the Patrol Officer 154
The Legacy of O. W. Wilson 155
Academic Studies of the Police Patrol Function 155
From the Foot Beat to the Patrol Car 159

Return to Foot Patrol 161
Why Walking Works Better Than Driving 162

Detective Operations 163
What Do Detectives Do? 163
The Detective Mystique 164

Police Traffic Operations 165

Police Special Operations 165
SWAT Teams 165
Emergency Service Units 166

Chapter Summary 167

Chapter 8
Police Operations: A New Approach 171

Introduction 172

Alternatives to Random Routine Patrol and Rapid Response to Citizens' 911 Calls 172
Directed Patrol 172
Split Force Patrol 174
Differential Response to Calls for Service 174

Alternatives to Retroactive Investigation of Past Crimes by Detectives 175
Improved Investigation of Past Crimes 176
Repeat Offender Programs (ROPS) 178

New, Proactive Tactics 178
Uniformed Tactical Operations 178
Decoy Operations 182
Stakeout Operations 183
Sting Operations 183
Civil Liability and Code Enforcement Teams 184
Efforts against Drunk Drivers 184

Undercover Operations 186
Police Undercover Investigations 186
Federal Undercover Investigations 186
Private Security Undercover Investigations 186
Drug Undercover Investigations 189

Entrapment 190

Chapter Summary 191

Chapter 9
Police and the Community 195

Introduction 196

The Need for Proper Police-Community Relationships 196

Human Relations, Public Relations, Community Relations 197

Public Opinion and the Police 198

Police and Minority Communities 200
Multiculturalism 200
The African-American Community 201
The Hispanic-American Community 202
The Asian-American Community 203
Native Americans 203
Women 203
The Gay Community 203
New Immigrants 204

Police and Special Populations 204
Senior Citizens' Programs 204
Programs for Young People 208
Assistance for the Homeless 214
Help for Crime Victims 216
Help for Disabled People 216

Community Crime Prevention Programs 217
Neighborhood Watch Programs 217
Crime Stoppers 218
Citizen Patrols 218
Citizen Marches 219
Citizen Volunteer Programs 219
Home Security Surveys and Operation Identification 220
National Night Out 220
Police Storefront Stations or Ministations 221
Mass Media Campaigns 221
Citizen Police Academies 222
Other Police-Sponsored Crime Prevention Programs 222

Police and Business Cooperation 222
AmeriCorps and Policing 222
Chapter Summary 224

Chapter 10
Community Policing: The Debate Continues 229

Introduction 230

Corporate Strategies for Policing 230

The Philosophy of Community Policing and Problem-Solving Policing 231

Community Policing 233

Problem-Solving Policing 237

Current Ways of Doing Community Policing 239
Resident Officer Programs—The Ultimate in Community Policing? 242

The Federal Government and Community Policing 245
The Crime Bill 245
Office of Community Oriented Policing Services (COPS) 245
Community Policing Consortium 247

Some Accomplishments of Community Policing 247

Not All Agree with Community Policing 248

Chapter Summary 249

Chapter 11
Police and the Law 253

Introduction 254

Crime in the United States 254
How Do We Measure Crime? 254
How Much Crime Occurs in the United States? 255
Arrests in the United States 256

The Police and the U.S. Constitution 256
Bill of Rights and the Fourteenth Amendment 256
Role of the Supreme Court in Regulating the Police 258
The Exclusionary Rule 259
Impact of the Exclusionary Rule on the Police 263

The Police and Arrest 263
Probable Cause 264
Reasonable and Deadly Force in Making Arrests 264
Stopping Vehicles 265

The Police and Search and Seizure 266
The Warrant Requirement and the Search Warrant 266
Exceptions to the Warrant Requirement 267

The Police and Custodial Interrogation 274
The Path to Miranda 274
The Miranda Ruling 276
The Erosion of Miranda 278
1990s and Miranda 280
Miranda in Retrospect 282

The Police and Identification Procedures 282
Lineups, Showups, and Photo Arrays 282
Other Identification Procedures 284

Chapter Summary 284

PART IV
CRITICAL ISSUES IN POLICING

Chapter 12
Police Ethics and Police Deviance 287

Introduction 288

Ethics and the Police 288

The Dilemma of Law Versus Order 290

Review of the Police 290

Police Corruption 291
Corruption Makes Good Books and Films 291
Examples of Police Corruption 292
Types and Forms of Corruption 293
Effects of Police Corruption 296
Reasons for Police Corruption 296
Responses to Police Corruption 297

Other Police Misconduct 298
Drug Abuse and Trafficking 298
Drinking and Alcohol Abuse 298
Cooping 299
Police Deception 299
Abuse of Authority 299

Police Brutality 300
Tradition of Police Brutality 300
Examples of Police Brutality 300
Is Brutality Really the Problem? 302
Police Department Responses to Police Brutality 303
Citizen Oversight 305

Chapter Summary 306

Chapter 13
Women and Minorities in Policing 311

Introduction 312

Discrimination in Policing 312
Discrimination against Women 312
Discrimination against Racial and Ethnic Minorities 314
Discrimination against Gay Officers 316

How Did Women and Minorities Achieve Equality? 316
Civil Rights Act of 1964 316
Equal Employment Opportunity Act of 1972 317
Federal Courts and Job Discrimination 317
Affirmative Action Programs 318

White Male Backlash 319

Can Women and Minorities Do the Job? 320
Academic Studies of Female Officers 320
Academic Studies of African-American Officers 323

Women and Minorities in Policing Today 323
Female Representation Today 324
African-American and Other Minority Representation Today 325

Problems Persist for Women and Minorities in Policing 326
Problems for Women 326
Problems for African-Americans and Other Minorities 328

Chapter Summary 329

Chapter 14
Technology in Policing 333

Introduction 334

Computers in Policing 334
Computer-Aided Dispatch (CAD) 334
Automated Databases 337
Automated Crime Analysis 338
Computer-Aided Investigation 338
Computer-Assisted Instruction 340
Administrative Uses of Computers 340
Computer Networks/The Internet 341

Innovations in Fingerprinting 342
Automated Fingerprint Identification Systems 343
Other Fingerprinting Innovations 345

Less-Than-Lethal Weapons 345
Chemical Irritant Sprays 346
The TASER and Other Stun Devices 346
Safety and Effectiveness of Less-Than-Lethal Weapons 346

Surveillance Technology 347
Surveillance Vans 348
Night Vision Devices 348

Advanced Photographic Techniques 348
Mug Shot Imaging 348
Age Progression Photographs 349
Composite Sketches 349

Modern Forensic or Criminalistic Techniques 350
The Modern Crime Lab 352
Crime Lab Accreditation 352
Some New Laboratory Criminalistic Techniques 353

DNA Profiling 354
The Blooding 355
The Castro Case 356
The Frye Test 356
The Debate Goes On 356

Videotaping 358

Robots 358

Fear of Technology by Civil Libertarians 358

Chapter Summary 359

Chapter 15
Specific Police Problems and Issues 363

Introduction 364

Police and Danger 364
Officers Killed in the Line of Duty 364
Officers Assaulted in the Line of Duty 368
Police and AIDS 369

Police Shootings: Use of Deadly Force 370
Number of Citizens Shot by the Police 370
Police Shooting Rates by City, Region, and State 370
Do Police Discriminate with Their Trigger Fingers? 370
Departure from the "Fleeing Felon" Rule 371

Police Automobile Pursuits 374
Studies Involving Police Pursuits 374
Establishment of Police Pursuit Policies 375

Police and Domestic Violence 376
Traditional Police Response to Domestic Violence 376
Minneapolis Domestic Violence Experiment 376
Police Response to Domestic Violence Today 377

Police and Radical and Hate Groups 378

Police Civil and Criminal Liability 381
State Liability 382
Federal Liability 382
Reasons for Suing Police Officers 382
Effects of Lawsuits on Police Departments and Officers 383

Chapter Summary 384

Appendix A
Sources of Employment Information in Law Enforcement 389

Appendix B
The "Law Enforcement Code of Ethics" and "The Police Code of Conduct" 393

Appendix C
The National Law Enforcement Officers Memorial, Washington, D.C. 397

Appendix D
Police-Related Associations and Organizations 399

Bibliography 405

Index 415

Photo Credits 430

Preface

★ To the Student

An Introduction to Policing, Second Edition, is an introductory text for college students who are interested in learning who the police are, what they do, and how they do it.

Who are the police? Are they the brutal people portrayed in the infamous Rodney King tape, or the heroic, virtuous crime fighters we see on television or in the movies? Or, are they simply people like you, motivated by the desire to contribute to their communities and to society in a special way?

What do they do? Are they primarily law enforcers who arrest offenders and show up when we call 911 (or, perhaps, show up unannounced when we wish they hadn't)? Or, are they public servants and peacekeepers who are dedicated to providing essential community and societal services?

How do they do what they do? Are the philosophies and operations of policing the same today as they were when Sir Robert Peel first introduced them in 1829 in London, England? Or, instead, is policing a dynamic, ever-changing undertaking that is shaped daily by the people who practice it and the communities they serve?

An Introduction to Policing explores these issues from the perspective of a practitioner, student, and teacher of policing. I wrote the text, in part, out of a desire to combine the practical experience gained from my twenty-four years of police work with the equally valuable insights gained from my years of formal education. It is designed to make students aware of who the police are, what they do, and how they do it, while also sensitizing them to the complexities and ambiguities of modern policing.

The text is intended to teach students about policing not only for their academic interest in the subject but, more importantly, to help them decide if police work is really what they want to do. After all, shouldn't college prepare students for making intelligent, well-informed career choices as well as teach them about life?

★ To the Instructor

In this Second Edition my overall philosophy, which focuses on the needs of students who wish to learn about policing in our society, still permeates the text. This is, above all, a text for students.

Changes to the Second Edition

Even more attention has been given to actual examples of specific police departments—small and large—throughout the nation and world. Each chapter has been thoroughly updated to include new research and applications.

A separate chapter on community policing has been added to reflect the growing importance of this topic. There is also increased coverage of such important topics as police ethics, rural policing, and state-of-the-art police technology. In addition, I've added some exciting new pedagogical features.

Pedagogical Features

Within each chapter, I have included the following pedagogical elements:

- *Chapter Goals.* These serve as chapter "road maps" to orient students to the main learning objectives of each chapter.
- *Chapter Introduction.* This section previews the material to be covered in the chapter.
- *Chapter Summary.* This section reinforces the major topics discussed in the chapter and helps students check their learning.
- *Learning Check.* These questions further test the student's knowledge of the material presented in the chapter.
- *Review Exercise.* These projects require students to apply their knowledge to hypothetical situations much like those they might encounter in actual police work. They can be assigned as final written or oral exercises or as the basis of lively class debates.
- *World Wide Web Exercises (new to this edition).* These exercises allow the student to research policing topics on the Internet.

Boxed Features

In an effort to increase student interest, I have included several types of boxed features in each chapter to supplement the main text:

- *You Are There.* These take the student back to the past to review the fact pattern in a particular court case or to learn the details about a significant event or series of events in history. They are intended to give the students a sense of actually being at the scene of a police event.
- *Dempsey's Law.* These recount personal experiences from my own police career or dialogues between students and myself in class. They are intended to provide a reality-based perspective on policing, including the human side of policing.
- *Patrolling the Net (new to this edition).* These provide general and specific information for students regarding the use of the Internet for academic and professional growth, as well as their own interest.
- *All in the Line of Duty (new to this edition).* These boxes depict actual police work being performed by officers nationwide, ranging from arrests and rescues to just walking the beat.

Appendices

Four appendices have been included:

- *Sources of Employment Information in Law Enforcement.* This gives students ideas on where and how to find jobs in policing and is a valuable resource for class assignments or personal job hunting.
- *The Law Enforcement Code of Ethics and the Police Code of Conduct.* These two documents provide a framework for the ethical foundations of the police profession—essential knowledge for any student of law enforcement. They can serve as background reading for dynamic and stimulating class discussions in police ethics.
- *National Law Enforcement Officers Memorial: Washington, D.C.* This section pays tribute to the memory of the heroic men and women who have paid the ultimate sacrifice to the police profession and their fellow citizens.
- *Police-Related Associations and Organizations.* This list of professional and academic associations and organizations provides a valuable resource for students who are interested in learning more about policing.

Supplements

The following supplements are available to adopters of *An Introduction to Policing,* Second Edition:

Instructors Manual: Chapter objectives, chapter outlines, teaching suggestions, testing items in a variety of formats: multiple choice, true/false, fill-in, short answer, and essay.

Computerized Test Bank: The questions in the IM are in computerized format for professors to generate their own tests. They can change the order of the questions as well as add to them. Available for Windows and Macintosh.

Crime Scenes: An Interactive Criminal Justice CD ROM: The first introductory criminal justice CD ROM available. This interactive CD ROM places the student in various roles as she explores all aspects of the Criminal Justice system: Policing/Investigations, Courts, Sentencing, and Corrections.

InfoTrac College Edition: Gives students access to full-length articles from over 600 scholarly and popular periodicals. Students can print complete articles or use the cut/paste and e-mail techniques. Includes readings from *U.S. News and World Report, Corrections Today, Prison Journal, American Criminal Law Review,* and much more.

Internet Investigator II: Includes new Criminal Justice-related web sites categorized by course for ease of use: policing, investigations, courts, corrections, research, juvenile delinquency, and much, much more! Save students money by bundling with the book.

Video Library: Qualified adopters may choose from over 200 videos to accompany their lectures. Please contact your local Wadsworth representative for more information.

Call-in Testing. Adopters of this title are eligible for our call-in testing service. Requests received before 12:00 P.M. EST will be processed within 72 business hours. For more information on this service, please contact Tammi Potter, Call-In Testing Administrator, at 1-800-423-0563, est. 5405 or tpotter@kdc.com.

Acknowledgments

So many people helped me make a successful transition from the world of being a street cop to the world of academia, and so many more helped in the publication of this book. I hope I do not forget anyone.

First, I have to thank again Albin Cofone and Robert Arrigon from Suffolk County Community College for taking a chance in hiring this kid from the Bronx who had never taught college. Also at Suffolk, I would like to thank my partners in the Criminal Justice Department, Mike Higginson, Rob Griffiths, and all of our dedicated and professional adjuncts who have brought their lessons from the street to the classroom. To those invaluable secretaries—Ellen Eichenholz, Fran Basile, Terry Spillett, and Marylou Radano—thanks for all you have done for me. To Dave Karnuth—thanks for your help in printing the manuscript.

I would also like to thank all the professors across the country, particularly those former women and men in blue who have made that transition from the streets to the classrooms, for their adoption of the first edition and their kind words and sage advice. They inspired me to prepare this second edition.

To my senior developmental editor Dan Alpert—not only did you always listen but you always had the right idea—truly, I could not have finished this edition without your support. You are a true professional. To senior acquisitions editor Sabra Horne—thanks for your faith, patience and constant assistance in this project. To the intelligent and excellent copy editing of Susan Brown and the able production efforts of Jennie Redwitz (of Wadsworth) and Jennifer Ballentine (of Professional Book Center)—my sincere thanks.

To the following reviewers of the Second Edition, my profound thanks for your advice, guidance, and particularly your respect for scholarship and our discipline: Elaine Bartgis, Fairmont State College; Joseph Bunce, Rockville Community College; Edmund Grosskopf, Indiana State University; John Harlan, Stephen F. Austin State University; Pamela Hart, Iowa Western Community College; Charles Kelly, Jr., Southeastern Louisiana University; Gary Keveles, University of Wisconsin–Superior; Tom Lenahan, Herkimer County Community College; Walter Lewis, St. Louis Community College at Meramec; David Mackey, St. Anselm College; Gregory Petrakis, University of Missouri–Kansas City; Albert Sproule, Allentown College; Gary Tucker, Sinclair Community College; William Vizzard, California State University–Sacramento.

I also wish to gratefully acknowledge the invaluable help provided by the reviewers of my previous edition: Frank P. Alberico, Joliet Junior College; David A. Armstrong, McNeese State University; Michael B. Blankenship, Memphis State University; Paul V. Clark, Community College of Philadelphia; Frank Cornacchione, Pensicola Junior College; Alvin A. Fuchsman, Northern Virginia Community College; Patrick J. Hopkins, Harrisburg Area Community College; Julius O. Koefoed, Jr., Kirkwood Community College; Kenneth L. Mullen, Appalachian State University; Hugh E. O'Rourke, Westchester Community College; David F. Owens, Onondaga Community College; Charles S. Purgavie, Ocean County Community College; Chester L. Quarles, University of Mississippi; Jayne T. Rich, Atlantic Community College; John P. Sargent, Jr., Kent State University; William A. Sposa, Bergen Community College; Sam Swaim, Indian Hills Community College; Roger Turner, Shelby State University.

To my buddy, Richie Haeg, great police officer and private investigator, my thanks for your friendship and assistance to my students. I have never finished a conversation with you without learning something new. To Professors Pat Ryan, Dave Owens, Donna Stuccio, and all the other former police officers who have shown me that we can work the classroom as well as we worked our beats—thanks for your companionship in my travels through the years. Pat—we have come a long way from the radio car in the 41. To my former partners in the NYPD, scholars Jim Fyfe and Bill Walsh—thanks for your example. To Dr. Harvey Kushner and the other great educators I have been fortunate enough to work with, thanks.

On a personal level, the inspiration for this work came from the many students who came to my office or class wanting to know about the material I have put in this text. This book is for you. To all the great men and women I worked with in the New York City Police Department, the heart of this book comes from you.

To my family—Marianne, my love and my best friend; my children, John, AnneMarie, Donna, and Cathy; and my daughter-in-law, Diane—thanks for putting up with me during these years of writing this book. Please forgive my absences and often mercurial personality. To Mae and Danny: You can never know how important you were to us. Finally, to Daniel Joseph, my first grandson, and to little Nicolette Ashley, my first granddaughter: Who loves you more than the Granddude, Dude and Dudette?

John S. Dempsey

1
Police History

Chapter Outline

Early Police
English Policing: Our English Heritage
  Early History
  Seventeenth Century and Thief-Takers
  Henry Fielding
  Peel's Police
American Policing: The Colonial Experience

American Policing: Eighteenth and Nineteenth Centuries
  The Urban Experience
  The Frontier Experience
American Policing: Twentieth Century
  Policing from 1900 to 1960
  Policing in the 1960s and 1970s
  Policing in the 1980s and 1990s

Chapter Goals

- To acquaint you with the rich, colorful history of policing.
- To show you how the U.S. police and, indeed, the entire U.S. criminal justice system evolved from the English law enforcement experience.
- To acquaint you with early American policing—both the urban and the frontier experiences.
- To introduce you to the history of policing in the early twentieth century.
- To acquaint you with the history and development of recent policing, from the 1960s through the 1990s.

Introduction

The word police comes from the Latin word *politia,* which means "civil administration." The word *politia* goes back to the Greek word *polis,* or "city." Etymologically, therefore, the police can be seen as those involved in the administration of a city. *Politia* became the French word *police.* The English took it over and at first continued to use it to mean "civil administration." The specific application of police to the administration of public order emerged in France in the early eighteenth century. The first body of public-order officers to be named police in England was the Marine Police, a force established in 1798 to protect merchandise in the port of London.[1]

The reference to the police as a "civil authority" is very important. The police represent the civil power of government, as opposed to the military power of government. We use the military in times of war. The members of the military, of necessity, are trained to kill and destroy. That is appropriate in war. However, do we want to use military forces to govern or patrol our cities and towns? I do not think so. Imagine that you and some of your classmates are having a party. The party gets a bit loud, and your neighbors call 911. Instead of a police car, an armored personnel carrier and tanks arrive at the party, and twenty soldiers come out pointing AK-47 assault rifles at you. Obviously, this is a silly example, but think about it. Surely we need a civil police, not the military, in our neighborhoods.[2]

This chapter will discuss early forms of policing and the direct predecessor of the American police, the English police. Then the discussion will turn to the United States, beginning with the colonial experience with policing. A summary of the eighteenth- and nineteenth-century experience will focus on urban and frontier police. The chapter will then turn to modern times—twentieth-century policing—and discuss the American police from 1900 to 1960, the turbulent decades of the 1960s and 1970s, and finally our generation, the 1980s and 1990s.

Early Police

We do not know much about the very early history of the police. Policing—maintaining order and dealing with lawbreakers—had always been a private matter. Citizens were responsible for protecting themselves and maintaining an orderly society. Uniformed, organized police departments as we think of them today were rare. In fact, as we'll see in this chapter, modern-style police departments didn't appear until the fourteenth century in France and the nineteenth century in England.

Around the fifth century B.C., Rome created the first specialized investigative unit, called *questors,* or "trackers of murder."[3] Around the sixth century B.C. in Athens and the third century B.C. in Rome, unpaid magistrates (judges), appointed by the citizens, were the only people we would consider law enforcement professionals. The magistrates adjudicated cases, but private citizens arrested offenders and punished them. In most societies, people in towns would group together and form a watch, particularly at night, at the town borders or gates to ensure that outsiders did not attack the town.

At about the time of Christ, the Roman emperor Augustus picked out special, highly qualified members of the military to form the Praetorian Guard. The Praetorian Guard could be considered the first police officers. Their job was to protect the palace and the emperor. At about the same time, Augustus also established the Praefectus Urbi (Urban Cohort) to protect the city. The Urban Cohort had both executive and judicial power. Augustus also established the Vigiles of Rome. The Vigiles began as fire fighters. They were eventually also given law enforcement responsibilities, and they patrolled Rome's streets day and night. The Vigiles could be considered the first civil police force designed to protect citizens. They were considered quite brutal, and it is from them that our word vigilante comes.[4]

Also in Rome in the first century A.D., public officials called *lictors* were appointed to serve as bodyguards for the magistrates. The *lictors* would bring criminals before the magistrates upon their orders and carry out the magistrates' determined punishments, including the death penalty. Their symbol of authority was a *fasces,* a bundle of rods tied by a red thong around an ax, which represented their absolute authority over life and limb.

During the twelfth and thirteenth centuries, kings on the European continent began to assume responsibility for the administration of the law. They began to appoint officials for that purpose to replace the watch and other private forms of self-defense. In the thirteenth century in Paris, Louis IX created a provost, who was assigned to enforce the law and supervise the night watch. The provost was assisted by investigating commissioners and sergeants. In 1356, France created a mounted military patrol, the Maréchausée, to maintain peace on the highways. The Maréchausée evolved into the Gendarmerie Nationale, which today polices the areas outside France's major cities.

English Policing: Our English Heritage

The American system of law and police was borrowed from the English. Therefore, we will now concentrate on the English police experience, which is colorful and related to the development of English society.

Early History

Sir Robert Peel is generally credited with establishing the first English police department, the London Metropolitan Police, in 1829.[5] However, the first references to an English criminal justice or law enforcement system appeared some 1,000 years earlier, in the latter part of the ninth century, when England's king, Alfred the Great, was preparing his kingdom against an impending Danish invasion. Part of King Alfred's strategy against the Danes was the maintenance of stability in his own country and the provision of a method for people living in villages to protect one another. To achieve this stability, King Alfred established a system of **mutual pledge** (a form of "society control" where citizens grouped together to protect each other), which organized the responsibility for the security of the country into several levels. At the lowest level were tithings, ten families who grouped together to protect one another and to assume responsibility for the acts of the group's members. At the next level, ten tithings, or 100 families, were grouped together into a hundred; the hundred was under the charge of a constable. People were supposed to police their own communities. If trouble occurred, a citizen was expected to raise the **hue and cry** (yell for assistance), and other citizens were expected to come to that citizen's assistance. The constable, who might be considered the first form of English police officer, was responsible for dealing with more serious breaches of the law.

Groups of hundreds within a specific geographic area were combined to form shires (the equivalent of today's county). The shires were put under the control of the king and were governed by a **shire-reeve**, or sheriff.

Over the centuries, as formal governments were established, early, primitive forms of a formal criminal justice system evolved in England. In 1285 A.D., the Statute of Winchester was enacted in England. It established a rudimentary criminal justice system in which most of the responsibility for law enforcement remained with the people themselves. The statute formally established (1) the watch and ward, (2) the hue and cry, (3) the parish constable, and (4) the requirement that all males keep weapons in their homes for use in maintaining the public peace.

The **watch and ward** required all men in a given town to serve on the night watch. The watch, therefore, can be seen as the most rudimentary form of metropolitan policing. The watch was designed to protect against crime, disturbances, and fire. The watchmen had three major duties:

1. Patrolling the streets from dusk until dawn to ensure that all local people were indoors and quiet and that no strangers were roaming about.
2. Performing duties such as lighting street lamps, clearing garbage from streets, and putting out fires.
3. Enforcing the criminal law.

Persons serving on the watch, if necessary, would pronounce the hue and cry, and all citizens would then be required to leave their homes and assist the watchmen. The Statute of Winchester made it a crime not to assist the watch. The statute also established the office of parish constable, who was responsible for organizing and supervising the watch. The parish constable was, in effect, the primary urban law enforcement agent in England.

In the early fourteenth century, we see the beginnings of a more formal system of criminal justice, with a separation of powers and a hierarchical system of authority. The office of the justice of the peace was created to assist the shire-reeve, or sheriff, in nonurban areas and the parish constable in urban areas. Eventually, the justices of the peace developed judicial functions and a status equal to that of the sheriff. Parish constables became subordinate to the justices of the peace and became their operational assistants. While retaining the duty of supervising the night watchmen, the parish constables also had the obligation to investigate offenses, serve summonses, execute warrants issued by the justices of the peace, and secure prisoners. The shire-reeve was busy with his other county duties, especially collecting taxes, and left most of the law enforcement duties to the justices of the peace and the constables.

Seventeenth Century and Thief-Takers

In seventeenth-century England, as before, law enforcement was seen as the duty of all the people, even though more and more officials were being charged with enforcing the law and keeping the peace. Already we see the beginnings of a tremendously fragmented and inept criminal justice system. The next criminal justice positions to be created were magistrates and beadles. Magistrates assisted the justices of the peace by presiding in courts, ordering arrests, calling witnesses, and examining prisoners. Beadles were assistants to the constables and walked the streets removing vagrants. The impact of the magistrates, constables, and beadles was minimal, and they were mostly corrupt.

The seventeenth-century English policing system also used a form of individual, private police. Called **thief-takers**, these private citizens, with no official status, were paid by the king for every criminal they arrested—similar to the bounty hunter of the American West. The major role of the thief-takers was to combat highway robbery committed by highwaymen, whose heroes were the likes of such legendary outlaws as Robin Hood and Little John. By the seventeenth century, highwaymen such as Jack Sheppard and Dick Turpin made traveling through the English countryside so dangerous that no coach or traveler was safe. In 1693, an act of Parliament established a monetary reward for the capture of any road agent, an armed robber. A thief-taker was paid upon the conviction of the highwayman and also received the highwayman's horse, arms, money, and property.

The thief-taker system was later extended to cover offenses other than highway robbery, and soon a sliding scale of rewards was established. Arresting a burglar or footpad (street robber), for example, was worth the same as catching a highwayman, but catching a sheep stealer or a deserter from the army brought a much smaller reward. In some areas, homeowners joined together and offered supplementary rewards for the apprehension of a highwayman or footpad in their area. In addition, whenever there was a serious crime wave, Parliament awarded special rewards for thief-takers to arrest particular felons.

Often a criminal would agree to become a thief-taker and catch another criminal to receive a pardon from the king for their own crime. Thus, many thief-takers were themselves criminals. Thief-taking was not always rewarding, because the thief-taker was not paid if the highwayman was not convicted. The job also could be dangerous, because the thief-taker had to fear the revenge of the highwayman and his relatives and associates. Many thief-takers would seduce young people into committing crimes and then have other thief-takers arrest the youths during the offenses. The two thief-takers would then split the fee. Others framed innocent parties by planting stolen goods on their persons or in their homes. Although some real criminals were apprehended by the professional thief-takers, the system generally created more crime than it suppressed.

Henry Fielding

Henry Fielding, the eighteenth-century novelist best known for writing *Tom Jones*, may also be credited with laying the foundation for the first modern police force. In 1748, during the heyday of English highwaymen, Fielding was appointed magistrate in Westminster, a city near central London. He moved into a house on Bow Street, which also became his office. Fielding, in an attempt to decrease the high number of burglaries, street and highway robberies, and other thefts, established relationships with local pawnbrokers. He provided them with lists and descriptions of recently stolen property and asked them to notify him should such property be brought into their pawnshops. He then placed the following ad in the London and Westminster newspapers: "All persons who shall for the future suffer by robber, burglars, etc., are desired immediately to bring or send the best description they can of such robbers, etc., with the time and place and circumstances of the fact, to Henry Fielding Esq., at his house in Bow Street."[6]

Fielding's actions brought about what we can call the first official crime reports. Fielding was able to gain the

---

All in the Line of Duty

Introduction to All in the Line of Duty

All in the Line of Duty is a series of features designed for this textbook. It is included to give today's college students who are interested in the field of policing an idea of what the men and women in our police departments do every hour of the day, every day of the week, every week of the year in the United States.

These are not television or movie reenactments or action pages of novels. They are simply examples of what our police officers do, all in the line of duty, whether on duty or off-duty, all the time.

cooperation of the high constable of Holborn and several other public-spirited constables. Together they formed a small investigative unit, which they called the Bow Street Runners. These were private citizens who were not paid by public funds but who were permitted to accept thief-taker rewards.

Eventually, Fielding's efforts were rewarded by the government, and his Bow Street Runners were publicly financed. In 1763, Fielding was asked to establish with public funds a civilian horse patrol of eight men to combat robbers and footpads on the London streets. The patrol proved successful but was disbanded after only nine months due to a lack of government support.

Londoners debated whether to have a professional police department. Although certainly enough crime occurred to justify forming a civil police force, most people did not want a formal, professional police department for two major reasons. Many felt that a police force would threaten their tradition of freedom. Additionally, the English had considerable faith in the merits of private enterprise, and they disliked spending public money.

Despite the widespread public fear of establishing a civil police force, a small, permanent foot patrol financed by public funds was established in London in 1770. In 1789, a London magistrate, **Patrick Colquhoun**, lobbied for the creation of a large, organized police force for greater London, but his ideas were rejected after much government and public debate.

In 1798, Colquhoun was able to establish a small, publicly financed special river or marine police, patterned after Fielding's Bow Street Runners, to patrol the Thames. Some consider Colquhoun's force the first civil police department in England.

In 1804, a new horse patrol was established for central London. It included two inspectors and fifty-two men who wore uniforms consisting of red vests and blue jackets and trousers, making them England's first uniformed civil police department. As the problems of London in the late eighteenth and early nineteenth centuries increased (the Industrial Revolution, poverty, public disorder, and crime), the people and Parliament finally surrendered to the idea that London needed a large, organized, civil police department.

Peel's Police

In 1828, **Sir Robert Peel**, England's home secretary, basing his ideas on those of Patrick Colquhoun, drafted the first police bill, the Act for Improving the Police in and near the Metropolis (the Metropolitan Police Act).

Sir Robert Peel was responsible, in London in 1829, for the first organized, large-scale police department.

Parliament passed it in 1829. This act established the first large-scale, uniformed, organized, paid, civil police force in London. Over 1,000 men were hired. Although a civil, as opposed to a military, force, it was structured along military lines, with officers wearing distinctive uniforms. The first London Metropolitan Police wore three-quarter-length royal blue coats, white trousers, and top hats. They were armed with truncheons, yesterday's equivalent of today's police baton. The police were commanded by two magistrates, later called commissioners. The control of the new police (called bobbies in honor of their founder, Sir Robert Peel) was delegated to the home secretary, a member of the democratically elected government. Thus, the police as we know them today were, from their very beginning, ultimately responsible to the public.

Peel's early police were guided by seven basic principles:

1. The police should be organized along military lines.
2. It is essential that the proper persons be hired and trained.

3. The police should be hired on a probationary basis and should be fired if they do not meet standards during their probationary period.
4. The police should be under the control of the civil government.
5. The police should be organized and deployed by time and area.
6. Police headquarters and leadership should be centrally located.
7. It is essential that police maintain records.[7]

As a result of the formation of the new police force, the patchwork of private law enforcement systems in use at the time was abolished. The English model of policing eventually became the model for the United States.

London's first two police commissioners were Colonel Charles Rowan, a career military officer, and Richard Mayne, a lawyer. Rowan believed that mutual respect between the police and citizens would be crucial to the success of the new force. As a result, the early bobbies were chosen for their ability to reflect and inspire the highest personal ideals among young men in early nineteenth-century England.

Unfortunately, the new police were not immediately well received. Some elements of the population saw the police as an occupying army, and open battles between the police and citizens occurred. The tide of sentiment turned in favor of the police, however, when an officer was viciously killed in the Cold Bath Fields riot of 1833. At the murder trial, the jury returned a not guilty

An English "bobbie" on foot patrol.

verdict, inspiring a groundswell of public support for the much-maligned police. Eventually, Peel's system became so popular that all English cities adopted his idea of a civil police department.

American Policing: The Colonial Experience

The American colonists did not have an easy life.[8] They were constantly at risk from foreign enemies, their brother and sister colonists, and Native Americans. Their only protection was their own selves and, at times, the military or militia. By the seventeenth century, the colonies started to institute a civil law enforcement system that closely replicated the English model. The county sheriff was the most important law enforcement official. However, in addition to law enforcement, he collected taxes, supervised elections, and had much to do with the legal process. Sheriffs were not paid a salary but, much like the English thief-taker, were paid

England's Early Experience with a Civil Police Department

1763	Fielding creates civilian horse patrol in London.
1770	Foot patrol is established in London.
1798	River or marine police to patrol the Thames is established by Patrick Colquhoun. (Some consider this to be England's first civil police department.)
1804	Horse patrol is established in London (England's first uniformed patrol).
1829	Peel's Police is established in London (England's first large-scale, organized, uniformed, paid, civil police department).

PATROLLING THE NET

Introduction to Patrolling the Net

Patrolling the Net is a special feature of this textbook and will be found a few times in each chapter. Most people refer to surfing the Net, but for obvious reasons, we'll call it patrolling the Net. The purpose of this feature is to show you how the Internet can be useful to students, police officers, and the public.

The Internet is fun, easy to use, and very useful in doing research and in finding jobs in policing and the criminal justice system.

Patrolling the Net will discuss computers, the Internet, the World Wide Web, and all related topics without using computer terms, as much as possible. I am not a computer person or an expert in anything about computers. As a matter of fact, just a few years ago I was computer phobic. I was even afraid to turn one on. Eventually, I learned how to use a word processing program on the computers at my school. I learned enough to type up my course outlines, my examinations, and even some speeches and personal letters.

Eventually, I wrote two textbooks on the computer, yet whenever anyone mentioned the Internet, I froze. I came from the pre-computer generation—we didn't even know what a computer was. In fact, when I went to grade school, we actually used fountain pens; we actually filled them up from an ink bottle on our desk. Then, the ballpoint pen came into fashion. We still had never heard of a computer.

How did I learn to use the Internet? One evening I approached my secretary, Colleen, and asked her to teach me. She smiled, turned on her computer, pressed some buttons, played with the mouse, and then started walking away. I yelled, "Hey, Colleen, where are you going? I don't know what I'm doing." She said, "Hey, you're a professor; you can figure it out!" I didn't see her again for three hours. By the time she came back, I knew the basics of the Internet. It's that easy, even for a professor, and it's a heck of a lot of fun. Hopefully, if you don't know how to use the Internet yet, or don't know how much it can help you with research, finding a job, or having fun, you'll start here. I really can't teach you how to do it. You have to just sit down and get started.

---

fees for each arrest they made. Sheriffs did not patrol but stayed in their offices.

In cities, the town marshal was the chief law enforcement official, aided by constables (called schouts in the Dutch settlements) and night watchmen. Night watch was sometimes performed by the military. The city of Boston created the first colonial night watch in 1631 and three years later created the position of constable. In 1658, eight paid watchmen replaced a patrol of citizen volunteers in the Dutch city of Nieuw Amsterdam. This police system was inherited by the British in 1664 when they took over the city and renamed it New York. By the mid-1700s, the New York night watch was described as follows: "a parcel of idle, drinking, vigilant snorers, who never quell'd any nocturnal tumult in their lives; but would perhaps, be as ready to joining in a burglary as any thief in Christendom."[9]

When serious breaches of the peace occurred, including riots or slave revolts, the governors called on the colonial militia or the British army. Many cities, including Fort Pontchartrain (Detroit), New Orleans, and Fort Washington (Cincinnati), were under martial law for much of their early existence.

Despite the presence of law enforcement officials in the colonies, law enforcement was still mainly the responsibility of the individual citizen, as it had been in early England. There was little law and order on the colonial frontier. When immediate action was needed, the frontier people took matters into their own hands, which led to an American tradition of vigilantism.

American Policing: Eighteenth and Nineteenth Centuries

Historically, American policing attempted to control crime and disorder in an urban and frontier environment. Although the urban and frontier experience differed in many ways, both could be classified as brutal and corrupt.

The Urban Experience

During the eighteenth century, the most common form of American law enforcement was the system of constables in the daytime and the watch at night. Crime, street riots, and drunkenness were very common, and law enforcement personnel were totally incompetent.

From 1790 to 1845, New York City's population rose from 33,000 to 370,000 people, and most were new immigrants. The increased population and poverty dramatically increased crime. An 1840 New York newspaper reported: "Destructive rascality stalks at large in our streets and public places, at all times of day and night, with none to make it afraid; mobs assemble deliberately. . . . In a word, lawless violence and fury have full dominion over us."[10] In 1842, a special citizens' committee of New Yorkers wrote: "The property of the citizen is pilfered, almost before his eyes. Dwellings and warehouses are entered with an ease and apparent coolness and carelessness of detention which shows that none are safe. Thronged as our city is, men are robbed in the street. Thousands that are arrested go unpunished, and the defenseless and the beautiful are ravished and murdered in the daytime, and no trace of the criminals is found."[11]

Early Police Departments The first organized American police department was created in Boston in 1838. In addition to police duties, until 1853 the Boston police were charged with maintaining public health. The first Boston Police Department consisted of only eight members and worked only in the daytime. By 1851, the night watch was assumed by the new Boston Police Department. In 1853, the office of police chief was created, and in 1854, police stations were constructed. The Boston police force was not fully uniformed until 1859, when members were required to wear blue jackets and white hats.

In 1844, the New York State legislature authorized communities to organize police forces and gave special funds to cities to provide twenty-four-hour police protection. In New York City, under the leadership of Mayor William F. Havermeyer, a London-style police department was created on May 23, 1845. The first New York City police officers were issued copper stars to wear on their hats and jackets but were not allowed to wear full uniforms until 1853. In fact, the first New York cops did not even want to wear their copper stars, because doing so made them targets for the city's ruffians. The New York City police were also in charge of street sweeping until 1881.

Philadelphia started its police department in 1854. By the outbreak of the Civil War, Chicago, New Orleans, Cincinnati, Baltimore, Newark, and a number of other large cities had their own police departments. The new police departments replaced the night watch system. As a result, constables and sheriffs were relieved of much of their patrol and investigative duties. However, they performed other duties in the fledgling criminal justice system, such as serving court orders and managing jails.

You Decide: How Did the Term "Cops" Come About?

Did "cops" refer to the copper stars worn by the first New York City police officers?

or

Was "cops" a shortened way of saying constables on patrol (COPs)?

YOU ARE THERE!

What a Police Officer's Uniform Means

The police badge—known in some departments as the shield, chest piece, or tin—is the outward symbol of a police officer's legal status and entitlement. It is symbolic of the authority vested in that individual by the public. The badge and other parts of the police officer's uniform are vestiges of the armor worn by government warriors centuries ago.

The badge's history can be traced back to two pieces of armor: the hand-held shield used to deflect blows and the chest plating intended to protect the warrior's chest from penetration. The shield often displayed the heraldry and symbols of the warrior's lord or head of state, just as today's badges reflect symbols of the officer's municipality, county, or state.

Shoulder epaulets or shoulder patches represent the shoulder plating worn to protect the warrior from the heavy, flat swords of the time. The officer's hat is reminiscent of helmets worn by warriors in battle. The hat badge or shield is a vestige of the plumage or insignia on the helmets.

Source: Adapted from *Police Chief*, September 1988, p. 66.

> ### YOU ARE THERE!
>
> #### Saved by the Badge
>
> A Kansas prosecutor literally owes his life to his badge. Eric Stonecipher, a special narcotics prosecutor for the Geary County, Kansas, attorney's office, was ambushed August 11, 1992, while driving on a Kansas highway. At least five bullets struck his car. Stonecipher's special prosecutor's badge, carried in his breast pocket, deflected a bullet that would have struck him in the heart. Three bullets struck his car headrest, one passed through his upper left arm, and the fifth bounced off his badge.
>
> Source: Adapted from "Saved by the Badge," *Law Enforcement News*, 30 September 1992, p. 4.

Politics in American Policing Nineteenth-century American policing was dominated by local politicians and was notorious for brutality, corruption, and ineptness: "In addition to the pervasive brutality and corruption, the police did little to effectively prevent crime or provide public services.... Officers were primarily tools of local politicians; they were not impartial and professional public servants."[12] In his 1991 book, *Low Life: Lures and Snares of Old New York*, Luc Sante says, "The history of the New York police is not a particularly illustrious one, at least in the nineteenth and early twentieth centuries, as throughout the period the law-enforcement agents of the city continually and recurrently demonstrated corruption, complacency, confusion, sloth and brutality."[13]

In 1857, political differences between the Democrats, who controlled New York City, and the Republicans, who controlled New York State, caused a full-scale police war. The corrupt New York City police, the Municipal Police, under the control of New York's mayor Fernando Wood, was replaced by the Metropolitan Police, created and controlled by Governor John A. King. Wood, however, refused to disband the Municipals. Thus, the city had two separate police departments, each under the control of one of the two enemies.

On June 16, 1857, the two police departments clashed at New York's City Hall. Fifty Metropolitan police arrived at City Hall with a warrant to arrest Wood. Almost 900 members of the Municipal Police attacked the Metropolitans, causing them to retreat. As the Metropolitans were retreating, the state called in the Seventh Regiment of the National Guard under the command of General Sandford. The members of the National Guard marched on City Hall and raised their weapons as if to fire at the Municipals and City Hall. Eventually Wood surrendered to arrest, and no shots were fired. In court, the mayor was released and the judge decided that the Metropolitan Police would be the official New York City police.

The primary job of nineteenth-century police was to serve as the enforcement arm of the political party in power, protect private property, and control the rapidly arriving foreign immigrants. In the late 1800s, police work was highly desirable, because it paid more than most other blue-collar jobs. The average factory worker earned $450 a year, whereas a police officer was paid, on average, $900.

Politics dominated police departments, and politicians determined who would be appointed a police officer and who would be promoted to higher ranks. Job

> ### YOU ARE THERE!
>
> #### First Urban U.S. Police Departments
>
> **Boston**
>
> | Year | Event |
> |---|---|
> | 1838 | Boston Police Department is created—comprising eight officers who only worked in the daytime. |
> | 1851 | Boston Police Department assumes the night watch. |
> | 1853 | First Boston police chief is appointed. |
> | 1854 | First Boston police stations are built. |
> | 1859 | Boston police officers receive first uniforms. |
>
> **New York**
>
> | Year | Event |
> |---|---|
> | 1845 | New York City Police Department is created—with officers on the job twenty-four hours a day, seven days a week. |
> | 1853 | New York City police are required to wear uniforms. |
> | 1857 | Police "civil war" erupts at New York City Hall. |
>
> **Philadelphia**
>
> | Year | Event |
> |---|---|
> | 1854 | Philadelphia Police Department is created. |
>
> Chicago, New Orleans, Cincinnati, Baltimore, Newark, and a number of other large cities created police departments around the time of the start of the Civil War.

PATROLLING THE NET

What Equipment Do I Need to Get Started on the Internet?

A computer, a modem, Internet software, a mouse, and that's about all.

What if you do not have a computer? A modem? Internet software? A mouse? Can't afford one? The majority of schools in our nation today have everything you need to get started and allow students to use them for free. Mine does. Your local library probably will give you free access to the Internet. Mine does. If all else fails, talk to your classmates; plenty of them have all you need to get started. Maybe you can wash their car for them or buy them lunch. It's that easy.

Get started. It's fun.

---

security was nonexistent, because when a new political party gained control of city government, it would generally fire all police officers and hire new ones.

Regarding the influence of politics on the hiring of police officers, Samuel Walker wrote:

> Ignorance, poor health, or old age was no barrier to employment. An individual with the right connections could be hired despite the most obvious lack of qualifications. Recruits received no formal training. A new officer would be handed a copy of the police manual (if one could be found) containing the local ordinances and state laws, and sent out on patrol. There he could receive on-the-job training from experienced officers who, of course, also taught the ways of graft and evasion of duty.[14]

Robert M. Fogelson wrote about the political impact of politicians on the police: "Most patrolmen who survived for any length of time quickly . . . learned that a patrolman placed his career in jeopardy more by alienating his captain than by disobeying his chief and more by defying his wardman, who regulated vice in the precinct than by ignoring [his sergeant]."[15]

According to one researcher, "They [the police] knew who put them in office and whose support they needed to stay there. Their job was to manage their beat; often they became completely enmeshed in the crime they were expected to suppress. Corruption, brutality, and racial discrimination, although not universal, were characteristic of most big city departments."[16]

The Early Police Officer's Job Police work was primitive. The role of the American urban police in the eighteenth and nineteenth centuries was varied and often not limited to law enforcement. The early police performed many duties they do not have today, including cleaning streets, inspecting boilers, caring for the poor and homeless, operating emergency ambulances, and performing other social services.

American police, in the English tradition, were not issued firearms. However, this changed quickly. In 1858, a New York City police officer shot a fleeing felon with a personal weapon. The case was presented to a grand jury, which did not indict the officer. Police officers in New York then began to arm themselves. A similar incident in Boston led to the arming of that police force. By the early 1900s, cities commonly issued revolvers to their police officers. Officers patrolled on foot with no radios, backup, or supervision. They relied on brute force and brutality to avoid being beaten up or challenged by local toughs. (See the description of the turn-of-the-century New York City police captain Alexander "Clubber" Williams in chapter 12.) Citizens had a tremendous hatred for nineteenth-century police officers and saw them as political hacks. The police were subjected to frequent abuse by street gangs, and suspects often had to be physically subdued prior to arrest.

Commenting on this lack of respect by citizens, Walker notes, "A tradition of police brutality developed out of this reciprocal disrespect. Officers sought to gain with their billy clubs the deference to their authority that was not freely given."[17] Regarding this brutality, the social reformer Lincoln Steffens wrote: "He saw the police bring in and kick out their bandaged, bloody prisoners, not only strikers and foreigners, but thieves too, and others of the miserable, friendless, troublesome poor."[18]

Corruption, mismanagement, and brutality were rampant. Consequently, between 1860 and 1866, the police forces of Baltimore, St. Louis, Chicago, Kansas City, Detroit, and Cleveland were placed under state control.

Boston was the first city to form a detective division to investigate past crimes. However, early detectives were as corrupt as their uniformed counterparts, private thief-takers, or bounty hunters.

In the latter part of the nineteenth century, we begin to see some practical and technological advances in policing. The public health and social welfare responsibilities that formerly were the province of the police, including sweeping sidewalks and housing the homeless, were transferred to newly created municipal agencies. in the 1850s, precincts began to be linked to central headquarters by telegraph machines. In the 1860s, telegraph signal stations were installed, first in Chicago and then in Cincinnati. These enabled officers, using Morse code, to check with their precincts for instructions or to call for assistance. In 1881, the Morse code signal system was replaced by telephone call boxes in Cincinnati. A police officer could now call from his beat for a patrol wagon to transport prisoners. A red light on the top of a call box could summons officers for messages from their precinct headquarters.

As primitive as the eighteenth and nineteenth century urban policing was, policing America's frontier was even more primitive, as we shall see in the next section.

The Frontier Experience

Life on the American frontier was not easy.[19] Early settlers faced tremendous problems from the weather, the terrain, Native Americans, and the criminals within their own ranks. Formal law enforcement on the frontier was rare. What little law enforcement existed in the Old West consisted mainly of the locally elected county sheriff and the appointed town marshal, and sometimes the U.S. marshal, the U.S. Army, or the state militia.

Sheriffs and Town Marshals The locally elected county sheriffs and the appointed town marshals (appointed by the mayor or city council) were usually the only law enforcement officers available on the frontier. Most of the sheriff's time was spent collecting taxes and performing duties for the courts.

If a crime spree occurred or a dangerous criminal was in an area, the sheriff would call upon the posse comitatus, a common law descendent of the old hue and cry. (The term **posse comitatus**, in Latin, means "the power of the county.") No man above the age of fifteen could refuse to serve as a member of a legally constituted posse. The posse was often little more than a legalized form of vigilantism. Vigilantism and lynch mobs were common in the Old West because of the

---

All in the Line of Duty

The Explosion Didn't Keep Them Out, and They Got Others Out

Sergeant Rod Hill, age 46, Oklahoma City Police Department, was among the first Oklahoma City police officers to arrive at the scene of the explosion in the Alfred P. Murrah Federal Building on April 19, 1995. The bombing destroyed the structure, killing 168 people and injuring 675 more. Sergeant Hill was trying to rescue survivors when firefighters warned of the possibility of another explosion. Hill was about to follow their advice and leave with other rescuers when he saw two women on the seventh floor of the building. "Don't leave us!" they pleaded. Hill decided to return to try to rescue the women and was followed by two other members of the Oklahoma City Police Department, Detective Sergeant Robert Campbell, age 39, and Officer Jim Ramsey, age 27.

Hill reached the seventh floor, crawled through a blown-out window, and came upon a fifteen-foot-wide pit. He could hear one of the two women trying to persuade her friend to jump from the window. Before either could jump, Hill yelled out that he was there. "I'll get you out!" he shouted.

Hill pulled himself up onto a window frame, then moved carefully over two blown-out windows to get closer to the women. He hoisted one onto a window frame as Campbell and Ramsey threw a piece of metal over a narrow strip of floor to give the women an extra foothold. Using the metal plate to regain his own footing, Campbell grabbed one woman from the window frame and pulled her across as Hill and Ramsey returned to rescue the other.

Source: Adapted from "Finding Heroes Among the Wreckage: Five Are Hailed for Actions in Oklahoma City Bombing Aftermath," *Law Enforcement News*, 15 December 1996, p. 7.

---

lack of professional law enforcement. Many famous town marshals, such as James Butler (Wild Bill) Hickok of Hays City, Kansas, and later, Abilene, Kansas, and Wyatt Earp of Dodge City, Kansas, were really semireformed outlaws. There was little to distinguish between the good guys and bad guys in the American frontier's criminal justice system.

Federal Marshals Federal marshals played a role in frontier law enforcement. The Federal Judiciary Act of

All in the Line of Duty

Almost Critically Injured in Blast, She Saved Others

Midwest City Police corporal Regina Bonny, age 36, an undercover narcotics officer, was present in the Alfred P. Murrah Federal Building at 9:05 a.m. on April 19, 1995, while assigned to work with the DEA on a case.

As Bonny walked down the hall to an office, she was knocked unconscious by the blast. When she came to, she saved the lives of several others trapped in the rubble.

Although suffering from serious injuries that left her with irreparable nerve damage, a brain injury, and hand and shoulder wounds, Bonny pulled Vernon Buster, an inspector with the Bureau of Alcohol, Tobacco and Firearms (ATF), from debris and removed a piece of metal from his arm. Then she went to the aid of Jim Staggs, also an ATF inspector, who was bleeding from a head wound. She tore off Staggs' shirt and wrapped it around his head to stop the flow of blood. As dust and smoke began to swirl around them, Bonny, who is five feet, four inches tall, guided Buster and dragged Staggs, who weighed 205 pounds, over a pile of concrete and to a staircase.

But Bonny didn't stop once she reached the street. She went back into the crumbling structure to search for her colleagues. All she found was a gaping chasm where nine floors of the building, including the DEA office, used to be. She continued her fruitless search, and learned a few days later that everyone with her when the blast occurred had perished.

In 1996, Bonny was recognized by *Parade Magazine* and the International Association of Chiefs of Police as Police Officer of the Year for her exploits in Oklahoma City.

Source: Adapted from "Finding Heroes Among the Wreckage: Five Are Hailed for Actions in Oklahoma City Bombing Aftermath," *Law Enforcement News*, 15 December 1996, p. 7.

1789, which created the office of the U.S. marshal, also gave the marshals the power to call upon the militia for assistance, a power formalized under federal posse comitatus legislation in 1792. The militia were technically members of the federal marshal's posse and aided him in performing his civil duties. In 1861, Congress passed a law empowering the president to call upon the militia or regular army to enforce the law when ordinary means were insufficient.

The Military After the Civil War, from 1867 to 1877, law enforcement duties were provided by the military in the military districts created from the Confederacy. U.S. marshals in occupied southern states often called upon federal troops to form a posse to enforce local laws. Once southern states regained representation in Congress, they tried to prevent such practices. In both the North and the South, the military was also used by civilian authorities. In the South, the army guarded polling places and curbed the actions of the Ku Klux Klan; in the North, the army was used to suppress labor disturbances. Excesses by the military in enforcing the law resulted in Congress passing the Posse Comitatus Act of 1879, forbidding the use of the military to enforce civilian law except where expressly authorized by law. Some of these exceptions applied in the Old West to prevent trespassing on Native American reservations or to enforce unpopular federal decisions regarding territories such as Arizona and New Mexico. The use of the military in the Old West ended around the last quarter of the nineteenth century.

State Police Agencies Some states and territories created their own police organizations. In 1823, Stephen Austin hired a dozen bodyguards to protect fellow "Texicans" from Native Americans and bandits. Austin's hired guns were officially named the Texas Rangers upon Texas's independence in 1835. The Texas Rangers served as a border patrol for the Republic of Texas, guarding against marauding Native Americans and Mexicans. When Texas was admitted to the Union in 1845, the Texas Rangers became the first U.S. state police agency.

Unlike present-day state police, the Texas Rangers and their counterparts, the Arizona Rangers (1901) and the New Mexico Mounted Patrol (1905), were primarily border patrols designed to combat cattle thievery and control outlaw activities on the Rio Grande. By the 1850s, they had received general police powers. The Rangers were disbanded during the post–Civil War reconstruction period but reemerged in 1874.

With Pennsylvania leading the way in 1905, non-southwestern states began to create their own state police agencies. The twentieth century saw the creation of state police agencies in each state, with the exception of Hawaii.

Private Police Private police were much more effective than public law enforcement agencies on the frontier. The private police acted in the same manner as the English thief-takers; however, the American private police were more professional and honest than the English version.

Allan Pinkerton, a native of Scotland, was a former police detective who established a detective agency in Chicago in 1850. The Pinkerton Agency first gained notoriety just before the Civil War, when it thwarted the alleged "Baltimore Plot" to assassinate president-elect Abraham Lincoln. By the 1880s, Pinkerton's National Detective Agency had offices in nearly two dozen cities. In the West, Pinkerton's customers included the U.S. Department of Justice, various railroad companies, and major land speculators. The agents arrested train robbers and notorious gangsters, including the James Gang in the 1880s, Robert Leroy Parker (Butch Cassidy), and Harry Longbaugh (the "Sundance Kid") in the early 1900s. The agents also arrested John and Simeon Reno, who organized the nation's first band of professional bank robbers. They were also hired in the East by mining and manufacturing companies to suppress labor organizations, such as the Molly Maguires in 1874 to 1875, as well as to suppress the Homestead Riots in Pittsburgh in 1892. The Pinkertons employed informants throughout the United States and its territories and offered cash rewards for information. The Pinkertons mainly protected the interests of the railroads, wealthy eastern bankers, and land speculators.

In competition with the Pinkerton Agency during the latter part of the nineteenth century was the Rocky Mountain Detective Association, which pursued and apprehended bank and train robbers, cattle thieves, murderers, and the road agents who plundered highways and mining communities throughout the Southwest and Rocky Mountain area.

Also in competition with the Pinkertons was Wells, Fargo and Company, started in 1852 by Henry Wells and William G. Fargo as a banking and stock association designed to capitalize on the emerging shipping and banking opportunities in California. It operated as a mail-carrying service and stage coach line out of more than a hundred offices in the western mining districts. Because the company carried millions of dollars in gold and other valuable cargo, it created a guard company to protect its shipments. The Wells-Fargo private security employees were effective in preventing robberies and thefts; moreover, criminals who were able to hold up its banks and carriers were relentlessly hunted down by specially trained and equipped agents.

American Policing: Twentieth Century

The first half of the twentieth century saw such dramatic negative events as the Boston Police Strike, National Prohibition, and the issuance of the Wickersham Commission Report. However, innovation and an increase in professionalism grew to characterize the American police force in part through the efforts of such early police professionals as August Vollmer, O. W. Wilson, and J. Edgar Hoover.

Policing from 1900 to 1960

As we have seen, American policing has historically been characterized by ineptness, corruption, and brutality.[20] At the start of the twentieth century, serious attempts were made to reform the police.

Even earlier, Theodore Roosevelt attempted reform as one of the New York City Board of Police Commissioners between 1895 and 1897. Roosevelt raised police recruitment standards and disciplined corrupt and brutal officers. However, despite much publicity and some superficial changes, Roosevelt's efforts failed when the corrupt Tammany Hall political machine was returned to power in 1897.

During the progressive era of American government, 1900 to 1914, attempts at reforming the police were originated outside police departments by middle-class, civic-minded reformers. For the most part, however, these attempts failed.

Technology In the twentieth century, the use of technology grew phenomenally in American police departments. By 1913, the police motorcycle was being used by departments in the Northeast. The first police car was used in Akron, Ohio, in 1910, and the police wagon was first used in Cincinnati in 1912. By the 1920s, the patrol car was in widespread use. The patrol car began to change police work by allowing the police to respond quickly to crimes and other problems, as well as by enabling each officer to cover much more territory.

The widespread use of the one-way radio in the 1930s and the two-way radio in the 1940s, combined

This 1920s police car was state-of-the-art transportation for its time.

with the growing use of the patrol car, began to revolutionize police work. A person could call police headquarters or a precinct, and a police car could be dispatched almost immediately, providing rapid response to calls for service and emergencies. Although this innovation was greeted with great joy by police administrators, motorized patrol eventually forced a separation of the police from the community and played a part in the serious problems in policing that arose in the 1960s.

The Boston Police Strike The Boston police strike of 1919 was one of the most significant events in the history of policing, and it increased interest in police reform. While other professions were unionizing and improving their standards of living, police salaries lagged behind, and the police were becoming upset with their diminished status in society. The fraternal association of Boston police officers, the Boston Social Club, voted to become a union affiliated with the American Federation of Labor (AFL). On September 9, 1919, 70 percent of Boston's police officers—1,117 men—went on strike. Rioting and looting immediately broke out, and Governor Calvin Coolidge mobilized the state militia. Public support went against the police, and the strike was broken. All the striking officers were fired and replaced by new recruits. The strike ended police unionism for decades. Calvin Coolidge became a national hero and went on to become president of the United States. Many say that his action in firing the Boston police propelled him to the presidency.

National Prohibition Another significant event in twentieth-century policing, and one that stirred up another police reform movement, was the experiment with the prohibition of alcohol in the United States. The **Volstead Act** (**National Prohibition**) was passed in 1919 and became law in 1920 with the adoption of the **Eighteenth Amendment** to the Constitution. It forbade the sale and manufacture of alcohol, attempting to make America a dry nation. Traditional organized crime (TOC) families received their impetus during this period as gangsters banded together to meet the tremendous demand of ordinary Americans for alcohol. When the Eighteenth Amendment was repealed in 1933 with the adoption of the Twenty-first Amendment, the organized crime families funneled the tremendous amount of capital that they had received in the alcohol trade into other vice crimes, such as illegal gambling, prostitution, loan sharking, labor racketeering, and later, drug dealing.

Local law enforcement was unable to stop the alcohol and vice operations of organized crime and became even more corrupt as many law enforcement officers cooperated with organized crime. As a result, between 1919 and 1930, twenty-four states formed crime commissions to study the crime problem and the ability of the police to deal with crime.

The Wickersham Commission In 1929, President Herbert Hoover created the National Commission on Law Observance and Enforcement with George W. Wickersham as its chair. The commission was popularly known as the **Wickersham Commission** and conducted the first national study of the U.S. criminal justice system. The commission issued a report in 1931, popularly known as the Wickersham Report. The report criticized the Volstead Act, which created Prohibition, saying it was not enforced because it was unenforceable. The following year National Prohibition was repealed.

The commission found that the average police commander's term of office was too short and that his responsibility to politicians made his position insecure. It said there was a lack of effective, efficient, and honest patrol officers, as well as no effort to educate, train, or discipline officers or to fire incompetent ones. The commission found further that police forces, even in the biggest cities, did not have adequate communication systems or equipment.

Two volumes of the Wickersham Report, *Lawlessness in Law Enforcement* (volume 2) and *The Police* (volume 14), concerned themselves solely with the police. *Lawlessness in Law Enforcement* portrayed the police as inept, inefficient, racist, and brutal, and accused them of committing illegal acts. The volume concluded that "the third degree—the inflicting of pain, physical or mental, to extract confessions or statements—is extensively practiced."[21]

The Wickersham Report blamed the shortcomings of the police on a lack of police professionalism. *The Police,* written primarily by August Vollmer, discussed methods that could be used to create a professional police force in the United States. The methods the commission advocated included increased selectivity in the recruitment of officers, better pay and benefits, and more education for police officers.

The Wickersham Report angered citizens and started another groundswell for police reform. With the onset of the Great Depression, however, police reform became less important than economic revival, and another attempt at police reform failed.

Professionalism An early attempt at police reform was the creation in 1893 of a professional society, the International Association of Chiefs of Police (IACP). Its first president was the Washington, D.C., chief of police, Richard Sylvester. The IACP became the leading voice of police reform during the first two decades of the twentieth century by consistently calling for the creation of a civil service police and for the removal of political influence and control over the police. The IACP remains a significant force in policing today.

Eventually a federal law, the **Pendleton Act**, was passed in 1883 to establish a civil service system that tested, appointed, and promoted officers on a merit system. The civil service system was later adopted by local governments, and political influence slowly evaporated from police departments. However, today not all U.S. police agencies are governed by civil service rules. Furthermore, despite civil service systems, politics continued to play some part in American law enforcement.

Several people were pioneers in modern policing, and two men, August Vollmer and O. W. Wilson, stand out in the twentieth century as the founders of police professionalism.

August Vollmer The chief of police in Berkeley, California, from 1905 to 1932 was **August Vollmer.** Vollmer instituted many practices that started to professionalize the U.S. police. Among those practices was incorporating university training as a part of police training. Also, Vollmer introduced the use of intelligence, psychiatric, and neurological tests to aid in the selection of police recruits and initiated scientific crime detection and crime-solving techniques. In addition, Vollmer helped develop the School of Criminology at the University of California at Berkeley, which became the model for programs related to law and criminal justice throughout the United States. Vollmer, as stated earlier, was also the author of the Wickersham Report's volume entitled *The Police.* Additionally, he trained numerous students who went on to become reform-oriented and progressive police chiefs. August Vollmer can certainly be considered the father of modern American policing.

O. W. Wilson A disciple of Vollmer's, **O. W. Wilson** pioneered the use of advanced training for police officers when he took over and reformed the Wichita, Kansas, police department in 1928. While there, Wilson conducted the first systematic study of the effectiveness of one-officer squad cars. Despite officers' complaints about risks to their safety, his study showed that one-officer cars were more efficient, effective, and economical than two-person cars. Wilson developed modern

PATROLLING THE NET

So, Now That I'm Interested, What's Next?

Now you have to sit down and get started. One of your friends at school must have access to the Internet and the patience to let you start working on it. If not, get new friends. If you do not want to do that, take a course at school that covers the Internet. There are many of them in colleges, school district evening programs, libraries, and the like. Some of these courses are free, and some charge. Just get started and have fun.

Once you get familiar with the Internet beat, you might want to look at a really good little book published by the company that published this textbook. It's only seventy pages and covers the basics of the Internet and some of the ways to use it to its fullest. Your professor probably has one. See Internet Guide for Criminal Justice, Daniel J. Kurland and Christina Polsenberg, Wadsworth Publishing Company, 1987.

---

management and administrative techniques for policing. He was the author of the first two textbooks on police management: the International City Management Association's *Municipal Police Administration* and his own text, *Police Administration*, which became the Bible of policing for decades.

Wilson was dean of the School of Criminology at the University of California at Berkeley from 1950 to 1960 and the superintendent of the Chicago police from 1960 to 1967. The core of Wilson's approach to police administration was managerial efficiency. He believed that police departments should maximize patrol coverage by replacing foot patrols with one-person auto patrols. He advocated rapid response to calls for service as a key criterion by which to judge the effectiveness of police departments.

Almost every U.S. police department since the 1950s has been organized around the principles espoused in Wilson's books. He developed workload formulas based on reported crimes and calls for service on each beat. Wilson's 1941 workload formula remained unchanged for decades.

Raymond Blaine Fosdick and Bruce Smith Other early pioneers in the movement toward police professionalism were Raymond Blaine Fosdick and Bruce Smith. Neither was a police officer. Fosdick is noted for the first scholarly research regarding the police. In 1915, he published *European Police Systems*, which examined the police structures and practices of Europe. In 1920, he published *American Police Systems* after studying the police of seventy-two U.S. cities.

Bruce Smith, a researcher and later manager of the Institute of Public Administration, also contributed to our early knowledge of the police. His efforts in surveying and researching police departments in approximately fifty leading American cities in eighteen states led to his noteworthy 1940 book *Police Systems in the United States*; a second edition was published in 1949.

John Edgar Hoover One cannot discuss law enforcement in the twentieth-century United States without mentioning John Edgar Hoover, more popularly known as **J. Edgar Hoover**. In 1921, Hoover, an attorney working for the U.S. Department of Justice, was appointed assistant director of the Bureau of Investigation, the forerunner of the Federal Bureau of Investigation (FBI) by President Warren G. Harding. In 1924, President Calvin Coolidge, upon the retirement of the bureau's director, appointed Hoover as the director. Over the next forty-eight years, Hoover was reappointed as director of the FBI by every U.S. president and remained director until his death in 1972.

Under Hoover's leadership, the FBI changed from an inefficient organization into what many consider to be the world's primary law enforcement agency. Among his major contributions were the hiring of accountants and lawyers as special agents; the introduction of the FBI Uniform Crime Reports, which since 1930 has been the leading source of crime and arrest statistics in the United States; the development of the National Crime Information Center (NCIC); the development of the FBI's Ten Most Wanted Criminals Program, otherwise known as Public Enemies; the development of the FBI Academy at Quantico, Virginia; and the popularizing of the FBI through the media as incorruptible, crime-fighting G-men.

During the past few decades, Hoover's reputation has diminished. Revelations have surfaced about his use of the media to build a myth about the FBI, his single-mindedness about Communism, and his domestic surveillance operations over prominent Americans.

Kefauver Committee In 1950, in response to fear about crime and the corruption of law enforcement officers, the U.S. Senate's Crime Committee, chaired by Senator Estes Kefauver, was created. The Kefauver Committee held televised public hearings that led to the discovery of a nationwide network of organized crime, a syndicate that has commonly been called the Mafia or Cosa Nostra. The hearings also revealed that many law enforcement officers nationwide were on the syndicate's payroll. The public was shocked over these tales of corruption, and another attempt at police reform began. David R. Johnson wrote about this decade:

> The 1950s marked a turning point in the history of professionalism. Following major scandals, reformers came to power across the nation. Politicians had real choices between the traditional and new models of policing because a number of professional police reformers were available for the first time. With an enraged middle class threatening their livelihoods, the politicians opted for reform.[22]

Policing in the 1960s and 1970s

The 1960s and 1970s, times of great tension and change, were probably the most turbulent era ever for policing in U.S. history. Numerous social problems permeated these decades, and the police were right in the middle of each one of the problems. In this era the struggle for racial equality reached its height, accompanied by marches, demonstrations, and riots. These riots burned down whole neighborhoods in U.S. urban centers. In this era the Vietnam War was reaching its height, soldiers were dying, and students across the United States were protesting the war and governmental policies. The Supreme Court decided in case after case to protect arrested persons from oppressive police practices. During this time, the police seemed to be more the targets of radical groups than the respected protectors of the people. In short, in this time of dramatic social change in the United States, the police were not only right in the middle of it all, but often were the focus of it all.

The police, because of their role, were always in the middle—between those fighting for their civil rights and the government officials (the employers of the police) who wanted to maintain the status quo, between demonstrating students and college and city administrators. The police received much criticism during these years. Some of it was deserved, but much of it was beyond their control.

James Q. Wilson perhaps described the decade of the 1960s best when he wrote, "It all began about 1963, that was the year, to over dramatize a bit, that a decade began to fall apart."[23]

This section briefly describes some of the problems experienced by the police during this period and some of the encounters between the police and what were seen at the time as rival groups. It should be noted that I served as a uniformed police officer in New York City during this time. During the day, I policed antiwar marches, civil rights demonstrations, and urban riots, and at night I attended college, sitting next to fellow students, many of whom I had encountered as adversaries on the street.

Supreme Court Decisions The 1960s saw the Warren Court at its height, a U.S. Supreme Court that focused dramatically on individual rights. Police actions, ranging from arrests to search and seizure and custodial interrogation, were being declared unconstitutional. (Chapter 11 will focus on these decisions.) The Court made dramatic use of the exclusionary rule, a Supreme Court ruling in 1914 that declared that evidence seized by the police in violation of the Constitution could not be used against a defendant in federal court, thus leading to the possibility that a guilty defendant could go free because of procedural errors by the police.

Many important police-related cases were decided in this era. *Mapp v. Ohio* (1961) finally, after much warning, applied the exclusionary rule to all states in the nation.[24] *Escobedo v. Illinois* (1964) defined the constitutional right to counsel at police interrogations.[25] *Miranda v. Arizona* (1966) required the police to notify a person who is in police custody and who is going to be interrogated of his or her constitutional rights.[26]

The Civil Rights Movement Legal segregation of the races finally ended with the landmark Supreme Court case of *Brown v. Board of Education of Topeka* (1954), which desegregated schools all over the nation. However, equal treatment of the races did not occur overnight. Numerous marches and demonstrations were to come before the Civil Rights Act of 1964 was passed.

> ## All in the Line of Duty
>
> ### She Rescued Him but Collared Him Too
>
> While responding to the robbery of a cab driver, Officer Julia Krebs of the Savannah, Georgia, Police Department observed a subject attempting to conceal himself along the riverfront. Upon seeing the officer, the subject ran and jumped into the Savannah River to elude apprehension. As he attempted to swim across the wide river, Officer Krebs saw that he was in danger of drowning. Without regard to the personal dangers, including swift river currents, commercial ship traffic, and limited nighttime visibility, she dove into the river and convinced the combative subject, who was drunk and 60 pounds heavier than her, to accept her assistance. She kept him afloat until both were picked up by a Coast Guard vessel. Officer Krebs both rescued and apprehended an escaping offender.
>
> Source: Adapted from *FBI Law Enforcement Bulletin*, June 1996, p. 33.

In the 1960s African-Americans and other civil rights demonstrators participated in freedom marches throughout the United States, particularly in the South. Because the police are the enforcement arm of government, they were used to enforce existing laws, which in many cases meant arresting and inhibiting the freedom of those marching for equality.

In 1960, the Freedom Riders left Washington, D.C., by bus to confront segregation throughout the South. The buses and protesters were harassed and were temporarily halted and attacked by violent white mobs in Anniston and Birmingham, Alabama. The police were again used to inhibit these marches for equality.

During the 1960s, the Reverend Martin Luther King, Jr., was at the forefront of the civil rights marches. In 1962, there were mass arrests of civil rights demonstrators in Albany, Georgia. Also in 1962, James Meredith became the first African-American to enroll at the University of Mississippi. President John F. Kennedy was forced to send U.S. marshals and the armed forces into Mississippi to protect Meredith against attacks by segregationists, because the local police were unable or unwilling to protect him.

In 1963, Dr. King led 25,000 demonstrators on a historic march on Washington that culminated in his "I have a dream" speech. During this speech, a defining moment of the movement, a white uniformed police officer stood behind King in a highly visible position, perhaps as a symbolic representation of the new role of the police in America's social history. Officers were to act as defenders rather than oppressors.

Also in 1963, in Birmingham, Alabama, four African-American girls were killed when a bomb exploded during a church service at the 16th Street Baptist Church.[27] In the same year, King led a peaceful march against segregation in Birmingham, Alabama, while Birmingham's sheriff Bull Connor unleashed hoses and police dogs against the demonstrators. The actions of police personnel like Bull Connor caused the police much negative press and has affected police–minority group relationships ever since.

In 1964, the Student Non-Violent Coordinating Committee (SNCC) launched the Mississippi Freedom Summer Project as thousands of students from northern campuses flocked to Mississippi for the summer voter registration drive, attempting to get African-Americans to register to vote. During that summer, three civil rights volunteers were brutally murdered in Philadelphia, Mississippi.

In 1965, African-Americans and other civil rights demonstrators attempted a peaceful march to Selma, Alabama. During the march, Alabama state police stopped the marchers at the Edmund Petus Bridge in Selma, where a Boston minister was murdered and many others were beaten by white toughs. A massive civil rights march then proceeded from Selma to Montgomery, Alabama, under the protection of the National Guard.

In 1966, activist Stokely Carmichael was elected chair of the SNCC and coined the term black power. In the same year, James Meredith, the first African-American student at the University of Mississippi, began a solitary March against Fear through Mississippi and was wounded by a sniper. African-American leaders continued Meredith's march using the slogan "Black Power." The "Black Power" slogan began to symbolize the movement toward equality for some African-Americans. Also in 1966, King led an antidiscrimination march in Chicago and was stoned by a hostile crowd.

The civil rights movement continued and succeeded in part by enrolling more minorities as voters, outlawing forms of government-sanctioned segregation, and ensuring that more minorities participated in government. Today, many of our large-city mayors and politicians are members of minority groups.

Although the civil rights movement was necessary in the evolution of our nation, the use of the police by government officials to thwart the movement left a wound in police-community relations that has still not healed. The 1991 beating of Rodney King in Los Angeles and the 1992 jury verdict acquitting the four Los Angeles police officers who where charged in King's beating (described later) angered people across the United States. The resultant riots in Los Angeles and other cities seemed to bring the United States back to the same strained racial conditions that existed in the 1960s.

Assassinations In the 1960s three of the most respected leaders in the United States were assassinated: President John F. Kennedy in 1963 in Dallas; his brother Robert Kennedy in 1968 in Los Angeles; and the Reverend Martin Luther King, Jr., also in 1968 in Memphis. These assassinations clearly reflected the turbulence of the decade.

Many say that the person who assassinated President Kennedy as he rode in a Dallas motorcade is still unknown. Lee Harvey Oswald was captured and charged with Kennedy's murder after shooting and killing a Dallas police officer, J. D. Tippett, an hour after the president was killed. Several days later, Oswald himself was shot and killed by Jack Ruby as Oswald was being led out of a Dallas police station. The debate over these incidents in Dallas continues today.

Anti–Vietnam War Demonstrations The Vietnam War was another turbulent, heartrending experience in American history, and again the police were used in a manner that tarnished their image. There were numerous and violent confrontations between opponents of the Vietnam War and the government's representatives—the police—on college campuses and city streets.

In 1967, hundreds of thousands of people using civil disobedience tactics marched in antiwar demonstrations in New York City, Washington, D. C., San Francisco, and numerous other cities around the nation, often clashing with the police, whose job it was to enforce the law and maintain order.

At the Democratic party presidential convention in Chicago in 1968, police-citizen violence occurred that shocked the nation and the world. With information that 10,000 protesters organized by antiwar groups, including the Youth International Party (Yippies), were coming to Chicago for the 1968 National Democratic Convention, Chicago's mayor, Richard J. Daley, mobilized the National Guard and the Chicago police. On August 28, the protesters attempted to force their way into the convention. Police and the National Guard chased the crowd through downtown Chicago. Many report that the police command structure broke down and that the police became a mob that ran through the streets and assaulted protesters, reporters, and bystanders. A study subsequent to the convention, the Walker Report, called the actions of the police a police riot.

There are many different viewpoints of the chaotic disturbances that occurred on the U.S. streets during this period. What some perceived as a police riot others perceived as the police doing their job. Many stress that the Yippies and other protesters were attempting to break up a lawfully gathered assembly by illegal means.

Eight members of the Yippies were charged with conspiracy for starting the disturbances in Chicago and were dubbed the "Chicago Eight." In 1969, the Chicago Eight trial began (it was later called the Chicago Seven trial due to the severance from the trial of Bobby Seales, the co-founder of the Black Panther Party). A Students for a Democratic Society (SDS) splinter group, the Weathermen, organized the Days of Rage in Chicago, which resulted in violent rampaging in the streets and more confrontation with the police. In 1970, all of the Chicago Eight were acquitted of conspiracy charges; convictions on lesser charges were later overturned as well.

Campus Disorders In addition to the civil rights movement of the 1960s, demonstrations, marches, and civil disobedience also took place on college campuses across the nation. These events protested a perceived lack of academic freedom, the Vietnam War, the presence of Reserve Officers' Training Corps (ROTC) units on campuses, and many other issues. Again, the police were used to enforce the law.

In 1960, the SNCC was organized to coordinate student civil rights protests. In 1961, the SDS held its first national convention in Port Huron, Michigan. These two groups had a tremendous impact on the 1960s. Teach-ins, rallies, student strikes, takeovers of campus buildings, and the burning of draft cards were some of the tactics used on the campuses.

The protests on the campuses caused college administrators to call in local police departments to maintain order. That, in turn, caused students to complain about the actions of the police. Again, the police became the focus of anger and attention.

In 1968, a state of civil disorder was declared in Berkeley, California, following recurring police-student confrontations. Protests, riots, and violent clashes be-

Dempsey's Law

What a Difference Eighteen Years Makes

In 1968, I was at Columbia University in Morningside Heights, New York City. I was not a student. I was a cop. My job: evict protesting students from the college buildings. I was doing my job, earning a paycheck.

For several nights, I was spit at and called a pig. I listened to chants calling my mother, and other cops' mothers, obscenities and had bags of human waste thrown at me.

In 1986, eighteen years later, I was at Harvard University, as a student. One day, in a large auditorium at the Kennedy School of Government, a woman started a conversation with me.

Hi, my name is Ardyth, I'm from Boise, Idaho.

Hi, I'm Jack, I'm from New York.

I never would have known that, with that accent! I went to school in New York, for a year.

Oh, where?

Barnard College.

Barnard College? That was the women's school at Columbia, right? [Would you believe that in those years, Columbia had different colleges for men and women?]

Yes.

What year did you go there?

1968.

1968! I was there, then, too.

What was your major?

No, I wasn't a student, I was a cop.

Were you the _____ _____ cop who threw me into the rose bushes and made my arm bleed?

Were you the girl who threw the bag of _____ at me?

During the year at Harvard, Ardyth and I became friends and discussed the sixties often. It was interesting. Now she seemed to understand the role of the cops back then, and now I seemed to understand why the kids were protesting. Isn't it interesting how smart we can get in eighteen years?

---

tween students and the police replaced education on many college campuses in the United States.

Probably the most widely publicized campus protest of the 1960s was the student takeover at Columbia University, in New York City, in the spring of 1968. Students employed every tactic that had been used in earlier campus protests, including teach-ins, rallies, picketing, sit-ins, a student strike, and the takeover of university buildings. As negotiations between the college administration and the student rebels broke down, the administration decided to call in the police.

In the early morning of April 30, 1968, after students had taken over many college buildings, 2,000 police officers moved onto the campus and methodically cleared five occupied buildings. The effort to clear the remaining buildings became violent. Finally, the police were able to secure all buildings by arresting 692 students. In late May, the students again took over two buildings on Columbia's campus. The administration again called the police. The Cox Commission, formed to investigate the violence at Columbia University, reported on the police action that followed:

Hell broke loose. One hundred students locked arms behind the barricades at Amsterdam Avenue. Hundreds more crowded close to the gate. The police swiftly dismantled the obstruction. The hundred broke and ran. But 2,000 students live in dormitories facing South Field. Many of them and hundreds of other people were crowded on the campus. For most, the character of the police action was a profound shock; neither they nor others in the Columbia community appreciated the extent of the violence which is the probable concomitant of massive police action against hundreds, if not thousands, of angry students. As police advanced, most students fled. . . . Some police first warned the students; others chased and clubbed them indiscriminately. But not all students went to their dormitories and some who fled came back out to attack the police. Bottles and bricks were hurled by students. A number of police were injured. The action grew fierce. . . . By 5:30 A.M. the campus was secured.[28]

The campus antiwar riots reached their height in 1970. The firebombing of a University of Wisconsin ROTC building began a wave of some 500 bombings or arsons on college campuses. Students rampaged through Cambridge's Harvard Yard; two students were

Police standing guard at Columbia University student takeover in 1968.

killed and nine wounded by police gunfire at Jackson State College in Mississippi; and four students were killed by the National Guard at a protest at Kent State University, causing many U.S. colleges and universities to close for the year. Again, clashes between the police and students caused wounds that were hard to cure.

Urban Riots Major riots erupted in the ghettos of many U.S. cities during the 1960s. Most started directly following a police action. This is not to say that the riots were the result of the police; rather, a police action brought to the surface numerous underlying problems, which many say were the actual causes of the riots.

In the summer of 1964, an off-duty white New York City police lieutenant shot an African-American youth who was threatening a building superintendent with a knife. This shooting precipitated the 1964 Harlem riot. Riots also occurred that summer in Rochester, Jersey City, and Philadelphia. In 1965, riots occurred in Los Angeles (the Watts district), San Diego, and Chicago. In 1966, riots again occurred in Watts, as well as in Cleveland, Brooklyn, and Chicago. In 1967, major riots occurred in Boston's Roxbury section, in Newark, and in Detroit.

The riot in Detroit was responsible for forty-three deaths, 2,000 injuries, and property damage estimated at over $200 million; 7,000 persons were arrested. The Watts riot was responsible for the deaths of thirty-four people, over 1,000 injuries, and the arrests of nearly 4,000 people. The Newark riot was responsible for twenty-six deaths and 1,500 injuries.

In 1968, riots occurred in cities all over the United States—including Baltimore, Boston, Chicago, Detroit, Kansas City, Newark, New York City, Washington, D.C., and scores of other cities—in the wake of the murder of the Reverend Martin Luther King Jr. The worst riot occurred in Washington, D.C., with twelve people killed, 1,200 injured, and 7,600 people arrested and

YOU ARE THERE! »

The Urban Riots

1964	Harlem (New York City), Rochester, Jersey City, Philadelphia
1965	Watts (Los Angeles), San Diego, Chicago
1966	Watts; Cleveland; Brooklyn, the Bronx, and the Barrio (New York City); Chicago
1967	Roxbury (Boston), Newark, Detroit
1968	Washington, D.C., and much of the urban United States

Dempsey's Law

It Was a Tough Time to Be a Cop
It Was a Tough Time to Be a Cop's Spouse

I was married in 1967. My wife, Marianne, was expecting our first child in either March, April, or May of 1968. On April 4, 1968, my day off, we went to see the obstetrician, on the Grand Concourse in the Bronx. It was about 4:45 p.m., and we heard on the radio in the doctor's waiting room that the Reverend Martin Luther King, Jr., had been assassinated in Memphis.

I said to Marianne, "I want to be around to help you when the baby comes. Have the baby right now, or you have to wait a couple of weeks, because America is going to burn and I won't have much time off."

I was called in for riot duty that night and worked 12-hour tours without a day off for two weeks. Marianne, the tough spouse that all cops need, held on until the riots were over. Our first child, a ten-pound boy, John Daniel, was born on April 19, 1968.

John Daniel's first child, a ten-pound, two-ounce boy, Daniel Joseph, was born on October 24, 1992. John Daniel did see the 1992 Los Angeles riot. It is my hope that Daniel Joseph never has to see a riot.

---

nearly $25 million in property damage. Nationwide, 55,000 federal troops and National Guards members were called out. Forty-six deaths resulted from the riots, and 21,270 people were arrested.

Again, the efforts of the police to maintain order during these massive shows of civil disobedience and violence caused wounds in police-community relations that have yet to heal. Problems between the minority communities and the police continued, as did the riots. Several radical groups, including the Black Panther party and the Black Liberation Army, waged urban warfare against the police, resulting in many deaths among their members and the police.

Creation of National Commissions In the wake of the problems of the 1960s, particularly the problems between the police and citizens, three national commissions were created. The first was the **President's Commission on Law Enforcement and Administration of Justice**, which issued a report in 1967 entitled *The Challenge of Crime in a Free Society* and a collection of *Task Force Reports* covering all aspects of the criminal justice system.

The second national commission was the National Advisory Commission on Civil Disorders (Kerner Commission), which released a report in 1968 that decried white racism and a rapidly polarizing society. The report stated, "Our nation is moving toward two societies, one black, one white, separate and unequal." The commission concluded that "abrasive relationships between police and Negroes and other minority groups, have been a major source of grievance, tension, and, ultimately, disorder."[29]

The third was the President's Commission on Campus Unrest. Its report, issued in 1970, called the gap between youth culture and mainstream society a threat to U.S. stability. These commissions are mentioned often in this text.

Corruption The corruption that has historically permeated American policing in the past has continued into the present. Approximately every twenty years, the nation's largest and most visible police department, the New York Police Department (NYPD), has been the subject of a major scandal involving police corruption: the Seabury Hearings in the 1930s, the Gross Hearings in the 1950s, and the Knapp Commission in 1970.

The Knapp Commission resulted from allegations made by New York City plainclothes police officer Frank Serpico and New York City police sergeant David Durk. Serpico was a Bronx plainclothes police officer (assigned to enforce antigambling laws) who was aware of widespread graft and bribe receiving in his unit. He took his tales of corruption to major police department officials, including the second highest ranking officer in the department; to the city's Department of Investigation; and eventually even to the mayor's office. When Serpico finally realized that no one was taking his claims seriously, he and Durk went to a *New York Times*

Police History 23

> ## Dempsey's Law
>
> ### Thank You, LEEP
>
> I started college in 1964 as a full-time student. However, finances forced me to leave school and work full time. In 1965, having been fortunate enough to obtain a position as a New York City police trainee, I applied for admission to the City University of New York and was accepted. My college was called the College of Police Science (now the John Jay College of Criminal Justice). My entire four-year college degree, which took me ten years to complete, was paid for by the Law Enforcement Education Program (LEEP). My first graduate degree, from Long Island University, was also paid for by LEEP. My second masters degree, from Harvard, was supported in part by New York City and the New York City Police Foundation.

reporter, who wrote a series of stories about corruption in the department that shocked the public. The *Times* articles forced the mayor, John Lindsey, to appoint a commission to investigate police corruption, which popularly became known as the Knapp Commission. Chapter 12 will focus on the Knapp Commission and police corruption and misconduct. The revelations of the Knapp Commission regarding widespread, systemic, organized corruption in the NYPD led to sweeping changes in the department's organization, philosophy, operations, and procedures.

Police Research The decades of the 1960s and 1970s saw tremendous research into policing, which brought about sweeping changes in thinking about how police work is done in the United States. One of the most significant developments in modernizing and professionalizing the police was the creation of the Law Enforcement Assistance Administration (LEAA) within the U.S. Department of Justice through Title 1 of the Omnibus Crime Control and Safe Streets Act of 1968. The LEAA spent over $60 million in its first year alone, and between 1969 and 1980 it spent over $8 billion to support criminal justice research, education, and training.

LEAA required each state to create its own criminal justice planning agency, which in turn was required to establish an annual, comprehensive, statewide criminal justice plan to distribute LEAA funds throughout the state. One of LEAA's primary benefits to police officers was its Law Enforcement Education Program (LEEP), which provided funds for the college education of police officers.

An independent organization, the Police Foundation, joined LEAA as a funding source for research on innovative police projects. The most significant of these projects were the Kansas City Preventive Patrol Experiment, the Rand Corporation's study of the criminal investigation process, the Police Foundation's study of team policing, and the Newark Foot Patrol Experiment. These innovative studies began to change the way we thought about policing in the United States.

As we will see later, traditional policing involved three major strategies: (1) routine random patrol, (2) rapid response to calls by citizens to 911, and (3) retroactive investigation of past crimes by detectives. Academic research, starting in the 1960s and 1970s and continuing to this day, has indicated that these three strategies have not worked. This research has led police administrators to implement the innovative approaches to policing that will be discussed in this text.

Policing in the 1980s and 1990s

The tremendous turmoil that permeated society and policing during the decades of the 1960s and 1970s gave way to somewhat more peaceful times in the 1980s and 1990s. The police, as always, were confronted by a myriad of issues and events that severely tested their professionalism and ability. Prominent among those events were terrorist bombings of New York City's World Trade Center and the Federal Building in Oklahoma City, Oklahoma. In these cases, police agencies from all over the nation performed numerous heroic and successful actions that saved lives and resulted in the eventual criminal prosecution of the offenders.

Police officer pushing back crowds moments after the bombing of the Alfred P. Murrah Federal Building in Oklahoma City in 1995.

Some of the many positive developments of the 1980s and 1990s included the development of a computer revolution in policing involving communications, record keeping, fingerprinting, and criminal investigations; a drastic reduction in violent crime; and the birth of two major new concepts of police work: community policing and problem-solving policing. Community policing and problem-solving policing can be seen either as new approaches to policing or as a return to the policing of the past—the cop on the beat. Chapter 10 of this text covers these concepts. The computer and technology revolution in policing is covered in chapter 14.

Some believe that the highlight of recent developments in policing is the significant crime reductions that occurred throughout the nation in the late twentieth century. In 1997, the FBI reported that serious crime for 1996 had declined 3 percent, the fifth annual decrease in a row since 1992. Violent crime, including homicide, robbery, rape, and aggravated assault, dropped 7 percent from the previous year. This decrease in violent crime was the largest in 36 years. The homicide rate was the lowest it had been nationwide since 1969.[30]

Some criminologists attributed this decline to a series of factors, including community policing, problem-solving policing, and aggressive zero-tolerance policing. Other factors mentioned were increased jail and prison populations; demographic changes in the numbers of crime-prone young people; and community efforts against crime.

The explanation, however, that has gained the most popularity among some law enforcement officials, politicians, and criminologists is that the reduced crime rates are the result of aggressive police tactics like those introduced in New York City by its former commissioner William J. Bratton. Bratton completely reengineered the NYPD to make reducing crime its primary objective.[31] The keynote behind Bratton's reengineering was a process known as **Compstat**.[32]

Compstat was originally a document, referred to as the "Compstat book," which included current year-to-date statistics for criminal complaints and arrests developed from a computer file called Compare Stats—hence Compstat. Central to Compstat are the semi-weekly crime-strategy sessions conducted at police headquarters. At each Compstat meeting, sophisticated computer-generated maps addressing a seemingly unlimited variety of the latest crime details confront and challenge the precinct commanders. The commanders are held responsible for any increases in crime and must present innovative solutions to address their precincts' crime problems. In these sessions, crime-fighting techniques are developed and expected to be implemented. The four-step process that is the essence of Compstat is

- timely and accurate intelligence;
- use of effective tactics in response to that intelligence;
- rapid deployment of personnel and resources; and,
- relentless follow-up and assessment.

One writer summed up the essence of NYPD's new policing strategy as follows:

> The multifaceted Compstat process is perhaps best known to law enforcement insiders for its high-stress, semiweekly debriefing and brain-storming sessions at police headquarters, but it is far more. . . . Compstat is enabling the NYPD to pinpoint and analyze crime patterns almost instantly, respond in the most appropriate manner, quickly shift personnel and other resources as needed, assess the impact and viability of anti-crime strategies, identify bright, up-and-coming individuals from deep within the ranks, and

transform the organization more fluidly and more effectively than one would ever expect of such a huge police agency.[33]

Only history will tell if the crime reductions of the mid-1990s can continue, and no one can attribute them solely to the police, but Bratton seems convinced: "We've changed course, and the course will be changed for all time."[34]

Despite all the successes of the police in the 1980s and 1990s, many of the problems of earlier decades carried over into this time. Some of the negative issues and problems confronting the police in our generation were the continuing debate over misconduct by the police and the continuing occurrence of riots in our communities.

The endemic corruption that has always characterized U.S. policing seemed to have subsided somewhat during the 1980s and 1990s, although there were sporadic corruption scandals. The most noticeable of these included the Miami River Cops scandal of the 1980s, involving murders, extortions, and drug violations, and New York City's 77th and 32nd Precincts and "Cocaine Cops" scandals, involving drug corruption. Many other police departments throughout the nation also suffered embarrassing corruption and misconduct scandals. Chapter 12 of this text covers this area in detail.

In 1991, the Rodney King incident in Los Angeles shocked the public and may have set the police back thirty years in the progress they had made in improving relationships with the community. A video camera captured on film the police beating of Rodney King, an African-American. King had taken the police on a 115-mile-per-hour chase throughout Los Angeles and, when finally stopped by the police, allegedly lunged at one of the officers. The videotape shows four Los Angeles police officers beating King with fifty-six blows from nightsticks while a dozen other officers stood by and watched. King seemed to be in a defenseless, prone position on the ground. Four of the officers were arrested and charged with the assault of King. They were originally acquitted in a criminal trial but were subsequently convicted in a federal trial.

The Rodney King incident was followed in 1997 with allegations that at least two police officers from New York City's 70th Precinct assaulted a Haitian-American prisoner, Abner Louima, by placing a wooden stick into his rectum and then shoving the blood- and feces-covered stick into his mouth. This incident shocked the world as the King incident did.[35]

In 1994, a criminal trial also brought negative attention to the police. Former football star Orenthal James (O.J.) Simpson was charged by the Los Angeles police with the brutal murder of his former wife, Nicole Brown, and her friend Ronald Goldman. The trial was covered on national television and captured the attention of the world. Two hundred and fifty days and 126 witnesses later, the jury, despite overwhelming scientific evidence to the contrary, voted to acquit Simpson of all charges. Many said the verdict was jury nullification; others said it was an indictment of the Los Angeles Police Department. The LAPD was accused of gross incompetence in its handling of the crime scene and forensic evidence, and one of its main witnesses, Detective Mark Fuhrman, later pled guilty to charges that he had lied while testifying in the trial.

In 1997, the Justice Department's inspector general reported that the FBI's renowned crime laboratory was riddled with flawed scientific practices that had potentially tainted dozens of criminal cases, including the bombings of the Federal Building in Oklahoma City and the World Trade Center in New York. The inspector general's findings resulted from an eighteen-month investigation that uncovered extremely serious and significant problems at the laboratory that had been a symbol of the FBI's cutting-edge scientific sleuthing.[36] The dramatic series of problems associated with the FBI and their alleged bungling of scientific evidence and criminal investigations led the national magazine *Time* to produce a cover article entitled, "What's Wrong at the FBI: The Fiasco at the Crime Lab."[37]

Riots again scarred our sense of domestic tranquility. The city of Miami experienced two major riots in its Overtown district in the 1980s. New York City experienced riots in the 1990s in Crown Heights and Washington Heights. Many other cities witnessed racial and civil unrest and skirmishes between the police and citizens.

Perhaps the worst riot in our nation's history occurred in 1992 in the wake of the not-guilty verdicts against the officers in the Rodney King case. The riot began in Los Angeles and spread to other parts of the country. By the second day of the riot, at least twenty-three people had been killed, 900 injured, and 500 arrested. Hundreds of buildings burned as the violence spread from south-central Los Angeles to other areas. Entire inner-city blocks lay in ruin. The riot quickly spread to Atlanta, San Francisco, Madison, and other cities. Fighting between African-Americans and whites

YOU ARE THERE!

The Nicole Brown Simpson and Ronald Goldman Murder Case

On Sunday, June 12, 1994, somewhere between the hours of 10:00 P.M. and 11:00 P.M., Nicole Brown Simpson (the ex-wife of former football star Orenthal James [O.J.] Simpson) and a male acquaintance, Ronald Goldman, were brutally murdered in front of Nicole's expensive town house in Brentwood, California.

Investigation by the Los Angeles Police Department revealed that Nicole and O.J. had attended a dance recital that day in West L.A., which they left at approximately 6:00 P.M. At approximately 6:30 P.M., Nicole, her two children, and other family members and friends dined at the trendy Mezzaluna Trattoria restaurant in Brentwood. O.J. was not invited to the dinner. At approximately 8:30 P.M. Nicole and her party left the restaurant, and Nicole returned home with her children. Later, she received a call from her mother stating that she might have left her eyeglasses at the restaurant. Nicole called the restaurant and was told the eyeglasses were located. Her friend, Ronald Goldman, a waiter at the restaurant, offered to bring the glasses to Nicole's home after he was off duty at the restaurant. At approximately 9:45 P.M. Goldman left the restaurant. At approximately midnight on June 12 the dead bodies of Nicole Simpson and Ronald Goldman were found by neighbors.

Detectives investigating the murder left the murder scene and responded to O.J. Simpson's $5-million mansion several miles away, also in Brentwood. While attempting to notify Simpson regarding the murder of his former wife, the detectives received no answer at his gate and then observed blood on the left door of Simpson's white Ford Bronco, which was parked outside the house. The detectives, fearing that there could be further injuries inside the Simpson property, entered the property without a search warrant and began to interview people residing there. While inside the property the detectives found evidence, including blood stains and a bloody glove that matched a bloody glove found at the murder scene.

At approximately 10:45 P.M., on the night of the murder, O.J. Simpson traveled from his residence to Los Angeles International Airport, where he boarded a flight to Chicago. At approximately 5:34 A.M., June 13, 1994, he arrived in Chicago and checked into a room at the O'Hare Plaza Hotel, where he had made reservations days earlier. That morning the police telephoned Simpson at his hotel room and notified him of his ex-wife's murder. He then flew back to Los Angeles. At approximately noon on Monday, Simpson was taken to L.A. police headquarters for several hours of questioning and then released.

During the week that followed there was intense media attention to the case, including reports of spousal abuse by Simpson against his ex-wife. These reports covered a 1988 arrest of Simpson for spousal abuse and a 1993 911 tape recording of a frantic call to the police by Nicole Brown Simpson with the angry voice of Simpson in the background.

On Friday, June 17, 1994, at 8:30 A.M. the LAPD called Simpson's attorney Robert Shapiro, saying they were ready to arrest Simpson for the murder of his ex-wife and Mr. Goldman. Shapiro reported that he would bring Simpson to police headquarters. At approximately 2:00 P.M., police reported that Simpson had not surrendered and was being considered a fugitive. At approximately 5:00 P.M., the police, responding to a citizen's tip, pinpointed Simpson as a passenger in his friend Al (A.C.) Cowlings' Ford Bronco, which was being driven on L.A. freeways. The police then proceeded on a nearly fifty-mile "low-speed pursuit" of Cowlings' car. During the pursuit, Simpson called 911 from the car cellular phone, stated he was armed, threatened to kill himself, and asked to talk to his mother. At approximately 8:00 P.M., Cowlings' car entered Simpson's property. After about forty-five minutes of hostage negotiations, police persuaded Simpson to leave the car and enter his house. After being searched, Simpson was allowed to call his mother, use the bathroom, and drink a glass of orange juice. The low-speed pursuit and negotiations were watched by approximately 90 million Americans on live television.

A six-day preliminary hearing held in late June and early July resulted in O.J. Simpson being bound over for a murder trial.

---

was reported at high schools in Maryland, Tennessee, Texas, and New York.

By the end of the second day, over 4,000 National Guard troops had entered Los Angeles, as well as over 500 U.S. Marines. Less than a week after the riot started, calm began to appear. The final toll of the Los Angeles riot revealed that 54 people were killed; 2,383 people were injured; 5,200 buildings, mostly businesses, were destroyed by arson; and over $1 billion in property damage occurred. The riot resulted in the loss of approximately 40,000 jobs. Almost 17,000 arrests were made.

Entire city blocks were burned out in the Los Angeles riot of 1992.

Beverly Hills, shouting, brandishing hatchets, crowbars and bottles, beating passersby and looting shops.

As night fell, what had been scattered pillars of smoke broadened to become a huge black cloud reminiscent of the burning oil wells of Kuwait during the Persian Gulf war.[38]

A special commission under the direction of William H. Webster (the former director of both the Federal Bureau of Investigation and the Central Intelligence Agency), created to study the causes of the Los Angeles riots, issued a report highly critical of the Los Angeles Police Department.[39]

Chapter Summary

This chapter covered over 2,000 years of recorded history in its discussion of the history of policing, and it concentrated on the past three centuries in England and the United States. The concept of preserving the peace and enforcing the law has moved from primitive forms like the watch and ward to highly organized, professional police departments. The history of policing has included brutality, corruption, incompetence, innovation, research, heroism, and professionalism.

Academic interest in policing began in earnest in the 1960s with programs in police science, which later were expanded to include the entire criminal justice system and renamed criminal justice programs. Courses similar to the one for which you are using this text were offered. Much of the impetus for these programs came from recommendations made by commissions investigating criminal justice agencies and violence in the United States. Many of the recommendations of these commissions have been implemented by governments and police agencies. Billions of dollars have been spent in an attempt to ameliorate the inequalities that were seen as the underlying problems that caused the violence and disorder of the 1960s. Police departments have been totally revamped since those days. Human relations training has been implemented. Better recruitment efforts and hiring practices have made police departments more reflective of the communities they serve. Community relations units and numerous programs have been in effect for three decades, attempting to improve relationships between the police and the community. Community policing and problem-oriented policing are being implemented throughout the United States to build relationships and partnerships between

The following is a vivid newspaper description of the events of the first days of the riot:

The violence in Los Angeles jumped a boundary from the South-Central area today, bringing racial conflict for the first time into the insulated, mostly white areas of West Los Angeles and Beverly Hills. Shops were looted and burned in Hollywood and nearby Santa Monica. A gunfight broke out this afternoon between Korean merchants and a group of black men in the Korea-town section, a sharp escalation in the tensions that have divided the groups in recent months. Tall plumes of smoke rose from burning shops in the neighborhood, just north of South-Central.

As fires, police sirens and pockets of violence spread, most of the city shut down, with offices and shops closing and public transport scaling back its operations early. As the guard members were taking up positions in the badly battered South-Central area, convoys of cars carrying young men headed out into affluent West Los Angeles and the police and the communities they serve, as well as to maintain order and fight crime.

Policing has changed dramatically since I first put on a police uniform in 1964. Great progress has been made in policing over the years, and the profession is much better today than it was—more technically sophisticated and professional. Certainly, the Rodney King and Abner Louima incidents have hurt the image of policing. Much will be said of these incidents in the rest of this text. Those of us who police our nation, or aspire to police it, cannot erase these incidents and the image they presented of our police to the world. What we can do, what we must do, and what we will do is accept that they happened while still regretting them and continue with the progress we have just read about. We must hope that by our study and by our example, incidents like these will not occur again.

Learning Check

1. Discuss the primary means of ensuring personal safety prior to the establishment of formal, organized police departments.
2. Talk about the influence of the English police experience on American policing.
3. Compare and contrast the urban and frontier experiences in eighteenth- and nineteenth-century U.S. policing.
4. Identify at least four people instrumental in the development of twentieth-century U.S. policing, and list some of their accomplishments.
5. Explain how the turbulent times of the 1960s and the early 1970s affected U.S. policing.

Review Exercise

As part of an honors program at your college, the chair of the social science division has nominated you to represent the Criminal Justice Department in a twentieth-century time capsule project. She is asking all departments to contribute material to be placed in a sealed, weatherproof container that will be buried on the campus grounds. The capsule will be opened on January 1, 2101.

The chair asks you to include at least ten simulated, representative documents or artifacts that reflect your study of the U.S. criminal justice system for the years 1900 to the present. What would you include?

Web Exercise

As part of your school's "Dawning of the New Millennium" conference, you have been asked by your department chair to represent the criminal justice department and present a brief history of your local police department. He asks that you gather your information from the World Wide Web and be prepared to give a twenty-minute oral presentation on it. If your local department is not on the web, find one close by, possibly your state's State Police.

Key Concepts

mutual pledge
hue and cry
shire-reeve
watch and ward
thief-takers
Henry Fielding
Patrick Colquhoun
Sir Robert Peel
posse comitatus
Volstead Act (National Prohibition)—
    Eighteenth Amendment
Wickersham Commission
Pendleton Act
August Vollmer
O. W. Wilson
J. Edgar Hoover
President's Commission on Law Enforcement
    and Administration of Justice
Compstat

Notes

1. John Ayto, *Dictionary of Word Origins* (New York: Arcade, 1990), p. 402.
2. Excesses by the military in enforcing the law in the American West led to the Posse Comitatus Act of 1879. See the discussion of the frontier experience later in the chapter.
3. The section on early policing is based on the following: William G. Bailey, ed., *The Encyclopedia of Police Science* (New York: Garland, 1989); John J. Fay, *The Police Dictionary and Encyclopedia* (Springfield, Ill.: Charles C. Thomas, 1988); Sanford H. Kadish, *Encyclopedia of Crime and Justice* (New York: Free Press, 1983); George Thomas Kurian, *World Encyclopedia of Police Forces and Penal Systems* (New York: Facts on File, 1989); Jay Robert Nash, *Encyclopedia of World Crime* (Wilmette, Ill.: Crime Books, 1990); and Charles Reith, *The Blind Eye of History: A Study of the Origins of the Present Police Era* (London: Faber, 1912).
4. "The word [vigilante] comes from the Latin vigilia, which was derived from the adjective vigil, meaning 'awake, alert.' Another derivative of the Latin adjective was vigilare, meaning 'keep watch,' which lies behind the English reveille, surveillance, and vigilant." Ayto, *Dictionary of Word Origins*, p. 559.

5. The section on the English roots of policing is based on the following: S. G. Chapman and T. E. St. Johnston, *The Police Heritage in England and America* (East Lansing, Mich.: Michigan State University, 1962); T. A. Critchley, *A History of Police in England and Wales,* 2d ed. rev. (Montclair, N.J.: Patterson Smith, 1972); Clive Emsley, *Policing and Its Context, 1750–1870* (New York: Schocken, 1984); A. C. Germann, Frank D. Day, and Robert R. J. Gallati, *Introduction to Law Enforcement and Criminal Justice* (Springfield, Ill.: Charles C. Thomas, 1969); W. E. Hunt, *History of England* (New York: Harper & Brothers, 1938); Luke Owen Pike, *A History of Crime in England* (London: Smith, Elder, 1873–1876); Patrick Pringle, *Highwaymen* (New York: Roy, 1963); Pringle, *Hue and Cry: The Story of Henry and John Fielding and Their Bow Street Runners* (New York: Morrow, 1965); Pringle, *The Thief Takers* (London: Museum Press, 1958); Reith, *Blind Eye of History;* Thomas Reppetto, *The Blue Parade* (New York: Free Press, 1978); Albert Rieck, *Justice and Police in England* (London: Butterworth, 1936); Robert Sheehan and Gary W. Cordner, *Introduction to Police Administration,* 2d ed. (Cincinnati: Anderson Publishing Co., 1989); and John J. Tobias, *Crime and Police in England, 1700–1900* (New York: St. Martin's Press, 1979).
6. Pringle, *Hue and Cry,* p. 81.
7. Germann, Day, and Gallati, *Introduction to Law Enforcement and Criminal Justice,* pp. 54–55, as cited in Sheehan and Cordner, *Introduction to Police Administration,* p. 5.
8. The sections on American colonial and eighteenth- and nineteenth-century policing are based on the following: Bailey, *Encyclopedia of Police Science;* Carl Bridenbaugh, *Cities in Revolt: Urban Life in America, 1743–1776* (New York: Knopf, 1965); Bridenbaugh, *Cities in the Wilderness: Urban Life in America, 1625–1742* (New York: Capricorn, 1964); Emsley, *Policing and Its Context;* Robert M. Fogelson, *Big City Police* (Cambridge, Mass.: Harvard University Press, 1977); Roger Lane, *Policing the City, Boston 1822–1885* (Cambridge, Mass.: Harvard University Press, 1967); Eric Monkkonen, *Police in Urban America: 1860–1920* (Cambridge, Mass.: Harvard University Press, 1981); Reppetto, *Blue Parade;* James F. Richardson, *The New York Police: Colonial Times to 1901* (New York: Oxford University Press, 1976); Richardson, *Urban Police in the United States* (Port Washington, N.Y.: Kennikat Press, 1974); Samuel Walker, *A Critical History of Police Reform: The Emergence of Professionalism* (Lexington, Mass.: Lexington Books, 1977); and Walker, *Popular Justice: History of American Criminal Justice* (New York: Oxford University Press, 1980).
9. Richardson, *New York Police,* p. 10.
10. Commercial Advisor, 20 August 1840, as cited in Richardson, *New York Police,* p. 31.
11. Cited in Richardson, *New York Police,* p. 31.
12. Walker, *Popular Justice,* p. 61.
13. Luc Sante, *Low Life: Lures and Snares of Old New York* (New York: Farrar, Straus & Giroux, 1991), p. 236.
14. Walker, *Popular Justice,* p. 61.
15. Fogelson, *Big City Police,* p. 25.
16. Richard A. Staufenberger, *Progress in Policing: Essays on Change* (Cambridge, Mass.: Ballinger Publishing, 1980), pp. 8–9.
17. Walker, *Popular Justice,* p. 63.
18. Lincoln Steffens, *The Autobiography of Lincoln Steffens* (New York: Harcourt Brace Jovanovich, 1958; originally published in 1931), p. 207.
19. The section on the frontier experience is based on the following: James D. Horan and Howard Swiggett, *The Pinkerton Story* (New York: Putnam, 1951); James D. Horan, *The Pinkertons: The Detective Dynasty That Made History* (New York: Crown, 1967); Edward Hungerford, *Wells Fargo: Advancing the American Frontier* (New York: Bonanza, 1949); David R. Johnson, *American Law Enforcement: A History* (St. Louis: Forum Press, 1981); Carolyn Lake, *Undercover for Wells Fargo* (Boston: Houghton Mifflin, 1969); Allan Pinkerton, *The Expressman and the Detective* (New York: Arno Press, 1976); Frank R. Prassel, *The Western Peace Officer: A Legacy of Law and Order* (Norman, Okla.: University of Oklahoma Press, 1972); Charles A. Siringo, *A Cowboy Detective: A True Story of Twenty-Two Years with a World-Famous Detective Agency* (Lincoln, Neb.: University of Nebraska Press, 1988); Bruce Smith, *Police Systems in the United States* (New York: Harper & Row, 1960); Smith, *Rural Crime Control* (New York: Columbia University Institute of Public Administration, 1933); and Walter Prescott Webb, *The Texas Rangers: A Century of Frontier Defense* (Boston: Houghton Mifflin, 1935).
20. The section on twentieth-century policing is based on the following: Jay Stuart Berman, *Police Administration and Progressive Reform: Theodore Roosevelt as Police Commissioner of New York* (New York: Greenwood Press, 1987); William J. Bopp and Donald D. Schultz, *A Short History of American Law Enforcement* (Springfield, Ill.: Charles C. Thomas, 1977); Fogelson, *Big City Police;* Richard Kluger, *Simple Justice* (New York: Vintage, 1977); Roger Lane, *Policing the City* (New York: Atheneum, 1975); Doug McAdam, *Freedom Summer* (New York: Oxford University Press, 1988); Wilbur R. Miller, *Cops and Bobbies: Police Authority in New York and London, 1830–1870* (Chicago: University of Chicago Press, 1977); Monkkonen, *Police in Urban America;* Edward P. Morgan, *The 60's Experience: Hard Lessons about Modern America* (Philadelphia: Temple University Press, 1991); Albert J. Reiss, *The Police and the Public* (New Haven, Conn.: Yale University Press, 1971); Richardson, *Urban Police in the United States;* Jerome H. Skolnick, *Justice without Trial: Law Enforcement in a Democratic Society,* 2d ed. (New York: Wiley, 1975); Jerome H. Skolnick and David H. Bayley, *The New Blue Line* (New York: Free Press, 1986); Milton Viorst, *Fire in the Streets:*

America in the 1960's (New York: Simon & Schuster, 1970); Walker, *Popular Justice*; Walker, *Critical History of Police Reform*; Juan Williams, *Eyes on the Prize: America's Civil Rights Years, 1954–1965* (New York: Penguin, 1983); and James Q. Wilson, *Varieties of Police Behavior* (Cambridge, Mass.: Harvard University Press, 1968).

21. National Commission on Law Observance and Enforcement, *Lawlessness in Law Enforcement*, vol. 2 of the Wickersham Report (Washington, D.C.: U.S. Government Printing Office, 1931).

22. Johnson, *American Law Enforcement*, p. 121.

23. James Q. Wilson, *Thinking about Crime* (New York: Basic Books, 1983), p. 5.

24. *Mapp v. Ohio*, 367 US 643 (1961).

25. *Escobedo v. Illinois*, 378 US 478 (1964).

26. *Miranda v. Arizona*, 384 US 436 (1966).

27. This 1963 case was initially closed with the arrest of one man, Robert E. Chambliss, a member of the Ku Klux Klan, despite a variety of evidence at the time that he had at least three accomplices. He was convicted in 1977, fourteen years after the explosion. He died in prison in 1985, at the age of 81, having never admitted his guilt. The case was reopened in 1980 and 1988, but no prosecutions ever ensued. On July 10, 1997, Federal agents and the Birmingham police reported that they reopened the investigation once again. [Rick Bragg, "FBI Reopens Inquiry into Landmark Crime of the Civil Rights Era," *New York Times*, 11 July 1997, p. A-13].

28. Cox Commission, *Crisis at Columbia: Report of the Fact-Finding Commission Appointed to Investigate the Disturbances at Columbia University in April and May 1968* (New York: Vintage, 1968), pp. 181–182.

29. National Advisory Commission on Civil Disorders, *Report of the National Advisory Commission on Civil Disorders* (New York: Bantam Books, 1967), p. 299.

30. Federal Bureau of Investigation, *Uniform Crime Reports: Crime in the United States* (Washington, D.C.: Federal Bureau of Investigation); Fox Butterfield, "Homicides Plunge 11 Percent in U.S., FBI Report Says: 'A Stunningly Low' Rate," *New York Times*, 2 June 1997, p. A1, B10; Michael Cooper, "As New York Homicides Fall, Rate of Solved Cases Goes Up," *New York Times*, 2 June 1997, pp. B-1, B-3; Michael Cooper, "Crime Reports Drop Sharply in New York: Murder and Car Theft Leads Declines in 1997," *New York Times*, 1 April 1997, pp. B-1, B-9.

31. Peter C. Dodenhoff, "LEN Salutes Its 1996 People of the Year, the NYPD and Its Compstat Process: A Total Package of Re-engineering and Strategy-Making That Has Transformed the Nation's Largest Police Force—as It Will Law Enforcement in General," *Law Enforcement News*, 31 December 1996, pp. 1, 4; "There's No Going Back to Old Ways: Cities Vie to Board Compstat Bandwagon," *Law Enforcement News*, 31 December 1996, p. 5; "What's on the Grill? In New York, It's Police Commanders," *Law Enforcement News*, 31 December 1996, p. 5; Eli B. Silverman, "Mapping Change: How the New York City Police Department Re-engineered Itself to Drive Down Crime," *Law Enforcement News*, 15 December 1996, pp. 10–12.

32. Howard Safir, Police Commissioner, City of New York, *The Compstat Process* (New York: New York City Police Department, no date); William J. Bratton, Police Commissioner, City of New York, "Great Expectations: How Higher Expectations for Police Departments Can Lead to a Decrease in Crime," Paper presented at the National Institute of Justice Research Institute's "Measuring What Matters" Conference, Washington, D.C., 28 November 1995; Rudolph W. Guiliani, Randy M. Mastro, and Donna Lynne, *Mayor's Management Report: The City of New York* (New York: City of New York, 1997).

33. Peter C. Dodenhoff, "LEN Salutes Its 1996 People of the Year," p. 4.

34. "There's No Going Back to Old Ways," p. 5.

35. Dan Barry, "A Clean Sweep for a Stained Station House: Heads of 70th Precinct Get New Assignment," *New York Times*, 15 August 1997, p. A-1, 13; James Barron, "A Father Finds Charges Hard to Believe," *New York Times*, 15 August 1997, p. A-13; David Firestone, "A Police Case in the Context of Elector Politics: A Mayor Closely Tied to Police Successes Faces a Police Problem," *New York Times*, 15 August 1997, p. A-13; Dan Barry, "2d Police Officer Charged in Attack on Arrested Man: Colleague Gave Details," *New York Times*, 16 August 1997, pp. 1, 24.

36. David Johnston, "Report Criticizes Scientific Testing at FBI Lab: Serious Problems Cited," *New York Times*, 16 April 1997, pp. A-1, D-23; Mireya Navarro, "Doubts about FBI Lab Raise Hopes for Convict: On Death Row, but Seeking a New Trial," *New York Times*, 22 April 1997, p. A-8.

37. "What's Wrong at the FBI?: The Fiasco at the Crime Lab," *Time*, 28 April 1997, pp. 28–35.

38. Seth Mydans, "23 Dead after 2d Day of Los Angeles Riot; Fires & Looting Persists Despite Curfew," *New York Times*, 1 May 1992, pp. Al, A20.

39. Seth Mydans, "Ex-Police Chief Blamed for Riot in Los Angeles: Gates Call the Authors of the Report 'Liars,'" *New York Times*, 22 October 1992, p. A12.

2

Organizing Public and Private Security in the United States

Chapter Outline

The U.S. Public and Private Safety Industry
Local Law Enforcement
  Metropolitan Law Enforcement
  County Law Enforcement
  Rural and Small Town Law Enforcement
State Law Enforcement
Federal Law Enforcement
  Department of Justice
  Treasury Department
  Department of the Interior
  Department of Defense
  General Services Administration
  U.S. Postal Service
  Department of Transportation
  Other Federal Enforcement Agencies
  Task Force Approach to Enforcement

International Police
Private Security
  What Is Private Security?
  History of Private Security
  Operations of Private Security Today
  Private Security and the Courts
  Current Problems of Private Security
  Licensing of Private Security
  Professionalization of Private Security
  Forecasts Regarding the Need for Private Security
Private Employment of Public Police
Community Self-Protection
  Target Hardening
  Neighborhood Watch Programs
Impact of Recession on Police Agencies and Police Consolidation

Chapter Goals

■ To acquaint you with the many and diverse local and state public agencies that attempt to enforce the law and ensure public safety in the United States.

■ To introduce the numerous federal law enforcement agencies that enforce federal laws and regulations and assist local and state police departments.

■ To describe the size, scope, and functions of law enforcement agencies in the private sector.

■ To explain methods that private communities can use to ensure their safety.

■ To acquaint you with the number and type of jobs available to you in policing.

31

Introduction

The public and private security industry—those institutions and people who attempt to maintain law and order and enforce the law in the United States—is enormous. We can almost say that it is a growth industry, expanding every year.

The U.S. security industry spends an immense amount of money and provides jobs for millions of people. The industry operates on all governmental levels: the local level (villages, towns, counties, and cities), the state level, and the federal level. The public agencies are funded by income taxes, sales taxes, real estate taxes, and other taxes. Additionally, the security industry is served by the private sector, which hires more people and spends more money than all the public agencies put together. Students interested in seeking a career in policing will find a vast number and types of law enforcement jobs from which to choose.

The U.S. Public and Private Safety Industry

Ensuring the safety of U.S. citizens by providing law enforcement services is an extremely complex and expensive undertaking. The American approach to law enforcement is unique when compared with the rest of the world. Japan and some western European countries, for example, Denmark, Finland, Greece, and Sweden, have a single national police force.[1] The United States does not have a national police force, although many people think of the FBI as being one. We will see later in this chapter that the FBI is an investigative agency, not a police agency.

U.S. law enforcement has developed over the years based on a philosophy of **local control**, the formal and informal use of local or neighborhood forms of control to deter abhorrent behaviors. To understand why, remember that the United States was built on the fear of a

---

Dempsey's Law

There Is More to Law Enforcement Than Policing

Professor Dempsey, I want a job in law enforcement, but I don't want to be a police officer. That's not the job for me—carrying a gun and working all those strange hours. Are there any jobs in law enforcement other than police officer?

The criminal justice field consists of more than the police. There are jobs in courts and corrections. Also, in law enforcement plenty of jobs do not require what we normally call police work. Let me give you examples of jobs that some of our criminal justice graduates have gotten.

Most of our graduates have become police officers, deputy sheriffs, or correction officers. However, many have gone on to four-year colleges and have gotten jobs as investigators in federal, state, and local enforcement agencies. One I remember well is Leanne, who now works for the U.S. Customs Service.

Some students have gotten police jobs not involving enforcement duties. For example, Paul is now a dispatcher with the county police department, and Mary Anne is a forensic technician with the city police department.

Some have gone on to law school after getting their baccalaureate. One who comes to mind right away is Rick Steinmann, who graduated in 1971. Rick went on to get a four-year degree and then graduated from law school. Besides legal work, Rick has been a criminal justice professor at colleges and universities in Ohio, Kentucky, Florida, and Missouri. He also has worked as a police officer and correctional counselor.

Another successful graduate is Joe Terry. Joe graduated from Suffolk Community College and then went to St. John's University in New York City, where he received his four-year degree in criminal justice. He started his career as a salesperson for West Publishing, selling criminal justice texts to colleges. He then became a developmental editor and then an acquisitions editor for West. Joe was one of the people instrumental in the publication of this book's first edition.

| Table 2.1 | Employees in State and Local Law Enforcement Agencies by Type of Agency, United States |

		Number of Employees					
		Full-Time			Part-Time		
Type of Agency	Number of Agencies	Total	Sworn	Civilian	Total	Sworn	Civilian
Total	17,120	828,435	622,913	205,522	87,875	42,890	44,985
Local police	12,361	474,072	373,554	100,518	58,146	28,186	29,960
Sheriff	3,084	224,236	155,815	68,421	19,660	11,048	8,612
State police	49	76,972	51,874	25,098	845	228	617
Special police	1,626	53,156	41,670	11,485	9,224	3,428	5,796

Note: These data are from the third Law Enforcement Management and Administrative Statistics (LEMAS) survey, which was conducted in 1993. The data were collected by the U.S. Bureau of Justice Statistics. The LEMAS survey collects data from a nationally representative sample of more than 17,000 publicly funded law enforcement agencies in the United States. A total of 854 State and local law enforcement agencies with 100 or more sworn officers were included in the survey. For agencies with fewer than 100 sworn officers, a nationally representative sample was drawn. A stratified random sample based on type of agency (local police, sheriff, or special police), size of population served, and number of sworn officers was used. A total of 3,028 agencies responded to the survey yielding a 93 percent response rate. The final database includes responses from 1,827 local police departments, 918 sheriffs' departments, 234 special police departments, and the 49 primary State police agencies. Hawaii does not have a State police agency. Data from agencies with fewer than 100 sworn personnel were derived from a sample and therefore subject to sampling variation. The pay period that included June 15, 1993 was the reference date for all personnel data and June 30, 1993 was used for all other items. A "local police" department ws defined as a general purpose police department operated by a municipal or county government. "Sheriffs" departments included were those operated by county or independent city governments. A "State police" department was defined as a general purpose State police agency operated by the State. "Local and State police" categories include only general purpose agencies. "Special police" agencies are both State and local agencies policing special geographic jurisdictions such as airports, parks, transit systems, public schools, and colleges and universities. Consolidated police-sheriff agencies are included under the local police category.

Source: Kathleen Maguire and Ann L. Pastore, eds., *Sourcebook of Criminal Justice Statistics 1996* (Washington, D.C.: U.S. Department of Justice, Bureau of Justice Statistics, U.S. Government Printing Office, 1997), Table 1.26, p. 39.

large central government, as had existed in England when the colonists came here. The primary responsibility for police protection still falls to local governments (cities, towns, and counties). Although we have state and federal law enforcement agencies, they are minuscule in size and importance when compared with the law enforcement agencies of local government.

Because of the tremendous number of law enforcement agencies and their employees in the United States and the lack of a unified system for the reporting of police personnel, it is very difficult to get a perfect picture of the U.S. law enforcement industry. The latest National Institute of Justice's (NIJ), Bureau of Justice Statistics (BJS), LEMAS (Law Enforcement Management and Administrative Statistics) Report attempts to paint this picture.[2] The report indicates that there are over 17,000 publicly funded state and local law enforcement agencies operating in the United States. These include approximately 12,300 general-purpose local police departments (mostly municipal and county departments); almost 3,100 sheriffs' departments; 49 state police departments; and over 1,600 special departments, including park police, transit police, and other special district police departments.

The report also indicates that nationwide there are approximately 828,000 full-time police employees and 88,000 part-time employees. Of the full-time employees, 623,000, or approximately 75 percent, are sworn officers with full police powers. The remainder are civilian, nonsworn officers who primarily perform nonenforcement duties. See Table 2.1.

The latest operating expenditures for the nearly 17,000 state and local law enforcement agencies in the United States amounted to approximately $44 billion, which was almost half of all the operating expenditures for the entire U.S. criminal justice system.[3]

The police represent the largest segment of the criminal justice system in terms of people employed and money spent. Nationwide, the police make up over 46 percent of the average state's criminal justice personnel budget.[4]

In addition to state and local law enforcement agencies and personnel, there are also approximately 75,000 full-time federal law enforcement employees. Addition-

PATROLLING THE NET

Try Some Sites

Here are some law enforcement–related web sites that were current when this text went to print: Try some!

Federal Bureau of Investigation
http://www.fbi.gov
U.S. Department of Justice
http://www.usdoj.gov
Law Enforcement Sites on the Web
http://www.ih2000.net/ira/ira.htm

Police Officer's Internet Directory
http://www.xensei.com/users/hubcom/police.htm
Cop Net & Police Resource List
http://police.sas.ab.ca
International Association of Chiefs of Police
http://www.amdahl.com/ext/iacp
National Sheriffs' Association
http://www.sheriffs.org

Source: Daniel J. Kurland and Christina Polsenberg, *Internet Guide for Criminal Justice* (Belmont, Calif.: Wadsworth, 1997), p. 72.

---

ally, the enormous private security industry in the United States employs 1.5 million people and spends $52 billion a year. The private security number of personnel and amount of expenditures will double by the year 2000. The amount of money spent by all levels of government for police protection has increased 416 percent in the past twenty years.[5]

Statistics can sometimes be cumbersome and confusing. When we translate them into words, however, we can make some generalizations about the U.S. law enforcement industry:

1. The size and scope of the U.S. law enforcement industry is enormous.
2. The U.S. law enforcement industry is tremendously diverse and fragmented.
3. The U.S. law enforcement industry is predominantly local.
4. There are many employment opportunities in U.S. law enforcement at the federal, state, local, and private levels.

In this chapter we will focus our attention on local police, including municipal police and sheriff's offices; state police; federal law enforcement agencies; and private security.

Local Law Enforcement

When we use the term local police, we are talking about the vast majority of all the law enforcement employees in the United States, including metropolitan and sheriff's offices. A 1996 LEMAS report indicated that during the latest reported fiscal year, local police departments had operating expenditures of $24.3 billion and employed over 474,000 people on a full-time basis. About 79 percent of the full-time employees were sworn officers with full enforcement powers, and the rest were civilian or nonsworn employees who performed administrative, support, and clerical services. (See chapter 3 for a discussion of sworn officers, nonsworn officers, and civilian employees.)[6] Most local police departments were very small, with about half employing fewer than ten sworn officers. About 91 percent of local police departments employed fewer than fifty officers, and 90 percent served a population of less than 25,000.[7]

Although most local police departments are very small, most police work for large local departments. Police departments in cities with a population of 1 million or more employed a fifth of all local police officers, and departments serving 100,000 or more residents employed half of all the sworn officers in the United States. Among sworn personnel in local police departments, 83.0 percent were white, 11.3 percent were African-American, 6.2 percent were Hispanic.

Local police departments paid officers an average starting salary of about $21,300 a year. Almost all local departments required officers to have at least a high school education and about 12 percent of local police departments required new recruits to have at least some college education. Most local police departments required an average of 640 hours preservice training for all recruits.

The vast majority of local police departments authorized the use of one or more types of semiautomatic sidearms by their officers. Fully 65 percent of local departments required all regular uniformed officers to wear protective body armor while on duty.

Nationwide, total local police department operating expenditures were about $131 per resident served. Overall, employee salaries and benefits accounted for about $6 of every $7 in operating expenses.[8]

Metropolitan Law Enforcement

The majority of police today work for metropolitan police departments. These departments can be extremely large.

Metropolitan police departments generally provide the duties and services we typically associate with the police. These include arresting law violators, performing routine patrol, investigating crimes, enforcing traffic laws (including parking violations), providing crowd and traffic control at parades and other public events, and issuing special licenses and permits.

Many larger metropolitan areas have overlapping police jurisdictions. For example, in New York City, the New York City Police Department (NYPD), the nation's largest police department with over 40,000 uniformed officers, is assisted by other federal, state, and local police and law enforcement agencies that police the city's public schools, colleges, hospitals, social service centers, parks, bridges and tunnels, airports, and the like. (The New York City Housing Authority Police, which patrols the city's numerous public housing projects, and the New York City Transit Authority Police, which patrols the New York City subways, merged into the NYPD in the mid-1990s. It should be noted that before the merger the separate transit and housing authority police departments were bigger than the police departments in the vast majority of the largest cities in the United States.) The Boston Police Department is assisted by the Metropolitan District Commission (MDC) police, which patrols public parks, public property, beaches, and parkways. Additionally, the Massachusetts State Police patrols the expressways and state roads leading into and out of the city. In Washington, D.C., there is a panoply of separate local and federal departments that have current jurisdiction throughout the city.

Most academic and professional studies of policing focus on municipal departments, because this is where "the action" is in the law enforcement world. This action includes problems with crime, budgeting and funding, politics, and population changes, as well as social problems, including homelessness, unemployment, drug addiction, alcoholism, and child abuse. Also, large municipal departments are highly visible because of their size, complexity, budgets, and innovative programs. In addition to attempting to control crime, municipal police have significant problems maintaining public order and solving quality-of-life problems that bother neighborhood residents. The police handle social problems that other public and private agencies either cannot or will not handle. In a big city, when there is a problem, citizens do not call the mayor's office; they call 911.

A Police Foundation report has focused its attention on the Big 6 police departments: New York City, Los Angeles, Chicago, Houston, Philadelphia, and Detroit. At the time of the study, these cities had 7 percent of the U.S. population but encountered 23 percent of the nation's violent crime, including 22 percent of all murders and 34 percent of all robberies. Additionally, these cities faced enormous financial problems and serious racial tension.[9]

County Law Enforcement

Most counties in the United States are patrolled by a sheriff's department under the command of an elected sheriff. A 1996 LEMAS report indicates that in the latest reporting year there were about 3,200 sheriff's departments in the United States and these employed approxi-

---

YOU ARE THERE! »

How Chicago Polices Its Subway System

The Chicago Transit System operates over 1,000 cars, which transport approximately half a million people daily. It has 140 stations and over 200 miles of track. The Public Transportation Section of the Chicago Police Department polices the system. Twenty-three percent of the personnel of the Public Transportation Section work the shift from midnight to 8:00 A.M., 34 percent of the personnel work the day shift, and 43 percent work the 4:00 P.M. to midnight shift. In addition to patrol personnel, each shift has canine units, tactical units, and crime assault teams (CATs). Only 5 percent of Chicago's crime occurs on the subways.

Source: Adapted from Robert W. Dart, "Urban Transportation Security," FBI Law Enforcement Bulletin, Washington, D.C., October 1991, pp. 1–3.

mately 224,000 full-time employees, of whom nearly 156,000 or 69 percent, were sworn officers with full enforcement powers.[10]

Most sheriff's departments were small: nearly two-thirds employed fewer than twenty-five sworn officers, and a third employed fewer than ten. Sheriff's departments had operating expenses of $10.7 billion. Demographically, 10 percent of employees of sheriff's offices were African-American and 5.8 percent Hispanic. Approximately 14.6 percent were women. The average starting salaries for new recruits was about $19,300. Approximately 97 percent of the departments required new recruits to have at least a high school diploma, and 8 percent required some college education, usually a two-year degree.

Approximately three-quarters of sheriff's departments authorized their officers to use semiautomatic sidearms; the 9-mm firearm was most frequently authorized. About 35 percent of the departments required all regular field officers to wear body armor while on duty.

The role of sheriff has evolved in several stages since the early English sheriff (shire-reeve), whose main duty was to assist the royal judges in trying prisoners and enforcing sentences. During the development of the West in the United States and until the development of municipal departments, the sheriff often served as the sole legal authority over vast geographical areas.

Today the duties of a county sheriff vary according to the size and urbanization of the county. The sheriff's office may perform the duties of coroners, tax assessors, tax collectors, keepers of county jails, court attendants, and executors of criminal and civil processes, as well as law enforcement officers.

There are several different types of sheriff's departments. Some are oriented exclusively toward law enforcement; some carry out only court-related duties; some deal exclusively with correctional and court matters and have no law enforcement duties; others are full-service programs that perform court, correctional, and law enforcement activities.[11]

Nearly all sheriffs' departments were responsible for performing court-related functions, such as serving civil process (97%) and providing court security (93%). About nine in ten investigated crimes (92%), responded to calls for service (91%), and provided routine patrol services (88%). Many sheriffs' departments also had primary responsibility for dispatching calls for service (80%), operating a jail (79%), drug enforcement (78%), traffic enforcement (77%), and search and rescue operations (65%).[12]

Rural and Small Town Law Enforcement

Sometimes, rural and small town police face different problems than large metropolitan and county police. The state of Wyoming, for example, has the lowest population in the United States (440,000 residents) and has vast open areas where one can drive over 100 miles between small towns. The 1,600 law enforcement officers in this state must routinely face the problem of not having immediate backup in most situations. As Mike Roy, the lead instructor at the Wyoming Law Enforcement Academy, says, "We deal with great distances out here and there is a different mentality. Every other pickup truck you stop out here has a rifle in a gun rack or a pistol in the glove box. Most of the problems we have in law enforcement centers around people—where you have people you will have problems." Regarding the lack of readily available backup, Roy says, "Everyone completing our academy is instructed not to get stupid by acting alone in known volatile situations. Officers are instructed to get used to waiting for the closest help to arrive even if it's 60 miles away."[13]

Although everyone seems aware of the drug problems and dangers to police in our large urban communities, many are not aware of the large-scale problems in the many small towns throughout America's heartland. Police officers searching a modest home on the outskirts of Kansas City, Missouri, encountered a perverse vision of middle-American domesticity:

> In the living room sat the computer where Dad had just been forging driver's licenses, while in another room Mom kept their towheaded children, 8 and 4 years old, away from the family's sawed-off shotgun and a crude laboratory that turned out methamphetamine from ingredients bought in local stores. Toxic waste from the illegal drug-making had been dumped down the drain. When officers looked in the kitchen, . . . a police detective [said], "we found several jars of meth in the freezer next to the children's popsicles."[14]

Authorities say that locally made methamphetamine, long popular on the West Coast, has become the small-town Midwest's drug of choice, similar to the scourge that crack or rock cocaine has been to the inner city. Methamphetamine is a stimulant variously called meth, crank, ice, and speed. For years it was made and distributed by outlaw motorcycle gangs, but today in the Midwest it is a "Mom and Pop" operation. Medical experts and some users say meth delivers a stronger, cheaper psychoactive kick than crack cocaine, unleashing ag-

PATROLLING THE NET

Here Are Some More Sites

Here are some law enforcement agency web sites that were current when this text went to print: Try some!

Anderson County, Tennessee, Sheriff's Office:
http://tn.areaguide.com/asco

Arroyo Grande, California, Police Department:
http://www.thegrid.net/agpd

Beaufort City, South Carolina, Police Department:
http://www.bftpolice.com

Chicago, Illinois, Police Department
http:///www.ci.chi.il.us

Davis, California, Police Department
http://www.den.davis.ca.us/go/dpd

Fairfield Township, New Jersey, Police Department
http://www.hicom.net/~fpd

Florida Office of the Attorney General Citizen Safety Center
http://legal.firn.edu/safe_cen.html

Fort Lauderdale, Florida, Police Department
http://paradise.net/online/police

King County, Washington, Police Department
http://www.metroke.gov

Lancashire Constabulary, Skelmersdale Police Station, United Kingdom
http://www.ehche.ac.uk/community/bluelight/forcei.htm

North Richland Hills, Texas, Police Department
http://web2.airmail.net/nrhjbc

Village of Olympia Fields, Illinois, Police Department
http://www.lincolnnet.net/users/lmolymp/ofpage.htm

Tempe, Arizona, Police Department
http://www.tempe.gov/police/pd_page2.htm

Wakefield, Massachusetts, Police Department
http://www.wakefieldpd.org

Source: Adapted from "FaxBack Response: Previous Question: How Has the Internet Helped Your Agency?," *FBI Law Enforcement Bulletin*, January 1997, pp. 23–25.

---

gression and leading to long binges that end with physical collapse.

In the first half of 1997, more than sixty clandestine methamphetamine laboratories were seized by the Jackson County drug task force, whose officers are drawn from seven towns from western Missouri. In 1996, over 300 labs were seized in the DEA field office covering small towns in Missouri, Kansas, Iowa, Nebraska, South Dakota, and southern Illinois. (In contrast, no labs were seized in New York and only one in New Jersey for the same period.)

In addition to the violence associated with meth users, their labs also prove dangerous to the police. A Missouri detective told of finding an overhead light bulb in a dark basement laboratory in Independence that was filled with tiny lead pellets and gunpowder, rigged to explode when the switch was turned on. He has also found a couple of pipe bombs and rattlesnakes, as well as toxic gasses in his raids on the labs.[15]

Rural and small town law enforcement agencies engage in mutual assistance programs with neighboring agencies and come to one another's aid when necessary.

Attention to the needs of rural law enforcement agencies gave birth to the National Center for Rural Law Enforcement (NCRLE), a part of the Criminal Justice Institute, located in Little Rock, Arkansas. To assist law enforcement officials throughout the United States, the NCRLE provides management education and training courses ranging from principles of supervision to detailed courses on the legal aspects of domestic violence. NCRLE also provides research and Internet assistance. In 1995, the NCRLE brought 181 sheriffs, police chiefs, citizens, and social service agency representatives together to discuss the needs of rural communities and explore the process of creating a community coalition.[16]

State Law Enforcement

Forty-nine of the fifty U.S. states have a state law enforcement agency. The only state without a state police agency is Hawaii. (This may surprise those who are familiar with the television series Hawaii 5–0, which was based on the fictional Hawaiian State Police.)

LEMAS reports indicate that the forty-nine state police departments had operating expenditures of $3.7 billion and employed 77,000 people full-time, 68 percent of them sworn officers.[17] Of the sworn employees, 87.1 percent were white, 7.5 percent were African-American, 4.4 percent were Hispanic, and 1 percent were other mi-

All in the Line of Duty

He Kept the Newborn Alive

In the early morning hours, Officer Forrest Davis of the Box Elder, South Dakota, Police Department received a request to assist a woman in labor. Officer Davis arrived as the woman gave birth, but took control when the newborn failed to start breathing. He cleared the airway and had to stimulate the child twice, as the baby stopped breathing after taking only a few breaths. Officer Davis kept the newborn breathing until an emergency medical team arrived and took the mother and child to an area hospital.

Source: Adapted from *FBI Law Enforcement Bulletin*, February 1994, p. 33.

---

norities. About 4.6 percent of sworn state police were women.

Approximately 18 percent of state police departments required new recruits to have some previous college education and required all recruits to have an average of 1,000 hours of preservice training. The average starting salary for new state police officers was about $22,800.

About 80 percent of state police departments authorized the use of one or more types of semiautomatic sidearms by their officers. About 12 percent required all regular field and patrol officers to wear protective body armor while on duty.

Historically, state police departments were developed to deal with growing crime in nonurban areas of the country, which was attributable to the increasing mobility of Americans, the proliferation of cars, and the ease of travel. The state police agencies were formed by governors and legislators to lessen reliance on metropolitan and county police departments, which were seen to be more closely linked with politics and urban and county corruption.

Generally, state police patrol small towns and state highways, regulate traffic, and have the primary responsibility to enforce some state laws. The state police also carry out many duties for local police agencies, such as the managing of state training academies, criminal identification systems, and crime laboratories.

At the state level, there are two distinct models of law enforcement agencies. The **centralized model of state law enforcement** combines the duties of major criminal investigations with the patrol of state highways. The centralized state police agencies generally assist local police departments in criminal investigations when requested and provide the identification, laboratory, and training functions for local departments.

The second state model, the **decentralized model of state law enforcement**, has a clear distinction between traffic enforcement on state highways and other state-level law enforcement functions. The states that use this model—many southern and midwestern, and some western, states—generally have two separate agencies, one a highway patrol and the other a state bureau of investigation. California, for example, has the California Highway Patrol and the California Division of Law Enforcement.

Although the duties of the various state-level police departments may vary considerably, the most common duties include highway patrol, traffic law enforcement, and the patrol of small towns.

Federal Law Enforcement

Although the U.S. Constitution created three branches of government—executive, legislative, and judicial—it did not create a national police force. However, it did give the national government power over a limited number of crimes.

Traditionally in the United States, the creation of laws and the power to enforce them have been matters for the states. The states have given much of their enforcement powers to local police agencies. Policing has largely been local. However, in recent years, the number of crimes included in the U.S. Criminal Code has multiplied greatly, as has the number of people assigned to enforce the crimes. In the latest reporting year, there were approximately 75,000 full-time federal law enforcement employees.[18]

The 1998 federal budget request, announced on February 6, 1997, sought a total of $19.3 billion, which would be used to add hundreds of federal law enforcement officers and boost efforts to fight youth violence, drug trafficking, terrorism, and illegal immigration.[19]

Several major U.S. departments administer federal law enforcement agencies: the Department of Justice, the Treasury Department, the Department of the Interior, the Department of Defense, the General Services Administration, and the Department of Transportation.

This text pays special attention to federal law enforcement agencies since many of these agencies require a four-year college degree for appointment.

Department of Justice

The U.S. Department of Justice is the primary legal and prosecutorial arm of the U.S. government. The Department of Justice is under the control of the U.S. Attorney General, the top law enforcement official in the United States, and is responsible for (1) enforcing all federal laws, (2) representing the government when it is involved in a court action, and (3) conducting independent investigations through its law enforcement services. The department's Civil Rights Division prosecutes violators of the federal civil rights laws, which are designed to protect citizens from discrimination on the basis of their race, creed, ethnic background, or gender. These laws apply to discrimination in education, housing, and job opportunity. The Justice Department's Tax Division prosecutes violators of the tax laws. Its Criminal Division prosecutes violators of the Federal Criminal Code, such as those engaged in bank robbery, kidnapping, mail fraud, interstate transportation of stolen vehicles, and narcotics and drug trafficking.

The Justice Department also operates the **National Institute of Justice (NIJ)** as its research arm. The National Institute of Justice maintains the **National Criminal Justice Reference Service (NCJRS)** as a national clearinghouse of criminal justice information. Associated clearinghouses operated as part of the NCJRS are the Juvenile Justice Clearinghouse for the Office of Juvenile Justice and Delinquency Prevention, the Justice Statistics Clearinghouse for the Bureau of Justice Statistics, the Bureau of Justice Assistance Clearinghouse for the Bureau of Justice Assistance, and the National Victims Resource Center for the Office for Victims of Crime.

Students interested in the study of crime in the United States can register at no cost with the NCJRS and receive a bimonthly publication. This publication announces NIJ's policy-relevant research results, publications, and initiatives. It also contains a calendar of criminal justice events nationwide, including conventions and seminars; describes new books and studies in criminal justice; and contains an order form for users to request some of the institute's publications, many of which are free. To become a regular user of NCJRS data, write to the National Institute of Justice/NCJRS User Services, Box 6000, Rockville, MD 20850. All of the NIJ publications and information is also available over the Internet.

Theodore Kaczynski being led out of court by federal law enforcement officers in 1996. Kaczynski was charged and pled guilty to the bombings ranging in date from 1978 to 1994 attributed to the "Unabomber."

The National Institute of Justice also conducts the National Crime Victimization Survey, a twice-yearly survey of a random sample of the American public that asks citizens about their criminal victimization. Finally, the Justice Department also maintains administrative control over the Federal Bureau of Investigation, the Drug Enforcement Administration, the U.S. marshals, and the Immigration and Naturalization Service.

Federal Bureau of Investigation The Federal Bureau of Investigation (FBI) is the largest federal law enforcement agency and the best known. The FBI has approximately 9,000 special agents and is the primary agency charged with the enforcement of all federal laws not falling under the purview of other federal agencies. The main headquarters of the FBI is in Washington, D.C. The FBI also has field offices located in major U.S. cities and in San Juan, Puerto Rico. The head of the FBI, known as the director, is appointed by the president of the United States, subject to confirmation by the Senate.

In addition to the 9,000 special agents, the FBI employs approximately 11,000 nonenforcement people, who perform such duties as fingerprint examinations, computer programming, forensic or crime laboratory analyses, and administrative and clerical duties.

All special agents must attend the FBI National Academy located on the U.S. Marine Corps base at Quantico, Virginia. The FBI Academy is also attended by other law enforcement officers and officers from some foreign governments.

YOU ARE THERE!

FBI's Violent Crimes and Major Offenders Program (VCMOP)

With the collapse of the former Soviet Union, the FBI started to concentrate more of its efforts on domestic crime. In June 1989, the FBI added crimes of violence to its list of national priorities. It also expanded cooperative efforts with state and local law enforcement, as well as with other federal law enforcement agencies, in an effort to reduce the increasing rate of violent crime. The FBI established the Violent Crimes and Major Offenders Program (VCMOP), which devotes its resources exclusively to the growing problem of violent crime.

In November 1991, the FBI unveiled Operation Safe Streets in Washington, D.C., as a component of its VCMOP. Since then, Operation Safe Streets has been expanded to thirty-nine cities nationwide. Operation Safe Streets is designed as a task force operation, which allows the FBI to join with other federal, state, and local agencies to combat organized criminal gangs.

Gangs are proliferating in the United States. Nationwide, there are 20,000 Jamaican Posse members, 50,000 outlaw motorcycle gang members and their associates, 34,000 Latin Kings and Black Gangster Disciples, 13,000 prison gang members, and an undetermined number of Asian gang members. In the Los Angeles area alone, there are 26,000 Crips, 10,000 Bloods, and 64,000 other street gang members. Recognizing this growing problem, in January 1992, the FBI transferred 300 agents from counterintelligence work to violent crime units that target violent street gangs. The FBI cooperates with state and local law enforcement agencies in this effort.

Source: Adapted from Andrew DiRosa, "The FBI's Violent Crimes and Major Offenders Program," *FBI Law Enforcement Bulletin*, Washington, D. C., July 1992, pp. 12–13.

Contrary to popular opinion, the FBI is not a national police force. It is an investigative agency that may investigate acts that are in violation of federal law. The FBI may also assist state and local law enforcement agencies and investigate state and local crimes when requested to do so by those agencies.

The FBI was created in 1908, when President Theodore Roosevelt directed the attorney general to develop an investigative unit within the Justice Department. It was first named the Bureau of Investigation; in 1935, it was renamed the Federal Bureau of Investigation. Its most prominent figure and longtime director from 1924 to 1972 was J. Edgar Hoover.

The FBI has had a colorful history. It captured the attention of the media during the Great Depression with nationwide searches and the capture of such notorious criminals as George "Machine Gun" Kelly in 1933, John Dillinger in 1934, and Charles "Pretty Boy" Floyd in 1934.

Critics, however, allege that the FBI under Hoover's regime ignored white-collar crime, organized crime, and violations of the civil rights of minority groups. After Hoover's death in 1972, it was discovered that under his direction, the FBI had committed many violations of citizens' constitutional rights, including spying, conducting illegal wiretaps, and burglarizing premises. These violations were mostly aimed at individuals and groups because of their political beliefs.[20]

Hoover's successors reoriented the mission of the bureau and put more emphasis on the investigation of white-collar crime, organized crime, and political corruption.[21] In addition to its investigative capacity, the FBI today provides many important services.

Identification Division   The FBI's Identification Division, created in 1924, collects and maintains a vast fingerprint file. This file is used for identification purposes by the FBI, as well as state and local police agencies.

National Crime Information Center   The National Crime Information Center (NCIC) is a tremendous computerized database of criminal information. It stores information on stolen property that has identifying information, such as serial numbers or distinctive markings. The NCIC also contains information on outstanding warrants and criminal histories.

FBI Crime Laboratory   The FBI Crime Laboratory, created in 1932, provides investigative and analysis services for other law enforcement agencies. It is the world's largest forensic, or criminalistic (scientifically crime related), laboratory and provides microscopic and chemical analyses, as well as spectrography and cryptography. Skilled FBI technicians examine such evidence as hairs, fibers, blood, tire tracks, and drugs.

Uniform Crime Reports   The Uniform Crime Reports (UCR) is an annual compilation that includes information on crimes reported to local police agencies, arrests, and police killed or wounded in the line of duty, along with other data. The Uniform Crime Reporting Program is a nationwide, cooperative statistical effort of approximately 16,000 city, county, and state law enforcement agencies voluntarily reporting data on crimes brought to their attention by the public and is published once a year as *Crime in the United States*. Since 1930, the FBI has administered the program and issued periodic assessments of the nature and type of crime in the nation. Although the program's primary objective is to provide a reliable set of criminal statistics for use in law enforcement administration, operation, and management, over the years its data have become one of the leading social indicators for the United States. The American public looks to the UCR for information on fluctuations in the level of crime. Criminologists, sociologists, legislators, municipal planners, the press, and students of criminal justice use the statistics for varied research and planning purposes.

The specific crimes measured by the UCR are called Part I—Index crimes. They are murder and non-negligent manslaughter, forcible rape, robbery, aggravated assault, burglary, larceny-theft, and motor vehicle theft. The latest addition to the UCR is the collection of hate crime statistics, mandated by the Hate Crime Statistics Act passed by the U.S. Congress and signed by President Bush in April 1990. This collection of data is being used to study crimes motivated by religious, ethnic, racial, or sexual orientation prejudice.[22]

Investigatory Activities Today, the FBI focuses its investigations on organized crime activities, including racketeering, corruption, and pornography; bank robbery; and white-collar crime, including embezzlement and stock and other business fraud.

Drug Enforcement Administration The Drug Enforcement Administration (DEA) was previously part of the Treasury Department and was called the Bureau of Narcotics. It was renamed and shifted to the Justice Department in 1973. The DEA is at the vanguard of the U.S. "war on drugs" by engaging in drug interdiction, conducting surveillance operations, and infiltrating drug rings. The agency also tracks illicit drug traffic, registers manufacturers and distributors of pharmaceutical drugs, tracks the movement of chemicals used in the manufacture of illegal drugs, and leads the nation's marijuana eradication program.

U.S. Marshals There are ninety-four U.S. marshals, one for each federal judicial district. They are appointed by the president of the United States, subject to confirmation by the Senate. The marshals are assisted by thousands of deputy marshals. The marshals perform many functions. Their primary functions are the transportation of federal prisoners between prisons and courts and the security of federal court facilities. The marshals also protect witnesses at federal trials, apprehend federal fugitives, execute federal warrants, operate the Federal Witness Security Program, and are in charge of handling the seizure and disposal of property resulting from criminal activity.

The Federal Witness Security Program, or Federal Witness Protection Program, is responsible not only for the protection of federal witnesses but also for the relocation and creation of new identities for witnesses who "turn" against former associates and testify against them in court. ("Turn" or "flip" means to cooperate with authorities and obtain or give evidence regarding former partners in crime.) Two notable criminals who have participated in the Federal Witness Protection Program are Henry Hill (the protagonist in Nicholas Pilegi's *Wiseguy: Life in a Mafia Family,* which served as the source of the 1991 movie hit *Goodfellas*) and Salvatore (Sammy the Bull) Gravano (the underboss of the Gambino crime family and the self-admitted participant in nineteen murders, whose testimony led to the conviction in 1992 of his boss, John Gotti).

Immigration and Naturalization Service The Immigration and Naturalization Service (INS) polices the thousands of miles of land and sea borders of the United States. The INS tries to prevent the entrance of illegal aliens and conducts investigations of smuggling rings that bring thousands of illegal immigrants into the United States each year. The INS is also in charge of admitting foreigners who qualify for U.S. citizenship. The branch of the INS that guards the U.S. borders is called the Border Patrol.

Problems relating to illegal immigration caused the federal government, in 1996, to add $2.8 billion to the federal budget to enforce immigration laws, including the hiring of 1,100 new Border Patrol agents.[23]

Treasury Department

The U.S. Treasury Department has administrative control over four very important federal law enforcement agencies: the Bureau of Alcohol, Tobacco, and Firearms; the Internal Revenue Service; the Customs Service; and the Secret Service.

U.S. Customs Service officer using her canine to inspect mail coming off planes at an airport.

Bureau of Alcohol, Tobacco, and Firearms The Bureau of Alcohol, Tobacco, and Firearms (ATF) is the primary agency for enforcing federal laws relating to alcohol, tobacco, and firearms violations. The ATF enforces laws pertaining to the manufacture, sale, and possession of firearms and explosives; attempts to suppress illegal traffic in tobacco and alcohol products; collects taxes; and regulates industry trade practices regarding these items.

The ATF assists other domestic and international law enforcement agencies by being the nation's primary agency for the tracing of weapons and explosives. It traces these weapons through records it maintains regarding manufacturers and dealers in firearms. The ATF also investigates cases of arson and bombings at federal buildings or other institutions that receive federal funds, as well as investigating arson-for-profit schemes. The ATF received much criticism for its 1993 raid on the compound of religious cult leader David Koresch but also suffered the ultimate in agency sacrifice, the murder of four agents.

Internal Revenue Service The Internal Revenue Service (IRS), the primary U.S. revenue collection agency, is also in charge of the laws regulating federal income tax and their collection. The investigative arm of the IRS is its Criminal Investigation Division (CID). CID investigators look into tax frauds, unreported income, and hidden assets.

In its efforts against organized crime figures and major drug dealers, the federal government often uses the CID to target these individuals with the goal of prosecuting them for tax evasion. Also, many other law enforcement agencies solicit the help of the CID in an attempt to prosecute major drug dealers and other criminals who are in possession of large amounts of undeclared income.

Customs Service The Customs Service conducts inspections and collects import duties and taxes at more than 300 ports of entry into the United States. The Customs Service also detects and intercepts illegal drugs, counterfeit consumer goods, and other contraband entering the United States. Additionally, Customs is charged with preventing strategic high technology from being smuggled outside the United States.

The Customs Service, the second largest federal law enforcement agency, also plays a major role in the war on drugs. The agency seizes and holds for civil forfeiture boats, planes, and other vehicles used to transport illegal drugs into the country. **Civil forfeiture** results in the owner's loss of legal ownership of their confiscated property and the individual must sue the government for its return.

Secret Service The Secret Service is responsible for protecting the president, the vice-president, and other government officials and their families, as well as former presidents. The Secret Service coordinates all security arrangements regarding official presidential visits, motorcades, and ceremonies with other federal government agencies and state and local law enforcement agencies. The Secret Service has uniformed and nonuniformed divisions.

The Secret Service is also responsible for the integrity of the federal government's money supply, including currency, checks, bonds, securities, and stamps. It investigates forgeries and counterfeiting of these items.

The Secret Service was created by Congress in 1865 as a bureau of the Department of the Treasury to deal with the counterfeiting and forgery of products of the government's monetary system. Because the Secret Service was the federal government's only general law enforcement agency at the time, its responsibilities were expanded to include smuggling, piracy, mail robbery, and land fraud. The Secret Service also conducted post–Civil War investigations of the Ku Klux Klan and served as intelligence and anti-espionage agents during the Spanish-American War and World War I.

In 1901, after the assassination of President William McKinley, the Secret Service was given the responsibility of protecting the president. Today the Secret Service also protects the vice-president, the immediate families of the president and vice-president, the president-elect and the vice-president–elect and their immediate families, former presidents and their wives and children up to the age of sixteen, major presidential and vice-presidential candidates, and visiting heads of foreign governments. Additionally, the Secret Service is currently actively involved in the investigation and efforts against the growing tide of computer fraud in the nation.

Department of the Interior

The Department of the Interior provides law enforcement for the property under its purview, such as the Fish and Wildlife Service and the National Park Service.

Fish and Wildlife Service Enforcement agents for the Department of the Interior's Fish and Wildlife Service are called Wildlife Law Enforcement Agents. They investigate people who are illegally trafficking in government-protected birds, such as falcons.

National Park Service Enforcement agents for the U.S. Park Police are known as park rangers. They are responsible for law enforcement, traffic control, fire control, and search and rescue operations in the 30 million acres of the National Park Service.

Department of Defense

Each branch of the U.S. military has its own law enforcement agency. The military police agencies are organized in a manner similar to the civil police, using uniformed officers for patrol duties on military bases and investigators to investigate crimes. The army's investigative arm is the Criminal Investigation Division (CID); the investigative arm of the navy and marines is

---

YOU ARE THERE! »

Focus on U.S. Park Rangers—Wildlife Patrol

The number of U.S. Park Service rangers—approximately 3,200—has remained relatively unchanged during the past fifteen years, even though the number of visitors to the U.S. park system has risen tremendously. Approximately 65 million people visited U.S. parks every year in the 1990s.

Only forty-four rangers patrol Alaska's national forest and park system, which encompasses 54 million acres. In Death Valley National Monument, a handful of rangers patrol an area the size of many states.

Often, the type of wildlife encountered by park rangers is the human kind. Kathleen Hambley, who works in Big Bend National Park in Texas, is typical of rangers who specialize in "visitor protection." She wears a bulletproof vest; is accompanied by a police dog; and is armed with an AR-15 semiautomatic rifle, a shotgun, and a service revolver. The chief ranger of Death Valley states, "Every one of my people now wears body armor—even in 128-degree temperatures."

The "wildlife" problems encountered by one ranger at Glen Canyon National Recreation Area over the 1991 Memorial Day weekend included two rapes, a case of domestic abuse, a dozen arrests for driving under the influence (DUI), and apprehensions for illegal drug and alcohol possession.

A lack of fiscal resources has made the rangers' jobs tougher. Night shifts have been virtually eliminated due to personnel shortages, and low pay is causing an exodus of rangers from the system and discouraging new recruits. Most are now required to receive certification in search and rescue, emergency services, fire fighting, and law enforcement. Despite specialization, however, the most a ranger can hope to make is about $30,000 a year.

Rangers are generally drawn to the job not for economic benefits but out of a love of nature. "You have to work hard and you don't get paid much," said Paul Henry, a ranger at California's Joshua Tree National Monument. "But they'd rather be here. I still don't believe I get paid to do this."

Source: Adapted from "As Nature of Job Changes, Park Rangers Face New Perils," *Law Enforcement News*, John Jay College of Criminal Justice, New York City, July/August 1991, p. 4.

All in the Line of Duty

An Almost Deadly Accident, but He Made It All Right

While driving off duty, Sergeant Brian D. Huffman, of the 9th Security Police Squadron, Beale Air Force Base, in California, observed a pickup truck go around a curve and swerve into an oncoming lane of traffic. The pickup truck collided with a log truck and then flew off the roadway, plunging down a steep embankment. Sergeant Huffman immediately pulled off the road and ran down the slope to where the vehicle had come to rest. He noticed that the driver was slumped unconscious over the steering wheel and that fuel was leaking from the damaged vehicle. With the assistance of two men from the log truck, Huffman freed the driver from the damaged vehicle just moments before it erupted into flames. After carrying the victim to safety, the sergeant checked the driver's vital signs and found that the man's heart had stopped. Sergeant Huffman, again assisted by the log truck operator, administered CPR until the man's heart began beating again and he resumed breathing. Paramedics transported the victim to an area hospital. It was later determined that the man was driving himself to the hospital after experiencing chest pains when he lost control and collided with the log truck.

Source: Adapted from *FBI Law Enforcement Bulletin*, May 1994, p. 33.

---

the U.S. Naval Criminal Investigative Service (NCIS); and the air force's is the U.S. Air Force Office of Special Investigation (OSI).

General Services Administration

The General Services Administration (GSA) is the government agency that manages government property and procures and distributes supplies. Its enforcement arm consists of federal protective officers who conduct routine patrol and law enforcement at government buildings and property.

U.S. Postal Service

The Postal Inspection Division of the U.S. Postal Service is one of largest federal law enforcement agencies. It is also one of the oldest, having been created in 1836. Postal Inspectors investigate illegal acts committed against the Postal Service and its property and personnel, such as cases of fraud involving the use of the mails; use of the mails to transport drugs, bombs, and firearms; and assaults upon postal employees while they are exercising their official duties.

Department of Transportation

The U.S. Coast Guard falls under the administrative control of the U.S. Department of Transportation. The Coast Guard is responsible for routine patrol and law enforcement, as well as lifesaving and rescue operations in U.S. waters. Additionally, the Coast Guard enforces boating safety, pollution, and fishery regulations.

The Coast Guard makes major efforts in the U.S. war on drugs as it searches for and boards ships suspected of smuggling drugs into the country. Using the civil forfeiture laws, it seizes numerous ships for violation of drug laws.

Other Federal Enforcement Agencies

Many other federal agencies have law enforcement responsibilities. The Food and Drug Administration (FDA) oversees the enforcement of the laws regulating the sale and distribution of pure food and drugs. The Office of Investigation of the Department of Agriculture investigates fraud in the areas of food stamps, aid to disaster victims, and subsidies to farmers and rural home buyers.

Criminal law enforcement divisions are also found in the Securities and Exchange Commission (SEC), the Interstate Commerce Commission (ICC), the Federal Trade Commission (FTC), the Department of Labor, the Department of Health and Human Services, and the Department of State. The Department of State's Bureau of Diplomatic Security was created in 1986 to investigate matters involving passport and visa fraud. The U.S. Supreme Court has its own police department, which employs approximately 200 officers. Even the National Gallery of Art has its own law enforcement unit.

Task Force Approach to Enforcement

In the 1970s, federal enforcement agencies implemented an innovative approach to law enforcement by using task forces involving local, state, and federal law enforcement officers acting as a team. In these task forces, investigators from local police departments and state police agencies are temporarily assigned to a federal law enforcement agency to work with federal agents in combating particular crimes. The local and state officers provide a knowledge of the area, local contacts, informants, and street smarts, and federal agents provide investigative experience and resources.

The Drug Enforcement Administration has been using joint drug enforcement task forces in many areas of the country since the early 1970s. The joint task force approach has also been used successfully in ongoing programs to investigate bank robbery, arson, kidnapping, and terrorism.

International Police

INTERPOL (the International Criminal Police Organization) is a worldwide organization established for the development of cooperation among nations regarding common police problems. INTERPOL was founded in 1923, and the United States became a member in 1938. The mission of INTERPOL is to track and provide information that may help other law enforcement agencies apprehend criminal fugitives, thwart criminal schemes, exchange experience and technology, and analyze major trends of international criminal activity. It attempts to achieve its mission by serving as a clearinghouse and depository of intelligence information on wanted criminals.

INTERPOL's main function is informational; it is neither an investigative nor an enforcement agency. A police official of any member country may initiate a request for assistance on a case that extends beyond his or her country's jurisdiction.

In January 1987, INTERPOL, showing its commitment to the struggle against international terrorism, created an antiterrorist unit at its General Secretariat. This unit provides communications and support facilities to member nations on a global and regional basis.

Currently, over 170 nations belong to INTERPOL. INTERPOL is headquartered in Lyon, France. The U.S. Treasury Department is the U.S. representative to INTERPOL.

Private Security

The preceding sections of this chapter showed the tremendous size and scope of the public law enforcement industry on the local, state, federal, and international levels. However, that was only the tip of the iceberg. Another cast of players is associated with providing safety and security in the United States. The vast industry that provides security to much of corporate America and, in-

---

Dempsey's Law

Jobs for College Students in Private Security

Professor Dempsey, are there many jobs for college students in private security?

You better believe it. There are plenty of private security jobs, full time and part time, in all types of industries in the immediate area. Let me give you a few examples. Rick supported himself and put himself through college by working as a security guard at a company that makes steering wheels for automobiles. He worked there during the hours that the factory was closed, so he also had plenty of time to study while working. He's now a sergeant with the city police. Sheila also worked for the same company while going to college. After graduating here, she went to John Jay College, became a police cadet, which paid for her college, and now is a city cop.

Although most of my students go on to become police officers, court officers, or correction officers, some choose to remain in private security. One who comes to mind right away is Nicolle, who graduated here, went on to graduate from a local four-year school, and then obtained a job as a loss prevention specialist at a large clothing store that has numerous branches in the area and in the city. She was so good that she was promoted to loss prevention specialist manager for the entire area. She has about twenty people working for her and seems to be headed for big things with this company.

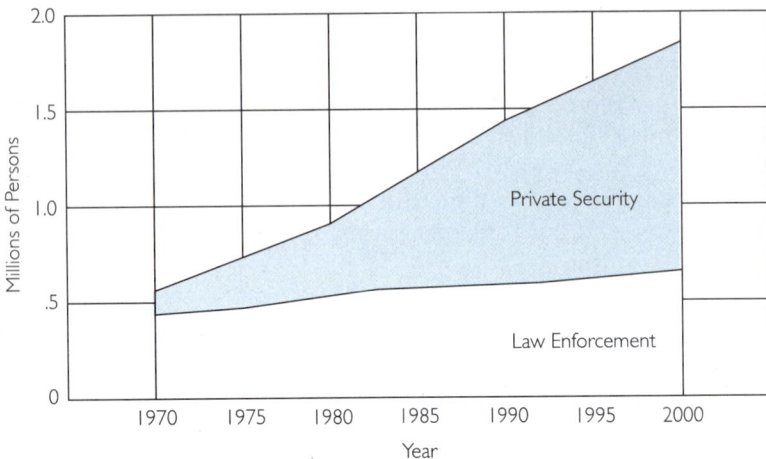

Figure 2.1
Private Security and Law Enforcement Employment
Source: Adapted from William C. Cunningham, John J. Strauchs, and Clifford W. Van Meter, *Private Security Trends, 1970–2000: The Hallcrest Report II* (Boston: Butterworth-Heinemann, 1990), p. 237.

creasingly, to much of public America is generally known as the **private security industry**.

In 1980, the National Institute of Justice commissioned Hallcrest Systems, Inc., to conduct a comprehensive study of the private security industry in the United States. Hallcrest's *The Hallcrest Report: Private Security and Police in America,* released in 1985, estimated that 1.1 million people were employed in private security and that almost $22 billion was spent for private security.[24]

Commissioned to do a follow-up report for the government, Hallcrest produced *The Hallcrest Report II: Private Security Trends: 1970–2000,* released in 1990. This report revealed that spending for private security had risen to $52 billion in 1990. Additionally, 1.5 million people were employed annually by private security agencies. Researchers estimate that private security expenditures will rise to $104 billion by the year 2000. Private policing is growing at a much faster rate than public policing (see figures 2.1 and 2.2).[25] As of 1997, it was estimated that the private security industry had a three to one employment ratio to public security, with approximately 1.8 million private security personnel and specialists in the United States. It is also estimated that private security responds to 50 percent of all crimes committed on private property.[26]

What Is Private Security?

Researchers have identified nine categories in the private security industry:

1. Proprietary (in-house) security. (Proprietary security means that a particular company has its own security department.)
2. Contract guard and patrol services. (Contract services are services that are leased or rented to another company.)
3. Alarm services.
4. Private investigations.
5. Armored car services.
6. Manufacturers of security equipment.
7. Locksmiths.
8. Security consultants and engineers.
9. Other, including such categories as guard dogs, drug testing, forensic analysis, and honesty testing.[27]

It must be noted that corporations are not the only source of funds for private security. The cost of the private guard standing in front of the corner jewelry store will necessarily be reflected in the price we pay for a bracelet we buy in that store. The cost of the undercover security agent who tries to apprehend shoplifters in a department store is reflected in the cost of everything we purchase in that store. In addition, governments at all levels are paying for private sector services through the increasing **privatization** of services. (Privatization is the use of the services of private industries to perform jobs previously under the care of government agencies.) In 1975, state and local government spending for private sector services was $27 billion; in 1982,

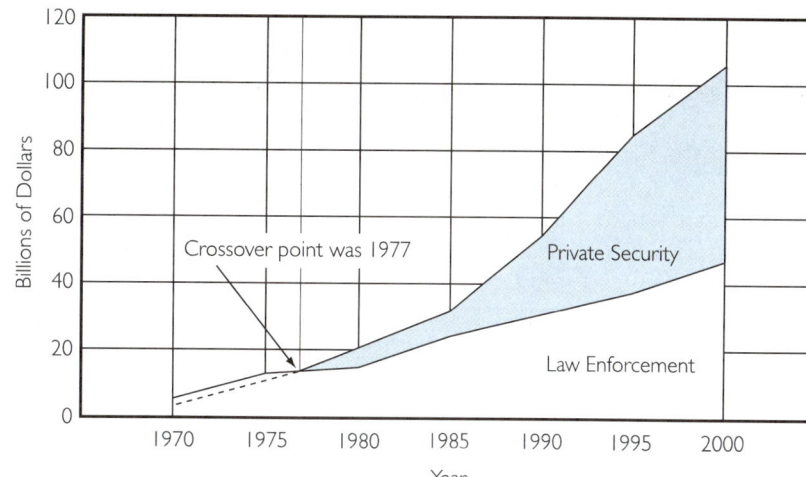

Figure 2.2
Private Security and Law Enforcement Spending
Source: Adapted from William C. Cunningham, John J. Strauchs, and Clifford W. Van Meter, *Private Security Trends, 1970–2000: The Hallcrest Report II* (Boston: Butterworth-Heinemann, 1990), p. 239.

it rose to $81 billion. Additionally, federal expenditures for private sector services in 1987 were $197 billion.[28]

History of Private Security

The history of private policing in the United States is a long and rich one. The original private security firms date back to the era before the Civil War and were connected with the westward expansion and the building of the railroads. The railroad companies hired private security forces to protect their property, goods, and shipments. As was discussed in chapter 1, the most notable of the early private security firms was the Pinkerton National Detective Agency, founded in 1850 by Scottish immigrant **Allan Pinkerton**, a former Chicago police detective. The agency advertised with the motto "We Never Sleep" and a logo of an open eye on its stationery and office doors.

The Wells Fargo Company was founded by **Henry Wells** and **William Fargo** in 1852. Next came the Brink's Company in 1859; Holmes Security, also in 1859; the William J. Burns International Detective Agency in 1909; and the Wackenhut Security Corporation in 1954. All these agencies are still in operation today.

Private security firms were responsible for many innovations in U.S. law enforcement. Allan Pinkerton invented the rogues' gallery—a collection of descriptions and photos of known criminals that could be shown to victims for positive identification. The Pinkerton Agency also is responsible for the term private eye, which has been widely used in the United States to designate a private investigator.[29]

Operations of Private Security Today

William C. Cunningham and Todd H. Taylor divide the private security industry into three distinct components: physical, information, and personnel security.[30]

The physical security component of the private security industry involves protecting people and property. Typical activities of physical security include guarding building entrances, preventing shoplifting, patrolling premises, and maintaining order.

The armored truck business is part of the lucrative private security industry in the United States.

> ## PATROLLING THE NET
>
> ### Hits on the Net
> The popularity of police homepages and other online sites is evidenced by the number of times citizens access (hit) them. Many small- to medium-sized agencies generate a surprisingly high level of citizen feedback (hits) with their sites.
> Here are some. Hit them.
>
> - Arroyo Grande, California, with a population of 15,500, has just over 700 local computers with Internet access. Still, the police department homepage averages 475 hits per month.
> - The Township of Fairfield, New Jersey, Police Department's homepage receives between 400 and 500 hits in any given month.
> - In its second week of operation, the Beaufort City, South Carolina, Police Department's web site recorded over 1,000 hits.
> - The Chula Vista, California, Police Department's homepage receives 700 hits per month.
> - The Davis, California, Police Department, serving a city with a population of 51,000, receives approximately 20,000 hits per month on its web site.
> - The Chicago Police Department receives 40,000 hits per month.
>
> Source: Adapted from "FaxBack Response: Previous Question: How Has the Internet Helped Your Agency?," *FBI Law Enforcement Bulletin*, January 1997, p. 25.

Information security involves protecting information. Typical activities of information security are protecting against the unauthorized use of computer programs and preventing the theft of corporate research and development plans.

Personnel security means protecting people. Activities of personnel security include being bodyguards for company executives or celebrities and conducting background investigations of prospective employees.

Most major corporations in the United States have private security forces performing overt and covert functions. Overtly they perform visible patrol designed to provide protection and loss prevention. Covertly, private security forces engage in surveillance or countersurveillance regarding trade secrets. The overt functions of private security are increasing. According to the Society of Competitor Intelligence Professions, over 80 percent of the Fortune 1000 companies have regular in-house "snoops" on the payroll. Corporate spying has reached the point where companies everywhere are now concerned with finding and eliminating spies and securing their files and corporate secrets.[31]

Private Security and the Courts

Private security officers are not restricted by the provisions of the U.S. Constitution in their duties, as the public police are. Private security officers do not have to give a suspect Miranda warnings before questioning, and the exclusionary rule does not apply to the evidence they seize. (Constitutional limitations on the police will be discussed in chapter 11.) However, private security officers must be very careful in their operations, as they can be sued and suffer monetary losses.

Current Problems of Private Security

Traditionally, there has been a lack of personnel standards and training for private security employees. A study by the Rand Corporation found that fewer than half of the private security guards in the United States were high school graduates, their average age was fifty-two years, and most were untrained and poorly paid. Rand provided the following stereotype of the "typical security guard": "an aging white male who is poorly educated and poorly paid—between 40 and 55; he has little education beyond the ninth grade; he has had a few years of experience in private security; he earns a marginal wage—some have retired from a low-level civil service or military career."[32]

Licensing of Private Security

Because of the proliferation of private security employees in the United States and their clouded history, a number of states have required a licensing process for them. Eleven states require training if the security guard is to be armed. Some states, however, require only an application and a minor fee.[33]

Professionalization of Private Security

In an effort to improve their image and increase their effectiveness, many private security firms have developed their own training programs. In 1955, a number of private security professionals developed a professional association to improve the image of private security—the **American Society for Industrial Security (ASIS)**. Membership in ASIS has increased over the years, and the group has definitely improved the image of the industry. ASIS has developed a comprehensive national examination to ensure that a private security professional merits the title professional. The exam requires a combination of study and experience before it can be taken by members of the security industry. Applicants who pass this examination earn the title of certified protection professional (CPP). ASIS also holds a yearly convention to discuss the latest security techniques and state-of-the-art equipment. Today there are several professional security magazines and a professional journal that enable security professionals to keep abreast of developments in the field.

In 1989, a first issue of *Security Journal* reported a survey that found that the education and experience characteristics of one proprietary security organization approached those of the local public police. This private security organization also employed more female officers and the staff had a greater diversity of ethnic backgrounds than did the local police department.[34]

In the 1980s, the International Association of Chiefs of Police, the National Sheriffs' Association, and the American Society of Industrial Security began joint meetings to foster better cooperation between the public and private sector. In 1986, these organizations, with funding from the National Institute of Justice, established the Joint Council of Law Enforcement and Private Security Associations.[35]

In 1976, only five colleges in the United States offered a bachelor's degree in private security, and no master's programs were available. By 1990, forty-six colleges offered a bachelor's degree, and fourteen offered a master's degree.[36]

The American Society for Industrial Security (ASIS) is seeking to professionalize the ranks of private security by appealing to college students. In 1997, ASIS had eight separate panels dealing with jobs in security at a career exposition at John Jay's College of Criminal Justice in New York City. It has distributed more than 30,000 "Careers in Security" booklets to universities, colleges, and career centers.[37]

Forecasts Regarding the Need for Private Security

Researchers have made the following predictions regarding economic crime and the size of the private security industry in the future.[38] More sophisticated white-collar

---

The CPP Examination

The CPP examination is a one-day, multiple-choice test consisting of two parts, a mandatory test administered in the morning and specialty subjects administered in the afternoon.

Mandatory Subjects
- Emergency Planning
- Investigations
- Legal Aspects
- Personnel Security
- Physical Security
- Protection of Sensitive Information
- Security Management
- Substance Abuse
- Loss Prevention
- Liaison

Specialty Subjects
- Banking and Financial Institutions
- Computer Security
- Credit Card Security
- Department of Defense Industrial Security Program Requirements
- Educational Institutions Security
- Fire Resources Management
- Health Care Institutions Security
- Manufacturing Security
- Nuclear Power Security
- Public Utility Security
- Restaurant and Lodging Security
- Retail Security
- Transportation and Cargo Security
- Oil and Gas Industrial Security
- Telephone and Telecommunications Security

The CPP certification is valid for three years and must be renewed thereafter.

Source: American Society for Industrial Security.

Dempsey's Law

There Are Jobs for College Students in Investigating

Students ask me this question often, particularly when I am teaching my Investigations course. I generally tell them the following story about two former students, Tony and Bill.

I was walking to my building getting ready to teach the second day of my course in Criminal Investigations when Tony and Bill called out to me from the parking lot. Tony and Bill had graduated our two-year program two years ago and were in their last year in a combined B.A./Master's program at a local university. I asked them how they were doing. They told me they were on their way to a surveillance in a neighboring town and wanted to stop by to say hello to me and some other former favorite professors. I asked them about their surveillance job. They told me they had been hired a few months ago by a local private investigations firm and were working about twenty-five to thirty hours a week, at $10 an hour, conducting surveillances. Their boss supplied them with a surveillance van, paid for the gas, and also supplied them with sophisticated camera equipment. That morning their goal was to take pictures of a man who had claimed that he was unable to work and was collecting disability payments from his employer. The former students' boss had received information that the man was actually feigning his injury and had been observed in his neighborhood not wearing the neck collar and not using the cane that he always used when he visited his doctor's office or his employer.

Tony and Bill followed me to my class where I introduced them to my thirty-four new students and asked them to tell the class about their job. The new students were impressed, but they were more impressed when I asked my former students where they had learned the techniques of surveillance. They both replied, "We learned it from you, right here in this classroom, Professor Dempsey." Needless to say, I had a captive audience from that class on.

---

crime will emerge in the later 1990s, with a higher loss of revenue than ever before. Computer crime will rise; however, most networks and systems are now protected by security devices and programs. Thus, computer threats will be a diminishing concern by the year 2000.

The rapid growth of closed-circuit television, sophisticated alarm systems, access control, and other technology will improve private security. This improvement will not necessarily lead to a reduction in the number of security personnel, because security personnel may perform different functions. By the year 2000, there will be an estimated 750,000 contract guards and 410,000 proprietary security personnel, of which 280,000 will be guards.

According to the U.S. Bureau of Labor Statistics (BLS), private security will remain one of the nation's fastest expanding industries through the year 2005. In 1997, the private security industry was ranked seventh, with an annual growth rate of 15 percent, according to BLS. The government projects the industry will create approximately 408,000 new and diverse jobs by 2005, including casino theft and fraud investigators; nuclear power disaster, fire, and life safety experts; systems integrators; and forensic accountants.[39]

According to Professor Robert McCrie, a noted private security expert,

> The statistics paint a bright future for private security and those students looking to enter the market. It also looks bright for those looking to make a career change.[40]

Private Employment of Public Police

A study disclosed that as many as 150,000 public police officers moonlight (work on their off-duty hours) as private security guards.[41] Almost all police departments re-

Dempsey's Law

More Jobs for Students in Private Security: Integrity Shoppers

Professor Dempsey, a friend of mine was just arrested and lost her job as a cashier at the Feel-Well drug store in town. She said that she was the victim of integrity shoppers. What's that?

Many retail businesses employ integrity shoppers to test employees' honesty and adherence to the rules and regulations established by the business. Let me give you the following scenario. It describes the actual operation of a team of integrity shoppers who were students of mine in a night class here at the college.

Mary, age 40, rushing through the busy aisles of a large pharmacy downtown, hurriedly selects an item of cosmetics costing $4.50. Clutching the item and a five dollar bill she passes other customers waiting on the check-out line and addresses the cashier in an excited manner: "I have to get back to work or I'll be fired. Look, take the five. That'll cover the tax." She then quickly places the five dollar bill on the counter in front of the cashier. Without waiting for a reply, she turns and rushes out of the store.

At the same time, Mary's daughter Linda, age 21, who is also Mary's partner, waits by the hair dye in the front of the store looking as if she cannot make up her mind which product to buy. Linda, in actuality, is carefully watching the cashier to determine what the cashier will do with the five dollar bill.

If the cashier puts the money into his or her pocket instead of ringing it up on the cash register, Linda signals her mother, who is waiting outside. The two women then approach the store manager, identify themselves as company security, and report the transaction. The cashier is removed from her or his station and brought to the manager's office.

Mary and Linda generally try to get the employee to prepare a written statement regarding her or his actions and any other previous illegal acts he or she has engaged in at the store. Because Mary and Linda are not police officers or government officials, they do not have to read the subject his or her Miranda Rights prior to questioning. Often the employee will give the names of other employees who steal from the store.

After obtaining the written statement, Mary and Linda notify the police, who respond and arrest the employee on the written complaint of the store manager.

Professor Dempsey, isn't that entrapment?

No! Providing someone an opportunity to commit a crime is not entrapment. The cashier did not have to pocket the five. He or she should have followed proper company procedures, which, no doubt, involved ringing up the sale or notifying the store manager to account for any cash overage or shortage.

quire an officer to obtain the department's permission before obtaining private security employment. In some departments, the officers must find their own private employer; in others, the police union serves as a broker in assigning off-duty officers to private employers. In some areas (for example, Boston, Colorado Springs, New Haven, and St. Petersburg), the police department itself actually serves as the broker between the private employers and the off-duty officers.[42]

The Seattle Police Department reported that 47 percent of its police officers had security work permits (department permission to work as private security officers while off duty). The Colorado Springs Police Department reported that 53 percent of its officers had work permits and worked a total of 20,000 off-duty hours in uniform, earning an average of $1,333 per officer. The Metro-Dade, Florida, police department reported that its uniformed off-duty officers made approximately $4 million in a year while working as private security guards.[43]

Three-quarters of the police departments that permit officers to perform private security on their off-duty

Dempsey's Law

More Jobs for Students in Private Security: Tom, the Store Detective

Professor Dempsey, I want to get into law enforcement, but I don't want to be a police officer. I want something more like a business or retail job. Can you tell us something about store detective work?

Sure, but why don't we ask Tom? He's a store detective, or more properly called a loss-prevention specialist, at that new clothing store in the area, Bobs. Tom, what do you do and how do you do it?

Well, professor, I've been working at Bobs since it opened last year. We have two store detectives working each shift. One works the cameras and one works the floor. Our job is to catch as many shoplifters as possible. After we catch them, we call the police and they arrest them.

Tom, what do you mean working the cameras and working the floor? Could you explain that better to your classmates?

Sure. We have video cameras all over the store. Some of them focus strictly on the cashiers so that we can monitor their actions, and some of them focus on the entire store. We have video monitors in the security office that we continually monitor. One of the security people sits in the office watching the video monitors and looks for people shoplifting. If he sees suspicious activity that indicates possible shoplifting, he notifies his partner who is working the floor by radio. The floor person then goes to that area and stands by as the camera person continues to monitor the video. If the person actually shoplifts, the camera person presses a button that provides an immediate photo of the activity and then notifies the floor person to move in to make an apprehension. The floor person is then assisted by the camera person and some other store personnel in making the apprehension.

Tom, is loss prevention always a two-person operation?

No, some stores only use one person. He or she walks around the store posing as a regular customer and makes discreet observations. That's not a good idea, however. It's always better to work with the cameras because they can give you direct evidence of the shoplifting. In this business there's no room for a bad stop, meaning apprehending someone who hasn't actually taken any property. If you make a bad stop, the store can be sued and you can be sued.

---

hours allow the officers to wear their uniforms. Also, many departments permit the off-duty use of other department equipment, including radios and vehicles.[44]

The use of public police as private security guards can lead to obvious problems. To whom is the officer responsible—the primary employer (the police department) or the private company? Who is responsible for the officer's liability in the event he or she makes a mistake? Should a police department continue to pay an officer who is out on sick report due to injuries sustained while working for a private firm? If an officer is guarding a local business and he or she observes a crime on the street, which obligation comes first—the obligation to the private business for security or the obligation to his or her oath of duty?

Community Self-Protection

Chapter 10 will discuss the two most current philosophies affecting police departments today, community policing and problem-solving policing. These two philosophies acknowledge that the police, by themselves, cannot eliminate or control crime; the community has to get involved. There must be a working relationship between the police and the community.

Chapter 9 will discuss numerous police-community partnerships. One is neighborhood watch, which involves neighborhood residents attempting to reduce crime and improve the quality of life in their communities. Two of the most effective strategies in community crime prevention are target hardening and neighborhood watch programs.

Target Hardening

One way citizens can protect themselves from crime is through **target hardening**—making a home or business as crime-proof as possible by installing locks, bars, alarms, and other protective devices. One survey of 11,000 households across the United States found that one-third of the households reported taking one or more crime prevention measures, including installing a burglar alarm (7 percent), participating in a neighborhood watch program (7 percent), or engraving valuables with an identification number (25 percent). Other commonly used crime prevention techniques included window bars, watchdogs, warning signs, fences or entrance barricades, guards or door attendants, and intercoms or surveillance cameras in building entrances.[45]

A National Institute of Justice report indicated that in the early 1980s, 2 to 5 percent of all homes in the United States were equipped with burglar alarms. This increased to 10 percent by 1990, and researchers predict that as alarm systems become less expensive and more readily available, residential alarm systems could double in number by the year 2000. However, this proliferation could cause a problem for the police, because police studies have consistently indicated that 95 to 99 percent of alarm calls are false.[46]

Neighborhood Watch Programs

A National Institute of Justice report discussed the various neighborhood patrol and block watch programs being created by communities and the police. These programs are designed so that people in communities watch for suspicious people, lobby for improvements like increased lighting, report crime to the police, conduct home security surveys, and generally work with the police to make neighborhoods safer. Chapter 9 will discuss this report and these programs in greater depth.[47]

Impact of Recession on Police Agencies and Police Consolidation

The economic recession of the late 1980s and early 1990s and the business concept of corporate downsizing has taken its toll on police agencies.

Consolidation of police services means combining small departments in adjoining areas into a super-

A Neighborhood Watch notice posted in a Washington, D.C., neighborhood informs residents of a crime committed that day. Such programs are common throughout the United States.

agency that serves the previously fragmented jurisdictions. Consolidation has the benefit of creating departments of sufficient size to use expanded services, such as training centers, communications centers, and emergency units, which are not generally cost effective in smaller departments. This consolidation has proved controversial because it requires that existing lines of political and administrative authority be changed drastically. Consolidation of departments or special services has been attempted in California, Massachusetts, New York, Illinois, New Jersey, and numerous other states.[48]

Some agencies have formed mutual aid pacts so that they can share infrequently used emergency services, such as SWAT and Emergency Response Teams, and some states have set up centralized data services to connect most local police agencies into a statewide information network.[49]

In New Jersey, many municipalities have "regionalized" their police departments by merging them with those of their neighbors. Others have disbanded their police agencies totally, opting instead for coverage by the state police. Of New Jersey's municipalities in 1992, eighty-two had no police departments, thirty-eight had agencies with one to five officers, and sixty-three had six to ten officers. The state police provides free law enforcement services for seventy-one municipalities—about one-quarter of the state's geographic area—and partial coverage for thirty-four other municipalities with small police departments.[50]

In 1997, the Essex County, New Jersey, Police Department, with a budget of nearly $2 million, was transferred along with the forty-officer department into the larger Essex County Sheriff's Department. With this merger, New Jersey has only two remaining county police departments as of 1997—Bergen and Union counties.[51] A few months before the Essex merger, the Hudson County Police Department was disbanded and its officers offered jobs with the county corrections department.[52]

In Ohio, in 1992, the St. Clair Township Police Department was virtually disbanded when its five part-time officers were laid off due to budgetary problems, leaving the police chief as the only officer in the township. The village of New Miami, Ohio, also virtually disbanded its police department, leaving the chief as the only law enforcer in the village. The Butler County (Ohio) Sheriff's Department has assumed law enforcement duties for these two communities and is feeling the pinch due to the additional duties.[53]

Departments all over the nation are starting to use contracting, which means that one government enters into a formal, binding agreement to provide all or certain specified law enforcement service to another government for an established fee. For example, a number of small towns in Florida have contracted with the Broward County Sheriff's Department to provide law enforcement for their communities, saving each town millions of dollars.[54]

Chapter Summary

This chapter discussed the public and private organizations that attempt to ensure safety and enforce the law in the United States. The public agencies are extremely complex and fragmented. Private security is rapidly overtaking public security in both numbers of people employed and amount of money spent. Although public law enforcement has seen considerable growth since the first U.S. police departments, the economic recession of the late 1980s and early 1990s has forced many localities to impose restrictions on their public safety agencies. Many agencies have been forced to reduce the services they offer to the public, lay off officers, and postpone hiring. No one knows if this trend will continue. We might see a reversal of the trend and an increased emphasis on public law enforcement as the recession dissipates and increased funds enter the public coffers. However, as we have seen in the past several decades, the private sector is ready to fill in what the public police cannot provide in meeting the need for security and law enforcement.

Learning Check

1. In terms of personnel and money spent, talk about how extensive the safety industry is in the United States.
2. Most police in the United States are local, as opposed to state and federal. Discuss why this is so.
3. Discuss how state police differ from local police.
4. Explain how federal law enforcement agencies differ from local and state police.
5. Discuss the scope of the private security industry in the United States.

Review Exercise

You have been given the opportunity to create a new town or city based on your specifications. To do this, you must also create the institutions that will govern this locality. What institutions would you create to ensure a safe and orderly environment? You must assume that crime and disorder is possible, even in your new city. Consider the qualifications you want these offices to possess, what power you would give them, and if you would design them as private or public.

Web Exercise

Patrol the Net to the National Institute of Justice's homepage and obtain the Bureau of Justice Statistics' latest update regarding the number of law enforcement agencies in the United States. Local departments? Sheriffs' offices? State police agencies? Federal law enforcement agencies?

Also, obtain the latest statistics on the number of sworn officers in local, state, and federal law enforcement agencies.

Key Concepts

local control
centralized model of state law enforcement
decentralized model of state law enforcement
National Institute of Justice (NIJ)
National Criminal Justice Reference Service (NCJRS)
civil forfeiture
private security industry
privatization
Allan Pinkerton
Henry Wells
William Fargo

American Society for Industrial Security (ASIS)
target hardening

Notes

1. David H. Bayley, *Forces of Order: Police Behavior in Japan and the United States* (Berkeley: University of California Press, 1976).
2. Kathleen Maguire and Ann L. Pastore, eds., *Sourcebook of Criminal Justice Statistics 1996* (Washington, D.C.: U.S. Department of Justice, Bureau of Justice Statistics, U.S. Government Printing Office, 1997), Table 1.25, p. 37. The numbers in the text are rounded off for ease of reading.
3. Maguire and Pastore, *Sourcebook of Criminal Justice Statistics 1996,* Table 1.2, p. 3.
4. Maguire and Pastore, *Sourcebook of Criminal Justice Statistics 1996,* Table 1.21, p. 26.
5. Maguire and Pastore, *Sourcebook of Criminal Justice Statistics 1995.*
6. Brian Reaves, *Local Police Departments—1993* (Washington, D.C.: National Institute of Justice, 1996).
7. Reaves, *Local Police Departments.*
8. Reaves, *Local Police Departments.*
9. The Police Foundation, *Annual Report, 1989* (Washington, D.C.: The Police Foundation, 1989), pp. 3–4.
10. Brian Reaves, *Sheriffs' Departments: 1993* (Washington, D.C.: National Institute of Justice, 1996).
11. Lee P. Brown, "The Role of the Sheriff," in *The Future of Policing,* ed. Alvin Cohn (Beverly Hills, Calif.: Sage Publications, 1978), pp. 237–240.
12. Reaves, *Sheriffs' Departments.*
13. John Hoffman, "Rural Policing," *Law and Order,* June 1992, pp. 20–24.
14. Christopher S. Wren, "The Illegal Home Business: 'Speed' Manufacture," *New York Times,* 8 July 1997, p. A-8.
15. Wren, "The Illegal Home Business."
16. Lee Colwell, "The National Center for Rural Law Enforcement: One Part of the Greater Whole," *Community Policing Exchange,* March/April 1997, p. 6. The author is the director of The Criminal Justice Institute, 7723B Asher Avenue, Little Rock, Arkansas 72204. For more information, contact him.
17. Maguire and Pastore, *Sourcebook of Criminal Justice Statistics 1996.*
18. Brian Reaves, *Federal Law Enforcement Officers, 1996* (Washington, D.C.: National Institute of Justice, 1997), p. 1.
19. "What Price Justice? For FY'98, the Tab Could Top Out at $19.3B," *Law Enforcement News,* 28 February 1997, pp. 1, 6.
20. See, for example, Althan Theorharis and John Stuart Cox, *The Boss* (Philadelphia: Temple University Press, 1988). There are a myriad of books in college libraries and local public libraries regarding the history and operations of the FBI and the history of Director Hoover. An interesting class project or research paper may be to compare and contrast the treatment of the FBI and Hoover in the books published before his death in 1972 and after his death. Most authors needed the prior approval of Hoover and his officials prior to publication. The books published after his death generally paint a much different picture of Hoover and the FBI.
21. See, for example, Tony Proveda, *Lawlessness and Reform: The FBI in Transition* (Pacific Grove, Calif.: Brooks/Cole, 1990).
22. Federal Bureau of Investigation, *Uniform Crime Reports,* p. 5.
23. "Once More, into the Breach," *Law Enforcement News,* 31 December 1996, p. 13.
24. William C. Cunningham and Todd H. Taylor, *The Hallcrest Report: Private Security and Police in America* (Portland, Oreg.: Chancellor Press, 1985).
25. William C. Cunningham, John J. Strauchs, and Clifford W. Van Meter, *The Hallcrest Report II: Private Security Trends: 1970–2000* (Boston: Butterworth-Heinemann, 1990). This report was also published by the National Institute of Justice, in summary form, for the government as: William C. Cunningham, John J. Strauchs, and Clifford W. Van Meter, *Private Security: Patterns and Trends* (Washington, D.C.: U.S. Government Printing Office, 1991). Also, see chapter 2 of John S. Dempsey, *An Introduction to Public and Private Investigations* (Minneapolis/St. Paul: West, 1996) for a full discussion of the private security industry in the United States and its investigative function and relationship with the public police. Figures 2.1 and 2.2 graphically depict this fact.
26. "ASIS Display Promotes Security Careers," *Security Management,* July 1997, pp. 137–138.
27. Cunningham, Strauchs, and Van Meter, *Private Security,* p. 2.
28. Bureau of Justice Statistics, *Report to the Nation on Crime and Justice,* 2d ed. (Washington, D.C.: National Institute of Justice, 1988), p. 118.
29. James D. Horan and Howard Swiggett, *The Pinkerton Story* (New York: G.P. Putnam's Sons, 1951) and James D. Horan, *The Pinkertons: The Detective Dynasty That Made History* (New York: Crown, 1967).
30. William C. Cunningham and Todd H. Taylor, *The Growth of Private Security* (Washington, D.C.: National Institute of Justice, 1984).
31. "George Smiley Joins the Firm," *Newsweek,* 2 May 1988, pp. 46–47.

32. James F. Kakalik and Sorrel Wildhorn, *Private Police in the United States,* vol. 2 (Washington, D.C.: National Institute of Justice, 1971), p. 133.
33. Joseph G. Deegan, "Mandated Training for Private Security," *FBI Law Enforcement Bulletin,* March 1987, pp. 6–8.
34. William Walsh, "Private/Public Police Stereotypes: A Different Perspective," *Security Journal* 1(1989): 21–27.
35. Cunningham, Strauchs, and Van Meter, *Private Security,* p. 2.
36. Cunningham, Strauchs, and Van Meter, *Private Security,* p. 4.
37. "ASIS Display Promotes Security Careers." For a free "Careers in Security" brochure, contact ASIS Customer Service at 703/522–5800. The information is also available on ASIS Online at http://www.asisonline.org.
38. Cunningham, Strauchs, and Van Meter, *Private Security,* p. 4.
39. "ASIS Display Promotes Security Careers."
40. "ASIS Display Promotes Security Careers."
41. Albert Reiss, *Private Employment of Public Police* (Washington, D.C.: National Institute of Justice, 1988).
42. Reiss, *Private Employment of Public Police.*
43. Reiss, *Private Employment of Public Police.*
44. Cunningham, Strauchs, and Van Meter, *Private Security,* p. 3. See the *New York Post,* 23 November 1997, p. 6, for the latest controversy involving a bill allowing New York City police officers to work in uniform for private employers.
45. Catherine Whitaker, *Crime Prevention Measures* (Washington, D.C.: National Institute of Justice, 1986).
46. Cunningham, Strauchs, and Van Meter, *Private Security,* pp. 2–3.
47. James Garofalo and Maureen McLeod, *Improving the Use and Effectiveness of Neighborhood Watch Programs* (Washington, D.C.: National Institute of Justice, 1988).
48. Thomas McAninch and Jeff Sanders, "Police Attitudes Toward Consolidation in Bloomington/Normal, Illinois: A Case Study," *Journal of Police Science and Administration* 16 (1988): 95–105.
49. Mike D'Alessandro and Charles Hoffman, "Mutual Aid Pacts," *Law and Order* 43 (1995): 90–93; and Leonard Sipes, Jr., "Maryland's High-Tech Approach to Crime Fighting," *Police Chief* 61 (1994): 18–20.
50. "Is the Who Equal to the Sum of Its Parts? Increasingly, Strapped N.J. Towns Consider Police Agency Mergers," *Law Enforcement News,* 30 September 1992, p. 4.
51. "Wedding Is on for NJ Agencies," *Law Enforcement News,* 15 May 1997, p. 5.
52. "Sheriffs Rule in New Jersey, as Another County PD May Vanish," *Law Enforcement News,* 15 March 1997, p. 5.
53. "As Local PD's Fold, Ohio Sheriff Feels Pinch of Added Workload," *Law Enforcement News,* 30 September 1992, p. 4.
54. Nick Navarro, "Six Broward County Cities Turn to the Green and Gold," *Police Chief* 59 (1992): 60.

3

Organizing the Police Department

Chapter Outline

Organizing the Department: Managerial Concepts
  Division of Labor
  Chain of Command (Hierarchy of Authority)
  Span of Control
  Delegation of Responsibility and Authority
  Unity of Command
  Rules, Regulations, and Discipline
Organizing by Personnel
  The Civil Service System
  Quasi-Military Model of Police
  Sworn and Nonsworn (Civilian) Personnel
  Rank Structure
  Other Personnel
  Some Personnel Issues
Organizing by Area
  Beats/Posts
  Sectors/Zones
  Precincts
Organizing by Time
  The Three-Tour System
  Tour Conditions
  Steady (Fixed) Tours
Organizing by Function or Purpose
  Line and Staff (Support) Functions
  Police Department Units

Chapter Goals

■ To acquaint you with the organizational and managerial concepts necessary to organize and operate a police department.

■ To acquaint you with the complexities of modern police organizations.

■ To show you how police departments are organized on the basis of personnel, area, time, and function.

■ To introduce you to the major ranks in a police department and to the responsibilities connected with those ranks.

■ To introduce you to the major units of a police department and the functions they perform.

57

Introduction

This chapter deals with organizing a police department. In any organization, someone must do the work the organization is charged with doing; someone must supervise those doing the work; and someone must command the operation. Certain commonly accepted rules of management must be followed to accomplish the goals of the organization. This chapter will include the organization of the police department by personnel (rank), area, time, and function or purpose. It will look at the various ranks in a police department and examine the responsibilities of the people holding those ranks. Then it will discuss how a police department allocates or assigns its personnel by area, time, and function or purpose. This chapter is designed to give you an awareness of the complexities involved in policing seven days a week, twenty-four hours a day.

Not all police organizations are as complex as what is described here. In fact, most police departments in the United States are small. The intent of this chapter, however, is to cover as many complexities of the police organization as possible to give you the broadest possible view of policing in the United States.

Organizing the Department: Managerial Concepts

Before discussing the organization of a police department, some managerial concepts common to most organizations should be understood. These concepts include division of labor; chain of command (hierarchy of authority); span of control; delegation of responsibility and authority; unity of command; and rules, regulations, and discipline.

Division of Labor

Obviously, all the varied tasks and duties that must be performed by an organization cannot be performed by one, a few, or even all of the members of the organization. The different tasks and duties an organization performs must be divided among its members in accordance with some logical plan.

In police departments, the tasks of the organization are divided according to personnel, area, time, and function or purpose. Work assignments must be designed so that similar (homogeneous) tasks, functions, and activities are given to a particular group for accomplishment. In a police department, patrol functions are separate from detective functions, which are separate from internal investigative functions. Geographic and time distinctions are also established, with certain officers' working certain times and areas. The best way to think of the division of labor in an organization is to ask the question, Who is going to do what, when, and where?

The division of labor should be reflected in an organization chart, a pictorial representation of reporting relationships in an organization (Figure 3.1). A good organizational chart is a snapshot of the organization. Workers can see exactly where they stand in the organization (what functions they perform, who they report to, and who reports to them).

Chain of Command (Hierarchy of Authority)

The managerial concept of chain of command (also called hierarchy of authority) involves the superior-subordinate or supervisor-worker relationships throughout the department, wherein each individual is supervised by one immediate supervisor or boss. Thus, the chain of command as pictured in the organizational chart shows workers which supervisor they report to; the chain of command also shows supervisors to whom they are accountable and for whom they are responsible. All members of the organization should follow the chain of command. For example, a patrol officer should report to his or her immediate sergeant, not to the captain. A captain should send his or her orders through the chain of command to the lieutenant, who disseminates the directions to the sergeants, who disseminate the information to the patrol officers (see Figure 3.2). Chain of command may be violated, however, when an emergency exists or speed is necessary.

Span of Control

The number of officers or subordinates that a supervisor can supervise effectively is called the span of control. Although no one can say exactly how many officers a sergeant can supervise or how many sergeants a lieutenant can supervise, most police management experts say the chain of command should be one supervisor to every six to ten officers of a lower rank. Nevertheless, it is best to keep the span of control as limited as possible so that the supervisor can more effectively

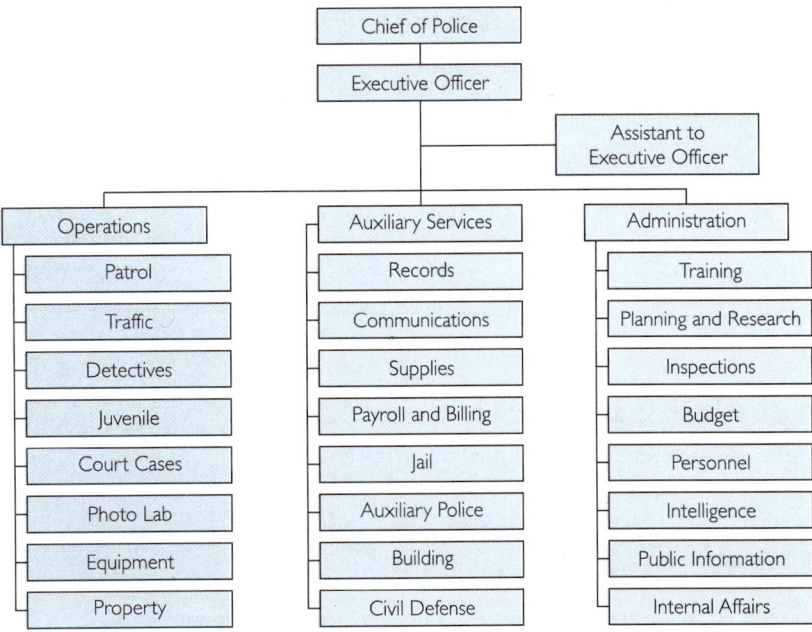

**Figure 3.1
Organization of a Police Department by Function**
Source: Adapted, with permission, from Anderson Publishing, Cincinnati, Ohio 45202. Robert Sheehan and Gary W. Cordner, *Introduction to Police Administration*, 2d ed. (Cincinnati: Anderson, 1989), p. 33.

supervise and control. The number of workers a supervisor can effectively supervise is affected by many factors, including distance, time, knowledge, personality, and the complexity of the work to be performed.

Delegation of Responsibility and Authority

Another important managerial concept in police organizations is delegation of responsibility and authority. Tasks, duties, and responsibilities are assigned to subordinates, along with the power or authority to control, command, make decisions, or otherwise act in order to complete the tasks that have been delegated or assigned to them.

Unity of Command

The concept of unity of command means that each individual in an organization is directly accountable to only one supervisor. The concept is important, because no one person can effectively serve two supervisors at one time. Unity of command may be violated in emergency situations.

Rules, Regulations, and Discipline

Most police organizations have a complex system of rules and regulations designed to control and direct the actions of officers. Most departments have operations manuals or rules and procedures designed to show officers what they must do in most situations they encoun-

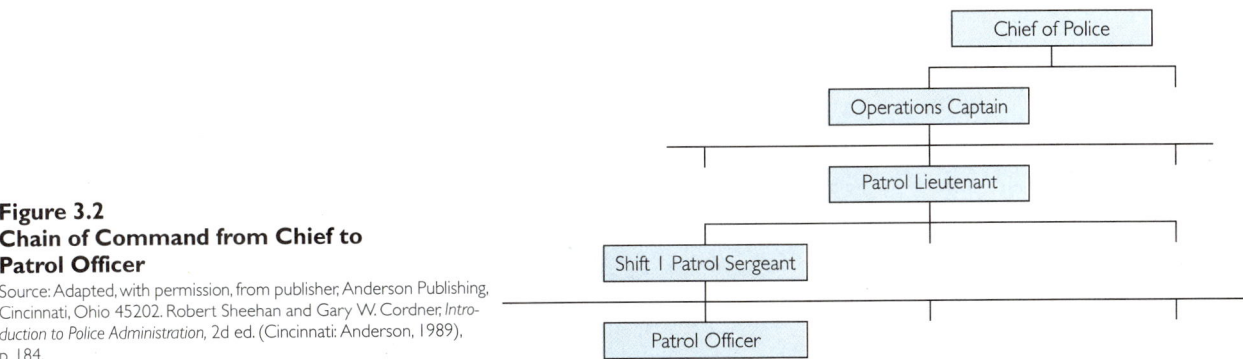

**Figure 3.2
Chain of Command from Chief to Patrol Officer**
Source: Adapted, with permission, from publisher, Anderson Publishing, Cincinnati, Ohio 45202. Robert Sheehan and Gary W. Cordner, *Introduction to Police Administration*, 2d ed. (Cincinnati: Anderson, 1989), p. 184.

ter. Rule books are often complex and detailed. In the New York City Police Department, the police rule book is over 1 foot thick.

Police departments have disciplinary standards that are similar to, but less stringent than, the military's. Violation of department standards in terms of dress, appearance, and conduct can lead to sanctions against officers in terms of reprimands, fines, or even dismissal from the department.

Organizing by Personnel

A police department faces the same organizational challenges as any organization, and a major challenge is personnel. The civil service system plays a large role in police hiring. This section will describe that role, along with the quasi-military model of police, sworn versus nonsworn personnel, rank structure, and other personnel issues.

The Civil Service System

The **civil service system** is a method of hiring and managing government employees that is designed to eliminate political influence, favoritism, nepotism, and bias. Civil service rules govern the hiring, promoting, and terminating of government employees. The Pendleton Act created a civil service system for federal employees in 1883, in the wake of the assassination of President James Garfield, who was killed in 1881 by a person who had been rejected for appointment to a federal of-

---

PATROLLING THE NET

The Dallas, Texas, P.D.—What's on Their Homepage?

The Dallas Police Department (DPD) launched a homepage on the World Wide Web in 1995. It contains information in the following areas:

- Crime statistics (dating back to 1992)
- Arrest statistics
- Recruiting information
- Budget allocations
- Police department contact information
- Calls for service statistics
- Crime prevention programs
- Staffing data
- Maps of the city, service areas, police sectors, and beats
- Links to other law enforcement–related sites on the World Wide Web

Lieutenant Walter W. Manning, who serves in DPD's Computer/Crime Analysis Unit, says:

If all this information were printed on paper, the package would be approximately 1-inch thick. The cost of printing this material in full process color, storing it, and mailing it to requestors would be staggering. In contrast, providing this volume of data via the Internet is exceptionally cost-effective.

Since the deployment of DPD's homepage, the site has averaged more than 260 visits each day. The department received 32,000 visitors to the web site during its first year, with more than 1,200 e-mail messages. Many of the e-mail messages from the public have shown the value of the department's Internet presence. Citizens have offered to work as volunteers with juvenile detainees and gang members, indicated an interest in joining the police reserves based on information posted about the program, and simply expressed appreciation for the department's work. One community member said, "Many possibilities are here to make your jobs easier and [the citizens] of Dallas safer. Glad to see that the Department is making use of all the advanced technology to work for all of our best interests."

Similar positive returns have been realized in the area of recruiting. The department posted information related to its hiring requirements, the hiring and training process, salary, benefits, and career opportunities. In the first twelve months, 500 people indicated an interest in employment via e-mail, and an unknown number of others might have called the Personnel Section's toll-free phone number, which is listed on the homepage.

Messages have not been limited to the United States. The DPD home page has received messages from England, Canada, Australia, South Africa, Taiwan, Germany, and Sweden.

Check out the DPD home page at: http://www.airmail.net/dpd/index.htm

Source: Adapted from Walter W. Manning, "Should You Be on the Net?" *FBI Law Enforcement Bulletin,* January 1997, pp. 18–22.

fice. Eventually, many state and local governments adopted their own civil service systems.

Today, over 95 percent of all government employees at the federal, state, and local levels are covered by the civil service system. Civil service has reduced political interference and paved the way for merit employment, a system in which personal ability is stressed above all other considerations. However, some civil service systems seem to guarantee life tenure in the organization and provide an atmosphere of absolute employee protection instead of stressing the merit that the system was initially designed to emphasize.[1]

Most police departments, particularly larger departments, are governed by civil service regulations. Some complain that the civil service system creates many problems for police administrators, because a chief or commissioner cannot appoint or promote at will but must follow the civil service rules and appoint and promote according to civil service lists. Additionally, it is often difficult to demote or terminate employees under the civil service system.[2] Although many criticize civil service rules, it must be remembered that they help eliminate the autocratic power of a supervisor to hire, fire, or transfer employees on a whim.

Quasi-Military Model of Police

As chapter 1 indicated, the U.S. police are a civil, as opposed to a military, organization. Despite this, our police departments are **quasi-military organizations** (organizations similar to the military). Like the military, the police are organized along strict lines of authority and reporting relationships; they wear military-style, highly recognizable uniforms; they use military-style rank designations; they carry weapons; and they are authorized by law to use force. Like the military, police officers are trained to respond to orders immediately.

Despite similarities, however, the police are far different from the military. They are not trained as warriors to fight foreign enemies but instead are trained to maintain order, serve and protect the public, and enforce the criminal law. Most important, the power of the police is limited by state laws and by the Bill of Rights.

Sworn and Nonsworn (Civilian) Personnel

People who work for police departments fall under two major classifications: sworn members of the department, or police officers, and nonsworn members of the department, or civilians.

All in the Line of Duty

40 Minutes of Hell in L.A.

On Friday, February 28, 1997, at 9:15 A.M. in North Hollywood, California, Police Officers Loren Farell and Martin Perello, Los Angeles Police Department (LAPD), were on routine patrol when they observed a "211" robbery in progress at the Bank of America. They had seen two men dressed like "Ninja Turtles" pushing a person into the bank. The officers took tactical cover and called for backup. Within five minutes the LAPD had the bank covered. Automatic weapons fire began to come out of the bank.

For forty minutes LAPD cops, officers from five other jurisdictions, and the citizens of North Hollywood were in their own version of hell, under attack by the perpetrators, who were wearing full body armor and armed with AK-47s. When the smoke cleared, the following details of the firefight emerged:

- Eleven LAPD officers (nine shot) and seven civilians (two shot) lay injured.
- Both suspects dead.
- Eight police cars damaged.
- 350 officers at the scene (five agencies).
- 1,500 rounds fired by the suspects.
- 500 rounds fired by police.
- Gunshot wounds to suspect #1: Eleven (one self-inflicted to head).
- Gunshot wounds to suspect #2: Twenty-nine.
- Dollars robbed from bank: $350,000 (all recovered).
- Dollars robbed from bank by these suspects in previous robberies: $2,000,000.

Upon their capture, officers found the following weapons in the perpetrators' possession:

- 3 Norinco rifles, full automatic.
- 1 Heckler and Koch rifle, full automatic.
- 1 Bushmaster rifle, full automatic.
- 1 Beretta pistol, semiautomatic.
- 1 Molotov cocktail.

Subsequent to the shoot-out, police found another arsenal of weapons in the perpetrators' home, including numerous rifles, pistols, 2,000 rounds of ammunition (including live incendiary rounds and armor-piercing rounds), do-it-yourself hand grenade kits, and numerous other deadly devices.

Source: Various news media, February, March, 1997.

Sworn Members **Sworn members** are those people in the police organization we usually think of as police officers, troopers, or deputy sheriffs. They are given traditional police powers by state and local laws, including penal or criminal laws and criminal procedure laws. Additionally, upon appointment, sworn members take an oath to abide by the U.S. Constitution and those sections of state and local law applicable to the exercise of police power.

The best example of police power is the power to arrest. Regular citizens also have the power to arrest (citizen's arrest). However, these powers differ.

As an example, the *Criminal Procedure Law* of New York State grants arrest powers to both police officers and ordinary citizens:

> Section 140.10 . . . a police officer may arrest a person for:
> (a) Any offense when he has reasonable cause to believe that such person has committed such offense in his presence; and
> (b) A crime when he has reasonable cause to believe that such person has committed such crime, whether in his presence or otherwise. . . .
>
> Section 140.30 . . . any person (citizen) may arrest another person:
> (a) for a felony when the latter has in fact committed such felony: and
> (b) for any offense when the latter has in fact committed such offense in his presence.[3]

The law is quite specific. Police officers need only to have probable cause (not definite proof) to make arrests for any crimes committed in their presence or not. They can make arrests for any offenses (including minor infractions) committed in their presence.

Probable cause is a series of facts that would indicate to a "reasonable person" that a crime is being committed or was committed and that a certain person is committing or did commit it. A good example of facts leading to probable cause follows:

1. At 3 A.M., screams from a female are heard in an alley.
2. An officer sees a man running from the alley.
3. Upon the officer's command, the man refuses to halt and rushes past the officer.

This gives the officer probable cause to stop the man, even though there is no "proof" yet of a crime. If it later turns out that no crime was committed, the officer has done nothing wrong, because he or she acted under probable cause.

Citizens, in contrast, cannot use probable cause, and the crimes must have actually happened. (In fact, this leaves citizens open for false arrest lawsuits.) Additionally, citizens can only arrest for offenses actually committed in their presence, unless that offense was a felony.

In addition to the power of arrest, the police officer has the power to stop temporarily and question people in public places, to stop vehicles and conduct inspections, and to search for weapons and other contraband. Additionally, the police officer has significantly more power to use physical force, including deadly physical force, than does the citizen.

Nonsworn (Civilian) Members **Nonsworn (civilian) members** of police departments are not given traditional police powers and can exercise only the very limited arrest power given to ordinary citizens. Thus, they are assigned to nonenforcement duties in the department. They serve in many different areas of a police organization and in many roles. When we think of nonsworn members, we usually think of typists, 911 operators, and police radio dispatchers. However, nonsworn members serve in many other capacities as well, including clerical, technical, administrative, and managerial jobs. Their rank structure is generally not as vertical as that of sworn officers.

Rank Structure

Sworn members generally have a highly organized rank structure (chain of command). The lowest sworn rank in the police organization is usually the police officer, although many organizations have lower-ranked sworn officers, such as cadets or trainees, who generally perform duties similar to nonsworn members or assist sworn members in performing nonenforcement duties. Many cadets or trainees aspire to an eventual sworn position or are in training for one. In most organizations, those in training at the police academy are known as recruits or cadets and generally have the same legal authority as regular officers, except that they are generally not assigned to enforcement duties while still in training.

To say the police officer is the lowest rank in a police department may sound demeaning to the rank. However, it only refers to the relative rank in the organizational chart, not to the police officer's power or to the quality and importance of the service performed.

The following sections describe the various ranks in the police organization using generic terms. Most departments use the titles police officer, detective, sergeant, lieutenant, and captain. However, some organizations, such as state police departments and county sheriff's offices, use different terms to describe their members. In a state police force, the rank of trooper is almost identical to the rank of police officer. In a sheriff's office, the rank of deputy sheriff is synonymous with the rank of police officer.

The police officer/trooper/deputy sheriff is the most important person in the police organization. He or she is the person who is actually working on the streets, attempting to maintain order and enforce the law. A police agency is only as good as the quality of the men and women it employs.

Police Officer Police officers serve as the workers in the police organization. The average police officer is assigned to patrol duties. (See chapters 7 and 8 for a complete discussion of the activities of patrol officers.) Police officers perform the basic duties for which the police organization exists. They are under the control of supervisors, generally known as ranking officers or superior officers. Ranking officers are generally known as sergeants, lieutenants, and captains. At the highest level in most police organizations are inspectors and chiefs. In some state police organizations, military ranks such as major and colonel are used instead of inspector and chief. In federal law enforcement organizations, nonmilitary terms are used to reflect rank structure, such as agent, supervisor, manager, administrator, and director.

Corporal or Master Patrol Officer Many police departments have established the corporal or master patrol officer rank as an intermediate rank between the police officer and the first-line supervisor, the sergeant. Often this rank is given to an officer as a reward for exemplary service or for additional services performed, such as training or technical functions.

Detective/Investigator Some police officers in a department are designated as detectives, investigators, or inspectors. (The various names for ranks may be confusing, since investigators in the San Francisco Police Department are called inspectors, whereas in the New York City Police Department, the rank of inspector is that of a senior manager.) Their role is to investigate past crimes. (See chapter 7 for a complete discussion of the role and activities of the detective.) Detectives exercise no supervisory role over police officers except at a crime scene (the location where a serious crime occurred and where possible evidence may be present),

Officers of all ranks are important in planning police operations. The officer to the left is a deputy inspector, the officer in the center is a captain, and the officer to the right is a police officer.

where they are in charge and make most major decisions.

The role of the detective is generally considered more prestigious than that of police officer. Detectives generally receive a higher salary and do not wear uniforms. They are usually designated detectives not through the typical civil service promotional examination but rather by appointment, generally for meritorious work. Often detectives do not possess civil service tenure and can be demoted back to the police officer rank without the strict civil service restrictions applicable to the other ranks in a police organization.

Sergeant The first supervisor in the police chain of command is the sergeant. The sergeant is the first-line supervisor and, as many will say, the most important figure in the police supervisory and command hierarchy. The sergeant has two main responsibilities in police operations. First, the sergeant is the immediate supervisor of a number of officers assigned to his or her supervision. This group of officers is generally known as a **squad.** (Generally, six to ten officers make up a squad, and several squads may work on a particular tour of duty.) The sergeant is responsible for the activities and conduct of members of his or her squad. Second, the sergeant is responsible for decisions made at the scene of a police action until he or she is relieved by a higher-ranking officer.

The sergeant is responsible for getting the job done through the actions of people. Thus, he or she must possess numerous important personal qualities, such as intelligence, integrity, and dedication. The sergeant also draws on numerous organizational, motivational, and communication skills.

Lieutenant Just above sergeant in the chain of command is the lieutenant. Whereas the sergeant is generally in charge of a squad of officers, the lieutenant is in charge of the entire **platoon**. The platoon consists of all of the people working on a particular tour (shift). Not only is the lieutenant in charge of employees; he or she also is in charge of all police operations occurring on a particular tour.

Captain Next in the chain of command above the lieutenant is the captain. The captain is ultimately responsible for all personnel and all activities in a particular area, or for a particular unit, on a twenty-four hour-a-day basis. The captain must depend on the lieutenants and sergeants under his or her command to communicate his or her orders to the officers and to exercise discipline and control over the officers.

Ranks above Captain Many larger municipal agencies have a hierarchy of ranks above the rank of captain. Inspectors generally have administrative control over several precincts or geographic areas, whereas assistant chiefs or chiefs have administrative control of major police units, such as personnel, patrol, or detectives.

Chief of Police/Police Commissioner The head of the police agency is usually termed the chief of police or the police commissioner. Chiefs of police and police

Dempsey's Law

Making Rank

Professor Dempsey, how do you make rank in a police department? How do you get promoted?

All police departments are different. Would you like me to tell you how I made rank in the NYPD?

Sure, that would be great.

I was appointed to the rank of police officer in 1966, after passing all the entry examinations, which we will discuss when we get to chapter 4. At that time, the entry-level rank in the NYPD was called patrolman instead of police officer. It was changed to police officer for reasons we will discuss when we get to chapter 13. I worked in the Forty-first Precinct, which was located in the South Bronx, until 1973, when I was transferred to the police academy as a recruit instructor. I was promoted to detective in 1973. There is no examination for the rank of detective; generally, officers make detective based on merit.

I was promoted to sergeant in 1974 and transferred to the Sixtieth Precinct in Coney Island, Brooklyn. Promotion to sergeant was based on a civil service examination and an assessment center. I spent my years as a sergeant in the 60 (Sixtieth Precinct) and the Organized Crime Control Bureau. Because of the city's financial crisis, there was no test for the next rank, lieutenant, until 1982.

I was promoted to lieutenant in 1983 and assigned to the 60 once again. Promotion to lieutenant involved a three-stage civil service examination, including administrative, operational, and oral exercises.

I was promoted to captain in 1985 and transferred to Patrol Borough Brooklyn North. Promotion to captain was also based on a three-stage civil service examination. I spent my years as a captain in Patrol Borough Brooklyn North; the Seventy-ninth Precinct in Bedford Stuyvesant, Brooklyn; the Civilian Complaint Review Board; and the Personnel Bureau.

Professor, you must have worked very hard to get all those promotions!

I sure did.

Was it worth it?

I would say so. My pension today and for the rest of my life is over $45,000 a year, and I had a great time.

PATROLLING THE NET

He's a Cyber Cop—One of Only a Few

Special Agent Jeffrey Herig, of the Florida State Police, is a cyber cop. It is reported that only about 200 cops nationwide have the knowledge and sophistication to deal with the computer criminals and the computer crime that is proliferating in our Information Age.

When regular cops "hit the field," everyone knows they are going out onto the street. Cyber cops don't go into the field; they go into "meat space," cybertalk for what other cops call the field. Agent Herig spends most of his time cruising hard-drive scenes for evidence. Generally, he does so without ever leaving the Tallahassee, Florida, lab he founded.

Some of his cases:

- One Medicaid swindler uploaded hundreds of phony claims, pocketing more than $200,000 in five months. He pled guilty.
- Criminals sent bogus faxes, with official government seals and signatures, to county jails authorizing the release of prisoners.
- Counterfeiters created fake driver's licenses, school transcripts, and price stickers.
- A Casio organizer belonging to a murdered drug-gang member revealed names and phone numbers that helped convict four men in a federal drug-conspiracy trial.

Herig has methods to recover deleted files from a hard drive—is that legal? The courts haven't had a case on that yet, but you can be sure there will be a Mapp- or Miranda-type decision in this field in the near future as this science moves forward. To avoid possible future constitutional and legal problems, Herig and his colleagues have developed their own standards for seizing data: They don't scan a seized hard drive itself but a "mirror" copy, to avoid suspicion of tampering and to prohibit untrained personnel from destroying or corrupting data.

Source: Adapted from Peter Katel, "Cybercrooks, Beware: Here Come the Cybercops," *Newsweek*, 9 June 1997, p. 86.

---

commissioners are generally appointed by the top official of a government (mayor, county executive, or governor) for a definite term of office. Generally, commissioners and chiefs do not have civil service tenure and may be replaced at any time.

One of the major exceptions to this lack of civil service tenure was the chief of the Los Angeles Police Department (LAPD). The LAPD chief of police is not subject to the direction of the Los Angeles mayor but rather to a board of officials called the Police Commission, who may remove the chief of police from duty, but only for cause. In effect, the chief had a permanent appointment.[4] This proved to be a complicating factor in the 1991 Rodney King case in that the Police Commission fired Chief Daryl Gates, who was then returned to his post by the Los Angeles City Council. Gates maintained his post, despite much pressure, during the 1992 Los Angeles riots.

Gates resigned after the riots and was replaced by former Philadelphia top cop Willie Williams, who was granted a five-year contract. Williams was instrumental in planning the city's strategy to deal with possible problems in the wake of the 1993 re-trial of the officers involved in the Rodney King case and was generally credited with maintaining order on Los Angeles streets during that time.

However, upon the end of his first term, Williams was refused the chance for a second five-year term. The Los Angeles Police Commission issued a twenty-two-page report explaining its actions and offered Williams a $375,000 severance package to persuade him to leave six weeks before his contract expired.[5] "This is in the best interest of the City of Los Angeles," said the Police Commission.[6]

Other Personnel

Police departments are increasingly using nonsworn employees and civilians to perform tasks in the police department. This effort can increase both efficiency in the use of human resources and cut costs. Community service officers and police auxiliaries also help some departments operate more effectively.

Civilianization The process of removing sworn officers from noncritical or nonenforcement tasks and replacing them with civilians or nonsworn employees is **civilianization**. Civilians with special training and qualifications

All in the Line of Duty

One Officer Remembers the LAPD's Finest Hour

The hellacious gunbattle on the streets of North Hollywood on February 28, 1997, will be remembered as one of the Los Angeles Police Department's finest hours. The courage that was demonstrated by so many officers—some, but not all of it, captured by news media video footage—ensures this legacy.

The video images of officers driving a police car into the line of fully automatic AK-47 fire, then climbing out to rescue a downed officer, are indelible.

Stories of officers exposing themselves to automatic gunfire to rescue citizens trapped and frozen in their own cars—not to mention on their own street, in front of their own bank—speak to the heroism that is proudly held in the highest traditions of the LAPD.

"We didn't do anything that any other cop wouldn't do," said Officer Loren Farell, who was one of the first officers at the scene along with his partner, Officer Martin Perello.

"The place was full of heroes that day."

Farell speaks of the tradition of finding and thanking officers that come to your aid when you need help. In this case, some of those officers were shot in the process.

When Farell visited them in the hospital, he told them, "Hey, thanks. But what good are you to me with bullets in you?" He says that approach brought a few much-needed smiles at the end of an incredibly stressful day.

They're going to have to build an extra-large stage for the LAPD's Medal of Valor ceremony this year. Apparently, the people of Los Angeles agree.

"There's so many flowers and so much food here that our station looks like a combination wedding chapel and delicatessen," said Farell with a laugh when asked about the community reaction to the shoot-out.

Source: Adapted from Lieutenant Greg Meyer, "Courage under Fire, LAPD Has One of Its Finest Hours," *Police*, April 1997, p. 22.

---

have been hired to replace the officers who formerly did highly skilled nonenforcement jobs (traffic control, issuing parking tickets, taking past-crime reports, and so on). Additionally, civilians with clerical skills have been hired to replace officers who were formerly assigned to desk jobs. Approximately one quarter of all local police department employees are civilians.

The replacement of sworn officers by civilians in nonenforcement jobs is highly cost effective for police departments, because civilian employees generally earn much less than sworn officers. This strategy also enables a department to have more sworn personnel available for patrol and other enforcement duties.

A study of civilianization programs found that managers and officers were favorably impressed with the use of civilians for nonenforcement duties. Many officers observed that civilians performed some tasks better than the sworn officers they replaced. Perhaps the civilians were not subject to rotation and emergency assignments and thus could concentrate better on their specific duties. Additionally, many officers tended to consider some of the noncivilianized jobs as confining, sedentary, a form of punishment, and not proper police work. Officers in the study felt that civilians want careers in police work, and a sizable number of officers recommended that more be hired.[7]

Community Service Officers The President's Commission on Law Enforcement and Administration of Justice recommended that three distinct entry-level police personnel categories be established in large and medium-size police departments: (1) police agents, (2) police officers, and (3) community service officers.[8] Police agents would be the most knowledgeable and responsible entry-level position. They would be given the most difficult assignments and be allowed to exercise the greatest discretion. The commission suggested a requirement of at least two years of college and preferably a bachelor's degree in the liberal arts or social sciences. Some departments have adopted this recommendation and give these officers the title of corporal or master patrol officer.

Police officers would be the equivalent of the traditional and contemporary police officer. They would perform regular police duties, such as routine preventive patrol and providing emergency services. The commission recommended that a high school degree be required for this position.

Community service officers (CSOs) would be police apprentices, youths seventeen to twenty-one years of age, preferably from minority groups. They would have no general law enforcement powers and no weapons. The commission reasoned that because of their social background and greater understanding of inner-city problems, community service officers would be good police-community relations representatives. The commission suggested that the CSOs work with youths, investigate minor thefts, help the disabled, and provide community assistance. The commission also recommended that the lack of a high school diploma and the existence of a minor arrest record not bar the CSOs from employment. It also recommended that the CSOs be allowed to work their way up to become regular police officers.

The Tulsa (Oklahoma) Police Department began a community service officer program. The CSOs received twelve weeks of training, compared with the sixteen weeks required for regular officers. A high school education is required for CSOs, whereas police officers need 108 hours of college. The salary is also lower. The community service program provides career opportunities for qualified young people who either cannot or prefer not to attend college. The CSOs in Tulsa are certified law enforcement officers; they carry guns, and they may arrest law violators.

The community service officers have provided excellent services in Tulsa. The system was designed to relieve some of the pressures on the time of other officers and to save the community money. The program supervisor said the program was designed "to relieve police officers of routine chores and place them back on field duty and to provide security at municipal facilities at a price less than what it would cost to use regular officers." The use of community service officers at the Tulsa airport alone saved $60,875 in one year.[9]

Police Reserves/Auxiliaries Personnel shortcomings in police departments may be perennial or seasonal, depending on the jurisdiction. Some resort communities face an influx of vacationers and tourists during a particular season that can more than double the normal size of the population. In response to this annual influx, some communities employ "summertime cops."

The use of the term **reserve officer** has been very confusing. In many jurisdictions reserve officers are part-time employees who serve when needed and are compensated. In other jurisdictions, reserves are not compensated. The key element regarding the reserve officer is that he or she is a nonregular but sworn member of the department who has regular police powers. Other volunteer officers, sometimes referred to as auxiliaries, do not have full police power. Perhaps the best definition of a reserve officer has been provided by the International Association of Chiefs of Police (IACP):

> The term "reserve police officer" usually is applied to a non-regular, sworn member of a police department who has regular police powers while functioning as a department's representative, and who is required to participate in a department's activities on a regular basis. A reserve officer may or may not be compensated for his or her services, depending on each department's policy.[10]

Police agencies in some communities employ part-time officers throughout the year. These men and women, sometimes referred to as reserve or auxiliary officers, are either unpaid volunteers or paid less than full-time officers. In Illinois and North Carolina, for example, they are sworn officers who carry firearms. In Arizona, the highway patrol has used unpaid reserve officers for more than thirty years. These troopers are fully certified state law enforcement officers. Regarding the Arizona Highway Patrol reserve troopers, two researchers have written, "the only distinguishing element of their uniform is the word 'Reserve' written on the badge. The public sees reserve officers as Highway Patrol officers, which, by statute and training, they are. Reserves issue traffic citations, effect felony or misdemeanor arrests, investigate accidents and perform all the functions of a full time officer."[11]

Reserve officers augment the regular force in police departments throughout the nation. Whether paid or not, they have full police powers. Many augment the traditional police force by providing law enforcement services, including patrol, traffic control, assistance at natural and civil disasters, crime prevention, dispatch operations, and numerous other functions.[12]

Each state varies in its requirements to become a reserve officer. South Carolina, for example, requires a minimum of sixty hours of police instruction and a firearms qualification conducted by a certified firearms instructor. The reserve candidate must then pass a rigid examination conducted by the South Carolina Criminal Justice Academy. The reserve officer in South Carolina cannot be paid.

In North Carolina, however, a reserve candidate must receive the same training as a full-time officer. He or she must attend the Basic Law Enforcement Training Course, which consists of 488 hours of instruction at a host of community colleges or at the central North Carolina Justice Academy at Salemburg, North Carolina. Upon completion of the basic training, the student must pass a state board examination. Reserve officers in North Carolina can receive a salary from their employer.

The following are some examples of successful reserve programs:

- Salem, Illinois, with 8,000 residents, has a full-time department of thirteen officers. Salem supplements its

Table 3.1 — Sample of Police Departments Allowing Lateral Transfers

Police Department	In-State Lateral	Out-of-State Lateral
Mesa (Arizona) Police Department	✔	
Alachua County (Florida) Sheriff's Office	✔	✔
Prince Georges County (Maryland) Police Department	✔	✔
Bethlehem (Pennsylvania) Police Department	✔	
Florence (South Carolina) Police Department	✔	

regular force with a reserve unit when necessary, especially during its annual Little Egypt Festival, which usually draws crowds of approximately 15,000.[13]

- Belding, Michigan, with a population of 5,800 and nine full-time officers, organized a ten-member reserve unit, which contributes over 6,000 hours of volunteer service a year. Under Michigan state law, reserve officers do not require any special or mandatory training. Consequently, the Belding Police Department trains all reserve officers at the department using the full-time officers as trainers.[14]

- Selma, North Carolina, a community 22 miles southeast of Raleigh, the state capital, has a permanent population of 6,000 and fifteen sworn police officers and five civilians. In 1990 it added six reservists. The reserves are required to perform a minimum of twelve hours service per month, mostly on Friday and Saturday evenings and during holidays. The department's normal three-car shift is boosted by up to five vehicles because of the reserves. Recently when the department added three new full-time officers, they were selected from the reserve force. Because all reservists eventually desire full-time appointment, the program is important in allowing the command staff to evaluate each reserve officer's performance under normal and emergency operating conditions.[15]

In some cities, auxiliary officers are unpaid volunteers. Although they wear police-type uniforms and carry nightsticks, these auxiliaries are citizens with no police powers, and they do not carry firearms. They usually patrol their own communities, acting as a deterrent force and providing the police with extra eyes and ears. New York City has more than 8,000 of these unpaid volunteer auxiliary officers. Chapter 9 of this text provides coverage of police volunteer programs.

Some Personnel Issues

Like all organizations with employees, police departments have a distinct set of personnel issues. Some important issues are lateral transfers, police unions, and other police affiliations (for example, fraternal organizations and professional organizations).

Lateral Transfers Lateral transfers, or lateral movement, in police departments can be defined as the ability and opportunity to transfer from one police department to another. Some states allow lateral transfers from one department in the state to another department and also allow lateral transfers from out-of-state departments. Some states allow only in-state lateral transfers, and some states do not allow lateral transfers at all. Table 3.1 lists some police departments that allow lateral transfers.

The major problem with lateral transfers is that many police pension systems are tied into the local government, and funds put into that fund cannot be transferred into other funds. Thus, lateral transfers in those departments can cause officers to lose all or some of their investments.

The President's Commission on Law Enforcement and Administration of Justice recommended developing a national police retirement system that would permit the transfer of personnel without the loss of benefits. A few experiments with portable police pensions have been tried.[16]

Police Unions Police unionism has a long and colorful history. Police employee organizations first arose as fraternal associations to provide fellowship for officers, as well as welfare benefits (death benefits and insurance policies) to protect police families. In some cities, labor unions began to organize the police for the purpose of collective bargaining, and by 1919, thirty-seven locals had been chartered by the American Federation of Labor (AFL). The Boston Police Strike of 1919, as we saw in chapter 1, was triggered by the refusal of the city of Boston to recognize the AFL-affiliated union. In response to the strike, Calvin Coolidge, then the governor of Massachusetts, fired all of the striking officers—almost the entire police department. Because of the Boston strike, the police union movement stalled until the 1960s, when it reemerged.[17]

Today, nearly 75 percent of all U.S. police officers are members of labor unions. About two-thirds of all the states have collective bargaining laws for public employees. In those states, the police union bargains with the locality over wages and other conditions of employment. In the states that do not have collective bargaining agreements, the police union serves a more informal role.[18]

Police unions are predominantly local organizations that bargain and communicate with the local police department and the mayor's or chief executive's office. Local unions often join into federations on a state or federal level to lobby state and federal legislative bodies. Some of the major national federations of local police unions are the International Union of Police Associations (IUPA), the Fraternal Order of Police (FOP), the International Conference of Police Associations (ICPA), and the International Brotherhood of Police Officers (IBPO). Some officers are also members of national federations of civil service workers, such as the American Federation of State, County, and Municipal Employees (AFSCME).

Unions exist in order to harness the individual power of each worker into one group, the union, which can then speak with one voice for all the members. The ultimate bargaining tool of the union has traditionally been the strike. Members of many organizations, such as the telephone company, the department store, the factory, and so on, strike to win labor concessions from their employers.

Should police officers be allowed to strike? Many feel that police officers are special employees and should not have the right to strike. In fact, most states have laws that specifically prohibit strikes by public employees. New York State has one of the toughest laws against strikes by public employees in the nation, the Taylor Law.

Despite the presence of the Taylor Law and similar laws, there have been strikes by police employees. In 1970, members of the New York City Police Department staged a wildcat strike, for which all officers were fined two days' pay for each day they participated in the strike. Police strikes have also been staged in Baltimore, San Francisco, and New Orleans.

To avoid the penalties involved in a formal police strike, police union members occasionally engage in informal job actions to protest working conditions or other grievances felt by the officers. These job actions include the **blue flu** (where officers call in on sick report) and a refusal to perform certain job functions, such as writing traffic summonses.

Other Police Affiliations Police officers affiliate on levels other than unions. The two major types of affiliations are fraternal and professional.

Fraternal organizations generally focus on national origin, ethnic, or gender identification. In the New York City Police Department, some examples include the Emerald Society (Irish-American officers), the Columbian Society (Italian-American officers), the Guardians Association (African-American officers), the Schomrin Society (Jewish officers), the Policewoman's Endowment Society (female officers), and the Gay Officers Action League (gay and lesbian officers).

The two major professional organizations for police officers, designed as a forum to exchange professional information and provide training, are the International Association of Chiefs of Police (IACP) and the Police Executive Research Forum (PERF), a research-oriented organization.

Organizing by Area

Police departments must be organized not only with regard to personnel but also with regard to the geographic area they serve. Each officer and group of officers must be responsible for a particular well-defined area. Geographic areas may be beats or posts, sectors or zones, and precincts. In very large police departments that have numerous precincts, the precincts may be grouped together to form divisions. Figure 3.3 shows a map of a precinct divided into sectors.

Beats/Posts

The beat or post is the smallest geographic area that a single patrol unit—one or two people in a car or on foot—can patrol effectively. A beat may be a foot beat, radio car beat, mounted beat, motorcycle or scooter

70   Chapter 3

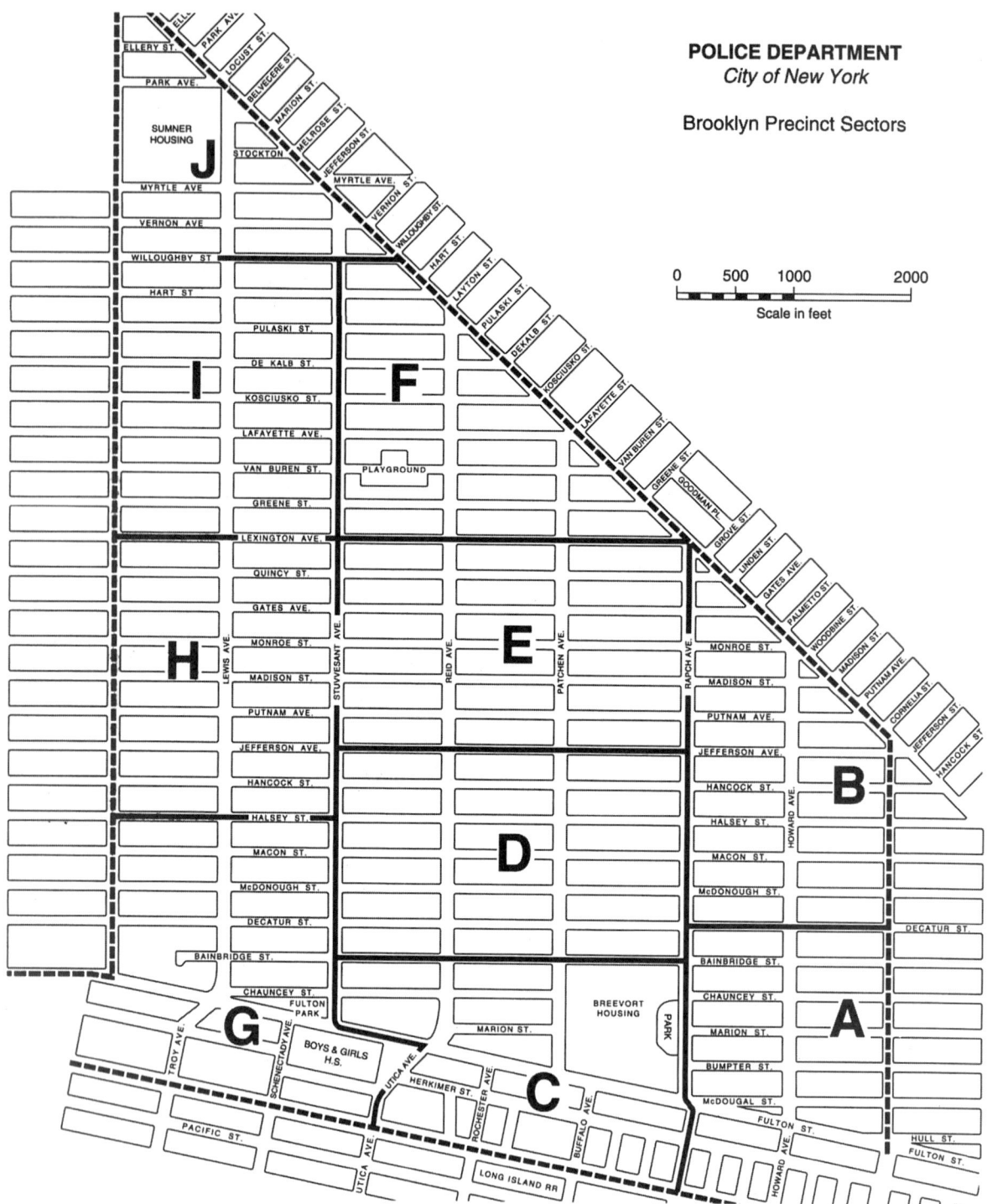

Figure 3.3
Map Dividing Precinct into Sectors
Source: Courtesy of New York City Police Department.

beat, or even bicycle beat. Obviously, radio car beats can be much larger than foot beats.

The beat officer ideally should know everyone living or doing business on his or her beat, as well as conditions and problems on the beat that require police assistance or concern. For this reason, a beat should be as geographically limited as possible, without being so small that it is nonproductive or boring to the officer.

Sectors/Zones

A sector or zone is a number of individual beats grouped together. A radio car sector may patrol several foot beats. A supervisor's zone may include numerous foot beats and several auto sectors.

Precincts

A precinct is generally the entire collection of beats and sectors in a given geographic area. In a small department, generally only one precinct serves as the administrative headquarters for the entire department. The Long Beach Police Department, in Nassau County, New York, which patrols a city of 35,000 people with seventy police officers, has one precinct. The Corning (Iowa) Police Department, which serves 2,100 people, has one precinct. The Suffolk County (New York) Police Department, which serves over 1.5 million people with about 2,000 officers, has six precincts geographically placed throughout the county. The city of Imperial Beach, California, policed by the San Diego County Sheriff's Office, has one precinct. The New York City Police Department, which serves over 8 million people with almost 40,000 officers, has seventy-six police precincts spread throughout the five boroughs of the city.

The building that serves as the administrative headquarters of a precinct is generally called a precinct house or station house. The station house usually contains detention cells for the temporary detention of prisoners awaiting a court appearance after an arrest, locker rooms in which officers can dress and store their uniforms and equipment, administrative offices, meeting rooms, and clerical offices.

The focus of the precinct or station house is the desk. The desk is usually an elevated platform near the entrance of the station house, where all major police business is carried on. Prisoners are booked at the desk, and officers are assigned to duty from it. A ranking officer, generally a sergeant or lieutenant, is assigned as the desk officer and supervises all activities in the station house. The desk officer is usually in charge of the police blotter, a record in chronological order of all police activities occurring in a precinct each day. The blotter traditionally has been a large bound book in which all entries are handwritten by the desk officer. Although some departments still maintain the classic handwritten blotter, that term is now used more generically as the written record of all activity in a precinct. The blotter can include typed and computerized reports.

Organizing by Time

In addition to being organized by personnel and by area, a police department must organize its use of time. The following discussion will describe the tour system, including the common three-tour system, tour conditions, and steady (fixed) tours.

The Three-Tour System

Common sense dictates that police officers, like other workers, can work only a certain number of hours and days before fatigue sets in and they lose their effectiveness. Tradition and civil service rules have established the police officer's working tour (also called the shift or platoon) as eight hours. The traditional police organization separates each day or twenty-four-hour period into three tours: (1) a midnight or night tour, which generally falls between the hours of 12 midnight and 8 A.M.; a day tour, which generally falls between the hours of 8 A.M. and 4 P.M.; and an evening tour, which generally falls between the hours of 4 P.M. and 12 midnight. Shifts or tours do not necessarily have to fall between these exact hours; they can be between any hours, as long as all twenty-four hours of the day are covered. Some departments have shifts that last longer than eight hours, and they use the overlapping time as training time. Also, some departments use variations of the three-tour system, including two 12-hour tours a day or four 10-hour tours a week.

Table 3.2 shows a duty chart, a schedule of assigned working tours for one year for all members of the New York City Police Department who work steady midnight-to-8 A.M. tours (the first platoon). The chart is divided into the three squads that work that tour, Squads 1, 2, and 3.

By a quick glance, officers can tell if they are working or off for any day of the year. For example, an officer from Squad 1 or 2 knows he or she is working on January 13 and January 28 (the first box after the word

Table 3.2 Patrol Duty Chart

First Platoon Duty Schedule
243 Appearances

	1	2	3	4	5	6	7	8	9	10	11	12	13	14	15
Squad No. 1	1	1	1	1	1			1	1	1	1	1			
Squad No. 2	1	1				1	1	1	1	1			1	1	1
Squad No. 3															
January	13–28	14–29	15–30	1–16–31	2–17	3–18	4–19	5–20	6–21	7–22	8–23	9–24	10–25	11–26	12–27
February	12–27	13–28	14	15	1–16	2–17	3–18	4–19	5–20	6–21	7–22	8–23	9–24	10–25	11–26
March	14–29	15–30	1–16–31	2–17	3–18	4–19	5–20	6–21	7–22	8–23	9–24	10–25	11–26	12–27	13–28
April	13–28	14–29	15–30	1–16	2–17	3–18	4–19	5–20	6–21	7–22	8–23	9–24	10–25	11–26	12–27
May	13–28	14–29	15–30	1–16–31	2–17	3–18	4–19	5–20	6–21	7–22	8–23	9–24	10–25	11–26	12–27
June	12–27	13–28	14–29	15–30	1–16	2–17	3–18	4–19	5–20	6–21	7–22	8–23	9–24	10–25	11–26
July	12–27	13–28	14–29	15–30	1–16–31	2–17	3–18	4–19	5–20	6–21	7–22	8–23	9–24	10–25	11–26
August	11–26	12–27	13–28	14–29	15–30	1–16–31	2–17	3–18	4–19	5–20	6–21	7–22	8–23	9–24	10–25
September	10–25	11–26	12–27	13–28	14–29	15–30	1–16	2–17	3–18	4–19	5–20	6–21	7–22	8–23	9–24
October	10–25	11–26	12–27	13–28	14–29	15–30	1–16–31	2–17	3–18	4–19	5–20	6–21	7–22	8–23	9–24
November	9–24	10–25	11–26	12–27	13–28	14–29	15–30	1–16	2–17	3–18	4–19	5–20	6–21	7–22	8–23
December	9–24	10–25	11–26	12–27	13–28	14–29	15–30	1–16–31	2–17	3–18	4–19	5–20	6–21	7–22	8–23

Note: 1 = 0001 to 0800 hours. Each tour consists of 8 hours and 35 minutes, as described in Operations Order 105S78.

Source: Courtesy of New York City Police Department.

January), whereas an officer from Squad 3 knows he or she is off duty. The number 1 in the box indicates the first platoon. If an administrator wants to know who is working January 1, he or she can immediately tell that Squads 1 and 3 are working and Squad 2 is off.

Officers take these charts very seriously, because they also affect their private lives. For example, Squad 3 has Christmas Day (December 25) off but must be back on duty at midnight after Christmas Day, at 0001 hours, December 26. Squad 3 members will consider themselves very fortunate in that they have the dreaded New Year's Eve off.

Using the traditional three-tour system, it takes three officers to cover each day, one on the night tour, one on the day tour, and one on the evening tour. When days off, vacation time, and sick time are factored into the three-tour system, approximately five officers are required to cover each beat twenty-four hours a day, seven days a week, 365 days a year. (Formulas to allocate personnel are available in police organization and management texts.)

Historically, police officers have been allocated evenly during the three tours of duty each day, with equal numbers of officers assigned to each of the tours. However, the academic studies of the police beginning in the 1960s discovered that crime and other police problems do not fit neatly into the three-tour system. Studies indicated that the majority of crime and police problems in the United States occurred during the late evening and early morning hours. Many police departments began to change their methods of allocating police personnel. Most now assign their personnel according to the demand for police services, putting more officers on the street during those hours when crime and calls for police officers are highest.

Many departments now distribute patrol officers according to a work load formula based on reported crimes and calls for service. The Dallas Police Department, for example, assigns 43 percent of its officers to the tour from 4 P.M. to midnight, 25 percent to the tour from midnight to 8 A.M., and 32 percent to the tour from 8 A.M. to 4 P.M.[19]

However, a survey by the Police Executive Research Forum found that some cities still routinely distribute one-third of all patrol officers to each shift. Some also assign the highest percentage of officers to the day shift rather than to the evening one.[20]

Tour Conditions

Each of the three shifts in the three-tour system has its own characteristics, as any police officer will tell you.

The midnight tour is sometimes called the graveyard shift. Most people are sleeping during this time, although in some large cities a good deal of commerce and business occurs. The most common problems for police officers during this tour are disorderly and intoxicated people at home and on the street, disorderly tavern patrons, commercial burglaries, prostitution, and drug sales. In addition to handling these specific problems, the police provide their normal duties, such as routine patrol, response to emergency calls, aiding the sick and injured, and solving disputes. Generally, the least amount of police activity occurs on this tour, and the lowest number of officers are on duty.

The day tour occurs during the normal business hours in the United States. Stores and offices are open, highway and construction crews are working, and children are in school and at play. The most common activities for police officers during this tour are facilitating the traffic flow and ensuring the safety of those traveling to and from work by enforcing parking and moving violations, ensuring the safety of children walking to and from school and entering and leaving school busses, preventing robberies and other property thefts in commercial areas, and providing other normal police services. Generally, the second highest amount of police activity occurs on this tour, and the second largest number of police officers are on duty.

The evening tour is generally the busiest for the police. The work day and school day are over; the sun goes down; and the hours of darkness are here. During the evening hours, normal adherence to acceptable ways of behavior often gives way to alcohol and drug abuse, fights, and disputes. The most common activities of the evening tour are facilitating traffic for the homeward-bound commuter; dealing with bar fights, violence at home, and violence on the streets; preventing and dealing with street and commercial robberies; and providing normal routine police services. The largest amount of police activity occurs on this tour, and the majority of officers are assigned to it.

Steady (Fixed) Tours

Traditionally, most police departments have assigned their officers to rotating tours of duty: one week of night tours, one week of day tours, and one week of evening tours. Officers' days off rotate to accommodate the three-tour system. This practice has caused tremendous problems for police officers in both their on-duty and off-duty lives. The strain of working a new shift every other week has a negative effect on eating, living, sleeping, and socializing. It creates tremendous levels of stress.

There has been a move in recent years, therefore, to place officers on steady, or fixed, tours of duty, much like most other workers in the United States. Today, officers in many jurisdictions are assigned to steady night tours, day tours, or evening tours based on seniority or the officer's own choice. Police administrators hope that these steady tours will make officers' on-duty and off-duty lives more normal, thus eliminating the many problems created by shift work.

Police officer "turning out" the school busses.

Table 3.3 Organizing a Police Department by Function or Purpose

Operations	Administration	Auxiliary Services
Patrol	Personnel	Records
Traffic	Training	Communications
Criminal investigations	Planning and analysis	Property
Vice	Budget and finance	Laboratory
Organized crime	Legal assistance	Detention
Juvenile services	Public information	Identification
Community services	Clerical/secretarial	Alcohol testing
Crime prevention	Inspections	Facilities
Community relations	Internal affairs	Equipment
	Intelligence	Supply
		Maintenance

Source: Adapted from Robert Sheehan and Gary W. Cordner, *Introduction to Police Administration*, 2d ed. (Cincinnati: Anderson, 1989), pp. 114–115.

★ Organizing by Function or Purpose

The best way to organize a police department in this way is to place similar functions performed by the police into similar units. Thus, all members of the department performing general patrol duties are placed into a patrol division, whereas all officers performing detective duties are placed into a detective division.

Line and Staff (Support) Functions

Police departments, like all organizations, must be organized by function or purpose. The first and simplest grouping of units or divisions of a department differentiates between line functions and staff (support) functions. Line functions are those tasks that directly facilitate the accomplishment of organizational goals, whereas staff (support) functions are those tasks that supplement the line units in their task performance.[21]

One of the organizational goals of a police department is order maintenance. Thus, the patrol officers who actually patrol the streets to preserve order would be grouped under a patrol unit or patrol division. Another organizational goal of a department is to investigate past crime. Thus, the detectives charged with investigating past crimes would be grouped together under a detective unit or detective division. Patrol and detective units directly facilitate the accomplishment of the organizational goals of a police department; thus, they perform line functions.

Staff (support) functions are those functions of the police department that are not directly related to the organizational goals of the department but nevertheless are necessary to ensure the smooth running of the department. Investigating candidates for police officers, performing clerical work, and handing out paychecks are examples of staff (support) functions.

Police Department Units

Robert Sheehan and Gary W. Cordner provide an excellent and comprehensive description of the basic tasks of a police department.[22] They describe thirty tasks or duties the police must perform to have an effective police department. They state that in very large police departments, separate units may be established to perform each task. In smaller departments, the tasks may be grouped together in various ways to be performed by certain units or people. Sheehan and Cordner divide the thirty tasks into three subsystems, which are similar to the previously mentioned division of line and staff functions. Their three task subsystems are operations, administration, and auxiliary services. Table 3.3 summarizes the Sheehan and Cordner system of organizing a police department by function or purpose.

Operational Units Operations are activities performed in direct assistance to the public. These are the duties most of us think about when we think of police departments, including crime fighting, crime detection, and providing service. Operational units include patrol, traffic, criminal investigations, vice, organized crime, juvenile services, community services, crime prevention, and community relations.

The patrol unit performs the basic mission of the police department: maintaining order, enforcing the law, responding to calls for assistance, and providing services to citizens. Patrol officers, who are usually on radio motor patrol or foot patrol, are the backbone of the police service. They are the most important people in police service. Police patrol will be the subject of chapters 7 and 8.

The traffic unit performs traffic control at key intersections and in other heavily traveled areas, enforces the traffic laws, and investigates traffic accidents. The police traffic function will be covered in chapter 7.

The criminal investigations unit investigates past crimes reported to the police in an effort to identify and apprehend the perpetrators of those crimes. Criminal investigations will be covered in chapter 7 of this text.

The vice unit enforces laws related to illegal gambling, prostitution, narcotics, pornography, and illegal liquor sales.

The organized crime unit investigates and apprehends members of criminal syndicates who profit from continuing criminal enterprises, such as the vice crimes just mentioned, extortion, loan sharking, and numerous other crimes.

The juvenile services unit provides a multitude of services to juveniles, including advice and referral to appropriate social agencies designed to assist youth, particularly youthful offenders. This function also investigates cases of child abuse and child neglect.

The community services unit provides a multitude of services to the community, including dispute resolution, crime victim assistance, counseling, and other routine and emergency services. Relationships between the police and the community, including numerous partnership programs between the police and the community, will be covered in chapter 9 of this text.

The police crime prevention unit attempts to organize and educate the public on methods people can take alone and with the police to make themselves at less risk to crime. Some techniques include target hardening, neighborhood watch programs, and operation identification programs. Crime prevention will be covered in chapter 9.

The community relations unit attempts to improve relationships between the police and the public so that positive police-community partnerships can develop to decrease crime and improve the quality of life in U.S.

Bicycle patrol places officers closer to members of the community.

neighborhoods. Community relations will be covered in chapter 9.

Administrative Units Administration in a police department is defined as those activities performed not in direct assistance to the public but for the benefit of the organization as a whole, usually from 9 A.M. to 5 P.M. five days a week. Administrative units include personnel, training, planning and analysis, budget and finance, legal assistance, public information, clerical/secretarial, inspections, internal affairs, and intelligence.

The personnel unit performs the duties generally associated with corporate personnel departments, including recruiting and selecting candidates for police positions and assigning, transferring, promoting, and

YOU ARE THERE!

What Cops Do, as Told by Cops

The police department is a service organization, open for business twenty-four hours a day, seven days a week. Dial their number and somebody has to answer, no matter what it is you want. As one officer put it, "People'll [sic] call us for everything. If their toilet runs over, they call the police before they call the plumber." A police officer deals with the desperate, the disturbed, and all those people out there who are just plain lonely in the middle of the night. His duties put him on intimate terms with the bizarre things people are doing to each other and to themselves behind all the closed doors and drawn shades in the community. While the rest of us look the other way, he carts away the societal offal we don't want to deal with—suicides, drunks, drug addicts, and derelicts. We call it keeping the peace, but the policeman often thinks of himself as humanity's garbageman. Every smart cop carries a pair of rubber surgical gloves in his car for handling dirt, disease, and death. He uses his gloves much more often than he uses his gun.

***

The woman who opened the door for me was just a medium-sized black female. The thing unique about her was that I could not see either one of her eyes. Her nose no longer existed. And she had a cavernous opening where there would have been a mouth and teeth. Her cheekbones were broken. In my entire career, I had never seen anybody who was so thoroughly battered. I asked her what the problem was and she said, "My husband beat me up." . . . I'm holding him by his left arm, escorting him down in handcuffs. As we stepped through the front door of the building, she tried to bury a twelve-inch butcher knife right between my shoulder blades. Kachunk! She hit me right in the old bulletproof vest. . . . It's human nature. When I walked in there she was upset because he beat her up so bad. When she saw her true love going out the door with the big bad police hauling him off, then no longer is he the villain. The police is the villain. It just tears your mind up. In spite of all that damage he did to her, she still loved him so much that she wanted me dead as opposed to taking him away.

***

So it goes, each shift ticked off by one stomach-curdling cup of coffee after another, enlivened only by the knowledge that something hairy just might happen. In those dead hours on the underbelly of the night when the orange glare of streetlights slowly gives way to the dawn, when the worst bar brawler is home in bed or sleeping it off in a cell and the ugliest hooker has made her quota, the hardest part of the job is staying awake until quitting time. By then the cop is running on residual adrenaline alone, struggling to remember that the next wife beater might have a deer rifle, that the next empty warehouse might not be empty after all, that the next underaged driver he stops for speeding might just be crazy enough to poke a pistol in a policeman's face and pull the trigger.

***

Police work is basically 99 percent pure bull____t, because there is just not that much going on. But it is punctuated by one percent of just sheer terror. And it happens just that quick. That's the reason a lot of policemen keel over from heart attacks, because of all that adrenaline pumping all of a sudden all of the time. Ulcers, too. You ride around for five or six shifts in utter boredom, worried to death about when the next time is going to happen.

Source: Adapted from Mark Baker, *COPS: Their Lives in Their Own Words* (New York: Simon & Schuster, 1985), pp. 41–44.

---

terminating police personnel. The training unit provides entry-level training to newly hired recruits and in-service training for veteran officers. Police training is covered in chapter 4 of this text.

The planning and analysis unit conducts crime analysis to determine when and where crimes occur in order to prevent them. This unit also conducts operational and administrative analysis to improve police operations and the delivery of police services.

The budget and finance unit of the police department is involved in the administration of department finances and budgetary matters, including payroll, purchasing, budgeting, billing, accounting, and auditing. The legal assistance unit provides legal advice to members of the department, including patrol officers.

The public information unit informs the public, through the news media, about police activities, including crime and arrests. This unit also informs the public about methods they can take to reduce their chances of becoming crime victims. The clerical/secretarial unit prepares the necessary reports and documents required to maintain police record keeping.

Dempsey's Law

Becoming a Police Detective/Investigator

Professor Dempsey, I want to become a detective with the city police, but I want to skip the uniform stuff. I want to just become a detective right away.

It doesn't work that way, Frank. Most police departments do not put new people in their detective units. Becoming a detective is a promotion from the uniformed patrol police officer, trooper, or deputy sheriff rank. It takes many years of experience and an outstanding record of achievement to be considered for promotion to detective or investigator.

The inspections unit conducts internal quality control inspections to ensure that the department's policies, procedures, and rules and regulations are being followed. The internal affairs unit investigates corruption and misconduct by officers. Corruption, misconduct, and internal affairs will be covered in chapter 12. Finally, the intelligence unit conducts analyses of radical, terrorist, and organized crime groups operating in a police department's jurisdiction.

Auxiliary Services Units Auxiliary services are defined as activities that benefit other units within the police department, but on a more regular and frequent basis than do administrative activities. Auxiliary services functions are usually available to assist the police officer twenty-four hours a day. Auxiliary services units include records, communications, property, laboratory, detention, identification, alcohol testing, facilities, equipment, supply, and maintenance.

The records unit of a police department maintains department records, including records of crimes and arrests, statistics and patterns regarding criminal activity, and records of traffic accidents. The communications unit answers incoming calls to the department's 911 telephone lines and assigns police units to respond to emergencies and other requests for police services. Communications will be discussed in chapter 14 of this book.

The property unit inventories and stores all property coming into the custody of the police, including evidence, recovered property, and towed and recovered vehicles. The laboratory unit examines and classifies seized evidence, including drugs, weapons, and evidence found at crime scenes (for example, fingerprints, fibers, and stains). The police laboratory will be discussed in chapter 14.

The detention unit provides temporary detention for prisoners awaiting their appearance in court. The identification unit fingerprints and photographs criminals, classifies prints, and maintains identification files. The alcohol testing unit administers driving-while-intoxicated tests for court prosecution.

The facilities unit of a police department maintains buildings designed for police use, such as station houses, offices, and detention facilities. The equipment unit maintains the numerous types of equipment necessary for the department's effective operation. The numerous supplies necessary for the proper operation of the department are purchased by the supply unit. Finally, the maintenance unit keeps all facilities and equipment serviceable.

Table 3.4 shows the breakdown, by rank and assignment, of a police department. By reading the top line of the chart and following it down to the bottom line ("Total"), one can easily see that there are a total of 165 employees in this department, with 82 police officers, 19 ranking officers (1 chief, 2 captains, 6 lieutenants, and 10 sergeants), 5 civilians, 2 coordinators, and 57 crossing guards.

By reading the details under "Police Officers" from the top line down, one can see that fifty-nine of the officers are assigned to the Patrol Bureau (twenty-one to 8-A.M.-to-4 P.M. tours, twenty-three to 4 P.M.-to-midnight tours, and fifteen to midnight-to-8 A.M. tours); six to the Detective Bureau; three to the Juvenile Bureau; eight to the Traffic Bureau; two to the Prosecutions Unit; one to the Planning and Records Bureau; one to the Payroll, Billing, and Budget Unit; and two to the Community Services and Training Unit.

Table 3.4 Staffing of a Police Department by Function and Time

	Chief	Captain	Lieutenant	Sergeant	Police Officer	Civilian	Coordinators	Crossing Guards	Total
Office of the Chief	1					1			2
Operations Division		1				1/2			1-1/2
Patrol Bureau									
8–4			1	3	21				25
4–Midnight			1	3	23				27
Midnight–8			1	3	15				19
Detective Bureau									
8–4			1		4				5
4–Midnight					1				1
6–2					1				1
Juvenile Bureau									
8–4			1		2				3
6–2									
Traffic Bureau									
8-4				1	3		2	57	63
4–Midnight					3				3
Midnight-8					2				3
Prosecutions Unit					2				2
Fingerprint and Photography Unit					None full-time				
Administration and Services Division		1	1			1/2			2-1/2
Planning and Records Bureau					1	2			3
Payroll, Billing, and Budget Unit					1				1
Community Services and Training Unit					2				2
Custodial Services					2				2
Total	1	2	6	10	82	5	2	57	165

Source: Adapted from Robert Sheehan and Gary W. Cordner, *Introduction to Police Administration*, 2d ed. (Cincinnati: Anderson, 1989), p. 38.

Chapter Summary

This chapter described the tremendous complexity involved in a police organization. The discussion covered managerial concepts relating to a police department, such as division of labor, chain of command, span of control, and delegation of responsibility and authority. The chapter described the civil service system, the quasi-military nature of the police, the police rank structure, civilianization, police auxiliaries, and police unions and other police affiliations.

The size of the geographic area many police agencies cover forces them to subdivide the area into beats (posts), sectors (zones), precincts, and sometimes divisions. Because of the responsibility of being available twenty-four hours a day, seven days a week, the police must employ a three-tour system.

The functions the police are charged with performing are complex and diverse. The primary responsibility of the police is to maintain order, enforce the law, and provide services to citizens. These functions are generally charged to a department's operational units—primarily patrol, criminal investigations, traffic, and community services units. The police also perform administrative duties and auxiliary services.

Dempsey's Law

So, You Want to Be a Criminalist!

Professor Dempsey, I love studying science and I love police work. I think I want to become a criminalist and work in a crime lab some day. What should I major in when I go on to my four-year school next year, criminal justice or science?

Well, several studies have been conducted to determine what crime laboratory managers look at when considering hiring new personnel.

In a 1986 study of 156 laboratory managers, the managers stated that chemical knowledge was the most important attribute they sought when hiring new employees. The vast majority of them preferred graduates from a traditional chemistry background. (K. Higgins and C. Selavka, "Do Forensic Science Graduate Programs Fulfill the Needs of the Forensic Science Community?" *Journal of Forensic Sciences* 33(4) 1988: 1015–1021.)

In a 1988 survey of members of the American Society of Crime Laboratory Directors, researchers discovered that these members expressed the strongest entry-level hiring preference for applicants with undergraduate science training plus a master's degree in criminalistics and the least preference for applicants with a baccalaureate in criminalistics. The same researcher also surveyed 125 forensic scientists employed by the Michigan State Police Forensic Science Division and found the majority stated that the best preparation for the job was a master's degree in criminalistics or in one of the physical or biological sciences. (J. Siegel, "The Appropriate Educational Background for Entry Level Forensic Scientists: A Survey of Practitioners," *Journal of Forensic Sciences* 33(4) 1988: 1065–1068.)

Also, in a 1992 survey of 351 members of the American Society of Crime Laboratory Directors, the majority of the respondents reported that when hiring people for their crime labs they preferred people with master's degrees in criminalistics or in physical or biological science. (C. A. Lindquist, "Criminalistics in the Curriculum: Some Views from the Forensic Science Community," *Journal of Criminal Justice Education* 5(1) 1994: 59–68.)

Well, Professor Dempsey, it looks like it's going to be graduate school for me when I finish my four-year degree!

Learning Check

1. Identify the major managerial concepts that must be considered when organizing a police department.
2. Discuss how police departments exercise their quasi-military nature.
3. Name some ways in which civilianization can benefit a police department.
4. Discuss the special problems that must be dealt with in organizing a police department that operates seven days a week, twenty-four hours a day.
5. Differentiate among operational units, administrative units, and auxiliary services units.
6. Identify the backbone of the police department, and tell why this is the most important person in police service.

Review Exercise

You have been appointed the new commissioner of the Anycity Police Department. Anycity is a suburban city sixty miles from a major U.S. city; it has a population of 30,000 people and a police department of one hundred officers. The major police problems in Anycity are disorderly teens making unnecessary noise at night, parking and traffic problems in Anycity's commercial district during business hours, and daytime residential burglaries.

The former commissioner's assistant informs you that the department has no organizational chart, no written rules and procedures, and "has always done a great job in the past."

Anycity's city manager, however, tells you that the former commissioner was incompetent and that the department is totally disorganized and ineffective. You review the department's personnel records and find that of the one hundred officers in the department, 30 percent are patrol officers, 30 percent are detectives, and 40 percent are supervisors. Additionally, the entire department is divided evenly into the three tours of duty.

In view of what you learned in this chapter, would you reorganize the department? Why or why not? If you would reorganize, how would you do it?

Web Exercise

Patrol the Internet and find information on civilian or nonsworn employment opportunities in several police departments. Select one department and one advertised employment opportunity and prepare a resume and cover letter applying for that position.

Key Concepts

civil service system
quasi-military organization
sworn member
nonsworn (civilian) member
squad
platoon
civilianization
reserve officer
lateral transfers
blue flu

Notes

1. Ronald J. Waldron, *The Criminal Justice System: An Introduction* (New York: Harper & Row, 1989), pp. 174–175.
2. George W. Griesinger et al., *Civil Service Systems: Their Impact on Police Administration* (Washington, D.C.: U.S. Government Printing Office, 1979); Dorothy Guyot, "Bending Granite: Attempts to Change the Rank Structure of American Police Departments," *Journal of Police Science and Administration* 7 (1979), pp. 253–284.
3. *Criminal Procedure Law* of the State of New York, Article 140, Sections 140.10, 140.30.
4. Leonard Ruchelman, *Who Rules the Police?* (New York: New York University Press, 1973).
5. B. Drummond Ayres Jr., "Los Angeles Chief of Police Is Refused a Second Term: Effort to Remake a Major Department Fails," *New York Times,* 12 March 1997, p. A-16.
6. "Los Angeles Offers Chief Severance Deal," *New York Times,* 23 April 1997, p. A-18.
7. National Institute of Law Enforcement and Criminal Justice, *Employing Civilians for Police Work* (Washington, D.C.: U.S. Government Printing Office, 1975), preface.
8. President's Commission on Law Enforcement and Administration of Justice, *Task Force Report: The Police* (Washington, D.C.: U.S. Government Printing Office, 1967), p. 123.
9. "Tulsa Police Officials Praise Community Service Program," *Tulsa World,* 15 September 1985, p. 4-B.
10. International Association of Chiefs of Police, *Operational Issues in the Small Law Enforcement Agency* (Arlington, Virginia: International Association of Chiefs of Police, 1990).
11. L. I. Deitch and L. N. Thompson, "The Reserve Officer: One Alternative to the Need for Manpower," *Police Chief,* May 1985, pp. 59–61.
12. Randall Aragon, "Does Your Agency Need a Reserve Officer Program?" *Police Chief,* November 1994, pp. 27–29. Note: The author is chief of police of Selma, North Carolina.
13. W. A. Krueger, "Another Concept of an Auxiliary Police Organization," *Police Chief,* May 1982.
14. Aragon, "Does Your Agency Need a Reserve Officer Program?"
15. Aragon, "Does Your Agency Need a Reserve Officer Program?"
16. President's Commission on Law Enforcement and Administration of Justice, *The Challenge of Crime in a Free Society* (Washington, D.C.: U.S. Government Printing Office, 1967), p. 112; and Geoffrey N. Calvert, *Portable Police Pensions Improving Inter-Agency Transfers* (Washington, D.C.: U.S. Government Printing Office, 1971).
17. Anthony V. Bouza, "Police Unions: How They Look from the Academic Side," in *Police Leadership in America,* ed. William A. Geller (New York: Praeger, 1985), p. 241.
18. Bouza, "Police Unions," p. 241.
19. Police Executive Research Forum, *Survey of Police Operational and Administrative Practice* (Washington, D.C.: Police Executive Research Forum, 1982), pp. 606–610.
20. Police Executive Research Forum, *Survey of Police Practice.*
21. Waldron, *Criminal Justice System,* p. 154.
22. Robert Sheehan and Gary W. Cordner, *Introduction to Police Administration,* 2d. ed. (Cincinnati, Ohio: Anderson Publishing, 1989), pp. 113–162.

4

Becoming a Police Officer

Chapter Outline

Finding Information on Jobs in Policing
The Recruitment Process
The Job Analysis
The Selection Process
  Characteristics of Good Police Officers
  Guidelines for the Selection Process
  Written Entrance Examination
  Oral Interview
  Psychological Appraisal
  Polygraph Examination
  Medical Examination
  Physical Agility Test
  Background Investigation
Standards in Police Selection
  Physical Requirements
  Age Requirements

Education Requirements
Prior Drug Use
Criminal Record Restrictions
Residency Requirements
Sexual Orientation
The Police Training Process
  Recruit Training
  In-Service, Management, and Specialized Training
  Training for the Police Corps
  Community Policing Training
  Probationary Period

Chapter Goals

■ To show you where you can find information on jobs in law enforcement.

■ To make you aware of the police selection process.

■ To acquaint you with the standards that must be met to be accepted for employment as a police officer.

■ To give you a sense of the type of individuals police departments are interested in employing.

■ To acquaint you with the police academy training, field training, community policing training, and probationary periods required in many police departments.

Introduction

Becoming a police officer is very different than obtaining most other jobs in the United States. The men and women applying for police jobs in the United States must be carefully screened to determine if they have the necessary attributes for this challenging position. Why? Because we trust these young women and men with our liberty and safety. We give them guns and enormous discretion.

Many of you reading this textbook are interested in becoming police officers. Some of you want to become officers because it is a secure job with a good salary and good benefits. Some of you are attracted to police work because you find the work exciting, or you may be interested in it because of the opportunity to aid your fellow human beings. If you are similar to the recruits interviewed by the researcher John Van Maanen in his fictionalized Union City, you are a special type of person. Van Maanen found that "virtually all recruits alluded to the opportunity afforded by a police career to perform in a role which was perceived as consequential or important to society."[1]

This chapter is designed to show how the average person begins a police career. It will discuss the recruitment process, the job analysis, the selection process, standards (necessary qualifications to become a police officer), the police training process, and the probationary period. The chapter contains several highlighted boxes giving the latest possible examples of standards, testing procedures, and requirements for selected police departments in the following areas: height and weight, vision, age, education, and physical agility. It also gives examples of current testing and selection procedures in selected departments.

The typical officer today is better educated, better trained, and more representative of the entire community than ever before. Educational levels have risen; training programs have improved; and there are more African-American, Hispanic, other minority, and female police officers than in the past.[2]

For many years, stereotypes have existed about police officers. The dominant stereotypes have fallen into two basic categories, both essentially undesirable. The negative stereotype views officers as uneducated, poorly trained, biased and prejudiced, violence prone, and corrupt. The positive stereotype views them as heroic saints who risk their lives in the face of hostility from the public, the media, and the courts.[3] Some police officers probably fall into these two stereotypes, but most do not. Most police officers are like you and your classmates: some good, some bad, but all human.

Finding Information on Jobs in Policing

Where do you find information about available jobs in policing or criminal justice in general? Many sources are available. One possible source is media advertising. Many police departments today are recruiting through radio, television, and newspaper advertising.

Civil service publications are another source. Many large cities have civil service weekly or monthly newspapers on sale in local stores. These newspapers carry information regarding openings in civil service jobs, and some even carry advertisements for courses to help you prepare for civil service exams.

Many cities have an office in their city hall or other government buildings that contain up-to-date job information on civil service jobs. You can also easily obtain information regarding the next police entrance examination or other information regarding the police by visiting or calling the local police station or headquarters.

Many police departments, in an effort to recruit college-educated men and women, participate in college job fairs. Additionally, many high school career days include representatives from local police departments or other criminal justice agencies.

Another source of information on jobs in policing is national publications. Appendix A of this text contains subscriber information for numerous publications that list police jobs and other criminal justice jobs in the United States. The most comprehensive is the *National Directory of Law Enforcement Administrators, Correctional Institutions and Related Agencies,* published by the National Police Chiefs and Sheriffs Information Bureau. This publication lists the names, mailing addresses, and the telephone number of criminal justice agencies in each state in the following categories:

- Municipal law enforcement agencies.
- County law enforcement agencies.
- Prosecutors' offices.
- Campus law enforcement agencies.
- State police agencies and highway patrols.
- State criminal investigation units.
- State correctional agencies.

- General state agencies.
- Airport and harbor police agencies.
- Federal (U.S.) law enforcement agencies.
- Military law enforcement agencies.
- General national law enforcement agencies.
- International law enforcement agencies.

Word-of-mouth advertising by family members and friends is a common way people receive information about jobs in policing and criminal justice. In a study conducted by the Los Angeles Police Department, researchers found that over 64 percent of new recruits surveyed received information on available positions within the department from police officers, friends, or relatives. Only a very small percentage of the recruits learned of job openings through the more traditional newspaper employment ads.[4] At the college where I teach, most students taking civil service tests or securing jobs in criminal justice agencies or private law enforcement received the information regarding those opportunities from professors who announced local opportunities in class.

Today, perhaps one of the best and easiest ways to obtain information on jobs in law enforcement is the Internet. Access to a computer and a modem and a few minutes of time can give one access to a myriad of job opportunities. Many police departments have their own web site on the World Wide Web and include job information among other information provided to the public. Appendix A of this text includes information regarding the role of the Internet in finding jobs in law enforcement.

Finally, many colleges and universities provide intern programs, in which students work for a local government agency for a semester while earning college credit. These programs are valuable for two major reasons: (1) students see firsthand what working in a particular agency is like and thus are better equipped to make well-informed decisions regarding future career plans, and (2) students may obtain inside information regarding job opportunities that may not be available to the general public.

The Recruitment Process

According to Robert Sheehan and Gary W. Cordner, police departments seem to discourage applicants from applying. Sheehan and Cordner also point to the low

All in the Line of Duty

The Flames Didn't Deter Them

Upon responding to the report of a raging house fire, Officers Brian Byrnes and John Trutt, Jr., of the Nassau County, New York, Police Department determined that at least one person was trapped in the burning residence. Officer Byrnes rushed in and assisted a man from the house, who informed the officer that his mother remained trapped somewhere inside. Both officers then entered the house and crawled through the smoke-filled hallway to the woman, as burning debris fell behind them, blocking their exit. Yet, the officers continued to search for a way out. When it appeared that all three would be trapped in the blaze, several volunteer firefighters arrived and were able to briefly beat back the flames using a water canister. The officers dove past the flames and escaped with the woman down the staircase. The woman was transported to a local hospital for treatment. Officers Byrnes and Trutt were treated for burns and released.

Source: Adapted from *FBI Law Enforcement Bulletin*, January 1997, p. 33.

esteem in which police are seen in some communities and the fictitious television image of the police as other factors that keep qualified applicants from applying for police jobs.[5] Another researcher states that many police departments prevent much of the available labor pool from passing through their evaluation process, thus compelling themselves to make their selection of officers from a much narrower segment of the population than would otherwise be necessary.[6]

To attract more qualified candidates, particularly among minority groups, the Commission on Accreditation for Law Enforcement Agencies has recommended a number of standards that departments should adhere to regarding recruiting candidates for selection as police officers. Among these standards are the following:

1. Individuals assigned to recruitment activities for a law enforcement agency should be knowledgeable in personnel matters, especially **equal employment opportunity regulations** and **affirmative action regulations** that affect the management and operations of the agency. Equal employment opportunity regulations are designed to ensure that members of minority groups are treated equally with members of dominant groups. These regulations should ensure

Police officers recruit young people at college job fairs.

that race, gender, ethnicity, and religion will not affect a person's chances of being hired or promoted. Affirmative action regulations are designed to achieve a ratio of minority group employees in approximate proportion to their makeup in the population of a locality, as well as to remedy past discriminatory employment and promotional practices. These concepts will be discussed at length in chapter 13.

2. The law enforcement agency should seek recruitment assistance, referrals, and advice from community organizations and leaders.
3. The agency should have an equal employment opportunity plan.
4. The agency should advertise as an equal opportunity employer on all employment applications and recruitment advertisements.
5. The agency's recruitment literature, if any, should depict women and minorities in law enforcement roles.[7]

Successful police recruiters recruit in high schools and colleges, among other places. Police Officer Paul Failla, a police officer in Suffolk County, New York, has recruited over 100,000 candidates for the 1992, 1994, and 1996 Suffolk County police entrance examinations through daily visits to high schools and colleges in the greater New York area. In an effort to attract minorities to his department, Failla also recruited at predominantly minority colleges throughout the Eastern Seaboard. Also, numerous departments throughout the United States use the local media (especially television and radio) to recruit for their examinations.

Rapid changes in U.S. demographics have made the recruiting of minorities for police careers more essential than ever before. Robert C. Trojanowicz and David L. Carter predict that by the year 2010, more than one-third of all U.S. children will be African-American, Hispanic-American, or Asian-American. Additionally, they predict that the white majority of today will become a minority within the United States in less than 100 years.[8]

Police departments in the United States, however, have had problems hiring qualified minority group members in a way that properly represents the racial, ethnic, and gender makeup of the community. Chapter 13 of this text shows how women, African-Americans, and Hispanic-Americans have used the federal courts and affirmative action programs to enter law enforcement positions and move up through the ranks.

In addition to the racial and ethnic changes occurring in the United States, the age of the population is changing tremendously. It has been estimated that the percentage of the population between the ages of sixteen and twenty-four (the ages most commonly recruited for police jobs) will shrink to 16 percent of the labor force in the year 2000, almost one-half that of a decade ago.[9]

Ralph S. Osborn, in a 1992 *FBI Law Enforcement Bulletin,* wrote that because of the changing demographics just discussed, "Recruitment strategies of the past will not be sufficient to provide agencies with quality applicants."[10] Osborn makes a number of recommendations

PATROLLING THE NET

The Net and Getting a Job/Recruiting

This topic is what first got me interested in finally learning about the Internet. In my college we really stress jobs. We tell students about all the sources of jobs in law enforcement: the civil service newspapers, the magazines, the recruiting drives, the career days, college intern programs, and the like. One day I was talking to my class about jobs and where and how to find them. One student, Dave, said to me, "Professor, what about the Net? That's where I get all my information." Then Troy raised his hand, then Julie, then about ten other students. And then they started to teach me about the best source of job information—the Internet.

I offered my students an option to their ordinary final class exercise. I told those interested to turn in a folder regarding police jobs they could find on the Internet. Include, I told them, at least, thirty different jobs. These students laughed. It was the easiest final assignment they ever had.

The Internet also can benefit police agencies in recruiting applicants for jobs. Today, the scarcity of qualified applicants, together with the growing costs associated with recruitment, make recruiting a perfect way to use the Internet.

Departments can post their hiring requirements, salary structure, and employment benefits on their homepages. Descriptions of various career opportunities can be included, complete with photographs and audio and video clips to make the presentation attractive and interesting. The multimedia effects possible with the World Wide Web have a punch that only a few traditional recruiting practices can match.

Many departments recruit heavily from colleges and universities all over the United States. The departments in my area certainly do. Most colleges and universities provide students with access to the Internet. Departments with a presence on the Internet can reach this group, whose members are preparing to make a career choice. By providing employment information to prospective applicants, departments enable them to make highly informed career decisions.

Not only students can benefit from recruitment efforts on the Internet. Police recruiters can assume that applicants who respond to information posted on the Internet are fairly serious about prospective employment. This results in a more efficient return on the investment of the recruiting staff's time and effort. Also, through the Internet, recruiters reach a larger number of potential applicants and cover greater distances without ever leaving the office. Also, many departments provide an online employment application, possibly saving staff time and expense, and speeding up the entire application process.

Source: Partially adapted from Walter W. Manning, "Should You Be on the Net?" *FBI Law Enforcement Bulletin*, January 1997, pp. 18–22.

---

that departments may implement to recruit properly for the year 2000. Among the recommendations are the following:

1. Try to understand the values of the current entry-level applicants and make changes in the department that will encourage these people to take pride in the department and have a sense of belonging in it.

2. Improve the retention of current officers by understanding the wants, needs, and desires of employees, thus decreasing the need to recruit an increasing number of individuals.

3. Examine the department's employee benefits package to determine whether it addresses issues that are important to women. During the next ten years, two of every three employees in all occupations will be women, and the police will need to obtain their fair share of them.

4. Increase recruitment in high schools, colleges, and the military.

5. Increase programs for young people, including police cadet and explorer programs. Allow youths to take the police entrance exam; the knowledge of a good career ahead may help young people stay out of trouble.

6. Develop programs aimed at changing traditional ethnic community attitudes toward law enforcement careers by showing newly arrived minority group members that the U.S. police are interested in providing services to them rather than in oppressing them, which may have occurred in their home countries.[11]

In recent years, a number of factors have resulted in better and more efficient police recruitment. The depressed job market in some areas has made the security

All in the Line of Duty

They Braved the Storm; One Family Is Grateful for That

During the middle of the night on January 17, 1993, a young couple and their daughter tried to cross the Tiajuana River into the United States seeking a new life. They would have lost their lives were it not for Officers Ed Sergott and Gene MacConagy, of the San Diego, California, Police Department's helicopter unit.

The three people were caught up in a torrent of unforgiving rapids in a major storm and were barely able to reach temporary sanctuary on an area of brush-covered dirt that rose out of the river like a small island. The rapidly moving waters would have eventually washed away their new place of refuge.

Officers Sergott and MacConagy, alerted to the family's plight, arrived at the scene and quickly realized they were their last hope. Working in the hellacious storm and just inches over the rampaging waters, the officers were able to get the child onto the skids of the helicopter and flew her to a waiting rescue crew. Two other successful attempts resulted in the rescues of both parents.

Sergott and MacConagy were awarded the Meritorious Service Medal, the second highest award possible for San Diego police officers.

Source: Adapted from Dale Stockton, "River Rescue Posed Dangerous Challenge," *Police*, May 1997, p. 68.

of a police career particularly inviting; the growing numbers of criminal justice programs in colleges and universities have attracted a pool of educated young people seeking careers in law enforcement. Also, the development of a competitive salary structure in some communities, with the addition of educational pay incentives, has provided new officers annual starting salaries in the neighborhood of $30,000. As an example of the move toward increased pay for officers, a private consulting firm in 1997 recommended that Fargo, North Dakota, police officers' salaries be raised by as much as $6,000.[12] Surveys indicate that candidates are attracted to the variety, pay, and public service aspects of a police career.[13]

Duane L. West, of the Tallahassee, Florida, Police Department writes of the new procedures used by his department in aggressively recruiting a diverse group of officers who meet the highest standards both personally and educationally, and who are also representative of the community they may serve. He reports that hiring benchmarks have been established based on both race and gender to ensure that the department mirrors the community's ethnic and gender demographics.[14]

The Job Analysis

Before the selection process for new members can actually begin, a police department must know what type of person it is interested in hiring. To determine this, the department must first decide what type of work is done by officers and then determine the type of person who would be most qualified to do that type of work. This **job analysis** identifies the important tasks that must be performed by police officers and then identifies the knowledge, skills, and abilities necessary to perform those tasks.

In the past, women and members of minority groups were rejected from police departments because they didn't meet certain standards, such as height, weight, and strength requirements. A good job analysis can avoid that situation by measuring what current police officers in a department actually do. From this study, the department then can establish the standards and qualifications necessary for its officers to perform the needed duties.

If a competent job analysis is performed, the knowledge, skills, and abilities necessary for performance in that department are judged to be **job related.** If a certain qualification is deemed to be job related, that requirement can withstand review by the courts, and the specific test measuring for that knowledge or those skills or abilities is nondiscriminatory.

The case of *Guardians Association of New York City Police Department v. Civil Service Commission of New York* (1980) is a landmark appellate court decision case regarding the job analysis.[15] In this case, the federal courts accepted the job analysis of the New York City Department of Personnel and the New York City Police Department. Two researchers have outlined these departments' procedures in preparing the job analysis, which were considered to be nondiscriminatory.

First, the Department of Personnel identified seventy-one tasks that police officers generally perform; the department based the choice of tasks on interviews with forty-nine officers and forty-nine supervisors.

Second, a panel of seven officers and supervisors reviewed the list of tasks in order to add any tasks that

PATROLLING THE NET

"On-Line Police Academy" Starts on the Net

A new law enforcement correspondence course is being offered by Millerville University in Lancaster, Pennsylvania, right online. The "academy" was developed by the commercial online service CompuServe. Workbooks, lectures, assignments, and tests are accessible through the CompuServe Law Enforcement Forum on the Internet. Instructors also schedule real-time conferences on line.

Participants who successfully complete the courses—Introduction to Law Enforcement; Media-Press Relations, and Introduction to Law Enforcement Education—receive a certificate and continuing education units that are recognized for noncredit college learning.

If interested in the program, click onto the program's web site, located at http://ourworld.compuserve.com/homepages/opacad/.

Source: Adapted from "The Virtual University: 'On Line Police Academy' Debuts in Pa.," *Law Enforcement News,* 28 February 1997, p. 5.

---

might have been omitted and to eliminate duplicate tasks and tasks not performed by entry-level officers. Certain tasks were combined, and some were added or deleted. This process resulted in a final list of forty-two tasks commonly performed by entry-level police officers.

Third, a questionnaire was sent to 5,600 officers requesting them to rate each of the forty-two tasks on the basis of frequency of occurrence, importance, and the amount of time normally spent on performing the task. The 2,600 responses received were analyzed by computer to yield a ranking of the forty-two tasks. The ranking was confirmed by observations made by professors from the John Jay College of Criminal Justice in New York City.

Next, the Department of Personnel divided the list of forty-two ranked tasks into clusters of related activities. Each one of the clusters was then analyzed by a separate panel of police officers to identify the **knowledge, skills, and abilities (KSAs)** for the cluster as a whole.[16] KSAs are a shortened way to indicate the knowledge, skills, and abilities needed to do police work. Candidates are not expected to know how to do police work, but they must have the KSAs to learn how to perform the duties of the profession. Some KSAs are the ability to read, write, reason, memorize facts, and communicate with others. Additional KSAs include physical ability, such as physical agility and endurance. The fact that this job analysis and the entrance examination based on it successfully passed the court's examination of job-relatedness shows that a police department must carefully construct its entrance examinations based on the duties actually performed by police officers.

The Selection Process

Becoming a police officer is much more difficult than getting a job as a security officer in a retail store. The **police selection process** is lengthy, difficult, and competitive. The police selection process is a series of examinations, interviews, and investigative steps designed to select the best candidate to appoint to a police department from the many who apply. As one criminal justice scholar has indicated, "In many cities the police receive large numbers of applications for admission to the force, but few applicants have the 'right' characteristics."[17]

The Pueblo County, Colorado, Sheriff's Office uses a thorough and fair selection process to ensure that only the most competent and qualified individuals are hired. Many police departments in the United States use similar selection criteria. An overview of their 1997 tests and procedures for hiring sworn personnel follows:

- A written test to measure the applicant's ability to learn the job
- A psychological test to assess emotional stability and the ability to endure stress and law enforcement work conditions
- A physical fitness test to measure an applicant's strength, agility, and endurance
- A background check to review traffic arrests and citations, moral character, and criminal history
- A polygraph exam to determine the applicant's honesty—any admissions of drug use or illegal activities

are reviewed by the bureau director, sheriff, and undersheriff and may or may not be disqualifying
- A medical exam to reveal problems that would prevent acceptable performance of assigned work
- Assessment center exercises to evaluate the applicant's decision-making and problem-solving abilities; aptitude for leadership and teamwork; writing, oral presentation, and interpersonal communications skills; and in-basket exercises to reveal how the applicant makes decisions and handles administrative tasks[18]

Pueblo focuses on the following four general goals and objectives in conducting their selection process: (1) achieving ethnic diversity, (2) developing selection criteria, (3) using the assessment center approach for final selection, and (4) maintaining a community organization.[19]

Timothy N. Oettmeier, of the Houston, Texas, Police Department, recently discussed the selection process in view of the increasing adoption of the community policing philosophy throughout the United States. He warned that departments must not radically change existing approaches to selecting the right personnel to adapt to this innovative policing philosophy,

> A commitment to community policing does not necessarily mean a department must make radical changes to its selection procedures. In fact, before implementing any changes, department members should reach consensus about an officer's role and responsibilities in a community-based department.[20]

He recommends departments take the following four general steps before restructuring the selection process for community policing:

- Redefine the role of the officer.
- Re-evaluate knowledge, skills and abilities.
- Place a new emphasis on marketing police positions.
- Proceed with caution.[21]

Characteristics of Good Police Officers

What are the "right characteristics" police administrators should look for when selecting future police officers? There have been a number of efforts to determine the specific criteria that predict future police performance, including a comprehensive analysis by Allan and Norma Roe.[22]

The Roes' data were reanalyzed and simplified in a subsequent study by researchers Bernard Cohen and Jan Chaiken.[23] Cohen and Chaiken found that performance on written civil service entrance tests was the best predictor of subsequent police performance. They identified this police performance as arrest activity, investigative skills, evidence gathering, and crime scene management. They also found that performance on written civil service exams was associated with future supervisory ratings and career advancement. Thus, the Cohen and Chaiken study indicates that police candidates who score best in written entrance exams become better police officers in terms of arrest and investigative activity, are seen as better officers by their supervisors, and have more successful careers. Cohen and Chaiken found that other factors, such as oral interviews, prior work experience, numerical ability, intelligence quotient (IQ), age, and education, also may predict above average performance as a police officer. They also found that unsatisfactory police performance was observed in officers with low educational levels, prior work problems, and poor probationary periods.[24]

It is interesting to note that Cohen and Chaiken had conducted an earlier study, in 1973, examining the background characteristics of 1,608 New York City police officers in an attempt to correlate these background characteristics with the officers' subsequent performance. These background characteristics included race, age, IQ, father's occupation, previous job history, exam score, recruit training score, military record, marital status, education, criminal record, and others for a total of thirty-nine factors. None appeared to predict subsequent performance except for the individual's recruit training score, which Cohen and Chaiken found was one of the most powerful and consistent predictors of later police performance.[25] The inconsistencies among the two Cohen and Chaiken studies and numerous other studies indicate the difficulty of predicting the future job performance of police officers and, thus, the difficulty in finding suitable measurement or selection tests.

Another researcher, Hrand Saxenian, a former professor at Harvard's Business School and a management consultant, also attempted to find which personal qualities eventually make a successful police officer. Saxenian determined that maturity is the single most important criterion in the selection process. He has attempted, with some success, to measure maturity by determining "the extent to which a man expresses his own feeling and convictions, with consideration for the thoughts and feelings of others." In an experiment conducted with a state police agency, Saxenian, using his own unique sys-

YOU ARE THERE!

Fort Lauderdale, Florida, Police Officer Examination Process

The City of Fort Lauderdale receives a large number of police officer applications, both local and out-of-state. Tests are conducted approximately four times during the year, alternating between local and out-of-state groups. The following list shows the order in which the tests are given and each test's weight in the final score.

1. Written Test; 40% of final score
2. Preliminary Background Investigation; Pass/Fail
3. Physical Agility Test; Pass/Fail
4. Oral Interview; 60% of final score
5. Polygraph Examination; Pass/Fail
6. Final Background Investigation; Pass/Fail
7. Psychological Examination; Pass/Fail
8. Medical Examination, including drug screen; Pass/Fail
9. Swim Test; Pass/Fail

Written Test
The written test covers such topics as the ability to learn and apply police information, the ability to remember details, verbal ability, the ability to follow directions, and the ability to use judgment and logic.

Applicants will also be required to answer job-related essay questions. Both content and writing ability (including spelling, grammar, and punctuation) will be evaluated. The essay questions will be evaluated at the oral interview.

Preliminary Background Investigation
This may be conducted for applicants who pass the written exam. The focus of the investigation will include, but not be limited to, verification of education and training, previous employment and work history, driving history, arrest and conviction record, and past or present use of drugs. Discrepancies found in the background investigation from information given at any other point in the selection process will be grounds for disqualification from the process.

Physical Agility Test
This test includes two parts:

Part I—Pursuit
1. Run a distance of one-half mile (5 minutes maximum allowed time).
2. Run the obstacle course (2 minutes or less).

Part II—Agility and Strength
1. Standing broad jump (be able to jump over your height).
2. 10 push-ups (back straight, touching cheek to floor).
3. 3 pull-ups (from dead-hang, palms facing away).
4. Vehicle push—20 feet (push from rear of vehicle).
5. Trigger pull—strong hand 18 times, weak hand 12 times.

Oral Interview
The interview is a formal, structured process. Applicants will be rated by a three-member panel (i.e., two ranking officers from the Police Department and a personnel representative). Applicants will be evaluated on characteristics important to the Police Officer position. Appropriate attire is required. Applicants will be evaluated on their command presence, integrity, initiative/interest, communicative ability, tolerance for stress, and judgment/decisiveness. The applicants' answers to the essay questions administered at the written exam will be evaluated at this time.

Medical Examination
Must successfully complete a medical examination by the City of Fort Lauderdale's licensed physician. Candidates will be required to meet specified body fat standards along with height/weight requirements. A drug screen test is part of this examination.

Vision Requirements
Must be free from color blindness and have no permanent abnormality of either eye; must have at least 20/50 vision in each eye without correction (glasses or contacts) and must have 20/20 vision in each separately with correction.

Swim Test
Swim fifty (50) yards (any recognized stroke) and tread water for three minutes.

Source: Fort Lauderdale, Florida, Police Department, 1997

---

tem for determining maturity, interviewed the fifty recruits in the twelve-week police academy. Each recruit was interviewed for a half hour. The recruits were then ranked from 1 to 50 based on Saxenian's system of measurement. At the end of the recruit training, the staff of the academy ranked the recruits from 1 to 50 based on overall performance. The two sets of rankings were remarkably similar and statistically showed a high rate of correlation. Several years later, follow-up studies verified the statistical validity of Saxenian's findings. Those

YOU ARE THERE!

Florida Highway Patrol Qualifications

Entrance Level Requirements
- U.S. citizenship.
- At least 19 years of age at the time of employment.
- High school diploma or GED
- *Employment preference* is given to qualified applicants who have completed 60 semester hours or 90 quarter hours of college course work at an accredited college or university.
- Possess a valid Florida driver's license.
- Willing to serve anywhere within the state.

Physical Requirements
- Weight in proportion to height.
- Vision must be 20/30 in each eye without correction or 20/100 in each eye corrected to 20/30 in each eye, normal color distinguishing capability, and 140 degree field of vision.
- Pass a physical examination prior to appointment.

Selection Process

The Florida Highway Patrol is committed to recruiting and selecting the most qualified applicants while maintaining a work force that reflects the community. Applicants are processed through three progressive phases and may be eliminated at any time during the process.

Phase I: Polygraph examination

Phase II: Background Investigation—will include a thorough check of each applicant's work, educational, credit, and residential history. Physical Examination.

Phase III: Psychological Examination—Drug screening and oral interview board.

Source: Florida Highway Patrol, 1997.

---

recruits identified by Saxenian as being the most mature were overwhelmingly the best officers.[26]

Despite these studies and probably many more studies in the future, the major difficulty in attempting to determine what characteristics make the best officer is the definition of the term best officer. Who is the best officer? The one who makes the most arrests, or the one with the best record in promoting goodwill in the community by doing such things as organizing local youths and forming after-school recreational programs?

Guidelines for the Selection Process

Despite the difficulties in predicting which characteristics produce the best police officers, most police departments in the United States use a combination of some of the following selection techniques in their selection process, according to a 1994 study: written entrance examinations, oral interviews, psychological appraisals, polygraph examinations, medical examinations, physical agility tests, and background investigations.[27] A candidate must pass each and every stage of the testing process before being appointed as a police officer.

The multiple testing process, which will be described in detail later, is designed to weed out all but the best possible candidates for police work. The process is so competitive that in New York City, only one out of every four candidates who successfully pass the written entrance examination ever qualifies for appointment to the department. In Suffolk County, New York, only one out of every eight to ten officers who pass the entrance exam ever qualifies for appointment. Once a candidate fails to qualify on the medical, psychological, or background investigation, he or she is dropped from the list and is no longer considered.

As an example of the typical police officer selection process in a major U.S. city, Cleveland's officer selection screening procedures follow.[28] Applicants are given a job-validated, nondiscriminatory paper-and-pencil examination. From this test, an eligibility list is generated. Raw scores are used to rank order, but additional points are given for city residency and military service. Applicants are given a personal history statement to complete and are scheduled for a medical examination. If they pass the medical test, psychological testing (Minnesota Multiphasic Personality Inventory, or MMPI) is done. Interviews are then arranged within the department. A background check is completed.

When an applicant passes all the above stages, an interview is scheduled with a psychologist or psychiatrist appointed by the Civil Service Commission. If the applicant is rejected by the mental health professional, a second opinion is sought. If the individual is again rejected, the department requests that the name be removed from the eligibility list.

The police department, using the eligibility list, makes a recommendation to the director of public safety, who then decides on the appointment of the applicant. If accepted, the individual is sent to the police academy.

YOU ARE THERE!

Indiana State Police Qualifications

Basic Eligibility Requirements:
1. Must be a United States citizen.
2. Must be at least 21 when appointed as a police employee.
3. Eye requirement: correctable to 20/50.
4. Must possess a valid driver's license.
5. Must be willing, if appointed, to reside and serve anyplace within the state of Indiana.
6. Applicants must have completed at least 60 semester or 90 quarter hours of credit from an accredited college or university and have at least a 2.0 grade point average based on a 4.0 grading scale and evidenced by a certified transcript.

Selection Process:
1. Submittal of completed application form.
2. Written tests.
3. Oral interview.
4. Polygraph.
5. Character investigation.
6. Fitness examination/psychological test/evaluation.

Source: Indiana State Police, 1997.

Although police departments have made significant progress in overhauling police selection procedures and have made them much more job related and less gender- and race-biased, as late as 1996, the Milwaukee, Wisconsin, Police Department was still under order by the U.S. Department of Justice to come up with a new set of rules governing race- and gender-based hiring. The Justice Department suggested that written and physical-agility tests given to applicants were still discriminatory and illegal. They ruled that the gap between the percentages of blacks and whites passing the written test and between the percentage of women and men passing the physical test was so wide that the tests have a clear adverse impact on blacks and women.[29]

In addition to uniformed or sworn members of law enforcement agencies, nonsworn or civilian members of many departments—for example, 911 operators and dispatchers—receive extensive pre-employment screening.[30]

See the boxes in this chapter for sample selection procedures in several police departments.

Written Entrance Examination

A police department's written entrance examination is usually a pen-and-pencil test administered in schools or police facilities near prospective candidates' homes. Some departments test at regular intervals, such as once a year or once every four years; other departments test continually as candidates appear.

Larry K. Gaines and his fellow researchers have stated that the written examination is the hurdle that screens out the most applicants and that has been the subject of most court litigation.[31] Many minority groups have claimed that most written entrance exams are discriminatory and biased. To reduce claims of discrimination, many innovative tests have been designed to eliminate bias.

Some testing professionals argue that most written police tests used to screen large numbers of entry-level candidates are incapable of bringing in the right types of applicants and culling from the field those who are ill-suited to perform the duties of today's police office, since these exams primarily test for cognitive abilities, rather than common sense. Stephen A. Lazer argues for better testing,

> Finding the perfect testing instrument may be a futile search, but seeking to improve existing tools is a worthy endeavor. Testing for common sense and public service orientation will go a long way towards identifying candidates who can cope with the demands placed on those ultimately selected to serve and protect. While no one test can do everything, entry-level law enforcement tests aimed at measuring more than just cognitive abilities are much needed and are likely to be well-received in the future.[32]

Some new tests incorporate features to eliminate bias and screen for common sense. Some have culturally equivalent language—language that does not discriminate against people on the basis of their cultural background. This change allows African-Americans to perform better than they did on the standard tests. Some measure candidates' ability to take quick and reasonable action in stressful situations, with correct answers determined by analyzing responses given by experienced, qualified police officers. Some tests provide candidates with job-related materials—memos, reports, and procedural guides—and ask them to make decisions on the basis of these materials.[33]

Additionally, some of the new exams use nonwritten group exercises that have candidates interact with one another in problem-solving situations. Candidates are asked to participate in role-plays that involve the need

> ## Sample Job Requirements in Policing
>
> ### Selection Procedures in Selected Police Departments
>
> **Mesa (Arizona) Police Department**
> - Written exam.
> - Written communication skills test.
> - Agility test.
> - Oral interview.
> - Polygraph exam.
> - Psychological appraisal.
> - Medical exam.
> - Background investigation.
>
> **Fort Lauderdale (Florida) Police Department**
> - Written exam.
> - Agility test.
> - Oral interview.
> - Medical exam.
> - Psychological appraisal.
> - Polygraph exam.
> - Background investigation.
> - Swimming test.
>
> **Spartanburg County (South Carolina) Sheriff's Office**
> - Written exam.
> - Oral interview.
> - Medical exam.
> - Background investigation.
>
> **Newport News (Virginia) Police Department**
> - Written exam.
> - Oral interview.
> - Agility test.
> - Medical exam.
> - Psychological appraisal.
> - Polygraph exam.
> - Background investigation.
>
> **Du Page County (Illinois) Sheriff's Office**
> - Written exam.
> - Agility test.
> - Oral interview.
> - Medical exam.
> - Psychological appraisal.
> - Background investigation.
>
> **Pennsylvania State Police**
> - Physical performance tests.
> - Polygraph examination.
> - Background investigation.
> - Medical evaluation.
> - Drug screening.
> - Psychological testing.
>
> **Marin County (California) Sheriff's Office**
> - Written test.
> - Physical performance test/obstacle course.
> - Interactive video test.
> - Oral interview.
> - Psychological assessment.
> - Polygraph exam.
> - Medical exam.
> - Thorough background investigation.
>
> **Detroit Police Department**
> - Written test.
> - Agility test.
> - Oral interview.
> - Background investigation.
> - Drug test.
> - Medical exam.
> - Psychological exam.

for leadership, problem-solving, and conflict-resolution skills.

Many departments use tests specifically developed for the police selection process. One such test, created by the International Personnel Managers Association, has been accepted by the courts as being job related. It tests for the knowledge and skills that are prerequisites for police work, using questions that are examples of actual police work.[34]

In 1991, the FBI announced plans to discontinue the test it used to screen applicants and to substitute one said to be free of cultural bias. As an FBI spokesperson said, "The world has changed, society has changed."[35] This decision to use a new test followed a federal court ruling in 1989 that the Bureau had systematically discriminated against its Hispanic-American agents by denying them promotional opportunities.[36]

Oral Interview

The oral interview in the police selection process can be conducted by a board of ranking officers, a psychologist, the police chief, or an investigator. The oral interview may merely discuss the candidate's application and background or may be used to test the candidate's ability to deal with stressful situations.

Psychological Appraisal

Psychological testing has become very important in the police selection process. According to three researchers, "Job-related stress is a major health problem, especially in law enforcement. There is an obvious need for a thorough background investigation, along with a comprehensive psychological-psychiatric evaluation, in order to eliminate candidates with psychiatric problems, personality disorders, problems with impulse control, substance abuse or questionable character."[37]

The Minnesota Multiphasic Personality Inventory (MMPI) and the California Personality Inventory (CPI) are administered to prospective police recruits in California and other states, as well as in some foreign countries, including Canada. These instruments measure personality dimensions, such as anxiety, sociability, personal adjustment, and social adjustment.[38] Police departments use these tests to screen out applicants who have maladjusted or problem personalities.[39]

Larger police departments often use sophisticated screening devices, such as the Wechsler Adult Intelligence Scale—Revised (WISC—R), to measure intelligence. They use the Inwald Personality Inventory (IPI), as well as the CPI and the MMPI, to evaluate personality structure and determine whether recruits have any disorders that would adversely affect their functioning.[40]

Some research has indicated that these tests, taken independently or used together with clinical interviews, can often be valid predictors of future police performance.[41] However, there is a continuing debate on the effectiveness of psychological testing. Some researchers report a growing consensus that psychological testing can determine the emotional and psychological fitness of recruits. Unfortunately, psychologists and psychiatrists often do not agree on what makes a good police officer. Therefore, they do not agree on what they are looking for in the prospective police officer, or how to test for it.[42]

Additionally, a number of researchers indicate that although psychological tests are valid, their predictive value tends to diminish over time.[43] A review of the literature by Elizabeth Burbeck and Adrian Furnham found not only significant methodological problems in the administration of psychological tests but also little success by most tests in distinguishing between good and bad police officers.[44] Consequently, some critics, such as Robin Inwald, have called for the development of guidelines to ensure that psychological profiles are used fairly and equitably.[45]

Polygraph Examination

The polygraph, or its more generic term, the lie detector, is a mechanical device designed to ascertain whether a person is telling the truth. It was first used by the Berkeley, California, police department in 1921. The polygraph records any changes in such body measurements as pulse, blood pressure, breathing rate, and galvanic skin response. The effectiveness of the polygraph is based on the belief that a person is under stress when telling a lie. Therefore, if a person lies, the machine will record that stress in the body measurements.

The use of the polygraph is an attempt to determine the truth through scientific instruments. The name polygraph means "many writings." During a polygraph test, several measurements of the body's activity are recorded on a visible graph. The three major sections of the polygraph are the pneumograph, which measures respiration and depth of breathing; the galvanograph, which measures changes in the skin's electrical resistance; and the cardiograph, which measures blood pressure and pulse rate. It is interesting to note that the

YOU ARE THERE! »

Sample Areas Covered in Polygraph Examination

1. Questions regarding the applicant's failure to disclose pertinent information on the application that would have an impact on the selection decision.
2. Questions regarding undetected felony acts of murder, rape, robbery, burglary, arson, etc.
3. Questions in regard to the current usage of drugs or narcotics (without prescription). Attention will be directed to the type of illegal usage, the number of times used and time frame of usage.
4. Questions regarding thefts: when, volume, how much dollar amount. Also to include deception type theft such as check fraud.
5. Questions regarding the omission of information from the application or deception in furnishing information during the background investigation or oral interview.
6. Questions regarding the sale and delivery, or participating in the sale or delivery of illegal drugs, narcotics, and marijuana.
7. Questions regarding current alcohol abuse.
8. Questions regarding *illegal* sexual conduct.

Source: Indiana State Police, 1997.

subject does not actually have to verbally answer a question for the machine to measure the mental and emotional response of the person to the question.

Some state that the polygraph, although not infallible, can detect physiological changes indicating deception anywhere from 75 to 96 percent of the time. Its accuracy depends on the subject, the equipment, and the operator's training and experience. In some cases, the polygraph may fail to detect lies because the subject may be on drugs, is a psychopathic personality, or makes deliberate muscular contractions.[46]

Formerly, the polygraph was used extensively within private industry for screening job applicants and preventing employee theft. The use of the polygraph in pre-employment screening was severely limited in the Employee Polygraph Protection Act (EPPA) signed into law June, 1988. The EPPA prohibited random polygraph testing by private sector employers and the use of the polygraph for pre-employment screening. However, the law exempts the United States government or any state or local government from its provisions and restrictions. The EPPA allows the use of the polygraph for pre-employment screening for police departments and other employers whose primary business is the provision of certain types of security services, companies that manufacture or dispense controlled substances, and for businesses doing sensitive work under contract to the federal government.[47]

Although, the results of polygraph tests are inadmissible in court, they are still used in the police selection process.[48] In one year, the Vermont State Police administered polygraph tests to 181 applicants and rejected 109 of them. The two major reasons for rejecting candidates were former drug offenses and undetected larcenies.[49] A 1993 study indicated that more than half of all police departments employ polygraphs to screen applicants and that about 22 percent of the 67,000 annual applicants for police jobs in this study were rejected because they were found to be deceptive on the polygraph testing.[50]

See the box on the previous page for sample areas of questioning on a polygraph examination in a certain police department.

Dempsey's Law

Some Advice on Becoming a Cop

Professor Dempsey, I'm taking the police test Saturday. Do you have any advice?

Professor Dempsey, I'm meeting my investigator for the first time next week. Do you have any advice?

These are questions I receive every day from my students. I do have advice for them.

- Make a test run. A few days before your appointment, go to the location where you are scheduled to appear. Know how long it will take you to get there. Learn where you can park; where to get coffee or a bite to eat; where you can find a public bathroom. If you are late, you may not be allowed to take the test. If you are late meeting your investigator, it will give him or her a very bad impression of you.
- Wear proper business attire. Whenever you are scheduled to meet your investigator, wear proper business attire. For a man, that is a conservative suit and tie. For a woman it is a simple dress or business suit. Select conservative colors—gray, blue, or black. Polish your shoes. Be neat.
- Take off the earring. You can always put it back after the interview. Accessories that are appropriate for the club scene are not appropriate for an interview. Men and women should eliminate jewelry of any type except for a functioning watch.
- If it moves, call it sir or ma'am. A friend of mine told me that when he was in the army, he was so afraid of getting in trouble for not saluting ranking officers that he would salute every person he saw. By doing that, he knew he could never make a mistake. You do not have to salute your investigator. However, whenever answering or asking a question, call your investigator sir or ma'am. In fact, while at your investigator's office, take my friend's advice: if it moves, call him sir and her, ma'am.

Medical Examination

Police departments generally want candidates who are in excellent health, without medical problems that could affect their ability to perform the police job. There are long-range and short-range reasons for using medical examinations in the police selection process. The short-range purpose is to ensure that candidates can do the police job. The long-range purpose is to ensure that candidates are not prone to injuries that may lead to early retirement and an economic loss to the department.

Gaines and his associates state that every applicant should be given a complete and thorough medical examination to detect any disqualifying diseases (such as diabetes, epilepsy, or heart disease) or any physical abnormalities or medical conditions (such as back problems or high blood pressure) that might later render the applicant physically unqualified for duty or allow the candidate to be able to retire early on a service disability.[51]

Territo, Swanson, and Chamelin, however, warn departments about carefully monitoring the medical examination. They cite examples where applicants took drugs to control hypertension (high blood pressure), used insoles to increase height, and obtained urine specimens from friends to conceal drug use or other medical ailments.[52]

The Americans with Disabilities Act (ADA), signed into law in 1990, extended the basic protection of the Rehabilitation Act of 1973 to government and private industry. This law took effect in 1992 and mandated that discrimination on the basis of disability is prohibited by all governmental entities and all but the smallest private employers.

The ADA prohibits discrimination of disabled persons who can perform the essential functions of the job in spite of their disability. If a police agency rejects a disabled person for employment, it must show that the disabled person cannot adequately perform the job. The law provides an affirmative duty on employers to reasonably accommodate qualified disabled persons unless doing so would create an undue hardship. Areas covered by ADA include physical agility tests, psychological tests, and drug testing.[53]

Physical Agility Test

Obviously, police departments are interested in candidates who are physically fit. However, in the past, physical agility testing has been criticized for discriminating against some candidates, particularly women. One researcher investigated the adverse impact of the physical agility testing for deputy sheriffs and found that women are four times more likely to fail these tests than men.[54] Another researcher argued that physical agility tests relate to aspects of the police job that are seldom performed.[55]

Physical agility tests are used by most departments. However, several tests have been declared invalid by the courts. The key to the validity of the agility testing is its job-relatedness. For example, in *United States v. Wichita Falls* (1988), the court found that the city of Wichita Falls, Texas, had adequately performed a job analysis and successfully linked the department's physical requirements with the work performed by police officers, thus ensuring that the test was job related.[56]

Most recently, physical agility tests have been based on the typical activities of local police officers; for example, how far they actually run in a critical incident, how many stairs they have to climb each day, and how many hours they spend on their feet. Strength tests are geared to how much the typical arrestee weighs and the amount of resistance he or she usually gives officers.[57] Such agility tests are much more likely to pass the job-relatedness standards for police testing.

See the boxes in this chapter for sample agility testing procedures in certain police departments.

> **YOU ARE THERE!**
>
> **Sample Agility Test—City of Lincoln, Nebraska**
>
> Vigorous physical activity, which includes dragging a 70 lb. weight a distance of 12 ft.; ascending and descending a stairway; entering/exiting through a window opening; climbing a 4 ft. 6 in. chain link fence; running a 76 yd. weaving course; and climbing a solid 4 ft. 2 in. barrier. All activities are done consecutively and against a time limit. The agility test is pass/fail.
>
> Source: Lincoln, Nebraska Police Department, 1997.

Background Investigation

In an effective background investigation, a candidate's past life, past employment, school records, medical records, relationships with neighbors and others, and military record are placed under a microscope. The investigator looks for evidence of incidents that might point to unfavorable traits or habits that in turn might affect the individual's ability to be a good police officer. Such factors are poor work habits, dishonesty, use of alcohol or drugs, or a tendency to violence.

Thomas H. Wright offers the following basics for a thorough background investigation:

1. Preliminary interview. In a preliminary interview, the investigating officer should advise the applicant of the details of the background investigation process and the facts about employment in the department, including salary, benefits, and responsibilities.
2. Background investigation booklet. Applicants should receive a booklet that contains questions for them to answer regarding all important aspects of their past, including residences, schools, jobs, military service, arrests or summonses, and any other information the department wishes to investigate. This booklet becomes the basic document for the background investigation.
3. Photographs and fingerprints. Photographs should be taken and used to show to neighbors and former employers in case they do not recognize the applicant by name. Fingerprints should be sent to the FBI and the local state criminal identification agency to determine any previous police record.
4. Education. The applicant's school experience should be investigated to determine attendance and disciplinary history.
5. Employment. The applicant's employment experience should be investigated to determine honesty, self-initiative, attitudes, job performance, absenteeism, tardiness, and use of sick leave.
6. Credit check. The applicant's credit history should be examined to ensure a previous history of fulfilling obligations.
7. Criminal history. Every police agency that covers areas where the applicant might have lived or attended school should be contacted to gather any available information regarding his or her conduct while living or attending school there.
8. Driving record. The applicant's record of traffic accidents and traffic summonses/citations should be investigated.
9. Military history. The applicant's military record should be investigated to determine any disciplinary actions or medical problems that may affect his or her police employment.[58]

Standards in Police Selection

Each police department sets standards, or necessary qualifications, that it requires in selecting its prospective police officers. In recent years these standards have changed to allow a greater number of females and minorities to become police officers, but they are still more stringent than standards in most other professions. The police standards cover physical, age, and education requirements, criminal record restrictions, and residency requirements.

Physical Requirements

At one time, the main requirement for becoming a police officer was the size of a young man's body and his physical strength and courage. Over the years, we have come to realize that brains are more important than brawn in police work. Also, the former physical requirements discriminated against women and minorities.

Today, physical requirements are still stringent. Two writers on police administration state that physical requirements in many police departments have been established at levels much higher than the requirements for entrance into the U.S. Military Academy (West Point), the U.S. Naval Academy (Annapolis), or the U.S. Air Force Academy (Colorado Springs).[59]

Height and Weight Requirements Height and weight requirements for police department applicants have changed dramatically in recent years. Only a few decades ago, nearly all police departments required officers

---

Sample Job Requirements in Policing

Height and Weight Standards in Selected Police Departments

- Mesa (Arizona): no height requirement; weight proportionate to height.
- Contra Costa County (California): no height requirement; weight proportionate to height.
- Los Angeles: height, 5'00" to 6'8"; weight proportionate to height.
- U.S. Capital Police (Washington, D.C.): no height requirement; weight proportionate to height.
- Largo (Florida): no height requirement; weight proportionate to height.
- Providence County (California): no height requirement; weight proportionate to height.

to be at least 5 feet 8 inches tall.[60] Because this is no longer so, women and minorities can enter the police ranks more easily. This change in height requirements is justified by research that has proved that routine police work rarely involves physical confrontations, and that officers gain the compliance of citizens in the vast majority of encounters without the need to use force.[61]

The old height requirements were challenged in court because it was believed that they discriminated against Hispanic-American and female applicants. Today, most departments have eliminated height and weight standards and now require that weight be reasonably related to height.[62]

See the boxes in this chapter for examples of height and weight standards in selected police departments.

Vision Requirements Many police departments require an applicant to have very good uncorrected vision that must be correctable to 20/20 vision with eyeglasses, as well as to be free from color blindness. These requirements have created a roadblock for many qualified candidates. Some contest this requirement, because many police officers wear glasses, and police work does not require perfect uncorrected vision. One researcher noted that a person with 20/200 uncorrected vision may be able to function adequately as a police officer, depending on the type of vision problem he or she had.[63] Other researchers noted that an applicant's specific vision problem should be considered before rejecting a candidate because of poor vision.[64]

Gaines and his associates explain that many police departments' vision requirements are based on tradition rather than need. It was long thought that a police officer should have relatively good vision because of the potential for officers to lose their glasses during an altercation with a suspect, which would render the officer helpless.[65] They tell us, however, that two researchers, Good and Augsburger, found that 50 percent of the police officers in a survey had experienced "spectacle dislodgement" (their glasses fell off), with an average of 4.09 occurrences during their career.[66] That rate does not appear to be a significant problem. Furthermore, the popularity of contact lenses makes this even less of a problem.

See the boxes in this chapter for examples of recent vision standards in selected police departments.

Age Requirements

Until recently, most police departments required that an officer be between the ages of twenty-one and twenty-nine at the time of appointment. Anyone over the age of twenty-nine was considered too old for employment. Sometimes, exceptions were made for those with previous military or police experience. The number of years a candidate served in the military or in previous police employment were added to the maximum age limit.

The percentage of departments with maximum age limits has dropped significantly in recent years. This decline is largely attributable to new laws barring discrimination on the basis of age.[67]

Many police departments, however, still do not want to accept candidates past a certain age. The New York City Police Department's age cap had once been set at age twenty-nine and then raised to age thirty-four in the 1990s to widen the applicant pool. New York, as well as many other localities, had exemptions under federal age discrimination laws in regard to hiring police officers.

Recently, several applicants who took an examination when they were under the age limit weren't called until much later, but still expected to be hired. However, on May 31, 1997, a Manhattan Supreme Court justice upheld the NYPD's policy of limiting new cops to applicants under age thirty-five. The judge said that age limits on public-safety jobs are acceptable exceptions to laws against age discrimination. The applicants had passed the necessary physical, psychological, and educational tests but were denied appointment at the last minute before they were to be appointed. A city law setting a maximum age of thirty-four for new recruits expired in 1993 and was not renewed, but the city ar-

---

Sample Job Requirements in Policing

Vision Standards in Selected Police Departments

- Los Angeles County (California): 20/70 correctable to 20/30.
- New Castle County (Delaware): 20/100 correctable to 20/20.
- New York State: 20/40 correctable to 20/20.
- Bethlehem (Pennsylvania): 20/50 correctable to 20/20.
- Hampton (New Hampshire): correctable to 20/20.
- Indiana State Police: correctable to 20/50.
- Maryland State Police: 20/70 uncorrected in each eye, correctable to 20/20 binocularly with soft contact lenses or safety glasses.

> **Sample Job Requirements in Policing**
>
> **Age Standards in Selected Police Departments**
>
> - Fort Lauderdale (Florida): minimum age, 19; maximum age, none.
> - Philadelphia (Pennsylvania): minimum age, 19; maximum age, 36.
> - Sioux Falls (South Dakota): minimum age, 21; maximum age, none.
> - Newport News (Virginia): minimum age, 20; maximum age, 63.
> - Salt Lake County (Utah): minimum age, 21; maximum age, none.
> - Pennsylvania State Police: minimum age, 21; maximum age, 40.
> - Charleston (West Virginia): minimum age, 21; maximum age, 35.
> - Maryland State Police: minimum age, 20; maximum age, 58.

gued that police work is stressful and physically demanding and therefore better left to people under thirty-five. Eighty passing applicants were denied appointment.[68]

Education Requirements

A recent study of the educational achievements of police officers in almost 700 U.S. police departments, sponsored by the Police Executive Research Forum, provided much new information about educational requirements for appointment as a police officer in the United States. The study also discussed the state of formal education in U.S. police departments.

The study discovered that the vast majority of U.S. police departments (86.1 percent) required a high school education or the equivalent for appointment. Only 0.4 percent required a four-year college degree, but 14 percent of all departments required some college. The authors of the study noted that the minimum high school diploma requirement may not necessarily reflect actual selection practices, because many departments favor applicants who meet more than the minimum standards. For example, the average recruit in the San Diego Police Department in the late 1980s had two years of college, despite the fact that there was no formal college education requirement.[69]

The study also found that the average level of education among police officers nationwide was fourteen years of schooling (high school plus two years of college). African-American and white officers had equal levels of education, and Hispanic-American officers had slightly less. Additionally, 65.2 percent of all sworn officers had some college education, and 22.6 percent had undergraduate or graduate degrees.[70]

As we saw earlier, many federal law enforcement agencies require a four-year college degree for employment.

In 1997, the New York City Police Department (NYPD) instituted a sixty-four college credit requirement for appointment to the police academy as a probationary police officer. The sixty-four-credit requirement is waived for candidates with two years of U.S. military experience. In the same year, the NYPD raised its minimum age requirement to the age of twenty-two.

The report also found that most departments had incentive programs to encourage their officers to continue their education. A program of tuition assistance or reimbursement was offered in 62 percent of the departments, whereas 53.7 percent offered incentive pay to officers with a college education. Nearly half (42.6 percent) of all departments surveyed allowed officers to adjust their assignments in order to pursue an education.[71]

The development of college programs for the police was first stimulated by the recommendations of the National Commission on Law Observance and Enforcement (Wickersham Report) in 1931, which discussed, among other police problems, the poor state of police training in the United States. However, the real impetus behind the relatively high levels of police education in recent decades was the Law Enforcement Education Program (LEEP), a federal scholarship and loan program operated by the U.S. Department of Justice between 1968 and 1976. LEEP spent more than $200 million in grants and loans to students in "law enforcement–related" college programs. LEEP funds supported more than 500,000 "student years" of college education. About 90 percent of the students in the program were in-service sworn officers.[72]

Considerable debate has arisen over the desirability of college education for police officers. Many experts believe that all police officers should have a college degree. As early as 1967, the President's Commission on Law Enforcement and Administration of Justice recommended, "The ultimate aim of all police departments should be that all personnel with general enforcement powers have baccalaureate degrees."[73]

Sample Job Requirements in Policing

Education Standards in Selected Police Departments

- Seattle (Washington): high school/General Equivalency Diploma (GED).
- Spartanburg County (South Carolina): high school/GED.
- Portland (Oregon): 60 college semester hours (90 quarter hours) or at least 45 quarter hours and 12 months of verifiable experience and/or community volunteer work.
- Florence (South Carolina): high school/GED.
- Alachua County (Florida): 2-year college degree.
- Pennsylvania State Police: Associates Degree or 60 semester hours in an accredited institution of higher education at the time of application. College requirement may be waived if active military for at least two years with an honorable discharge, or, prior employment for at least two years as a full-time police officer with completion of Basic Training Courses as approved by the Municipal Police Officers' Education and Training Commission.
- Indiana State Police: 60 semester or 90 quarter hours of credit from an accredited college or university with at least a 2.0 grade point average based on a 4.0 grading scale.
- University of Vermont Police Services: Associate's degree and 2 years of law enforcement experience or an equivalent combination of education and experience, which may include a bachelor's degree.
- Ventura County (California): high school/GED.
- Shawano City (Wisconsin): Associate degree in police science or related field required; a Bachelor's degree in criminal justice or a related field is highly desirable, but not required.

Some studies have shown that college-educated officers receive fewer citizen complaints and have better behavioral and performance characteristics than those without college.[74] Higher levels of education have also been associated with fewer on-the-job injuries, fewer injuries by assault, fewer disciplinary actions from accidents, fewer sick days per year, and fewer physical force allegations.[75] Other research has shown that higher education results in higher aspirations; decreased dogmatism, authoritarianism, rigidity, and conservatism; fewer disciplinary problems; fewer citizen complaints; increased promotions; greater acceptance of minorities; decreased use of discretionary arrests; increased perception of danger; and a better ability to tolerate job-related excitement.[76]

In a 1992 article, Mitchell Tyre and Susan Braunstein reported on two studies they conducted regarding higher education and ethics in policing. In one study, the authors found that educational levels had a direct positive effect upon all individuals in the survey and that the correlation between a college degree and ethical decisions was twelve times greater for police officers than for the control group. In another study, the authors found that officers who had not attained a two-year college degree were approximately four times more likely to be brought before the Florida Department of Law Enforcement for decertification proceedings.[77]

However, the report of the National Advisory Commission on Higher Education for Police Officers, often called the Sherman Report, stated that there is some evidence that officers with more education become dissatisfied with policing as a career more often than officers with less education. Additionally, the report said that the lack of career opportunities for the educated and ambitious officer is a serious problem in law enforcement agencies, and that new officers with college degrees are often resented by veteran officers with no college experience. Additionally, the report concludes that there is evidence that some departments punished officers with more education by denying them career opportunities.[78]

The Sherman Report criticized current police higher-education programs for "servicing the status quo." It suggested that higher-education programs for the police should offer them a "broadening" experience, which would enable them to expand their ability to deal with their professional problems. The Sherman Report also recommended recruiting college-educated young people rather than sending recruits to college. It also argued that police departments should recruit students from liberal arts programs rather than law enforcement programs.[79]

One of the most common objections to requiring some college education for police officers is that this practice limits the pool of applicants and has a negative impact on racial minorities who may have been the victims of inferior schooling. Also, some argue that there is no conclusive evidence that officers with college degrees perform more effectively than those without degrees.[80]

Regarding their objections to the college requirement for police officers, Robert Sheehan and Gary W. Cordner write the following:

Education is very often seen as a vehicle for professionalization.... Yet a demand that all police applicants be college graduates necessarily narrows the field from which the applicants may be drawn. By establishing the college degree as an entrance level required input the police administrator precludes thousands of capable prospective applicants from applying for entrance-level positions.[81]

Some departments have instituted college education requirements for promotion to higher ranks. For example, since 1988, the New York City Police Department has required sixty-four college credits for promotion to the rank of sergeant; ninety credits for the rank of lieutenant, and a bachelors degree for the rank of captain. The San Diego Police Department requires two years of college work for promotion to the rank of sergeant, and the Sacramento, California, police department requires a four-year degree as a requirement for promotion to lieutenant.[82]

See the boxes in this chapter for recent examples of educational requirements and educational pay incentives in various departments.

Prior Drug Use

Departments have continually faced the problem of a candidate's prior drug use. Should a candidate be disqualified because of prior drug use? Is experimentation with marijuana enough to dismiss a candidate? What about cocaine? How many prior uses of drugs are acceptable? In 1997, the Maryland Legislature passed a bill that established minimum standards on prior drug use by those seeking certification as law enforcement officers. The bill was proposed to replace patchwork of policies throughout the state.[83] According to Michael Canning, deputy executive director of the Maryland Sheriffs Association, which proposed the legislation,

> Drugs are such a devastating factor in today's society, and right now, there aren't any minimum standards. There was a consensus that there should be at least a minimum standard, which would leave some flexibility for individual situations.[84]

Samples of Incentives for Officers

Education in Selected Police Departments

- Clinton (Massachusetts): Pay differential—10% associate's degree; 20% bachelor's degree; 25% master's degree in criminal justice.
- Arlington County (Virginia): Tuition reimbursement—up to $800 per year.
- Ventura County (California): Possible educational incentive of $47-$131 per month based on completion of associate's/bachelor's/master's degree.
- Charleston (West Virginia): Fifty cents ($.50) for each semester hour in an approved field, up to a maximum of $59 per month.
- Shawano (Wisconsin): Professional improvement program that pays $5 per month for every three college credits up to a maximum of thirty credits.
- Baltimore County: Educational Assistance Program.

Criminal Record Restrictions

Obviously, people wishing to become police officers must respect the rules of our society and must adhere to these rules. The lack of a significant criminal record is a requirement to become a police officer. However, many police departments recognize that people may make mistakes, especially when young, that might result in an arrest. Also, police departments distinguish between arrests and convictions.

A Justice Department survey discovered that 95 percent of all police departments reject applicants with an adult felony conviction, and 75 percent reject those with a juvenile felony conviction. Only 30 percent, however, reject applicants with either an adult or a juvenile misdemeanor conviction. Twenty percent of departments reject those with an adult felony arrest but no conviction, and 25 percent reject those with a juvenile arrest but no conviction.[85] Remember that in the U.S. criminal justice system, a person is not considered guilty until convicted in court.

Residency Requirements

Nineteen percent of all departments and 30 percent of those in the largest cities (populations of 500,000 to 1 million) require their officers to live within the geographic area the department serves.[86] The majority of larger departments have dropped their residency re-

---

Sample Job Requirements in Policing

No Smoking Policy

- Clinton (Massachusetts): No use of tobacco products.
- Arlington County (Virginia): Must be a nonsmoker.
- Pinecrest (Florida): Applicants must be nonsmokers.

quirements and recruit nationwide, whereas many of the smallest departments recruit only within their own local community—possibly a reflection on local politics. Some experts believe that a department should recruit from the largest possible area to maximize the potential of the qualified applicant pool.[87]

Sexual Orientation

One of the more controversial police personnel practices during the past decade has been the active recruitment of gay and lesbian officers by the San Francisco Police Department. Frank Schmalleger reports a side benefit to this recruitment: a reduced fear of reporting crimes among many city homosexuals, who for years had been victims of organized assaults by bikers and street gangs.[88]

As far back as 1969, the International Association of Chiefs of Police rescinded its policy of opposing the employment of homosexual officers. It has been estimated that today, 20 percent of the sworn officers in the San Francisco County Sheriff's Department and perhaps 10 percent of the officers in the Los Angeles Police Department are homosexuals.[89]

Some police administrators have decided not to make an issue of sexual orientation on the background investigation. Charles R. Swanson, Leonard Territo, and Robert W. Taylor believe that this decision may be the result of an overall change in society's social and sexual mores, as well as a concern by police administrators that if they do not voluntarily take the lead, the federal courts may be called upon to intercede on the behalf of homosexuals, as the courts have already done in the case of minorities and women.[90] In 1993, the Dallas Police Department, in the aftermath of a state supreme court ruling, lifted a ban on hiring homosexual police officers.[91]

The federal courts, however, have not been sympathetic to gay and lesbian law enforcement employees. In 1987, in *Padula v. Webster,* a federal appeals court upheld the FBI policy of not hiring homosexuals on the grounds that agents must be able to work in any state in the country, and half of the states have criminal laws prohibiting homosexual acts or sodomy.[92] In 1988, in *Todd v. Navarro,* a federal court upheld the dismissal of thirteen lesbian deputies from the Broward County (Florida) Sheriff's Department, citing that homosexuals are not a subject class accorded strict scrutiny under the Fourteenth Amendment.[93]

The Police Training Process

Police training today is critical. As Steve Bunting, the executive director of the American Society of Law Enforcement Trainers (ASLET), said, "Training will have to increase. . . . After O.J. [Simpson] and L.A. [Rodney King], law enforcement has had a loss of credibility."[94] Bunting stresses training in ethics and better use of force, as well as other traditional training.

Once an individual has been chosen to be a member of a police department, he or she begins weeks—and usually months—of intensive training. Recruit training and in-service training programs vary from department to department, as the following overview will illustrate. In addition, police training never really ends. Veteran police officers continue their educations in firearms training programs, as well as through in-service training, management training, and specialized training programs.

Recruit Training

Recruit training is the initial training a police officer receives. It serves to orient new officers to the department, teach them about the department's goals and objectives, and provide them with necessary skills and knowledge required to do the police job.[95] In most police departments, new officers must attend a formal training course at an academy operated by, or associated with, the department. Training courses run from two-week sessions involving handling firearms and target practice to more academic four- to six-month programs.[96] The first police training school in the United States was developed in 1908 by the Berkeley, California, chief of police, **August Vollmer**.[97]

Variations in Training Requirements A recent report by the Missouri Governor's Commission on Crime points to the disparity in police training requirements in the United States. The state of Missouri mandates a minimum of 120 hours for most law enforcement officers, the lowest number of hours in the nation. However, the number of training hours in the state of Missouri varies from 1,000 hours for state highway patrol officers to 600 hours for police officers in Kansas City and St. Louis, to no required training in cities of less than 2,000 and departments with less than four police officers.[98]

The majority of big cities in the United States have their own police academies. About 85 percent of cities

Sample Job Requirements in Policing

Academy Training Requirements in Selected Police Departments

- South Carolina Highway Patrol: 12-week police academy; officers are paid to attend.
- Sioux Falls (South Dakota): 8-week police academy; officers are paid to attend.
- Rockford (Illinois): 10-week police academy; officers are paid to attend.
- Sarasota County (Florida): 5-week police academy; officers are paid to attend.
- University of Georgia: 6-week police academy; officers are paid to attend.
- Los Angeles: 6-month police academy; officers are paid to attend.
- Charleston (West Virginia): 15-week academy; officers are paid to attend.

YOU ARE THERE!

Recruit Training in the NYPD

Recruit training in the New York City Police Department consists of almost nine months of training at its police academy and in the field. The program consists of (1) academic training, (2) physical training, (3) firearms training, (4) emergency first aid training, (5) driver training, and (6) field training.

The academic training is broken into three divisions: police science, law, and social science. The majority of this training takes place in the classroom. Students must pass four examinations in each division (a passing grade is 70) and must pass an exam on the use of deadly physical force (a passing grade is 100).

The physical training, which takes place at the academy's gymnasium, consists of physical conditioning; use of the police baton; and handcuffing, searching, and self-defense techniques. Students also learn water safety and lifesaving techniques at the academy's pool. Students must successfully complete a physical fitness test and show proficiency in everything taught in the physical training program.

The five-day firearms training takes place at the department's firearms range in Rodman's Neck, in the Bronx. The training includes safety training and the use of firearms in combat situations. Students must show a proficiency in firearms, which is measured by their accuracy in timed firing.

Emergency first aid training consists of basic lifesaving techniques, such as cardiopulmonary resuscitation (CPR) and the Heimlich maneuver (for choking victims). Techniques for the temporary treatment and transport of the injured are also stressed.

The driver training consists of five days at the department's Driver Training School at Floyd Bennet Field in Brooklyn. This training emphasizes driver and pedestrian safety, as well as defensive and emergency driving techniques. Students must successfully pass a timed course to graduate.

Training in the NYPD receives much attention and is constantly being updated to address current concerns. In the wake of a controversial shooting by a police officer, former Police Commissioner Benjamin Ward emphasized in a *New York Times* article that New York City police needed "more training in subduing violent people without using guns and in 'overcoming a mindset' that makes them reluctant to retreat."

---

with a population of 250,000 or more and approximately half of cities with a population between 100,000 and 250,000 operate their own police academies.[99] Localities without their own academy use a nearby state or county academy. Regional academies are increasingly serving the training needs of several departments in an area. Also, many academies are now operated by community colleges on a contract basis or using police personnel as staff.

A recently published history of the Northern Virginia Criminal Justice Academy (formerly called the Northern Virginia Police Academy) illustrates the evolution in police training of many police academies over the last quarter of a century. The Northern Virginia Police Academy was established in 1965 to train police from Arlington County, the city of Alexandria, and Fairfax County. In the academy's early years, the training consisted of eleven weeks divided into academic, firearms, physical, and driver training.[100]

The academic training consisted of an introduction to police science (police methods and techniques), government and law, police and community life, and laboratory techniques. The firearms and physical training curricula consisted of learning to fire a service revolver and shotgun, as well as calisthenics, judo, and close order drill (military-type marching and calisthenics). The driver training consisted of driving around traffic cones on a simplified course.

Police academy instructors show recruits the mechanics of searching a suspect.

In 1970, the state of Virginia formed its first training commission to promulgate mandatory requirements governing both basic and in-service training. The commission insisted that all sworn officers receive 160 hours of training during the first year of employment and that each veteran officer attend 40 hours of in-service training every two years. As a result of the new regulations, the academy added blocks of instruction on community relations, crisis intervention, tactical decisions, judgmental shooting, officer survival, crisis management, advanced driver training, and sensitivity training.

Police training has come a long way in recent years. A study of police training discovered that in the 1950s, training was considered a minor position in the department, whereas in the 1980s, most big city academies had been elevated to a higher level within the organization.[101] Gaines and his associates tell us that the 1970s and 1980s saw a dramatic increase in the quality and quantity of police training, and that departments are now paying more attention to curriculum, training methods, and the development of training facilities.[102]

Perhaps the improvement in police training can be traced to the 1967 recommendation by the President's Commission on Law Enforcement and Administration of Justice that police departments provide "an absolute minimum of 400 hours of classroom work spread over a four-to-six month period so that it can be combined with carefully selected and supervised field training." The commission also recommend in-service training at least once a year, along with incentives for officers to continue their education.[103] In 1996, it was reported that the number of hours required for the basic police academy in the state of Texas had been raised from 480 hours to 620 hours.[104]

Gaines and his associates call recruit training a critical part of personnel administration, because if recruits are not properly trained, they will not function adequately as police officers. As an example of a good training program, Gaines and his associates describe the state of Kentucky's training curriculum, which is based on a statewide police job analysis. The program attempts to provide future police officers with the necessary knowledge, skills, and abilities. The Kentucky curriculum consists of the following:

- Introduction to law enforcement: 8 hours.
- Police and community service: 6.5 hours.
- Criminal law: 75 hours.
- Police patrol function: 68 hours.
- Traffic: 30 hours.
- Defensive driving: 16.5 hours.
- First aid: 12 hours.
- Firearms: 56.5 hours.
- Criminal investigation: 17 hours.
- Simulated field exercises: 12.5 hours.
- Special police investigations: 6.5 hours.

- Functional fitness and health: 21 hours.
- Mechanics of arrest, restraint, and control: 24 hours.[105]

The federal government provides training for all federal law enforcement agencies (with the exception of the FBI, which has its own training academy in Quantico, Virginia) at the Federal Law Enforcement Training Center (FLETC) in Glynco, Georgia.[106]

See the boxes in this chapter for training academy procedures in various police departments.

Field Training Field training is on-the-job training of recently graduated recruits from the police academy. The training is provided by specially selected patrol officers and is designed to supplement the theory taught at the police academy with the reality of the street.

The San Jose (California) Police Department created a field training program as early as 1972 that has been adopted by many police departments across the country. The San Jose program consists of two phases of training: (1) sixteen weeks of regular police academy classroom training and (2) fourteen weeks of field training. During the field training phase, a recruit is assigned to three different field training officers (FTOs). Each FTO works with the recruit on patrol for four weeks. The recruit then returns to the first FTO for the last two weeks. Each recruit receives a daily evaluation report by his or her FTO and a weekly evaluation report by the FTO's supervisor.[107]

A survey found that nearly two-thirds (64 percent) of departments had a field training program. More than half indicated that their program was directly modeled after the innovative San Jose program.[108] In fact, so widespread is field training that in 1992, the National Association of Field Training Officers (NAFTO) held its first annual conference in Monterey, California. The organization was chartered for the purpose of furthering and representing the interests of law enforcement, corrections, and communications field training officers. The association expects to establish chapters in all fifty states.[109]

The New York City Police Department field training consists of six months in a local precinct training squad under the direct supervision of a training sergeant. Assignments vary from foot patrol to radio car patrol. Each recruit is evaluated several times by the training sergeant and must complete field training with a positive evaluation before being assigned to a regular squad.

> **YOU ARE THERE!**
>
> **Law Enforcement Training at FLETC**
>
> The Federal Law Enforcement Training Center (FLETC), established by Congress in 1970, is located on the site of the former Glynco Naval Air Station near Brunswick, Georgia. This center provides training for officers from fifty-nine federal agencies, with the exception of the FBI and DEA, which have their own training academies. Since 1983, the FLETC also has provided the opportunity for advanced or specialized training for state and local police through its National Center for State and Local Law Enforcement Training, also located on the FLETC campus. Each year, more than 20,000 students graduate from the FLETC, including nearly 4,000 state and local officers. The average training curriculum consists of legal studies, enforcement techniques, behavioral science, enforcement operations, computer/economic crime, firearms, and physical techniques. For more information on these programs, see Summary of Operations and Programs (available from the Federal Law Enforcement Training Center, Glynco, Georgia).
>
> One of the major benefits of the FLETC concept is that each agency does not have to operate its own training unit and thus can save significant funds through consolidated training. The cost of such a facility would be prohibitive for a single agency to staff and maintain.
>
> Source: Adapted from Charles F. Rinkevich, "The FLETC Concept," *FBI Law Enforcement Bulletin*, Washington, D.C., January 1992, pp. 6–7.

Firearms Training In the 1960s, most police firearms training in the United States consisted of firing at bull's-eye targets. Later, training became more sophisticated, using more realistic silhouette targets shaped like armed adversaries. The FBI's Practical Pistol Course began to modernize firearms training; the course required qualification not only from different distances but also from different positions, such as standing, kneeling, and prone positions. As firearms training progressed, shoot/don't shoot training was introduced using **Hogan's Alley** courses. Targets depicting "good guys" and "bad guys" would pop up, requiring officers to make split-second decisions. Today, many agencies have replaced Hogan's Alley programs with computer-controlled visual simulations.[110]

Police recruits get a chance to encounter simulated situations at "Hogan's Alley."

The Goldsboro (North Carolina) Police Department added a new twist to firearms training. Like many departments, the Goldsboro department had allowed its officers to wear nonuniform clothing to the range because of the possibility of inclement weather, dirt, and gun residue. Now, however, the Goldsboro Police Department, in an effort to strive for more realism at the range, requires its officers to shoot in clothing normally worn in conjunction with their duties, because clothes and accessories can affect shooting accuracy. Detectives must wear professional attire, and patrol officers must wear uniforms, including protective vests.[111]

In-Service, Management, and Specialized Training

Police training generally does not end at the recruit level. In many departments, in-service training is used to regularly update the skills and knowledge base of veteran officers. Because laws and developments in policing are constantly changing, officers need to be kept up-to-date.

In addition to in-service training, many departments use management training programs to teach supervisory and management skills to newly promoted supervisors and managers. The New York City Police Department sends newly promoted sergeants to a four-week Basic Management Orientation Course (BMOC). It also sends newly promoted lieutenants and captains to two-week orientation courses.

Many departments also offer specialized training programs for officers assigned to new duties. The New York City Police Department sends newly assigned detectives to a four-week Criminal Investigation Course (CIC). It sends other specialists to training courses relevant to their specialties.

See the table in this chapter for specific in-service training courses throughout the United States

Training for the Police Corps

The Police Corps, which has been proposed for over thirty years by Adam Walinsky, since he was an aide to former New York Senator Robert F. Kennedy, finally came to fruition in March 1997. This program models training after the military's successful Reserve Officer Training Corps (ROTC). As part of the 1994 Federal anticrime law, $10 million was appropriated for six states to develop these programs. The programs reimburse as much as $30,000 in educational costs to college graduates who agree to serve four years in a participating police agency. The largest award went to the Baltimore Police Department for three classes of forty recruits.[112] In addition to Maryland, South Carolina, Oregon, North Carolina, Arkansas, and Nevada received money from this program.

Proponents of the Police Corps say it will transform policing, not just by attracting college graduates, but by having these older, better-educated recruits trained in a different way. They will have a new curriculum focus-

> **YOU ARE THERE!**
>
> **Training and Conferences around the United States**
>
> *Law and Order* runs a monthly calendar of events listing law enforcement training programs and conventions. The following is a sample of such events listed in the June 1997 issue.
>
> **July 1997**
> 14–18 OC Instructor Certification; Reno, Nevada
> 16–18 Riot Control; Wayne, New Jersey
> 19–20 Tactical Folding Knife Instructor Course; Columbus, Ohio
> 20–23 National Conference on Criminal Justice Research; Washington, D.C.
> 21–25 Less-Lethal Weaponry Instructor Certification; Portsmouth, New Hampshire
> 22–24 9th Annual Symposium on Alcohol and Drug Enforcement; St. Petersburg, Florida
> 28–8/1 Law Enforcement Tactical Shooting Instructor Development; Quantico, Virginia
> 28–8/1 Electronic Surveillance Methods for Law Enforcement Investigators; Chesterfield, Virginia
>
> **August 1997**
> 1–5 Underwater Search and Evidence Recovery; Evanston, Illinois
> 2–3 Tactical Folding Knife Instructor Course; Sacramento, California
> 4–6 Street Survival; Anaheim, California
> 4–8 Crime Scene Investigation: From Scene to Courtroom; Biloxi, Mississippi
> 11–15 Firearms Instructor Development; Oregon City, Oregon
> 11–15 Less-Lethal Weaponry Instructor Certification; Seattle, Washington
> 12–14 Street Survival; New Orleans, Louisiana
> 13–15 Tactical Chemical Weapons; Akron, Ohio
>
> Source: Adapted from "Calendar of Events," *Law and Order*, June 1997.

ing on the community and emphasizing leadership, sensitivity, and social skills as tools to break down the friction and distrust that officers often encounter. To deal with these problems, recruits will learn not only regular police procedures but also the demographics of neighborhoods and communication and note-taking skills. Role playing will also be a major part of training.

Community Policing Training

Numerous departments throughout the United States have begun to develop low-cost and effective local and regional community policing training to inculcate community awareness into its recruits and in-service personnel.[113]

The U.S. Department of Justice, Office of Community Oriented Policing Services (COPS), funds training provided by the Community Policing Consortium, a group of five of the leading policing organizations in the United States: the International Association of Chiefs of Police (IACP), the National Organization of Black Law Enforcement Executives (NOBLE), the National Sheriff's Association (NSA), the Police Executive Research Forum (PERF), and the Police Foundation. This consortium delivers free community policing training to all recipients of COPS grants under the 1994 Crime Bill in the form of regional training. Sessions include community policing orientation, sheriff-specific training, cultural diversity/building community partnerships, problem solving, personnel needs and managing calls for service, and train-the-trainer courses.[114]

Probationary Period

A **probationary period** is the period of time that a department has to evaluate a new officer's ability to perform his or her job effectively. Generally, a probationary officer can be dismissed at will without proof of specific violations of law or department regulations. Once officers are off probation, civil service rules often make it very difficult to dismiss them.

Probationary periods can last anywhere from six months to three years. Today, the average probationary period nationwide is twelve months. About 7 percent of recruits either resign or are dismissed during this period.[115] The probationary period in policing has been called the "first true job related test . . . in the selection procedure."[116]

Chapter Summary

Numerous jobs are available in policing on the federal, state, local, and private levels. The police selection process can be complicated and time consuming. Before selection actually begins, a department must conduct a job analysis to determine the type of candidate the department wants to hire. Next comes the actual selection process. This process can include a written entrance examination, an oral review, a psychological appraisal, a polygraph examination, a medical examination, a physical agility test, and a background investigation.

The standards required to become a police officer have changed significantly in recent years to allow more females and minorities entry into policing. The standards, however, are still high. The major standards are physical, age, and education requirements; lack of a significant criminal record; and residency requirements.

Newly hired police officers generally receive academy training and field training. A probationary period must then be served. In addition, officers continue their educations throughout their careers through in-service, management, and specialized training programs.

Learning Check

1. Discuss why the job analysis is such a vital phase in the police hiring practice.
2. Explain the typical selection process most police departments use to identify and select qualified police officers.
3. Explain the standards most police departments use to select qualified police officers.
4. Discuss why field training programs and probationary periods are vital phases in the police training practice.
5. In your own words, describe the average newly hired U.S. police officer, in view of the police recruitment and selection process.

Review Exercise

Based on your reading of this chapter, prepare a resume and cover letter designed to request your employment in a police department. If you have never prepared a resume and cover letter, this may be the time to go to the library and obtain information on the process.

Web Exercise

Patrol over to several police department web sites that you may be interested in and research their standards and selection procedures. Contact the agency online and request an application and information on their next examination. If you cannot contact them online, call or write them.

Key Concepts

equal employment opportunity regulations
affirmative action regulations
job analysis
job related
Guardians Association of New York City Police Department v. Civil Service Commission of New York
knowledge, skills, and abilities (KSAs)
police selection process
United States v. Wichita Falls
Padula v. Webster
Todd v. Navarro
August Vollmer
field training
Hogan's Alley
probationary period

Notes

1. John Van Maanen, "Observations on the Making of Policemen," *Human Organization* 32 (1973): 407–418.
2. James J. Fyfe, "Police Personnel Practices, 1986," in *Municipal Yearbook 1987* (Washington, D.C.: International City Management Association, 1987), pp. 15–23.
3. Arthur Niederhoffer, *Behind the Shield: The Police in Urban Society* (Garden City, N.Y.: Anchor Books, 1967), p. 1.
4. Ralph S. Osborn, "Police Recruitment: Today's Standard—Tomorrow's Challenge," *FBI Law Enforcement Bulletin,* June 1992, pp. 21–25.
5. Robert Sheehan and Gary W. Cordner, *Introduction to Police Administration,* 2d ed. (Cincinnati: Anderson, 1989), p. 220.
6. S. W. Gellerman, *Motivation and Productivity* (New York: American Management Association, 1963), p. 238.
7. Sheehan and Cordner, *Introduction to Police Administration,* p. 222.
8. Robert C. Trojanowicz and David L. Carter, "The Changing Face of America," *FBI Law Enforcement Bulletin,* January 1990, p. 6. Also see Osborn, "Police Recruitment," pp. 21–25; Martha Farnsworth Riche, "America's New Workers," *American Demographics,* February 1988, p. 64; and Marvin J. Cetron, Wanda Rocha, and Rebecca Luckins, "Into the 21st Century: Long-Term Trends Affecting the United States," *Futurist,* July/August 1988, p. 64.
9. Cetron, Rocha, and Luckins, "Into the 21st Century," p. 64.
10. Osborn, "Police Recruitment," p. 23.
11. Osborn, "Police Recruitment," p. 23.
12. "Across the USA: News from Every State," *USA Today,* 13 August 1997, p. 10-A. See also: "Money Matters: Starting Pay Is Great, but Raises Don't Add Up," *Law Enforcement News,* 30 June 1997, p. 4.
13. Harold Slater and Martin Reiser, "A Comparative Study of Factors Influencing Police Recruitment," *Journal of Police Science and Administration* 16 (1990): 168–176.
14. Duane L. West, "Officer Looks Back at Recruitment Process—Things Have Changed," *Community Policing Ex-*

change, March/April 1997, p. 3. The author is a lieutenant with the Tallahassee, Florida, Police Department's Neighborhood Services Division.

15. *Guardians Association of NYC Police Department v. Civil Service Commission of New York,* 23 FEP 909 (1980).

16. D. Thompson and T. Thompson, "Court Standards for Job Analysis in Test Validation," *Personnel Psychology* (35): 865–874.

17. George F. Cole, *The American System of Criminal Justice,* 6th ed. (Pacific Grove, Calif.: Brooks/Cole, 1992), p. 233.

18. Dave Pettinari and Dan Corsentino, "Quality Begins with Selection," *Community Policing Exchange,* March/April 1997, p. 5. The authors are, respectively, commander and sheriff of the Pueblo County Sheriff's Office, Pueblo, Colorado.

19. Pettinari and Corsentino, "Quality Begins with Selection."

20. Timothy N. Oettmeier, "Perspectives on Selection Procedures," *Community Policing Exchange,* March/April 1997, p. 1. The author is a lieutenant in the Houston P.D.'s police academy.

21. Oettmeier, "Perspectives on Selection Procedures."

22. Allan Roe and Norma Roe, *Police Selection: A Technical Summary of Validity Studies* (Ogden, Utah: Diagnostic Specialties, 1982).

23. Bernard Cohen and Jan Chaiken, *Investigators Who Perform Well* (Washington, D.C.: National Institute of Justice, 1987), pp. 16–20.

24. Cohen and Chaiken, *Investigators Who Perform Well,* p. 20.

25. Bernard Cohen and Jan M. Chaiken, *Police Background Characteristics and Performance* (Lexington, Mass.: Lexington Books, 1973), pp. 87, 90–91.

26. H. Saxenian, "To Select a Leader," *MIT Technology Review* 72 (1970): 55–61.

27. Mark Hogue, Tommie Black, and Robert Sigler, "The Differential Use of Screening Techniques in the Recruitment of Police Officers," *American Journal of Police* 13 (1994): 120. Also, see Frank Horvath, "Polygraphic Screening Candidates for Police Work in Large Police Agencies in the United States: A Survey of Practices, Policies, and Evaluative Comments," *American Journal of Police* 12 (1993): 67–86. For a complete analysis of police background investigations, see: John S. Dempsey, *An Introduction to Public and Private Investigations* (Minneapolis/St. Paul: West, 1996), pp. 122–125. Also, see Thomas H. Wright, "Pre-Employment Background Investigations," *FBI Law Enforcement Bulletin,* November 1991, pp. 16–21.

28. Francis L. McCafferty, Godofredo D. Domingo, and Lawrence Palahunic, "Screening Out Psychologically Unsuitable Officers," *Police Chief,* February 1989, p. 24.

29. "Milwaukee PD Hiring Rules Get Overhaul—with Push from DoJ," *Law Enforcement News,* 15 December 1996, p. 1.

30. "Pre-employment Screening May Cut Dispatcher Attrition," *Law Enforcement News,* 30 June 1997, pp. 1, 9.

31. Larry K. Gaines, Mittie T. Southerland, and John E. Angell, *Police Administration* (New York: McGraw-Hill, 1991), p. 275.

32. Steven A. Lazer, "Common Sense, Can It Be Measured by Police Tests?" *Police Chief,* April 1997, pp. 157–158.

33. See James Kriebe, "Selection, Training, and Evaluation Ensure Success," *Police Chief* 62 (1994): 26–29. Also, see T. Kenneth Moran, "Pathways toward a Nondiscriminatory Recruitment Policy," *Journal of Police Science and Administration* 16 (1988): 274–287.

34. Gaines, Southerland, and Angell, eds. *Police Administration,* p. 275. See also Harvey Rachlin, "Nassau County's Police Entrance Exam," *Law and Order,* July 1997, pp. 77–90.

35. "FBI Plans to Abandon Its Entry-Level Test in Favor of New, Bias-Free Exam," *Law Enforcement News,* 30 November 1991, p. 1.

36. "FBI to Abandon Entry-Level Test," p. 1.

37. McCafferty, Domingo, and Palahunic, "Screening Out Psychologically Unsuitable Officers," p. 24.

38. G. E. Hargrave, "Using the MMPI and CPI to Screen Law Enforcement Applicants: A Study of Reliability and Validity of Clinician's Decisions," *Journal of Police Science and Administration* 13 (1985): 221–224.

39. Jack Aylward, "Psychological Testing and Police Selection," *Journal of Police Science and Administration* 13 (1985): 201–210.

40. George Pugh, "The California Psychological Inventory and Police Selection," *Journal of Police Science and Administration* 3 (1985): 172–177.

41. George Hargrave and Deidre Hiatt, "Law Enforcement Selection with the Interview, MMPI and CPI: A Study of Reliability and Validity," *Journal of Police Science and Administration* 15 (1987): 110–114.

42. Robert D. Meier and Richard E. Maxwell, "Psychological Screening of Police Candidates: Current Perspectives," *Journal of Police Science and Administration* 15 (1987): 210–215.

43. Alan Brenner, "Psychological Screening of Police Applicants," in *Critical Issues in Policing,* ed. Roger Dunham and Geoffrey Alper (Prospect Heights, Ill.: Waveland Press, 1989), pp. 72–87.

44. Elizabeth Burbeck and Adrian Furnham, "Police Officer Selection: A Critical Review of the Literature," *Journal of Police Science and Administration* 13 (1985): 58–69.

45. Inwald, "Administrative, Legal and Ethical Practices," pp. 367–372.

46. Wayne W. Bennett and Karen M. Hess, *Criminal Investigation*, 4th ed. (Minneapolis/St. Paul: West, 1994), p. 248.
47. F. Lee Bailey, Roger E. Zuckerman, and Kenneth R. Pierce, *The Employee Polygraph Protection Act: A Manual for Polygraph Examiners and Employers* (Severna Park, Md.: American Polygraph Association, 1989). See also James J. Kouri, "Federal Polygraph Law: A Blow to Private Security," *The NarcOfficer,* May 1989, pp. 37–39; Hugh E. Jones, "The Employee Polygraph Protection Act: What Are the Consequences?" *The NarcOfficer,* May 1989, pp. 41–42; and Norman Ansley, "A Compendium on Polygraph Validity," *The NarcOfficer,* May 1989, pp. 43–48.
48. For a discussion on the use of the polygraph in police testing, as well as testing for other jobs and the Employee Polygraph Protection Act (EPPA) of 1988, see Dempsey, *An Introduction to Public and Private Investigations,* pp. 173–175.
49. L. E. Prior, "Polygraph Testing of Vermont State Police Officer," *Polygraph* 14 (1985): 256–257.
50. Frank Horvath, "Polygraphic Screening Candidates for Police Work in Large Police Agencies in the United States: A Survey of Practices, Policies, and Evaluative Comments, *American Journal of Police* 12 (1993): 67–86.
51. Gaines, Southerland, and Angell, *Police Administration,* p. 276.
52. L. Territo, C. R. Swanson, and N. C. Chamelin, *The Police Personnel Selection Process* (Indianapolis: Bobbs-Merrill, 1977).
53. Paula Rubin, *The Americans with Disabilities Act and Criminal Justice: Hiring New Employees* (Washington: D.C.: National Institute of Justice, 1994). Also see Michael Smith and Geoffrey Alpert, "The Police and the Americans with Disabilities Act—Who Is Being Discriminated Against?" *Criminal Law Bulletin* 29 (1993): pp. 516–528; T. Schneid and L. Gaines, "The Americans with Disabilities Act: Implications for Police Administrators," *American Journal of Police* 10(1) (1991): 47–58.
54. Gaines, Southerland, and Angell, *Police Administration,* p. 274.
55. P. Maher, "Police Physical Agility Tests: Can They Ever Be Valid?" *Public Personnel Management Journal,* vol. 13, pp. 173–183.
56. *United States v. Wichita Falls,* 47 FEP 1629 (N.D. Texas, 1988).
57. Ken Peak, Douglas Farenholtz, and George Coxey, "Physical Abilities Testing of Police Officers: A Flexible, Job-Related Approach," *Police Chief* 59 (1992): 51–56.
58. Thomas H. Wright, "Pre-employment Background Investigations," *FBI Law Enforcement Bulletin,* November 1991, pp. 16–21.
59. Sheehan and Cordner, *Introduction to Police Administration,* p. 220.
60. President's Commission on Law Enforcement and Administration of Justice, *The Challenge of Crime in a Free Society* (Washington, D.C.: U.S. Government Printing Office, 1967).
61. Albert Reiss, *The Police and the Public* (New Haven, Conn.: Yale University Press, 1971).
62. Fyfe, "Police Personnel Practices," pp. 17–18.
63. J. E. Sheedy et al., "Recommended Vision Standards for Police Officers," *Journal of the American Optometric Association,* October 1983, pp. 925–928.
64. T. C. Cox et al., "A Theoretical Examination of Police Entry-Level Uncorrected Visual Acuity Standards," *American Journal of Criminal Justice,* November 1987, pp. 199–208.
65. Gaines, Southerland, and Angell, *Police Administration,* p. 271.
66. G. W. Good and A. R. Augsburger, "Uncorrected Visual Acuity Standards for Police Applicants," *Journal of Police Science and Administration,* December 1987, pp. 18–23.
67. Fyfe, "Police Personnel Practices," pp. 17–18.
68. Mike Pearl, "'Age' Ruling Backs Cops in Battle of Blue & Grey," *New York Post,* 31 May 1997, p. 12; "Age before Duty? Police Brass Alter Ground Rules, Leaving Some Over-35 NYPD Rookies Standing at the Altar," *Law Enforcement News,* 30 April 1997, p. 5.
69. David L. Carter, Allen D. Sapp, and Darrel W. Stephens, *The State of Police Education: Policy Direction for the 21st Century* (Washington, D.C.: Police Executive Research Forum, 1989), p. 84.
70. Carter, Sapp, and Stephens, *State of Police Education,* p. 38.
71. Carter, Sapp, and Stephens, *State of Police Education,* p. 61.
72. James B. Jacobs and Samuel B. Magdovitz, "At LEEP's End: A Review of the Law Enforcement Education Program," *Journal of Police Science and Administration* 5 (1977):1–17. LEEP was also discussed in chapter 1 of this text.
73. President's Commission on Law Enforcement and Administration of Justice, *Challenge of Crime,* p. 110.
74. B. E. Sanderson, "Police Officers: The Relationship of a College Education to Job Performance, *Police Chief* 44 (1977): 62.
75. Wayne Cascio, "Formal Education and Police Officer Performance," *Journal of Police Science and Administration* 5 (1977): 57–60.
76. Lee Bowker, "A Theory of Educational Needs of Law Enforcement Officers," *Journal of Contemporary Criminal Justice* 1 (1980): 17–24.
77. Mitchell Tyre and Susan Braunstein, "Higher Education and Ethical Policing," *FBI Law Enforcement Bulletin,* June 1992, pp. 6–10.

78. Lawrence Sherman et al., *The Quality of Police Education* (San Francisco: Jossey-Bass, 1978), pp. 185–188.
79. Sherman et al., *Quality of Police Education*, pp. 185–188.
80. Sherman et al., *Quality of Police Education*, pp. 185–188.
81. Sheehan and Cordner, *Introduction to Police Administration*, p. 221.
82. Carter, Sapp, and Stephens, *The State of Police Education*.
83. "How Much Is Too Much? Prior Drug Use at Issue," *Law Enforcement News*, 28 February 1997, p. 5. Also see "Md. Recruits Drug History Eyed," *Law Enforcement News*, 15 April 1997, p. 5.
84. "How Much Is Too Much?"
85. George W. Griesinger et al., *Civil Service Systems: Their Impact on Police Administration* (Washington, D.C.: National Institute of Justice, 1979), p. 102.
86. Fyfe, "Police Personnel Practices," p. 20.
87. Gaines, Southerland, and Angell, *Police Administration*, p. 270.
88. Frank Schmallenger, *Criminal Justice Today: An Introductory Text for the Twenty-first Century* (Englewood Cliffs, N.J.: Prentice-Hall, 1991), p. 213.
89. *Law Enforcement News*, 15 October 1990.
90. Charles R. Swanson, Leonard Territo, and Robert W. Taylor, *Police Administration: Structures, Processes, and Behavior*, 2d ed. (New York: Macmillan, 1988), p. 224.
91. "Dallas PD to Open Doors to Gay Recruits," *Law Enforcement News*, 15 June 1993, p. 6.
92. *Padula v. Webster* 822 F.2d 97 (1987).
93. *Todd v. Navarro*, 698 F.Supp. 871 (1988).
94. Lois Pilant, "Law Enforcement Training," *Police Chief*, November 1996, pp. 28–37.
95. Larry K. Gaines and C. W. Forester, "Recruit Training Processes and Issues," in *The Police Personnel System*, ed. C. Swank and J. Conser (New York: Wiley, 1983).
96. Cole, *American System of Criminal Justice*, p. 225.
97. Harold Backer and Jack E. Whitehouse, *Police of America: A Personal View: Introduction and Commentary* (Springfield, Ill.: Charles C. Thomas, 1980), pp. 49–51.
98. "Missouri Urged to Try Once Again to Raise Minimum Training Standards for Police," *Law Enforcement News*, 15 December 1991, p. 1.
99. Brian Reaves, *Local Law Enforcement*, (Washington, D.C.: National Institute of Justice, 1996), p. 4.
100. Thomas Shaw, "The Evolution of Police Recruit Training: A Retrospective," *FBI Law Enforcement Bulletin*, January 1992, pp. 2–6.
101. Thomas M. Frost and Magnus J. Seng, "The Administration of Police Training: A Thirty-Year Perspective," *Journal of Police Science and Administration*, March 1984, pp. 66–73.
102. Gaines, Southerland, and Angell, *Police Administration*, p. 279.
103. President's Commission on Law Enforcement and Administration of Justice, pp. 112–113.
104. Pilant, "Law Enforcement Training," p. 28.
105. Gaines, Southerland, and Angell, *Police Administration*, pp. 280–281.
106. See Larry Tully and Brad Smith, "FLETC Adopts Unified Approach to Training," *Police Chief*, November 1996, pp. 45–47.
107. "Law Enforcement Training Week Resolution Awaits Passage in House," *CJ Update* 21 (1992): 10.
108. Michael S. Campbell, *Field Training for Police Officers: State of the Art* (Washington, D.C.: National Institute of Justice, 1986).
109. Jack B. Molden, "Training Officer Notes: Training as a Management Function," *Law and Order*, September 1992, pp. 17–18.
110. James P. Morgan, Jr., "Police Firearms Training: The Missing Link," *FBI Law Enforcement Bulletin*, January 1992, pp. 14–15.
111. Morgan, "Police Firearms Training," p. 15.
112. Michael Janofsky, "Baltimore Tries Training Police in a New Way," *New York Times*, 30 March 1997, p. 12.
113. See, for example, "Kick-Start Training Strategies," *Community Policing Exchange*, March/April 1997, p. 4; Howard Lebowitz, "Academy Training Curriculum Emphasizes Moral Decision Making," *Community Policing Exchange*, March/April 1997, p. 2; John Gentile, "Recruit and In-Service Training: The Diversity Factor," *Community Policing Exchange*, March/April 1997, pp. 6–7; Clair Young, "Ohio Organizes Statewide Training," *Community Policing Exchange*, March/April 1997, p. 7; and Danny Shell, "State Makes Vision for Unity a Reality," *Community Policing Exchange*, March/April 1997, p. 8.
114. "Free Community Policing Training Available to COPS Grantees," *Community Policing Exchange*, March/April 1997, p. 2. The Community Policing Consortium can be reached at 1726 M Street N.W., Suite 801, Washington, D.C. 20036. 800–833–3085; Fax 202–833–9295. The consortium can also be clicked onto at its Web site at www.communitypolicing.org.
115. Fyfe, "Police Personnel Practices," p. 20.
116. O. W. Wilson and Roy Clinton McLaren, *Police Administration*, 4th ed. (New York: McGraw-Hill, 1977), p. 270.

5

The Police Role and Police Discretion

Chapter Outline

The Police Role
  Crime-Fighting Role
  Order Maintenance Role
  Ambiguity of the Police Role
Goals and Objectives of Policing
  Primary Goals and Objectives
  Secondary Goals and Objectives
Police Operational Styles
  Broderick's Police Operational Styles
  Wilson's Police Operational Styles

Police Discretion
  What Is Discretion?
  How Is Discretion Exercised?
  Why Is Discretion Exercised?
  What Factors Influence Discretion?
  How Can Discretion Be Controlled?

Chapter Goals

- To explore the police role and its many interpretations.

- To introduce you to the goals and objectives of policing.

- To explore various operational styles of the police.

- To introduce you to the concept of police discretion.

- To explore the concept of police discretion, seeking to understand how and why discretion is exercised and the methods that have been used to control it.

Introduction

The role of the police and the exercise of police discretion are among the most important issues in policing. Who are the police? What do they do? How do they do what they do? What should they do instead?

This chapter will look at the role of the police in society, including the crime-fighting role, the order maintenance role, and the ambiguity of the police role. It will discuss the goals and objectives of the police, as well as various police operational styles discovered by researchers who study the police. Additionally, the chapter will discuss police discretion. It will examine what discretion is, how and why discretion is exercised, what factors influence discretion, and how discretion can be controlled by police administrators.

The Police Role

Who are the police in the United States? What do they do? What should they do? These are very difficult questions to answer. Herman Goldstein warns, "Anyone attempting to construct a workable definition of the police role will typically come away with old images shattered and a new-found appreciation for the intricacies of police work."[1]

Two major views of the role of the police exist:

1. The police are crime fighters concerned with law enforcement (**crime fighting**).
2. The police are order maintainers concerned with keeping the peace and providing social services to the community (**order maintenance**).

Crime-Fighting Role

Movies and television shows about the police emphasize the police crime-fighting role. If we believe these stories, the police engage in numerous daily gunfights, car chases, and acts of violence, and they arrest numerous people every day. Fictional books about police work also emphasize the crime-fighting role. Even the news media emphasize this role; television news shows and newspaper headlines dramatize exciting arrests and action by the police.

The police themselves also emphasize their role as crime fighters and play down their job as peacekeepers and social service providers. As a former professor turned police officer, George L. Kirkham, states:

The police have historically overemphasized their role as crime fighters and played down their more common work as keepers of the peace and providers of social services, simply because our society proffers rewards for the former (crime fighting) but cares little for the latter (peace-keeping and providing services). The public accords considerable recognition and esteem to the patrol officer who becomes involved in a shoot-out with an armed robber or who chases and apprehends a rapist, and therefore so do the officer's peers and superiors."[2]

At first glance, there appears to be some truth to the belief that police are primarily crime fighters. Recently, the U.S. police have made over 15 million arrests for all criminal infractions a year, not including traffic violations.[3]

An analysis of the arrests, however, shows a different perspective. Almost 3 million of the 15 million arrests were for the FBI's Index or Part I crimes: serious crimes of violence (murder, forcible rape, robbery, and aggravated assault) accounted for about 796,000 of the arrests, whereas property crimes (burglary, larceny/theft, and motor vehicle theft) accounted for approximately 2.1 million of the arrests. However, the following accounted for the other 11 million arrests:

1. Driving under the influence (DUI) or driving while intoxicated (DWI)—1,436,000 arrests.
2. Drug abuse violations—1,476,000 arrests.
3. Misdemeanor assaults—1,290,000 arrests.
4. Liquor law violations, drunkenness, disorderly conduct, vagrancy, and loitering—2,214,000 arrests.
5. A large variety of lesser offenses excluding traffic offenses.

From the analyses of the arrests made by police, we can see that the vast majority of the arrests are not serious Index crimes but rather what we might call crimes of disorder or actions that annoy citizens and negatively affect their quality of life (for example, offenses involving drugs and alcohol). Even the vast majority of crime fighting the police do is related to order maintenance rather than serious crime.

The Police Role

crime fighting (law enforcement)
or
order maintenance (peacekeeping)?

Police officer attempting to maintain order at the United Parcel Service Distribution Center in Warwick, Rhode Island during the 1996 UPS strike.

Order Maintenance Role

If police are not primarily crime fighters, then, what are they? In an effort to determine the proper role of the police, researchers have conducted numerous studies to determine what it is that police do and why people call on their services. A summary of the key studies follows.

In a study of patrol activities in a city of 400,000, John Webster found that providing social service functions and performing administrative tasks accounted for 55 percent of police officers' time and accounted for 57 percent of their calls. Activities involving crime fighting took up only 17 percent of patrol time and amounted to about 16 percent of the calls to the police.[4]

A study by Robert Lilly found that of 18,000 calls to a Kentucky police department made during a four-month period, 60 percent were for information, and 13 percent concerned traffic problems. Less than 3 percent were about violent crime, and about 2 percent were about theft.[5]

In the Police Services Study (PSS), a survey of 26,000 calls to police in twenty-four different police departments in sixty neighborhoods, researchers found that only 19 percent of calls involved the report of a criminal activity.[6] Table 5.1 shows a breakdown of all citizens' calls for service in this study by general problem types. Similar studies were conducted by Michael Brown in California, Norman Weiner in Kansas City, and Albert J. Reiss in Chicago, with similar results.[7] Additionally, Steven Meagher analyzed the job functions (duties) of 531 police officers in 249 municipal depart-

Table 5.1	Analysis of Citizens' Calls for Service
Nonviolent crime	17
Interpersonal conflict	7
Medical assistance	3
Traffic problem	9
Dependent person	3
Public nuisances	11
Suspicious circumstances	5
Assistance	12
Citizen wants information	21
Citizen wants to give information	8

Source: Adapted from Eric J. Scott, *Calls for Service: Citizen Demand and Initial Police Response* (Washington, D.C.: U.S. Government Printing Office, 1981), pp. 28–30.

All in the Line of Duty

Not Just Routine Patrol

Within minutes of receiving a report of a vehicle being driven erratically, Trooper Matthew Hunter of the Pennsylvania State Police located and pulled the vehicle over. As Trooper Hunter approached the auto, the driver suddenly exited with drawn pistol and began firing. Trooper Hunter immediately took cover, first behind the passenger's side of the assailant's vehicle and then behind his patrol car, where he returned fire with the gunman. Upon realizing that passing motorists were in the line of fire, Trooper Hunter maneuvered into his vehicle and backed it about 50 feet to a point offering greater safety and a better line of fire. After calling for backup, the trooper removed a shotgun from the back seat, exited his vehicle and again returned fire, fatally wounding the assailant.

Source: Adapted from *FBI Law Enforcement News*, March 1997, p. 33.

ments and found that regardless of their size, most police agencies and police officers have similar functions and do pretty much the same thing.[8]

The academic studies clearly indicate that what the police do is maintain order and provide services. People call the police to obtain services or to get help in maintaining order.

Ambiguity of the Police Role

The police role is extremely diverse and dynamic. We must remember that England's Sir Robert Peel, who organized the first paid, full-time, uniformed police department, conceived of the police role as a conspicuous community-oriented patrol designed more for prevention and deterrence than for enforcement. Peel designed the police to be an alternative to the repression of crime and disorder that could have been achieved through military might and severe legal sanctions.

The early American settlers brought Peel's ideas on the role of the police to our shores. As Alan Coffey tells us, however, as the United States began to pass more and more statutory laws, the police role expanded from maintaining order to enforcing the law. Coffey states, "It is this combination of role expectations that generates controversy, particularly with those who emphasize the peacekeeping segment of police work as opposed to actual enforcement."[9]

One way of defining the police role may be to say that it is whatever the community expects the police to be. However, we must remember that most communities consist of many diverse groups with different goals and interests. One group in the community may expect police to do something entirely different from what another group expects. For example, older people in a community or store owners may want the police to hassle teenagers hanging out on the street, yet the teenagers, for their part, may feel that if the police do hassle them, the officers are abusing them. Parents in a community may want the police to search and arrest drug dealers and drug users yet not want the police to search their own children. In these and many other ways, the police are often in a no-win situation.

One researcher, George Pugh, writing on the expansive and varied role of the police, states that a good police officer must have the qualities of common sense and mature judgment, and must react quickly and effectively to problem situations. A good police officer, Pugh says, must be able to adopt the appropriate role of policing to the situation he or she encounters. Common roles include law enforcer, maintainer of social order, and public servant. Finally, a good police officer must have the appropriate concepts of policing that guide and prioritize the role the officer should employ in particular situations. These concepts governing police work, Pugh says, are the following: (1) an effort to improve the welfare of the community and (2) a respect for the individual's rights, worth, and dignity.[10]

Robert Sheehan and Gary W. Cordner, using the work of previous scholars, offer the following synopsis of the police role:

1. The core of the police role involves law enforcement and the use of coercive force;
2. the primary skill of policing involves effectively handling problem situations while avoiding the use of force;
3. skillful police officers avoid the use of force primarily through effective, creative communication.[11]

In summing up the police role, we might agree with Joseph J. Senna and Larry J. Siegel. They say that the police role has become that of a social handywoman or handyman called to handle social problems that citizens wish would simply go away.[12]

Egon Bittner has stated that from its earliest origins, police work has been a "tainted occupation": "The taint that attaches to police work refers to the fact that policemen are viewed as the fire it takes to fight fire, that in

Dempsey's Law

Should I Search Her Book Bag, or Should We Take the Chance That She'll Shoot Us? The Inherent Conflict

Diane: Professor, you always talk about a police officer's responsibility to protect people's individual rights under the U.S. Constitution, but my mom says that an officer's job is to protect society's rights, and the heck with criminals' rights.

Diane, your mother and I are both discussing the biggest problem in the criminal justice system: the inherent conflict between the rights of the individual, including the criminal, and the rights of society. Let's try an experiment. I hear that Dawn here has a gun in her book bag. If I'm an officer, I should search it, right? [Dempsey takes Dawn's book bag from the floor in front of her desk and acts as if he is going to open it and look in it.] What do you think about that, Dawn?

Dawn: I don't think that's right, Professor Dempsey. An officer can't just look into anyone's property. I don't think you should look into my bag.

What's your problem, Dawn? You have a gun in here?

Dawn: No!

You have drugs in here?

Dawn: No!

But what about Diane's mother's feelings? What about the rights of the students in this society—in this classroom? Do you people want Dawn to pull a gun out of this bag and shoot you?

Dawn: Yeah, Professor, but what about my rights? What about the Fourth Amendment?

That's the whole issue. There is an inherent conflict between the rights of the individual as expressed in our Bill of Rights and the rights of society to be free of crime. There is the conflict between Dawn's right that I not search her property unreasonably, based on a hunch, and the rights of the students here not to be shot by Dawn, if she does have a gun. Does anyone know the source of this inconsistency?

Mike: Yes, our founding fathers created the Bill of Rights, or the first ten amendments to the Constitution, to ensure that government would not violate their rights. They were afraid that the government oppression they faced in England could appear here, too.

Exactly right, but our founding fathers placed us in a dilemma. There is an inherent conflict between the rights of the individual and the rights of society. Crime is the price we pay for this conflict. The police must balance that conflict.

Police officers have a very special obligation to protect society and also to protect everyone's individual rights. I remember one afternoon when I was assigned to the Plaza Hotel in Midtown Manhattan. President Reagan was in town, and he always stayed at the Plaza. I was in charge of about a hundred officers who were assigned to the demonstration area in front of the hotel. Our job was to ensure that the demonstration was orderly and that there was no conflict between the demonstrators protesting President Reagan's foreign policy and onlookers. It was raining tremendously, and there was only one demonstrator. He obviously had a mental problem. It was 1985, and this man was holding up signs and screaming, "U.S. get out of Vietnam! Stop the Vietnam War! Reagan is a war criminal!" The man obviously had a problem. Then I saw one of my officers engaged in a rather loud argument with this sole demonstrator. I pulled the officer aside and asked him what the problem was between him and the man. He said to me, "Lieutenant, this man is a nut. Do you hear what he is saying about the president? I told him to stop or I would arrest him, and he started to argue with me about his First Amendment rights." Seeing that the officer had his priorities a little mixed up, I asked if he knew what his role in the demonstration was. He replied, "I'm here to protect the president from this nut." I replied, "Officer, you are here to protect everyone, including this nut."

Diane: Yeah, professor, I understand all that, but who is right? You or my mom? I respect you both, but who is right?

John: Diane, they are both right. The job of the police is to strike a balance between the rights of society and the rights of the individual. Right, Professor?

You got it, John. And it's not an easy job!

the natural course of their duties they inflict harm, albeit deserved, and that their very existence attests that the nobler aspirations of mankind do not contain the means necessary to insure survival."[13]

★ Goals and Objectives of Policing

Much study and research has gone into determining the proper goals and objectives of a police department. This topic can be discussed more easily by thinking in terms of primary goals and objectives and secondary goals and objectives.

Primary Goals and Objectives

The two primary goals and objectives of police departments, according to Sheehan and Cordner, are maintaining order and protecting life and property.[14] These are among the most basic roles of government, and government hires the police to perform these services. To achieve these goals, the police perform a myriad of duties. As Senna and Siegel say,

> Police are expected to perform many civic duties that in earlier times were the responsibility of every citizen: keeping the peace, performing emergency medical care, and dealing with civil emergencies. Today, we leave those tasks to the police. Although most of us agree that a neighborhood brawl must be broken up, that the homeless family must be found shelter, or the drunk taken safely home, few of us want to jump personally into the fray; we'd rather "call the cops."[15]

Secondary Goals and Objectives

Sheehan and Cordner also list six secondary goals and objectives toward which police resources and activities are used to meet the primary two objectives:

1. Preventing crime.
2. Arresting and prosecuting offenders.
3. Recovering stolen and missing property.
4. Assisting the sick and injured.
5. Enforcing noncriminal regulations.
6. Delivering services not available elsewhere in the community.[16]

The police attempt to prevent crime by trying to create a sense of omnipresence (the police are always there) through routine patrol; responding to calls by

Police officers assist a woman who had been trapped in the World Trade Center bombing in New York City in 1992.

citizens to deal with problems that may cause crime; and establishing and participating in police-citizen partnerships designed to prevent crime.

Arresting offenders and assisting prosecutors in bringing charges against defendants is one of the primary methods used by the police to maintain order and protect life and property.

When people find property on the street, they generally bring it to a police officer or to a police station. The police then attempt to find the owner. If that is not possible, they store the property in the hopes that the rightful owner will come in to claim it. When people lose property, they generally go to the police station in the hopes that someone has turned it in. Besides all of their other duties, then, the police serve as society's foremost lost and found department.

Because they are available seven days a week and twenty-four hours a day and because they are highly mobile, the police generally are the closest government agency to any problem. In many jurisdictions, the police are called to emergency cases of sickness and injury to assess the situation before an ambulance is dispatched, or they are called to assist ambulance, paramedical, or other emergency response personnel.

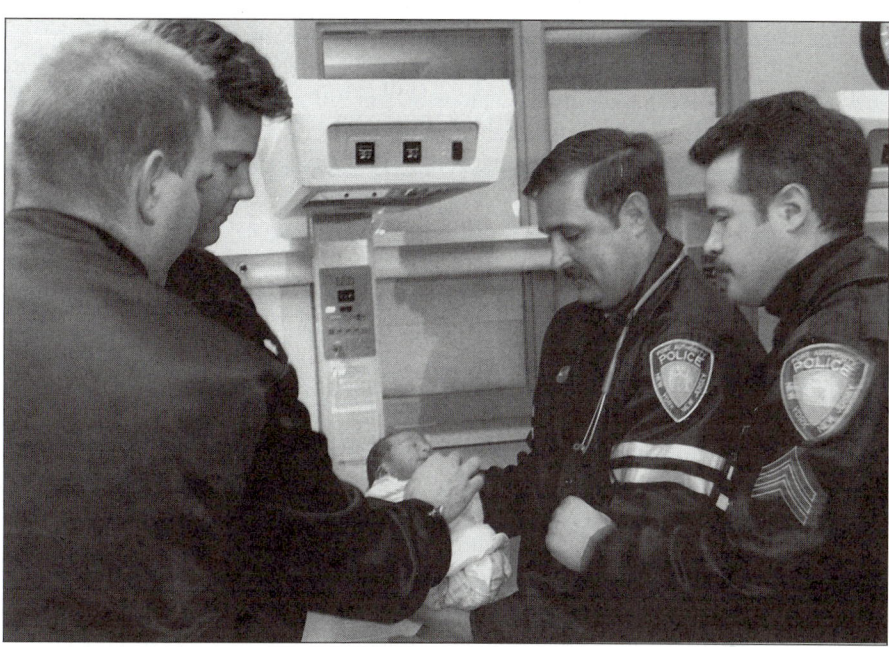

Police officers admire the baby they helped deliver at a New York City airport in 1997.

In the absence of other regulatory personnel or during the times they are not available, the police enforce numerous noncriminal regulations, including traffic and parking regulations, liquor law regulations, and many others.

The police are generally the only government officials available every day, round the clock. When government offices close, the police become roving representatives of the government who assist people with problems no one else is available to handle. When the lights go off in an apartment building, people call the police. When the water main breaks, people call the police. When your neighbor's dog barks all night and keeps you awake, who do you generally call? You call the police. After all, who else can you call at 3:00 in the morning? The police respond and take whatever action they can to ameliorate problems and deal with emergencies. They direct traffic, evacuate residents, and decide who to call for assistance.

Police Operational Styles

People who research the police write about **police operational styles**—styles adopted by police officers as a way of thinking about the role of the police and law in society and how they should perform their jobs. The findings of two leading researchers, John J. Broderick and James Q. Wilson, will be discussed here.

The concept of operational styles is useful in analyzing the police role and police behavior. However, it must be remembered that no officer conforms solely to one of these styles to the exclusion of the others. Many officers show characteristics of several of these styles.

Broderick's Police Operational Styles

John J. Broderick, in his *Police in a Time of Change*, presents four distinct police operational styles: enforcers, idealists, realists, and optimists.[17]

Enforcers Many officers believe that their major role is maintaining order on their beat, keeping society safe, and protecting society by arresting criminals. These "enforcers" place less value on the rights of the individual and on the due process of law granted under the U.S. Constitution than they do on their perceived role, which is maintaining social order and keeping society safe. Enforcers are critical of police administrators, politicians, and the court decisions that favor the rights of the individual over the rights of society.

Enforcers do not like their jobs. They spend much of their time arresting people and then watching these people win court cases based on what the enforcers see as legal technicalities. Furthermore, they often see offenders receiving probation or being released from prison. Enforcers are resentful, cynical, and distrustful, and they tend to stereotype individuals. They seek to return to the "good old days" when, they believe, there was more respect for law and order and the cop on the beat.[18]

Idealists The officers Broderick calls idealists are similar to enforcers, yet they place a higher value on individual rights and the adherence to due process as required by the U.S. Constitution. Idealists believe that it is their responsibility to keep the peace, to protect citizens from criminals, and to preserve the social order. Idealists tend to be cynical, because they see a system of justice with significant problems. They would like understanding and respect for their contributions to society, but they find that they do not receive it and feel that the public is against them. Idealists would like to be in a position to have some impact on the problems they constantly encounter. Seeing no chance of that, however, they tend to feel powerless.[19]

Realists Broderick's realists suffer many of the same resentments and dissatisfactions with the criminal justice system as enforcers and idealists, but they are more secure in themselves and less frustrated with their role in life. They place a relatively low emphasis on both social order and individual rights. Realists see due process of law as being an obstacle to criminal justice. They believe that the goals and objectives of the police (maintaining order and protecting life and property) are impossible, so they concentrate their efforts on the concept of police loyalty and the mutual support of their fellow officers. They are complete cynics and do not make attempts to change or affect the system.[20] As Broderick says, "Realists do not try to change the world, the offenders, or even the police department. They learn that if you cannot succeed at the job, because of politicians, offenders, and ordinary citizens who do not understand, then the hell with it—just don't let it get to you."[21]

Optimists Finally, Broderick describes the optimists—officers who place a relatively high value on individual rights and see their job as people oriented, as opposed to crime oriented. Optimists concentrate their efforts on helping people in trouble rather than on keeping society safe. They tend to like their jobs and are not cynical.[22] Figure 5.1 summarizes Broderick's four police operational styles.

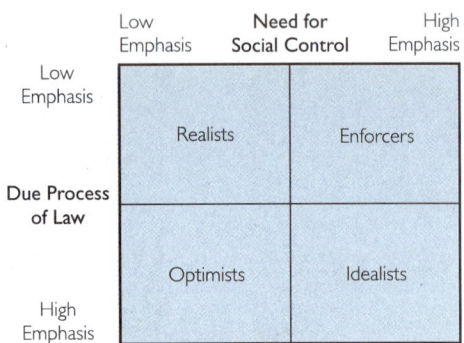

**Figure 5.1
Differences among Broderick's Police Operational Styles.**
Source: Based on John J. Broderick, *Police in a Time of Change*, 2d ed. (Prospect Heights, Ill.: Waveland Press, 1987), pp. 21–116.

Wilson's Police Operational Styles

In his seminal work *Varieties of Police Behavior: The Management of Law and Order in Eight Communities*, **James Q. Wilson** described three distinct styles of policing that a police department can deploy in maintaining order and responding to less serious violations of law. (Within each style, the police treat serious felonies similarly.) Wilson discussed the watchman style, the legalistic style, and the service style.[23] He found that the political culture of a city, which reflects the socioeconomic characteristics of the city and its organization of government, exerts a major influence on the style of policing exercised by the police.

Watchman Style Departments that operate using the watchman style are primarily concerned with order maintenance—maintaining order and controlling illegal and disruptive behavior. Officers in a watchman-style department exercise a great deal of discretion (see the section entitled "Police Discretion") and ignore many minor violations, especially those involving juveniles and traffic. These departments tolerate a certain amount of vice and gambling.

Watchman-style departments maintain order, when necessary, through informal police intervention. Officers use persuasion and threats, or even "hassle" or "rough up" disruptive people, instead of making formal arrests. This style, Wilson says, is generally found in working-class communities with partisan mayor–city council forms of government.

PATROLLING THE NET

Problems on the Net

Every few days, it seems, television newscasts and newspapers carry reports of unspeakable acts conducted over the Internet. Pedophiles and maybe even prisoners trade pornography and tips on kidnapping, while trying to seduce children in electronic chatrooms. Right-wing lunatics post recipes for explosives and rouse their members with paranoid visions of immense conspiracies that only they can overthrow.

In 1995, a California man was convicted of luring a thirteen-year-old girl from Kentucky through a computer network to engage in unlawful sexual activity.

From 1995 to 1997, the Federal Bureau of Investigation arrested thirty-five adult solicitors.

In March 1997, a Long Island, New York, man was accused by the Suffolk County District Attorney of using the Internet to conspire with an accomplice in North Carolina to take turns raping, torturing, and sodomizing a fourteen-year-old girl. A day later, a Minnesota prison inmate was indicted by a federal grand jury for conspiracy to traffic in child pornography over the Internet.

In March 1997, the U.S. Supreme Court held oral arguments on the constitutionality of the Communications Decency Act of 1996, which made it a crime to leave indecent material out on the Net where children can find it. The Communications Decency Act was ruled unconstitutional.

Source: Adapted from George Johnson, "Old View of Internet: Nerds. New View: Nuts," *New York Times*, 30 March 1997, Section 4, p. 1; and Amy Harmon, "For Parents, a New and Vexing Burden," *New York Times*, 27 June 1997, p. A-21.

Legalistic Style Legalistic departments, according to Wilson, enforce the letter of the law. They issue many summonses and make many misdemeanor arrests. They proceed vigorously against illegal enterprises. The legalistic style of enforcement envisions a single standard of conduct in a community and ensures that all members of the community live up to this standard. This style does not make allowances for juveniles, minorities, or intoxicated people. The legalistic style of enforcement, Wilson says, occurs in reform administrations' government styles. Furthermore, this style often occurs in the aftermath of a scandal in a watchman type of department that results in the hiring of a "reform" police chief.

Service Style Wilson's service departments stress servicing the needs of the community. The officers see themselves more as helpers than as soldiers in a war against crime. Service-oriented departments work hand in hand with social service agencies to provide counseling for minor offenders and to assist community groups in preventing crimes and solving problems. Service departments take all requests for service, law enforcement, or order maintenance seriously. They have a high rate of police intervention, but without the arrests and summonses found in legalistic departments. The service style, Wilson says, is generally found in more affluent suburban areas.

Police Discretion

The use of discretion is one of the major challenges facing U.S. police today. The following sections will discuss the meaning of police discretion, how and why it is exercised, what factors influence discretion, and how it can be controlled.

What Is Discretion?

Discretion means the availability of a choice of options or actions one can take in a situation. We all exercise discretion many times every day in our lives. At a restaurant, we have discretion in selecting a steak dinner or a fish dinner. At the video store, we have discretion in picking a mystery or a comedy to view. Discretion involves making a judgment and a decision. It involves selecting one from a group of options.

The criminal justice system involves a tremendous amount of discretion. A judge exercises discretion in sentencing. He or she can sentence a defendant to a prison term or to probation. A judge can release a defendant on bail or order the defendant incarcerated until trial. Prosecutors exercise discretion: they can reduce charges against a defendant or drop the charges entirely. Parole boards exercise discretion: they can parole a person from prison or order him or her to serve the com-

> ## YOU ARE THERE!
>
> **You Decide**
> Think about what you would do as a police officer under the following circumstances. This is a perfect example of a case calling for the exercise of police discretion.
>
> **Facts**
> You receive a call to respond to a boy who is bleeding on the street. You arrive at the location, and you find a fourteen-year-old Asian boy, naked and with blood on his buttocks; a male in his late twenties or early thirties; and two women. The two women tell you that the man must be trying to kill the boy. The boy is too dazed to respond and remains mute. The man tells you that he and the boy are homosexual lovers and were having an argument.
>
> **What Would You Do?**
> If you were the police officer at the scene, which of the following actions would you take?
>
> - Further question all parties at the scene.
> - Bring all parties to the station house for further investigation.
> - Request that your supervisor or the detectives meet you at the scene.
> - Arrest the man for assault and sexual relations with a minor.
> - Ignore the situation and let these people solve their own problems.
>
> **The Actual Case**
> The previous facts are from an actual case you probably recognize. Shortly after midnight on May 27, 1990, two women saw a man chasing a fourteen-year-old Asian boy, naked and with blood on his buttocks, down an alley behind the Oxford Apartments in a low-income area of Milwaukee, Wisconsin. The women called the police. Two police officers arrived in a patrol car. The man told the police officers that he and the boy were gay lovers having a spat. The officers told all parties to go home and resumed patrol.
>
> The boy was later identified as Konerak Sinthasomphone after his remains were found amid the carnage at Apartment 213 of the Oxford Apartments in 1991. The man was later identified as Jeffrey Dahmer. When the police searched Dahmer's apartment, they found parts of at least eleven bodies. These included three severed heads in the refrigerator; decomposed hands and a genital organ in a lobster pot; five full skeletons; and the remains of six other bodies, three of which were in a chemical-filled, 57-gallon plastic drum in the basement. Dahmer later confessed to the murder of seventeen males.

plete sentence. The entire criminal justice system is based on the concept of discretion.

Why is there so much discretion in the U.S. system of criminal justice? In our system, we tend to treat people as individuals. One person who commits a robbery is not the same as another person who commits a robbery. Our system takes into account why the person committed the crime and how he or she committed it. Were there any mitigating or aggravating circumstances? The U.S. system is interested in the spirit of the law, in addition to the letter of the law.

When a judge, a prosecutor, or a parole board member exercises discretion, each generally has sufficient time and data necessary to make a careful, reasoned decision. The judge can read the presentence report prepared by the probation department or consult with the probation department staff member preparing the report. The judge can also consult with the district attorney or the defense attorney. The prosecutor and parole board member also have sufficient data and time in which to decide what action to take in a case.

However, the majority of the most crucial decisions made in the criminal justice system do not take place as described in the previous paragraph. The most important decisions do not take place within an ornately decorated courtroom or a wood-paneled conference room. They take place on the streets. They take place any time of the day or night, and generally without the opportunity for the decision makers to consult with others or to carefully consider all the facts. These split-second decisions are often based on little information. They take place at the very lowest level in the criminal justice system. The police officer is generally the first decision maker in the U.S. criminal justice system and is often the most important.

James Q. Wilson described the police officer's role in exercising discretion as being "unlike that of any other occupation . . . one in which sub-professionals, working alone, exercise wide discretion in matters of utmost importance (life and death, honor and dishonor) in an environment that is apprehensive and perhaps hostile."[24]

Two researchers state, "The police really suffer the worst of all worlds: they must exercise broad discretion behind a facade of performing in ministerial fashion; and they are expected to realize a high level of equality and justice in their discretionary determinations though they have not been provided with the means most commonly relied upon in government to achieve these ends."[25] Kenneth Culp Davis, an expert on police discretion, says, "The police make policy about what law to enforce, how much to enforce it, against whom, and on what occasions."[26]

Not much happens in the U.S. criminal justice system without the use of discretion by the police. How does a police officer exercise discretion on the street?

How Is Discretion Exercised?

The police exercise discretion to perform the following crucial actions:

- To arrest.
- To stop, question, or frisk.
- To use physical force.
- To use deadly force.
- To write traffic summonses.
- To use certain enforcement tactics (harassment, moving loiterers, warning, and so on).
- To take a report on a crime.
- To investigate a crime.

The extent of police discretion is indicated by the following research findings. Donald Black found that only 58 percent of adults suspected of felonies were arrested.[27] John A. Gardiner found that Dallas police officers wrote traffic tickets at a rate twenty times higher than that of Boston police.[28] The Police Foundation noted that the police in Birmingham, Alabama, shot and killed citizens at a rate of 25 per 1,000 officers, compared with 4.2 per 1,000 in Portland, Oregon.[29]

Why Is Discretion Exercised?

Discretion is an extremely necessary part of police work. Sheehan and Cordner tell us that there are seven reasons why the police exercise discretion:

1. If the police attempted to enforce all the laws all the time, they would be in the station house or court all the time and would not be on the street maintaining order and protecting life and property.
2. Because of political realities, legislators pass some laws that they do not intend to have strictly enforced all the time.
3. Lawmakers pass some laws that are vague and ill-defined, making it necessary for the police to interpret these laws and decide when to apply them.
4. Most violations of the law are minor (for example, traffic violations) and do not require full enforcement.

All in the Line of Duty

On Duty, Even When Off Duty

While en route to work in the early morning hours and waiting at a traffic light, Sergeant Robert Shearer of the Harrisburg, Pennsylvania, Bureau of Police observed two men running through the snow-covered street, with one man attempting to assault the other.

Sergeant Shearer pulled his personal vehicle over and, opening his civilian overcoat to reveal his uniform and badge, identified himself as a police officer. The assailant, who had caught the other man and began stabbing him frantically with a large kitchen knife, ignored Sergeant Shearer's repeated commands to drop the knife. Hoping to avoid the use of deadly force, Sergeant Shearer rushed the assailant and knocked him off the critically injured victim. Instead of discontinuing his attack, the assailant raised the knife and began advancing toward the victim again. Sergeant Shearer fired one shot, which struck the 6'8", 260-pound assailant but failed to slow his advance. He fired two more shots, which finally stopped the man, who subsequently died in the emergency room of a local hospital. Though critically wounded, the victim, who had come to the aid of his wife and child when the assailant attacked the woman as she prepared to leave for work, made a full recovery.

Source: Adapted from *FBI Law Enforcement Bulletin*, June 1997, p. 33.

5. The complete enforcement of all the laws all the time would alienate the public from the police and the entire criminal justice system.
6. The full enforcement of all the laws would overwhelm the courts, jails, and prisons.
7. The police have so many duties to perform and such limited resources that good judgment must be exercised in when, where, and how they enforce the law.[30]

What Factors Influence Discretion?

We know that officers practice discretion, and we know that discretion is necessary. Are there factors, however, that cause the police to exercise discretion in a certain way? Scholars have been studying this issue for quite a while.

PATROLLING THE NET

No More Ex-Cons on the Net

In 1997, the United States Parole Commission, alarmed by some of the information they had seen on the Net from parolees and aimed at parolees, added a new item to the list of things federal parolees can be kept from doing: owning firearms, drinking to excess, consorting with criminals, and now, using a computer to access the Internet.

Source: Adapted from George Johnson, "Old View of Internet: Nerds. New View: Nuts," *New York Times*, 30 March 1997, Section 4, p. 1.

Herbert Jacob says that four major factors influence police officers in determining the exercise of discretion:

1. Characteristics of the crime. A serious crime leaves the police less freedom or ability to ignore it or exercise discretion regarding it.
2. Relationship between the alleged criminal and the victim. Generally, the police tend to avoid making arrests when a perpetrator and a victim have a close relationship. In recent years, however, many departments have limited discretion in family-related assault cases and have adopted proarrest policies. Family-related assault cases will be discussed in chapter 15.
3. Relationship between police and the criminal or victim. Generally, a respectful, mannerly complainant is taken more seriously and treated better by the police than an antagonistic one. In the same way, a violator who acts respectfully to the police is also less likely to be arrested than an antagonistic one.
4. Department policies. The preferences of the police chief and city administration, as expressed in department policy, generally influence the actions of the officer.[31]

In *Varieties of Police Behavior*, Wilson found that an officer's discretion varied depending on the type of situation he or she encountered. Wilson found that police have wide latitude in self-initiated situations, such as the enforcement of traffic or drug violations, because there is usually no complainant or victim demanding police action. However, in citizen-initiated situations, an officer has less discretion, and the preferences of the citizen will often influence the officer's decision whether to arrest or not to arrest.[32]

Research has identified five other specific factors that may influence police discretion to arrest: the subject's offense, attitude, race, socioeconomic status, and gender. Studies of police discretion have shown that the most significant factor in the decision to arrest is the seriousness of the offense committed. This factor is supplemented by other information, such as the offender's current mental state, the offender's past criminal record (when known to the arresting officer), whether weapons were involved, the availability of the complainant, and the relative danger to the officer involved.[33]

Irving Pilavin and Scott Briar found that the subject's attitude greatly influenced an officer's discretion to arrest. With the exception of offenders who had committed serious crimes or who were wanted by the police, the disposition of juvenile cases depended largely on how a youth's character was evaluated by the officer. This evaluation and the decisions that followed from it were limited to information gathered by police during their encounter with the juveniles.[34]

Numerous studies have looked at discretion to arrest as it relates to the race of the offender and the race of the victim. A study by Dennis Powell found that a community's racial makeup may influence police discretion. Powell studied five adjacent police jurisdictions and found that the police in predominantly African-American, urban communities demonstrated a higher use of discretion and were more punitive toward whites than toward African-Americans, whereas police in predominantly white areas were significantly more punitive toward African-American offenders than toward white offenders.[35] Dale Dannefer and Russel Schutt found that racial bias was often present in the patrol officer's decision to arrest juveniles and bring them to juvenile court.[36]

Some studies have indicated that the victim's race rather than the criminal's race was the key to racial bias in the use of discretion. It was discovered that the police are more likely to take formal action when the victim of a crime is white than they are when the victim is a minority group member.[37] Cecil Willis and Richard

Wells found that police were more likely to report child abuse involving white families than African-American families.[38]

There is also evidence that the influence of race on police discretion varies from jurisdiction to jurisdiction and may be a function of the professionalism of the individual department.[39] However, a number of studies have produced data indicating that racial bias does not influence the decision to arrest and process a suspect.[40]

Douglas Smith and Jody Klein found that the socioeconomic status of a neighborhood had a great deal of influence on police discretion in domestic violence cases. The researchers found that the police were much more likely to arrest spouse abusers in lower-class neighborhoods than in middle- and upper-class neighborhoods. They also found that a person's income level influenced whether the police took a complaint seriously.[41]

As for a subject's gender, Douglas Smith and Christy Visher found that males and females were equally likely to be arrested and formally processed for law violations when encountered by the police.[42] However, other researchers have found evidence of gender bias in police discretion, but they find that this bias has been decreasing in recent years.[43]

Some studies have found that more than one of the factors just discussed affects police decision making. For example, Christy Visher found that police were more likely to arrest women whose attitude and actions deviated from the stereotype of "proper" female behavior. Visher also found that older white female suspects were less likely to be arrested than younger African-American women.[44]

Studies on factors influencing police discretion and police decision making continue. A review of recent literature points to the tremendous complexity of the issue and the concern we all should have regarding it.[45]

How Can Discretion Be Controlled?

In recent years, much attention has been given to the need to prepare police for the appropriate use of discretion.[46] Most experts believe that discretion itself is not bad, but that the real problem is uncontrolled or unregulated discretion. The experts feel that discretion cannot and should not be abolished but believe that police departments should attempt to control or regulate it.[47]

Most researchers believe that discretion should be narrowed to the point where all officers in the same agency are dealing with similar issues in similar ways. They feel there should be limits on discretion that reflect the objectives, priorities, and operating philosophy of the department. The limits on discretion should be sufficiently specific to enable an officer to make judgments in a wide variety of unpredictable circumstances in a proper, unbiased manner that will achieve a reasonable degree of uniformity in handling similar incidents in the community.[48]

One approach to managing police behavior involves requiring obedience to a formal set of policies or guidelines that can ensure the just administration of the law. The New York City Police Department established written policies regarding the use of deadly force as far back as the early 1970s. These policies dramatically reduced the number of shootings of civilians by the police, as well as reduced the number of officers shot by civilians. In the 1980s, the NYPD established formal procedures for dealing with emotionally disturbed persons and other issues.

Wilson tells us that controlling discretion involves more than just establishing policies and ensuring that they are obeyed. Managing discretion involves an effort by management to instill a proper value system in officers. According to Wilson, controlling discretion "depends only partly on sanctions and inducements; it also requires instilling in them a shared outlook or ethos that provides for them a common definition of the situations they are likely to encounter and that to the outsider gives to the organization its distinctive character or 'feel.'"[49]

Chapter Summary

This chapter has concerned the role of the police in the United States. It discussed two major ways of looking at the police role—the crime-fighting role (law enforcement) and the order maintenance role (peacekeeping and providing social services)—as well as the ambiguity of the police role.

Two primary goals and objectives of police departments are maintaining order and protecting life and property. Secondary goals may include preventing crime, arresting and prosecuting offenders, recovering stolen and missing property, assisting sick and injured people, enforcing noncriminal regulations, and delivering services not available elsewhere in the community.

Police officers adopt a police operational style in thinking about the role of police and law in society and how they should do their jobs. John J. Broderick identifies these styles as enforcers, idealists, realists, and optimists. James Q. Wilson describes three styles police departments adopt: the watchman, legalistic, and service styles.

An important aspect of a police officer's job is the exercise of discretion. The chapter examined what discretion means, how and why it is exercised, what factors influence the use of discretion by the police, and how police departments can attempt to control discretion.

Learning Check

1. Explain the basic difference between the crime-fighting role and the order maintenance role of the police.
2. List the major goals and objectives of the police.
3. Compare and contrast each of James Q. Wilson's police department operational styles.
4. Discuss some of the major ways police exercise discretion.
5. Identify some of the major factors that influence police discretion.

Review Exercise

Interview or ride with officers from your local police or sheriff's department. Determine the following:

1. To which role—crime fighting or order maintenance—do the officers seem to subscribe?
2. Which of Broderick's police operational styles do the officers' styles most resemble?
3. Which of James Q. Wilson's styles does the department seem to resemble?
4. What factors influence the decisions the officers make regarding stopping, summonsing, and arresting people?

Web Exercise

Patrol the Net and click onto a police department's home page of your choice. Review and analyze the content of their web site and determine which role this department seems to reflect: the crime-fighting role or the order maintenance role.

Key Concepts

crime fighting
order maintenance
police operational styles
John J. Broderick
James Q. Wilson
discretion

Notes

1. Herman Goldstein, *Policing a Free Society* (Cambridge, Mass.: Ballinger Press, 1977), p. 21.
2. George L. Kirkham and Laurin A. Wollan, Jr., *Introduction to Law Enforcement* (New York: Harper & Row, 1980), p. 336.
3. Kathleen Maguire and Ann L. Pastore, eds., *Sourcebook of Criminal Justice Statistics, 1996* (Washington, D.C.: U.S. Department of Justice, Bureau of Justice Statistics, U.S. Government Printing Office, 1997), Table 4.1, p. 368; U.S. Department of Justice, Federal Bureau of Investigation, *Crime in the United States, 1995* (Washington, D.C.: 1996), p. 208. All numbers are approximate and rounded off for ease of reading.
4. John Webster, "Police Task and Time Study," *Journal of Criminal Law, Criminology, and Police Science* 61 (1970): 94–100.
5. Robert Lilly, "What Are the Police Now Doing?" *Journal of Police Science and Administration* 6 (1978): 51–53.
6. Eric J. Scott, *Calls for Service: Citizen Demand and Initial Police Response* (Washington, D.C.: National Institute of Justice, 1981), pp. 28–30.
7. Michael Brown, *Working the Street* (New York: Russell Sage Foundation, 1981); Norman Weiner, *The Role of Police in Urban Society: Conflict and Consequences* (Indianapolis: Bobbs-Merrill, 1976); and Albert J. Reiss, *The Police and the Public* (New Haven, Conn.: Yale University Press, 1971).
8. Steven Meagher, "Police Patrol Styles: How Pervasive Is Community Variation?" *Journal of Police Science and Administration* 13 (1985): 36–45.
9. Alan Coffey, *Law Enforcement: A Human Relations Approach* (Englewood Cliffs, N.J.: Prentice-Hall, 1990), p. 247. The author cites as an excellent example Bruce J. Terris, "The Role of Police," *Annals of the American Academy of Political and Social Science,* November 1967.
10. George Pugh, "The Police Officer: Qualities, Roles, and Concepts," *Journal of Police Science and Administration* 14 (1986): 1–6.
11. Robert Sheehan and Gary W. Cordner, *Introduction to Police Administration,* 2d ed. (Cincinnati: Anderson, 1989), p. 62. In stating this core role, the authors cite the work of Egon Bittner, *The Functions of the Police in Modern Society* (Washington, D.C.: U.S. Government Printing Office, 1970); Carl B. Klockars, ed., *Thinking about Police: Contemporary Readings* (New York: McGraw-Hill, 1983), pp. 227–231; and W. K. Muir, Jr., *Police: Streetcorner Politicians* (Chicago: University of Chicago Press, 1977).
12. Joseph J. Senna and Larry J. Siegel, *Introduction to Criminal Justice,* 5th ed. (St. Paul: West, 1990).
13. Bittner, *Functions of the Police,* p. 8.

14. Sheehan and Cordner, *Introduction to Police Administration,* p. 16.
15. Senna and Siegel, *Introduction to Criminal Justice,* p. 217.
16. Sheehan and Cordner, *Introduction to Police Administration,* pp. 16–21.
17. John J. Broderick, *Police in a Time of Change,* 2d ed. (Prospect Heights, Ill.: Waveland Press, 1987).
18. Broderick, *Police in a Time of Change,* pp. 21–46.
19. Broderick, *Police in a Time of Change,* pp. 47–74.
20. Broderick, *Police in a Time of Change,* pp. 75–95.
21. Broderick, *Police in a Time of Change,* p. 93.
22. Broderick, *Police in a Time of Change,* pp. 97–116. Figure 5.1 summarizes Broderick's four police operational styles.
23. The discussion of Wilson's police operational styles is based on James Q. Wilson, *Varieties of Police Behavior: The Management of Law and Order in Eight Communities* (Cambridge, Mass.: Harvard University Press, 1968).
24. Wilson, *Varieties of Police Behavior,* p. 187.
25. Michael R. Gottfredson and Don M. Gottfredson, *Decision Making in Criminal Justice: Toward the Rational Exercise of Discretion* (Cambridge, Mass.: Ballinger Press, 1980), p. 87.
26. Kenneth Culp Davis, *Police Discretion* (St. Paul: West, 1975).
27. Donald Black, *The Manners and Customs of the Police* (New York: Academic Press, 1980), p. 90.
28. John A. Gardiner, *Traffic and the Police: Variations in Law Enforcement Policy* (Cambridge, Mass.: Harvard University Press, 1969).
29. Catherine H. Milton et al., *Police Use of Deadly Force* (Washington, D.C.: The Police Foundation, 1977).
30. Sheehan and Cordner, *Introduction to Police Administration,* pp. 52–53.
31. Herbert Jacob, *Urban Justice* (Boston: Little, Brown, 1973), p. 27.
32. Wilson, *Varieties of Police Behavior,* pp. 83–89.
33. Larry J. Siegel, Dennis Sullivan, and Jack R. Greene, "Decision Games Applied to Police Decision Making," *Journal of Criminal Justice,* Summer 1974, pp. 132–142.
34. Irving Pilavin and Scott Briar, "Police Encounters with Juveniles," *American Journal of Sociology* 70 (1964): 206–214.
35. Dennis Powell, "Race, Rank, and Police Discretion," *Journal of Police Science and Administration* 9 (1981): 383–389.
36. Dale Dannefer and Russel Schutt, "Race and Juvenile Justice Processing in Court and Police Agencies," *American Journal of Sociology* 87 (1982): 113–132.
37. Douglas Smith, Christy Visher, and Laura Davidson, "Equity and Discretionary Justice: The Influence of Race on Police Arrest Decisions," *Journal of Criminal Law and Criminology* 75 (1984): 234–249.
38. Cecil Willis and Richard Wells, "The Police and Child Abuse: An Analysis of Police Decisions to Report Illegal Behavior," *Criminology* 26 (1988): 695–716.
39. Wilson, *Varieties of Police Behavior.*
40. William Willbanks, *The Myth of a Racist Criminal Justice System* (Monterey, Calif.: Brooks/Cole, 1987); Douglas Smith and Jody Klein, "Police Control of Interpersonal Disputes," *Social Problems* 31 (1984): 468–481.
41. Smith and Klein, "Police Control of Interpersonal Disputes," pp. 468–481.
42. Douglas Smith and Christy Visher, "Street-Level Justice: Situational Determinants of Police Arrest Decisions," *Social Problems* 29 (1981): 167–177.
43. Marvin Krohn, James Curry, and Shirley Nelson-Kilger, "Is Chivalry Dead? An Analysis of Changes in Police Dispositions of Males and Females," *Criminology* 21 (1983): 417–437.
44. Christy Visher, "Arrest Decisions and Notions of Chivalry," *Criminology* 21 (1983): 5–28.
45. For an interesting review of the literature on police discretion since 1980, see Eric Riksheim and Steven Cermak, "Causes of Police Behavior Revisited," *Journal of Criminal Justice* 21 (1993): 353–382. For additional interesting and insightful studies see Larry Miller and Michael Braswell, "Police Perception of Ethical Decision Making: The Ideal vs. the Real," *American Journal of Police* 11 (1992): 27–45; David Klinger, "Demeanor or Crime? Why 'Hostile' Citizens Are More Likely to be Arrested," *Criminology* 32 (1994): 475–493; Richard Lundman, "Demeanor or Crime? The Midwest City Police-Citizen Encounters Study," *Criminology* 32 (1994): 631–653; Sandra Lee Browning et al., "Race and Getting Hassled by the Police: A Research Note," *Police Studies* 17 (1994): 1–10; and, Darlene Conley, "Adding Color to a Black and White Picture: Using Qualitative Data to Explain Racial Disproportionality in the Juvenile Justice System," *Journal of Research in Crime and Delinquency* 31 (1994): 135–148.
46. See, for example, Davis, *Police Discretion.*
47. Davis, *Police Discretion;* and Herman Goldstein, "Police Discretion: The Ideal vs. the Real," *Public Administration Review* 23 (1963): 148–156.
48. Goldstein, *Policing a Free Society,* p. 112.
49. Wilson, *Varieties of Police Behavior,* p. 33.

6
The Police Culture: Personality and Stress

Chapter Outline

The Police Culture or Subculture
The Police Personality
  What Is the Police Personality?
  Are They Born Like That, or Is It the Job?
Police Cynicism
The Dirty Harry Problem
Police Stress
  What Is Stress?
  Nature of Stress in Policing

Factors Causing Stress in Policing
Effects of Stress on Police Officers
Stress and Police Families
Police Departments Dealing with Stress
Testing for Ability to Handle Stress
Police Suicide

Chapter Goals

■ To acquaint you with the research indicating the existence of a distinct police culture or subculture.

■ To familiarize you with studies of the police personality, including attempts made to define the police personality and to determine whether it comes from officers' own personalities or from the occupation.

■ To present studies of police cynicism.

■ To familiarize you with the Dirty Harry problem: Do good endings justify the use of bad means to achieve those endings?

■ To discuss one of the most serious police problems, police stress, and to see why it occurs, how it is exhibited, and what means can be taken to deal with it.

■ To discuss the serious and sad problem of police officer suicide and what can be done about it.

Introduction

Many experts and researchers studying the police write about such concepts as a distinct police culture or subculture and a distinct police personality. Are the police different from most other people? Much research indicates that they are. If they are different, were they born that way, or did police work make them like that?

This chapter will discuss such concepts as the police culture or subculture, the police personality, police cynicism, the Dirty Harry problem, and police stress. Police stress is one of the most serious problems facing the police. Therefore, this chapter will attempt to define it and to show why it occurs, how it exhibits itself, and how police agencies can deal with it. The chapter will also discuss police suicide and how this problem can be dealt with.

The Police Culture or Subculture

Numerous academic studies have indicated that the nature of policing and the experiences officers go through on the job cause them to band together into their own subculture, which many researchers call the **police culture** or **police subculture**.[1] For example, if someone who was not a police officer walked into a bar at 1:00 A.M. and overheard a group of men and women engaged in animated conversation using such words as collars, mopes, skells, perps, edps, and shooflies, he or she would have great difficulty understanding. However, to the off-duty police officers having a few drinks and talking about their previous tour of duty, each word has a precise meaning.

The police subculture, like most subcultures, is characterized by clannishness, secrecy, and isolation from those not in the group. Police officers work with other police officers during their tours of duty. Many socialize together after work and on days off, often to the exclusion of others—even old friends and family. When socializing, off-duty officers tend to talk about their jobs.

Working strange shifts of duty—especially 4 to 12s (4:00 P.M. to 12:00 midnight) and midnights (12:00 midnight to 8:00 A.M.)—and working weekends and holidays make it difficult for the police officer to socialize with the average person, who works a 9-to-5 job Monday through Friday. Many police officers find it difficult to sleep after working a tense, busy evening tour. If officers want to socialize or relax after work instead of going home to a house whose inhabitants have to get up at 6:00 A.M. to go to regular jobs, they tend to socialize with their comrades from the precinct. When officers work weekends, their days off fall during the average person's workweek, so again, many tend to socialize with other officers. Police wives or husbands tend to socialize with other police wives and husbands, and police families tend to associate with other police families. After a while, the police world (the job) is the only world for many officers.

Studies indicate that police officers protect one another from outsiders, often even refusing to aid police superiors or other law enforcement officials in investigating wrongdoing of other officers. This protective barrier is called the **Blue Wall of Silence**. Also, the police subculture involves maintaining a tough, macho image and being distrustful of outsiders.[2] Writing about the police subculture and the Blue Wall of Silence, Egon Bittner says, "Policing is a dangerous occupation and the availability of unquestioned support and loyalty is not something officers could readily do without."[3]

Michael K. Brown, in *Working the Street*, tells us that police officers create their own culture to deal with the recurring anxiety and emotional stress that is endemic to policing. Brown believes that the police subculture is based on three major principles: honor, loyalty, and individuality.[4]

Honor is given to officers for engaging in risk-taking behavior. (An example of risk-taking behavior is being the first one in the door to challenge an armed adversary when taking cover and waiting for backup would have been the more prudent course of action.)

Loyalty is a major part of the police subculture and police loyalty is extremely intense. The word backup occurs often in police officer conversations. Backup involves not only assisting other officers in emergency situations but also coming to their aid when they are challenged, criticized, or even charged with wrongdoing. Brown explains the importance of backup by pointing out that the violence that police must deal with and the strong bonding that occurs among police officers "places the highest value upon the obligation to back up and support a fellow officer."[5]

Individuality is the third component of the police subculture. The officers who are the most autonomous, aggressive, and able to take charge of any situation are generally considered the best officers in a department or precinct.

The ideal officer, then, according to the police subculture, takes risks (honor), is first on the scene to aid a fellow police officer (loyalty), and is able to handle any situation by doing it his or her own way (individuality).

The idea of danger permeates the police subculture. George L. Kirkham, a college professor who became a police officer to better understand his police students, discusses the police mistrust of civilians and police reliance upon their own peer group support to survive on the streets: "As someone who had always regarded policemen as a 'paranoid lot,' I discovered in the daily round of violence which became part of my life that chronic suspiciousness is something that a good cop cultivates in the interest of going home to his family each evening."[6]

Bittner also has said that an *esprit de corps* develops in police work as a function of the dangerous and unpleasant tasks police officers are required to do. Police solidarity, a "one for all, and all for one" attitude, Bittner says, is one of the most cherished aspects of the police occupation.[7]

However, Robert Sheehan and Gary W. Cordner write about how the police subculture can destroy the reputation and integrity of a police department: "The influence of dominant police subcultural role expectations can have a devastating effect on a police department. In fact the existence of such unofficially established, negative, institutionalized role expectations is the primary reason that so many police departments are held in such low esteem by the public."[8]

Sheehan and Cordner give two examples of how the police subculture can adversely affect a police department in two fictional cities, Cod Bay and Tulane City.[9] In Cod Bay, a police sergeant is dealing with an irate motorist whose car was towed because it was parked illegally. As the sergeant talks to the officer who wrote the summons that caused the car to be towed, the sergeant realizes that the motorist's car was indeed parked legally, and the towing was in error. The sergeant, however, following the dominant police subcultural expectation that he must back the officer whether he was right or wrong, tells the motorist that in order to get his car back, he must pay the towing charge.

In Sheehan and Cordner's other fictional city, Tulane City, politics rules the police department. A police chief who is appointed by local politicians accepts corruption, incompetence, and brutality by his officers because he realizes that when another mayor takes office, that mayor will select his own police chief, and he himself will return to the department in a lower rank. If he

All in the Line of Duty

Even Off Duty, She Gets Involved

While driving her personal vehicle home from work, Officer Lisa Bratton of the Kansas University Medical Center Police Department in Kansas City observed a vehicle swerve to the curb in front of her. Officer Bratton then saw the male driver begin to batter the female passenger. As the vehicle drove on, the officer followed and used her hand-held radio to call for assistance. Two marked police units responded immediately. Relying on Officer Bratton's radio transmissions, the officers located and stopped the vehicle. Officer Bratton joined them and assisted in the arrest of the subject. The woman later told police that she had been victimized repeatedly by the subject and if Officer Bratton had not intervened, she feared that the offender would have killed her.

Source: Adapted from *FBI Law Enforcement Bulletin*, November 1996, p. 33.

had tried to reform the police department while chief, he would be ostracized by officers when he returned to a lower status. Failing to adhere to the existing police subculture would have been dangerous to the chief in the future.

The Police Personality

The police subculture leads to what scholars call the **police personality**, or traits common to most police officers. Scholars have reported that this personality is thought to include such traits as authoritarianism, suspicion, racism, hostility, insecurity, conservatism, and cynicism.[10]

This text will attempt to describe the characteristics of the police personality, what shapes the police personality, and the causes and effects of police cynicism.

What Is the Police Personality?

The scholar Jerome Skolnick coined the term "working personality of police officers."[11] Skolnick stated that the police officer's "working personality" is shaped by constant exposure to danger and the need to use force and

PATROLLING THE NET

Nabbing Pedophiles on the Net

Detective Daryl Rowland of the Huntington Beach, California, Police Department is one of the few police investigators in the nation proficient enough on a computer to successfully track pedophiles using the Internet.

Rowland spends his days cruising chat rooms, using a variety of alter egos he's developed to attract sex offenders. In one case, he's a 24-year-old man looking for pictures of underage girls. In another, he poses as a father who molests his own son and offers him to other men. Then, he's a thirteen-year-old boy excited by the possibilities offered by the chat rooms.

In 1996, Rowland arrested a 39-year-old Pennsylvania man who tried to arrange oral sex with a twelve-year-old boy. Rowland met and arrested the man in a Huntington Beach hotel.

A week later, Rowland arrested a prominent California businessman on suspicion of distributing child pornography. The suspect had more than 100 computer files with images of children engaged in sexual activity.

Source: Adapted from "Net Proceeds," *Law Enforcement News* 31 January 1997, p. 4.

---

authority to reduce and control threatening situations.[12] Skolnick wrote,

> The policeman's role contains two principal variables, danger and authority, which should be interpreted in the light of a "constant" pressure to appear efficient. The element of danger seems to make the policeman especially attentive to signs indicating a potential for violence and lawbreaking. As a result the policeman is generally a "suspicious person." Furthermore, the character of the policeman's work makes him less desirable as a friend since norms of friendship implicate others in his work. Accordingly the element of danger isolates the policeman socially from that segment of the citizenry whom he regards as symbolically dangerous and also from the conventional citizenry with whom he identifies."[13]

Skolnick's description seems to validate the concept that there does exist a police subculture in which officers tend to associate only with other officers.

Further evidence of the police subculture is William Westly's classic study of the Gary (Indiana) Police Department, in which he found a police culture that had its own customs, law, and morality. Westly says that the attitudes and values that make up the police personality produce the **Blue Curtain**—a situation in which police officers only trust other police officers and do not aid in the investigation of wrongdoing by other officers. Westly calls the Blue Curtain a barrier that isolates police officers from the rest of society.[14]

Elizabeth Burbeck and Adrian Furnham have identified three important features of an officer's working environment that can account for the police personality: danger, authority, and isolation from the public.[15] Additionally, Burbeck and Furnham reviewed the literature comparing the attitudes of police officers with those of the general population and found that police officers place a higher emphasis on terminal values (such as family security, mature love, and a sense of accomplishment) than on social values (such as equality).

One example of the studies Burbeck and Furnham looked at was the Rokeach study. Social psychologist Milton Rokeach and his colleagues studied police officers in Lansing, Michigan. He compared their personality traits with a national sample of private citizens and concluded that police officers seemed more oriented toward self-control and obedience than the average citizen. Also, police were more interested in personal goals, such as "an exciting life," and less interested in social goals, such as "a world of peace." Rokeach also compared values of veteran officers with those of recruits and discovered no significant differences. Rokeach believed police officers have a particular value orientation and personality before they start their police career.[16]

Many social scientists have attempted to duplicate the Rokeach study to see if the recruit police officer has values that differ from those of the ordinary citizen. Results have been mixed and inconclusive. Some researchers have found that police officers are actually psychologically healthier, less depressed and anxious, and more social and assertive than the general population.[17]

Are They Born Like That, or Is It the Job?

Two opposing viewpoints on the development of the police personality exist. One says that police departments recruit people who by nature possess those traits that we see in the police personality. The second point of view holds that officers develop those traits through their socialization and experiences in the police department.[18]

Edward Thibault, Lawrence M. Lynch, and R. Bruce McBride tell us that the majority of recent studies have found that the police working personality derives from the socialization process in the police academy, field training, and patrol experience.[19] John Van Maanen also asserts that the police personality is developed through the process of learning and doing police work. In a study of one urban police department, he found that the typical police recruit is a sincere individual who becomes a police officer for the job security, salary, belief that the job will be interesting, and the desire to enter an occupation that can benefit society.[20] Van Maanen found that at the academy, highly idealistic recruits are taught to have a strong sense of camaraderie with fellow rookies. The recruits begin to admire the exploits of the veteran officers who are their teachers. From their instructors, the recruits learn when to do police work by the book and when to ignore department rules and rely on personal discretion.[21]

Van Maanen says that the learning process continues when the recruits are assigned to street duty and trained by field training officers. The recruits listen to the folklore, myths, and legends about veteran officers and start to understand police work in the way the older officers desire them to. By adopting the sentiments and behavior of the older officers, the new recruits avoid ostracism and censure by their supervisors and colleagues.[22]

Richard J. Lundman says that the formal training at the police academy—courses in law and criminal procedure—do not teach the recruits what they really want to know. Recruits, according to Lundman, want to know the following: "What is it really like out there on the streets? How do I arrest someone who doesn't want to be arrested? Exactly when do I use my nightstick and how do I do it? What do the other patrol officers think of me?"

To answer these questions, Lundman says, instructors tell war stories. Most of the war stories stress police defensiveness (the distrust police officers have of outsiders, or non-police officers) and police depersonation (the tendency of police officers to treat violence, victims, and other unpleasant experiences in a matter-of-fact way in an attempt not to get emotionally affected by all the human misery they see).[23] By stressing the danger of police work and the need for officers to group together and defend themselves from civilians, the instructors reinforce the police subculture and help to create the police personality.

Conversely, a number of researchers have found little evidence that a "typical" police personality actually exists. Studies by sociologists Larry Tifft, David Bayley and Harold Mendelsohn, and Robert Balch indicate that even experienced police officers are quite similar to the average citizen.[24] Nevertheless, the weight of existing evidence generally points to the existence of a unique police personality that develops from the police socialization process.

All in the Line of Duty

On Foot, They Catch Their Man

Officers Doug Pann and Brad Shelton of the Rockford, Illinois, Police Department responded to a bank robbery alarm at a local shopping center. As the officers pulled into the bank parking lot, they were confronted immediately by the assailant, who ran from the bank firing a semi-automatic machine pistol at them. The officers pursued the gunman on foot and were joined by deputy Robert L. Humphries of the Winnebago County, Illinois, Sheriff's Office, who was off duty in the area and responded to shots being fired. During a lengthy foot pursuit, Officers Pann and Shelton and Deputy Humphries repeatedly exchanged gunfire with the subject and were able to wound and apprehend him without injury to others. The man was later charged with bank robbery and attempted murder of police officers.

Source: Adapted from *FBI Law Enforcement Bulletin*, September 1994, p. 33.

Dempsey's Law

Do Any of You Have Parents Who Are Police Officers?

We have just discussed the police personality. Does anyone in the class have a parent who is a police officer—who might have displayed aspects of the police personality?

Neill: My father was an officer for twenty years. He's retired now, and he's slowed down a lot. But when he was a cop, he was really wired up. If a car he didn't recognize drove down the block, he would really stare down the driver. And once when I was sixteen, I got a speeding ticket. You know how sometimes parents will ground a kid—take away driving privileges—for a while over something like that. Well, he told me I was grounded until I was twenty-one.

Sounds reasonable to me. Cathy, how about you? I know your mom is a deputy sheriff with the county. Is she different from other moms?

Cathy: Well, she's very suspicious. Whenever I'm going out, she wants to know where I'm going, who I'm going with, and what I'm doing. She's always warning me about bad things that can happen to me when I go out. And her hours are terrible. Every week she has to work different tours, and also weekends and holidays. Even though she tried, she could never go to my high school plays or my band recitals. Most of the other kids had their parents there. I know she loves her job, but in a way, she's kind of sad she can't be like most moms.

Sue: Professor, my father's a cop in the city, and because of him I couldn't even get a date to my senior prom. Every time a guy would come to the house, my dad would interrogate him—ask him questions like, Where did he work? Where did he go to school? Why was his car so noisy? He always had something to say about their clothes. When the guys would leave, he would interrogate me, like "Who was that kid?" "How come his hair was so long?" Guys don't want to hang out with a girl who has a father like that.

I find that quite reasonable conduct for a father, Sue. Let me tell you about my daughter Anne-Marie's first date. This young man asked her to go to a dance with him in Great Neck, which is quite a distance from our home. She was about seventeen, and it was her first formal date. Knowing my police personality, I guess, she told me he was coming over Saturday afternoon to meet me before their date the following Friday night. Saturday afternoon he shows up in a three-piece suit, and it was a hot summer day. I can just imagine what Anne-Marie told him about me.

When I interrogated him—I mean talked to him—I asked him how they were going to get to Great Neck. He said that he didn't have a car, so they would take the railroad. I said to him, "Instead of taking the railroad and paying all that money, I'll drive you to the dance." He didn't object. On the following Friday, he showed up to pick up my daughter, and I drove them to the dance. I sat in my car outside until it was over, and I drove the young man back to his house and then took my daughter home. He never called her again. I wonder . . .

Ralph: Now that you are retired, Professor Dempsey, has anything about your personality or conduct changed?

That's a good question, Ralph. I think I'm much less suspicious than I was. I remember my wife used to get very annoyed whenever we went out to a restaurant for dinner. I always had to sit in a chair with my back to a wall and in a position where I could see whoever was coming into the restaurant. Whenever people came in the door, I would check them out. My wife thought I was ignoring her. The other night we went out to eat, and I sat with my back to the door. She noticed it and remarked about it to me. But it took a long time to change. I've been retired over eight years now.

Police Cynicism

Police cynicism is an attitude that there is no hope for the world and a view of humanity at its worst. This is produced by the police officer's constant contact with offenders and what he or she perceives as miscarriages of justice, such as lenient court decisions and plea bargaining.

Arthur Niederhoffer described police cynicism as follows:

> Cynicism is an emotional plank deeply entrenched in the ethos of the police world and it serves equally well for attack or defense. For many reasons police are particularly vulnerable to cynicism. When they succumb, they lose faith in people, society, and eventually in themselves. In their Hobbesian view, the world becomes a jungle in which crime, corruption and brutality are normal features of the terrain.[25]

Niederhoffer, a former New York City Police Department lieutenant and then professor at John Jay College of Criminal Justice, wrote what is possibly the best-known study of the police personality, *Behind the Shield: The Police in Urban Society*. Niederhoffer examined the thesis that most police officers develop into cynics as a function of their experience as police officers.[26] Niederhoffer tested Westly's assumption that police officers learn to mistrust the citizens they are paid to protect as a result of being constantly faced with keeping people in line and believing that most people are out to break the law or injure a police officer.[27] Niederhoffer distributed a survey measuring attitudes and values to 220 New York City police officers. Among his most important findings were that police cynicism increased with length of service in the police department, that police officers with a college education became quite cynical if they were denied promotion, and that quasi-military police academy training caused new recruits to become cynical about themselves quickly. For example, Niederhoffer found that nearly 80 percent of first-day recruits believed that the police department was an "efficient, smoothly operating organization." Two months later, less than a third held that belief. Also, half the new recruits believed that a police superior was "very interested in the welfare of his subordinates." Two months later, that number declined to 13 percent.[28]

Robert Regoli and Eric Poole found evidence that police officers' feelings of cynicism intensify their need to obtain the respect of citizens and increase their desire to exert authority over others. Regoli and Poole note, however, that as police escalate the use of authority to obtain respect, citizens learn to mistrust and fear them. In turn, the citizens' feelings of hostility and anger create feelings of potential danger among police officers, resulting in "police paranoia."[29] Regoli and Poole also found that negative attitudes of the police contribute to their tendency to be very conservative and resistant to change—factors that interfere with the efficiency of police work.[30]

Cynicism may hurt the relationship between the police and the public, but it may help advance an officer in his or her career within the department. In a longitudinal study of police officers in Georgia, Richard Anson, J. Dale Mann, and Dale Sherman found that the officers with the most cynical attitudes were the ones most likely to get high supervisory ratings. The researchers concluded, "Cynicism is a valued quality of the personality of the police officer and is positively evaluated by important individuals in police organizations."[31]

The Dirty Harry Problem

Police officers are often confronted with situations in which they feel forced to take certain illegal actions to achieve a greater good. Indeed, one of the greatest and oldest ethical questions people have ever faced is, Do the good ends ever justify the bad means?[32]

Carl B. Klockers has dubbed this moral dilemma of police officers as the **Dirty Harry Problem**, from the 1971 film *Dirty Harry*, starring Clint Eastwood as Detective Harry Callahan. In the film, a young girl has been kidnapped by a psychopathic killer named Scorpio, who demands $200,000 in ransom. Scorpio has buried the girl with just enough oxygen to survive a few hours. Harry eventually finds Scorpio, shoots him, and tortures him to find out where the girl is. Finally, Scorpio tells Harry where the girl is. Harry finds her, but she has already died from lack of oxygen.

Let's change the plot of the movie and say that Harry's action resulted in his finding the girl and saving her life. This would be a great Hollywood ending, but think about it. Harry had a good end in mind (finding the girl before she dies), but what about the means (torturing Scorpio and not giving him his constitutional rights prior to interrogation)?

Actor Clint Eastwood portrays "Dirty Harry" Callahan.

Harry was wrong, right? He violated police procedure. He violated the precepts of the Fifth Amendment to the U.S. Constitution, which he swore an oath to obey. He has committed crimes, the most obvious of which is assault.

Harry was wrong, right? If Harry had used proper police procedure, had not violated the law, had not violated the Constitution of the United States, and had advised Scorpio of his right to an attorney, and if Scorpio had availed himself of one, there is no doubt the attorney would have told him to remain silent, and the little girl would have died.

Which is more wrong morally? Is it more wrong to (1) torture Scorpio, thereby violating the police oath of office and legal obligations but therefore finding the girl and saving her life, or (2) act in accordance with the rules of the system and not make every effort, illegal or not, to force Scorpio to talk and thus permit the girl to die?

Sure, this is only Hollywood. You would never be faced with this dilemma as a police officer, would you? As Klockars writes:

In real, everyday policing, situations in which innocent victims are buried with just enough oxygen to keep them alive are, thankfully, very rare. But the core scene in *Dirty Harry* should only be understood as an especially dramatic example of a far more common problem: real, everyday, routine situations in which police officers know they can only achieve good ends by employing dirty means. Each time a police officer considers deceiving a suspect into confessing by telling him that his fingerprints were found at the scene or that a conspirator has already confessed, each time a police officer considers adding some untrue details to his account of probable cause to legitimate a crucial stop or search . . . that police officer faces a Dirty Harry Problem.[33]

We can sympathize with Harry Callahan, and surely we can sympathize with the plight of the little girl about to die. However, despite Hollywood portrayals, police officers must operate within the boundaries of the law, because the law is what the people, through their representatives, want to be governed by. The police cannot make their own laws. Harry Callahan, although he attempted to save the life of the child, was wrong. In our system of law, we cannot use unlawful means to achieve worthy goals. Police work is a tough business. Tough choices must be made. As Klockars says,

Dirty Harry Problems are an inevitable part of policing. They will not go away. The reason they won't is that policing is a moral occupation which constantly places its practitioners in situations in which unquestionable good ends can only be achieved by employing morally, legally, or politically dirty means to their achievements.

The effects of Dirty Harry Problems on real police officers are often devastating. They can lead officers to lose their sense of moral proportion, fail to care, turn cynical, or allow their too passionate caring to lead them to employ dirty means too readily or too crudely. They make policing the most morally corrosive occupation.[34]

Is the Dirty Harry Problem a serious ethical problem facing our police? It certainly is. Police officers must be always alert to the fact that bad means never justify good ends. The police swear allegiance to their oath of office and the U.S. Constitution and their state constitution. Although it may be tempting, police cannot solve all the problems of this world and they certainly cannot solve them by violating their oath of office and their dedication to the Constitution of our land. Much more will be discussed regarding ethics in chapter 12.

YOU ARE THERE! »

Real-Life Dirty Harry Problems

Dirty Harry problems—the police officer's moral dilemma about whether illegal actions justify good ends—are common and inevitable in policing. Think about the following two scenarios. Did the police officers make the "right" decisions?

Lying to Get Him to Confess
The Facts: A boy's mother and father are murdered. The police suspect that the boy did it and bring him in for questioning.

Police Action: Detectives questioning the boy make believe that they are on the telephone. After hanging up the phone and reentering the interrogation room, a detective says to the boy, "Marty, I just got off the phone with the hospital; they just pumped your father full of adrenaline, and he came back to life—he was never dead like we thought—and he said you did it."
Result: The boy confesses to the murder.

Lying to Close Down a Cutting Operation
The Facts: An informant tells Officer Grant that apartment 7A at 923 Fox Street is being used, right now, to cut and package cocaine. The officer realizes he will not have time to obtain a warrant to enter and search the premises.

Police Action: Officer Grant, who is riding in Sector 41-Frank, using a disguised voice, telephones 911 from a pay phone. He states, "Ma'am, I live at 923 Fox, seventh floor. I just heard gunshots come from the apartment next door, 7A. They're shooting at each other. I'm scared. Please come fast."

Result: The dispatcher assigns Sector 41-Frank to respond to 923 Fox Street on a report of "Shots Fired in Apartment 7A." Three additional sector cars report that they are backing up Sector 41-Frank. The police arrive at the location, break down the apartment door, and find six naked females mixing two piles of white powder with playing cards. The police, because of their experience, realize they are mixing cocaine. They arrest the women and seize the cocaine.

Police Stress

Police officers are faced with stressful situations often during a routine tour of duty. The dispatcher assigns them to respond to a "gun run." (A gun run is a dispatcher's order to patrol units to respond to a certain location because of a report over 911 that a person has a gun in his or her possession. These calls receive immediate police response.) Citizens stop them to report a crime or dangerous condition. Officers find an open door to a factory and search for a possible burglar. They wait in a stakeout for an armed felon to appear. Police officers are always ready to react. Their bodies' response to these stressful situations is good in that it prepares them for any emergency, but the stress response takes its toll on officers' physical and mental states.

What Is Stress?

Stress is the body's reaction to internal or external stimuli that upset the body's normal state. A stimulus that causes stress (stressor) can be physical, mental, or emotional. The term stress is used to refer to both the body's reaction and the stimuli that caused it.

The body's reaction to highly stressful situations is known as the **flight-or-fight response**. Under stressful circumstances, quantities of adrenaline, a hormone produced by the adrenal glands, are released into the bloodstream. This stimulates the liver to provide the body with stored carbohydrates for extra energy. It also results in quickened heartbeat and respiration, as well as increased blood pressure and muscle tension. The body is getting prepared for extraordinary physical exertion; this is good. However, if the need for this extraordinary exertion does not materialize, the frustrated readiness may cause headache, upset stomach, irritability, and a host of other symptoms.[35]

Some experts say that stress alone probably does not cause illness, but it contributes to circumstances in which diseases may take hold and flourish. Stress weakens and disturbs the body's defense mechanisms and may play a role in the development of hypertension; ulcers; cardiovascular disease; and as recent research indicates, probably cancer.[36] Table 6.1 lists some of the mental and physical problems associated with stress.

Nature of Stress in Policing

Although most people have stress in their careers or lives, studies have found evidence of particularly high

Table 6.1	Mental and Physical Problems Associated with Stress

Psychiatric problems:
Post-trauma stress syndrome
Neuroses
Transient situational disturbances
Immunologic problems:
Reduced resistance to infection
Tumor problems
Cardiovascular problems:
Heart attacks
Coronary artery disease
Hypertension
Stroke
Genitourinary problems:
Failure to menstruate
Impotence
Incontinence
Gastrointestinal problems:
Ulcers

Source: Adapted from Edwin S. Geffner, ed., *The Internist's Compendium of Patient Information* (New York: McGraw-Hill, 1987), sec. 30.

rates of stress in certain professions. Some have called policing the most stressful of all professions. The American Institute of Stress ranked police work among the top ten stress-producing jobs in the United States.[37]

A reporter riding with the police addressed the stress that officers experience:

> The world inside the patrol car is a world of its own, two officers who are slave to the dispatcher on the crackling radio who can send them speeding into adrenaline overdrive racing to catch a suspect with a gun and then can order "slow it down" after enough cars are already at a crime scene. The result is an emotional up and down in just six blocks.[38]

Some studies indicate that police have higher rates of divorce, suicide, and other manifestations of stress than other professions.[39] One writer said, "It would be difficult to find an occupation that is subject to more consistent and persistent tension, strain, confrontations and nerve wracking than that of the uniformed patrolman."[40]

Researchers have identified four general categories of stress with which police officers are confronted:

1. External Stress. Stress produced by real threats and dangers, such as responding to gun runs and other dangerous assignments and taking part in auto pursuits.

2. Organizational stress. Stress produced by elements inherent in the quasi-military character of the police service, such as constant adjustment to changing tours of duty, odd working hours, working holidays, and the strict discipline imposed on officers.

3. Personal stress. Stress produced by the interpersonal characteristics of belonging to the police organization, such as difficulties in getting along with other officers.

4. Operational stress. Stress produced by the daily need to confront the tragedies of urban life: the need to deal with derelicts, criminals, the mentally disturbed, and the drug addicted; the need to engage in dangerous activity to protect a public that appears to be unappreciative of the police; and the constant awareness of the possibility of being legally liable for actions performed while on duty.[41]

Compounding the stress problems of police officers is the phenomenon known as **suicide by cop**, in which a person wishing to die deliberately places an officer in a life threatening situation, causing the officer to use deadly force against that person. Such a case occurred on a Long Island, New York, expressway in November 1997, when a nineteen-year-old man, despondent over a gambling debt, forced police to pull him over for driving erratically and then pulled a "very real-looking gun" on them. Police shot and killed the youth. Inside the youth's auto were good-bye cards for his friends and a chilling suicide note addressed "To The Officer Who Shot Me" in which he apologized for getting the police involved.[42]

The "suicide by cop" phenomenon became widely reported in 1996 by a Canadian police officer, Richard Parent, in a landmark report, "The Phenomenon of Victim-Precipitated Homicide." Parent, who interviewed cops after they were involved in such incidents, said many quit the police department, got divorced, and abused drugs or alcohol after the killings.[43]

Factors Causing Stress in Policing

According to researchers, factors leading to stress in police work include poor training, substandard equipment, poor pay, lack of opportunity, role conflict, exposure to brutality, fears about job competence and safety, and lack of job satisfaction. Researchers also say that the pressure of being on duty twenty-four hours a day leads to stress and that the police learn to cope with

The Police Culture: Personality and Stress 137

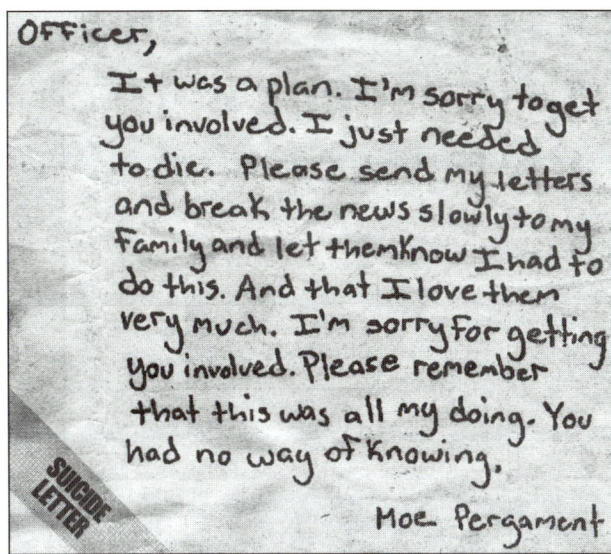

"Suicide by Cop." After police officers were forced to defend themselves by shooting a youth pointing a weapon at them on a busy Long Island, New York, expressway in 1997, they found this "suicide letter" in his car.

6. Judicial contradictions, irregularities, and inconsistent decisions tend to negate the value of police work in officers' lives.[46]

Table 6.2 presents an extensive list of sources of stress for those in law enforcement. These include both external and internal stressors, stressors in law enforcement work itself, and stressors confronting the individual officer.

Effects of Stress on Police Officers

Too much stress affects health, as Table 6.1 showed. Police officers face the stress created by always being ready for danger day in and day out. In addition, the working hours of police officers and the resultant living conditions have a further negative effect on their that stress by becoming emotionally detached from their work and the people they are paid to serve.[44]

One researcher attributes stress problems to a lack of emphasis on physical fitness once an officer leaves the police academy: "Without police fitness standards, a police department has too many 'loose wires' to account for. It is unfair to place the burden of quality effectiveness on each individual without presenting a plan that will achieve these goals."[45]

Leonard Territo and Harold J. Vetter have attempted to explain the high rates of suicide among police officers. The stressors they identify shed a light on the particularly stressful nature of police work:

1. Police work is a male-dominated profession, and men have higher suicide rates than women.
2. The use, availability, and familiarity with firearms by police in their work make it fairly certain that suicide attempts will be successful.
3. There are psychological repercussions to being exposed to potential death on a constant basis.
4. Long and irregular working hours do not promote strong friendships and strain family ties.
5. There is constant exposure to public criticism and dislike toward the police.

Table 6.2 Sources of Law Enforcement Stress

External stressors:
Lack of consideration by courts in scheduling officers for court appearances
Public's lack of support
Negative or distorted media coverage
Internal stressors:
Policies and procedures that are offensive
Poor or inadequate training and inadequate career development opportunities
Lack of identity and recognition
Poor economic benefits and working conditions
Excessive paperwork
Inconsistent discipline
Perceived favoritism
Stressors in law enforcement work itself:
Rigors of shift work
Role conflict
Frequent exposure to life's miseries
Boredom
Fear
Responsibility for protecting other people
Fragmented nature of the job
Work overload
Stressors confronting the individual officer:
Necessity to conform
Necessity to take a second job
Altered social status in the community

Source: Adapted from Richard M. Ayres and George S. Flanagan, *Preventing Law Enforcement Stress: The Organization's Role* (National Sheriff's Association funding agency: Bureau of Justice Assistance, 1990).

Police officers, who are expected to handle everyone's problems, often suffer from stress themselves.

health. One writer reports that police officers may be among those with the most unhealthy diets in the United States, due to a very high rate of consumption of fast food and junk food.[47] In fact, Dorothy Bracey, in a 1988 study, found that due to a poor diet and lack of exercise, a significant sample of U.S. police possessed a body composition, blood chemistry, and general level of physical fitness greatly inferior to that of a similarly sized sample of prison convicts.[48]

One study of 2,300 police officers in twenty U.S. police departments revealed that 37 percent had serious marital problems; 36 percent, health problems; 23 percent, problems with alcohol; 20 percent, problems with their children; and 10 percent, drug problems.[49] Other researchers estimate that between 20 and 30 percent of all police officers have an alcohol problem. The typical drinker is single, over forty years of age, with fifteen to twenty years of police experience.[50]

Professors at Michigan State University have found that officers who have had to kill someone in the line of duty suffer postshooting trauma that may lead to severe problems, including the ruin of their careers. Studies indicate that 70 percent of these officers leave the police force within seven years after the shooting.[51]

Stress and Police Families

Police work not only affects officers; it also affects their families, loved ones, and friends: "police work . . . affects, shapes, and at times, scars the individuals and families involved."[52] Studies of stress in the immediate families of police officers reveal that between 10 and 20 percent of all police wives are dissatisfied with their husband's job and would like to see their husbands leave the police department.[53] In addition, rotation shift work interferes with planning and celebrating holidays and important family events, such as birthdays and anniversaries. Rotating shifts also makes it difficult for a spouse to pursue another career.[54]

Ellen Scrivner, the director of the Psychological Services Division of the Prince George's County (Maryland) Police Department and president of the Psychologists in Public Service Division of the American Psychological Association, identified a number of job-related issues that contribute to family dysfunction in police families:

1. Family disruption due to rotating shifts. Problems caused by rotating shifts include providing child care; unavailability on holidays and at other family events; and physical problems caused by overtime and shift work, which causes irritability and increased tension.

2. **Unpredictable work environment.** The constantly changing work setting of the police officer leads to crisis and emergency responses, as well as fear of death or injury and of being the target of internal investigations.
3. **Job-related personal change and family relationships.** An officer is forced to see much human tragedy and is always personally affected. Changes in the officer's personality and attitudes, in turn, affect the family.
4. **Community expectations and demands.** The public seems to hold police officers to a higher standard of behavior in comparison with other workers. Neighbors often expect their police officer neighbors to take care of neighborhood problems and be available for emergencies.
5. **Intrusion into family life.** The police officer may have to carry parts of his or her job home. For example, police officers generally carry weapons, which they must secure in a safe place at home. Officers also must be available twenty-four hours a day.[55]

Police Departments Dealing with Stress

A report by the U.S. Commission on Civil Rights emphasized the need to provide stress management programs and services for police. The commission noted that most police departments lack such programs, despite the recent emphasis on stress as "an important underlying factor in police misconduct incidents." The commission recommended the following: "Police officials should institute comprehensive stress management programs that include identification of officers with stress problems, counseling, periodic screening and training on stress management."[56]

YOU ARE THERE!

The Police and Hurricane Andrew: Symbols of Order, Yet Victims Too

In late August 1992 in southern Florida, police officers faced the dilemma of being victims of Hurricane Andrew yet being forced to forget their own problems in order to deal with the problems of others.

Before dawn Monday, as the hurricane howled around her, Sgt. Kathy Sours of the Coral Gables Police Department lifted the dining room wall that had fallen on her husband, Randy; dragged him into the bathroom; prayed; and wondered how their two young children, gone on vacation, would live without them. Tuesday night, staying with fellow detective Kathy Williams, Sergeant Sours spent the long hours until dawn brandishing her gun at looters who terrorized elderly neighbors and tried to break into what was left of William's house.

Like the 235 other officers in the twenty-nine police departments that serve Dade County, Sergeant Sours, thirty-six years old, was caught in a wrenching psychological bind. Professionally, she was a symbol of order in chaotic times. Personally, she was a victim of the same chaos.

As Ed Hudak, a narcotics detective who heads the Patrolmen's Benevolent Association, put it,

> We're working 12 to 16 hours a day. We can only be victims when we're off duty. We're always supposed to be in control. Because we work in such a controlled environment, when we can't stop and control our destinies, it's the ultimate sort of helplessness for a police officer. Here we're victimized by the same out-of-control force that victimized everyone, but we're supposed to go back in the same old control mode. We have no time to adjust to the devastation.

In the middle of the storm, Patrol Officer David Henghold was crouching in a closet with his wife, his sixteen-year-old son, his twenty-one-year-old daughter, and his daughter's boyfriend when there was a knock on the window. "The little sixteen-year-old girl next door, her mother was hysterical," Officer Henghold said. "She wanted help. I couldn't believe she went out in it, but I went and got her mother, and they stayed with us."

When he goes back to work, Officer Henghold said, he turns his thoughts to the people of Coral Gables whom he is sworn to protect. He tries not to forget that their burdens feel heavy and their problems are vexing. Still, he said, "If they could come down here and see what happened to us, they might feel differently. We might not get the same calls, like 'There's flashlights in the backyard' or 'When will they pick up our tree?'"

For some officers the hardest thing is the capricious quality of the destruction. Like survivors of a war zone, they are puzzled or irritated by lesser complaints. They leave houses without roofs or walls to take others' complaints about loss of electricity and the lack of garbage collection.

Source: Adapted from Felicity Barrenger, "Protectors and Victims Both: Police Officers Lose Homes," *New York Times*, 27 August 1992, p. A-1.

Recently, police departments have started to pay attention to the stress problems of their members. Today, at least seventy-five U.S. police departments have their own stress unit programs that sponsor workshops by department psychologists, outside consultants, or local college professors and offer counseling to members involved in traumatic incidents.[57]

For example, the New York City Police Department responded to the problem of police suicides by training one hundred officers as peer counselors. The NYPD also established telephone hotlines in four precincts; officers needing help in stressful situations could call for help twenty-four hours a day, seven days a week.[58]

Scrivner describes the Prince George's County Police Department's Psychological Services Division, which was initiated by a 1980 grant from the Maryland Governor's Commission on Law Enforcement. According to Scrivner, the program provides a wide range of psychological services to the department, including research, training, and management consultation services. The keystone of the program is the confidential counseling services provided to sworn and civilian police personnel and their families. The counseling services are free and offered at a nonpolice facility. An employee or family member can contact the service, receive an initial assessment of the problem, and receive follow-up therapeutic intervention. The program also offers a twenty-four-hour crisis intervention service and a critical incident response (an immediate response to an emergency situation) for personal or job-related problems for officers and their families.[59]

Officers who perform as hostage negotiators experience a great deal of stress. In the California counties of Riverside and San Bernardino, hostage negotiators receive four hours of training from a psychologist. The topics of instruction include sources and symptoms of stress and techniques officers can use to reduce stress both during and after negotiations.[60]

Stress management has a physical as well as a psychological component. The FBI's Training Division Research and Development Unit mailed a training needs survey packet to 2,497 police agencies across the nation. The survey results indicated that handling personal stress and maintaining an appropriate level of physical fitness ranked first and second in programs most requested by police officers. In another survey, 90 percent of the nearly 2,000 officers questioned reported that they were in favor of a department-sponsored physical fitness program.[61]

Some departments have instituted health and fitness programs to ensure their officers' physical and emotional well-being. For example, the Ohio State Patrol has implemented a mandatory health and fitness program for all its officers. The Ohio program is designed to ensure a "high quality of life during the troopers' active career period and into retirement." Incumbent troopers who failed minimum fitness standards were subject to discipline as of March 1991; new recruits are subject to the entire program upon graduation from the police academy.[62]

Speaking of the need for physical fitness, James J. Ness and John Light state:

> The adverse effects of the lack of fitness are overwhelming, while the positive benefits of fitness are often overlooked. Being physically fit diminishes stress, promotes self-esteem, improves firearms accuracy, increases an officer's confidence in confrontations, makes him more effective with impact weapons and defense tactics, and generally improves his quality of life.[63]

Testing for Ability to Handle Stress

At least forty-two states administer psychological tests to police applicants to avoid the appointment of officers who may overreact to law enforcement stress.[64] Some departments also routinely test current officers for their ability to handle stress.

The Officer at Risk Examination (ORE) is a paper-and-pencil test recently developed to detect individual police officers who may tend to get into trouble on the job by being overaggressive or underaggressive. Based on test results, officers can receive individual counseling, reassignment, or department sanctions. The examination consists of 143 multiple choice questions and takes twenty minutes to administer. It contains a built-in reliability index and consists entirely of law-enforcement-specific questions designed to minimize falsification. The test has been administered to law enforcement officers in Alabama, California, Florida, Michigan, and Wisconsin. According to its developers, William Nagler and David Carlington, the examination is so specific to police officers that most officers actually enjoy taking the examination: "Many laugh with self-recognition while taking the test and discuss the ORE and its results for days after."[65]

The New York City Police Department has established a policy requiring all police officers applying for a specialized assignment to undergo additional psychological testing. Prior to the implementation of this policy, the NYPD conducted psychological testing only as a part of the preemployment screening process. The psychological testing consists of a battery of written tests and an oral interview. Qualities measured or identified include reaction time, psychosomatic disorders, ability to concentrate without distraction, decision-making ability, impulsivity, manual dexterity, perceptual abilities, distortion of reality, organic brain damage, and possible violent or psychotic personalities. In short, the testing provides an up-to-date assessment of a police officer's mental well-being.

Police Suicide

Closely associated with the problem of stress in policing is the problem of **police suicide**. The problem of police suicide seems to worsen over the years. Despite all the programs existing to deal with officer problems that may cause suicide, the toll continues to mount. During 1994, of the total of thirteen police homicides in the New York City Police Department, eleven were suicides. Studies indicate that the suicide rate among police officers is three times higher than that of the

Dempsey's Law

Why Did He/She Do It? Is There Any Hope?

Professor Dempsey, I have been reading the academic research on police suicides. It disturbs me since I want to be a police officer. Am I going to be subjecting myself to this potential problem? Do you have any firsthand experience with the problem? Do you have any advice for me?

Yes, Emily. Unfortunately, I certainly do. During my career in policing I have lost some friends and numerous acquaintances through suicide. All the stressors and problems discussed in the academic studies were present in each case. The biggest factors were the tremendous stress that goes with policing, the sense of frustration and helplessness in experiencing and watching what human beings do to each other, the sense of isolation from the public and sometimes the officer's own family, and the reluctance of police officers to admit they have personal problems in dealing with the experience of policing. Certainly, when you combine these stressors with other conditions police officers face in regular life—problems with relationships, alcohol, and the ready, immediate access to firearms—the problem is compounded.

The problem, however, Emily, can be dealt with. For all the personal tragedies I have encountered in this area, there have also been successes. It all depends on the officers' peers and supervisors. They must attend to fellow officers' problems and warning signs. As a police manager, I felt compelled numerous times to recommend officers for psychological counseling. On a couple of occasions I even removed an officer's firearms. Sure, the immediate reaction was that I had damaged the officer's career; however, in the long run, those officers and others understood and thanked me for caring enough to intercede and get them the help they needed.

I can never forget _____, a terrific cop who worked for me in a Brooklyn precinct. He was a great cop, but his productivity had recently declined and he had become the subject of much station house gossip about what many considered his bizarre behavior. When I confronted him, he admitted to me that he was having tremendous marital problems. He said that his wife was pregnant but he believed he was not the father. He said that he was drinking heavily but didn't feel he needed any help. I removed his firearms and drove him myself to the department's psychological unit for counseling. At first, he hated me for this, but eventually I think he understood. When I retired, I received a call from him. He thanked me for caring about him and told me, "You know, Captain, if you hadn't removed my gun that night, I would have blown my _____ brains out when I got home." There is always hope, Emily, but people have to pay attention and they have to care.

general population, and the rate of police suicides has doubled in the 1990s.⁶⁶

> In January 1996, a New York City police officer shot herself at the City Island home she shared with her boyfriend, another New York police officer.

> In September, 1996, authorities in Texas found the body of a former deputy in the reserve unit of the county sheriff's department. A handgun was found beside the body, which had what looked like a bullet wound to the head.

> An Oklahoma City police sergeant was found dead in May 1997, an apparent suicide. He was up for a medal of valor last year for rescuing people from the bombing of the Federal Building.⁶⁷

Dr. John M. Violanti, a professor in the Criminal Justice Department of the Rochester Institute of Technology in Rochester, New York, and a member of the Department of Social and Preventive Medicine, University of New York at Buffalo, works on the problem of police suicide under a National Institute of Mental Health grant.⁶⁸ Dr. Violanti, who also served twenty-three years with the New York State Police, notes that the police culture and the reluctance of police officers to ask for help complicates the problem of police suicide. His study revealed that police are at higher risk for committing suicide for a variety of reasons, including access to firearms, continuous exposure to human misery, shift work, social strain and marital difficulties, drinking problems, physical illness, impending retirement, and lack of control over their jobs and personal lives. Violanti's work indicates that police commit suicide at a rate up to 53 percent higher than other city workers.⁶⁹

Traditionally, no matter what their problems, police officers refrain from asking for help. There are various reasons for this reluctance. The primary reason, however, is that officers do not wish to appear weak or vulnerable in front of their peers. Individuals who perceive themselves as problem solvers often have great difficulty admitting that they have problems of their own. As a result, some officers who feel that they can no longer tolerate psychological pain choose to solve the problem themselves through suicide rather than by asking others for help.⁷⁰

Stressing the role of police management in developing programs for dealing with police suicides, Thomas E. Baker writes,

> A suicide prevention program can work only if members of the department feel free to take advantage of it. Police administrators and supervisors must play a nonpunitive role. They must communicate to officers four clear messages: (1) seeking help will not result in job termination or punitive action; (2) all information will be respected and kept confidential; (3) other ways exist for dealing with a situation, no matter how hopeless it seems at the time; and (4) someone is available to help them deal with their problems. Police training and departmental policy, as well as the everyday examples set by police leaders, must communicate these four messages consistently.⁷¹

Doctor Violanti, who feels that a stress-management program needs to be a key part of any effort to prevent police suicides, also believes that police management must address the problem. He echoes Baker's feelings,

> [Denial of the problem] runs right through an entire organization. Middle management is probably a perfect place to train sergeants, lieutenants and captains about how to recognize this problem.⁷²

Chapter Summary

This chapter addressed the police culture or subculture, the police personality, police cynicism, the Dirty Harry Problem, and police stress. Most researchers believe that there is a distinct police subculture and police personality. Most believe that this subculture and this personality arise from the type of socialization specific to police work rather than from police departments recruiting only people who already have the attributes of the police subculture and personality. Police cynicism is very common and seems to get more intense the longer a person stays in policing.

The Dirty Harry Problem is the conflict over whether to use illegal means to accomplish good ends. It is a problem that seems to permeate many aspects of policing.

Finally, the chapter looked at the issues of police stress and police suicide. It discussed what stress is, what factors produce it, the results of stress, the effects of stress on police families, and efforts on the part of departments to deal with stress among their ranks. Many police departments test candidates and in-service members on their ability to handle stress. The problem of police suicide and its causes was also discussed.

Learning Check

1. Explain what the police subculture is and how it expresses itself.
2. Define the police personality and how it expresses itself.

3. List some reasons for the existence of a police subculture and a police personality.
4. Give some reasons why police officers experience high levels of stress.
5. Discuss what police departments can do to deal with the high levels of stress present in their officers.

Review Exercise

You are confronted with the following Dirty Harry Problem. Your friend Bill became a police officer in your hometown, the city of Bigproblems. During Bill's academy training and field training, he was very happy about the job and constantly conveyed this to you. However, after his first month on patrol as a community beat officer in a high-crime public housing development, Bill's personality seems to be changing. You begin to worry about him, and one night when you are out to dinner together, you ask him if anything has happened.

Bill confides in you that he had arrested a twenty-year-old resident, Bigman Doper, for dealing drugs on his beat several weeks ago and had been disappointed that the court had only sentenced Bigman Doper to probation, even though it was his second drug arrest.

You tell Bill that you understand his disappointment. However, you caution him to remember that the actions of courts are beyond his control and that he should just continue to do his job.

Bill then tells you that the court's decision is not his major concern. He relates that he had been complaining in the locker room about the court decision and had been approached by Hotshot Cassidy, a twenty-year veteran of the department, who said, "Hey kid, don't worry about it. I'll fix Bigman for you." Bill says that a week later, he observed Bigman walking through the streets of the development and noticed that he had been the victim of a vicious beating. Later, at the station house, Cassidy approached Bill and said, "You see what I did to Bigman, kid?"

Bill asks your advice.

Web Exercise

Use the Internet to get onto some police officer–related web sites. Find out what officers there are talking about. Do their stories and comments remind you of anything you have read about in this chapter?

Key Concepts

police culture or police subculture
Blue Wall of Silence
police personality
Blue Curtain
police cynicism
Dirty Harry Problem
flight-or-fight response
suicide by cop
police suicide

Notes

1. See, for example, Egon Bittner, *The Functions of Police in Modern Society* (Cambridge, Mass.: Oelgeschlager, 1980); Michael K. Brown, *Working the Street* (New York: Russell Sage Foundation, 1981); and Malcolm Sparrow, Mark Moore, and David Kennedy, *Beyond 911: A New Era for Policing* (New York: Basic Books, 1990). A subculture may be defined as the culture of a particular group that is smaller than, and essentially different from, the dominant culture in a society. The police subculture, then, is a combination of shared norms, values, goals, career patterns, life styles, and occupational structures that is substantially different from the combination held by the rest of society.
2. See Richard Harris, *The Police Academy: An Inside View* (New York: Wiley, 1973); Jonathan Rubenstein, *City Police* (New York: Ballentine Books, 1973); and John Van Maanen, "Observations on the Making of a Policeman," in *Order Under Law,* ed. R. Culbertson and M. Tezak (Prospect Heights, Ill.: Waveland Press, 1981), pp. 111–126.
3. Bittner, *Functions of Police,* p. 63.
4. Brown, *Working the Street,* p. 82.
5. Brown, *Working the Street,* p. 82.
6. Gorge L. Kirkham, "A Professor's Street Lessons," in *Order Under Law,* ed. R. Culbertson and M. Tezak (Prospect Heights, Ill: Waveland Press, 1981), p. 81.
7. Bittner, *Functions of Police,* p. 63.
8. Robert Sheehan and Gary W. Cordner, *Introduction to Police Administration,* 2d ed. (Cincinnati: Anderson, 1989), p. 286.
9. Sheehan and Cordner, *Introduction to Police Administration,* pp. 286–289.
10. Richard Lundman, *Police and Policing* (New York: Holt, Rinehart & Winston, 1980); see also Jerome Skolnick, *Justice without Trial: Law Enforcement in a Democratic Society* (New York: Wiley, 1966).
11. Skolnick, *Justice without Trial.*
12. Skolnick, *Justice without Trial.*
13. Skolnick, *Justice without Trial.*
14. William Westly, *Violence and the Police: A Sociological Study of Law, Custom, and Morality* (Cambridge, Mass.: MIT Press, 1970).
15. Elizabeth Burbeck and Adrian Furnham, "Police Officer Selection: A Critical Review of the Literature," *Journal of Police Science and Administration* 13 (1985): 58–69.

16. Milton Rokeach, Martin Miller, and John Snyder, "The Value Gap between Police and Policed," *Journal of Social Issues* 27 (1971): 155–171.
17. Bruce Carpenter and Susan Raza, "Personality Characteristics of Police Applicants: Comparisons across Subgroups and with Other Populations," *Journal of Police Science and Administration* 15 (1987): 10–17; Richard Lawrence, "Police Stress and Personality Factors: A Conceptual Model," *Journal of Criminal Justice* 12 (184): 247–263; and James Teevan and Bernard Dolnick, "The Values of the Police: A Reconsideration and Interpretation," *Journal of Police Science and Administration* 1 (1973): 366–369.
18. Richard Bennett and Theodore Greenstein, "The Police Personality: A Test of the Predispositional Model," *Journal of Police Science and Administration* 3 (1975): 439–445.
19. Edward A. Thibault, Lawrence W. Lynch, and R. Bruce McBride, *Proactive Police Management* (Englewood Cliffs, N.J.: Prentice-Hall, 1985).
20. Van Maanen, "Observations on the Making of a Policeman."
21. Van Maanen, "Observations on the Making of a Policeman," p. 68.
22. Van Maanen, "Observations on the Making of a Policeman," p. 66.
23. Lundman, *Police and Policing,* pp. 73, 82.
24. Larry Tifft, "The 'Cop Personality' Reconsidered," *Journal of Police Science and Administration* 2 (1974); David Bayley and Harold Mendelsohn, *Minorities and the Police* (New York: Free Press, 1969); and Robert Balch, "The Police Personality: Fact or Fiction?" *Journal of Criminal Law, Criminology, and Police Science* 63 (1972): 117.
25. Arthur Niederhoffer, *Behind the Shield: The Police in Urban Society* (Garden City, N.Y.: Doubleday, 1967), pp. 41–42.
26. Niederhoffer, *Behind the Shield,* pp. 41–42.
27. Westly, *Violence and the Police.*
28. Niederhoffer, *Behind the Shield,* pp. 216–220.
29. Niederhoffer, *Behind the Shield,* p. 43.
30. Niederhoffer, *Behind the Shield,* p. 44.
31. Richard Anson, J. Dale Mann, and Dale Sherman, "Niederhoffer's Cynicism Scale: Reliability and Beyond," *Journal of Criminal Justice* 14 (1986): 295–307.
32. Carl B. Klockars, "The Dirty Harry Problem," *Annals,* November 1980, pp. 33–47.
33. Klockars, "Dirty Harry Problem," pp. 33–47.
34. Klockars, "Dirty Harry Problem," pp. 33–47.
35. Edwin S. Geffner, ed., *The Internist's Compendium of Patient Information* (New York: McGraw-Hill, 1987), sec. 30.
36. Geffner, *Internist's Compendium,* sec. 30.
37. "Stress on the Job," *Newsweek,* 25 April 1988, p. 43.
38. Alison Mitchell, "A Night on Patrol: What's Behind Police Tensions and Discontent," *New York Times,* 19 October 1992, pp. B-1, B-2.
39. W. Clinton Terry, "Police Stress: The Empirical Evidence," *Journal of Police Science and Administration* 9 (1981): 67–70. This article has a substantial bibliography and discussion of the issue of police stress.
40. Clement Milanovich, "The Blue Pressure Cooker," *Police Chief* 47 (1980): 20.
41. Robert J. McGuire, "The Human Dimension in Urban Policing: Dealing with Stress in the 1980's," *Police Chief,* November 1979, p. 27; and Joseph Victor, "Police Stress: Is Anybody Out There Listening?" *New York Law Enforcement Journal,* June 1986, pp. 19–20.
42. Denise Buffa, Linda Massarella, et al. "Suicide Teen Tricked Tops into Shooting Him: Dear officer . . . Please Kill Me," *New York Post,* 17 November 1997, pp. 1–3.
43. John O'Mahony, "'Suicide by Cop' Not So Odd: Docs," *New York Post,* 17 November 1997, p. 3.
44. Nancy Norvell, Dales Belles, and Holly Hills, "Perceived Stress Levels and Physical Symptoms in Supervisory Law Enforcement Personnel," *Journal of Police Science and Administration* 6 (1978): 402–416.
45. B. Healy, "The Aerobic Cop," *Police Chief,* February 1981, pp. 67–70.
46. Leonard Territo and Harold J. Vetter, "Stress and Police Personnel," *Journal of Police Science and Administration* 9 (1981): 200.
47. Sue Titus Reid, *Criminal Justice,* 3d. ed. (New York: Macmillan, 1993), p. 230.
48. Dorothy Bracey, "The Decline of the Vaccination Model: Criminal Justice Education for a Changing World," *CJ, The Americas,* April 1988, p. 1.
49. John Blackmore, "Are Police Allowed to Have Problems of Their Own?" *Police* 1 (1978): 47–55.
50. Charles Unkovic and William Brown, "The Drunken Cop," *Police Chief,* April 1978, p. 20.
51. *Justice Assistance News* 4 (1983): 5.
52. Jerry Dash and Martin Resier, "Suicide among Police in Urban Law Enforcement Agencies," *Journal of Police Science and Administration* 6 (1978): 18.
53. David Rafky, "My Husband the Cop," *Police Chief,* August 1984, p. 65.
54. Peter Maynard and Nancy Maynard, "Stress in Police Families: Some Policy Implications," *Journal of Police Science* 10 (1980): 309.
55. Ellen Scrivner, "Helping Police Families Cope with Stress," *Law Enforcement News,* 15 June 1991, p. 6.
56. U.S. Commission on Civil Rights, *Who Is Guarding the Guardians? A Report on Police Practices* (Washington, D.C.: U.S. Government Printing Office, 1981).

57. *USA Today,* 15 September 1986, p. 3.
58. *New York Times,* 15 September 1986, p. 14.
59. *New York Times,* 15 September 1986, p. 10.
60. Nancy K. Bohl, "Hostage Negotiator Stress," *FBI Law Enforcement Bulletin,* August 1992, pp. 23–26.
61. James J. Ness and John Light, "Mandatory Physical Fitness Standards: Issues and Concerns," *Police Chief,* August 1992, p. 74.
62. Ness and Light, "Mandatory Physical Fitness Standards," p. 77.
63. Ness and Light, "Mandatory Physical Fitness Standards," p. 75.
64. Robin E. Inwald and Elizabeth J. Shusman, "The IPA and MMPI as Predictors of Academy Performance for Police Recruits," *Journal of Police Science* 12 (1984): 1.
65. William Nagler and David Carlington, "Officer Fitness: The Officer at Risk Examination," *Law and Order,* September 1992, p. 21.
66. Recently, significant attention is being addressed to police suicide and the stresses that can be attributed to it. See, for example: Thomas E. Baker and Jane P. Baker, "Preventing Police Suicide," *FBI Law Enforcement Bulletin,* October 1996, pp. 24–27. See also John M. Violanti, "The Mystery Within: Understanding Police Suicide," *FBI Law Enforcement Bulletin,* February 1995, pp. 19–23; Steven R. Standfest, "The Police Supervisor and Stress," *FBI Law Enforcement Bulletin,* May 1996, pp. 7–10; Arthur W. Kureczka, "Critical Incident Stress," *FBI Law Enforcement Bulletin,* February/March 1996, pp. 10–16; "What's Killing America's Cops? Mostly Themselves, According to New Study," *Law Enforcement News,* 15 November 1996, p. 1; and, "The Greatest Threat to Cops' Lives—Themselves," *Law Enforcement News,* 31 December 1997, p. 22.
67. "The Greatest Threat to Cops' Lives—Themselves."
68. J. M. Violanti and J. E. Vena, "Epidemiology of Police Suicide," NIMH Grant MH47091–02.
69. "What's Killing America's Cops?"
70. Violanti, "The Mystery Within: Understanding Police Suicide," p. 22.
71. Baker and Baker, "Preventing Police Suicide," p. 25.
72. "What's Killing America's Cops?"

7

Police Operations: The Traditional Approach

Chapter Outline

Traditional Methods of Police Work
Evaluating the Effectiveness of Police Work
Random Routine Patrol: The Kansas City Study
   The Kansas City Study in Brief
   Results of the Kansas City Study
   Critiques of the Kansas City Study
   Value of the Kansas City Study
Rapid Response to Citizens' 911 Calls
   Early Studies of Rapid Response
   Later Studies of Rapid Response
Retroactive Investigation of Past Crimes by
   Detectives

Police Patrol Operations
   Activities of the Patrol Officer
   The Legacy of O. W. Wilson
   Academic Studies of the Police Patrol Function
   From the Foot Beat to the Patrol Car
   Return to Foot Patrol
   Why Walking Works Better Than Driving
Detective Operations
   What Do Detectives Do?
   The Detective Mystique
Police Traffic Operations
Police Special Operations
   SWAT Teams
   Emergency Service Units

Chapter Goals

■ To acquaint you with the three traditional methods of doing police work and examine their effectiveness.

■ To introduce you to police patrol—what the police do on patrol and how they do it.

■ To supply you with basic information regarding police detective operations.

■ To acquaint you with police traffic operations and special operations.

Introduction

This chapter is about police operations: what the police do and how they do it. It covers police patrol operations, detective operations, traffic operations, and special operations. The traditional methods used by the police to fulfill their mission of maintaining order and enforcing the law in our society are (1) random routine patrol, (2) rapid response to citizens' calls to 911, and (3) retroactive investigation of past crimes by detectives.

The chapter will discuss the academic studies of the 1960s and 1970s, particularly the Kansas City Study, which has changed our understanding of the effectiveness of the traditional methods of doing police work. The Kansas City Study, as well as other studies, forced academics and progressive police administrators to look closely at their operations to see if there were better, more effective ways to do police work.

Most of this chapter will be related to police patrol operations, the "backbone" of policing. Patrol operations involve the activities and role of the patrol officer and the various methods of doing patrol work, including motorized and foot patrol. Additionally, the chapter will discuss detective operations; traffic operations; and special operations, including SWAT teams and emergency service units.

Traditional Methods of Police Work

Robert Sheehan and Gary W. Cordner identify the following three traditional methods of doing police work: (1) random routine patrol, (2) rapid response to calls by citizens to 911, and (3) retroactive investigation of past crimes by detectives.[1]

The average U.S. police officer arrives at work at the beginning of his or her shift and receives the keys and the patrol car from the officer who used it on the previous tour. The officer then drives around a designated geographic area (**random routine patrol**). When the officer receives a call from the police dispatcher, he or she responds to the call and performs whatever police work is required—an arrest, first aid, breaking up a fight, taking a crime report, and so on (**rapid response to citizens' calls to 911**). If the call involves a crime, the officer conducts a preliminary investigation and often refers the case to a detective, who conducts a follow-up investigation of the crime (**retroactive investigation of past crimes by detectives**). As soon as the officer is finished handling the call, he or she resumes patrol and is ready to respond to another call.

These are the methods of traditional police work. However, are random routine patrol, rapid response to citizens' calls to 911, and retroactive investigation of past crimes by detectives the proper ways for the police to safeguard our communities? Are these methods effective? Is this combination of methods the only way to do police work? This chapter will attempt to answer these questions.

Evaluating the Effectiveness of Police Work

Evaluating the effectiveness of police work is very difficult. If a city has a high crime rate, does it follow that its police department is not effective? If a city has a low crime rate, does it follow that its police department is an effective one? When we talk about crime, we are talking about many different and complex variables. The police cannot control all the variables that might produce crime, such as social disorganization; anger; poverty; hostility; revenge; psychological, social, or biological problems; and the desire to commit crime as an alternative to the world of work.

Despite the difficulties and problems associated with conducting academic and scientific research in policing, the research has been influential in the development of policing strategies over the last two decades. As Joan Petersilia, one of the early researchers, has written,

> Although systematic research on policing began less than 15 years ago, it has already influenced major changes in the way police departments operate and in public perceptions of policing. Changes in policy and practice around the country suggest that research has had particularly important conceptual and operational effects in patrol operations, criminal investigation, and specialized offense and offender operations.[2]

One of the problems in conducting scientific studies of policing involves attempting to set up controlled experiments. When scientists conduct academic studies of the effects of a variable on something—for example, to see if a particular drug cures a particular illness—they conduct a controlled experiment. In a controlled experiment, two categories of groups are used. One group is the experimental group, and the other is the control group. The experimental group, in the drug example, is given the drug, whereas the control group is not given the drug. If the drug is effective, the experimental group will recover from the illness, and the control group will not.

Another example of a controlled experiment could be changing the packaging of a particular product sold in a store to see if putting a product in a red package results in more people's buying the product than the same product in a blue box. The new red packages would be the experimental group, and the old blue packages would be the control group. If we leave all other variables the same (the price, where the packages are located in the store, and so on) and the red boxes sell at a better rate than the blue boxes, it can be said that the red boxes make a difference.

Can we have controlled experiments to see if a police department is effective? Can we eliminate police patrols from one neighborhood and compare the crime rate in that neighborhood with the crime rate in the neighborhood where there are police patrols? Obviously, a myriad of problems accompany controlled experiments with crime. Is such experimentation ethical? Is it legal? This chapter will look at several controlled experiments with crime and see how they have affected our traditional concepts of doing police work.

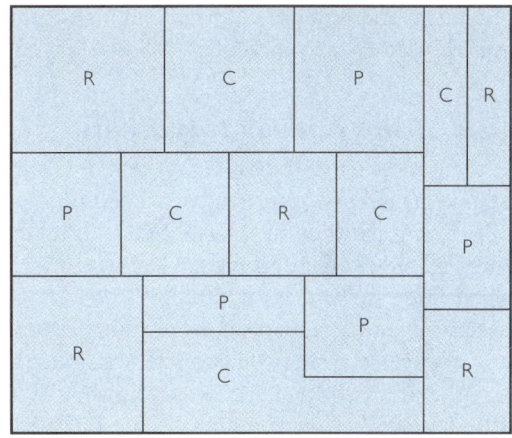

P = Proactive   C = Control   R = Reactive

Figure 7.1
A Schematic Representation of the Kansas City Patrol Experiment. In the proactive areas routine random police patrol was increased; in the control areas it remained the same; and in the reactive areas it was eliminated.
Source: Adapted from George L. Kelling et al., *The Kansas City Patrol Experiment: A Summary Report* (Washington, D.C.: Police Foundation, 1974), p. 9.

Random Routine Patrol: The Kansas City Study

Random routine patrol, otherwise known as preventive patrol, involves a police officer's driving around and within a community when he or she is not on an assignment from the radio dispatcher or a supervisor. Tradition has held that random routine patrol creates a sense of omnipresence and deters crime, because a criminal will not chance committing a crime if a police officer might be just around the corner. It was also felt that random routine patrol enabled police officers to catch criminals in the act of committing their crimes. Just how effective is random routine patrol? The **Kansas City Study** was the first attempt to actually test the effectiveness of random routine patrol.

The Kansas City Study in Brief

During 1972 and 1973, the Kansas City Police Department, under the leadership of Police Chief **Clarence Kelly** (who later became the director of the FBI) and with the support of the Police Foundation, conducted an experiment to test the effects of routine preventive patrol. This year-long experiment has been both influential and controversial.

Fifteen patrol beats in Kansas City's South Patrol Division were used for the study (see Figure 7.1). Five of these beats were assigned to a control group with no changes in normal patrol staffing or tactics. Five other beats were chosen as reactive beats, and all preventive patrolling was eliminated. Outside patrol units handled calls in the reactive beats, and units left the beats once they had handled the calls. The final five beats in the experiment were proactive beats, in which two to three times the usual level of preventive patrolling was provided. Thus, the reactive beats (with all routine patrol eliminated) and the proactive beats (with routine patrol increased) were the experimental groups. If random routine patrol is an effective way of policing our communities, we should expect to see changes in the reactive and proactive beats.

Prior to the outset of the experiment, researchers collected data on reported crime, arrests, traffic accidents, response times, citizen attitudes, and citizen and business victimization for each of the fifteen beats. The researchers collected similar data after the conclusion of the year-long experiment. During the experiment, the activities of the police officers assigned to the beats were observed and monitored. No one in the community was advised of the experiment.[3]

Results of the Kansas City Study

When the Kansas City Study was finished, the researchers concluded, "Decreasing or increasing routine preventive patrol within the range tested in [the] experiment had no effect on crime, citizen fear of crime, community attitudes toward the police on the delivery of police service, police response time or traffic accidents."[4] In effect, the study failed to demonstrate that adding or taking away police patrols from an area made any difference within the community (see Table 7.1). At the end of the experiment, no one in the community had any idea that an experiment regarding policing had been conducted in their community.

The conclusions of the Kansas City Study shocked many people and differed from all the assumptions we had always made regarding police patrol. It had been commonly believed that putting more officers on patrol would cause a decrease in crime, and taking away police would cause an increase in crime. The Kansas City Study told us that this basic assumption about police work was wrong. Or did it?

Critiques of the Kansas City Study

In an evaluation of the Kansas City Study, James Q. Wilson cautions that the results should not be misinterpreted: "The experiment does not show that the police make no difference and it does not show that adding more police is useless in controlling crime. All it shows is that changes in the amount of random preventive patrol in marked cars does not, by itself, seem to affect over one year's time in Kansas City, how much crime occurs or how safe citizens feel." Wilson says that very different results might have occurred if changes had been made in how the police were used and not merely in the number of marked patrol cars placed in one area.[5]

Joseph D. McNamara, who succeeded Kelly as chief of the Kansas City Police Department in 1974 and later served as chief of the San Jose (California) Police Department, warned that "a great deal of caution must be used to avoid the error that the experiment proved more than it actually did. One thing the experiment did not show is that a visible police presence can have no impact on crime in selected circumstances." McNamara stressed the fact that the experiment seemed to show that police officers' uncommitted time (time they are not responding to calls to 911 or doing self-initiated po-

Table 7.1	Results of the Kansas City Study

No change in crime
No change in citizen fear of crime
No change in community attitudes toward the police
No change in police response time
No change in traffic accidents

Source: Adapted from George L. Kelling et al., *The Kansas City Preventive Patrol Experiment: A Summary Report* (Washington, D.C.: Police Foundation, 1974), p. 16.

lice work)—approximately 50 percent of their time—could be used more effectively. Uncommitted time probably should be devoted to activities with more specific objectives than routine patrol.[6]

George Kelling, director of the Kansas City Study, said that it would be a mistake to conclude that patrol was completely unnecessary or that police departments could manage with far fewer resources. He argued that "the experiment has demonstrated that the time and staff resources do exist within police departments to test solutions to the many complex and interrelated problems of police service."[7] Thus, it seems to Kelling that the police can actually experiment with ways to do better work.

Richard C. Larson, in contrast, reported that he found serious flaws in the research design of the experiment. He noted that when police cars in the reactive beats entered the area in response to calls, they made a visible police presence. In the eyes of citizens and potential criminals, this was the same as routine patrol. Larson also pointed out that police vehicles from other specialized units (who were not part of the experiment) operated in the reactive beats, thereby creating a visible police presence. Larson found other differences in the reactive beats. Officers undertook a higher rate of self-initiated activities (such as vehicle stops), and they used sirens and lights more often in responding to calls. Furthermore, there was a higher incidence of two or more cars responding to a call for service.[8]

The major proponent of the effectiveness of patrol, O. W. Wilson, and his associate Roy Clinton McLaren, argued that despite the conclusions of the researchers, the value of police patrol cannot be measured by a statistical study like the Kansas City one and must be evaluated based on historical experience. Wilson and McLaren stated, "The fact remains that in the few situations in recent history in which police response was

All in the Line of Duty

A Routine Traffic Stop on I-35? The Feds Took the Credit but Charley Caught Him

Police Officer Charles J. Hanger, of the Oklahoma Highway Patrol was on patrol on Interstate 35 in Oklahoma, sixty miles north of Oklahoma City, on April 19, 1995, when he observed a yellow 1977 Mercury Marquis in the opposite lane of traffic with no license plates. Hanger pursued the auto and stopped it, something he had done thousands of times in his police career.

When the driver reached for his license at the trooper's request, Hanger saw a bulge under his jacket. The bulge reminded Hangar of one of the dangers of his job—the armed felon. He ordered the driver from the automobile and retrieved a loaded Glock semiautomatic pistol, two clips of ammunition, and a knife from under his jacket. The pistol had a live round in the chamber—a black talon bullet. The driver was arrested for driving without license plates, having no insurance, and carrying a concealed weapon. The time of the arrest was approximately ninety minutes after the infamous bombing of the Alfred P. Murrah Federal Building in which 168 persons were killed and over 600 injured. Trooper Hanger testified at the driver's trial on April 29, 1997. In June 1997, the driver was sentenced to death.

The driver was Timothy J. McVeigh.

We all know how the government cracked the case and charged McVeigh with the greatest terrorist attack against the United States of America. Would he have been apprehended if Hanger had not made a routine traffic stop on I-35?

Source: Adapted from Jo Thomas, "Officer Describes His Arrest of a Suspect in the Oklahoma Bombing," *New York Times*, 28 April 1997, p. A-13; Peter Annin and Evan Thomas, "Judgment Day: As Tim McVeigh Goes on Trial for His Life, a *Newsweek* Investigation Uncovers the Inside Story of How the Feds Managed to Crack the Conspiracy to Bomb Oklahoma City," *Newsweek*, 24 March 1997, pp. 41–46.

obviously not immediately available . . . wholesale looting and lawlessness have been the result."⁹

Wilson made that statement in 1977. In 1992, the absence of police patrols by the Los Angeles Police Department was blamed for the rioting and looting in the area near the intersection of Florence and Normandy after the not guilty verdict in the Rodney King trial. Was Wilson prophetic? It must be remembered however, that a myriad of reasons led to the riots in addition to the paucity of police patrols.

To date, only one attempt has been made to replicate the Kansas City experiment. A similar study in Albuquerque, New Mexico, reached essentially similar conclusions.¹⁰

A 1981 analysis revealed that the relationship between crime and the time police spend on patrol may be more complex than previously recognized. For example, in some instances, the rates of robbery have actually increased when police patrol has increased. This may be because citizens are more likely to report robberies when they know that police are concentrating more time and effort on detecting that crime.¹¹

Value of the Kansas City Study

Sheehan and Cordner describe the value of the Kansas City Study by saying that the study did not result in the elimination of preventive or random routine patrol but rather set the stage for further experimentation with alternative patrol strategies and tactics. Because of the study, police executives realized that they could try alternative patrol tactics without fearing that reduced random routine patrol would result in calamity.¹² In that regard, Samuel Walker says, "It seems to indicate that possibilities exist for more flexible and creative approaches to the use of patrol officers."¹³

In summary, the Kansas City Study indicated that our traditional three cornerstones of policing might not be the most effective way to do police work. The Kansas City Study definitely set the stage for the academic study of policing, which in turn has caused tremendous changes in our thinking about policing. A later section of this chapter will further explore police patrol—what patrol officers do and how they do it. Chapter 8 will look at new approaches to police work that resulted from the Kansas City Study.

Rapid Response to Citizens' 911 Calls

Rapid response to citizens' calls to 911 has traditionally been thought of as a way in which the police could catch criminals while they were in the act of committing their crimes or as they were escaping from their crimes. The ideal scenario is this: A citizen observes a person committing a crime and immediately calls 911. The police respond in seconds and arrest the perpetrator. This sounds great, but it rarely works that way.

Another scenario follows: A citizen is mugged and, just after the mugging, immediately calls 911 and reports the crime. The police respond in seconds and catch the perpetrator as he or she is at the crime scene or in immediate flight from it. This also sounds great, but again, it rarely works that way.

The traditional approach of rapid response to 911 calls was based on unexamined assumptions about police patrol. Research over the past twenty years has pointed out that we cannot depend on this television portrayal of police work.

Early Studies of Rapid Response

In 1967, the President's Commission on Law Enforcement and Administration of Justice, in its *Task Force Report: Science and Technology,* found that quick response to a citizen's report of a crime to 911 made an arrest more likely. However, the commission emphasized that only extremely quick response times were likely to result in arrest. The commission discovered that when police response time was one or two minutes, an arrest was likely, and improvements in the response time of even fifteen to thirty seconds greatly improved the likelihood of an arrest. In contrast, when response time exceeded three or four minutes, the probability of an arrest dropped sharply.[14]

The U.S. National Advisory Commission on Criminal Justice Standards and Goals in 1973 recommended that "urban area response time . . . under normal conditions should not exceed 3 minutes for emergency calls and 20 minutes for non-emergency calls." The commission stated that "when the time is cut to 2 minutes, it can have a dramatic effect on crime."[15]

Later Studies of Rapid Response

In time, further studies of rapid response to citizens' calls to 911 were carried out. These studies took into account the complexity of response time, which the earlier research by the two commissions had failed to do. Total response time (from the moment of the crime to the arrival of the first police officer) consists of three basic components:

1. The time between the crime and the moment the victim or a witness calls the police.
2. The time required for the police to process the call (answer the phone, obtain details from the citizen, and dispatch a patrol car).
3. Travel time from the moment the patrol car receives the call from the dispatcher until it arrives at the scene.[16]

Two later studies looked even more carefully at response time and at the different types of situations that spur calls to 911 for police assistance. These studies found that victims often delay calling the police after a crime or other incident occurs. Sometimes no phone is available; sometimes the victims are physically prevented from calling by the perpetrator. Often, victims of crime are temporarily disoriented, frightened, ashamed, or even apathetic. Some people in one study reported that they first called parents, insurance companies, or their doctors. The later studies reported that the average citizen delay in calling the police for serious crimes was between five and ten minutes. The discovery that citizens often wait several minutes before calling the police puts response time in a different light and suggests that rapid response may not be as significant as was once thought.[17]

The later studies also made an important distinction between involvement crimes and discovery crimes. In involvement crimes, the victim is actually present when the crime occurs. Rapid response might be productive if the citizen has not delayed too long before calling 911. In discovery crimes, a citizen comes home (from work or vacation, for example) and discovers that a burglary has occurred. In this case, rapid police response is unlikely to matter, because the crime probably occurred a long time before the call to the police. Frequently, then, the actual time of occurrence may be hours or days earlier, making even instantaneous police arrival irrelevant.[18]

The emphasis on rapid response time (one or two minutes) makes no sense for several reasons. First, citizens generally cannot or do not report crimes immediately. Second, it is unlikely that a police car can get to a given location in one or two minutes. Consider the delay in calling the police, the time involved in processing the call by the 911 operator, and the distance the available police car has to travel and the traffic with which the car's driver has to contend.

Obviously, we will always need some type of rapid police response to citizens' calls to 911, even though we have to realize that a one- or two-minute response is highly unrealistic. We will always need rapid response to take people injured in traffic accidents to hospitals, to respond to violent arguments and fights, to deliver babies when their mothers cannot get to the hospital, and to respond to those crimes where rapid response

Dempsey's Law

Does It Help When the Police Get There Really Fast?

For the past nine years, I have performed an experiment in my "Introduction to Policing" class to determine the validity of studies that indicate that police response time is not critical in apprehending perpetrators of past crimes. I generally pose the following scenario to a female student:

It's 1:00 A.M. You have just left the Noisy Barn (a local college-age nightclub known for a rowdy, drunken crowd; in my generation we called these places buckets of blood). As you are walking to your car, you get pushed to the ground, and a person you never see takes your purse. You get back on your feet. What do you do?

The students in my classes give a variety of answers:

"I'd chase him."

"I'd scream. Maybe someone would come and help me."

"I don't know."

"I'd call my boyfriend."

"I'd call my insurance company."

"I'd call my dad."

"I'd call 911."

"I'd call 911" is rarely the answer. When a student gives that answer, I generally ask a follow-up question: "Where do you find a phone, and if you do, do you think the 911 operator can hear you?" Think about your last evening at your local Noisy Barn! Also, think about the description you would give the police of your attacker!

Is rapid response to citizens' calls to 911 really an effective way for the police to apprehend criminals?

---

may be effective (the victim or witness calls immediately, and the perpetrator is still on the scene or is in immediate flight from it). Also, quick response improves the chances for finding and interviewing possible witnesses and securing and retrieving physical evidence for analysis. However, as the academic studies have indicated, alternative strategies to rapid response to citizens' calls to 911 are needed to make better use of police officers.

Retroactive Investigation of Past Crimes by Detectives

Prior to the Rand Study of the Criminal Investigation Process, the investigation of almost all felonies and of some misdemeanors was the sole responsibility of the detective division of a police department.[19] The patrol officer merely obtained information for a complaint or incident report and referred the case to the detectives for follow-up investigation. Theoretically, detectives would interview each complainant and witnesses again, respond to the scene of the crime, and search for clues and leads that could solve the crime.

In 1975, the Rand Corporation think tank found that much of a detective's time was spent in nonproductive work—93 percent of their time was spent on activities that did not lead directly to solving previously reported crimes—and that investigative expertise did little to solve cases. The Rand report said that half of all detectives could be replaced without negatively influencing crime clearance rates.[20]

The single most important determinant of whether or not a case will be solved is the information the victim supplies to the immediately responding patrol officer. If information that uniquely identifies the perpetrator is not present at the time the crime is reported, the perpetrator, by and large, will not be subsequently identified. Of those cases that are ultimately cleared but in which the perpetrator is not identifiable at the time of the initial police incident report, almost all are cleared as a result of routine police procedures. . . .

Our data consistently reveal that an investigator's time is largely consumed in reviewing reports, documenting files and attempting to locate and interview victims on cases that experience shows will not be solved. For cases that are solved (i.e., a suspect is identified), an investigator spends more time in post-clearance processing than he does in identifying the perpetrator.[21]

The effectiveness of detectives was also questioned by a study conducted by the Police Executive Research Forum (PERF) in 1981. Data from the study disclosed that if a crime is reported while it is in progress, police have about a 33 percent chance of making an arrest. However, the probability of arrest declines to about 10 percent if the crime is reported one minute later and to 5 percent if more than fifteen minutes elapse before the crime is reported. In addition, as time elapses between the crime and the arrest, the chances of a conviction are reduced, probably because the ability to recover evidence is lost. Once a crime has been completed and the investigation is put into the hands of detectives, the chances of identifying and arresting the perpetrator diminish rapidly.[22]

The Rand and PERF findings were duplicated in a study of detective work by Mark Willman and John Snortum in 1984. The researchers analyzed 5,336 cases reported to a suburban police department. They found that the majority of cases that were solved were solved when the perpetrator was identified at the scene of the crime; scientific detective work was rarely necessary.[23]

These early studies of detective operations indicate that detectives are not very successful in the criminal investigation process. Chapter 8 will explore better techniques police departments have developed to investigate past crimes.

Police Patrol Operations

When we think of the police, our first image is that of the man or woman in uniform driving a police car, at rapid speeds with lights and siren, to the scene of a crime or an accident. We also may think of the uniformed officer on foot patrol ("walking a beat") in a downtown business area, moving a drunk and disorderly citizen away from a group of ordinary shoppers. (**Foot patrol** is a method of deploying police officers that gives them responsibility for all policing activity by requiring them to walk around a defined geographic area.) We may think of a police officer on horseback or one on a motorcycle. All these officers have one thing in common: they are patrol officers.

Since the time of Robert Peel (the promoter of the first organized, paid, uniformed police force in London in 1829), patrol has been the most important and visible part of police work to the public. Peel's major innovation and contribution to society was the idea of a continuous police presence throughout a community that is organized and delivered by means of regular patrol over a fixed beat by uniformed officers. Patrol is the backbone of policing.

Activities of the Patrol Officer

Former Minneapolis police chief Anthony Bouza described the patrol division of a police department as follows: "The patrol forces are the backbone of the agency. They are the uniformed troops, the infantry. They do the bulk of what is known as 'police work': responding to calls, handling emergencies, policing events or demonstrations and just simply being available."[24]

According to Samuel Walker, the basic purpose of patrol has not changed since 1829. Patrol has the following purposes:

1. The deterrence of crime.
2. The maintenance of a feeling of public security.
3. Twenty-four-hour availability for service to the public.[25]

The American Bar Association offers the following as the major purposes of police patrol:

1. To deter crime by maintaining a visible police presence.
2. To maintain public order.
3. To enable the police department to respond quickly to law violations or other emergencies.
4. To identify and apprehend law violators.
5. To aid individuals and care for those who cannot help themselves.
6. To facilitate the movement of traffic and people.
7. To create a sense of security in the community.[26]

The patrol officer is the police department's generalist and foremost representative to the public. He or she performs numerous and varied duties in and for the community. Patrol officers face numerous complex problems on a daily basis and see things that most human beings never see. As W. Clinton Terry III wrote,

> Patrol officers respond to calls about overflowing sewers, reports of attempted suicides, domestic disputes, fights between neighbors, barking dogs and quarrelsome cats, reports of people banging their heads against brick walls until they are bloody, requests to check people out who have seemingly passed out in public parks, requests for more police protection from elderly ladies afraid of some-

one entering their residence, and requests for information and general assistance of every sort.[27]

The word patrol may be derived from the French word *patrouiller*, which originally meant "to tramp about through the mud of a military camp."[28] This translation reflects the feelings of one authority, who has called patrol a function that is "arduous, tiring, difficult, and performed in conditions other than ideal."[29]

The majority of police patrol today is performed by uniformed officers in radio-equipped patrol cars or on foot. Police also patrol on motorcycles, scooters, boats, planes, helicopters, horses, and bicycles. Officers also patrol in golf carts, in all-terrain vehicles, and on roller skates. In 1997, the city of Philadelphia actually started a patrol unit using officers on in-line skates.[30]

Some police patrol wearing civilian clothes; they try to blend into the community in an effort to catch criminals in the process of committing crimes. Chapter 8 will discuss civilian clothes patrol in detail.

The Legacy of O. W. Wilson

Until the 1970s, most of what we knew about patrol was written by O. W. Wilson, former dean of the School of Criminology at the University of California at Berkeley and a former police chief in Wichita (Kansas) and Chicago, and his associate Roy C. McLaren, in the classic *Police Administration*.[31] Wilson called patrol "the backbone of policing" and stated that patrol is designed to create "an impression of omnipresence," which will eliminate "the actual opportunity (or the belief that the opportunity exists) for successful misconduct."[32] The word omnipresence can be defined as "the quality of always being there." Thus, if the police are "always there" or seem to be always there, criminals cannot operate. Wilson's patrol ideas were designed to make the police appear to be as omnipresent as possible.

Wilson defined the distribution of patrol officers as the "assignment of a given number of personnel according to area workload, time or function."[33] Under Wilson's theory, some police officers work the day shift; others, the evening shift; and others, the night shift. They are assigned to certain areas based on the work load (number of crimes, arrests, and calls for service) in a particular area. Patrol officers are also assigned according to the type of work they perform—foot, radio car, traffic, canine, or some other type of patrol function. Professional police management has consistently followed Wilson's ideas emphasizing the rational distribution of patrol officers according to a work load formula.

Academic Studies of the Police Patrol Function

Prior to the 1960s, there was little study of the police patrol function—what patrol officers do and how they do it. For years, O. W. Wilson's writings were the Bible of policing.[34] It took many years of study to realize that much of what Wilson had taught us about police patrol was wrong and was based on faulty assumptions. Despite the fact that many of Wilson's ideas were replaced by new ideas and concepts based on the subsequent research revolution in policing, we still owe a tremendous thanks to him as the first researcher to really study and write on police operations. As three of the leading police researchers of the 1980s and 1990s, James J. Fyfe, Jack R. Greene, and William F. Walsh, said in their 1997 revised edition of Wilson's classic *Police Administration*:

> Other materials in this edition also are new and, in some cases, actually in conflict with information included in past editions. These conflicts, however, do not indicate that Fyfe, Greene, and Walsh are in disagreement with the Wilson/McLaren tradition. The Wilson/McLaren tradition is to present readers with the state of the art of police administration, rather than to perpetuate information that may be time-locked in earlier years. The fact is that the state of the art has changed since 1976: It is our honor to continue in the tradition of O.W. Wilson and Roy C. McLaren by attempting to present the state of the art as it exists at this writing.[35]

What do the police hope to accomplish through the use of patrol? William Gay, Theodore H. Schell, and Stephen Schack define the goals of patrol as follows: "crime prevention and deterrence, the apprehension of criminals, the provision of non-crime related service, the provision of a sense of community security and satisfaction with the police and the recovery of stolen property."[36] They then divide routine patrol activity into four basic functional categories:

1. Calls for services. Responding to citizens' calls to 911 relative to emergencies or other problems accounts for 25 percent of patrol time.

2. Preventive patrol. Driving through a community in an attempt to provide what O. W. Wilson described as omnipresence accounts for 40 percent of patrol time.

3. Officer-initiated activities. Stopping motorists or pedestrians and questioning them as to their activities account for 15 percent of patrol time.

4. Administrative tasks. Paperwork accounts for 20 percent of patrol time.[37]

Examples of various types of patrol operations engaged in by officers, including dirigible, marine, horse or mounted, and three-wheel scooter.

James Q. Wilson's pioneering work, *Varieties of Police Behavior: The Management of Law and Order in Eight Communities,* attempted to study what police officers do. Wilson concluded that the major role of the police was "handling the situation." Wilson believed that the police encounter many troubling incidents that need some sort of "fixing up." He says that enforcing the law might be one tool a patrol officer uses; threats, coercion, sympathy, understanding, and apathy might be others. Most important to the police officer, Wilson says, "is keeping things under control so that there are no complaints that he is doing nothing or that he is doing too much."[38]

For many years, the major role of police patrol was considered to be law enforcement. However, research conducted in the 1960s and 1970s by academics showed that very little of a patrol officer's time was spent on crime-fighting duties.

Patrol Activity Studies To determine what police actually do, researchers have conducted patrol activity studies. This research involved studying four major sets of data: data on incoming calls to police departments (calls to 911), calls radioed to patrol officers, actual activity by patrol officers, and police-citizen encounters.

The nature of incoming calls to police departments reveals the kinds of problems or conditions for which citizens call 911. Data from these calls can usually be retrieved from telephone logs or from recordings of conversations between callers and 911 operators.

The nature of the calls radioed to patrol officers, or assignments given to police patrol units by 911 dispatchers, reveals not only the types of problems for which people call the police but also the types of problems the police feel deserve a response by patrol units. These data can usually be retrieved from telephone logs or tapes of transmissions between 911 operators and patrol units.

The collection of data regarding the actual activity of patrol officers during each hour of their tour is probably the best answer to the question, What do police officers do? This information includes activities the police are directed to perform from the 911 dispatcher, as well as the officers' self-initiated activities. These data can usually be retrieved from officers' activity reports and observations by researchers riding with police patrol officers.

Data on what occurs when an officer encounters a citizen—either when the officer is on assignment from the dispatcher or is on self-initiated activities—can best be retrieved from observations by researchers riding with police patrol officers.[39]

The following sections summarize findings by researchers in each of the categories just described.

Studies of Calls to 911 Robert Lilly found that of 18,000 calls to the Newport (Kentucky) Police Department made over a four-month period, 60 percent were requests for information and 13 percent concerned traffic problems. Only 2.7 percent of the calls were about violent crime; 1.8 percent of the calls concerned theft.[40] In a survey of 26,000 calls to the police in twenty-one different jurisdictions, George Antunes and Eric Scott found that only 20 percent of the calls involved the report of criminal activity.[41] James Q. Wilson conducted a study of all calls to the Syracuse (New York) Police Department during a six-day period. He discovered that only one-tenth of the calls involved incidents in which the police would have to perform a law enforcement function.[42]

Albert Reiss monitored all calls to the Chicago Police Department over a twenty-eight-day period. Of all the calls, 58 percent were in regard to criminal or potentially criminal matters. Of these calls, 26 percent involved breaches of the peace; 16 percent, offenses against property; 6 percent, offenses against persons; 5 percent, violations regarding automobiles; and 3 percent, suspicious persons. Reiss noted that the Chicago police themselves categorized as noncriminal some 83 percent of the incidents reported to them.[43]

Summarizing these studies of calls to 911, Cordner reports that most of the calls to police departments are requests for information, requests for services, and reports of disputes and disturbances.[44]

Studies of Calls Radioed to Patrol Officers Bercal analyzed a sample of over 200,000 calls dispatched to patrol officers in Detroit and St. Louis. He discovered that in Detroit, 39 percent of the calls involved predatory crimes; 35 percent, public disorder; 12 percent, accidents; and 15 percent, service-related requests. In St. Louis, 51 percent of the calls involved predatory crimes; 27 percent, public disorder; 10 percent, accidents; and 12 percent, service-related requests.[45]

Tien, Simon, and Larson discovered that 57 percent of dispatched calls in Wilmington, Delaware, dealt with crime; 14 percent, with traffic; 8 percent, with alarms; 3 percent, with medical problems; and 18 percent, with miscellaneous matters.[46] In 1987, Lawrence Sherman analyzed over 300,000 dispatches in Minneapolis and discovered that 32 percent involved conflict management; 28 percent, property crime; 19 percent, traffic problems; 13 percent, service; 5 percent, miscellaneous; and 2 percent, stranger-to-stranger crime.[47]

Cordner states that these studies show that a much greater portion of calls handled by patrol officers are crime related than earlier studies regarding only calls to 911 had suggested. He also points out that sizable portions of patrol workload are calls regarding order maintenance, traffic, and service responsibilities.[48]

Studies of Actual Activity by Patrol Officers Reiss found that the average police officer's typical tour of duty does not involve a single arrest.[49] Egon Bittner found that patrol officers average about one arrest per month and only three Index crime arrests per year.[50] O'Neill and Bloom found that patrolling and nonduty activities accounted for 45 to 50 percent of patrol time in eighteen California cities.[51] Finally, Kelling and his associates in the Kansas City Study found that 60 percent of patrol time in Kansas City was uncommitted.[52]

Cordner, commenting on these studies, writes that the majority of patrol work involves not doing anything very specific, but rather taking breaks, meeting with other officers, and engaging in preventive patrolling. He states that administrative duties are the most common in police patrol, and the remaining time is divided among police-initiated activities (33 percent) and calls from the police dispatcher (67 percent). Cordner says the police-initiated activities are mostly related to law enforcement (particularly traffic enforcement). The calls from the dispatcher involve a blend of crimes, disputes, traffic problems, and service requests, with crimes and disputes being the most common.[53]

Studies of Police-Citizen Encounters The Police Services Study examined patrol work in sixty different neighborhoods. Observers accompanied patrol officers on all shifts in twenty-four different police departments. The observers collected information on each encounter between a police officer and a citizen, detailing nearly 6,000 encounters. The study found that only 38 percent of all police-citizen encounters dealt primarily with crime-related problems. Most of these were nonviolent crimes or incidents involving suspicious circumstances. The next most common kinds of encounters were disorder problems and traffic-related matters, each accounting for 22 percent of the total. Finally, 18 percent of the police-citizen encounters were primarily of a service nature.

The Police Services Study data also indicated that the police invoked the law relatively rarely, making arrests in only 5 percent of the encounters and issuing tickets in less than 10 percent of the encounters. Additionally, officers used force or the threat of force in only 14 percent of the encounters, with force actually used in only 5 percent of the encounters. Most of this force involved only handcuffing or taking a suspect by the arm.[54]

The Greene and Klockars Study Jack R. Greene and Carl B. Klockars have described a survey of a full year's worth of computer-aided dispatch (CAD) data for the Wilmington (Delaware) Police Department. Their survey has given us a new look at police activity.[55] Greene and Klockars also describe many of the previous studies regarding police activity and note that most of these studies, as we have seen, reveal that much of police work deals with problems that are not related to crime.

The study revealed that the police spent 26 percent of their time on criminal matters, 9 percent on order maintenance assignments, 4 percent on service-related functions, 11 percent on traffic matters, 2 percent on medical assistance, and 12 percent on administrative matters. Five percent of their time, they were unavailable for service, and almost 30 percent of the time was clear or unassigned, when the officers performed random routine patrol (see Tables 7.2 and 7.3).

Two of the significant findings of this study follow. First, when the percentage of time involved in unavailable, administrative, and clear time is excluded from the data, the data indicate that the police spent almost 50 percent of their time on criminal matters, 16 percent on order maintenance, 8 percent on service, 21 percent on traffic, and 4 percent on medical assistance. Second, 47 percent of the officers' time was spent on activities other than actual assignments.

Observations on the Studies We have seen that the police spend their time performing numerous types of duties. They spend significant time on criminal matters, but the measurement of this time varies depending on the study.

Looking at all the police activity studies, it is obvious why most experts today agree that the great bulk of police patrol work is devoted to what has been described as random routine patrol, administrative matters, order maintenance, and service-related functions. Sheehan and Cordner state that although the studies performed a valuable function by challenging the crime-

Table 7.2	Distribution of Police Patrol Time
Activity	Percentage of Time
Criminal matters	26
Order maintenance matters	9
Service-related matters	4
Traffic matters	11
Medical assistance	2
Administrative matters	12
Unavailable for patrol	5
Random routine patrol	30

Source: Adapted from Jack R. Greene and Carl B. Klockars, "What Police Do," in *Thinking about Police: Contemporary Readings*, 2d ed., ed. Carl B. Klockars and Stephen D. Mastrofski (New York: McGraw-Hill, 1991), pp. 273–284.

Table 7.3	Why Police Are Not on Assignment
Activity	Percentage of Time
Administrative time: Traveling to and from headquarters, hospitals, or courts	12
Unavailable time: meals, personal time	5
Clear time: random routine patrol	30

Source: Adapted from Jack R. Greene and Carl B. Klockars, "What Police Do," in *Thinking about Police: Contemporary Readings*, 2d ed., ed. Carl B. Klockars and Stephen D. Mastrofski (New York: McGraw-Hill, 1991), pp. 273–284.

Dempsey's Law

College Intern Programs Are Great

Has anyone in this class participated in the college's intern program with the county police?

I have, Professor Dempsey.

OK, Troy, tell us about it.

Well, we have to work 100 hours with the police, attend a weekly seminar with the other students where we talk about what we are doing on our jobs, and write a fifteen-page paper on our experiences. We get 4 credits for it.

Troy, what do you do with the police?

We get to work in many different units. I spent one tour on patrol in the radio car and went to all the calls the officer went on. One day I worked with the precinct detectives and another day, with the precinct crime control team, where we busted some prostitutes and raided a crack house. That was cool! Another day I worked with speed enforcement on the expressway. Man, I'll never speed again. I worked another tour at the Equipment Bureau, but that was just administrative work.

Just administrative work? They don't let you do police work, do they?

Sure, but we have to sign a waiver that we won't sue the department and the county if we get hurt. When we were at the crack house, the perps thought I was a cop. One called me officer; another called me sir.

Troy, we have had a lot of students who have worked the intern program with the police. Some have decided that police work wasn't for them after their experiences. How about you?

Mr. Dempsey, I want it more than ever, now!

---

fighting image of police work, by the late 1970s, many police chiefs and scholars carried them too far and began to downplay and deemphasize the crime-related and law enforcement aspects of police work.[56] James Q. Wilson noted that he would "prefer the police to act and talk as if they were able to control crime."[57]

Sheehan and Cordner sum up all the studies on "what do cops do" as follows:

> Taking all of these studies into consideration, we think a middle of the road position is advisable. It is obvious now, that police work is not so completely dominated by crime-fighting as its public image and media misrepresentations would suggest. However, it is equally clear that crime-related matters occupy an appreciable portion of the police work load. The available research conclusively demonstrates that those who have been arguing that police work has little or nothing to do with crime know little or nothing about police work.[58]

A former police chief gives a vivid description of police patrol work that may point more to the truth of the matter than can academic studies:

> Cops on the street hurry from call to call, bound to their crackling radios, which offer no relief—especially on summer weekend nights. That is the time when the ghetto throbs with noise, booze, violence, drugs, illness, blaring TVs, and human misery. The cops jump from crisis to crisis, rarely having time to do more than tamp one down sufficiently and leave for the next. Gaps of boredom and inactivity fill the interims, although there aren't many of these in the hot months. Periods of boredom get increasingly longer as the night wears on and the weather gets colder.[59]

From the Foot Beat to the Patrol Car

Patrol allocation models give the police answers as to where and when to assign officers. However, over the years, different methods of deploying police officers have been used. The two major deployments are motorized patrol and foot patrol.

Police patrol, as we saw in chapter 1, is a historical outgrowth of the early watch system. The first formal police patrols were on foot, and the cop on the beat became the symbol and very essence of policing in the United States. Furthermore, the cop on the beat became the embodiment of American government to most citizens. However, as early as the 1930s—even before the automobile had become an integral part of American

YOU ARE THERE!

What Do Cops Do? A Reporter Finds Out!

Reporter Alison Mitchell tells some tales of her days riding with police officers:

They hurtled up three steep flights of stairs, six police officers racing to answer a 911 call about a deranged man with a knife. What they found in the small Brooklyn apartment was a skinny man sitting quietly, surrounded by frantic family members.

"We don't want him to get hurt—he's real passive," a nephew said. But when the officers suggested that the relatives should bring the man to a hospital themselves, the story changed. "He's dangerous—he's walking around with this," said a stepson, grabbing a large steak knife to demonstrate how the man had been threatening to kill Fidel Castro.

After several minutes of argument, the officers—two women and four men—cuffed the man's hands behind his back and led him downstairs to await an ambulance. There, as neighbors watched from nearby stoops, the bewildered man began struggling and officers forced him to lie on his stomach on the sidewalk.

"They're kicking him," a spectator holding a bagged beer cried, though, in fact, the officers had done nothing more than stand in a protective circle since putting the man on the ground.

It was a typical call on a typical night on patrol. . . .

On busy nights, the 911 calls are as likely to involve domestic disputes as crime. Police Officer Hanna Tonuzi, 27, and her partner, Officer Nicole Medico, 23, were on the 4-to-midnight tour on a recent balmy Saturday evening when they received the call about the man with the knife.

But they had scarcely any time to dwell on the case, which was sandwiched somewhere between the brother who beat his sister so savagely that her blood was splattered on the floor outside their apartment, and a 911 report of a woman with a gun.

The gun call was the one that left them talking. Seven officers responded, only to find that it was in reality a woman with an infant. The long-haired redhead in black-tights outfit had shown up to confront her child's father at his home, where he and his wife also had a newborn. A screaming fracas was under way between the women. The police quickly separated everyone. The girlfriend was pulled into the yard. The man and his wife were quizzed in their home.

Officer Tonuzi, her blond hair in a ponytail, calmed the girlfriend with down-home feminist advice: forget him. "I'm sure you still love him," she said to the intruder who was in tears and would get a desk-appearance ticket for harassment. "To come here is not good. She's going to fight you because she's here too." . . .

He [Police Officer Louis Marino] was speeding toward a burglary when a new call of officer needing assistance sent him into reverse. His patrol car pulled up where two plainclothes officers, Eddie Mattera and Carlos Pacheco, had just arrested a nineteen-year-old carrying a .25 caliber semi-automatic pistol. The young man was handcuffed. The only problem was his dog.

The uniformed officers pulled the animal into their car, to return it to the man's mother. She wasn't home, but a young neighbor was. They told him his friend was under arrest. "His dog's under arrest too," Officer Marino deadpanned. They handed over the dog with instructions that it be returned to his owner's mother, along with the news that her son could be found at the precinct station house.

"I don't know the dog's name," the teenager called back to the officers.

"Call him Pistol," Officer Tomasi answered.

Source: Reprinted with permission from Alison Mitchell, "A Night on Patrol: What's behind Police Tensions and Discontent," *New York Times*, 19 October 1992, pp. B-1, B-2. Copyright © 1992 by The New York Times Company.

---

life—foot patrols were beginning to vanish in favor of the more efficient and faster patrol car.[60]

By the late 1930s and 1940s, police management experts stressed the importance of motorized patrol as a means of increasing efficiency. The International City Management Association (ICMA) reported that the number of cities using motorized patrols increased from 840 in 1946 to 1,000 in 1954, and to 1,334 in 1964.[61]

By the 1960s, the efficiency of the remaining foot patrols was being challenged. Foot patrols were considered geographically restrictive and wasteful of personnel. Foot officers, who at the time had no portable radios (these did not become available until the 1970s), were not efficient in terms of covering large areas or being available to be signaled and sent on assignments. Thus, to management experts, foot patrols were not as efficient as the readily available radio cars.

In 1968, the District of Columbia Crime Commission, criticizing the District of Columbia's continued use of foot patrol, stated: "The department's continued reliance on foot patrol is an inefficient and outdated utilization of manpower resources. . . . As long as the Department uses foot patrol as the primary method of patrol, however, available economics will not be realized and the city will not be provided the best possible police service."[62]

At about this time, many cities—including Kansas City, Missouri; Dallas; Phoenix; Omaha; Oklahoma City; Birmingham, Alabama; and other large cities—had shifted almost totally away from foot patrols, replacing them with more deployable two-person, motorized patrol cars. However, as a report of the Kansas City (Missouri) Police Department pointed out, in 1966, the number of foot patrol beats per shift in Boston, Baltimore, Pittsburgh, and other major urban centers still remained in the hundreds.[63]

At almost the same time these reports from Kansas City and the District of Columbia were prepared, the International Association of Chiefs of Police (IACP) went one step further, strongly advocating the idea of a conspicuous patrol that conveyed a sense of police omnipresence. The association felt that this could be best achieved using a highly mobile force of one-person cars:

> The more men and more cars that are visible on the streets, the greater is the potential for preventing a crime. A heavy blanket of conspicuous patrol at all times and in all parts of the city tends to suppress violations of the law. The most economical manner of providing this heavy blanket of patrol is by using one-man cars when and where they are feasible.[64]

The change from foot to motor patrol revolutionized U.S. policing. It fulfilled the expectations of the management experts by enabling police departments to provide more efficient patrol coverage—that is, covering more areas more frequently and responding more quickly to calls for service.[65] However, one major unforeseen consequence of the shift to motorized patrol continues to haunt us to this very day. As William A. Westly pointed out in 1970, "In contrast to the man on the beat, the man in the car is isolated from the community."[66]

Motor patrol was very efficient in terms of coverage, but it involved a trade-off in terms of the relationship between the police and the community. Now police officers had few contacts with ordinary citizens in normal situations; most calls involved problems, either crime or order maintenance problems. A growing rift began to develop between the police and the public. Few people noticed this change in policing until the riots of the 1960s dramatized the problem of police-community relations.[67]

As early as 1968, experts began to realize the problems created by the emphasis on the efficiency of the patrol car. They realized the absence of the foot officer's closeness to the community. The Task Force on the Police of the President's Commission on Law Enforcement and Administration of Justice noted, "The most significant weakness in American motor patrol operations today is the general lack of contact with citizens except when an officer has responded to a call. Forced to stay near the car's radio, awaiting an assignment, most patrol officers have few opportunities to develop closer relationships with persons living in the district."[68]

Despite the drawbacks, by 1978, the Police Practices Survey found that more than 90 percent of all beats were handled by motor patrol. Foot patrol accounted for less than 10 percent.[69]

Return to Foot Patrol

Obviously, police officers on motorized patrols are more efficient than foot officers. Cars get to locations much more quickly; they can cover much larger areas; and they provide the officers more comfort in inclement weather. However, as we have seen, some police managers and other experts feel that automobile patrolling had led to a police alienation from neighborhoods and a loss of the feelings of safety by citizens that is generated by foot patrol.[70]

In the mid-1980s, in an attempt to get the police closer to the public and to avoid the problems caused by the alienation of radio car officers from the community, an emphasis on foot patrol began to return to many cities. By 1985, foot patrol had returned to Newark, Oakland, Los Angeles, Detroit, Flint (Michigan), Houston, Boston, New York City, Atlanta, Tampa, Minneapolis, Cincinnati, and many other cities. A 1984 survey revealed that approximately two-thirds of medium-sized and large police departments utilized foot patrol in some form.[71]

Researchers arrived at the following conclusions about the reinstitution of foot patrol in Newark and Flint:

1. When foot patrol is added in neighborhoods, levels of fear decrease significantly.
2. When foot patrol is withdrawn from neighborhoods, levels of fear increase significantly.

3. Citizen satisfaction with police increases when foot patrol is added in neighborhoods.
4. Police who patrol on foot have a greater appreciation for the values of the neighborhood residents than do police who patrol the same area in automobiles.
5. Police who patrol on foot have greater job satisfaction, less fear, and higher morale than do officers who patrol in automobiles.[72]

A thorough study conducted in Newark regarding foot patrols was unable to demonstrate that either adding or removing foot patrol affected crime in any way. However, Newark citizens involved in this study were less fearful of crime and more satisfied with services provided by officers on foot patrol than service by officers on motorized patrol. Also, Newark citizens in this study were aware of additions and deletions of foot patrol from their neighborhoods, in contrast to the Kansas City Study, where citizens did not perceive changes in the level of motorized patrol.[73] Thus, the Newark foot patrol studies do not prove that foot patrols actually reduce crime but that foot patrols actually make citizens feel safer. Experience indicates that citizens clearly want to see a return to the old "cop on the beat."

The best evidence that citizens want foot patrols may have been shown in Flint. Despite the highest unemployment rate in the nation, citizens there voted in 1982 and 1985 to increase their taxes to extend foot patrol to the entire city.[74]

Interviews over a four-year period disclosed that the Neighborhood Foot Patrol program in Flint improved relationships between the police and the community. Residents of the community indicated their belief that the police on foot patrol were more responsive to their needs than had been the case before the experimental program.[75]

Research has indicated that more active citizen involvement in policing has occurred where foot patrol programs have been implemented. In Boston, for example, citizens actively participate with police officers on neighborhood crime and street patrol committees.[76] In Atlanta, a Bureau of Police Services Partnership against Crime program has actively involved citizens with police in devising ways of attacking crime through more aggressive prevention and control.[77]

A Tampa, Florida, patrol experiment, the Permanent Patrol Assignment system, was supplemented with golf cart patrols. Like foot patrols, golf cart patrols can get closer to the people, but they are more mobile than foot patrol. The golf car patrols responded more rapidly to citizen calls and increased dispatcher efficiency in dealing with citizen complaints.[78]

Why Walking Works Better Than Driving

Citizens want and like foot patrol officers. Why does this more expensive form of policing seem more effective than traditional radio car patrol?

Researchers have found that foot patrol officers pay more attention to disorderly behavior and minor offenses than do motor patrol officers. Foot patrol officers are in a better position to manage their beats—to see, understand, and deal with threatening or inappropriate behavior. They are more likely to pay attention to derelicts, petty thieves, disorderly persons, vagrants, panhandlers, noisy juveniles, and street people—people who are not committing serious crimes but are causing concern and fear among many citizens.[79]

The existence of the foot patrols themselves does not seem to be the critical factor that makes them effective. Rather, it is the actions of the officer on the foot post. As Robert C. Trojanowicz, evaluator of the Flint experiment, points out, "If an officer's walking along in the traditional way, he won't affect the crime rate. Patrolmen who operate that way are just motorized officers without a car. Basically, they're doorshakers. But when the officers becomes actively involved in the community, that's when crime problems begin to be solved."[80]

James Q. Wilson and George L. Kelling, in "'Broken Windows': The Police and Neighborhood Safety," talk about a Newark street cop they call "Kelly," with whom Kelling spent many hours walking a beat:

> As he saw his job, he was to keep an eye on strangers; and make certain that the disreputable regulars observed some informal but widely understood rules. Drunks and addicts could sit on the stoops, but could not lie down. People could drink on side streets, but not at the main intersection. Bottles had to be in paper bags. Talking to, bothering, or begging from people waiting at the bus stop was strictly forbidden. . . . Persons who broke the informal rules, especially those who bothered people waiting at bus stops, were arrested for vagrancy. Noisy teenagers were told to keep quiet.[81]

Kelly obviously separated the people on his beat into strangers versus regular people and reputable versus disreputable people, and he created rules to enforce a distance between them. By walking around and enforcing the rules, Kelly maintained peace and a sense of equilibrium on his beat.

★ Detective Operations

Most of the activities of a police department involve police patrol operations. However, as we saw in chapter 3, the police engage in numerous other activities. Detective operations are an important part of police work.

What Do Detectives Do?

The detective division of a police department is charged with solving, or clearing, reported crimes. In traditional detective operations, detectives conduct a follow-up investigation of a past crime after a member of the patrol force takes the initial report of the crime and conducts some sort of preliminary investigation.

According to police tradition, a detective or investigator reinterviews the victim of the crime and any witnesses, collects evidence, and processes the crime scene (searches the scene of a crime for physical evidence, collects the evidence, and forwards it to the police laboratory for analysis). The detective or investigator also conducts canvasses (searches of areas for witnesses); interrogates possible suspects; arrests the alleged perpetrator; and prepares the case, with the assistance of the district attorney's or prosecutor's office, for presentation in court.

The detective generally begins an investigation upon receipt of an incident report (complaint report) prepared by the officer who conducted the initial interview with the victim. The incident report contains identifying information regarding the victim, details of the crime, identifying information regarding the perpetrator (or perpetrators) or a description; and identifying information regarding any property taken.

As the detective begins the investigation, he or she maintains a file on the case, using follow-up reports for each stage of the investigation. The incident report and the follow-up reports are generally placed in a case folder and serve as the official history of the crime and its investigation. The case folder is then used by the prosecutor to prosecute the case in court. (To prosecute means to conduct criminal procedures in a court of law against a person accused of committing criminal offenses. The people performing this duty are generally called prosecutors. They are also called, in various jurisdictions, district attorneys, state attorneys, or U.S. attorneys.) The incident report and the follow-up reports may also be subpoenaed by a defendant's defense attorney under the legal process known as discovery, which allows a defendant, prior to a trial, to have access to the

The 1994 Nicole Brown/Ronald Goldman crime scene in Brentwood, California.

information the police and prosecutor will use at the trial.

Detective units may be organized on a decentralized or centralized basis. In a decentralized system, each precinct in a city has its own local detective squad, which investigates all crimes occurring in the precinct. Detectives or investigators in a decentralized squad are considered generalists.

In a centralized system, in contrast, all detectives operate out of one central office or headquarters and are each responsible for certain particular types of crime in the entire city. These detectives are considered specialists. Some departments separate centralized or specialty squads into crimes against persons squads and crimes against property squads. Some departments operate specialized squads for most serious crimes—for example, they may have a homicide squad, sex crime squad, robbery squad, burglary squad, forgery squad, pickpocket squad, and bias crimes squad (which investigates crimes that are motivated by bigotry or hatred of a person's race, ethnic origin, gender, or sexual orientation).

Some cities use both decentralized and centralized investigatory units. The decentralized squads operate out of a local precinct and refer some of their cases to the specialized centralized squads, such as sex crime, homicide, or arson squads. The decentralized squads then investigate less serious cases themselves.

The Detective Mystique

Detectives work out of uniform, perform no patrol duties, and are generally paid at a higher rate than regular uniformed officers. The assignment to detective duties is generally considered a promotion. Detectives generally enjoy much greater status and prestige than patrol officers. They have historically been seen as the heroes of police work in novels, television, and the movies—consider Sherlock Holmes, Inspector Clouseau, Cagney and Lacey, V. I. Warshawski, Crokett and Tubbs, Dirty Harry Callahan, and other fictional detectives. Are real-life detectives as heroic, smart, individualistic, tough, hardworking, and mysterious as their fictional counterparts? Or is there a mystique attached to the detective position?

The **detective mystique** is the idea that detective work is glamorous, exciting, and dangerous, as it is depicted in the movies and on television. In reality, however, detectives spend most of their time filling out reports and reinterviewing victims on the telephone. Commenting on the detective mystique, Herman Goldstein has written the following:

> Part of the mystique of detective operations is the impression that a detective has difficult-to-come-by qualifications and skills, that investigating crime is a real science, that a detective does much more important work than other police officers, that all detective work is exciting and that a good detective can solve any crime. . . . [In] the context of the totality of police operations, the cases detectives solve account for a much smaller part of police business than is commonly realized. This is so because in case after case, there is literally nothing to go on: no physical evidence, no description of the offender, no witness and often no cooperation, even from the victim.[82]

Prior to the Rand Study of the Criminal Investigation Process, which will be discussed in chapter 8, the detec-

Boulder, Colorado police working at the crime scene in the 1996 JonBenet Ramsey homicide.

tive mystique was considered to be an accurate representation of reality. It was believed that each crime was completely investigated, that all leads and tips were followed to their logical conclusion, and that each case was successfully solved. This was not true, as we will see when we discuss the Rand study. The reality of detective work usually has little in common with its media representations.

Because of the Rand study and other studies, police administrators can now make some generalizations about detective operations. First, the single most important determinant of whether or not a crime is solved is not the quality of the work performed by the detectives but the information the victim supplies to the first patrol officer who reports to the scene of the crime.[83] Next, detectives are not very effective in solving crimes. Nationally, police are only able to clear (solve) about 21 percent of all serious crime reported to them.[84] (It must be remembered however, that this 21 percent clearance figure refers to all crimes and that the police have much higher clearance rates in the most serious crimes, such as murder, rape, and aggravated assault). Furthermore, because only about one-third of all crimes are ever reported to the police at all, the real clearance rate of crime is much lower than 21 percent. (Police cannot clear crimes not reported to them.)[85] Finally, patrol offi-

PATROLLING THE NET

Are They Serious? More for the Police to Worry about on the Road

The Microsoft computer company, eager to take advantage of the time that most of us spend in our cars, is reported to be developing programs for dashboard-mounted computers that would allow drivers to use the Internet while driving. They could check their e-mail, buy and sell stocks, and even surf the Net using cellular telephone technology.

Microsoft is talking with several car makers. Obviously, some in the auto industry fear there will be safety problems if drivers are distracted while driving because they are surfing the Net. Microsoft says it intends to use voice commands and automated synthesized voices so drivers will not have to take their eyes off the road to look at a screen. With studies already showing higher accident rates among drivers using cellular phones, is this a good idea?

Source: Adapted from "Computers in Cars: 'Sorry, Officer, I Was Downloading,'" New York Times, 6 July 1997, Section 3, p. 2.

cers, not detectives, are responsible for the vast majority of all arrests. In fact, in one study, patrol officers made 87 percent of all arrests.[86]

Police Traffic Operations

Controlling the movement of vehicular traffic and enforcing the traffic laws is another one of the important activities the police engage in. The proliferation of automobiles, motorcycles, and trucks in the United States has been accompanied by a tremendous amount of traffic fatalities, injuries, and property damage. In 1990, a total of 44,529 people died, 3.2 million people were injured, and $74 billion in economic loss occurred due to traffic accidents.[87] In 1995, 43,900 died in traffic accidents.[88]

The states have enacted numerous laws dealing with vehicle use, and it falls upon the police to enforce those laws. Thibault, Lynch, and McBride define the traffic role of the police as follows:

1. The elimination of accident causes and congestion.
2. The identification of potential traffic problems and hazards.
3. The regulation of parking on street and municipal facilities.
4. The investigation of property damage and personal injury automobile accidents.
5. Directing public awareness toward the proper use of automobiles, bicycles, and motorcycles.
6. The arrest of offenders.[89]

The vast majority of local and state law enforcement agencies have the responsibility of enforcing state and local traffic laws and ordinances. Some states have a state highway patrol, whose primary duties are the enforcement of traffic laws. Many police departments create a special unit, such as a traffic division, to pay special attention to traffic problems. However, the enforcement of traffic regulations is generally the duty of all officers in a department. In some municipalities, nonsworn officers or civilians are hired for traffic control and the enforcement of local parking regulations.

Police Special Operations

One type of police work that has increased greatly in recent years includes special weapons and tactical teams (SWAT) and emergency service units (ESUs). SWAT teams and ESUs address specific emergency and lifesaving situations that regular officers on routine patrol do not have the time or expertise to handle.

SWAT Teams

SWAT teams were created in many cities during the 1960s, generally in response to riots and similar disturbances. The first SWAT team was the Philadelphia Police Department's 100-officer Special Weapons and Tactics (SWAT) squad, which was organized in 1964 in response to the growing number of bank robberies throughout the city.[90]

Members of SWAT teams are carefully chosen and trained in the use of weapons and strategic invasion tactics. SWAT teams are used in situations involving hos-

This photo of police emergency service vehicles and equipment shows the many services emergency services units perform.

tages, serious crimes, airplane hijackings, and prison riots, as well as in other situations requiring specialized skills and training.

A recent study by Professors Peter B. Kraska and Victor E. Kappeler, of Eastern Kentucky University, said that paramilitary police units are becoming a standard feature of American policing, even in small- and medium-sized departments. Their study found that from 1982 to 1995, the proportion of police agencies with SWAT teams in departments servicing populations of 50,000 residents had risen from 59 percent to 89 percent.[91]

Emergency Service Units

Police departments provide numerous emergency services, including emergency first aid to sick and injured citizens, rescues of people trapped in automobiles at accident scenes, rescues of those trapped in burning or collapsed buildings, and often rescues of people attempting to commit suicide by jumping from buildings and bridges. These duties involve specialized training and, often, sophisticated rescue equipment. The first aid and rescue services are often provided by patrol officers as part of their routine services. Many larger cities or counties, however, provide special patrol units whose primary responsibility is to respond to these emergencies. Often these emergency duties are merged into a department's SWAT operations or are provided by specialized emergency service units with sophisticated rescue and lifesaving equipment.

The New York City Police Department has had its Emergency Service Unit (ESU) since 1930. This unit of 250 officers spends most of its time on rescue missions, as well as on performing traditional hostage and SWAT operations. An emergency service volunteer recruit described his training as follows:

> [The ESU recruit] is schooled in a staggering syllabus of skills. He is trained as a marksman so he can play a key role when an armed perpetrator takes cover or a terrorist takes hostages. Then he is taught the psychology of barricaded criminals so he can avoid using his marksmanship talents. He is certified as an emergency medical technician and can administer cardiopulmonary resuscitation and oxygen to victims of coronaries, respiratory ailments, smoke inhalation and asphyxiation. He is versed in the art of extrication and rescues people trapped in not only elevators but also vehicles, heavy machinery and cave-ins. He knows how to secure dangerous cornices and scaffolds, repair downed electrical wires and poles . . . and navigate an armored personnel carrier for rescuing people pinned down by gunfire.[92]

Police emergency service officers and equipment at the scene of a crane collapse in New York City. A woman who was trapped under the crane was rescued by officers.

Chapter Summary

This chapter has discussed the traditional methods of doing police work: random routine patrol, rapid response to citizens' 911 calls, and retroactive investigation of past crimes by detectives. Prior to the academic studies of the 1960s and 1970s—particularly the Kansas City Study—most of what we knew about police work, and most of the way police work was done in the United States, relied on untested assumptions. We assumed that adding more police to a community reduced crime. Routine random patrol by officers driving in and around a neighborhood in marked police cars, rapid response to citizens' calls to 911 for assistance, and retroactive investigations of past crimes by detectives were the only ways we did police work, and we assumed they were effective. The Kansas City Study forced academics and progressive police administrators to look closely at police operations to see if there were better, more effective ways to do them. This chapter looked at some of the academic studies regarding policing.

Most of the chapter involved police patrol operations—the "backbone" of policing. The text discussed the activities and role of the patrol officer and the various methods of doing patrol work, including motorized and foot patrol. Additionally, the chapter discussed detective operations; traffic operations; and special operations, including SWAT teams and emergency service units.

Chapter 8 will look at new ways of policing based on the academic studies and experiences of police administrators discussed in this chapter.

Learning Check

1. Name the three basic methods used by the police to fulfill their mission.
2. Discuss whether the three basic methods used by the police to fulfill their mission are effective. If they are effective, why? If they are not effective, why not?
3. Identify the major value of the Kansas City Study.
4. Explain what the academic studies regarding police patrol revealed about what the police do while on patrol.
5. Discuss what the academic studies regarding police detective operations revealed about what detectives do.

Review Exercise

Your professor in this course is attending the annual national convention of the Academy of Criminal Justice Sciences (ACJS) in March and has invited you and your fellow students to accompany her. She has indicated that students may present student papers at the convention on any issue in policing. The paper must be ten pages long, double spaced. In addition to preparing the paper, the student will be required to present it to an assembled panel of other students from all over the United States in a ten- to fifteen-minute oral report.

Your professor has recommended that you select one of the following topics and write a report on it:

1. Traditional methods of policing—What are they? How effective are they?
2. Police patrol operations—What do patrol cops do?
3. Police detective operations—What do detectives do?

Web Exercise

Patrol the Internet and find several examples of police departments using foot patrols and describe what these departments say about their benefits.

Key Concepts

random routine patrol
rapid response to citizens' calls to 911
retroactive investigation of past crimes by detectives
Kansas City Study
Clarence Kelly
George Kelling
foot patrol
detective mystique

Notes

1. Robert Sheehan and Gary W. Cordner, *Introduction to Police Administration,* 2d ed. (Cincinnati: Anderson, 1989), p. 365.
2. Joan Petersilia, "The Influence of Research on Policing," in *Critical Issues in Policing: Contemporary Readings,* ed. Roger G. Dunham and Geoffrey P. Albert (Prospect Heights, Ill.: Waveland Press, 1989), pp. 230–247.
3. George L. Kelling et al., *The Kansas City Preventive Patrol Experiment: A Summary Report* (Washington, D.C.: Police Foundation, 1974).
4. Kelling et al., *Kansas City Preventive Patrol Experiment,* p. 16.
5. James Q. Wilson, *Thinking about Crime* (New York: Vintage Books, 1975), p. 99.
6. Kelling et al., *Kansas City Preventive Patrol Experiment,* pp. v-vi.
7. Kelling et al., *Kansas City Preventive Patrol Experiment,* pp. 48–49.
8. Richard C. Larson, "What Happened to Patrol Operations in Kansas City? A Review of the Kansas City Preventive Patrol Experiment," *Journal of Criminal Justice* 3 (1975): 267–297.
9. O. W. Wilson and Roy Clinton McLaren, *Police Administration,* 4th ed. (New York: McGraw-Hill, 1977), p. 4.
10. *Criminal Justice Newsletter,* 27 August 1979, p. 4.
11. Herbert Jacob and Michael J. Rich, "The Effects of the Police on Crime: A Second Look," *Law and Society Review* 15 (1980–1981): 109–122.
12. Sheehan and Cordner, *Introduction to Police Administration,* pp. 367–368.
13. Samuel Walker, *The Police in America: An Introduction* (New York: McGraw-Hill, 1983), p. 118.
14. H. H. Isaacs, "A Study of Communications, Crimes, and Arrests in a Metropolitan Police Department," in President's Commission on Law Enforcement and Administration of Justice, *Task Force Report: Science and Technology* (Washington, D.C.: U.S. Government Printing Office, 1967).
15. U.S. National Advisory Commission on Criminal Justice Standards and Goals, *Police* (Washington, D.C.: U.S. Government Printing Office, 1973), p. 194.
16. Walker, *Police in America,* pp. 119–120.
17. Kansas City Police Department, *Response Time Analysis: Executive Summary* (Washington, D.C.: U.S. Government Printing Office, 1978); and William Spelman and D. K. Brown, *Calling the Police: Citizen Reporting of Serious Crime* (Washington, D.C.: Police Executive Research Forum, 1981).
18. Gary W. Cordner, Jack R. Greene, and T. S. Bynum, "The Sooner the Better: Some Effects of Police Response Time," in *Police at Work: Policy Issues and Analysis,* ed. R. R. Bennett (Beverly Hills: Sage Publications, 1983).
19. Peter W. Greenwood and Joan Petersilia, *The Criminal Investigation Process: Summary and Policy Implications* (Santa Monica, Calif.: Rand Corporation, 1975).
20. Greenwood and Petersilia, *Criminal Investigation Process,* p. vi.
21. Greenwood and Petersilia, *Criminal Investigation Process,* p. vii.
22. Spelman and Brown, *Calling the Police.*
23. Mark Willman and John Snortum, "Detective Work: The Criminal Investigation Process in a Medium-Size Police Department," *Criminal Justice Review* 9 (1984): 33–39.
24. Anthony V. Bouza, *The Police Mystique: An Insider's Look at Cops, Crime, and the Criminal Justice System* (New York: Plenum Press, 1990), p. 27.
25. Walker, *Police in America,* p. 103.
26. American Bar Association, *Standards Relating to Urban Police Function* (New York: Institute of Judicial Administration, 1974), Standard 2.2.
27. W. Clinton Terry III, *Policing Society: An Occupational View* (New York: Wiley, 1985), pp. 259–260.

28. John Ayto, *Dictionary of Word Origins* (New York: Arcade, 1990), p. 386.
29. Samuel G. Chapman, *Police Patrol Readings,* 2d ed. (Springfield, Ill.: Charles C. Thomas, 1970), p. ix.
30. American Society for Industrial Security, "Innovations in Patrol," *The Educator,* Spring/Summer 1997, p. 3.
31. O. W. Wilson, *Police Administration* (New York: McGraw-Hill, 1950). Later editions of this book, which was considered to be the "Bible of Policing," prior to the research revolution of the 1960s and 1970s, were published in 1963, 1972, and 1977. This book served as the college text for many of today's police chiefs and scholars, as well as for the author of this text. A new edition was published in 1997 as *Police Administration,* 5th ed., by McGraw-Hill. The publishers selected three of the major researchers of policing in the 1980s and 1990s to rewrite this classic text: James J. Fyfe, Jack R. Greene, and William F. Walsh.
32. Wilson and McLaren, *Police Administration,* pp. 320–321.
33. Wilson and McLaren, *Police Administration,* p. 320.
34. Wilson and McLaren, *Police Administration.*
35. James J. Fyfe, Jack R. Greene, William F. Walsh, O. W. Wilson, and Roy Clinton McLaren, *Police Administration,* 5th ed. (New York: McGraw-Hill, 1997), p. xxiii. Fyfe is professor of criminal justice and Senior Public Policy Research Fellow at Temple University, Philadelphia. Greene is professor of criminal justice at Temple University. Walsh is the director of the Southern Police Institute and associate professor in the Department of Justice Administration at the University of Louisville.
36. William G. Gay, Theodore H. Schell, and Stephen Schack, *Routine Patrol: Improving Patrol Productivity,* vol. 1 (Washington, D.C.: National Institute of Justice, 1977), p. 2.
37. Gay, Schell, and Schack, *Routine Patrol,* pp. 3–6.
38. James Q. Wilson, *Varieties of Police Behavior: The Management of Law and Order in Eight Communities* (Cambridge, Mass.: Harvard University Press, 1968), p. 31.
39. Gary W. Cordner, "The Police on Patrol," in *Police and Policing: Contemporary Issues,* ed. Dennis Jay Kenney (New York: Praeger, 1989), pp. 60–71.
40. Robert Lilly, "What Are the Police Now Doing?" *Journal of Police Science and Administration* 6 (1978): 51–53.
41. George Antunes and Eric Scott, "Calling the Cops: Police Telephone Operations and Citizen Calls for Service," *Journal of Criminal Justice* 9 (1981): 165–174.
42. Wilson, *Varieties of Police Behavior.*
43. Albert Reiss, *The Police and the Public* (New Haven, Conn.: Yale University Press, 1971).
44. Cordner, "Police on Patrol," p. 62.
45. T. Bercal, "Calls for Police Assistance," *American Behavioral Scientist* 13 (1970): 267–277.
46. J. Tien, J. Simon, and R. Larson, *An Alternative Approach in Police Patrol: The Wilmington Split Force Experiment* (Washington, D.C.: National Institute of Justice, 1978).
47. Lawrence Sherman, *Repeat Calls to Police in Minneapolis* (Washington, D.C.: Crime Control Institute, 1987).
48. Cordner, "Police on Patrol," p. 63.
49. Reiss, *Police and the Public,* p. 19.
50. Egon Bittner, *The Functions of the Police in Modern Society* (Washington, D.C.: U.S. Government Printing Office, 1970), p. 127.
51. M. O'Neill and C. Bloom, "The Field Officer: Is He Really Fighting Crime?" *Police Chief,* February 1972, pp. 30–32.
52. Kelling et al., *Kansas City Preventive Patrol Study.*
53. Cordner, "Police on Patrol," p. 65.
54. G. P. Whitaker, "What Is Patrol Work?" *Police Studies* 4 (1982): 13–22.
55. Jack R. Greene and Carl B. Klockars, "What Police Do," in *Thinking about Police: Contemporary Readings,* 2d ed., ed. Carl B. Klockars and Stephen D. Mastrofski (New York: McGraw-Hill, 1991), pp. 273–284. This chapter for *Thinking about Police* was written for the book and is actually part of a larger resource allocation study published in Carl B. Klockars, Jack R. Greene, and S. Wissman, *An Evaluation of Resource Allocation in the Wilmington Police Department* (Wilmington, Del.: Office of the Director of Public Safety, 1988).
56. Sheehan and Cordner, *Introduction to Police Administration,* pp. 57–58.
57. Wilson, *Thinking about Crime,* p. x.
58. Sheehan and Cordner, *Introduction to Police Administration,* pp. 57–58.
59. Bouza, *Police Mystique,* p. 84.
60. Bruce Smith, *Police Systems in the United States* (New York: Harper & Brothers, 1949), p. 14.
61. President's Commission on Law Enforcement and Administration of Justice, *Task Force Report: The Police* (Washington, D.C.: U.S. Government Printing Office, 1967), p. 55, Table 1.
62. President's Commission on Crime in the District of Columbia, *A Report on the President's Commission on Crime in the District of Columbia* (Washington, D.C.: U.S. Government Printing Office, 1966), p. 53.
63. Police Department of Kansas City, *1966 Survey of Municipal Police Departments* (Kansas City, Mo.: Police Department of Kansas City, 1966), p. 53.
64. International Association of Chiefs of Police, *A Survey of the Police Department of Youngstown, Ohio* (Washington, D.C.: International Association of Chiefs of Police, 1964), p. 89.
65. Walker, *Police in America,* p. 107.

66. William A. Westly, *Violence and the Police* (Cambridge, Mass.: MIT Press, 1970), p. 35.
67. Walker, *Police in America,* p. 107.
68. President's Commission on Law Enforcement and Administration of Justice, *Task Force Report: The Police,* p. 54.
69. John Heaphy, ed., *Police Practices: The General Administrative Survey* (Washington, D.C.: Police Foundation, 1978), p. 11.
70. Edward A. Thibault, Lawrence M. Lynch, and R. Bruce McBride, *Proactive Police Management,* 2d ed. (Englewood Cliffs, N.J.: Prentice-Hall, 1990), p. 209.
71. Robert C. Trojanowicz and Dennis W. Banas, *Perceptions of Safety: A Comparison of Foot Patrol versus Motor Patrol Officers* (East Lansing, Mich.: National Neighborhood Foot Patrol Center, School of Criminal Justice, Michigan State University, 1985); and Trojanowicz and H. A. Harden, *The Status of Contemporary Community Policing Programs* (East Lansing, Mich.: National Neighborhood Foot Patrol Center, School of Criminal Justice, Michigan State University, 1984).
72. Kelling, *Foot Patrol* (Washington, D.C.: National Institute of Justice, 1987).
73. Police Foundation, *The Newark Foot Patrol Experiment* (Washington, D.C.: Police Foundation, 1981).
74. Trojanowicz and Banas, *Perceptions of Safety.*
75. Trojanowicz and Banas, *The Impact of Foot Patrol on Black and White Perceptions of Policing* (East Lansing, Mich.: National Neighborhood Foot Patrol Center, School of Criminal Justice, Michigan State University, 1988).
76. G. Graves et al., *Developing a Street Patrol: A Guide for Neighborhood Crime Prevention Groups* (Boston: Neighborhood Crime Prevention Council, Justice Resource Institute, 1985).
77. George Napper, "Partnerships against Crime: Sharing Problems and Power," *Police Chief,* February 1986, pp. 45–46.
78. S. Morrill, "Tampa Likes Sector Patrolling," *Law and Order* 32 (1984): 37–40.
79. James Q. Wilson and George L. Kelling, "'Broken Windows': The Police and Neighborhood Safety," *Atlantic Monthly,* March 1982, pp. 29–38.
80. Ben Davis, "Foot Patrol," *Police Centurion,* June 1984, p. 41.
81. Wilson and Kelling, "'Broken Windows,'" p. 30.
82. Herman Goldstein, *Policing a Free Society* (Cambridge, Mass.: Ballinger, 1977), pp. 55–56.
83. Greenwood and Petersilia, *Criminal Investigation Process,* p. vii.
84. Federal Bureau of Investigation, *Uniform Crime Reports.*
85. Bureau of Justice Statistics, *Special Report: Reporting Crimes to the Police* (Washington, D.C.: U.S. Government Printing Office, 1985).
86. Reiss, *Police and the Public,* p. 104.
87. Earl M. Sweeney, "Community-Oriented Traffic Policing," *Police Chief,* July 1992, p. 13.
88. "Slow Down, You're Movin' Too Fast: Traffic Deaths Creep Upward," *Law Enforcement News,* 15 December 1996, p. 5.
89. Thibault, Lynch, and McBride, *Proactive Police Management,* p. 154.
90. *Philadelphia Bulletin,* 28 March 1976, Sec. 3, p. 1.
91. "Paramilitary Police Units Are More Popular Than Ever," *Law Enforcement News,* 15 May 1997, p. 9.
92. Joseph Mancini, "NYPD's Hero Cops," *National Centurion,* August 1983, p. 22.

8

Police Operations: A New Approach

Chapter Outline

Alternatives to Random Routine Patrol and Rapid Response to Citizens' 911 Calls
  Directed Patrol
  Split Force Patrol
  Differential Response to Calls for Service
Alternatives to Retroactive Investigation of Past Crimes by Detectives
  Improved Investigation of Past Crimes
  Repeat Offender Programs (ROPS)
New Proactive Tactics
  Uniformed Tactical Operations
  Decoy Operations
  Stakeout Operations
  Sting Operations
  Civil Liability and Code Enforcement Teams
  Efforts against Drunk Drivers
Undercover Operations
  Police Undercover Operations
  Federal Undercover Operations
  Private Security Undercover Operations
  Drug Undercover Investigations
Entrapment

Chapter Goals

■ To acquaint you with alternatives to the traditional methods of random routine patrol and rapid response to citizens' 911 calls, as discussed in chapter 7.

■ To introduce you to alternatives to retroactive investigation of past crimes by detectives, as discussed in chapter 7.

■ To acquaint you with the most recent proactive tactics being used by the police to fight crime, including tactical operations, decoy operations, sting operations, civil liability and code enforcement teams, and new efforts against drunk drivers.

■ To acquaint you with undercover operations, including police, federal and private security operations, and undercover drug operations.

■ To define entrapment and show how it relates to police tactical and undercover operations.

Introduction

Despite the unprecedented crime decreases of the mid-1990s, as discussed in chapter l, public and media attention to crime has intensified. In fact, in August 1997, a study by the Washington, D.C.-based Center for Media and Public Affairs showed that the amount of network news devoted to stories regarding murder cases in the United States soared 721 percent from 1993 to 1996.¹ Police operations and efforts against crime, therefore, remain a critical component of policing.

Chapter 7 discussed the three traditional methods of police work—random routine patrol, rapid response to citizens' calls to 911, and retroactive investigation of past crimes by detectives—and why they are not very effective. Police departments throughout the nation have learned that they must be more specific and focused in addressing crime and disorder problems. They have created new policies, procedures, and units to address these concerns. This chapter will discuss and examine some of these innovations.

Despite all of the criticism of traditional police patrol methods by academic researchers, no one is calling for the elimination of police patrol. Rather, researchers and police administrators are exploring various innovative alternatives to supplement traditional methods of patrol. These alternatives involve organizational and procedural changes in the makeup and use of the patrol force.

The first three alternatives—directed patrol, split force patrol, and differential response to requests for service—are modifications of normal routine preventive patrol and rapid response to calls for service. Traditional detective operations have also been modified in response to academic studies that have indicated that new methods can be used in the investigation of past crimes and the apprehension of career criminals. Improved investigations of past crimes include changes made in detective operations in response to research conducted by the Rand Corporation and other think tanks. Increased attention to career criminals has led to a proliferation of repeat offender programs (ROPS) throughout the United States.

Additionally, new tactics and operations have been developed over the past two decades in an attempt to provide more effective policing. The tactics discussed in this chapter include uniformed tactical operations, including aggressive and saturation patrol; decoy operations; stakeout operations; sting operations; code enforcement teams; and efforts against drunk drivers.

The chapter also discusses the major types of undercover operations, including police, federal, and private security undercover operations. The chapter concludes with a discussion of the legal aspects of entrapment and how it relates to undercover work and other law enforcement tactics.

Alternatives to Random Routine Patrol and Rapid Response to Citizens' 911 Calls

The current popular alternatives to random routine patrol and rapid response to citizens' 911 calls are directed patrol, split force patrol, and differential response to calls for service. These innovative approaches to policing are designed to make better use of officers' patrol time, as well as to make better use of a department's resources.

Directed Patrol

An alternative to random routine patrol is **directed patrol,** in which officers are given specific directions to follow when they are not responding to calls. The directed patrol assignments are given to officers before they begin their tour and are meant to replace uncommitted random patrol time with specific duties that police commanders believe will be effective. Directed patrol assignments can be based on crime analysis, specific problems, or complaints received from the community.

Several studies present some evidence that target crimes were reduced by directed patrol. By basing directed patrol assignments on statistical studies, many of the inadequacies of random, unstructured patrol may be overcome. The data suggest that citizen satisfaction and crime control efforts increase when patrol is based on a systematic analysis of crime.²

A significant recent example of a directed patrol program that achieved positive results was the "Kansas City Gun Experiment." Working with the University of Maryland, the Kansas City, Missouri, Police Department focused extra directed patrol attention to gun crimes in a "hot spot" area that was determined by computer analysis. Two 2-officer patrol cars focused exclusively on gun detection from 7 P.M. to 1 A.M., seven days a week. They focused on the directed patrol assignment and did not respond to any radio calls or service assignments.³

During the course of the twenty-nine-week experiment, the officers worked a total of 200 nights involving over 4,500 officer hours and over 2,200 patrol car hours (70 percent of their time was spent processing arrests and performing other necessary duties). During the twenty-nine-week experiment, the gun patrol officers made thousands of car and pedestrian checks, traffic stops, and over 600 arrests. They confiscated twenty-nine guns; an additional forty-seven weapons were seized by other officers in the experimental area. The gun seizures represented a 65 percent increase over the number of guns seized in the target area during the previous six months.

The gun patrol efforts also affected crime rates. There were 169 gun crimes in the target beat in the twenty-nine weeks prior to the experiment, but only 86 during the experimental period, a decrease of 49 percent. Drive-by shootings and homicides decreased significantly. Interestingly, none of the seven contiguous beats showed a significant increase in gun crime, indicating that there was little crime displacement effect. Community surveys conducted before and after the program was initiated indicated that citizens in the target area were less fearful of crime and more satisfied with their neighborhood than residents in companion areas. After the extra directed patrols were ended, crime rates went back to their normal levels.

Regarding this experiment, Senna and Siegel indicated,

> The Kansas City gun patrol experiment suggests that a modest police patrol effort targeting a specific crime problem can produce dramatic effects on the crime rate. Whether such efforts should be made part of general police policy remains to be seen. They could produce risks to officer safety, provoke hostile reactions from citizens, and make people subject to police searches hostile and angry. These risks may be acceptable if aggressive police action could significantly reduce the threat of gun violence.[4]

Dempsey's Law

A Typical Directed Patrol Assignment

Professor Dempsey, What does directed patrol mean? Who directs what? Can you give me an example?

Directed patrol is designed to address specific problems when police are not involved in any other police work. It is an alternative to routine random patrol. Based on a review of a precinct's crime statistics, complaints from the community, and other data, the precinct commander prepares a list of directed patrol assignments that officers can concentrate on when they are not on assignment from the radio dispatcher. The assignments are then given to the officers who patrol that particular area at that particular time when they report for duty.

Consider the following example of a typical police problem. Outside a local rock club, the Sundance Heavy Metal Trash Club, numerous fights have broken out in the parking lot during the hours when the club is open (Friday and Saturday nights between 9 P.M. and 4 A.M.). Generally, police respond, bring the victims to the hospital for first aid, and sometimes arrest the perpetrator. But the problem does not go away. The precinct does not have the personnel to assign directly to the lot due to the need to answer emergency calls.

A directed patrol assignment might be used to correct this condition. The following instructions could be given to two or three patrol cars on the Friday and Saturday evening and night tours: "Between 9 P.M. and 4 A.M., while not on assignment, sit in the parking lot of the Sundance Heavy Metal Trash Club, located at 711 Sunrise Highway, to prevent fights between youths."

Possible combatants might feel the police presence and realize the police were serious about this problem. At the same time, the police would still be available for rapid response to emergencies.

Think about it. If you had a dispute at a club and decided to go outside and settle it, would the presence of several police cars make you think more rationally? Think about some problems in your own community that could benefit from directed patrol.

> **YOU ARE THERE!**
>
> **Examples of Conditions Suitable for Directed Patrol**
> - Disorderly youths gathering at Oak and Pine streets between 10 P.M. and 1 A.M.
> - Burglaries at the Tudorville Industrial Park on weekends.
> - Sale of beer to minors at the convenience store at Mill Pond Lane and North Street.
> - Students leaving Northville High School at 3 P.M. weekdays who paint graffiti on trees and fences.
> - Purse snatches at the Steubenville railroad station between 5 and 7 P.M.

Split Force Patrol

As we have just seen, directed patrol is designed so officers can pay particular attention to specific crimes and disorder while they are not on assignment from the police dispatcher. One of the problems with directed patrol, however, is that calls for service often interrupt the performance of directed patrol assignments. **Split force patrol** offers a solution to this problem. One portion of the patrol force is designated to handle all calls dispatched to patrol units. The remaining portion of the officers working that tour are given directed patrol assignments with the assurance that except for serious emergencies, they will not be interrupted.

The most extensive test of the split force strategy was conducted in Wilmington, Delaware. The evaluation of the experiment found that this patrol improved both call-handling productivity and patrol productivity while also enhancing patrol professionalism and accountability.[5]

The Houston Police Department, faced with a spiraling crime rate, implemented a form of split force patrol called the high-intensity patrol (HIP). HIPs are an effort to put more officers on the streets in different parts of the city during peak crime hours. The Houston patrols, funded from a $2 million overtime account, are staffed by as many as thirty-five officers working on their days off or outside their regular duty hours. The HIP officers perform highly visible patrol in specific areas to emphasize the police presence. They are directed not to answer 911 calls but to remain patrolling in their assigned areas.[6]

Some critics of the Houston program state that it is mismanaged and a waste of time and money. They say that calls for service are put on hold and accumulated because there are not enough regular patrol officers to respond to them. Some officers have jokingly referred to the HIPs as "the drive-by-and-wave program." One officer stated, "Meanwhile, the calls for service just continued to pile up. It was unbelievable. The regular officers were really upset because they are running from one call to another while the other guys weren't doing anything. The guys in the HIP weren't to blame. They were ordered not to answer calls."[7] More studies are needed to reveal whether Houston's is an effective program.

Differential Response to Calls for Service

Differential response to calls for service is a policy that abandons the traditional practice of responding to all calls for service. In differential response, responses to citizens' calls to 911 for service are matched to the importance or severity of the calls. Reports of injuries, crimes, or emergencies in progress, as well as reports of serious past crimes, continue to receive an immediate response by sworn police. However, less serious calls are handled by alternative methods. Table 8.1 lists some typical calls to 911 and how they are handled under differential response.

Conditions for which delayed or alternative responses are appropriate include the following:

- Past burglaries, larcenies, or other thefts.
- Lost property.
- Crimes reported merely for insurance purposes.
- Past assaults without injuries.

Differential response alternatives can replace sending a patrol unit to investigate a past crime. A patrol unit can be sent later, when there are fewer calls for service. The caller can be asked to come into the precinct headquarters to report the crime. The call can be transferred to a nonsworn member, who then takes the report over the phone. Finally, the dispatcher can make an appointment for a nonsworn member to respond to the caller's home to take a report.

Differential response to calls for service is designed to reduce and better manage the work load of patrol officers. It gives patrol officers more time to devote to directed patrol, investigations, or crime prevention programs.[8]

Table 8.1 Assessment of Responses to 911 Calls

Complaint to 911 Operator	Immediate Response	Alternative Response	Rationale
"I got home from work three hours ago, but I just found out that $20 is missing from the drawer I keep my money in."		✓	Past crime
"I just got home from work, and my front door is open. I'm afraid to go in."	✓		Possibility that someone is still in there
"A man with red hair just drove off with my Toyota."	✓		Crime in progress
"The guy in apartment 5C sells crack. He's been doing it for years."		✓	Not an emergency right now
"The other night, Richie Green punched out my son Frank. I want him arrested."		✓	Past crime
"Come quick! Richie Green is beating up my son Frank with a bat."	✓		Crime in progress

Differential response is based on the research described in chapter 7 on the effectiveness of rapid response to citizens' calls to 911. The policy arises from an evaluation of questions such as these: Is there any value in sending a patrol unit immediately to a past burglary, particularly when the owner has just returned from a week-long vacation? Must a patrol unit be sent right away when the likelihood of the arrest of the perpetrator or the obtaining of leads to solving the crime is extremely low, even with an extremely rapid response of one to two minutes?

Perhaps rapid response is good for police public relations—"See how fast we respond when you call!"—but the allocation of scarce patrol resources should depend on police effectiveness rather than public relations. Research has shown that most citizens will accept explanations of alternative police responses if the explanations are politely and logically presented. However, researchers have suggested that providing such explanations goes beyond the traditional role of police communications personnel and requires additional training and supervision.[9]

Tests of differential response programs have yielded promising results. Some departments have successfully implemented such a program and diverted up to 50 percent of their calls to alternative responses without suffering any reduction in citizen satisfaction.[10]

Departments suffering from financial difficulties that prevent them from hiring additional officers may benefit most from differential response. They can spread out the work load while still ensuring that all emergency calls are responded to and all reports to past crimes and incidents are recorded and investigated.

Alternatives to Retroactive Investigation of Past Crimes by Detectives

Current popular alternatives to retroactive investigation of past crimes by detectives are improved investigation of past crimes and repeat offender programs. These in-

YOU ARE THERE! »

Differential Response Works in Canada

Police in the Toronto suburb of Scarborough are dispatching fewer cars and handling more calls by phone. The program, Alternate Response, allows officers to handle low-priority calls on the phone so they remain free to handle emergencies in person. In the first month of operation, seventeen constables and two sergeants on the Alternate Response Unit handled 1,700 calls, including 241 parking complaints, 286 thefts, and 118 break-ins. Without the program, the group could have handled only about 425 calls in person.

Source: Adapted from "International News: Calls Handled by Phone," *Law and Order*, August 1992, p. 6.

novative techniques are designed to concentrate investigative resources on crimes that have a high chance of being solved.

Improved Investigation of Past Crimes

The National Advisory Commission on Criminal Justice Standards and Goals has recommended the increased use of patrol officers in the criminal investigation process. The commission recommended that every police agency direct patrol officers to conduct thorough preliminary investigations and recommended that agencies establish written priorities to ensure that investigative efforts are spent in a manner that best achieves organizational goals. The commission further recommended that investigative specialists (detectives) only be assigned to very serious or complex preliminary investigations.[11]

As a consequence of the Rand Study of the Investigative Process and other studies discussed in chapter 7, the Law Enforcement Assistance Administrative (LEAA) funded research that led to the publication and wide dissemination of a new proposal regarding methods that should be used to investigate past crimes.[12] The proposal, **Managing Criminal Investigations (MCI)**, offers a series of guidelines that recommend (1) expanding the role of patrol officers to include investigative responsibilities and (2) designing a new method to manage criminal investigations by including solvability factors, case screening, case enhancement, and police and prosecutor coordination.[13] Solvability factors and case screening will be covered in this part of the chapter, and case enhancement and police and prosecutor coordination will be discussed in the next section, "Repeat Offender Programs."

Under an MCI program, the responding patrol officer is responsible for a great deal of the follow-up activity that used to be assigned to detectives. These duties include locating and interviewing the victim and witnesses, detecting physical evidence, and preparing an initial investigative report that will serve as a guide for investigators. This report must contain proper documentation to indicate whether the case should be assigned for continued investigation or immediately suspended for lack of evidence.[14]

The other major innovation under MCI involves the use of a managerial system that grades cases according to their solvability; detectives then work only on cases that have a chance of being solved. Some solvability factors follow:

1. Is there a witness?
2. Is a suspect named or known?
3. Can a suspect be identified?
4. Will the complainant cooperate in the investigation?

PATROLLING THE NET

Watch TV, Use the Net, Solve Cases

A new television show, "Cold Cases," first airing on a major television network in 1997, gave armchair detectives a real chance to solve unsolved murder cases by using the Internet to collect clues and follow up on leads by visiting its World Wide Web site at http://www.coldcase.com.

This web site features crime scene photographs, detectives' case notes, and other information that couldn't fit on the one-hour show, hosted by veteran television actor Richard Crenna. According to producers, "Cold Cases" is the first broadcast program that logically merges the Internet into its programming. The idea behind "Cold Cases" grew from a fifteen-year-old murder case solved by a Los Angeles-area homicide detective, Jon Perkins.

The case involved a U.S. suspect who fled to the Philippines. Perkins contacted the local authorities, who did not have the jurisdiction to make an arrest but did offer Perkins some important information. They said that the suspect's daughter was about to be married and that the father might be returning to the United States to attend the wedding.

Perkins began to examine bridal registries on department store web sites and discovered the suspect's daughter's name at a major store's site, where he also learned the address of the church where the wedding was to take place. He arrived at the rehearsal with flowers, then arrested the bride's father for the murder.

Source: Adapted from "'Net Gain," *Law Enforcement News*, 30 April 1997, p. 4.

Each solvability factor is given a numerical weight. In the next process, case screening, the total weight of all solvability factors—the total score—determines whether the case will be investigated or not.[15]

The MCI method of managing investigations is designed to put most of an investigator's time and effort into only very important cases and cases that actually can be solved.

Research conducted by numerous police departments has demonstrated that scoring systems using checklists and point scores successfully screen out cases with a low probability of being solved and identify promising cases.[16]

Even with all the changes recommended by the Rand and other studies, and even though police departments have implemented many changes in the investigatory process, the police are still not very successful in clearing by arrest (also just referred to as clearing, a police term for solving) crimes reported to them. Only 21 percent of the serious crimes called to police attention are cleared.[17] (It must be remembered again, as was stated in chapter 7, that the 21 percent clearance rate refers to all crime and that the police have much higher clearance rates in the very serious crimes of murder, rape, and felonious assault.) The improved methods of investigation, however, have resulted in less waste and more

All in the Line of Duty

They Saved the City

The police officers who patrol New York City, the New York City Police Department (NYPD), are called the Finest, an accolade they deserve every day. The finest of the Finest has to be the NYPD's elite Emergency Service Unit. These are the men and women who risk life and limb to climb to the tops of the city's myriad bridges and skyscrapers to rescue potential "jumpers" from themselves, enter blazing buildings, and breathe the life back into cardiac victims and other people near death. The NYPD's ESU is also the city's SWAT team. They are the Marine Corps of the city called in daily with their automatic weapons to combat highly armed terrorists and maniacs. Their action on July 31, 1997, was just one of the heroic things cops in New York did that day, but it saved the city from certain disaster.

The events began unfolding with the frantic waving of a man along a darkened Brooklyn street. A Long Island Rail Road police officer, on patrol in his radio car, observed a man acting irrationally at 10:45 p.m. July 30, 1997. He was repeatedly screaming in Arabic, "Bomba" and cupping his hands and moving them apart to mimic an explosion. The officer took the man to the 88th precinct station house in Fort Greene, Brooklyn, where an interpreter determined that there were bombs and plans to blow up New York City subways at a house at 248 Fourth Avenue in Park Slope, Brooklyn. Just before dawn on July 31, the police closed off scores of blocks in Park Slope and called upon the ESU to enter the building. The officers entered the cramped apartment, led by hero cops, Joseph Dolan, age 34, and David Martinez, age 38, shouting, "Police, don't move," whereupon one man reached for one of the officers' weapons, while another reached for one of four toggle switches on a pipe bomb. Officers Dolan and Martinez shot both suspects before any actions against them could be taken. A nine-inch pipe packed with gunpowder and nails, and a device in which four pipes had been wrapped together and equipped with toggle-switch detonators were among the explosives removed by the police. Further investigation revealed that the men were Middle-Eastern terrorists who had planned to engage in a suicide bombing of the NYC subways on that very day. The police action came a day after a suicide bombing in a Jerusalem market had killed and injured scores. The lives of over a million New York City commuters and residents were disrupted by the police action and investigation, but no injuries or deaths ensued. Says Officer Martinez, "I felt a little sick when I woke up the next day. I started to realize I almost wasn't here. I started to think of the magnitude of what these people were going to do. They would have killed hundreds of people, little children, mothers, people they don't even know. It's a great feeling to know in some way you helped alter the future." The city's mayor, Rudolph Giuliani, said, "They prevented a major terrorist attack from taking place."

Source: Adapted from "They Saved the City: New York Would Be Counting Its Dead If These Hero Cops Had Not Acted," *New York Post*, 3 August 1997, p. 1; Rocco Parascandola, "Hail Storm for City's Finest of Heroes: Danger They Faced Just Now Sinking in, Say Ace Cops," *New York Post*, 3 August 1997, pp. 1–3; "Heroes of Bomb Scare: Courageous Cops of Emergency Unit Honored," *Daily News*, 3 August 1997, p. 3; William K. Rashbaum and Patrice O'Shaugnessy, "Raiders Knew Lethal Risk: With Seconds to Spare, Cops Nearly 'Naked' vs. Bomb," *Daily News*, 3 August 1997, pp. 2–3; Dan Barry, "Police Break up Suspected Bomb Plot in Brooklyn: A Tip Leads to Finding of Explosive Devices as 3 Are Arrested, *New York Times*, 1 August 1997, pp. A-1, B-4.

efficiency in police detective operations and have allowed departments to use personnel in more proactive policing.

Repeat Offender Programs (ROPS)

U.S. criminologist Marvin Wolfgang discovered that only a few criminals are responsible for most of the predatory street crime in the United States. Most Americans do not commit street robberies; only a relatively small group of people do, but they commit a tremendous amount of crime each year. Borrowing from Wolfgang's research, police started to address their investigative resources to the career criminal using **repeat offender programs (ROPS)**. These programs can be conducted in two major ways.

First, police can identify certain people to be the target of investigation. Once a career criminal is identified, the police can use surveillance techniques, follow the criminal, and wait to either catch the person in the act of committing a crime or catch him or her immediately after a crime occurs.

The second way police can operate a repeat offender program is through case enhancement. Specialized career criminal detectives can be notified of the arrest of a robbery suspect by other officers and then determine from the suspect's conviction or arrest rate whether or not the arrest merits enhancement. If the case is enhanced, an experienced detective assists the arresting officer in preparing the case for presentation in court and debriefs the suspect to obtain further information. A major tactic behind case enhancement is liaison with the district attorney's office to alert the prosecuting attorney to the importance of the case and to the suspect's past record. Such information helps ensure zealous efforts by the prosecutor.

A study in Washington, D.C., found that a proactive repeat offender unit was successful in arresting targeted offenders. In addition, those offenders who were apprehended had much more extensive and serious prior records than other arrested offenders. The tactics of this unit included conducting surveillances of active offenders, locating wanted serious offenders, acting on tips from informants, and employing decoy and sting methods.[18]

Marcia Chaiken and Jan Chaiken in their report *Priority Prosecutors of High-Rate Dangerous Offenders*, distinguished among persistent offenders (those who commit crimes over a long period of time), high-rate offenders (those who commit numerous crimes per year), and dangerous offenders (those who commit crimes of violence).[19]

Chaiken and Chaiken suggest that the most accurate way to identify high-rate dangerous offenders is through the use of a two-stage screening process. The first stage, they say, should look for evidence of a serious previous felony conviction, failure to complete a previous sentence, arrests while in pretrial release, or a known drug problem. The authors state that defendants falling into three of these categories have a 90 percent chance of being high-rate dangerous offenders and should be further screened. The second screening involves looking for evidence of the following: use of a weapon in the current crime, one or more juvenile convictions for robbery, or status of wanted for failure to complete a previous sentence.[20] The presence of any of these aggravating factors would cause the defendant to be considered a high-rate dangerous offender. The authors suggest that any defendant considered a high-rate dangerous offender should receive special attention by investigators and prosecutors.

New, Proactive Tactics

In addition to alternatives to random routine patrol, rapid response to citizens' 911 calls, and retroactive investigation of past crimes by detectives, police departments are using new, proactive tactics to supplement traditional patrol techniques. These innovations include uniformed tactical operations, decoy operations, stakeout and sting operations, code enforcement teams, and efforts against drunk drivers.

Uniformed Tactical Operations

Uniformed tactical operations involve the use of traditional patrol operations in a more aggressive manner. The two basic kinds of uniformed tactical operations are aggressive patrol tactics and saturation patrol.

Uniformed tactical units are officers who are relieved of routine patrol responsibilities, such as random routine patrol and handling calls for service, in order to concentrate on proactive crime control. Uniformed tactical units often saturate an area that is experiencing a serious crime problem. The tactical units are aggressive and make numerous pedestrian and vehicle stops to increase the likelihood of encountering offenders. These specially assigned officers make numerous field interrogations (FIs). An FI is a contact with a citizen initiated

Officers conducting a field interrogation (FI).

by a patrol officer who stops, questions, and sometimes searches a citizen because the officer has reasonable suspicion that the subject may have committed, may be committing, or may be about to commit a crime. One researcher says that field interrogations "serve to generate information about the activities of probable suspects and, more importantly for deterrence, they make the suspects aware that the police know of their presence in a given area, regard them as suspicious and are watching them closely."[21]

Among the most controversial, and perhaps the forerunner, of these tactical groups was New York City's Tactical Patrol Force (TPF), a unit of rapidly moving officers trained in mob control. They were selected from the very best of police academy recruits. During the 1960s and early 1970s, the 1,000-member TPF viewed itself as the elite of incorruptible law enforcement. In addition to mob and riot control, TPFs swept into high-crime areas to hunt down muggers and robbers, often using a variety of decoy units that readily blended into life on the street.[22]

Although New York City's Tactical Patrol Force was successful in reducing crime, it was frowned on by many citizens, especially in minority communities. Eventually the unit's name was changed to Tactical Patrol Unit to avoid the connotations of the word force. In the 1980s, the Tactical Patrol Unit was discontinued altogether. One can only wonder whether highly mobile, aggressive units like the TPF could have reduced the numerous civilian and police injuries that resulted from civil disorders in the early 1990s—for example, the disturbances on the streets of Chicago in 1992 and 1993 in the wake of the Chicago Bulls National Basketball Association championships; or the disturbances in Montreal after the Canadians won hockey's 1993 Stanley Cup; or the 1992 street riots in south central Los Angeles in the wake of the not guilty verdicts in the Rodney King case; or the disturbances on the streets of Crown Heights, Brooklyn, in 1991 and Washington Heights, Manhattan, in 1992.

Aggressive Patrol Tactics Uniformed tactical operations make use of aggressive patrol tactics: stopping numerous people and vehicles in an attempt to find evidence that they may have committed a crime or may be committing a crime. Aggressive patrol tactics using field interrogations can be very effective in reducing crime. However, they often cause problems with the community due to their potential for abusing citizens' rights.

A study in San Diego tested the effects of field interrogations. In this study, field interrogation activity was suspended for nine months in one experimental area but maintained at normal levels in two control areas. Crime in the area where field interrogations were suspended increased by a substantial amount and remained about the same in the control areas where field interrogations continued to be used. With the resumption of FI activity in the experimental area, crime decreased to about the same level it had been before the experiment.[23]

Another study used the number of traffic citations issued by police as a measure of patrol aggressiveness and developed a sophisticated mathematical model to determine the relationship between aggressive patrol and the robbery crime rate. The analysis suggested that aggressive patrol contributes to a higher robbery arrest rate, which in turn leads to a lower robbery crime rate.[24]

For quite some time it was believed that police action had little deterrent effect or, if it did, that the effect was short-lived.[25] However, some academic studies have proved otherwise.

Researchers James Q. Wilson and Barbara Boland found that proactive, aggressive law enforcement styles may help reduce crime rates. They found that jurisdictions that encourage patrol officers to stop motor vehicles to issue citations and to aggressively arrest and detain suspicious persons experience lower crime rates than jurisdictions that do not follow such proactive policies.[26] Robert Sampson and Jacqueline Cohen found that departments that more actively enforced disorderly conduct and traffic laws also experienced lower robbery rates.[27]

In a study using data acquired in Scandinavia, Perry Shapiro and Harold Votey found that an arrest for drunk driving can actually reduce the probability of offender recidivism. Arrests apparently increase people's beliefs that they will be rearrested if they drink and drive and also heighten their perceptions of the unpleasantness associated with an arrest.[28] Similarly, Douglas Smith and Patrick Gartin's research shows that getting arrested reduces the likelihood that a novice offender will repeat criminal activity. Their study also shows that experienced offenders have reduced future offending rates after an arrest.[29]

Lawrence W. Sherman's review of eighteen case studies of varying types of police crackdowns revealed that the effects of these crackdowns "began to decay after a short period, sometimes despite continued dosage of police presence or even increased dosage of police sanctions."[30] Jay S. Albanese and Robert D. Pursley report that law enforcement "sweeps" are essentially mass arrests of gang members on minor charges, and that they are similar to an enforced curfew in that they take young people off the streets at night and release them by the next day.[31]

Some of the innovative aggressive tactics regarding crime are based on research that indicates that a great deal of urban crime is concentrated in a few "hot spots." Lawrence Sherman, Patrick Gartin, and Michael Buerger have found that a significant portion of all police calls in Minneapolis came from a relatively few locations: bars, malls, the bus depot, hotels, and certain apartment buildings. They believed that concentrating police resources on these hot spots of crime could appreciably reduce crime.[32]

Many claim that the drastic drop in crime rates in the mid-1990s, particularly in cities like New York, were the results of aggressive, zero-tolerance anticrime policies. During this period, New York City's crime rates dropped to 30-year lows under the administration of then Police Commissioner William Bratton. As part of his crime-fighting strategy he ordered his officers to crackdown on such minor offenses as public urination, loitering, loud radios, and unlicensed street vending to improve the city's quality of life. He told his uniformed street officers to resume making low-level drug arrests and not leave them to specialized units, which the NYPD had done for many years for fear of corruption scandals. Under his policies all minor offenders were frisked for guns and checked for outstanding warrants. Computer-plotted maps were made daily to track crime every day on each and every block in the city. Bratton said, "I want to challenge the old idea that policing can't make a substantial impact on social change. American policing has been swatting at mosquitoes for 20 years. In New York we've learned how to drain the swamp."[33]

Fugitive and warrant programs have been added to the aggressive patrol actions of police departments. In Houston, in 1996, warrant enforcement generated 8,860 arrests and cleared over 38,000 cases. In New York City, the NYPD, with help from the U.S. Marshals Service and the FBI, began going after as many as 87,000 fugitive felons and 403,000 misdemeanor offenders.[34]

Regarding aggressive policing techniques, Marie Simonetti Rosen wrote,

> Clearly, 1996 was the year of the crackdown, but perhaps the most common approach was a crackdown on quality-of-life crime. In city after city, quality-of-life enforcement became a priority, in part because such a focus was desired by the community, but as important, because evidence increasingly points to the fact that going after minor violators contributes directly to reductions in major crime. . . . In growing numbers, police executives are convinced that effective policing can decrease crime, and even a growing cohort of criminologists is conceding that police work is responsible for the recent notable decline in crime. Nation-

wide, there are clear signs of departments reorganizing, refocussing and implementing anti-crime strategies, targeting problems and attacking them with verve. And from all indications it appears that their efforts are paying off, as 1996, like the years immediately preceding it, witnessed significant drops in the crime rate.[35]

The evidence seems to suggest that proactive, aggressive police strategies are effective in reducing crime, at least in target areas. However, many believe that aggressive patrol tactics breed resentment in minority areas; citizens there often believe they are the target of police suspicion and reaction. There is evidence that such aggressive police tactics as stop and frisk and rousting teenagers who congregate on street corners are the seeds from which police-citizen racial conflict grows.[36]

This leads to a serious conflict for police administrators. Do they reduce crime rates by using effective, yet aggressive police techniques and therefore risk poor relationships with lawful members of the community?

It must be stated, however, that despite the credit paid to the police in reducing crime, many criminologists and other students of crime and criminal justice point to other possible reasons for crime reduction, including the aging of the criminal-age-prone population, the increased prison and jail populations, the increased commitment of community groups in addressing crime conditions, and other such issues.

Saturation Patrol Another kind of uniformed tactical operation is saturation patrol. A larger number of uniformed officers than normal is assigned to a particular area to deal with a particular crime problem. The results of this type of strategy are mixed, according to several studies involving saturation patrol. In a study of a New York City precinct, researchers concluded that a 40 percent increase in patrol personnel resulted in 30 to 50 percent decreases in street crime.[37] A study that analyzed New York subway robberies in relation to increased patrol over an eight-year period also found that saturation patrol reduced crime. In this instance, the deployment of substantially more subway patrol officers in the evening hours resulted in a decrease in subway robberies during the hours of the patrols. After a brief decrease, however, daytime robberies increased steadily.[38]

In a study of saturation patrol in Nashville, Tennessee, three patrol areas experiencing high burglary incidences during daylight hours were given increased patrols between 8:00 A.M. and 4:00 P.M. The level of saturation raised the number of patrol cars per area from one to between four and eight. During the five weeks of the study, the number of burglary arrests increased, but there were no changes in the incidence of burglary.[39] A year later, in Nashville, four high-crime areas were given increased patrol, two during daytime hours and two during evening hours. Patrol in all areas during the saturation times was increased from one to five cars. The results indicated that daytime saturation patrols had no effect on crime, but that evening saturation patrols did decrease crime.[40]

One of the most effective tactical operations employed by the New York City Police Department during the 1980s was Operation Pressure Point. Located in the city's Lower East Side, Operation Pressure Point involved using numerous young rookie officers on foot patrol. The officers were encouraged to use aggressive field interrogation techniques and undercover opera-

---

YOU ARE THERE! »

Some Examples of Aggressive Patrol Tactics

Washington, D.C.
In the late 1980s, Washington, D.C., conducted Operation Clean Sweep. This crackdown involved more than a hundred officers who conducted roadblocks, surveillance, undercover buys, and seizures affecting fifty-nine street-corner "drug markets." In the first eighteen months, 30,000 arrests were made at a rate of approximately sixty per day. A postoperation evaluation concluded that the operation was "well-executed" and that fewer drug markets operated openly. However, drug use was found to have increased substantially, drug markets were displaced to other nearby areas, and there was a dramatic rise in homicides.

Philadelphia
A police crackdown in Philadelphia, called Cold Turkey, targeted fifty-six corner drug markets. In four days, 1,000 people were stopped and searched by a task force of 450 officers. One-third of the people stopped were arrested for disorderly conduct, and approximately 20 percent were arrested on narcotics charges. The operation was terminated in the wake of significant public protest and hostility.

Source: Adapted from Peter Reuter et al., *Drug Use and Drug Programs in the Washington Metropolitan Area* (Santa Monica, Calif.: Rand Corporation, 1988); and Mark A. R. Kleiman, "Crackdowns: The Effects of Intensive Enforcement on Retail Heroin Dealing," in *Street Level Drug Enforcement: Examining the Issues*, ed. M. Chaiken (Washington, D.C.: National Institute of Justice, 1988).

Undercover New York City police officer Mary Glatzle earned such a reputation for her decoy work that she was dubbed "Muggable Mary." Here she waits, in costume with a gray wig, for potential muggers.

tions to combat the sale and possession of drugs, which had ravaged the neighborhood for years.[41] Operation Pressure Point was so successful that real estate prices began to skyrocket, turning the Lower East Side into a gentrified, high-rent section of the city. Although crime was reduced in the target area, it actually was merely displaced to adjoining neighborhoods.

Decoy Operations

One of the primary purposes of police patrol is to prevent crime through the creation of a sense of omnipresence; potential criminals are deterred from crime by the presence or potential presence of the police. Obviously, omnipresence does not work well. We have crime both on our streets and in areas where ordinary police patrols cannot see crime developing, such as the inside of a store or the hallway of a housing project. Additionally, we have seen that retroactive investigations of crimes, with the intent to identify and arrest perpetrators, is not very effective.

During the past two decades, an innovative proactive approach to apprehending criminals in the course of committing a crime has developed—**decoy operations**. Decoy operations take several forms, among them blending and decoy.

In **blending**, officers dressed in civilian clothes try to blend into an area and patrol it on foot or in unmarked police cars in an attempt to catch a criminal in the act of committing a crime. Officers may target areas where a significant amount of crime occurs, or they may follow particular people who appear to be potential victims or potential offenders. In order to blend, officers assume the roles and dress of ordinary citizens—construction workers, shoppers, joggers, bicyclists, physically disabled persons, and so on—so that the officers, without being observed as officers, can be close enough to observe and intervene should a crime occur.

In decoy, officers dress as, and play the role of, potential victims—drunks, nurses, businesspeople, tourists, prostitutes, blind people, isolated subway riders, or defenseless elderly people. The officers wait to be the subject of a crime while a team of backup officers is ready to apprehend the violator in the act of committing the crime.

Decoy operations are most effective in combating the crimes of robbery, purse snatching, and other larcenies from the person; burglaries; and thefts of and from automobiles.

Descriptions of decoy operations in major cities contain numerous successful applications.[42] A successful decoy operation was begun by the Miami Police Department in 1991 with the establishment of an undercover decoy operation targeting tourist robberies, known as STAR (Safeguarding Tourists Against Robberies). Members of this twelve-officer unit pose as tourists sitting in parked rental cars near busy areas. When robbers strike, a backup team moves in to assist in the arrest. STAR has resulted in a 33 percent decrease in tourist robberies.[43]

The NYPD's Street Crime Unit (SCU) has been extremely successful and has served as a model for numerous other police agencies. The SCU consists of experienced volunteer officers who are aggressive and street smart. The SCU members, who receive extensive training in decoy techniques, are assigned to high-crime areas.[44] Each of New York City's seventy-six patrol precincts has its own decoy unit, called anticrime unit, composed of volunteer officers with high arrest records.

Among the more effective decoy and blending operations was another NYPD unit, the Taxi-Truck Surveillance Unit, which was organized to combat the growing number of nighttime assaults on truck and cab drivers. For a period of five years, specially equipped officers from both patrol and detective units were selected to play the roles of cabbies and truckers. This undercover approach ultimately reduced assaults and robberies of cabbies and truckers by almost 50 percent.[45]

An interesting recent decoy program in New York City to combat a rash of robberies at McDonald's and other fast-food restaurants involved officers donning McDonald's uniforms and posing as employees. In one case, a robber was apprehended by the store's "cleaners" when he passed a hold-up note to a cashier.[46]

Another recent use of disguises involved a police officer in Paulsboro, New Jersey, who was facing a growing list of persons wanted on arrest warrants. On Halloween evening, 1995, he donned a clown's outfit over his bulletproof vest and went trick-or-treating. As his subjects opened their doors, they had a real surprise. They were arrested. The officer cleared 12 warrants by arrest that evening.[47]

Anticrime and decoy strategies focus on reducing serious and violent street crimes, apprehending criminals in the act, making quality arrests, and maintaining a high conviction record. In achieving successful prosecutions in their cases, decoy operations overcome the problem police encounter when witnesses and victims are reluctant to cooperate with police and prosecutors because of fear, apathy, or interminable court delays.[48]

A San Francisco police sergeant successfully defined the goals and operations of a decoy program: "The underlying theory . . . is that the type of criminal that is responsible for the most violent street crime is an opportunist. The criminal walks the streets looking for a victim that is weaker than himself, looking for an opportunity to make a 'score' without any danger to himself, or any danger of apprehension. The decoy program is intended to respond to this type of criminal."[49]

There has been some criticism of decoy operations. As one former police commander says, "Decoy operations are often seen as entrapment, even though they rarely come close to it."[50] Also, decoy programs, in which officers dress and assume the roles of victims, can be very dangerous to the officers involved.

Stakeout Operations

Many crimes occur indoors, where passing patrol officers cannot see their occurrence. A stakeout consists of a group of heavily armed officers who hide in an area of a store or building waiting for an impending holdup. If an armed robber enters the store and attempts a robbery, the officers yell "Police!" from their hidden areas. If the perpetrators fail to drop their weapons, the officers open fire.

Stakeouts are effective in cases in which the police receive a tip that a crime is going to occur in a commercial establishment or in which the police discover or come upon a pattern. A typical pattern would be a group of liquor stores in a certain downtown commercial area that have been robbed at gunpoint with a type of consistency that indicates that it might happen again.

Stakeouts are extremely expensive in terms of police personnel. They are also controversial, because they invariably involve death or serious injury to the perpetrator. Detroit, which once had a stakeout unit called STRESS (Stop the Robberies, Enjoy Safe Streets), disbanded it because of the many deaths of perpetrators and the public furor that attended a series of highly publicized killings of robbers.[51]

Sting Operations

Sting operations, which have become a major law enforcement technique in recent years, involve using various undercover methods to apprehend thieves and recover stolen property. For example, the police rent a storefront and put the word out on the street that they will buy any stolen property—no questions asked. The police set up hidden video and audio recorders that can be used to identify "customers," who are then located and placed under arrest several months later. The audio and video recorders make excellent evidence in court.

There are numerous examples of successful stings. An FBI-run high-tech electronics store in Miami was used by drug traffickers to purchase beepers, cellular phones, and computers. The seventeen-month operation resulted in ninety-three arrests.[52]

Another FBI sting in New Jersey, in which agents posed as fences who bought 170 stolen trucks and luxury cars worth $9 million over a two-year period, netted thirty-five arrests.[53]

Another type of sting operation is directed against people wanted on warrants. These wanted persons are mailed a letter telling them that they have won an award (such as tickets to an important ball game) and that they should report to a certain location (usually a hotel) at a certain time to pick up the prize. When the person appears, he or she is arrested.

Studies of sting operations have found that they account for a large number of arrests and the recovery of a significant amount of stolen property. However, the studies have failed to demonstrate that the tactic leads to reductions in crime.[54]

A major drawback to sting operations is that they can serve as inducements to burglary and theft, because they create a market for stolen goods. Additionally, sting operations can lead to questions regarding ethics. Consider the congressional Abscam operations. Abscam was a 1978–1980 sting conducted by FBI agents against members of Congress. The agents, posing as Arab sheikhs, offered bribes to members of Congress in order to receive favors. The sting resulted in the conviction of seven members of Congress and other officials, as well as harsh criticism (by some) of the FBI for its undercover methods.

Civil Liability and Code Enforcement Teams

Many cities have turned to civil liability enforcement to attempt to deal with local problems that have a negative effect on the quality of life in their communities. These cities use civil, as well as criminal laws, to force landlords and others in control of premises to correct illegal conditions. These cities have established code enforcement teams, which consist of a number of agents from different municipal agencies working together using local ordinances and codes, as well as the criminal law, in an attempt to solve particular problems.

Fort Lauderdale, Florida, has established a code enforcement team consisting of one member each from the police, fire, building, and zoning departments. In a three-year period, Fort Lauderdale's code enforcement team demolished 124 crack cocaine houses and boarded up another 587. They collected $600,000 in fines from 300 landlords and property managers of substandard housing. Additionally, they pressured landlords into spending $5.7 million on repairs to deteriorating properties. Drug activity in the code enforcement team's targeted area dropped 57 percent. In the most recent reported year, the code enforcement team inspected approximately 2,500 dwellings, resulting in over 21,600 citations for code violations and more than sixty structures being boarded up or demolished.[55]

Milwaukee formed an interagency team to combat crack houses in the city. Representatives from the city's police department, building inspection department, city attorney's office, and Community Outreach joined forces to attack drug houses in the community. In its first year, the team closed 264 drug houses. A key to the success of the programs, says Milwaukee's police chief, was the information provided by citizens calling a community hotline.[56]

In 1997, a zero-tolerance program targeting drug houses in Worcester, Massachusetts, was so successful that it had rid neighborhoods of locations where drug activity flourished. At least sixty drug houses were driven out of business, and police made hundreds of arrests in the interagency effort. The city put pressure on landlords to clean and make repairs to their properties. The owners were also put on notice that they could lose their properties under the city's nuisance laws if criminal activity reoccurs.[57]

Worcester uses very aggressive methods to conduct their zero tolerance program. Uniformed and undercover police officers flood the streets of the target areas, making arrests and maintaining a high-profile presence that keeps potential drug buyers away from the area.

The following is a very graphic example of the squalid and dangerous conditions code enforcement teams are designed to combat,

> Vacant apartments have become a maze of traps, meant to block out drug dealers' rivals and the police. Electrified wires have been stretched across window frames. Holes have been smashed in the walls and floors to provide easy escape routes. And hallway floors have been smeared with Vaseline to trip unwary intruders.
>
> They spray-painted in the hallways where you could buy drugs. They later spray painted that they would kill all the informers.[58]

Efforts against Drunk Drivers

During the 1990s, much attention has been paid to the tremendous damage done on our highways by drunk drivers. Efforts by such groups as Mothers Against Drunk Driving (MADD) and Students Against Drunk

Police officer conducting a field sobriety test at a mobile field sobriety checkpoint.

Driving (SADD) have caused the police to pay particular attention to the problem.

In 1995, according to the National Safety Council, alcohol-related fatalities rose to 17,274 from 16,589 in 1994. (Total number of driving fatalities in 1995 was 43,900.) The worst-ever year for alcohol-related fatalities was 1986 when 24,045 deaths occurred.[59]

Patrol officers cannot be expected to deal effectively with the problem of drunk drivers, because so much of the officers' time is occupied by other duties. To enforce the laws against driving while intoxicated (DWI) or driving under the influence (DUI), the police have resorted to sobriety checkpoints. The following describes the typical DWI checkpoint or roadblock:

> Officers conducting a roadblock may stop all traffic or some numerically objective number, like every fifth vehicle. After a vehicle is directed to the side of the road, an officer may request to see an operator's license and vehicle registration and may ask several questions to observe the driver's demeanor. If the officer detects the signs of inebriation, the motorist may be directed to move the vehicle to a secondary area, step out, and submit to a roadside sobriety coordination or breathalyzer test. The failure to pass either test constitutes sufficient probable cause for arrest.[60]

YOU ARE THERE! »

Sobriety Checkpoints

In an effort to control driving under the influence of alcohol and drugs, the director of the Michigan Department of State Police appointed state and local police officials, prosecutors, and the University of Michigan's transportation researchers to a Sobriety Checkpoint Advisory Committee. This committee created guidelines governing the following issues regarding sobriety checkpoints: site selection, publicity, and police procedures while conducting the sobriety checks.

Under Michigan's program, checkpoints were set up at selected sites, and all drivers passing through the checkpoints were stopped and briefly examined for signs of intoxication. Drivers who showed evidence of being under the influence were directed out of the traffic flow for a license and registration check and further sobriety tests. If the tests showed intoxication, arrests were made.

One court case that arose from Michigan's policy was *Michigan Department of State Police v. Sitz*. The checkpoint at issue in the case conformed to the guidelines just described and operated for one hour and fifteen minutes, during which the state police stopped 126 individuals for an average delay of twenty-five seconds each. Officers detained two drivers for field sobriety testing, one of whom they arrested for driving under the influence (DUI). A third motorist, who drove through the checkpoint without stopping, was pulled over by an officer in an observation vehicle and arrested for DUI.

To determine the constitutionality of the sobriety checkpoint in this case, the court focused on (1) the gravity of the public concerns addressed by the checkpoint, (2) the effectiveness of the checkpoint, and (3) the severity of the checkpoint's interference with individual liberty. The court found that Michigan's procedures were constitutional.

Source: *Michigan Department of State Police v. Sitz* 110 S.Ct. 2481 (1990); and Louis DiPietro, "Sobriety Checkpoints: Constitutional Considerations," *FBI Law Enforcement Bulletin*, Washington, D.C., October 1992, pp. 27–32.

Undercover Operations

An **undercover investigation** may be defined as a form of investigation in which an investigator assumes a different identity in order to obtain information or achieve another investigatory purpose. The undercover investigator generally plays the role of another person.

In an undercover investigation there are many things the investigator can be doing, including merely observing or performing certain actions that are designed to get other people to do something, or to react to, or interact with the investigator in a certain way. The primary function of the investigator in these cases is to play a role without anyone realizing that he or she is playing a role. In policing, the primary purpose of the undercover operation most often is the collection of evidence of crimes.

Gary T. Marx has identified several general types of undercover investigations, including police undercover investigations, federal undercover investigations, and private security undercover investigations.[61] This section will discuss these types of investigations and operations and will pay particular attention to the drug undercover investigation. Other types of investigations and police proactive tactics that could be described as undercover investigations, sting operations, decoy operations, and stakeouts were previously discussed in depth in this chapter.

Police Undercover Investigations

These investigations generally include drug undercover investigations; stings, including warrant stings and fencing stings that involve the buying and selling of stolen goods and other contraband; decoy operations targeted against the crimes of robbery, burglary, and assault; antiprostitution operations; and operations involving the infiltration and arrest of people involved in organized crime, white collar crime, and corruption.

Police undercover officers have a dangerous yet often rewarding job. In a 1994 news article, some of the 200 undercover officers of the New York City Transit Authority Police Department talked about their jobs.

> "Undercovers are a better breed—more gutsy," said Officer William Diaz, a 34-year-old transit officer in an elite anti-crime unit in downtown Brooklyn. To conceal his identity from the criminals who work the stations he patrols, he continually grows a beard, cuts it off and grows it again.
>
> Officer Diaz's 33-year-old partner, Denise James, said her commitment to undercover work arose from seeing crime's toll on her own neighborhood. She said, "I got tired of people taking crack and robbing people in hallways. I wanted to make a small dent on crime in my neighborhood.
>
> "What I like is surprising people," she said. "You get the perpetrator. The victim is thankful. When you make the collar, the criminal says, 'You're a cop?' That's what I call satisfying."[62]

Federal Undercover Investigations

These investigations generally include efforts at detecting and arresting people involved in political corruption, insurance fraud, labor racketeering, and other types of organized conspiracy-type crimes.

Perhaps the classic case of a successful undercover investigation was the work of FBI Special Agent Joseph D. Pistone who assumed the cover identity of Donnie Brasco. Pistone began his infiltration of La Cosa Nostra (the American Mafia) in 1976 and continued it for six years. Pistone was so completely accepted by the Mafia that he was able to move freely among all the Mafia families and learn their secrets. He was so effective that he had to terminate his undercover operations because he was about to be inducted into the Mafia as a "made man" and was expected to kill another Mafiosi. As a result of Pistone's work more than one hundred federal criminal convictions were obtained, dealing a severe blow to Mafia operations throughout the United States.

An FBI undercover investigation shows the success of the undercover investigation concept. For two years, FBI agents conducted Operation Road Spill, in which they established a bogus company, Southern Leasing Systems of South Kearny, New Jersey. The agents posed as shady business people who were willing to pay cash for stolen BMWs, Acura Legends, and other luxury cars. During the investigation they bought 120 stolen cars for a fraction of their value.[63]

Private Security Undercover Investigations

According to Marx, these investigations generally involve inventory losses, pilferage, willful neglect of machinery, unreported absenteeism, "general employee attitudes," and "delicate investigations."[64] In addition to Marx's categories, many other categories can be added to private security undercover investigations, including criminal, marital, civil, and child custody cases, to name only a few. This section will cover four important private security undercover investigations: shopping

Dempsey's Law

But She Was 6 Feet Tall and Looked Like She Was 23!

Professor, you're talking about proactive and covert investigations—are they, like, stings?

Yes, Daniel. Stings are generally proactive and covert investigations, meaning that they are police initiated and secret or undercover.

My father was the victim of a sting last night. He owns a deli and this young woman came in about 6 p.m. She took a six-pack of Bud from the box, paid my father for it, and immediately left the deli. Five minutes later the police came in and told my father that he had just sold beer to a minor and issued him a summons.

Dan, business owners have to be very careful selling beer, alcohol, or cigarettes to youthful-looking people. The police in your father's area are very aggressive in enforcing the laws regarding beer, alcohol, and cigarette sales. Many of the students in our criminal justice program volunteer to work with the police participating in these sting operations.

Yeah, Professor, but my father said she looked like she was about 23 years old, not 19, like the police told him. He said she was about 6 feet tall, real foxy, and dressed to the nines. Doesn't the fact that my father thought she looked older relieve him of criminal responsibility?

Not in this state, Dan. We have a legal concept called strict liability regarding certain laws. Sale of alcohol is one of those laws. Strict liability means that the prosecutor does not have to prove criminal intent on the part of the person committing a crime. Just the mere fact that he sold her the alcohol and the fact that she was less than 21 is enough to charge him with the crime.

Professor Dempsey, I probably shouldn't admit it, but I think I'm the one Dan is talking about. Sorry about that, Dan. I didn't know that was your father's store.

Kimberly, you were volunteering with the 6th Precinct again yesterday evening?

Yeah, we hit 8 delis and two liquor stores on Route 25. I was only carded in one place and I couldn't make a buy because I didn't have proof and the guy refused to sell me the beer. The police gave summonses in the other nine places because they sold to me without carding me.

Note: Kimberly is actually Kimberly Dean of East Setauket, New York. Kimberly, who does stand 6 feet tall, was actually 19 years old when this event occurred.

Kimberly volunteered many hours working with the Suffolk County Police Department doing proactive, covert sting operations regarding the illegal sale of alcohol. Regarding her work with police, Kimberly says, "It definitely makes store owners aware of who they are selling alcohol to. Fifteen-year-olds can go in and get beer sometimes—it's pathetic."

Kimberly's parents, Marie and Sandy, are proud of their daughter's involvement with the police and say, "Kimberly is certainly aware of the important issues in our community, and we couldn't be more proud of her." Kimberly is pursuing her college career and is considering law enforcement as a career choice.

---

services, silent witness programs, internal intelligence programs, and the store detective.

Shopping Services Wackenhut Investigations offers prospective business clients its "Integrity Testing" and other "Shopping Services." Wackenhut calls its integrity analysis the single most important element of a shopping service. This test of employees' honesty is performed by "shoppers" (undercover agents) posing as customers and is designed to act as a deterrent to inventory shrinkage, detect dishonest employees, and provide evidence for prosecuting employees caught stealing.[65]

> ## YOU ARE THERE! »
>
> ### The Legality of Police Undercover Drug Investigations
>
> ***Gordon v. Warren Consolidated Board of Education***
> High-school officials had placed an undercover officer into regular classes to investigate student drug use. After the investigation, several students were arrested and convicted of participating in the drug trade. They appealed their convictions claiming that the actions of the school officials violated their rights under the First Amendment of the United States Constitution. Their appeal was dismissed by appellate courts ruling that the presence of the police officer working undercover did not constitute any more than a "chilling" effect on the students' First Amendment rights, since it did not disrupt classroom activities or education and it did not have any tangible effect on inhibiting expression of particular views in the classroom.
>
> Source: Based on *Gordon v. Warren Consolidated Board of Education*, 706 F.2d 778 6th Cir. (1983).

Silent Witness Programs Wackenhut also offers prospective corporate clients its "Silent Witness" program. The function of the Silent Witness Program is to provide a method for honest, dedicated employees who are concerned about wrongdoing in the workplace to volunteer helpful information without compromising themselves. Wackenhut reports that it created the program because of its conviction that the vast majority of employees are honest, that they are disturbed by the threat of illegal activities to their employer, their own morale, and their jobs—but are reluctant to speak out because they fear being revealed as an informer.[66]

The Wackenhut program uses some techniques familiar to the Neighborhood Crime Watch and media TIPS programs. Silent Witness utilizes a telephone number readily available to employees throughout the facility or company. Materials explain the program and guarantee anonymity, and all calls are monitored by trained Wackenhut personnel in its Communications Center. Wackenhut simply acts as a third-party conduit, accepting the volunteered information and passing it on to the client employer. The employee is never asked for his or her name or for other information that would lead to the caller's identity, is invited to call again, and is given a way to claim any reward offered.

Internal Intelligence Program Private investigative firms offer corporations undercover internal intelligence programs in which they plant undercover agents into a corporation's business operations to make observations and report back to the company.

Wackenhut reports its internal intelligence program has been used successfully in combating theft of funds and merchandise, use of alcohol or drugs on the job, gambling, sabotage, and planned disruption by anti-management activists.

Pinkerton Inc. reports that one of the most effective ways to combat avoidable losses is through undercover investigations. It describes its undercover operations in the following way:

> [S]pecially selected and trained individuals are temporarily hired as members of the work force. They mix into the company in ordinary capacities, then observe and report activities to their supervisor. . . . The net result of an effective investigation should be an objective and unbiased assessment of employee behavior, morale and supervisory competence. In the best undercover work, both good and bad information is reported by individuals with the experience and objectivity to find the truth under difficult circumstances.[67]

The Store Detective One of the most common types of undercover private investigations is the store detective (also known as a loss prevention specialist). Shoplifting is one of the most common crimes in the United States. Statistics available through the U.S. Department of Justice reveal that shoplifting is the fastest-growing crime in the larceny-theft category—up 22 percent between 1986 and 1990, with more than one million arrests reported each year since 1989. However, these figures may be only the tip of the iceberg; some experts speculate that for every shoplifter caught, as many as 10 to 20 others go undetected.[68]

Shrinkage is a major problem for retailers. The term "shrinkage" is used by retailers to describe the difference between inventory on hand at the beginning of the year and inventory on hand at year-end, taking into account the year's sales. In a national retail security survey, the average shrinkage for surveyed department stores was 2.09 percent. Using this rate, a department store chain with merchandise sales of $1 billion would have shrinkage of almost $21 million. In the judgment of the survey's respondents, 38.4 percent of all shrinkage was caused by shoplifting.[69] Another major cause of shrinkage is employee theft.

The goal of the store detective is to apprehend persons stealing property from the store. After apprehending the shoplifter, the store detective retrieves the stolen property. In many cases the police are called to arrest the violator and process him or her through the criminal justice system.

Some stores use sophisticated camera equipment to scan the store for people stealing merchandise, whereas other stores rely on a store detective "roaming" the store, appearing to look like an ordinary shopper.

Many college students work their way through college by working as store detectives or loss prevention specialists. Store detective is also a good entry-level job in private security from which employees can work their way up to security management.

Drug Undercover Investigations

At least three general methods can be used in conducting drug undercover investigations. The first involves infiltrating criminal organizations that sell large amounts of drugs. The method of that kind of undercover operation is to buy larger and larger amounts of drugs to reach as high as possible into the particular organizational hierarchy. Lower members of the criminal hierarchy have access only to a fixed quantity of drugs. To obtain larger amounts they have to introduce the investigator to their source or connection, who is generally someone in the upper echelon of the organization or a member of a more sophisticated organization. These operations generally require sophisticated electronic surveillance measures and large sums of money. Also, they can be very lengthy and dangerous to undercover investigators.

The next method that can be used to attack drug syndicates or drug locations is the process of "staking out" (a fixed surveillance) a particular location and making detailed observations of the conditions that are indicative of drug sales, such as the arrival and brief visit of numerous autos and people. These observations are best if recorded on video to establish probable cause for obtaining a search warrant. If a judge agrees with the

PATROLLING THE NET

The Drug Culture Flourishes on the Net

As parents, teachers, police, and others are trying to dissuade young people from using illegal drugs, the Internet may be emerging as an alluring shopping mall where anyone with a computer and access to the Net can find out how to get high on LSD, eavesdrop on what it is like to snort heroin or cocaine, find the going price for marijuana, or copy the chemical formula for methamphetamine or speed.

Although many are concerned about pornography and free speech on the web, few have bothered to worry about the growing drug culture on the Net and how it might influence young people. Sophisticated graphics, alluring cartoons, relative anonymity, fun interactive sites, and freedom to browse make the Internet a dangerous place for young people seeking to experiment in drugs.

High Times, a monthly magazine that has popularized the drug culture for over two decades, has created its own web site. The magazine's homepage is receiving 200,000 visitors a month. *High Times* dispenses an array of online advertising and other profit-motivated services that give such advice as coaching on how to beat a drug test. They even advertise a related telephone service that gives advice on drugs at $1.95 a minute.

"We're really losing the war on the Internet," says a spokesperson for the Community Anti-Drug Coalitions of America.

Some of the scariest aspects of the drug culture comes from the chatrooms:

- In response to a query over whether it was safe to mix methamphetamine with alcohol—a dangerous combination: "Yeah, you can drink on speed and drink and drink."
- Suggestions for first-time users of ecstasy.
- Explicit instructions for growing, processing, and consuming drugs.
- Do-it-yourself guides to drug use.
- Endorsements of marijuana and other drugs.
- How to get high legally.
- Growing hallucinogens.
- "Cannabis alchemy."
- "Cooking with cannabis, and other 'trippy, phat, groovy things.'"

Source: Adapted from Christopher S. Wren, "A Seductive Drug Culture Flourishes on the Internet," *New York Times,* 20 June 1997, p. A-1, 22.

probable cause, he or she can issue a search warrant, which can then be executed against a particular person, automobile, or premise. These investigations can be very lengthy and involve extensive sophisticated electronic surveillance.

The third method is the undercover "buy and bust." The undercover drug "buy and bust" is an operation in which an undercover police officer purchases a quantity of drugs from a subject, then leaves the scene, contacts the backup team and identifies the seller. The backup team, in or out of uniform, responds to the location of the sale and arrests the seller, based on the description given by the undercover officer. The legal basis of the arrest is probable cause to believe that a crime was committed and that the subject is the perpetrator of the crime. Based upon the legal arrest, the backup team can search the subject and seize any illegal drugs. If the arrest occurs inside a premise, the backup team can seize any illegal substances that are in plain view. The undercover officer then goes to the police facility the subject was brought to and makes a positive identification of the subject from a hidden location, generally through a one-way mirror or window. By viewing the suspect through the one-way mirror or window, the undercover officer cannot be seen and can be used again in the same role.

The buy and bust is generally utilized in low-level drug operations that receive numerous complaints from the community. The purpose is to take the person into custody as quickly as possible to relieve the quality of life problem in the neighborhood.

A sufficient number of officers is extremely important in undercover "buy and bust" operations. The basic players in the game are

1. The undercover officer (U/C).
2. The ghost officer. This officer closely shadows or follows the U/C as she or he travels within an area and approaches the dealer.
3. The backup team. This should consist of at least five officers, if possible, who can watch from a discreet location to ensure the safety of the U/C and ghost and who can move in when ready to arrest the dealer.
4. The supervisor. He or she is the critical member of the team. He or she plans and directs the operation and makes all key decisions.

The arrest in the buy and bust operation can also be delayed until the officers obtain an arrest warrant.

Entrapment

Often people believe that undercover operations by the police are entrapment. What is entrapment? **Entrapment** is defined as inducing an individual to commit a crime he or she did not contemplate, for the sole purpose of instituting a criminal prosecution against the offender.[70] Entrapment is a defense to criminal responsibility that arises from improper acts committed against an accused by another, usually an undercover agent. Inducement is the key word; when police encouragement plays upon the weaknesses of innocent persons and beguiles them into committing crimes they normally would not attempt, it can be deemed improper as entrapment and the evidence barred under the exclusionary rule.

The police, by giving a person the opportunity to commit a crime, are not guilty of entrapment. For example, an undercover officer sitting on the sidewalk, apparently drunk, with a ten dollar bill sticking out of his or her pocket is not forcing a person to take the money even though he or she is giving a person the opportunity to take the money. If a person takes advantage of the apparent drunk and takes the money, he or she is committing a larceny. The entrapment defense is not applicable to this situation. However, when the police action is outrageous and forces an otherwise innocent person to commit a crime, the entrapment defense may apply.

The U.S. Supreme Court in *Jacobson v. U.S.* (1992) ruled that the government's action of repeatedly, for two and a half years, sending a man advertisements of material of a sexual nature, causing the man to order an illegal sexually oriented magazine constituted entrapment. It ruled that law enforcement officers "may not originate a criminal design, implant in an innocent person's mind the disposition to commit a criminal act, and then induce commission of the crime so that the government may prosecute."[71]

Regarding this case, Thomas V. Kukura in a recent article in the *FBI Law Enforcement Bulletin* made the following recommendations:

> To ensure that undercover investigations do not give rise to successful claims of entrapment or related defenses, all law enforcement offices should consider the following three points before conducting undercover investigations. First, while reasonable suspicion is not legally necessary to initiate an undercover investigation, officers should nonethe-

YOU ARE THERE!

Jacobson v. United States 1992

In February 1984, a 56-year-old Nebraska farmer (hereinafter the defendant), with no record or reputation for violating any law, lawfully ordered and received from an adult bookstore two magazines that contained photographs of nude teenage boys. Subsequent to this, Congress passed the Child Protection Act of 1984, which made it illegal to receive such material through the mail. Later that year, the U.S. Postal Service obtained the defendant's name from a mailing list seized at the adult bookstore, and in January 1985, began an undercover operation targeting him.

Over the next two and a half years, Government investigators, through five fictitious organizations and a bogus pen pal, repeatedly contacted the defendant by mail, exploring his attitudes toward child pornography. The communications also contained disparaging remarks about the legitimacy and constitutionality of efforts to restrict the availability of sexually explicit material, and finally, offered the defendant the opportunity to order illegal child pornography.

Twenty-six months after the mailings to the defendant commenced, Government investigators sent him a brochure advertising photographs of young boys engaging in sex. At this time, the defendant placed an order that was never filled.

Meanwhile, the investigators attempted to further pique the defendant's interest through a fictitious letter decrying censorship and suggesting a method of getting material to him without the "prying eyes of U.S. Customs." A catalogue was then sent to him, and he ordered a magazine containing child pornography.

After a controlled delivery of a photocopy of the magazine, the defendant was arrested. A search of his home revealed only the material he received from the Government and the two sexually oriented magazines he lawfully acquired in 1984.

The defendant was charged with receiving child pornography through the mail in violation of 18 U.S.C. 2252(a)(2)(A). He defended himself by claiming that the Government's conduct was outrageous, that the Government needed reasonable suspicion before it could legally begin an investigation of him, and that he had been entrapped by the Government's investigative techniques. The lower Federal courts rejected these defenses, but in a 5-4 decision, the Supreme Court reversed his conviction based solely on the entrapment claim.

In Jacobson, the Supreme Court held that law enforcement officers "may not originate a criminal design, implant in an innocent person's mind the disposition to commit a criminal act, and then induce commission of the crime so that the Government may prosecute."

Source: Based on *Jacobson v. United States*, 112 S.Ct. 1535 (1992); and, Thomas V. Kukura, J.D., "Undercover Investigations and the Entrapment Defense: Recent Court Cases," *FBI Law Enforcement Bulletin*, April 1993, pp. 27–32.

less be prepared to articulate a legitimate law enforcement purpose for beginning such an investigation. Second, law enforcement officers should, to the extent possible, avoid using persistent or coercive techniques, and instead, merely create an opportunity or provide the facilities for the target to commit a crime. Third, officers should document and be prepared to articulate the factors demonstrating a defendant was disposed to commit the criminal act prior to Government contact.[72]

Chapter Summary

This chapter discussed new approaches to traditional police operations. Alternatives to random routine patrol and rapid response to citizen's calls to 911 for service include directed patrol, split force patrol, and differential response to calls for service. Alternatives to retroactive investigation of past crimes by detectives include improved detective operations and career criminal or repeat offender programs.

New proactive tactics in police operations include uniformed tactical operations (aggressive patrol and saturation patrol), decoy operations, stakeout operations, sting operations, code enforcement teams, and efforts against drunk drivers.

The chapter also discussed undercover operations, including police, federal, and private security undercover operations. It also discussed the legal concept of entrapment and how it affects undercover operations and proactive tactics.

Learning Check

1. Name and describe three alternatives to random routine patrol and rapid response to citizens' calls to 911.
2. Discuss the innovations to police detective operations motivated by the Rand Study and other studies.
3. Name some of the new proactive tactics employed by the police to deal with crime problems and criminals.
4. Discuss the rationale behind repeat offender programs (ROPS) and give some examples.
5. Describe the three major types of undercover drug operations.
6. Define entrapment and give some examples.

Review Exercise

After you receive your degree in criminal justice, you are hired by the Averagetown Police Department as an assistant and consultant to the police commissioner. Averagetown has several crime problems, including robberies at its fast food restaurants, thefts from autos in public parking lots, burglaries, and some low-level drug dealing in the town's commercial area and at the local high school. Of the department's 100 officers, 10 are assigned to the detective unit to investigate past crimes, 5 are assigned to traffic duties, 5 are assigned to administrative duties, and the rest are assigned to the uniformed patrol force.

Based on your reading of this chapter, what would you advise the police commissioner to do?

Web Exercise

Patrol over to the National Institute of Justice's web site. Find recent studies regarding innovative police proactive programs, such as decoy operations, civil liability and code enforcement teams, and the like. Describe several of these programs and evaluate them regarding their effectiveness in crime control.

Key Concepts

directed patrol
split force patrol
differential response to calls for service
Managing Criminal Investigations (MCI)
repeat offender programs (ROPS)
decoy operations
blending
sting operations
undercover investigations
entrapment

Notes

1. Peter Johnson, "Crime Wave Sweeps Networks Newscasts," *USA Today,* 13 August 1997, p. 3-D.
2. J. W. Warren, M. L. Forst, and M. M. Estrella, "Directed Patrol: An Experiment That Worked," *Police Chief,* July 1979, pp. 48–49; Gary W. Cordner, "The Effects of Directed Patrol: A Natural Quasi-Experiment in Pontiac," in *Contemporary Issues in Law Enforcement,* ed. James J. Fyfe (Beverly Hills, Calif.: Sage, 1981), pp. 242–261; George J. Sullivan, *Directed Patrol* (Kansas City, Mo.: Kansas City Police Department, Operations Resource Unit, 1976).
3. Lawrence Sherman, James Shaw, and Dennis Rogan, *The Kansas City Gun Experiment* (Washington, D.C.: National Institute of Justice, 1994).
4. Joseph Senna and Larry Siegel, *Introduction to Criminal Justice,* 7th ed., (Minneapolis/St. Paul: West, 1996), p. 269.
5. James M. Tien, James W. Simon, and Richard C. Larson, *An Alternative Approach in Police Patrol: The Wilmington Split-Force Experiment* (Cambridge, Mass.: Public Systems Evaluation, 1977).
6. "Faced with a Crime Wave, Houston Cops 'Wave Back': Intensive Patrols Hit the Streets, But Union Blasts Directive Not to Field Calls for Service," *Law Enforcement News,* 15 December 1991, p. 3.
7. "Houston Cops 'Wave Back,'" p. 3.
8. Michael T. Farmer, ed., *Differential Police Response Strategies* (Washington D.C.: Police Executive Research Forum, 1981). Also, see Robert Worden, "Toward Equity and Efficiency in Law Enforcement: Differential Police Response," *American Journal of Police* 12 (1993): 1–24.
9. Robert Sheehan and Gary W. Cordner, *Introduction to Police Administration,* 2d ed. (Cincinnati: Anderson, 1989), p. 554.
10. Michael F. Cahn and James M. Tien, *An Alternative Approach in Police Response: The Wilmington Management of Demand Program* (Cambridge, Mass.: Public Systems Evaluation, 1981); and J. Thomas McEwen, Edward F. Connors III, and Marcia J. Cohen, *Evaluation of the Differential Police Responses Field Test* (Washington, D.C.: National Institute of Justice, 1986).
11. National Advisory Commission on Criminal Justice Standards and Goals, *Police* (Washington, D.C.: U.S. Government Printing Office, 1973).
12. Donald F. Cawley et al., *Managing Criminal Investigations: Manual* (Washington, D.C.: National Institute of Justice, 1977).
13. Ilene Greenberg and Robert Wasserman, *Managing Criminal Investigations* (Washington, D.C.: National Institute of Justice, 1975); and Cawley et al., *Managing Criminal Investigations.*

14. Greenberg and Wasserman, *Managing Criminal Investigations.*
15. Greenberg and Wasserman, *Managing Criminal Investigations.*
16. John E. Eck, *Managing Case Assignments: The Burglary Investigation Decision Model Replication* (Washington, D.C.: Police Executive Research Forum, 1979).
17. Federal Bureau of Investigation, *Uniformed Crime Reports: Crime in the United States* (Washington, D.C.: Federal Bureau of Investigation).
18. Susan E. Martin and Lawrence W. Sherman, "Selective Apprehension: A Police Strategy for Repeat Offenders," *Criminology,* February 1986, pp. 155–173.
19. Marcia Chaiken and Jan Chaiken, *Priority Prosecutors of High-Rate Dangerous Offenders* (Washington, D.C.: National Institute of Justice, 1991), as cited in Stephen Goldsmith, "Targeting High-Rate Offenders: Asking Some Tough Questions," *Law Enforcement News,* July/August 1991, p. 11.
20. Goldsmith, "Targeting High-Rate Offenders."
21. Stephen Schack, Theodore H. Schell, and William G. Gay, *Specialized Patrol: Improving Patrol Productivity,* vol. 2 (Washington, D.C.: National Institute of Justice, 1977), p. 1.
22. Charles Whited, *The Decoy Man* (New York: Playboy Press, 1973), p. 12.
23. J. E. Boydstun, *San Diego Field Interrogation: Final Report* (Washington, D.C.: Police Foundation, 1975).
24. James Q. Wilson and Barbara Boland, *The Effect of Police on Crime* (Washington, D.C.: National Institute of Justice, 1979).
25. H. Lawrence Ross, *Deterring the Drunk Driver: Legal Policy and Social Control* (Lexington, Mass.: D.C. Heath, 1982); and, Samuel Walker, *Sense and Nonsense about Crime* (Monterey, Calif.: Brooks/Cole, 1985), pp. 82–85.
26. James Q. Wilson and Barbara Boland, "The Effect of Police on Crime," *Law and Society Review* 12 (1978): 367–384.
27. Robert Sampson and Jacqueline Cohen, "Deterrent Effects of the Police on Crime: A Replication and Theoretical Extension," *Law and Society Review* 22 (1988): 163–191.
28. Perry Shapiro and Harold Votey, "Deterrence and Subjective Probabilities of Arrest: Modeling Individual Decisions to Drink and Drive in Sweden," *Law and Society Review* 18 (1984): 111–149.
29. Douglas Smith and Patrick Gartin, "Specifying Specific Deterrence: The Influence of Arrest on Future Criminal Activity," *American Sociological Review* 54 (1989): 94–105.
30. Lawrence W. Sherman, "Police Crackdowns: Initial and Residual Deterrence," in *Crime and Justice: A Review of Research,* vol. 12, ed. M. Tonry and N. Morris (Chicago: University of Chicago Press, 1990), p. 1–48.
31. Jay S. Albanese and Robert D. Pursley, *Crime in America: Some Existing and Emerging Issues* (Englewood Cliffs, N.J.: Regents/Prentice-Hall, 1993), p. 210.
32. Lawrence Sherman, Patrick Gartin, and Michael Buerger, "Hot Spots of Predatory Crime: Routine Activities and the Criminology of Place," *Criminology* 27 (1989): 27–55. Also, see Dennis Roncek and Pamela Maier, "Bars, Blocks, and Crimes Revisited: Linking the Theory of Routine Activities to the Empiricism of 'Hot Spots'," *Criminology* 29 (1991): 725–753.
33. *Law Enforcement News,* 31 October 1995, p. 1. Also, see John S. Dempsey, *Criminal Justice Update* (Minneapolis/St. Paul: West, April 1996), p. 3.
34. Marie Simonetti Rosen, "Forget Events in the Spotlight—Local PD's Are Where the Action Is," *Law Enforcement News,* 31 December 1996, p. 1.
35. Rosen, "Forget Events in the Spotlight."
36. Lawrence Sherman, "Policing Communities: What Works," *Crime and Justice,* ed. A. J. Reiss and Michael Tonry (Chicago: University of Chicago Press, 1986), pp. 366–379.
37. S. J. Press, *Some Effects of an Increase in Police Manpower in the 20th Precinct of New York* (New York: Rand Institute, 1971).
38. J. M. Chaiken, M. W. Lawless, and K. A. Stenson, *The Impact of Police Activity on Crime: Robberies in the New York City Subway System* (New York: Rand Institute, 1974).
39. J. P. Schnelle et al., "Social Evaluation Research: The Evaluation of Two Police Patrolling Strategies," *Journal of Applied Behavior Analysis* 8 (1975): 232–240.
40. J. P. Schnelle et al., "Patrol Evaluation Research: A Multiple-Baseline Analysis of Saturation Police Patrolling during Day and Night Hours," *Journal of Applied Behavior Analysis* 10 (1977): 33–40.
41. Lynn Zimmer, "Proactive Policing against Street-Level Drug Trafficking," *American Journal of Police* 9 (1990): 43–65.
42. ABT Associates, *New York City Anti-crime Patrol: Exemplary Project Validation Report* (Washington, D.C.: National Institute of Justice, 1974); and Gary T. Marx, "The New Police Undercover Work," in *Thinking about Police: Contemporary Readings,* ed. Carl B. Klockars (New York: McGraw-Hill, 1983), pp. 201–202.
43. "Miami Seeks to Aid Tourist-Crime Target," *Law Enforcement News,* 31 October 1991, p. 4.
44. Andrew Halper and Richard Ku, *New York City Police Department Street Crime Unit* (Washington, D.C.: National Institute of Justice, n.d.).
45. Patrick J. McGovern and Charles P. Connolly, "Decoys, Disguises, Danger—New York City's Nonuniform Street Patrol," *FBI Law Enforcement Bulletin,* October 1976, pp. 16–26.

46. *New York Post,* 23 December 1995, p. 7. Also, see Dempsey, *Criminal Justice Update,* p. 2.
47. *Newsday,* 2 November 1995, p. A-7. Also, see Dempsey, *Criminal Justice Update,* p. 2.
48. "Miami Seeks to Aid Tourist-Crime Targets," p. 4.
49. Bernard Edelman, "Blending," *Police,* September 1979, pp. 53–58.
50. Anthony V. Bouza, *The Police Mystique: An Insider's Look at Cops, Crime, and the Criminal Justice System* (New York: Plenum Press, 1990), p. 93.
51. Bouza, *Police Mystique,* pp. 92–93.
52. Jeannie DeQuine, "High-Tech Drug Sting Zaps 93," *USA Today,* 7 December 1988, p. 3.
53. "Car Ring Sting," *USA Today,* 13 July 1988, p. 3.
54. Carl B. Klockars, "The Modern Sting," in *Thinking about Police: Contemporary Readings,* ed. Carl B. Klockars (New York: McGraw-Hill, 1983), pp. 217–226.
55. Joseph M. Donisi, "Police Practices: Ft. Lauderdale's Code Enforcement Team," *FBI Law Enforcement Bulletin,* March 1992, pp. 24–25.
56. Philip Arreola and Edward N. Kondracki, "Cutback Management, Cost Containment and Increased Productivity," *Police Chief,* October 1992, p. 118.
57. "Expanding Zero Tolerance (The Crackdown, Not the Tolerance)," *Law Enforcement News,* 30 April 1997, pp. 1, 10.
58. John Sullivan, "Taking Back a Drug-Plagued Tenement, Step One: Get the Dealers Out," *New York Times,* 16 August 1997, pp. 25–26.
59. "Slow Down, You're Movin' Too Fast: Highway Traffic Deaths Creep Upward," *Law Enforcement News,* 15 December 1996, p. 5.
60. Jerome O. Campane, "The Constitutionality of Drunk Driver Roadblocks," *FBI Law Enforcement Bulletin,* July 1984, pp. 24–31.
61. Gary T. Marx, "The New Police Undercover Work," *Urban Life,* January 1980, pp. 399–446.
62. Clifford Krauss, "Undercover Police Ride Wide Range of Emotion: Boredom and the Adrenaline Rush," *New York Times,* 29 August 1994, p. B-3.
63. Robert D. McFadden, "F.B.I. Sting: Hot Cars, Great Deals, 30 Suspects," *New York Times,* 9 September 1994, p. B-1.
64. Marx, "The New Police Undercover Work."
65. Wackenhut Investigations Division, *Integrity Testing and Other Shopping Services* (Coral Gables, Fla.: The Wackenhut Corporation, 1995).
66. Wackenhut Investigations Division, *Investigative Services* (Coral Gables, Fla.: The Wackenhut Corporation, 1995).
67. Pinkerton, *Pinkerton Reference Guide to Investigation Services,* 3rd ed. (Encino, Calif.: Pinkerton Security and Investigation Services, 1995), p. 10.
68. John McNamara, "Helping Merchants Mind the Store," *Police Chief,* October 1993, pp. 90–92.
69. McNamara, "Helping Merchants Mind the Store."
70. George E. Rush, *The Dictionary of Criminal Justice,* 4th ed., (Guilford, Conn.: Dushkin Publishing Group, 1994), p. 124.
71. *Jacobson v. U.S.* 112 S.Ct. 1535 (1992); and Thomas V. Kukura, "Undercover Investigations and the Entrapment Defense: Recent Court Cases," *FBI Law Enforcement Bulletin,* April 1993, pp. 27–32.
72. Kukura, "Undercover Investigations and the Entrapment Defense."

9

Police and the Community

Chapter Outline

The Need for Proper Police-Community Relationships
Human Relations, Public Relations, Community Relations
Public Opinion and the Police
Police and Minority Communities
   Multiculturalism
   The African-American Community
   The Hispanic-American Community
   The Asian-American Community
   Native Americans
   Women
   The Gay Community
   New Immigrants
Police and Special Populations
   Senior Citizens' Programs
   Programs for Young People
   Assistance for the Homeless
   Help for Crime Victims
   Help for Disabled People
Community Crime Prevention Programs
   Neighborhood Watch Programs
   Crime Stoppers
   Citizen Patrols
   Citizen Marches
   Citizen Volunteer Programs
   Home Security Surveys and Operation Identification
   National Night Out
   Police Storefront Stations or Ministations
   Mass Media Campaigns
   Citizen Police Academies
   Other Police-Sponsored Crime Prevention Programs
Police and Business Cooperation
AmeriCorps and Policing

Chapter Goals

- To show you the meaning of police community relations and its importance to the safety and quality of life in a community.

- To explore public attitudes regarding the police.

- To describe some minority populations and their specific problems and interactions with the police.

- To explore the problems of some special populations, including senior citizens, young people, the homeless, crime victims, and disabled people, and show how the police assist them.

- To acquaint you with current community crime prevention programs that focus on crime reduction and improving the quality of life in communities.

★
Introduction

This chapter deals with relationships between the police and the citizens they are paid to protect: the community. This chapter, along with chapter 10, forms the focus of the police and community section of this text. Because chapter 10 will deal with the philosophies of community policing and problem-solving policing, this chapter will discuss the relationships between the police and the public. It will discuss numerous programs that assist the police in helping the public, especially certain groups of the public with special needs.

The chapter emphasizes the need for proper relationships between the police and the community and presents definitions of police human relations, police public relations, and police community relations. It also explores public opinion of the police and the problems and opportunities of multiculturalism. It will also explore the relationships between the police and minority communities (including African-American, Hispanic-American, Asian-American, and Native-American communities; women; and the gay community). It will also look at relationships between the police and some special populations, including senior citizens, young people, the homeless, crime victims, and disabled people. Additionally, the chapter will discuss community crime prevention programs, including Neighborhood Watch programs, Crime Stoppers, citizen patrols, citizen marches, citizen volunteer programs, home security surveys, Operation Identification, National Night Out, police storefront stations or ministations, citizen police academies, mass media campaigns, and other police-sponsored crime prevention programs.

★
The Need for Proper Police-Community Relationships

No one would argue that the police are not needed in the United States. There will always be criminals, and we need the police to arrest them. We also need the police to handle emergencies, maintain order, regulate traffic, and give us a sense of security. However, the police must be a part of the community. They cannot be viewed as mercenaries or as an army of occupation. When the police see themselves as an occupying army or are seen as one by the community, urban unrest results. An example is South Africa, where the police are seen as an occupying army.

All in the Line of Duty

The Fire and Smoke Didn't Stop Her

Officer Shirley M. Atherton of the Pinellas Park, Florida, Police Department responded to a call of people trapped inside a burning house. When Officer Atherton arrived on the scene, she observed a woman covered with soot exiting the front door. The woman was able to tell the officer that her husband was still inside the house. Although smoke was billowing from the windows and doors, Officer Atherton entered the residence to search for the man. As she crawled under the smoke, she heard someone coughing, followed by what sounded like a body falling to the floor. Atherton located the victim but was unable to revive him. She then dragged the unconscious man out of the house onto the lawn, where she revived him. Hospital personnel later determined that the man had suffered a stroke and probably would have perished in the blaze if not for the actions of Officer Shirley Atherton.

Source: Adapted from *FBI Law Enforcement Bulletin*, September 1995, p. 33.

The police cannot do its job without the support and assistance of the public, and the public cannot have peace and order without the police. Police-community relationships must be two-way partnerships. Additionally, in a democratic society, the legitimacy of the police depends on broad and active public acceptance and support.

Police chiefs or police commissioners have the responsibility and obligation to educate the public about the many causes of crime and the inability of the police, acting alone and on their own, to control crime. Former New York City police commissioner Lee P. Brown (also former police chief of Houston and Atlanta) has said that the police chief must "take the lead in addressing broadened local social service needs that could, if neglected, produce greater crime problems."[1]

The leadership of the chief in reaching out to the community is essential. As R. C. Davis says, "Initiating positive interaction with the community generally results in increased citizen support, higher morale in the work force, protection against or insulation from many hostile external forces, and increased resources."[2]

Although it is very important for a chief to seek the support and cooperation of the public to improve efforts to police the community, the most important person in the police department, in terms of improving

The most important aspect of police human relations is the treatment of each citizen by the individual police officer. Here an officer comforts and assists an injured child.

police community relations, is the individual police officer. Most people receive their impression of a particular police department through the actions of the police officers they encounter. If a person has a bad experience with a particular officer, he or she may believe that the entire department mirrors that officer. The Police Foundation has stated that "it is imperative that every . . . officer see a great deal of community relations as part of his daily patrol or investigative assignment."[3]

★ Human Relations, Public Relations, Community Relations

A tremendous emphasis on police community relations has arisen since the civil disorders of the 1960s. Numerous textbooks and courses exist on police community relations and police human relations. What do these terms mean? Are they interchangeable? Are community relations and human relations the same as police public relations?

Steven M. Cox and Jack D. Fitzgerald perhaps best define these terms. They define **police human relations** as follows: "In the most general sense, the concept of human relations refers to everything we do with, for, and to each other as citizens and as human beings."[4] Human relations thus connotes treating others with respect and dignity and following the Golden Rule—acting toward others as you would want others to act toward you. Cox and Fitzgerald define **police public relations** as "a variety of activities with the express intent of creating a favorable image of themselves . . . sponsored and paid for by the organization."[5] Then, using these two definitions, they define **police community relations** as follows:

> **Community relations** are comprised of the combined effects of human and public relations. Police community relations then encompass the sum total of human and public relations, whether initiated by the police or other members of the community. . . . Police community relations may be either positive or negative, depending upon the quality of police interactions with other citizens (human relations) and the collective images each holds of the other (which are derived from public as well as human relations).[6]

The President's Commission on Law Enforcement and Administration of Justice, in 1967, reported that "police relations with minority groups had sunk to explosively low levels."[7] The commission defined police community relations in its summary report, *The Challenge of Crime in a Free Society*:

> A community relations program is not a public relations program "to sell the police image" to the people. . . . It is a long-range, full-scale effort to acquaint the police and the community with each other's problems and to stimulate action aimed at solving these problems.[8]

Louis A. Radelet, a pioneer in studying the role of the police in the community, traced the development of the **police community relations (PCR) movement** to an annual conference begun in 1955.[9] However, some be-

All in the Line of Duty

They Knew What to Do and They Saved His Life

Officers Kathy Salava and Tracey Schofield of the Pinellas Park, Florida, Police Department were investigating a complaint at a local shopping mall when a mall security guard told them that a man had collapsed in a department store restroom. The officers immediately proceeded to the location, where they found an unconscious elderly man lying on the floor. The officers saw that the victim was bleeding from the head and that his face was turning blue. They also observed heart tablets on the floor. Officer Salava and Schofield initiated CPR and continued their resuscitation efforts until paramedics arrived and were able to get the victim's heart beating on its own. The quick, decisive action of Salava and Schofield saved the victim's life.

Source: Adapted from *FBI Law Enforcement Bulletin*, November 1995, p. 33.

---

lieve that the PCR movement grew out of the riots and civil disorders of the 1960s.

The PCR movement should not be confused with today's community policing. The PCR movement involved assigning a few officers in a department as community affairs or community relations specialists. These officers attended community meetings and tried to reduce tensions between members of the department and the public. Some of the programs were shams or merely public relations attempts. The PCR movement had no real effect on the philosophy or culture of most police departments.

Egon Bittner has said that for PCR programs to be effective, they need to reach to "the grassroots of discontent," where citizen dissatisfaction with the police exists.[10] In short, police human relations skills are needed.

Since the urban disorders of the 1960s, training in human relations has become part of the police academy and in-service training in many departments. Sensitivity training—sometimes referred to as T-groups, or encounter groups—is designed to provide participants an opportunity to learn more about themselves and their impact on others, as well as to learn to function more effectively in face-to-face situations. In a typical encounter group, officers may engage in a role-play face to face with a group of minority citizens, teenagers, or others who have had problem relationships with the police. The police officers play the role of the other group, and the members of the other group play the role of the police. Research evaluating sensitivity training indicated short-term positive changes in the participants' attitudes, but long-term benefits were more difficult to substantiate.[11]

Cox and Fitzgerald tell us that human relations training in police departments has focused on the police and youth, women, and the elderly, in addition to racial and ethnic minorities. This training uses films, lectures, discussion sessions, and the analysis of written case studies.[12]

Public Opinion and the Police

No one can doubt that the police have a difficult job. No one is sure, either, what it is we want the police to do. (Recall the question of the ambiguity of the police role in chapter 5.) Some people think of the police as crime fighters; some, as order maintainers; and others, as service providers. Whatever we believe the police role to be, most citizens, in this author's police experience, believe that we need more police.

Given the difficult job the police have, it is easier for them to perform their duties if they have the support of the public. The media often portray a police force that is not liked by the public. However, this is a false perception.

In a nationwide poll asking people how much respect they have for the police in their neighborhood, 60 percent answered "a great deal," 32 percent answered "some," 7 percent replied "hardly any," and 1 percent had no opinion.[13] See Table 9.1.

The public's opinion of the police has remained relatively constant over time, with the vast majority of the public giving favorable ratings to the police. Whites and older citizens generally give the police better ratings than do African-Americans and younger people.[14]

In a 1997 poll, when citizens were asked how much confidence they had in selected institutions in American society, the percentage reporting that they had a "great deal" or "quite a lot" of confidence in the police was 59 percent, a little less than the military (60 percent), but more than church or organized religion (56 percent), the U.S. Supreme Court (50 percent), banks

Table 9.1 Reported Respect for Police in Own Area

	Great Deal	Some	Hardly Any	No Opinion
National	60%	32%	7%	1%
Sex				
Male	58	34	8	< 1
Female	62	30	7	1
Age				
18 to 29 years	49	40	11	0
30 to 49 years	61	32	7	< 1
50 years and older	67	26	6	1
Race				
White	62	31	6	1
African-American	51	32	17	0

Source: Adapted from Timothy J. Flanagan and Kathleen Maguire, eds., *Sourcebook of Criminal Justice Statistics–1991* (Washington, D.C.: Bureau of Justice Statistics, 1992), Table 2.15, p. 180.

and banking (41 percent), and much more than public schools (40 percent), the presidency (49 percent), newspapers (35 percent), organized labor (23 percent), big business (28 percent), Congress (22 percent), and the criminal justice system (19 percent).[15] See Table 9.2. Whites and older persons reported more confidence in the police than did non-whites and younger persons.[16]

In a 1995 survey asking respondents, "In your view, are the police in your community paid too much, too little, or about the right amount," 5 percent reported too much, 40 percent too little, 44 percent about right, and 11 percent didn't respond.[17]

James Q. Wilson has said, "The single most striking fact about the attitudes of citizens, black and white, toward the police is that in general these attitudes are positive, not negative."[18] The polls mentioned here clearly indicate that Wilson was right. The police, however, feel that the public does not like them or support them. William A. Westly found that 73 percent of officers questioned thought that the public was against the police or hated the police. Only 12 percent of the officers felt that the public liked the police.[19] Wilson, acknowledging the fact that most police officers feel that the public does not like or appreciate them, concluded that the police "probably exaggerate the extent of citizen hostility."[20]

Perhaps one reason many officers believe the public does not like them is that officers, particularly in high-crime areas, spend a significant proportion of their time dealing with criminals and unsavory-type people.

Table 9.2 Reported Confidence in Selected Institutions (United States, 1997)

Question: "I am going to read you a list of institutions in American society. Please tell me ho much confidence you, yourself, have in each one—a great deal, quite a lot, some, or very little."

	Percent saying "a great deal" or "quite a lot"
Church or organized religion	56%
Military	60
U.S. Supreme Court	50
Banks and banking	41
Public schools	40
Congress	22
Newspapers	35
Big business	28
Television	NA
Organized labor	23
Police	59
Criminal justice system	19
Presidency	49

Source: Kathleen Maguire and Ann L. Pastore, eds., *Sourcebook of Criminal Justice Statistics–1996.* (Washington, D.C.: U.S. Department of Justice, Bureau of Justice Statistics, U.S. Government Printing Office, 1997), Table 2.8, p. 117.

Police and Minority Communities

One of the most significant problems facing the police over the past three decades has been the tension, and often outright hostility, between the police and minority group citizens. Most of this tension has focused on relationships between African-Americans and the police. However, tension has existed between police and Hispanic-Americans, Native Americans, Asian-Americans, and other minority groups, including women and the gay community.

One of the best ways to improve relationships between the police and minority groups is to ensure that minority groups are adequately represented in a jurisdiction's police department. Recently, minority representation has increased significantly in U.S. police departments. This should improve relationships between the police and minority communities. However, as chapter 13 will discuss, African-Americans, Hispanic-Americans, and other minorities (including women) are still seriously underrepresented in U.S. police departments.

Multiculturalism

In 1994, the Police Executive Research Forum (PERF) conducted a cultural diversity conference. Sherman Block, Sheriff of Los Angeles County, California, serving as the keynote speaker, stated in regard to cultural diversity in his community,

> The merging of cultures and ethnic backgrounds produced both a richness of diversity and a myriad of problems. The richness of diversity is evident in the new communities that have evolved from people relocating here in hopes of establishing a better life for their families.... The myriad of problems are as diverse as the mix of individuals who now comprise Los Angeles. Each ethnic community strives and struggles to overcome life's challenges to acquire part of the American Dream—the dream to be free to live, work, worship and pray as it sees fit. However, the cultural mix itself can cause problems.... When internal cultures conflict, it can be as destructive as a collision between an iceberg and an ocean liner. Misunderstanding between two cultural groups can lead to conflict and, taken to the extreme, physical confrontations.[21]

To improve relations between his department and their multicultural clientele, Block instituted a 36-hour block of multicultural training in his academy. He also established a "Host a Deputy Program" in which families within the community voluntarily host a deputy in their homes for an evening.[22]

A study of how police departments in four California cities responded to demographic changes that took pace in their communities between 1980 and 1994 revealed

---

YOU ARE THERE! »

Knowledge of Cultural Diversity Is Important

Gary Weaver, a professor of international and intercultural communications in the School of International Service at the American University in Washington, D.C., in an article on law enforcement in a culturally diverse society, asserts that the criminal justice community cannot afford to ignore the diversity of cultures in U.S. society or within the profession itself. Weaver asserts that police professionals need to understand the cultural aspects of communication and need to realize that they cannot eliminate diversity but must rather learn how to manage it and learn from it.

Weaver debunks four assumptions about cultural diversity:

1. As society and the work force become more diverse, differences become less important. No, differences usually become more apparent, and hostilities can increase during encounters among people of different cultures.

2. We are all the same in the American melting pot. No, the pot never really melted. Many people prefer to maintain the right to be different within a pluralistic society.

3. Proper relationships among citizens from different cultures are just a matter of communication and common sense. No, most messages we send to one another are not communicated verbally, but rather by posture, facial expressions, gestures, tone of voice, and other nonverbal messages. These nonverbal messages are different in all cultures, and they shape our attitudes and feelings toward others. People subconsciously learn the meaning of these messages while growing up in their own culture.

4. Conflict is conflict, regardless of the culture. No, conflict is handled differently in different cultures. Among members of certain ethnic groups, inflammatory words are often used for effect, not intent.

Source: Adapted from Gary Weaver, "Law Enforcement in a Culturally Diverse Society," *FBI Law Enforcement Bulletin*, September 1992, pp. 1–7.

that the four departments, San Jose, Long Beach, Stockton, and Garden Grove, have embraced the diverse communities they serve by innovative new strategies in recruitment and hiring, citizen participation, training programs both for employees and community members, community outreach initiatives, and community policing. African Americans, Asians, and Hispanics represented almost 50 percent of the population of these cities in 1994, an increase of 17 percent over 1980.[23]

Numerous training programs have been developed to address the issues of cultural diversity. Two recent examples include the following:

- The International Association of Chiefs of Police (IACP) offers two 2-day training courses in this area to departments throughout the nation, "Cultural Diversity Training for Law Enforcement Personnel," and "Development of Cultural Diversity Training: Train the Trainer."[24]
- The Long Beach, California, Police Department, collaborating with the National Conference of Christians and Jews, has developed a forty-hour cultural awareness training course for all department employees.[25]

Despite progress in multicultural training, however, a 1995 survey of 206 police training institutes in the United States revealed that of the average 638 hours devoted to basic police training, only about 13.5 hours are devoted to multicultural training.[26]

The African-American Community

The 1990 U.S. Census reports that there are almost 30 million African-Americans in the United States, 12.1 percent of the total population.[27] African-Americans have historically faced discrimination in U.S. society. Not until 1954, with the landmark Supreme Court case of *Brown v. Board of Education of Topeka,* was legal segregation of the races officially declared unconstitutional.[28] This case overturned the old "separate but equal" doctrine regarding race and public schools. A decade later, the Civil Rights Act of 1964 was passed by Congress, strengthening the rights of all citizens regardless of race, religion, or national origin.

Access to equal rights did not come easily. The 1950s and 1960s saw demonstrations, marches, and protests by minority groups to win these rights. Often the police, being the official agents of government bodies seeking to block equality for all people, were forced to enforce laws against minority groups, sometimes by arresting them and breaking up their gatherings. Additionally, the police were also forced to confront protests by people opposing equality for all. The police were constantly in the middle of those striving for equality and those expressing "white backlash."

Although some might disagree, police contacts with African-Americans were not the only—and perhaps not even the major—cause of the urban riots in the 1960s. However, police actions generally were the immediate precipitators or the precipitating events of these riots. The riots in Harlem, Watts, Newark, and Detroit were all precipitated by arrests of African-Americans by white police officers.[29]

In the wake of the 1960s riots, police departments throughout the United States established community relations programs designed to improve relationships with minority members of the community. Police departments increased their recruitment and hiring of African-American officers. The 1980s and 1990s saw the election of African-American mayors and other officials in many large cities, as well as the appointment of African-American police commissioners in many of the largest U.S. police departments.

Despite the elimination of legal racism and the increased acceptance of minorities into mainstream society, however, the problems of African-Americans did not disappear. Racism and hatred still exist in our society. Many African-Americans in the inner cities remain unemployed or underemployed. Many live below the poverty level and remain in a state of chronic anger or rage. It is this rage that many say led to the 1992 Los Angeles riots.

Cox and Fitzgerald, writing in 1992 (before the Los Angeles riots), seem to have been prophetic. After discussing the urban riots of the sixties, they state the following:

> We have the distinct impression that the horrors of the 1960s have receded into the backs of the minds of many police administrators; the same appears to be true of the general public. There is little doubt in our minds, however, that the same tensions that found temporary release on the streets of the urban centers of our country still exist. The growing "underclass" of minority-group members presents a real and present problem which we cannot afford to ignore. Well-thought-out, well-planned police minority relations programs are essential if the mistakes of the 1960s are not to be repeated.[30]

If police administrators had heeded the advice of Cox and Fitzgerald, they might have been more prepared for the 1992 Los Angeles incident.

Serious problems still remain between the police and the African-American community. In a 1996 survey by the Joint Center for Political and Economic Studies, about 43 percent of the African-Americans polled said police brutality and harassment were serious problems where they live, whereas only 13 percent of the general population responded similarly. A 1995 report by the Sentencing Project, a public-interest group that advocates sentencing reform, reported that one in every three young black males in the United States are imprisoned, on probation, or on parole. A similar study in 1991 had found that one out of every four young black men were under similar types of criminal justice supervision. The new figure represents an increase of 31 percent.[31]

Special Agent Ronnie A. Carter of the U.S. Bureau of Alcohol, Tobacco and Firearms wrote in a 1995 article regarding police relations with minorities:

> Officers must attempt to understand the attitudes of all community members, including those of minority residents. By joining with the many citizens who want fair and equitable law enforcement, police officers will find that the real minority is not defined by race or class. The real minorities are comprised of the few criminals who victimize society with little fear of being brought to justice.[32]

The Hispanic-American Community

The 1990 census reported that there were over 22 million citizens of Hispanic descent in the United States, 9 percent of the total U.S. population.[33] Hispanic-Americans have suffered discrimination, and many are also handicapped by language and cultural barriers. Their relationships with the police have often been as tense as the relationships between the police and the African-American community.

Considerable attention has been given to recruiting and hiring Hispanic-Americans as police officers. In addition, affirmative action programs have been used to appoint and promote Hispanic-Americans to higher ranks, and many police departments offer courses to teach their employees how to speak Spanish.

The following are two recent examples of departments offering Spanish-language training:

- The Los Angeles Police Department sent nineteen officers to Guadalajara, Mexico, for a ten-day crash course in Spanish language and culture. According to LAPD Deputy Chief Mark Kroeker, "Officers learn enough Spanish in the Academy to give basic commands to suspects. We also need to be able to say, 'How's your family? or How's work?'"[34]

- The Phoenix, Arizona, Police Department, in 1995, provided Spanish-language training courses for all its officers. It also has a program enabling Spanish-speaking translators to ride on patrol with Phoenix police officers. Five of the first ten translators were Arizona State University students.[35]

YOU ARE THERE! »

Learning to Speak Other Languages

The Northern Virginia Criminal Justice Academy, a regional police academy serving over twenty police departments, offers a two-day "Survival Spanish" course for those being trained at the facility. The course consists of verbal, visual, and practical exercises and concentrates on commonly used phrases and questions. During the course, students learn the vocabulary needed during an encounter with a Spanish-speaking person. They learn to identify certain Spanish words and phrases, including those that might show hostile intent. At the end of the class, they receive a cassette tape of what was taught so they can continue to practice their language skills.

The training academy also offers a cultural sensitivity workshop that addresses the differences between the current mainstream culture of the United States and the cultures of both Latin America and Asia. This course covers such areas as "body space," "machismo," and "touching," among others. Another course currently under consideration is a Spanish course designed specifically for telecommunications operators. This course would concentrate on the proper words and phrases needed to obtain information necessary for the police to respond to calls for services.

The Flagstaff (Arizona) Police Department is also encouraging its officers to learn to speak foreign languages. It has developed, with Coconino County Community College, a course in Spanish for police officers. Included in the curriculum are key words and phrases an officer needs in interacting with Spanish-speaking individuals. The course is given one evening each week and is accredited. Sheriff's deputies, highway patrol officers, and officers from other police departments also attend the course. The Flagstaff Police Department is also considering developing a Navaho language class.

Source: Adapted from Anita L. Colvard, "Foreign Languages: A Contemporary Training Requirement," *FBI Law Enforcement Bulletin,* Washington, D.C., September 1992, pp. 20–22; and Harvey Rachlin, "Meeting the Demands of Foreign Languages in Small and Medium-Sized Communities," *Law and Order,* September 1992, pp. 99–102.

Unfortunately, however, a 1995 survey of police departments revealed that most responding agencies do not provide foreign language training.[36]

Despite some improvements in the recruitment of Spanish-speaking officers, the president of the Washington, D.C., Hispanic Police Association charged in 1995 that the department has still done little to recruit more Hispanic or bilingual officers.[37]

The Asian-American Community

The Asian-American population is one of the fastest-growing ethnic groups in the United States, with an estimated 7 million people counted in the 1990 census, or almost 3 percent of the population. The Asian-American population is very diverse, with people from China, Japan, Vietnam, Laos, and many other countries of the Far East. Chinese-Americans are among the most visible of the Asian-American community, with Chinatowns in many large U.S. cities. The Chinese community has traditionally been viewed as relatively crime-free. However, as Delbert Joe and Norman Robinson stated as far back as 1980, "Over the past decade and a half Chinatowns in the major urban centers of North America have ceased to be lands of law and order and have instead become places in which crime is increasingly prevalent."[38]

As crime and social problems increase in Asian-American communities, some departments are making special efforts to recruit and hire Asian-Americans. For example, the San Jose, Long Beach, Garden Grove, and Stockton, California, Police Departments have taken affirmative steps to recruit and hire more Asian-American personnel.[39]

Native Americans

In the 1990 census, Native Americans classified as American Indians numbered almost 1.9 million or a little under one percent of the U.S. population.[40] Indian nations, reservations, colonies, and communities with criminal jurisdiction have traditionally been policed in two ways: use of federal officers from the Bureau of Indian Affairs (BIA), or by use of their own police departments like any other governmental entity. In a few cases, tribes contract police services with a local or state agency or the U.S. Bureau of Land Management. The trend in recent years is for tribes to assume their own police responsibilities and phase out reliance on BIA police and investigators.[41] As indicated in recent investigations by the U.S. Congress, police have traditionally had problems with Indian communities and much more needs to be done regarding police–Native American relationships.[42]

Women

Women have often been critical of police methods of handling domestic violence cases. They also have often complained of insensitivity by the police in rape and other sexual assault cases.

As chapter 15 will explain, the police have heeded complaints regarding the handling of domestic violence cases by the increasing adoption of proarrest policies in these cases. During the past two decades, the police have also been much more sensitive to women in rape and sexual assault cases. Numerous police departments have formed special investigating units to handle sex crimes (often using female investigators). Many departments conduct sensitivity sessions to help officers understand the concerns of women. Also, today, much of the prior discrimination against women in terms of hiring and promotions in police departments has been officially eliminated and women are active members of law enforcement agencies throughout much of the nation. However, as chapter 13 will show, women still face problems in law enforcement agencies.

The Gay Community

In cities with large gay populations, such as San Francisco and New York, there are numerous verbal and physical attacks on members of the gay community (sometimes called "gay bashing"). Police departments across the United States have created bias units to investigate crimes that are the result of racial, religious, ethnic, or sexual orientation hatred. In addition, as we saw in chapter 4, the International Association of Chiefs of Police has rescinded its policy of opposing the employment of gay and lesbian officers. Many police departments have not discriminated against homosexuals in recruiting and hiring officers, and some cities have made special efforts to recruit future officers from the gay community. These efforts have certainly improved relationships between the police and this minority population.

One author has even indicated that the special efforts of the San Francisco Police Department to recruit homosexuals have reduced fears of reporting crimes among many members of that city's gay community, who for years had been victims of organized assaults by bikers and street gangs.[43] Despite efforts by the police,

Los Angeles County deputies converse with Russian immigrants. Working with immigrant communities requires sensitivity to different cultures.

however, crimes against homosexuals are increasing in some communities and are still a sad reflection on our society.[44]

Police departments must also face the problems of discrimination against gay officers in their own ranks. Over the years, many officers have been forced to resign because of pressures placed on them because of their sexual preference. Gays in police departments have formed organizations to protect themselves. In the 1970s, gay officers in California started the Golden State Peace Officers Association (GSPOA). In 1995, when GSPOA held its second annual conference in Los Angeles, they attracted more than 500 gay and lesbian police officers from around the world. One of the nation's first gay officers' associations was the New York City Police Department's Gay Officers Action League (GOAL), which in 1996 had about 1,000 members in New York and fourteen branches nationally, as well as one in Hong Kong and one in Australia.[45]

New Immigrants

As new immigrants move to the United States every year to create a new life for themselves, they also impact upon the police. As early as a decade ago, the New York City Police Department created a New Immigrants Unit to establish a working liaison with representatives of new immigrant groups in the city. This action was prompted by census surveys showing that approximately 25 percent of the city's population was foreign born. Many of these immigrants come from countries where the role of the police is much different from ours. Part of the mission of the New Immigrants Unit is to inform these newcomers to the United States that our police operate differently than the police in their former lands and to make sure that they understand that here, the police serve the people. The unit is staffed by a group of ethnically and culturally diverse uniformed officers, who participate in hundreds of community meetings annually.[46]

Police and Special Populations

As we have seen, the community the police serve is extremely diverse. Special populations offer unique challenges for police departments. Some of the groups with special needs are senior citizens, young people, the homeless, crime victims, and the disabled.

Senior Citizens' Programs

Senior citizens experience particular problems that necessitate special attention from the police. Although seniors have the lowest criminal victimization rates of all age groups, they experience a tremendous fear of crime, often refusing to leave their homes because of the fear of being a victim. Additionally, many senior citizens are infirm and require emergency services. Often police provide special programs and services for senior citizens.

The population of the United States is aging rapidly. It is projected that by the year 2030, there will be 66 million older people in our society. The increasing number of older persons, coupled with their fear of victimization, yields new problems for law enforcement. Fear of victimization and perceptions of rising crime rates rank high among the concerns of the elderly.[47]

Today, numerous special programs have been created by police departments to deal with the problems of seniors. One such program is TRIAD, a joint partnership between the police and senior citizens to address specific problems seniors encounter with safety and quality-of-life issues. TRIAD was started by the International Association of Chiefs of Police (IACP) in cooperation with the American Association of Retired Persons (AARP) and the National Sheriff's Association (NSA). The three associations have designated members to serve as a national TRIAD policy board, which is responsible for providing guidance and technical support to local TRIADS.[48]

One example of a TRIAD program involves the plight of some seniors in personal care homes in Columbus, Georgia. The local TRIAD council devised a strategy to investigate elder abuse with the assistance of the sheriff's office and the police and health departments. They obtained a search warrant for the homes, arranged for proper lodging and care for those seniors living in unhealthy and unsafe conditions, and planned for more careful monitoring of such homes.[49]

Triads are also involved in training police officers to deal with seniors. In Illinois, "elder service officers" from local police agencies are given forty hours training in issues related to the elderly. Similar programs exist in Rhode Island, Florida, and Georgia.[50]

Other programs offer assistance to the elderly:

- The St. Martin Parish Sheriff's Department in Louisiana has created an "Adopt a Senior" program. Deputies are made "adoptive grandchildren" for isolated seniors and are assigned two or three elderly people to visit once or twice each week.[51]

- Police agencies in the Tampa Bay area of Florida pay special attention to the needs of senior citizens. Hillsborough County has a "First Responder's Program" to assist police agencies in dealing with seniors. Also, they provide a myriad of services for police officers to aid the elderly and for the elderly to educate and aid themselves.[52]

YOU ARE THERE!

Law Enforcement Gerontology

Gerontology, the science of researching and explaining the human aging process, and their practitioners, gerontologists, concentrate on many of the problems of our elderly, particularly their physical and mental problems. One problem, however, that they have passed over is the crime problem faced by seniors. To overcome this seeming neglect, some progressive police departments have turned to gerontology and created an innovative, specialized position within their agencies—the law enforcement gerontologist. Law enforcement gerontology is the branch of law enforcement science concerned with the crime- and abuse-related problems of aged persons and with creating the opportunity for older persons to assist the police with their crime prevention mission.

Law enforcement gerontologists work cooperatively with senior citizen communities. By developing a rapport with the elderly, officers assigned to this position can pinpoint specific problems that affect the senior population and then recommend ways to minimize the risk of victimization. They can also alert the senior community to ongoing scams being committed against them and involve them in volunteer programs.

The State of Illinois became the first state in the United States to train officers to become specialists in law enforcement gerontology. Several other states, including Rhode Island, Florida, and Delaware, followed their lead. Also, the National Crime Prevention Institute in Louisville, Kentucky, offers a forty-hour training program for law enforcement gerontologists. Its course on crime and abuse against the elderly offers information on developing and implementing a law enforcement gerontologist program and communication with the elderly. The course also addresses the demographics, myths, and facts of aging; assault and abuse by family, health care providers, and others; and guardianship, fiduciary, and health care fraud. The course also educates attendees on traditional con games and street crimes that target the elderly, such as roof repairs and telemarketing schemes, legislative issues (defining crimes of abuse and neglect), and senior volunteer services. A special focus is placed on the methods criminals use to enter residences of the elderly and ways to prevent situations conducive to elderly rapes and assaults.

Source: Adapted from Wilbur L. Rykert, "Law Enforcement Gerontology," *FBI Law Enforcement Bulletin*, February 1994, pp. 5–9. See also Evel J. Younger, "The California Experience: Prevention of Criminal Victimization of the Elderly," *Police Chief*, February 1996, p. 30; and Ronet Bachman, "Elderly Victims," *Bureau of Justice Statistics, Special Report*, U.S. Department of Justice, October, 1992, p. 1.

YOU ARE THERE!

Elder Abuse—What a Shame

Officers of the Austin, Texas, Police Department discovered the partially clothed body of a sixty-eight-year-old woman in an apartment she shared with her son. The woman wore a diaper fashioned from a vacuum cleaner bag and was found on the kitchen floor in a fetal position. Police later discovered that the victim did not die of any aggressive action—she died of starvation.

An eighty-one-year-old woman received treatment in a hospital emergency room twice in one month for serious wounds and abrasions. The woman admitted that her two sisters beat her. Although hospital officials counseled her on filing criminal charges, she refused. The woman died a month later. The coroner's inquest found that the victim had died from unnatural causes due to the intentional and unlawful conduct of her sisters.

A deputy found an elderly man abandoned by his children with no heat or hot water in his home. The bed was saturated with urine, and the man was covered with his own excrement. His body was a mass of lesions and sores that were infested with maggots. A foot had to be amputated.

Officials closed down the Riverside Nursing Home in Tampa and removed nineteen residents on stretchers after the administrators ignored repeated citations and scores of deficiencies. One resident restricted to soft foods died from choking on a hot dog. Another was treated for dehydration and malnutrition after not being fed for five days.

A home health aide—previously convicted of dealing in stolen property and grand theft—was assigned by a hospital in Sun City, Florida, to care for an eighty-six-year old man after open heart surgery. The woman and her husband systematically drained his assets to buy cars and gamble. They took out a $22,000 mortgage on his home and attempted to divert his direct deposit checks to their use before they were finally caught. The bank threatened foreclosure, but—after public pressure—announced that "no further actions will be taken for thirty days."

These are only a few stories from the myriad of sad tales of elder abuse by relatives and loved ones. Incidents of elder abuse in domestic settings are estimated at 1.5 million cases per year, yet only one out of eight cases comes to the attention of state elder abuse reporting systems. Because many older persons wish to maintain their privacy, they either do not report the abuse and neglect or they tell practitioners they do not wish to take any action against the abuser. Mel E. Weith of the St. Clair County Sheriff's Department, Belleville, Illinois, argues for more attention by police to education regarding this dramatic problem,

> Proper training regarding basic gerontology and the problems that face our elders on a daily basis is greatly needed. If it is not provided, we are failing to address the issues that concern a large segment of our "at risk" population. Through education of law enforcement personnel, we have the potential to eliminate this fear and guarantee that the elder population does more than just survive.

Sources: Adapted from Mel E. Weith, "Elder Abuse: A National Tragedy," *FBI Law Enforcement Bulletin*, February 1994, pp. 24–26; Ronald J. Getz, "Protecting Our Seniors: Elder Abuse and Neglect Is Coming out of the Closet as Police Network with Social Agencies to Improve the Quality of Life for Senior Citizens," *Police*, September 1995, pp. 40-41; Douglas A. Campbell, "Elder Abuse: The Needless Death of Cassandra," *50 Plus*, 1988, pp. 18–19; D. Quirk, "Agenda for the Nineties and Beyond," *Generations* 15, 1991, p. 25.

- One typical program is the "Wanderer's Program," developed by the Alzheimer's Association in cooperation with law enforcement, which identifies people afflicted with the disease and returns them to safety if they become lost. The program provides a registry for patients suffering from memory disorders that have a tendency to wander. An engraved ID bracelet or necklace lists the patient's name, a code number, and the words "memory impaired" with a central telephone number for the county. See Figure 9.1 for guidelines developed for police officers who encounter Alzheimer's victims.

- In Unionville, Indiana, senior citizens work with the police in a project called "55 Plus," where senior volunteers respond to calls from other seniors in non-emergency situations. The volunteers also go door to door to check on the well-being of seniors whose friends or relatives have called to express concern.[53]

- Another program is "Operation Senior Safe Shopping," which began as a response to robberies of seniors in Coney Island, Brooklyn. The local police tried numerous strategies to reduce robberies, including increased car and foot patrol, career criminal programs, and de-

YOU ARE THERE!

Alzheimer's Disease Victims

Many of our seniors face the dreaded Alzheimer's disease. This disease was first described by Dr. Alois Alzheimer in 1906. There are about 4 million Alzheimer's victims in the United States, with 19 million Americans having a family member afflicted and 37 million saying they know someone with the disease. Most victims are older than sixty-five, but this disease can strike people in their forties and fifties. It is found in 10 percent of persons over sixty-five years old and in nearly half of those over age eighty-five. A patient can live from three to twenty years after the onset of symptoms but the average is eight years. It is the fourth leading cause of death among adults. As our population ages, it has been estimated that the number of people affected will reach 14 million by the middle of the next century unless a cure or treatment is found.

Symptoms of Alzheimer's include gradual memory loss, decline in the ability to perform routine tasks, disorientation, difficulty in learning, loss of language skills, impairment of judgment, and personality changes. Patients have been known to wander aimlessly.

Now there is help for law enforcement agencies in dealing with Alzheimer's. In 1994, the Alzheimer's Association developed the Safe Return program, which provides a national registry for people with Alzheimer's or who suffer memory impairment for other reasons. Since its inception, more than 400 patients who were lost were returned safely. About 15,000 people are currently registered in the program. Through Safe Return, caregivers register their loved ones or patients through the Alzheimer's Association, providing their name, address, phone number, characteristics, distinguishing features, and other information, as well as names and phone numbers of contact persons. The registrant receives an identity bracelet or necklace, wallet cards, and clothing labels with their Safe Return ID number and Safe Return's 24-hour toll-free number. If a registrant is found, Safe Return is contacted and, through the ID number, his or her information is provided. Also, if a registrant is reported missing, Safe Return notifies the National Crime Information Center (NCIC) so law enforcement agencies are alerted to the missing person and his or her medical condition.

A special agency, the Elderly Services Officer Association (ESOA), a national group for law enforcement and social service professions, as well as other advocates for the elderly, teaches students at police academies and veteran officers about Alzheimer's and other dementias and how to handle people suffering from them. The forty-hour ESOA course includes such topics as the Graying of America, Myths and Facts of Aging, Communication Skills, Criminal Law and Elderly Victimization, Fear of Crime, Con Games, Elder Abuse, Neglect and Financial Exploitation, Crime Prevention and Services from the American Association of Retired Persons (AARP), and TRIAD.

Source: Adapted from Sheila Schmitt, "'Safe Return' Program Assists Alzheimer's Disease Victims and Police," *Law and Order,* June 1996, pp. 60–64.

When confronting an apparent Alzheimer's victim, a police officer should:

- Identify him or herself as a police officer.
- State why he or she is there, even if it appears obvious.
- Speak slowly and use a low-pitched voice.
- Use short, familiar words.
- Use "yes or no" questions.
- Ask one question at a time, allowing sufficient response time.
- If necessary, repeat questions using the same words. A victim may have only comprehended part of the question.
- Maintain eye contact.
- Use nonverbal communication if necessary.
- Avoid the use of restraints if possible, they may trigger an increase in the victim's symptoms. Restraints should only be used as a last resort to ensure the safety of the victim, officers, and others.

Figure 9.1
How to Deal with an Alzheimer's Victim

School children are special targets for police programs, such as this gang-resistance program in Boston.

coy programs. Despite increased arrests due to proactive anticrime programs, the seniors remained fearful. Many refused to leave their apartments, even to go shopping for food and other necessities. Operation Senior Safe Shopping is a twice-a-week program in which a special police van driven by a uniformed police officer picks up senior citizens at designated bus stops, drives them to shopping malls in the area, and returns them to their residences. Uniformed officers patrol the areas of the bus stops and the shopping malls on foot, ensuring the seniors' safety and even helping them by carrying their packages and other belongings.[54]

■ Another innovative program is the San Antonio, Texas, Police Department's "Operation Blue," in which officers transport a temporary banking facility to the elderly who reside in the city-owned housing projects.[55]

■ In Bridgeport, Connecticut, seniors participate in a weekly "Senior Safe Walk Program," where they get exercise and hear crime prevention presentations. The seniors learn about safe ways to carry money and valuables, home security, or carjacking prevention. Often, the appeal of companionship and exercise draws seniors who might otherwise not hear these presentations.[56]

■ The AARP has cooperated with law enforcement by publishing several brochures on crime prevention for the elderly. The brochures contain practical advice on how to reduce criminal opportunity.[57]

■ The Colorado Springs, Colorado, Police Department has the "Senior Victim Assistance Team" (SVAT). SVAT members have assisted at car accident scenes, listened to the fears and frustrations of robbery victims, transported domestic violence victims to a safehouse, and referred seniors to other appropriate agencies.[58]

Programs for Young People

Young children are a special target of police community relations programs because they are impressionable, and it is believed that if children learn something early enough in life, it will stay with them forever.

The problem of crime and young people is very serious. Over a recent ten-year period, the number of juveniles arrested for violent crimes increased by 68 percent, whereas the change in the number of adults arrested for violent crime was 46 percent. More shockingly, the number of juveniles arrested for murder for this ten-year period increased by nearly 168 percent, whereas the number of adults arrested for murder increased by only 13 percent.[59] Youths are also victims of serious crimes. Approximately three million official reports of child abuse and neglect are filed in the United States yearly.[60]

In a 1996 nationwide poll of police chiefs, 92 percent said that government must invest in programs that help children and youth if it is really serious about reducing crime.[61] Regarding this poll, former Chicago, Illinois, Police Superintendent Matt Rodriquez said,

Police Explorer Cindy Grob engaging in police duties at summer police camp.

Every day, police officers in Chicago and across the country see gangs and drug dealers competing with parents and law-abiding citizens for the allegiance of America's youth—bidding to recruit our children for their army, investing in our kids to lead them down a path to disaster. If we are going to win the fight for the souls of America's children, if we are going to make America safe for our families, then we are going to have to invest in the services that help kids get the right start they need in life.[62]

Former New York City Police Commissioner Patrick Murphy said,

> When I hear someone say we can't afford investments in programs that help kids get the right start, I see more bright yellow crime-scene tape, more prisons, hundreds of police officers and thousands of good men and women and boys and girls lying in pools of blood, more families crying. I've seen too much of that.[63]

There are numerous special police programs for young people. The most important, perhaps, are antidrug programs.

Antidrug Programs for Young People Currently, the most popular antidrug program aimed at children is **Drug Abuse Resistance Education (DARE)**. In DARE programs, police officers teach students in their own classrooms about the dangers of drug abuse. The program is designed to help youths (1) build self-esteem, (2) build self-confidence, (3) manage youthful stress, (4) redirect behavior to viable alternatives, and (5) see police officers as positive role models.

The DARE curriculum is organized into seventeen classroom sessions conducted by a police officer, coupled with suggested activities taught by the regular classroom teacher. The course includes classroom lectures, group discussions, role-plays, workbook exercises, and questions and answers.[64]

Nationwide, DARE is in 70 percent of the nation's school districts and reached 25 million students in 1996. About 25,000 police officers are trained to teach DARE courses. By 1996, DARE had reached 44 countries.[65]

A 1994 study confirmed the popularity of DARE and revealed that its appeal cuts across racial, ethnic, and socioeconomic lines. It indicated considerable support for expansion of the program, yet reported that DARE had little, if any, statistical impact on drug use by young people.[66]

Although DARE has been popular, some believe that it is not an effective use of resources in combating drug use among young people and point to other programs that are more effective.[67]

For example, in 1996, police officials in Seattle and Spokane, Washington, decided to shelve their DARE programs in favor of less-costly, home-grown, antidrug programs aimed at their schoolchildren.[68]

However, the executive director of DARE America, a national information and resource clearinghouse for local DARE programs, downplayed the Seattle and

YOU ARE THERE!

DARE Helps Kids

The following letter from a DARE program participant shows the impression the police officer made on the child and indicates the value of the program:

```
Dear Chief Gates,

I really enjoyed the DARE program be-
cause the officers were very nice and
made you feel comfortable when you
asked dumb questions. Thank you for
telling the officers to come to our
school and for giving us the nicest
ones!
    I really think that the DARE pro-
gram is a super neat thing and I will
resist drugs and will not get ad-
dicted for as long as I live. I will
always remember the nice officers who
came to our school.

                    Never Using Drugs,

                    Olga, Sixth Grade
```

Source: Adapted from William DeJong, *Project DARE: Teaching Kids to Say "NO" to Drugs and Alcohol* (Washington, D.C.: National Institute of Justice, March 1986), p. 4.

Spokane decisions, saying that their scrapped programs represent only a very small percentage of all of the DARE officers in Washington State. Parsons emphasized that 300 to 400 police departments add DARE programs each year. He praised the New York City Police Department, which in 1996 budgeted $8.8 million for the program, in which 101 officers teach the seventeen-week curriculum to 600,000 students in 1,100 schools.[69]

Other Programs for Young People Police programs for young people exist to address concerns other than drugs. The following are some of the most popular programs:

- Officer Friendly and other programs designed to help children see and talk to police officers are popular with schools and police administrators alike. The intent of the Officer Friendly programs is to encourage young children to view police officers as friends by getting to know some.[70]

- Musical programs attract young people. One is the Fayetteville, North Carolina, Police Department's Roll'rz Band, which performs for elementary schools, public housing projects, civic events, and community meetings in an effort to prevent drug use and violence.[71]

- Police explorer programs are very popular. (See Dempsey's Law in this section.) The Fontana, California, Police Department has an Explorer post whose primary function is emergency preparedness. These explorers have been used during actual emergency responses, including hazardous material spills, earthquakes, floods, major accidents, and a plane crash.[72]

- Police trading cards are popular police-youth programs today. For example, the Waterloo, Iowa, Police Department produces trading cards that feature the pho-

YOU ARE THERE!

Cops, Kids, and Rock and Roll

The Dayton (Ohio) Police Department has its own youth-oriented, antidrug rock and roll band. Members of its target audience, children in kindergarten through eighth grade, report that they "can scarcely believe their eyes or ears" when the band comes on stage. One fifth-grade boy, looking on in obvious amazement, exclaimed, "These guys are cops?" "These guys" are Dayton PD's COP'RZ, a rock and roll band of police officers who have made more than fifty school appearances, challenging some 50,000 young listeners to adopt a drug-free lifestyle. They even served as the opening act for LaToya Jackson at the 1991 Montgomery County Fair in downtown Dayton.

Two comments from school principals about the rock band and its message show its value. One said, "We have experienced many anti-drug messages and programs during the past few years, but this was undoubtedly the best. Not only do the children have a good time, but they receive an excellent message and see police officers in a very positive role." Another principal commented, "Your concert/program drew rave reviews from staff and students. I have been trying for four years to achieve that level of acceptance to my sermons and programs. The COP'RZ concert got everyone's vote in one grand effort."

Source: Adapted from Patricia Bork, "COP'RZ," *Law and Order*, December 1991, pp. 29–32.

YOU ARE THERE!

"I'll Trade You Two Officer Joneses for One Officer Smith": Police Officer Trading Cards

In an effort to capitalize on young people's interest in baseball trading cards, several police departments, including the Holland (Michigan) Police Department and the Santa Clarita station of the Los Angeles County Sheriff's Department, have given out police officer trading cards to children they encounter on patrol. The cards have the officers' names and photographs on the front and information about the officers and their duties on the back. They also carry antigang or crime prevention messages from the officers.

In Campbell, California, schoolchildren are encouraged to flag down officers, meet them, and ask for a card. Police Chief James Cost said, "Because collecting baseball cards is so popular with children, it seemed a natural way for the officers to attract the attention of kids who otherwise would have avoided them."

Even the U.S. Customs Service has issued trading cards that feature drug-sniffing canines.

Source: Adapted from "Police Trading Cards a Big Hit: How Many Sergeants for One Chief?" *Law Enforcement News*, October 1992, p. 6; and "Police Trading Cards," *Law and Order*, December 1991, p. 4.

---

tographs and personal information of officers in the department. Young people often go to the police station in order to find officers from whom they want a card or autograph.[73]

Other departments that have had success in using their police officer trading cards are the Campbell and Santa Fe, California, Police Departments. The Campbell department has printed and distributed 250,000 cards. Chief Jim Cost reports, "We even use them as business cards. I haven't given out a real business card in four years. . . . When an angry citizen comes in, I say, 'Here, let me give you my card,' and it starts the conversation with a smile."[74]

■ A big hit with kids are robots that teach crime prevention and safety programs. The robots are lifelike and come in all sizes, shapes, and colors. Some police-robotic programs are "P.C. the Patrol Car," "Safety Sam," and a 9-foot-tall "Officer Friendly."[75]

■ The school resource officer, a position designed to combat the increase of juvenile crime and improve relationships between school children and the police, has proven to be effective. This program assigns uniformed police officers to schools, generally junior and senior high schools, to provide a wide variety of service.[76]

The Phoenix, Arizona, Police Department, has such a program. A three-year study revealed that the truancy rate at schools with the officers dropped by 73 percent and crimes committed at the schools and in the surrounding neighborhoods decreased significantly.[77]

■ Anti-child abduction programs are also very popular. The U.S. Department of Justice estimates that more than a million children run away or are reported missing every year. Many law enforcement agencies provide parents with free photo ID documents and crucial information on safety for their children.[78]

■ Many organizations, such as the National Hot Rod Association,[79] the National Crime Prevention Council,[80] and the National Rifle Association,[81] have programs helping the police to work with youths.

■ Student-ride-alongs impress young people. In an effort to show students the dangers of drinking and driving, the Maryland State Police have established a program allowing high school students to ride with troopers on Friday and Saturday nights. Students see how troopers detect a drug or alcohol impaired driver

---

PATROLLING THE NET

Libraries Have to Watch Out for Guys Like This

In July 1997, a man was accused of using the Lakewood, Ohio, town library's computer to access an Internet site with pictures of nude boys. He then loaded the images onto a floppy disk. He was arrested on a charge of illegally using a minor in nudity-related material.

Workers at the library told police that the man had been coming into the library for the last three weeks to log onto the World Wide Web.

Source: Adapted from *Newsday*, 6 July 1997, p. A-43.

PATROLLING THE NET

CyberMom on Patrol

Joanne Fazel is a cybermom. As a paid surfer (patroller) for Microsystems Software, a Framingham, Massachusetts-based company that produces screening software, she spends her days hunting for material she feels doesn't belong on the web for children. The product she patrols for is called Cyber Patrol and has an enormous distribution. Eighty-five percent of people online have free access to the software via commercial providers such as America Online—if you don't have it for free, you can get it for $29.95. Its approved or not-approved list is huge. Cyber Patrol automatically blocks distasteful web sites (CyberNOTs—about 18,000 to date) and points toward some 40,000 CyberYes sites that the staff deems suitable.

To maintain their vigilant patrol, Microsystems employs seven women and five men who roam (patrol) cyberspace day and night, looking for pornography, violence, and cult ravings.

Source: Adapted from "Mom-and-Pop Web Cops," *New York Times Sunday Magazine*, 11 May 1997, p. 15.

---

and what happens when such a driver is pulled over. The students also respond with troopers to accidents and often see the deadly consequences of DWI.[82]

■ Police athletic programs or police athletic leagues (PALS) have long been one of the most popular programs involving the police and youth. These programs include boxing, baseball, football, and basketball leagues (including the more recent Midnight Basketball) and summer camps. The basic goals of these programs, according to Cox and Fitzgerald, include "teaching youth athletic skills and good sportsmanship, while encouraging both the juveniles and the officers involved to view one another as individuals deserving of respect."[83]

Some prominent former members of PALs around the nation include boxers Mohammed Ali and Evander Holyfield and entertainer Bill Cosby. As of 1994, there were over 300 chapters of PAL, serving 3 million youths nationwide.[84]

■ Police department/college intern programs are also common throughout the nation. A good example of a police/college intern program is that of the Spring Lake Park, Minnesota, Police Department. The program spans ten weeks; interns participate for 200 to 400 hours and prepare a research project or paper on a topic approved by the college and the department. Interns work on routine and proactive patrol. On their own, they handle calls for motorist assists, complaints about animals, and vehicle lock outs. They also work with investigators, tour jails and crime labs, spend a shift at the communications center, and observe district and municipal court proceedings.[85]

PATROLLING THE NET

Who's Out There on the Net

People concerned about the growing popularity of pornography and the drug culture on the Net are justified in their concern.

The Center for Media Education, a Washington group that monitors Internet content, reports that nearly 5 million children from two to seventeen years of age used online services in 1996 and that more than 9 million college students use the Internet regularly. "We really are witnessing the development of the most powerful medium that has ever existed, in terms of its ability to attract and interest young people," said its executive director.

Source: Adapted from Christopher S. Wren, "A Seductive Drug Culture Flourishes on the Internet," *New York Times*, 20 June 1997, p. A-1, 22.

Dempsey's Law

Check It Out! Police Exploring

Professor Dempsey, I think I want to be a police officer, but I'm not sure. How can I tell if it's for me?

I get this question every day. I tell students that there are several ways they can find out firsthand what police work is all about.

If your school has an intern program with the local government, try to get into it, and request to work with the police department. If your police department has an auxiliary program that allows you to contribute your time to the department, try that out. If your police department has a "ride-along" program, take advantage of it.

I tell the students about these programs and also about one of my former students, Cindy Grob, who was a Police Explorer [see photo, page 209]. Grob, of Port Jefferson Station, New York, had been a member of the Sixth Precinct Explorers in Suffolk County, New York, since the age of fourteen. She said, "Being a Police Explorer has made me more aware of the needs and problems of my community. The program has strengthened my direction in wanting to become a police officer." Grob, who rose to the rank of captain in the Explorers, hoped to use the experience she gained as an Explorer in a law enforcement career.

Grob's parents, Jack and Judy Grob, also had positive feelings about the Explorer program. They said, "Cindy's involvement with the Police Explorers has enhanced her direction toward choosing the occupation she wants to pursue. We are very proud to have a daughter who has set her standards high and has chosen the field of law enforcement."

The Law Enforcement Exploring program involves young men and women, ages fourteen through twenty years, in a hands-on look at law enforcement as a potential career. Youths interested in Law Enforcement Exploring join posts sponsored by a law enforcement agency. The law enforcement agency provides a sworn officer as the post leader. There are approximately 2,100 posts, with more than 23,000 members nationwide. More than half the posts are sponsored by local police and sheriff's departments; the rest are sponsored by state police agencies, federal law enforcement agencies, and schools and civic organizations. Liability insurance is provided by the Boy Scouts of America (BSA), which offers Law Enforcement Exploring as a program for older youths. The BSA also operates regional and national events for Explorers.

In a typical post, Explorers are required to work approximately twenty hours a month to maintain their eligibility, but they may work more hours if they wish. The following are some of the ways in which Explorers work with the police:

- Assisting the police in crowd, traffic, and parking control at parades and festivals.
- Staging crime prevention programs for neighborhood associations and assisting with Operation Identification by marking citizens' valuables.
- Assisting the police in performing clerical functions.
- Serving as role models for younger children and assistants for officers teaching DARE.

Explorers can attend regional events in which they compete in pistol shooting, crime scene searches, hostage negotiations, report writing, traffic accident investigations, and other events based on aspects of law enforcement. Every other year, a national conference with interpost competition is held. According to the BSA, approximately 40 percent of Explorers become either law enforcement officers or lawyers.

Note: In 1996, Cindy Grob was hired by the U.S. Customs Service, under the Federal Government's Outstanding Scholars Program. Cindy had achieved 4.0 grade point averages in our school and her four-year school. In 1997, Cindy, after extensive training, became a Customs Service canine operator. She now monitors people and cargo at New York City's Kennedy Airport. Regarding her job, Cindy says, "I love it."

Source: Used with permission from personal communication with Cindy Grob, Jack Grob, and Judy Grob, 1993, 1997; and Ordway Burden, "Law Enforcement Exploring: An Effective Intro to Policing," CJ The Americas, August/September 1992, pp. 9–10.

PATROLLING THE NET

Ways to Keep the Kids from the Smut on the Net

According to published reports, the following are some suggestions for parents concerned about what their children can see on the Net. They have several options to filter out adult material.

Sit with Children
The foolproof way to filter is to supervise the children while they are online.

Install Software
Software has been written to filter the web by blocking sites known to harbor explicit material. Some examples of commercially available blocking software are Cyber Patrol, Surf Watch, Net Shepherd, Cybersitter, and Triple Exposure.

Use Online Services
All of the major online services offer parental control options for no additional cost beyond standard subscription fees.

Source: Adapted from "A Primer: Just Click 'No'," *New York Times* 27 June 1997, p. A-21; and Lou Dolinar, "Software That Filters Smut," *Newsday,* 27 June 1997, p. 43.

Assistance for the Homeless

Police departments are generally the only agency available twenty-four hours a day, seven days a week. Therefore, the police are frequently called to deal with alcoholics, the mentally ill, and the homeless (street people). Tremendous numbers of people live on the streets today. Many of these people are often in drug or alcoholic stupors or frenzies, or they exhibit wild and chaotic behavior. The roots of the homeless problem include the policy in the 1960s and 1970s of releasing the institutionalized mentally ill, today's jail overcrowding, the decriminalization of public intoxication, and the lack of affordable housing.

Community residents often call the police and insist they remove homeless people from their streets. Residents do not realize, do not understand, and perhaps do not care that the police have very few options for dealing with these unfortunate members of the community.

One group of researchers has reported the following: "Handling the mentally ill is, perhaps, the single most difficult type of call for law enforcement officers. . . . Police officers usually found themselves saddled with sole responsibility for suspected mentally ill persons whose public behavior warranted some form of social intervention."[86]

A 1990 U.S. Supreme Court case, *Zinermon v. Burch,* may add another barrier to those already impeding the treatment of the mentally ill.[87] In this ruling, the Court held that all patients must be "competent" to sign themselves voluntarily into a mental hospital. Because of this ruling, patients who are marginally competent may have to be admitted involuntarily and have their treatment validated by the courts.

The homeless in the 1990s have special problems, as Allan Coffey pointed out at the beginning of the decade. Coffey writes, "The homeless are no longer the group of vagrants that police have traditionally encountered. Although hobos are still among the homeless in America, many urban areas are witnessing the inclusion of women and children, even whole families, in this group."[88]

The following gives a sense of the problems encountered by the homeless in the dangerous environs of the New York City subway system: "An indeterminate number of the homeless . . . have sought refuge underground in the city's hundreds of miles of subway tunnels. There, they face other dangers beyond the routine perils of homelessness—the possibility of being electrocuted by rails crackling with 600 volts of electricity, and the risk of being crushed by several tons of fast-moving subway trains."[89]

Who are the homeless? The National Institute of Justice reported that 25 to 45 percent of the people living on the streets are alcoholics, and that about 30 percent of all homeless people suffer from severe mental disorders. Many more homeless suffer from less severe psychological disorders that may prevent them from holding stable jobs. It also reports that a surprising number of homeless people are military veterans. Runaways also account for many of the homeless. Others are neither alcoholic nor suffering from mental illness, but they have instead experienced economic hard times or cannot afford housing.[90]

YOU ARE THERE!

Police Networking Arrangements with Mental Health Professionals

Police departments across the United States have set up networking systems with social service agencies to assist the mentally ill, alcoholics, and the homeless. For example, a networking arrangement has been established between the Los Angeles Police Department, the Los Angeles County Department of Mental Health, and fourteen other appropriate agencies and organizations. The LAPD requires its officers to call an emergency Mental Evaluation Unit for assistance twenty-four hours a day in handling, screening, and transporting suspected mentally ill people. The mental evaluation unit is staffed by nine detectives, who receive approximately 600 calls a month from patrol officers. The unit's detectives prescreen the cases and either go to the scene or advise the officer on how to handle the call. Sometimes they advise the officer to bring the individual to the unit's offices. If they advise the officer to bring the individual to a hospital, an immediate examination is made by the emergency ward psychiatrist there, who knows the case has been prescreened by the Mental Evaluation Unit. A case generally consumes only thirty minutes of the patrol officer's time and fifteen minutes of the Mental Evaluation Unit's time. Other municipalities have established programs similar to the Los Angeles Mental Evaluation Unit, including Rochester, New York; Birmingham, Alabama; Galveston, Texas; and Fairfax, Virginia.

A networking arrangement has also been established between the Boston Police Department, the state department of public welfare, and Boston's largest shelter for the homeless (the Pine Street Inn). This arrangement allows the police in the city's downtown precincts to take any homeless people (including intoxicated and mentally ill street people) to the shelter at any hour of the night. The state department of public welfare provides the funds to station an off-duty officer, on overtime, at the shelter during each shift to assist other officers in handling problem people and in maintaining order at the shelter.

Source: Adapted from Peter E. Finn and Monique Sullivan, *Police Response to Special Populations: Handling the Mentally Ill, Public Inebriate, and the Homeless* (Washington, D.C.: National Institute of Justice, January 1988), p. 1; and James Janik, "Dealing with Mentally Ill Offenders," *FBI Law Enforcement Bulletin*, July 1992, Washington, D.C., pp. 22–26.

YOU ARE THERE!

The Transit Police Homeless Outreach Program

To deal with the problem of the homeless people sleeping in stations in New York City's subway system, the Transit Authority Police Department has established a Homeless Outreach Program. The transit officers offer the homeless a ride to a city shelter with a free meal en route.

The officers worry about the safety of those sleeping along the tracks, but the following is an example of the response they often get:

> A man named Gary, in his forties, has transformed a passageway—part of an emergency exit leading out of the tunnel to the street—into his home. A makeshift clothesline holds clothes on hangers. A bedroll lays on the concrete floor.
>
> Gary is in no mood tonight to be told to move. "I told you to stay away from me, man!" he tells Officer Alan Logan, a four-year police veteran who has worked in the unit for two years.
>
> "Gary, I'm your friend. You know that," Logan replies calmly.
>
> "You're not my friend; I told you to stay away from me. I don't want nothing to do with you. You come by here every night bothering me. Every night you come by with the same s—, man. I ain't got nothin' to say to you. Stay the f—away from me! Quit shinin' lights on me!" . . .
>
> Despite the cursing and grumbling, Gary pulls on his coat and is escorted to the exit. He stumbles down the street still muttering about being forced out of his lair. "He'll be back in a few hours," [another officer] predicts.

Source: Adapted from Jacob R. Clark, "Be It Ever So Humble . . . NY Transit Cops Reach Out to Those Who Would Make the Subways Their Home," *Law Enforcement News*, 15 March 1992, p. 11.

Some of the homeless who come to the attention of the police survive on the streets by begging or theft and often become victims themselves. A recent study revealed that 27 percent of all calls for police service in Santa Monica, California, involved homeless persons, either as victims or suspects. In addition, the homeless represented 35 percent of all jail bookings.[91] The police are caught in the middle of the homeless problem, pressured by private citizens, merchants, and government officials to address the problem and "do something."

A proactive approach to these problems has been taken in Reno, Nevada, which has instituted a Homeless Evaluation Liaison Program (HELP), with the goal of uniting the police with various social service agencies in order to find alternatives to jailing the homeless.[92]

Help for Crime Victims

In recent years, police have instituted numerous programs to deal with crime victims, particularly victims of rape and sexual abuse. Many police departments have created special investigatory units to deal specifically with victims of sexual abuse. Many of these units use female investigators to ease the interview process with both adult and juvenile victims.

Many police departments use **anatomically correct dolls**—dolls made to resemble actual people and their body parts, including sexual organs—in an effort to facilitate interviews of child victims of sexual abuse. These dolls can be useful in reducing stress, establishing rapport, determining competency, and learning the child's sexual vocabulary. Great care is needed, however, in the use of anatomically correct dolls; experts warn that the improper use of dolls can block communication and cause severe case problems for prosecutors.[93]

One successful police assistance program for crime victims is the Police Crisis Intervention Unit in Scottsdale, Arizona. The program provides twenty-four-hour crisis intervention, interviews with victims to offer support and assistance, referrals to appropriate agencies, orientation to court procedures, and transportation of victims to court. The staff also provides emotional support to many victims during municipal court proceedings, and city judges often call the unit when victims become upset in court. Police refer victims for assistance, even after regular business hours, by telephoning the specialists at home or by paging them on beepers.[94]

Marion County, Indiana, has established the Child Advocacy Center, where children can be questioned in cases of possible child abuse and molestation. The center maintains child-friendly, toy-filled, cheerful playrooms where investigators can question and assist children. Since the child-friendly atmosphere was created, the number of cases handled by the center's detectives has risen almost 50 percent, and the clearance rate has risen to over 97 percent. Most of the detectives agree that it is the center's atmosphere, which makes children feel comfortable and at ease, that has led to this extraordinarily high clearance rate. The detectives claim that when children feel at ease, they are much more willing to talk about their abuse.[95]

Help for Disabled People

Depending on the definition of disabled, there are between 40 million and 70 million disabled people in the United States. They include the deaf and hard of hearing; those who use wheelchairs, walkers, canes, and other mobility aids; the blind and visually impaired; those with communication problems; the mentally ill; and the retarded.

There are special problems for the police when dealing with hearing impaired people. These people can be found in any type of police situation, from traffic stops to murder investigations, and as victims, complainants, or perpetrators of crime. Police officers should have some knowledge of the various methods used by the hearing impaired to communicate their disability and the various types of communication they use. Departments should have interpreters available around-the-clock to communicate with the hearing impaired.[96]

Police Officer Elizabeth Cook has a talent only a few other officers have—the ability to use sign language. In 1996, as a deaf and mute man climbed to a ledge of a 32-story building and threatened to jump, the call went

YOU ARE THERE! »

How a Hearing Impaired Person May Communicate His or Her Disability

How does a police officer determine if someone is hearing impaired? The most likely indications are the following:

The subject might say, "I am deaf." Many hearing impaired people can speak, but it should not be assumed that because they can speak that they can also hear. Their speaking ability may range from normal to unintelligible.

A manual sign may be given to indicate deafness. This may be a movement of the hand pointing first to the ear and then to the mouth, or by pointing to the heart and putting their two hands together in front of them.

The hearing impaired person may have a printed card that states that he or she is deaf and how a person can best communicate with him or her.

Source: Adapted from Suzanne M. Youngblood and Thomas W. Lynch, "Officer, I Can't Hear You!," *Law and Order*, February 1995, pp. 51–53.

out for Officer Cook. "I'm here to help you," Cook signed, "Tell me what happened." The man indicated to Cook that he was despondent over the death of his girlfriend in a car accident the previous week. Cook counseled the man and reminded him of the friends and relatives who loved him and how he had the power to change his life. Within a half-hour the man surrendered to the police. Previously, Cook had used sign language to deal with crime victims but this was the first time she had used it to save a life.[97]

Diabetics also have significant problems of which the police should be aware. Because of the prevalence of drug abuse in our society, officers frequently confront people who are in the possession of hypodermic syringes and needles or are actually involved in the use of a hypodermic needle. Some, however, may be people suffering from and treating themselves for diabetes. People with diabetes often wear some form of easily recognizable identification alerting first responders and police to the fact that they have insulin-treated diabetes. Officers might also encounter diabetics in situations in which they appear to be suffering from drug- or alcohol-related impairment or are unconscious or are suffering from seizure activity.[98]

Community Crime Prevention Programs

Police expert George L. Kelling has written that citizens have "armed themselves, restricted their activities, rejected cities, built fortress houses and housing complexes both inside and outside the cities, and panicked about particular groups and classes of citizens."[99] Surely, citizens are worried about crimes and have taken measures to isolate or protect themselves against it. However, the police have an obligation to help citizens protect themselves against crime.

It is obvious that the police cannot solve the crime and disorder problems of the United States by themselves, and they cannot let citizens take the law into their own hands. To address these problems, the police must turn to the public for its support and active participation in programs to make the streets safer and make the quality of life better. As Wesley G. Skogan has written, "Voluntary local efforts must support official action if order is to be preserved within realistic budgetary limits and without sacrificing our civil liberties."[100] Community crime prevention programs include Neighborhood Watch, Crime Stoppers, citizen patrols, citizen volunteer programs, home security surveys, Operation Identification, National Night Out, police storefront stations or ministations, mass media campaigns, and other police-sponsored programs.

Neighborhood Watch Programs

Citizen involvement in crime prevention programs has increased greatly in the past decade. The National Institute of Justice has reported that one family in five lives in a neighborhood with a crime prevention program. In those neighborhoods, 38 percent of the citizens participate in the program.[101] Another report indicates that more than 6 million U.S. residents are members of citizens' crime watch groups. In Detroit, Neighborhood Watch is organized on 4,000 of the city's 12,000 blocks. In New York City, 70,000 homes are involved in Blockwatcher programs, and in Dade County, Florida, 175,000 members belong to the Citizen Crime Watch.[102]

Crime prevention programs in which community members participate have different names in various parts of the country. Examples are Crime Watch, Block Watch, Community Alert, and, most commonly, **Neighborhood Watch**.[103] Neighborhood Watch groups engage in a wide range of specific crime prevention activities, as well as community-oriented activities. Citizens watch over activities on their block and alert the police to any suspicious or disorderly behavior. Neighborhood Watch blocks have clear signs alerting people that the block is protected by a Neighborhood Watch group.

It has been reported that Neighborhood Watch programs can produce at least short-term reductions in certain crimes—particularly house burglaries—and are more likely to be effective when they are part of general-purpose or multi-issue community groups rather than when they only address crime problems.[104]

Voluntary community organizations are often more successful in middle-class or high-income neighborhoods. Community watch programs are less likely to be found in poor neighborhoods, areas in which disorder is generally high. Skogan has found that in lower-income areas, "residents typically are deeply suspicious of one another, report only a weak sense of community, perceive they have low levels of personal influence on neighborhood events, and feel that it is their neighbors not 'outsiders' whom they must watch with care."[105]

As of 1997, Lansing, Michigan, has organized 151 neighborhood watches, which serve more than 11,500 households. Two officers are responsible for establishing new groups, facilitating existing ones, and disseminating information to all.[106]

One neighborhood watch program that has shown positive results using the latest in high-tech cellular telephone technology is the Dade County, Florida, Neighborhood Cellular Watch Project. This program, which put cellular phones in the hands of Citizen Crime Watchers, has led to a dramatic overall decrease in burglaries, robberies, and thefts during a nine-month study period in 1995.[107]

In 1996, President Clinton, during a ceremony for more than 100 crime-fighting volunteers, announced the donation of 50,000 cellular phones for use by neighborhood crime watch groups.[108]

Citizen's crime watch programs also work in Canada. Sharp-eyed and alert citizens, trained and coordinated by officers from the Vancouver Police Department, have located more than 660 stolen vehicles from 1993 to 1996. Volunteers patrol a minimum of six hours a month in their own vehicle and broadcast reports to two mobile police coordinators who evaluate the information and respond accordingly.[109]

Crime Stoppers

Crime Stoppers originated in 1975 in Albuquerque, New Mexico, and quickly spread across the country. In the typical Crime Stoppers program, the police ask television and radio stations to publicize an "unsolved crime of the week." Cash rewards are given for information that results in the conviction of the offender.[110]

Today there are an estimated 600 Crime Stoppers programs in the United States. Approximately 950 Crime Stoppers programs worldwide have resulted in the resolution of more than 400,000 cases and the recovery of more than $2 billion in stolen property and illegal drugs. This averages out to $1 paid in rewards to anonymous callers for every $77 dollars of property or narcotics recovered.[111]

Virginia Beach, Virginia, had a successful Crime Stoppers program for years. In a ten-year period ending in 1992, Virginia Beach made over 3,000 arrests (with a 98 percent conviction rate), closed over 6,400 cases, and recovered $6.5 million in property and illegal drugs as a result of Crime Stoppers tips.[112] By 1995, Virginia Beach's recovery of property and illegal drugs had risen to nearly $13 million and, in that year alone, the program cleared 700 cases.[113]

Similar to Crime Stopper programs are anonymous tip programs that provide citizens the opportunity to leave anonymous tips regarding crimes and criminals for the police. Wausau, Wisconsin, a city of 38,000, has had such a program since 1990. The program, called A-TIP, provides a direct, anonymous, and confidential telephone link to the Wausau Police Department.[114]

Citizen Patrols

Citizen patrols are very popular around the nation. They involve citizens patrolling on foot or in private cars and alerting the police to possible crimes or criminals in the area, thus being the eyes and ears of the police.

The most well-known citizen patrol is the Guardian Angels. The group, begun by Curtis Sliwa in 1977 to patrol New York City subway cars and stations, now has chapters in many other parts of the United States. The Angels are young people in distinctive red berets and T-shirts who patrol on buses, subways, and streets. Their main function is to act as an intimidating force against possible criminals or potentially disruptive people. Many people report that the mere presence of the Guardian Angels reassures them. Despite their popularity with citizens, however, the Guardian Angels have not been welcomed by police executives, who argue that only well-trained officers can maintain order.[115] In 1996, however, the Guardian Angels finally received official acceptance by the NYPD when it was announced the department will train twelve Guardian Angels in civilian crime-fighting techniques and make them part of a police-sponsored rollerblade patrol to improve safety in New York City's famed Central Park.[116]

Researcher Susan Pennell evaluated the Guardian Angels' impact on crime in San Diego and twenty other local areas in the United States. The impact of the Angels on crime was inconclusive. However, the study revealed that a majority of citizens knew that the Guardian Angels were patrolling their neighborhood, and most of those who knew about the Angels felt safer as a result of their presence.[117]

Another noted citizen patrol group is the Nation of Islam Security Agency, which is affiliated with the Reverend Louis Farrakhan's Nation of Islam. In 1992, the Los Angeles Police awarded the group a permit to patrol fifteen drug-ridden apartment buildings. Some African-American residents praise the idea, saying, "The Nation carries respect because they give it, they are courteous and we know they won't just look the other way," and "People out here, even the drug dealers, respect the Nation. More than the police."[118] In Washington, D.C., the Nation of Islam Security Agency is credited by tenants with improving conditions at two housing projects that the agency has been patrolling for about four years.[119]

As part of the latest trend in citizen crime patrols, cable television workers in Loudoun County, Virginia, are reporting crimes and emergencies they witness to the police as part of the "Eyes and Ears" program. Eyes and Ears is similar to two programs launched elsewhere in the nation during 1995. In Operation Waste Watch, sanitation workers in Mississippi were trained to notice suspicious activity on their routes and notify police. In Nashville, Tennessee, mail carriers were given cellular telephones to report crimes and emergencies they witness while on the streets.[120]

Citizen Marches

Increasingly, citizens in many communities have taken to their own streets to motivate criminals and drug users to leave their neighborhoods. As one example, Florida citizens in Boynton Beach, as well as Pompano Beach, Key West, Tampa, Orlando, and Fort Myers take to the streets every weekend night conducting noisy, high-profile protests against drug dealers and their customers. They chant such anti-drug slogans as "Up with hope, down with dope," and other "in-your-face" efforts to rid their neighborhoods of drugs and the negative problems they produce. Most local police chiefs agree that the marchers' efforts help forge closer ties between police and residents. Marchers are often accompanied by police to ward off possible violence from those they encounter.[121]

Citizen Volunteer Programs

Citizen volunteer programs—in which citizens volunteer to do police jobs, thus freeing police officers to return to patrol duties—have become numerous and popular, involving about 600,000 citizens in numerous U.S. police departments. Citizens perform such jobs as crime analysis, clerical work, victim assistance, and crime prevention. Ordway P. Burden reports that although police unions are often critical of volunteers, the volunteers typically are accepted by the police officers with whom they work once their ability to do the job has been demonstrated.[122]

In addition, as was discussed in chapter 3, numerous citizens patrol in uniform as auxiliary police officers in their own communities. This serves to increase visible police patrol in the community.

In Tampa, Florida, in 1995, volunteers donated over 2,000 hours doing clerical work for the Tampa Police Department. Services performed by these volunteers include answering phones, taking messages, and assisting

> ### YOU ARE THERE! »
>
> **Examples of How Volunteers Help Shoulder the Load for the Lakewood, Colorado, Police Department**
>
> **Volunteer Surveillance Team**
> A neighborhood house occupied by an elderly couple is believed by local teenagers to be haunted. In the past, the couple's home has been vandalized during the weeks preceding Halloween. In 1994, however, the Volunteer Surveillance Team kept watch over the home in October. The team spotted several groups of mischievous teens around the house, and police intervened before any damage was done. The Volunteer Surveillance Team's work prevented the home from being vandalized and sent a strong message to local teenagers that such behavior will not be tolerated in the community.
>
> **Gang Graffiti Enforcement and Eradication Team**
> In the seven months from April through October 1994, volunteers spent ninety-two hours taking 392 reports of graffiti, which saved the department nearly $1,800 (based on the mid-range salary of a sworn officer).
>
> **Victim Assistance Program**
> On February 5, 1994, while on routine patrol, the Victim Assistance Mobile Unit responded to the location of a drive-by shooting. There, volunteers found paramedics loading a juvenile male into an ambulance. He had been shot twice. Officers asked the volunteers to notify the victim's parents and accompany them to the hospital.
>
> The volunteer crisis counselors explained to the parents what had happened, assisted officers with their interviews, and acted as a bridge between the parents and the detectives. The parents had prior contact with the department regarding their son's affiliation with gangs, and the relationship between the parents and the detectives was initially very hostile. The volunteers calmed the situation and established an environment that enabled medical personnel to perform their duties and detectives to conduct a thorough investigation.
>
> Source: Robert J. Liddell, "Volunteers Help Shoulder the Load," *FBI Law Enforcement Bulletin*, August 1995, pp. 21–25.

community service officers in crime prevention programs.[123]

Over 33,000 volunteers assisted the Detroit, Michigan, Police Department in patrolling the streets during the three days surrounding Halloween in 1996, in an effort to stem the malicious and macabre tradition of "Devil's Night" fires that have plagued the city for

PATROLLING THE NET

Angels Help Patrol the Net but under Attack by Darkspace

Law enforcement agencies have received help patrolling the Net. Angels have arrived.

The CyberAngels, a branch of the Guardian Angels, the anticrime volunteers originally formed by Curtis Sliwa to prevent crime on New York City subways, have begun patrolling the Net, looking for pedophiles who may try to lure children.

The CyberAngels were formed in 1995 when Sliwa mentioned his e-mail address on his radio show and received more than 300 messages from concerned parents. The CyberAngels went global in 1995 when it was offered a web site by an organization that helps parents monitor their children's Internet surfing.

The CyberAngels, who claim they have discovered gangs and death threats on the Net, have come under fire from other groups who use the Net and are apparently wary of policing efforts. One such group, calling itself "Darkspace," has launched a campaign against the CyberAngels, nearly shutting down their system at one point by sending them over 13,000 e-mail messages.

Source: Adapted from "Patrolling Cyberspace, Looking for Clues and Crimes," *Law Enforcement News*, 29 February 1996, p. 7.

---

nearly a decade. The record number of "Devil's Night" fires was in 1984 with 810 fires. Thanks to extensive police patrols and the help of the volunteers, the number of fires dropped to 142 in 1996.[124]

Home Security Surveys and Operation Identification

Target-hardening programs have become very popular in the last few decades. Target hardening involves installing burglar alarms, installing protective gates, and using other devices and techniques to make it more difficult for criminals to enter premises to commit crime. To facilitate target hardening, numerous police departments offer home security surveys and business security surveys free of charge.

Operation Identification programs involve engraving identifying numbers (usually Social Security numbers) onto such property as bicycles, televisions, and other personal electronic items with the goal of returning the property to owners if it is stolen and then recovered by the police. The program also involves displaying decals on windows announcing that a house is equipped with an alarm or has participated in an Operation Identification program.

National Night Out

Every year citizens are encouraged to turn on all outside lighting and step outside their homes between 8 P.M. and 9 P.M. on a well-publicized, designated night, called National Night Out. In addition, a growing number of residents are expanding their participation

YOU ARE THERE!

Home Security Surveys, Downers Grove, Illinois

An innovative home security survey program, using modern telemarketing techniques, is run by the Downers Grove (Illinois) Police Department, which offers a home security survey performed by members of the department's Crime Prevention Unit (CPU). In the past, the Crime Prevention Unit performed home security surveys when they were requested by citizens. This resulted in only thirty to forty home surveys annually, despite an area population of about 46,000. In October 1988, the unit began having messages printed on all water bills forwarded to Downers Grove residents encouraging residents to call the police department to make appointments for free home security surveys. In 1989, the number of home security surveys performed increased to 258.

In 1990, the CPU started a telemarketing program by having the unit's community support assistant telephone residents to explain the survey and make appointments. During the home security survey, which lasts an hour, a crime prevention practitioner evaluates home security risks—such as exterior lighting, landscaping, doors, windows, and locks—and gives advice to owners. In 1990, the number of home security surveys performed increased to 380.

Source: Adapted from David I. Rechenmacher, "Telemarketing Crime Prevention," *FBI Law Enforcement Bulletin*, October 1991, Washington, D.C., p. 9.

by staging parades and concerts and securing corporate sponsors for the annual event.

One of the program's primary objectives is to enable neighbors to get to know one another so suspicious people and activities can be detected and reported as soon as possible. Other objectives include the generation of community support for, and participation in, local anticrime efforts, the strengthening of community spirit, and the placing of criminals on notice that neighborhood residents are watching them.[125]

Police Storefront Stations or Ministations

In an effort to get closer to the public, many police departments operate **police storefront stations or ministations.** In these programs, a small group of police officers are assigned to patrol in the immediate area of a ministation or storefront station and to engage in crime prevention programs with members of the community.

The city of Elizabeth, New Jersey, operates a ministation precinct program that doubles as an antidrug education program. Each ward in the city has a ministation staffed by patrol officers and civilian volunteers. Under this program, the officers and volunteers visit each school within their ministation precincts and present an antidrug program.[126]

In East Dallas, Texas, four sworn Dallas police officers and three civilian employees operate the East Dallas Police Storefront, which has forged a lasting bond with the community for over nine years. The East Dallas Storefront is one of five in the Central Patrol Division.[127]

Although they would not be considered ministations, many businesses, such as 7-11, McDonald's, and the pharmacy chain CVS, are opening up their stores to the local police to use as temporary community police stations. In Providence, Rhode Island, some officers are assigned to work full eight-hour shifts in local 7-11 stores that are equipped with telephones and copying machines, which allow officers to file reports from their beats. Similar work stations are provided in CVS stores in Providence.

In Horry County, South Carolina, which includes the town of Myrtle Beach, twelve McDonald's restaurants created workstations (actually tables near the front of the store) that each have a sign saying "Police Work Station."[128]

Some police departments, including the Baltimore, Maryland, Police Department, have recently borrowed an idea that has worked for the Japanese police for

Police officer in front of a Tampa, Florida ministation.

years—the "koban" or kiosk-style police ministation. In 1995, the Baltimore version of the koban opened up in the city's popular Market Center shopping district. The 8-by-12-foot steel and bulletproof glass structure is equipped with telephones, a fax machine, a computer, closed-circuit television monitors, and a bathroom. It is staffed by a police officer for twelve to sixteen hours a day. The koban provides a high-visibility post for officers who can monitor areas of the district by closed-circuit cameras. Other officers in the area can drop by to write reports or make phone calls.[129] The major difference between the Baltimore koban and the Japanese one is that Japanese officers live in their kobans, which are usually two stories tall and staffed around the clock.

Mass Media Campaigns

Mass media campaigns, such as the "Take a Bite Out of Crime" advertisements in newspapers, magazines, and on television, provide crime prevention suggestions for citizens. The "Take a Bite Out of Crime" national media campaign features the crime dog McGruff, the trench-coated cartoon figure. McGruff advises readers or viewers of actions they should take when they witness criminal activity.

Citizen Police Academies

Many police departments have established citizen police academies. Through these academies, police agencies seek to educate community members about the roles and responsibilities of police officers and to familiarize the public with the departments and how they work within the community.[130] The goal of most citizen's police academies is not to provide civilians trained in law enforcement but to create a nucleus of citizens who are well informed about a department's practices and services.

The Farmington, Connecticut, Police Department has had a ten-week citizens' police academy since 1993 with the goal of improving communication with the community and serving as a valuable problem-solving resource.[131] The Lakewood, Colorado, Police Department offers a nine-week Citizen Police Academy that educates community members about various aspects of policing, such as basic law, patrol procedures, drugs, vice investigations, SWAT, K-9, officer survival, firearms, arrest control, and building searches.[132]

In Piqua, Ohio, nearly 150 citizens have graduated from the department's eleven-week academy, gaining a better understanding of what life is like for members of the department. In 1996, the department started its first Junior Citizen's Police Academy for the city's junior high schools.[133]

Other Police-Sponsored Crime Prevention Programs

To allow citizens to get an inside look at how the police perform their jobs and to help them understand the police better, many police departments offer such programs as ride-alongs and tours of precincts and other police facilities. In the ride-along programs, citizens actually ride in patrol cars with police officers and respond to calls for police services with the officers. Citizens get a firsthand look at the activities the police perform and the special problems they encounter. Police departments providing ride-along programs require participants to sign a waiver freeing the jurisdiction from civil liability if a participant gets injured.

Many departments also provide tours of police stations, police headquarters buildings, shooting ranges, and other facilities to allow citizens to see how their tax dollars are spent.

Police and Business Cooperation

Businesses throughout the United States have recently begun to take a proactive role in assisting their local police departments. The following are some examples:

- The Crown Point, Indiana, Police Department was able to refurbish nineteen of its patrol vehicles in 1995 with help from local business sponsors.[134]
- In East St. Louis, Missouri, advertising on patrol cars pays for the local drug awareness programs.[135]
- In 1995, the Alliance for a Safer L.A. donated thirty computers to the Los Angeles Police Department.[136]
- In South Florida, weekly newspapers print trading cards for law enforcement officers to distribute to children.[137]
- In Norfolk, Virginia, local businesses fund the police department's twenty-one-officer bicycle patrol.[138]
- The five-person Hesston, Kansas, Police Department, in an effort to alert citizens to the need to wear seat belts, cooperates with a local printing company and local restaurants in obtaining place mats bearing the slogan, "We care, Buckle up." The police also lecture in classrooms about the importance of seat belt safety and provide free T-shirts and McDonald Happy Meal certificates donated by local businesses. The Hesston police also provide free year-round meals to needy citizens by picking up food from merchants and restaurants and discreetly dropping it off with needy families.[139]

AmeriCorps and Policing

AmeriCorps is a program that uses the services of thousands of Americans of all ages and backgrounds to perform vital functions in communities across the nation. In exchange for either one or two years of service, AmeriCorps members earn a small living allowance and an education award to help finance a college education or vocational training, or to pay back student loans. Many departments throughout the nation are using AmeriCorps members in programs designed to prevent and control crime and violence and prevent fear. In 1996, AmeriCorps members were walking the beat with

YOU ARE THERE!

Sample of AmeriCorps Public Safety Programs—1997

Aspira of New York
AmeriCorps members work in the South Bronx, New York City, to improve relationships between community youth and law enforcement officers. They also create safe corridors and assist victims of domestic violence.

Bridgeport Police Department
AmeriCorps members conduct home security assessments, install locks, and assist the department's Victim Services Unit in a "target hardening" program.

Enterprise Foundation
AmeriCorps members in York, Pennsylvania; Charlotte, North Carolina; and Columbus, Ohio, participate in the Community Safety Project, launched by the Enterprise Foundation in Columbia, Maryland. The project's goals include improving the physical environment in low-income areas; reclaiming sites with illegal drug activity and closing crack houses; and mobilizing communities to enhance safety. Members work closely with the local police to identify crime problems in targeted communities.

Kansas City Police Department
AmeriCorps members working in cooperation with the YMCA of Greater Kansas City and the Kansas City Police Department is sponsoring the Blue Hills Together AmeriCorps program. In Kansas City's Blue Hills neighborhood, members mobilize the community, close drug houses, recruit neighborhood block captains, and work with community policing officers.

Harlem Peacemakers
AmeriCorps members operating as Harlem peacekeepers help to develop school safety plans, create safe corridors, and teach conflict resolution for Centers for Children and Families in Central Harlem and Brooklyn, New York.

Macon Police Department
AmeriCorps members participate in the Macon, Georgia, Police Department's Police Cadet program, in which they conduct bicycle patrols in neighborhoods as part of the department's community policing initiative, establish neighborhood watch programs, and establish a senior victim assistance helpline to provide information and referrals.

Montgomery County Police Department
AmeriCorps members work with the Montgomery County Police Department as victim assistance counselors and community mobilizers. They provide victim assistance; conduct outreach to neighborhoods, community residents, and organizations to address public safety problems; and train senior citizens in crime prevention techniques through the TRIAD program.

New Hampshire Victim Assistance Program
AmeriCorps members, in conjunction with the New Hampshire Coalition Against Domestic and Sexual Violence and the State Attorney General's Office, serve as victim/witness coordinators in five major police prosecutors' offices, orienting victims to the criminal justice system and referring them to legal and social services. Members also serve in seventeen district courts to help victims obtain protective orders and stay informed of court proceedings and in fourteen crisis centers throughout the state to assist victims and their children.

New York City Police Department
The New York City Police Department has created an AmeriCorps Cadet Unit that supports community policing in high-crime areas. AmeriCorps members directly assist patrol officers on the beat and design and implement community-oriented problem-solving initiatives.

St. Louis Safety Service Corps
AmeriCorps members, in partnership with the American Youth Foundation and the St. Louis Police Department, sponsor an AmeriCorps program to support community-oriented policing in fifteen new community education centers located throughout the city.

St. Petersburg Junior College
AmeriCorps members serve in the St. Petersburg and Clearwater Police Departments on community policing efforts. Other members assist detention deputies at the Pinellas County jail in partnership with the sheriff's office.

U.S. Department of Justice
AmeriCorps members serve in the department's "Just Serve Program" in five Weed and Seed sites. They support community policing efforts, expand safe haven activities, teach conflict resolution, and assist crime victims.

Wilmington Police Department
AmeriCorps members work with the Wilmington, North Carolina, Police Department's Community Policing Partnership in four neighborhood area base stations to support its community policing efforts. Members meet victims' needs and assist them with the criminal justice system, institute neighborhood crime prevention programs, and improve neighborhood safety.

Source: Adapted from Harris Wofford, "AmeriCorps: An Important Resource for Police Executives," *Police Chief*, May 1996, pp. 59–62.

police officers in New York City; supporting neighborhood policing centers in Wilmington, North Carolina; targeting crack houses for closure in Kansas City, Missouri; conducting safety escorts for seniors in St. Louis, Missouri; hardening targets in high-crime areas of Bridgeport, Connecticut; augmenting community policing in Clearwater and St. Petersburg, Florida; assisting victims of domestic violence in New Hampshire; and expanding safe havens in five Weed and Seed sites across the nation.[140]

Chapter Summary

This chapter discussed the importance of positive relationships between the police and the public and the concepts of police human relations, police public relations, and police community relations. Public opinion and the police and the relationships between the police and minority communities and special groups were covered. Police programs involving young people appear to have the greatest potential for success in creating positive relationships with the police and causing youths to develop positive ways of behaving that will lead to future success.

The chapter also discussed community crime prevention programs, including Neighborhood Watch, Crime Stoppers, citizen patrols, citizen volunteer programs, home security surveys, and other programs designed to fight crime and improve the quality of life in U.S. communities.

As we move on to chapter 10 and cover the philosophies of community policing and problem-solving policing and their importance in dealing with the entire community, let us not forget the lessons learned in this chapter, specifically that particular groups of people, such as minorities, young people, seniors, the homeless, and the disabled, have special needs and require special attention from the police.

Learning Check

1. Explain why it is essential that the police maintain positive relationships with the community.
2. Discuss why there has been a tradition of negative relationships between the police and the African-American community.
3. Explain the rationale behind DARE programs.
4. Discuss how effective community crime prevention programs are.
5. Identify some special populations and how the police help them with their problems.

Review Exercise

You are the president of Smalltown's police community council, a group of citizens who work with the police to improve the quality of life and the quality of police-citizen relationships in Smalltown. Two days ago, a Smalltown police officer was captured on a video camera while brutally beating a Smalltown resident, who remained motionless on the ground. The tape was turned over to a local cable station, which has played it numerous times each day, causing many residents to complain openly of police brutality and harassment. Smalltown police officers have reported that numerous teenagers are screaming insults at them as they pass in their police cars. One officer reported that a teenager openly challenged him to a fight.

The police chief has called the police community council into session and asks for advice in correcting the rapidly deteriorating relationship between the police and the community. What measures would you recommend to the chief?

Web Exercise

Patrol the Web and find some examples of police programs that help citizens help themselves in preventing crime in their neighborhoods.

Key Concepts

police human relations
police public relations
police community relations
police community relations (PCR) movement
Drug Abuse Resistance Education (DARE)
anatomically correct doll
Neighborhood Watch
Crime Stoppers
Operation Identification
police storefront station or ministation

Notes

1. Lee P. Brown, "Police–Community Power Sharing," in *Police Leadership in America: Crisis and Opportunity,* ed. William A. Geller (New York: Praeger, 1985), p. 71. See also Lee P. Brown, "Violent Crime and Community Involvement," *FBI Law Enforcement Bulletin,* May 1992, pp. 2–5.

2. R. C. Davis, "Organizing the Community for Improved Policing," in *Police Leadership in America: Crisis and Opportunity,* ed. William A. Geller, pp. 84–85, p. 85.
3. Police Foundation, *Experiments in Police Improvement: A Progress Report* (Washington, D.C.: Police Foundation, 1972), p. 28.
4. Steven M. Cox and Jack D. Fitzgerald, *Police in Community Relations: Critical Issues,* 2d ed. (Dubuque, Iowa: William C. Brown, 1992), p. 4.
5. Cox and Fitzgerald, *Police in Community Relations,* p. 7.
6. Cox and Fitzgerald, *Police in Community Relations,* p. 8.
7. President's Commission on Law Enforcement and Administration of Justice, *The Challenge of Crime in a Free Society* (Washington, D.C.: U.S. Government Printing Office, 1967), p. 100.
8. President's Commission on Law Enforcement and Administration of Justice, *Challenge of Crime.*
9. Louis A. Radelet, *The Police and the Community* (Encino, Calif.: Glencoe, 1980).
10. Egon Bittner, "Community Relations," in *Police Community Relations: Images, Roles, Realities,* ed. Alvin W. Cohn and Emilio C. Viano (Philadelphia: Lippincott, 1976), pp. 77–82.
11. Ray Bull, "An Evaluation of Police Recruit Training in Human Awareness," in *Police Selection and Training: The Role of Psychology,* ed. John C. Yuille (Dordrecht, The Netherlands: Martinus Nijhoff Publishers, 1986).
12. Cox and Fitzgerald, *Police in Community Relations,* p. 50.
13. Timothy J. Flanagan and Kathleen Maguire, eds. *Sourcebook of Criminal Justice Statistics—1991* (Washington, D.C.: U.S. Department of Justice, Bureau of Justice Statistics, U.S. Government Printing Office, 1992), Table 2.14, p. 179.
14. Flanagan and Maguire, *Sourcebook of Criminal Justice Statistics—1991,* Table 2.15, p. 180.
15. Kathleen Maquire and Ann L. Pastore, eds., *Sourcebook of Criminal Justice Statistics—1996* (Washington, D.C.: U.S. Department of Justice, Bureau of Justice Statistics, U.S. Government Printing Office, 1997), Table 2.8, p. 117.
16. Maguire and Pastore, *Sourcebook 1996,* Table 2.11, p. 119.
17. Maguire and Pastore, *Sourcebook 1995,* Table 2.23, p. 143.
18. James Q. Wilson, *Thinking about Crime,* 2d ed. (New York: Basic Books, 1983), p. 91.
19. William A. Westly, *Violence and the Police* (Cambridge, Mass. MIT Press, 1970), p. 93.
20. James Q. Wilson, *Varieties of Police Behavior* (New York: Atheneum, 1973), p. 28.
21. Sherman Block, "Policing an Increasingly Diverse America," *FBI Law Enforcement Bulletin,* June 1994, pp. 24–26.
22. Block, "Policing an Increasingly Diverse America."
23. Brad R. Bennett, "Incorporating Diversity: Police Response to Multicultural Changes in Their Communities," *FBI Law Enforcement Bulletin,* December 1995, pp. 1–6.
24. International Association of Chiefs of Police, *1996 Training Catalog: IACP Educational Programs* (Alexandria, Va.: International Association of Chiefs of Police, 1996), pp. 22–23. For more information on IACP training programs, contact the International Association of Chiefs of Police (IACP) at 515 N. Washington Street, Alexandria, Virginia, 22314-2357, or call IACP at 1-800-THE-IACP or fax 1-703-836-4543.
25. Bennett, "Incorporating Diversity."
26. Michael P. Brown and James E. Hendricks, "Multicultural Training for Police: A National Survey," *Police Chief,* November 1995, pp. 44–48.
27. U.S. Bureau of the Census, *1990 Census of Population: General Population Characteristics of the United States* (Washington, D.C.: U.S. Government Printing Office, 1991).
28. *Brown v. Board of Education of Topeka,* 347 U.S. 483 (1954).
29. National Advisory Commission on Civil Disorders, *Report of the National Advisory Commission on Civil Disorders* (Washington, D.C.: U.S. Government Printing Office, 1968); and Allen D. Grimshaw, *Racial Violence in the United States* (Chicago: Aldine, 1969), pp. 269–298.
30. Cox and Fitzgerald, *Police in Community Relations,* p. 130.
31. "Blacks and Criminal Justice—a Grim Picture," *Law Enforcement News,* 30 November 1995, p. 11.
32. Ronnie A. Carter, "Improving Minority Relations," *FBI Law Enforcement Bulletin,* December 1995, pp. 14–17, p. 17.
33. U.S. Bureau of Census, *1990 Census of Population.* Hispanic groups are quite diverse, with Mexican-Americans in our nation's Southwest, Puerto Rican-Americans in the Northeast, and Cuban-Americans in Florida. The Hispanic-American population had increased over 30 percent from the previous decade.
34. "LAPD Spices Things Up with a Little Mexican Flavor," *Law Enforcement News,* 30 April 1996, p. 1.
35. "Policing in Phoenix Gets a Little More Latin Flavor," *Law Enforcement News,* 30 June 1995, p. 5.
36. "FaxBack Response: April 1995 Question: Does Your Department Provide Foreign Language Training to Its Officers?" *FBI Law Enforcement Bulletin,* August 1995, p. 12.
37. "Law Enforcement around the Nation, 1995," *Law Enforcement News,* 31 December 1995/15 January 1996, p. 13.
38. Delbert Joe and Norman Robinson, "Chinatown's Immigrant Gangs: The New Warrior Class," *Criminology* 18 (1980), p. 337.
39. Bennett, "Incorporating Diversity," p. 2.
40. U.S. Bureau of Census, *1990 Census of Population.*

41. Alan Mentzer, "Policing in Indian Country: Understanding State Jurisdiction and Authority," *Law and Order,* June 1996, pp. 24–29. For further information on law enforcement and Indians, see B. T. Baker, *Law Enforcement within Indian Country: An Introduction* (Artesia, N.M.: Federal Law Enforcement Training Center, 1993); Bureau of Indian Affairs, Division of Law Enforcement, *Indian Law Enforcement History* (Washington, D.C.: U.S. Government Printing Office, 1975); *Indian Law Enforcement Reform Act of 1990, Public Law 101-379;* International Association of Chiefs of Police, Indian Country Law Enforcement Section, *A Report by the Indian Country Section of the International Association of Chiefs of Police* (Alexandria, Va.: International Association of Chiefs of Police, 1994).
42. Jacob R. Clark, "Brutality, Abuse and Neglect: BIA Grapples with Chronic Problems," *Law Enforcement News,* 15 May 1996, p. 18.
43. Frank Schmallenger, *Criminal Justice Today: An Introductory Text for the Twenty-first Century* (Englewood Cliffs, N.J.: Prentice-Hall, 1991), p. 213.
44. "The State of the Union: From Alabama to Wyoming, State-by-State Highlights of the Year in Policing," *Law Enforcement News,* 31 December 1995/15 January 1996, p. 9.
45. Sara Roen, "Coming Out: The Closet Is Opening a Bit Wider for Homosexuals in the Work Force," *Police,* February 1996, pp. 57–59, 78–79, 82.
46. New York City Police Department, *Annual Report—1985,* p. 50.
47. Betsy Cantrell, "Triad: Reducing Criminal Victimization of the Elderly," *FBI Law Enforcement Bulletin,* February 1994, pp. 19–23.
48. William D. Miller, "The Graying of America: Implications towards Policing," *Law and Order,* October 1991, pp. 96–97.
49. Cantrell, "Triad: Reducing Criminal Victimization of the Elderly."
50. Ordway P. Burden, "Adaptable, Low-Cost, Effective: That's Triad," *Law Enforcement News,* 30 April, 1995, p. 17.
51. Burden, "Adaptable, Low-Cost, Effective."
52. Ronald J. Getz, "First Responder: A Lifeline for Older Americans," *Law and Order,* October 1996, pp. 50–58.
53. Kathryn Lemmon, "S.A.L.T.: Seniors and Lawmen Together," *Law and Order,* December 1996, pp. 29–31.
54. John S. Dempsey, "Operation Senior Safe Shopping," *Law and Order,* December 1989, pp. 31–33.
55. Ann Worrell, "Operation Blue: Cops Become Bankers to Aid Elderly Citizens," *Law and Order,* December 1993, pp. 27–30.
56. Cantrell, "Triad: Reducing Criminal Victimization of the Elderly." See also Burden, "Adaptable, Low-Cost, Effective."
57. "Bulletin Reports: Crime and the Elderly," *FBI Law Enforcement Bulletin,* May 1994, p. 12. Note: Up to fifty copies of each brochure are available to law enforcement agencies, without charge, from AARP, ATTN: CJS B-5, 601 E Street, NW, Washington, D.C. 20049. Allow four to six weeks for delivery.
58. Lynne Bliss, "Assisting Senior Victims," *FBI Law Enforcement Bulletin,* February/March 1996, pp. 6–9.
59. Federal Bureau of Investigation, *Uniform Crime Reports: Crime in the United States, 1993* (Washington, D.C.: U.S. Government Printing Office), 1994.
60. Barbara Allen Hagen and Melissa Sickmund, *Juveniles and Violence Fact Sheet* (Washington, D.C.: Office of Juvenile Justice and Delinquency, 1996).
61. "Ounces of Prevention: Chiefs Call for More Investment in Youth Programs," *Law Enforcement News,* September 1996, p. 1.
62. "Ounces of Prevention," p. 10.
63. "Ounces of Prevention."
64. William DeJong, *Project DARE: Teaching Kids to Say "No" to Drugs and Alcohol* (Washington, D.C.: National Institute of Justice, March 1986), p. 4.
65. "Truth and DARE: Wash. Cities Shelve Anti-drug Curriculum," *Law Enforcement News,* 30 November 1996, pp. 1, 15.
66. National Institute of Justice, *The D.A.R.E. Program: A Review of Prevalence, User Satisfaction, and Effectiveness* (Washington, D.C.: National Institute of Justice, 1994).
67. See Samuel Walker, *Sense and Nonsense about Crime and Drugs: A Policy Guide,* 4th ed. (Belmont, Calif.: Wadsworth/West, 1998), pp. 256–257.
68. "Truth and DARE."
69. "Truth and DARE."
70. Cox and Fitzgerald, *Police in Community Relations,* p. 164.
71. "The Cops Are Rockin' with the Roll'rz Band," *Law and Order,* December 1996, pp. 54–55.
72. R. John Schmidt, "Emergency Services Explorers, *Law and Order,* December 1994, pp. 37–39.
73. Bernal F. Koehrsen, Jr., and Dennis L. Damon, "Police Practices: Collectible Cop Cards, *FBI Law Enforcement Bulletin,* February 1993, pp. 4–5.
74. Lois Pilant, "Promoting Community Awareness," *Police Chief,* May 1995, pp. 36–42, p. 40.
75. Pilant, "Promoting Community Awareness," p. 41.
76. Michael K. Ahrens, "School Resource Officers: Community Outreach Benefits Everybody," *Law and Order,* July 1995, pp. 81–83. See also, "Keeping Kids in School," *FBI Law Enforcement Bulletin,* August 1992, pp. 10–11; Bill Zalud, "Back to School: Back to Security," *Security,* September 1994, p. 7; and "T.A.S.R.O.: Texas Association of School Resource Officers," *Texas Police Journal,* August 1993, p. 7.

77. Ahrens, "School Resource Officers," pp. 81–83.
78. Betsy Showstack Young, "Project KidCare: Photo IDS and Safety Information Arm Parents against Child Abduction," *Law and Order,* December 1995, pp. 22–24. For more information on Project KidCare, contact Polaroid at 1-800-662-8337, ext. 558.
79. Jan Hogan, "The Super Challenge Car Racing Event," *Law and Order,* December 1995, pp. 18–21. For further information, contact the National Hot Rod Association in California at 1-818-914-4761.
80. "Publication for Preschoolers," *FBI Law Enforcement Bulletin,* November 1995, p. 26.
81. Pilant, "Promoting Community Awareness," p. 39.
82. Alan Harman, "Students Patrol with Troopers: Operation Night Ride Is Reality-Based Training," *Law and Order,* December 1993, pp. 48–49.
83. Cox and Fitzgerald, *Police in Community Relations,* p. 162.
84. "Inner-City Youths Get Fighting Chance," *Law and Order,* December 1994, pp. 33–36.
85. Kevin W. Dale, "College Internship Program: Prospective Recruits Get Hands-On Experience," *FBI Law Enforcement Bulletin,* September 1996, pp. 21–24. See also "NCO Participants Learn Police Work," *Law and Order,* June 1995, p. 33.
86. Peter E. Finn and Monique Sullivan, *Police Response to Special Populations: Handling the Mentally Ill, Public Inebriate, and the Homeless* (Washington, D.C.: National Institute of Justice, January 1988), p. 1.
87. *Zinermon v. Burch,* 110 S.Ct. 975 (1990).
88. Alan R. Coffey, *Law Enforcement: A Human Relations Approach* (Englewood Cliffs, N.J.: Prentice-Hall, 1990), pp. 136–137.
89. Jacob R. Clark, "Be It Ever So Humble . . . NY Transit Cops Reach Out to Those Who Would Make the Subways Their Home," *Law Enforcement News,* 15 March 1992, p. 11.
90. Peter Finn, *Street People: Crime File Study Guide* (Washington, D.C.: National Institute of Justice, 1988), p. 1.
91. Barney Melekin, "Police and the Homeless," *FBI Law Enforcement Bulletin,* November 1990, pp. 1–6.
92. Ronald W. Glensor and Ken Peak, "Policing the Homeless: A Problem-Oriented Response," *Police Chief,* October 1994, pp. 101–103.
93. Kenneth R. Freeman and Terry Estrada-Mullaney, *Using Dolls to Interview Child Victims: Legal Concerns and Interview Procedures* (Washington, D.C.: National Institute of Justice, January/February 1988).
94. Peter Finn and Beverly N. W. Lee, *Establishing and Expanding Victim-Witness Assistance Programs* (Washington, D.C.: National Institute of Justice, August 1988).
95. Robert Snow, "Agencies Turned Advocate," *Law and Order,* January 1992, pp. 285–287.
96. Suzanne M. Youngblood and Thomas W. Lynch, "Officer, I Can't Hear You!" *Law and Order,* February 1995, pp. 51–53.
97. "In Any language," *Law Enforcement News,* 15 May 1996, p. 4.
98. Lori M. B. Laffel and Cynthia Pasquarello, "Diabetes and Law Enforcement," *Police Chief,* December 1996, p. 60.
99. George L. Kelling, "On the Accomplishments of the Police," in *Control of the Police Organization,* ed. Maurice Punch (Cambridge, Mass.: MIT Press, 1983), p. 164.
100. Wesley G. Skogan, *Disorder and Decline: Crime and the Spiral of Decay in American Neighborhoods* (New York: Free Press, 1990), p. 125.
101. James Garofalo and Maureen McLeod, *Improving the Use and Effectiveness of Neighborhood Watch Programs* (Washington, D.C.: National Institute of Justice, 1988), p. 1.
102. Figgie International, *The Figgie Report, Part 4: Reducing Crime in America—Successful Community Efforts* (Willowby, Ohio: Figgie International, 1983).
103. Garofalo and McLeod, *Improving Neighborhood Watch Programs,* p. 1.
104. Garofalo and McLeod, *Improving Neighborhood Watch Programs.*
105. Skogan, *Disorder and Decline,* p. 130.
106. Mark Alley and Dr. Mark Lanier, "Community Evaluates Neighborhood Watch, Makes Improvements," *Community Policing Exchange,* May/June 1997, p. 4.
107. Gerald S. Rudoff, "Crime Watchers Use Cellular Phones: Program in Dade County Succeeds in Reducing Crime," *Law and Order,* December 1995, pp. 32–33.
108. "Staying in Touch," *Law Enforcement News,* 30 September 1996, p. 6.
109. Alan Harman, "Citizens' Crime Watch," *Law and Order,* December 1996, pp. 41–44.
110. Dennis P. Rosenbaum, Arthur J. Lurigio, and Paul J. Lavrakas, *Crime Stoppers: A National Evaluation* (Washington, D.C.: National Institute of Justice, 1986).
111. "IACP News: Crime Prevention Efforts Encouraged," *Police Chief,* June 1992, p. 78. Note: Crime Stoppers International can be reached by telephoning 1-800-245-0009.
112. "IACP News: Crime Prevention Efforts Encouraged."
113. Tina R. DiSalvo, "Police and Resort Community Respond to Tragedy," *Law and Order,* December 1996, pp. 37–40.
114. Dennis McCauley, "Tipped Off: 845-A-TIP Line Allows Citizens and Police to Team Up and Tap In on Crime," *Police,* August 1995, pp. 49–50.
115. Dennis Jay Kenney, "The Guardian Angels: The Related Social Issues," in *Police and Policing: Contemporary Issues,* ed. Dennis Jay Kenney (New York: Praeger, 1989), pp. 376–400.

116. Philip Messing, "Cops to Wing It with Angels in Park: Taking First Step Together—on Skates," *New York Post,* 1 December 1996, p. 6.
117. Susan Pennell et al., "Guardian Angels: A Unique Approach to Crime Prevention," *Crime and Delinquency,* July 1989, pp. 376–400.
118. "Los Angeles Complex Calls in Muslim Guards," *New York Times,* 11 October 1992, p. A-38.
119. "Los Angeles Complex Calls in Muslim Guards."
120. "Cable TV Crews Tune In to Crime-Fighting," *Law Enforcement News,* 31 October 1995, p. 5.
121. "An Outraged Citizenry Targets Crime: Floridians Stage Noisy Nighttime Marches to Take Back Their Streets," *Law Enforcement News,* 30 November 1996, p. 7.
122. Ordway P. Burden, "Volunteers: The Wave of the Future?" *Police Chief,* July 1988, pp. 25–26.
123. Adele Woodyard, "A Volunteer Program That Works: CVAP (Civilian Volunteers to Assist Police) Program Helps Out in Tampa," *Law and Order,* November 1995, pp. 96–99.
124. Robyn Meredith, "Civic Angels Curb Detroit 'Devil's Night' Fires," *New York Times,* 3 November 1996, p. 40.
125. Houston Police Department, *Multiyear Report—1983–1987* (Houston: Houston Police Department, 1988), p. 25.
126. "Mobile Precincts: Police on Wheels," *FBI Law Enforcement Bulletin,* April 1992, p. 14.
127. Jeff Siegel, "The East Dallas Police Storefront," *Law and Order,* May 1995, pp. 53–55.
128. *Law Enforcement News,* 15 September 1995. Also see John S. Dempsey, *West Home Page,* "Criminal Justice Update," April 1996; and Irving Molotsky, "Stores Invite Police to Stop By," *New York Times,* 24 September 1997, p. A-12.
129. *Law Enforcement News,* 15 May 1995. Also, see Dempsey, *West Home Page.*
130. Bennett, "Incorporating Diversity."
131. Tracy Enns, "Citizens' Police Academies: The Farmington Experience," *Police Chief,* April 1995, pp. 133–135.
132. Robert J. Liddell, "Volunteers Help Shoulder the Load," *FBI Law Enforcement Bulletin,* August 1995, pp. 21–25.
133. John Graham, "Arming Citizens with Guns (Radar Guns, That Is)," *Law and Order,* December 1996, p. 59.
134. "Law Enforcement around the Nation, 1995," p. 7.
135. "Law Enforcement around the Nation, 1995," p. 27.
136. "Law Enforcement around the Nation, 1995," p. 10.
137. Cheryl DuPree Kravetz, "Investing in Positive Community Relations: Newspaper's Police Trading Card Program Brings Cops and Kids Together," *Police,* January 1997, pp. 18–19.
138. Pilant, "Promoting Community Awareness," p. 37.
139. Harvey Rachlin, "Something for Nothing: Making an Impact on the Community on a Zero Budget," *Law and Order,* December 1996, pp. 24–28.
140. Harris Wofford, "AmeriCorps: An Important Resource for Police Executives," *Police Chief,* May 1996, pp. 59–62. Note: For information about applications or programs in your area, contact the AmeriCorps Office of Public Liaison at 1-202-606-5000, ext. 260, or contact your state commission.

10

Community Policing: The Debate Continues

Chapter Outline

Corporate Strategies for Policing
The Philosophy of Community Policing and Problem-Solving Policing
Community Policing
Problem-Solving Policing
Current Ways of Doing Community Policing
　Resident Officer Programs—The Ultimate in Community Policing?
The Federal Government and Community Policing
　The Crime Bill
　Office of Community Oriented Policing Services (COPS)
　Community Policing Consortium
Some Accomplishments of Community Policing
Not All Agree with Community Policing

Chapter Goals

■ To acquaint you with the most current thinking about corporate strategies for policing, including strategic policing, community policing, and problem-solving policing.

■ To explore the philosophy and genesis of the current corporate strategies of community policing and problem-solving policing.

■ To discuss the effect of community policing and problem-solving policing on current policing.

■ To discuss the implementation of community policing strategies, including the most recent methods, the role of the federal government, and some recent community policing successes.

■ To explain why some scholars and practitioners do not agree with the implementation of community policing strategies.

Introduction

Chapter 9 discussed police and the community. Specifically, it explored the concepts of police community relations, public relations, and human relations; public opinion and the police; and problems and relationships between the police and many specific populations, including minority groups and such special populations as senior citizens, young people, the homeless, the disabled, and crime victims. It also discussed numerous forms of crime-prevention services the police offer the community and numerous partnerships between the police and the community to deter crime and improve the quality of life in our communities.

This chapter continues discussing relationships between the police and the community, but deals with more philosophical and strategic issues about reducing crime and improving our quality of life. It addresses the concepts of community policing and problem-solving policing, concepts that many consider a new strategy of policing. Others feel these concepts are not a new strategy, but rather a return to the policing of the past.

In 1988, the scholar, George Kelling, stated:

> A quiet revolution is reshaping American policing. Police in dozens of communities are returning to foot patrol. In many communities, police are surveying citizens to learn what they believed to be their most serious neighborhood problems. Many police departments are finding alternatives to rapidly responding to the majority of calls for service. Many departments are targeting resources on citizen fear of crime by concentrating on disorder. Organizing citizen's groups has become a priority in many departments. Increasingly, police departments are looking for means to evaluate themselves on their contribution to the quality of neighborhood life, not just crime statistics. Are such activities the business of policing? In a crescendo, police are answering yes.[1]

By 1998, many said the face of policing had changed dramatically. Community policing and problem-solving policing had been practiced for over a decade and had proven to be tremendously popular with some citizens, academics, politicians, and police chiefs. Many believe that community policing and problem-solving policing could be the best strategies to use in policing our nation. These two ideas emphasize community involvement and the building of partnerships between the police and the community. In many areas where community policing and problem-solving policing have been implemented, crime rates have gone down, quality of life has been improved, and people have felt safer.

Many, however, are not enthusiastic about this new philosophy and argue over its definition and implementation. This chapter is intended to present the facts, explore the issues, and continue the debate.

The chapter will discuss three corporate strategies for modern policing: strategic policing, community policing, and problem-solving policing. It will discuss the underlying philosophy and the genesis of the thinking about community policing and problem-solving policing and then discuss some examples of how these concepts can be translated into action.

The chapter will also discuss the federal government and its influence over community policing, including the 1994 Crime Bill, the Office of Community Policing Services, and the Community Policing Consortium. It will present some empirical and anecdotal evidence of the accomplishments of community policing, but will also show how some scholars and practitioners do not agree with these policing strategies.

It is hoped that by presenting the issues and exploring them we may continue the process begun by Sir Robert Peel in 1829 of making the police an essential part of life in the community.

Corporate Strategies for Policing

Police chiefs and academics throughout the United States are discussing changes in the traditional methods of policing that were discussed in chapter 7—random routine patrol, rapid response to citizens' calls to 911, and retroactive investigation of past crimes by detectives. Since the mid-1980s, Harvard University's prestigious John F. Kennedy School of Government has held periodic meetings to discuss the current state of policing in the United States. These Executive Sessions on Policing were developed and administered by the Kennedy School's Program in Criminal Justice Policy and Management. Under the leadership of Professor Mark H. Moore, the chair of Harvard's program, leading police administrators and academics gathered at Harvard to focus and debate on the use and price of such strategies as strategic policing, community policing, and problem-solving policing.

Beginning in 1988, the National Institute of Justice and Harvard produced a series of monographs that have shaped the current state of police thinking. These monographs discussed community policing, problem-oriented policing, police values, corporate strategies of policing, crime and policing, policing and the fear of crime, the history of policing, police accountability, and drugs and the police.[2]

Harvard's Executive Sessions on Policing identified three "**corporate strategies for policing**" that are presently guiding U.S. policing: (1) strategic policing, (2) community policing, and (3) problem-solving policing.[3]

Strategic policing involves a continued reliance on traditional police operations, but with an increased emphasis on crimes that are not generally well controlled by traditional policing (for example, serial offenders, gangs, organized crime, drug distribution networks, and white-collar and computer criminals). Strategic policing represents an advanced stage of traditional policing using innovative enforcement techniques, including intelligence operations, electronic surveillance, and sophisticated forensic techniques. Much of this textbook, particularly the chapters on police operations and technology, deals with strategic policing issues.

Community policing is an attempt to involve the community as an active partner with the police in addressing crime problems in the community.

Problem-solving policing emphasizes the fact that many crimes are caused by underlying social problems. It attempts to deal with those underlying problems instead of just responding to each criminal incident.

Community policing and problem-solving policing are very similar approaches to the crime and disorder problems in our communities. Most departments adopting a community policing program also follow many of the tenets of problem-solving policing.

The Philosophy of Community Policing and Problem-Solving Policing

In the 1960s, increases in crime, technological advances, and changes in police management thinking led to the abandonment of police foot patrols and their resultant ties to the community. They were replaced by a highly mobile police department able to drive from one incident to another in minutes.

At about the same time, many urban communities were experiencing drastic demographic changes. Longtime community residents were moving from the inner city to newly opened suburbs and being replaced by newly arrived people from rural areas and Caribbean and Latin American countries. These newly arrived peo-

All in the Line of Duty

He Kept Her Up Until Help Arrived

While on patrol, Officer Charles R. Gunning of the Lincoln, Illinois, Police Department responded to the report of a woman trapped in an overturned vehicle. Officer Gunning located the vehicle resting upside down in several feet of water at the bottom of an embankment. The woman was unable to remove her seatbelt and was having great difficulty keeping her head above the water. Officer Gunning got into the freezing water and held the woman's head above the waterline until other rescue units arrived. He then assisted responding emergency units in freeing the woman from the vehicle.

Source: Adapted from *FBI Law Enforcement Bulletin*, August 1994, p. 33.

ple were not used to urban life and the culture, norms, and mores of their newly adopted neighborhoods. Often there was a language barrier between the immigrants and older members of the community. These changes brought severe social problems to our cities and, of course, problems to our police. In addition, the heroin epidemic hit the United States in the 1960s, causing crime, social disorganization, and fear and mistrust. Recall the descriptions of the urban riots of the late 1960s described in chapter 1 of this text.

Many problems developed between the police and the newly arrived citizens as rapidly moving police mobile units, with flashing lights and roaring sirens, arrived in a community to answer someone's request for assistance or report of a crime. Often a lack of communication and mistrust ensued because of the police's need to take quick action and get violent people off the street as soon as possible, and then to return to more serious emergencies. The police were no longer seen as members of the community, as the old beat cop had been; they were more and more seen as an invading army or an army of occupation. As a result, many police departments began to establish community relations units to address problems between the police and the community. The units were part of what was called the Police Community Relations movement (PCR).

The police community relations units were supposed to address this communication gap. These units were not effective, however, because they usually appeared

Burned out and abandoned buildings, like these in the Charlotte Street section of the South Bronx, are an example of the concept behind the "broken windows model" of policing.

only after an ugly incident. Although the community relations units were well intentioned, in reality they could not work. The real responsibility for proper police-community relations, as any professional, experienced police officer knows, rests with each and every police officer, not a select, small group of community relations officers. Today's community policing is completely different from the earlier community relations movement and should not be confused with it.

Modern community policing, as compared to the PCR movement, entails a substantial change in police thinking. As Albert J. Reiss, Jr., says, the change must be "one where police strategy and tactics are adapted to fit the needs and requirements of the different communities the department serves, . . . and where there is considerable involvement of the community with police in reaching their objectives."[4]

Many believe that the modern stage of community policing began with the seminal 1982 article in the *Atlantic Monthly* by **James Q. Wilson** and **George Kelling**, "'Broken Windows': The Police and Neighborhood Safety." Theirs has come to be known as the **broken windows model** of policing.[5] The Wilson and Kelling article made several very critical points.

First, disorder in neighborhoods creates fear. Urban streets that are often occupied by homeless people, prostitutes, drug addicts, youth gangs, and the mentally disturbed, as well as regular citizens, are more likely than other areas to have high crime rates. Second, certain neighborhoods send out "signals" that encourage crime. A community in which housing has deteriorated, broken windows are left unrepaired, and disorderly behavior is ignored may actually promote crime. Honest and good citizens live in fear in these areas, and predatory criminals are attracted. Third, community policing is essential. If police are to reduce fear and combat crime in these areas, they must rely on the cooperation of citizens for support and assistance. Wilson and Kelling argued that community preservation, public safety, and order maintenance—not crime fighting—should become the primary focus of police patrol.[6] From this concept, many believe, the modern concept of community policing began.

Expanding on the work of Wilson and Kelling, Wesley G. Skogan surveyed numerous neighborhoods and identified two major categories of disorder that affect the quality of life in the community: human and physical disorder. The human behaviors found to be extremely disruptive to the community were public drinking, corner gangs, street harassment, drugs, noisy neighbors, and commercial sex. The physical disorders that Skogan found extremely destructive to the community were vandalism, dilapidation and abandonment, and rubbish.[7]

Using the Wilson and Kelling and Skogan ideas as a philosophical and practical framework, many scholars and progressive police chiefs jumped onto the community policing bandwagon.

Community Policing

Robert C. Trojanowicz, director of the National Center for Community Policing in East Lansing, Michigan, said that community policing can play a vital role in reducing three important kinds of violence in the community: (1) individual violence, ranging from street crime to domestic abuse to drug-related violence; (2) civil unrest, which can often include gang violence and open confrontations among various segments of society, specifically the police; and (3) police brutality.[8]

Scholars Jerome Skolnick and David Bayley have pointed out the following in regard to community policing: "Among the world's industrial democracies, community-oriented policing represents what is progressive and forward-looking in policing. In Western Europe, North America, Australia, New Zealand, and the Far East, community policing is being talked about as the solution to the problems of policing. Papers exploring it have become a cottage industry."[9]

In 1997, Jeremy Travis, Director of the National Institute of Justice, speaking about community policing strategies in response to the dramatic decreases in crime during the mid- to late-1990s, noted,

> The dramatic decline in crime occurring in many of our nation's cities has generated an intense public debate over the cause or causes. . . . It is interesting to note that many authorities—among them a number of eminent criminologists—have credited much of the drop in crime to better and smarter policing.
>
> In fact, after a long period of reluctance to say the police can prevent crime, a consensus is emerging that gives at least partial credit for lower crime to the transformation in policing.[10]

Community policing mandates that the police work with the community, not against it, to be effective. The foot patrol experiments described in chapter 7 in Newark, New Jersey, and Flint, Michigan, are examples of the community policing model suggested by Wilson and Kelling in their "broken windows" approach to policing.

The scholar Herman Goldstein offers the following list of the most important benefits of community policing:

1. A more realistic acknowledgment of police functions.
2. A recognition of the interrelationships among police functions.

YOU ARE THERE!

Academic Research Resulting in Today's Emphasis on Community Policing

The academic research regarding policing, discussed in chapters 1, 7, and 8 of this text, revealed many facts about policing that have led to the current emphasis on community policing. According to Professor David L. Carter, the research indicates the following:

- Random, marked patrol does not prevent crime.
- Patrol officers have a notable amount of "uncommitted" time.
- Quick response to citizen calls does not increase the probability of apprehending criminals.
- Fulfillment of citizen expectations of response time—not the actual speed of response—shapes citizen satisfaction with the police.
- Call management plans, such as Differential Response to Calls for Service, can increase the efficiency and effectiveness of policing without sacrificing citizen safety.
- Assigning patrol officers to geographic locations based on population ratios does not meet the variability of demands for police service.
- Meaningful deployment of patrol officers requires careful analysis of environmental factors, thus calling for service that can fluctuate according to season, time of day, and geographic location.
- Because most citizen calls can be handled effectively by one officer, single-officer patrol cars are significantly more efficient than two-officer units.
- One-officer patrol cars do not pose undue threats to officer safety.
- Teams of police officers working in a cooperative effort toward commonly defined goals can provide more comprehensive police service than nonteam efforts.
- Unique patrol deployment schemes, or specialized patrols, can be useful in handling special circumstances and problems.
- Patrol officer job enlargement and job enrichment helps increase job satisfaction, thus fostering an environment in which officers become more productive.
- Citizen demands for police assistance and problem solving related to noncriminal matters must be addressed.

Source: Adapted from David L. Carter, *Community Policing and DARE: A Practitioner's Perspective* (Washington, D.C.: National Institute of Justice, 1995), p. 2.

PATROLLING THE NET

The Net and Community Policing—How Can It Help?

The philosophy of community policing has hit the Internet. Community policing focuses on solving problems at the neighborhood level by involving government organizations, citizens, and community groups in an effort to help to improve the quality of life in a neighborhood. The Internet provides a great opportunity to establish an information resource for the community and to solicit citizens' comments and questions.

For example, statistical information related to criminal offenses, arrests, and calls for police service are of considerable interest to individual community members, as well as community and business groups. Linking statistics to maps provides a graphical connection to this data.

Crime prevention material and information about agency programs also can be provided efficiently via the web. Photographs can be published with textual information that duplicates—or even surpasses—the quality of printed material. Some police departments publish an electronic list of most wanted fugitives with digitized photographs, physical descriptions, and details of the crimes for which they are wanted.

Many departments, to support the goal of improving access and communication between the agency and the community, publish a directory of all its units. Such a directory can be updated in a few minutes at any time and could include unit addresses, telephone numbers, the names of commanders or contact persons, and the like.

E-mail links from this directory can make it even easier for citizens to send messages to the right people or places to deal with most particular problems.

Source: Adapted from Walter W. Manning, "Should You Be on the Net," *FBI Law Enforcement Bulletin,* January 1997, pp. 18–22.

---

3. An acknowledgment of the limited capacity of the police to accomplish their jobs on their own and of the importance of an alliance between the police and the public.
4. Less dependence on the criminal justice system and more emphasis on new problem-solving methods.
5. Greatly increased use of the knowledge gained by the police of their assigned areas.
6. More effective use of personnel.
7. An increased awareness of community problems as a basis for designing more effective police response.[11]

Community policing seeks to replace our traditional methods of police patrol with joint community and police efforts to find proactive, innovative solutions to crime and disorder on our streets. In *Beyond 911: A New Era for Policing,* Malcolm K. Sparrow, Mark H. Moore, and David M. Kennedy offer the following observation on community policing: "Community policing, with its emphasis on openness and partnerships . . . has broadened police awareness and extended police capabilities. The police have been willing to accept community help in both setting priorities and carrying out operations."[12]

YOU ARE THERE! »

Different Communities Have Different Names for Community Policing Initiatives, But It's All Basically the Same

Municipality	Program
Aurora, Col.	Police Area Representative
Aurora, Ill.	Resident Officer
Baltimore County, Md.	Citizen-Oriented Police Experiment
Detroit, Mich.	Ministation
Flint, Mich.	Neighborhood Foot Patrol
Ft. Worth, Tex.	Code Blue
Houston, Tex.	Neighborhood-Oriented Policing
Jackson, Tenn.	Community-Oriented Policing
Kansas City, Mo.	Target-Oriented Policing
Madison, Wis.	Quality Policing
Newport News, Va.	Problem-Oriented Policing

Source: Adapted from David L. Carter, *Community Policing and DARE: A Practitioner's Perspective* (Washington, D.C.: National Institute of Justice, 1995), p. 2.

Some examples of very early attempts at community policing involved the experiences of the following three cities: Detroit, New York City, and Houston.

In Detroit, one innovative approach developed by community policing advocates was the development of decentralized neighborhood-based precincts that serve as "storefront" police stations. One well-known program is the Detroit Mini-Station Program, which established over thirty-six such stations around the city. At first, the community did not accept the program because the officers assigned to the ministations seemed to lack commitment. Later, however, officers were chosen for ministation duty on the basis of their community relations skills and crime prevention ability; since then the program has met with much greater community acceptance.[13]

YOU ARE THERE! »

What Is Community Policing? What Is a CPO?

Robert Trojanowicz and Bonnie Bucqueroux, in *Community Policing: A Contemporary Perspective*, define community policing as follows:

Community Policing is a new philosophy of policing, based on the concept that police officers and private citizens working together in creative ways can help solve contemporary community problems related to crime, fear of crime, social and physical disorder, and neighborhood decay. The philosophy is predicated on the belief that achieving these goals requires that police departments develop a new relationship with the law-abiding people in the community, allowing them a greater voice in setting local police priorities and involving them in efforts to improve the overall quality of life in their neighborhoods. It shifts the focus of police work from handling random calls to solving community problems. . . .

The community policing philosophy is expressed in a new organizational strategy that allows police departments to put theory into practice. This requires freeing some patrol officers from the isolation of the patrol car and the incessant demands of the police radio, so that these officers can maintain direct, face-to-face contact with people in the same defined geographic (beat) area every day. This new Community Policing Officer (CPO) serves as a generalist, an officer whose mission includes developing imaginative, new ways to address the broad spectrum of community concerns. . . . The goal is to allow CPOs to own their beat areas, so that they can develop the rapport and trust that is vital in encouraging people to become involved in efforts to address the problems in the neighborhoods. . . . The CPO not only enforces the law, but supports and supervises community-based efforts aimed at local concerns. The CPO allows people direct input in setting day-to-day local police priorities, in exchange for the cooperation and participation in efforts to police themselves.

Source: Adapted from Robert Trojanowicz and Bonnie Bucqueroux, *Community Policing: A Contemporary Perspective* (Cincinnati: Anderson, 1990), p. 5.

YOU ARE THERE! »

Critical Attitudes Associated with Community Policing: What the Community Police Officer Needs

1. A sense of personal responsibility for an area and its people.
   A feeling of ownership for what happens.
2. Belief in the importance of attempting to improve conditions within an area.
   A desire to assess what you have control over and act responsibly as it relates to crime and disorder.
3. Belief that the concerns of neighborhood residents matter.
   Recognizing that police do not always know what citizens want and are not afraid to ask.
4. Belief that citizens possess information necessary for police to do their jobs well.
   An understanding that police are heavily dependent on assistance from citizens to be successful.
5. Commitment to educating and empowering citizens to act.
   A desire to teach citizens how to help themselves.
6. Belief in working with citizens to solve problems.
   Recognizing limitations and a willingness to pursue alternative courses of action.
7. Belief in working with other government or community agencies to solve problems.
   Understanding the importance and being capable of working in teams to accomplish results.
8. Willing to make "extra efforts."
   Is willing to go above and beyond what is normally expected.

Source: Mary Ann Wycoff and Thomas Oettmeier, *Evaluating Patrol Officer Performance Under Community Policing: The Houston Experience* (Houston, Texas: Houston Police Department, 1993).

Dempsey's Law

Professor: What Is Community Policing? Did You Ever Do That Stuff?

I get this question each semester in my policing course.

When I first started as a police officer in the 41st Precinct in the Bronx, in 1966, I was a foot patrol cop, as were most of us. During my first two years there, there were only four RMP (Radio Motor Patrol) sector cars in the entire precinct and the sergeant's car. Our foot patrol beats generally covered five or six blocks. Early in my career there, the precinct earned the nickname Fort Apache because of the wild conditions and crime that permeated the precinct. It was considered the busiest and most dangerous precinct in the City of New York, and probably the world, in the 1960s and 1970s. Later, a movie was made, staring Paul Newman, called *Fort Apache—the Bronx*, detailing life as a police officer in the days I was there. You can still see the movie on TV or get it from your video store. Believe me, the movie made the place seem too tame. It was much crazier than that.

My foot patrol post was called Post 28 and covered all of Westchester Avenue from Southern Boulevard to Kelly Street, both sides of the streets and all of the side streets including Simpson Street, Fox Street, Tiffany Street, and Kelly Street. Westchester Avenue, under the el, was the commercial hub of the area and all of the side blocks were covered by wall-to-wall five-story tenements. It was the height of the heroin crisis in New York City and crime and disorder was rampant. I patrolled this post alone without the portable radio you see officers carry today. I loved it. I made hundreds of collars [arrests], mostly gun collars and junk [drug] arrests. I also broke up fights, delivered babies, brought kids home to their parents, directed traffic, gave comfort and advice, and helped as many people as I could. Whatever the time, day or night, whenever I was working, people knew they could talk to me. Whenever they had a problem, they would come to me. The good people on my post loved me—they called me their amigo. The people who wanted to annoy the good people on my post learned to avoid me—they went someplace else. The criminals . . . well, they didn't like me too much. I put them in jail. In summary, I was the COP. Everyone knew me. I was part of the life of that community, part of the life of that little spot of the world—Patrol Post 28 of the 41st Precinct.

We didn't have a concept known as community policing then. We were all just cops, doing our job. As the years went by, the number of patrol car sectors assigned to the precinct increased and increased until by 1970 we had over fourteen sectors, almost four times the number we had when I started. I guess this was due to new management thinking in the department: A radio motor patrol unit can cover so much more territory than a foot cop, thus officers in a car are more economical, cost-effective, and efficient. Also, 911 had taken over the NYPD by then. We would race from one 911 call to another—handle one incident after another—do what we had to do and then do it all over again, time after time. No longer did we deal with problems. We just dealt with incidents.

Although this change from foot patrol to the more cost-effective motorized patrol may have been necessary because of 911, I think it was a big mistake. Most of us were assigned to regular seats in the radio cars and never walked our foot beats again. What we gained in efficiency, we lost in closeness to the community. Many of the people on my beat felt they had lost their amigo—I was always busy running around the entire precinct handling 911 jobs.

Today's community police officer, I believe and hope, is a return to the past. A return to the cop on the beat who knows everyone and everyone knows him or her. The major difference between today's community officer and the beat cop of my day is structure. Today, the officers receive training and support from the department and other city agencies. They have offices and answering machines and fill out paper work. Hopefully, they also become what I was on Post 28 in the 41st Precinct—part of life in that little part of the world—the good people's amigo.

Community Policing: The Debate Continues   237

Door-to-door community surveys are an important component of community policing.

A study in Houston that involved patrol officers' visiting households to solicit viewpoints and information on community problems reported both crime and fear decreases in the study area.[14]

The New York City Police Department began a Community Patrol Officer Program (CPOP) in 1984. CPOP officers did not respond to calls from 911 but instead were directed to identify neighborhood problems and develop short- and long-term strategies for solving them. Each officer kept a beat book in which he or she was expected to identify major problems on his or her beat and list strategies to deal with them. Officers thus were encouraged to think about problems and their solutions.[15]

David L. Carter, of Michigan State University, explains that community policing did not suddenly materialize as a new idea; rather, it evolved from research conducted by a wide range of scholars and police research organizations. Beginning primarily in the early 1970s, a great deal of research was conducted on police patrol.[16]

Regarding community policing, Joseph E. Braun, of the U.S. Department of Justice, wrote in 1997,

> The traditional role of law enforcement is changing.... Community policing allows law enforcement practitioners to bring government resources closer to the community. Hence, participation and cooperation are key.... we cannot expect law enforcement to solve crime and social disorder problems alone. Community involvement is imperative.... With the implementation of community policing practices, officers and deputies still retain their enforcement duties and powers. Community policing does not mean that authority is relinquished; rather, its proactive nature is intended to reduce the need for enforcement in the long term as problems are addressed up front and much earlier. This can only occur with the cooperation and participation of the community.[17]

It must be noted here that community policing is not a totally new concept. As we saw in chapter 1 of this text, policing, from its early English roots, has always been community oriented. As one officer reminded us in 1997,

> The concept of community policing goes as far back as London's Sir Robert Peel, when he began building his public police in 1829. In his original principles, he said, "The police are the public and... the public are the police: the police being only the member of the public that are paid to give full-time attention to duties which are incumbent on every citizen in the interests of community welfare and existence.[18]

Problem-Solving Policing

The idea of problem-solving policing can be attributed to **Herman Goldstein**, a law professor at the University of Wisconsin, who had spent a great deal of time in the trenches with different police departments. The problem-solving approach to policing was first mentioned by Goldstein in a 1979 article calling for a new kind of policing, which he termed problem-oriented policing.[19]

In traditional policing, most of what the police do is incident driven—they drive to incident after incident, dealing with each one and then responding to another. Problem-solving policing, or problem-oriented policing, however, forces the police to focus on the problems that cause the incidents.

Commenting on incident-driven policing, John E. Eck and William Spelman stated:

> Often officers tend to respond to similar incidents at the same location numerous times—burglaries in a certain

YOU ARE THERE!

Problem-Solving Policing Solves Problems

Newport News, Virginia, is a Navy town of 155,000 citizens that has many of the same crime problems as other major cities. It was the location of one of the first studies of problem-solving policing. The following selection shows how Newport News used the problem-solving approach, dealing with its robbery problem as a general problem rather than as a series of incidents.

At 1:32 A.M., a man identified as Fred Snyder dials 911 from a downtown corner phone booth. The dispatcher notes his location and calls the nearest patrol unit. Police Officer Knox arrives four minutes later.

Snyder says he was beaten and robbed twenty minutes earlier but did not see the robber. Under persistent questioning, Snyder admits he was with a prostitute he picked up in a bar. Later, in a hotel room, he discovered the prostitute was actually a man, who then beat Snyder and took his wallet.

Snyder wants to let the whole matter drop. He refuses medical treatment for his injuries. Knox finishes his report and lets Snyder go home. Later that day, Knox's report reaches Detective Alexander's desk. She knows from experience that the case will go nowhere, but she calls Snyder at work. Snyder confirms the report but refuses to cooperate further. Knox and Alexander go on to other cases.

Months later, reviewing the crime statistics, the city council deplores the difficulty of attracting business or people downtown. Midnight-watch patrol officers are tired of taking calls like Snyder's. They and their sergeant, James Hogan, decide to reduce prostitution-related robberies, and Officer James Boswell volunteers to lead the effort.

First, Boswell interviews the twenty-eight prostitutes who work the downtown area to learn how they solicit, what happens when they get caught, and why they are not deterred. They work downtown bars, they tell him, because customers are easy to find, and police patrols do not spot them soliciting. Arrests, the prostitutes tell Boswell, are just an inconvenience; judges routinely sentence them to probation, and probation conditions are not enforced.

Based on what he has learned from the interviews and his previous experience, Boswell devises a response. He works with the Alcohol Beverage Control Board and local bar owners to move the prostitutes into the street. At police request, the commonwealth's attorney agrees to ask the judges to put stiffer conditions on probation: convicted prostitutes would be given a map of the city and told to stay out of the downtown area or go to jail for three months.

Boswell then works with the vice unit to make sure that downtown prostitutes are arrested and convicted and that patrol officers know which prostitutes are on probation. Probation violators are sent to jail, and within weeks all but a few of the prostitutes have left the downtown area.

Then Boswell talks to the prostitutes' customers, most of whom do not know that almost half the prostitutes working the street are actually men posing as women. He intervenes in street transactions, formally introducing the customers to their male dates. The U.S. Navy sets up talks for him with incoming sailors to tell them about the male prostitutes and the associated safety and health risks.

In three months, the number of prostitutes working downtown drops from twenty-eight to six, and robbery rates are cut in half. After eighteen months, neither robbery nor prostitution show signs of returning to their earlier levels.

Source: Adapted from John E. Eck et al., *Problem Solving: Problem-Oriented Policing in Newport News* (Washington, D.C., Police Executive Research Forum, 1987), pp. 100–101.

---

housing project—car thefts in a certain parking lot. Because the police have traditionally focused on incidents, rarely have they sought to determine the underlying causes of these incidents. Problem-oriented policing tries to find out what is causing citizen calls for help.[20]

Sparrow, Moore, and Kennedy explain the need for problem-solving policing:

> By relying on patrol to prevent crime and rapid response to catch criminals police had backed themselves into an isolated, reactive corner. The beat officers of old had naturally seen crime on their beats in terms of patterns: they were responsible for all incidents on their turf, and a rash of burglaries or overdoses signaled a burglar or a dealer who needed to be dealt with. Modern officers, tied to their radios, saw crime as an endless string of isolated incidents. Fourteen burglaries in the same neighborhood might draw fourteen different cars.[21]

The Newport News, Virginia, and Baltimore County, Maryland, Police Departments have gained national recognition for their implementation of problem-solving policing. Their programs involved officers and the com-

Figure 10.1
Problem-Solving Technique—SARA

munity working together to find solutions that would reduce crime, disorder, and fear.

The problem-oriented policing strategy consists of four distinct parts: scanning, analysis, response, and assessment (see Figure 10.1). Problem-oriented policing practitioners call this scanning, analysis, response, and assessment process by the acronym SARA. In the scanning process, groups of officers discuss incidents as "problems" instead of as specific incidents and criminal law concepts, such as "robberies" or "larcenies." A robbery, which used to be thought of as a single incident, in the scanning process is thought of as being part of a pattern of robberies, which in turn might be related to another problem, such as prostitution-related robberies in a particular area of the city.

After defining the problem, officers begin analysis. They collect information from a variety of sources, including nonpolice sources, such as members of the business community, other city agencies, or local citizens. The officers then use the information to discover the underlying nature of the problem, its causes, and options for solutions.

After scanning and analysis, the police begin response. They work with citizens, business owners, and public and private agencies to prepare a program of action suitable to the specifics of the particular problem. Solutions may include arrest but also may involve action by other community agencies and organizations.

In the assessment process—after the police make their response to the problem—they evaluate the effectiveness of the response. They may use the results to revise the response, collect more data, or even to redefine the problem.[22]

Problem-oriented policing involves officers' thinking, not just responding to yet another call for duty. It involves officers dealing with the underlying causes of incidents to prevent those incidents from happening again, and it involves officers' using all sources, not only police department sources, to deal with problems. Sparrow, Moore, and Kennedy offer the following commentary on problem-oriented policing: "Problem-solving policing, with its emphasis on thoughtful police work . . . has challenged police to pay renewed attention to the causes and patterns of crime. It has also added to their arsenal new techniques of analysis, dispute resolution, and crime prevention, and an increased willingness to engage in productive cooperative relationships with other municipal agencies."[23]

Current Ways of Doing Community Policing

The concepts of community policing and problem-solving policing have merged in the past decade and can generally be looked at as one philosophy. There have been several names that have been given to this philosophy in addition to community policing and problem-solving policing, including community oriented policing. Whatever the name given to this philosophy, the concept is the same—the involvement of the community as a partner in the policing process and an emphasis on proactive, problem-oriented policing as opposed to incident-driven policing. This section will address several of the methods, techniques, or ways of implementing community oriented policing.

The police have implemented the philosophy of community policing with numerous methods. Primary among these is the refocusing of a department's overall philosophy and operations in order to view the community not only as a partner but as a consumer of the department's products.

Accordingly, Harvey Rachlin, a freelance writer who reports prolifically on police programs, wrote in 1997:

> Community policing has grown to be more than just a philosophy calling for police to cooperate with the public in addressing crime problems. Today, police agencies are beginning to mirror financial, telecommunications, and other industries and institutions by offering various "products" other than their core service to satisfy the ever-changing public.[24]

Rachlin then presents a staggering list of creative community policing "products" offered by a number of police departments in the state of Kansas. This list includes over thirty specific programs that focus on the consumers of the police product, including young people and other members of the community. Many of his

YOU ARE THERE!

Using Community Policing to Fight Gangs—Gilroy, California

To deal with a growing youth gang problem in the central California city of Gilroy, a community of 32,000 residents, the police instituted a Gang Suppression Program emphasizing community policing techniques. The program mobilized the entire community at all levels, including the school district, businesses, business leaders, the Chamber of Commerce, and churches.

Police Chief Sumisaki explains how he involved the community in the program:

> We educate them on the gang phenomenon, talk about where the situation stands in our community from a police perspective, and what we would like from them. We want their involvement and commitment to help us address the gang problem.

The community responded to the problem:

- The Chamber of Commerce started an "Adopt a School" program aimed at getting on a one-to-one basis with the youngsters.
- A major symphony orchestra provided music at a function held at a Gilroy park that drew 500 children. The music carried a super hero theme, with the slogan "Be a Super Hero—Say No to Drugs and Gangs."
- The manager of an apartment unit supplied 100 gallons of paint and painted over graffiti all over town.
- A martial arts instructor and hundreds of his students raised $800 for materials and participated in Gilroy's first "Paint Out Day," in which community members volunteered to cover graffiti.
- Gilroy's main newspaper, *The Dispatch*, regularly carries front page stories on the police department and community efforts against drugs.
- In Gilroy's eight elementary schools, the teachers help Corporal Joe Ramirez, who teaches twelve-week DARE programs, alerting children to ways to say no to drugs and to gangs.

The League of California Cities awarded Gilroy a prestigious award for excellence in 1991, stating that the town, ". . . saw the problem and jumped on it." A town near Gilroy, about the same size and with the same demographics, didn't react as quickly. According to Chief Sumisaki,

> If you look at their statistics versus ours, their robbery rates are almost double, and their murder rate is six times ours. They tried a different approach to gangs. We took an earlier approach. We were lucky that we stepped in, and attacked it immediately. They can't go back and start over—they're stuck with the problem.

Source: Adapted from Lynda Bloom, "Community Policing Nips Gang Problem in the Bud," *Law and Order*, September 1992, pp. 67–70.

---

products were referred to and discussed in chapter 9 of this text.

Elgin, Illinois, a community of 77,000 residents located thirty-five miles northwest of Chicago, has refocused its department on numerous products that have supported a comprehensive, innovative community policing philosophy. This philosophy emphasizes that policing is done by everyone in the community and that police officers are the paid professionals who facilitate it. Its refocusing includes many of the programs discussed in chapter 9 and the philosophies discussed in this chapter. Among their programs are the following:

- A Gang Unit that tracks gang activity and saturates areas manifesting an increase in gang crime.
- A Community Action Group that works directly with citizens to prevent crime and search for creative solutions to issues that affect the quality of life in the community.
- A citizen contact program that requires each patrol officer to make a meaningful community or problem-oriented contact each day with ordinary citizens.
- An elderly liaison officer who works with senior services and the local crisis center to enhance services through better criminal investigation, information, and education.
- School liaison officers who provide support for the schools, teach gang resistance education and awareness training programs, and attend students' social and sporting activities.
- A victim assistance coordinator who offers immediate assistance to victims of crime and counsels troubled youth.
- A "community resolution" specialist, whose task is to unearth the root causes of problems in troubled neighborhoods.

YOU ARE THERE!

What Some Community Policing Cops Do in Dallas

In 1997, Dallas police officers, along with employees from animal control, code enforcement, the fire department, the Dallas County Sheriff's Department, and the FBI, worked with residents living in the River Bottoms section of the city to remove junk motor vehicles and demolish more than thirty dilapidated buildings (many of which were used for drug trafficking). Officers carried employment applications from neighborhood businesses and were able to find work for sixty residents. The police officers also made friends with youths and senior citizens at neighborhood recreation centers in the area. Eight months later, Part I criminal offenses had decreased 47 percent in the River Bottoms neighborhood.

—

Dallas officers coordinated a graffiti paintout in the southwest section of the city. Dozens of citizen volunteers painted a concrete quarter-mile-long retaining wall. The effort was possible because of those volunteers and the eighty-four gallons of paint that a neighborhood store donated.

—

In the northeast part of Dallas, officers coordinated a Juneteenth Celebration that was attended by more than 500 citizens and included cultural dancing, story telling, African art, an exhibit about black inventors, a parade, and ethnic food. The day of fun went a long way to blend cultures and tear down barriers.

Source: Adapted from Ben Click, "Changed Perceptions, Expectations Spell Success," *Community Policing Exchange*, July/August 1997, p. 1.

YOU ARE THERE!

Community Policing Helps Prince George's County, Maryland

The Prince George's County, Maryland, Police Department has had such success with its community policing program that it expanded its cadre of community policing officers five-fold. Since community policing has been in effect, robberies dropped from 371 to 285 a year. In one neighborhood, the number of drug-related calls to the police dropped 45 percent from 4,046 to 2,247. In the Capitol Heights section, the number of crack houses decreased from forty-eight to eighteen.

The evidence of the success of community policing goes beyond crime statistics. Two years ago, attendance at nighttime church functions had dropped sharply, and area residents reported having cars stolen, being awakened regularly by gunshots, and having drug dealers take over the streets. One church leader said, "Two years ago, I'd have been embarrassed to invite you to this church. At night, I would have advised you to bring a SWAT team."

Community policing in Prince George's County includes clearing abandoned cars off the streets, encouraging landlords to provide playgrounds and pools for children, and helping the public obtain government services.

Source: Adapted from "Success Story: Prince George's County Moves to Expand Community Policing Program," *Law Enforcement News*, 30 June 1992, p. 5.

- Community outreach workers who offer special services to the city's Laotian and Hispanic population.
- A phone line for reporting crime anonymously.
- Crime prevention/community relations programs, including Neighborhood Watch, Citizens Patrol, and other volunteer activities.
- Police officer involvement on numerous community boards and committees that are working to prevent crime, drug use, and gang activity.
- Use of an AT&T language line that provides language translation for more than 200 foreign languages.[25]

The keystone, perhaps, of the Elgin program is their Resident Officer Program (ROPE), in which an officer is assigned to live and work in a neighborhood that has been identified as needing direct police attention due to criminal and social issues. Elgin's was the first such program in the United States. Resident officer programs are becoming very popular throughout the nation, as we will see later in this chapter.

Elgin's police chief, Charles A. Gruber, emphasizes the role of the police and citizens together in improving the quality of life of members of the community. Speaking of conditions that cause neighborhood deterioration, Gruber said,

> Neighborhoods do not decay overnight. They decay one apartment or one home at a time, and the only way to recover that is to take them back one at a time, and bring about a stabilization to where people can believe that the government is going to meet its public-safety requirements.[26]

> ### YOU ARE THERE!
>
> **A Sample of Community Policing Programs in Kansas**
>
> - Handicapped Parking Enforcement
> - Youth Summer Camps
> - Ride-Alongs
> - Trading Cards
> - Police Chief for a Day
> - Open House
> - Rewarding Good Behavior
> - Adopt-a-House
> - Safety Town
> - Radio Broadcasting
> - Children I.D.
> - Print Publications for Youth
> - Newsletters
> - McGruff House
> - Junior Police Academy
> - Block Watch
> - Community Surveys
> - Police Play Day
> - Solidarity Marches
> - Student Youth Forum
> - Crime Prevention Unit
> - Citizens Police Academy
> - Sports Competitions
> - Crime Line
> - Training Videos
> - Bubblegum Handouts
> - Bicycle Safety Rodeos
> - Bicycle Patrols
> - Safety Incentive Giveaways
> - Leadership Programs
>
> Source: Adapted from Harvey Rachlin, "Creative Community Policing Programs," *Law and Order*, April 1997, pp. 24–34.

Regarding the successes of his community policing programs and residents' attitudes toward police, Gruber says,

> It's changed dramatically. On occasion, you'd go out and have to fight with people to make an arrest. Now we go out, bust a drug house or a drug dealer on the corner, and people come out and clap. They're working with us to get that done.[27]

Chicago's Alternative Policing Strategy (CAPS), one of the nation's most ambitious community policing initiatives, also embodies the philosophies discussed earlier in this chapter. In an average month, some 6,000 Chicagoans connect with their beat officers through the 230 community meetings held throughout the city. The purpose of the beat officer is to identify and resolve problems of crime and disorder in Chicago's neighborhoods. Both the police and community members have been trained in problem solving and partnership building, resulting in the formation of meaningful partnerships. Other city agencies have been brought into the process to address quality-of-life issues. Beat officers work the same neighborhood and watch for one year to ensure they become a familiar presence in the community.[28]

Although most of the academic and professional writing about policing centers on our nation's big cities, many crime and disorder problems occur in small towns. Community-oriented policing strategies have also been directed toward these small towns. Consider the example of Sagamore Hills, Ohio, a small rural community with a population of 10,000 and a police department of eight full-time and eleven part-time officers, who cover a jurisdiction of sixteen square miles. The department transitioned to community policing in 1995.

The benefits of its community policing focus can be seen in the following results of a 1996 citizen perception survey:

- In 1995, 18 percent of the population surveyed stated they always felt safe, whereas in 1996, 53 percent stated the same.
- In 1995, 29 percent of the citizens reported that crime had increased. In 1996, only 9 percent reported that crime increased.
- In 1995, 26 percent of citizens reported knowing someone in Sagamore Hills who had been a victim of crime. In 1996, this dropped to 4 percent.[29]

According to a Sagamore Hills officer,

> Before 1995, the department did little to squash rumors, inform citizens of arrests, or arrange meetings to discuss neighborhood problems. As the department transitioned to community policing, however, management recognized that giving citizens ownership in the process would instill a sense of stability and security.[30]

Resident Officer Programs— The Ultimate in Community Policing?

Numerous initiatives generally known as **resident officer programs** have sprung up around the nation since the early 1990s. Key proponents of the programs, such as Elgin's Chief Gruber, believe resident officer pro-

Senior Patrolman Tom Olson, of Elgin's ROPE program, addresses a group of school children.

grams capture the essence of community policing: improved relationships between police and their neighbors, who team together to fight crime and address quality-of-life conditions that contribute to crime.

Elgin's ROPE program, which started in 1991 with three officers, grew to six officers by 1995. The ROPE officers, living in donated or subsidized homes or apartments, normally work an eight-hour day, but for all practical purposes are on 24-hour-a-day call because residents call them at all hours for assistance. In addition to a residence, the city provides the officers with utilities, a bicycle and squad car for patrol, an answering machine, and whatever expenses are necessary for special needs in the neighborhood. The officers cost the city more money than regular officers. About $31,000 extra is spent on each officer yearly for rent and utilities. Because the federal government has deemed that their rent-free status is taxable income, they also receive a slightly higher pay rate to compensate for additional taxes they pay. The officers decide on their own how to improve the quality of life in their neighborhood so residents can live without fear of drugs, gangs, prostitution, and crime, as long as their methods are legal, moral, and ethical.[31]

Generally, the stated term of an officer in the program is two years; however, most end up staying longer because of the bond that forms between the officers and residents. One officer reports, "When I first started, I'd go out in the morning and there'd be anonymous notes under my car's wipers, tipping me to crimes in the area. Now, people come up to me and tell me in person."[32]

The program's effectiveness can be seen by the change in answers to a survey distributed to one area's residents. When ROPE first started in the neighborhood, a questionnaire asked what problems concerned the residents. "Drugs and gangs" were the major problem then; two years later the same residents answered that loud stereos and speeding cars were now their biggest concern.

Elgin's Chief Gruber reports that ROPE has made a tremendous difference for the better in targeted neighborhoods, helping to reduce violent crime by as much as 60 percent since its inception. He says of the officers,

> They're expected to work with the neighborhood to come up with solutions to problems, whether it's gangs, drugs or kids littering, working with public works to get new sidewalks, visiting schools or working with kids—whatever it takes. . . . They work whenever they need to work; they work for the neighborhood.[33]

The Macon, Georgia, Police Department also implemented a resident officer program in 1995 in which officers agree to live in rent-free, city-owned housing in exchange for working with at-risk youths for twenty-four-hours a month.[34]

Columbia, South Carolina, has created resident officer programs by establishing the Police Homeowners Loan Program, which offers officers low-interest, no-

YOU ARE THERE!

Some Examples of Resident Officer Programs

Police departments all over the United States are creating innovative community policing and problem-solving policing programs to allow police to become closer to the citizens they serve.

Elgin, Illinois's ROPE

The Elgin (Illinois) Police Department has established a Resident Officer Program (ROPE) involving officers who volunteered to move into troubled neighborhoods with their families to maximize police presence. Elgin is a community of 77,000 residents located thirty-five miles northwest of Chicago. The Resident Officer Program moved Police Officer Terrance Allen and his family into a federally subsidized housing unit, Illinois Court, which was overrun with gangs, shootings, and drug dealing. Allen is the consummate beat cop—his beat is also his own neighborhood. Allen states,

> When I moved in, people were pretty skeptical. I didn't get any cooperation, but I never felt uncomfortable. When I'd come upon a group sitting out in front of their apartments drinking, I started telling them I didn't want to see alcohol on the court anymore—and they moved along. Gradually as people saw I was serious, they began to help me. One resident even asked his guests to leave because they were causing trouble. Now we don't have congregations of people out here anymore. The kids are able to come out and play in the summer.

> To help improve his new neighborhood, Allen gave residents a questionnaire asking them to identify problems. Learning that the biggest complaint was unsupervised children, he initiated programs to help the unemployed find jobs and to keep the children busy. He took children camping and on field trips.

One resident says of Officer Allen, "I have five kids and it used to be pretty bad around here, but Officer Allen has made a big difference, especially to the kids."

Columbia, South Carolina's Homeowners Loan Program

Many people in low-income neighborhoods complain that the police do not care for them because they do not live in the neighborhood. The city of Columbia, South Carolina, has addressed this problem by establishing the Police Homeowners Loan Program, which offers police officers low-interest, no-money-down mortgages to buy houses in neighborhoods that have high crime rates, deterioration, or both. The mortgages include renovation costs, so officers and their families can live in newly rehabilitated homes they otherwise may not be able to afford. At the same time, the officers are a physical presence to deter crime.

Patrolman James Brown, age twenty-five, who has been on the force for three years, bought his new brick house for $70,000 in a neighborhood that had problems with break-ins. Brown reports, "My neighbors say they see a big difference since we moved in. They tell me they feel safer and people look out for each other now. I come home from work late and look around. My neighbors say they sleep feeling safer, knowing I'm living here with them. I think the program is great for me and the city."

Source: Adapted from Charles A. Gruber, "Resident Officers," *Law and Order*, August 1992, pp. 44, 53; and Walter Oleksy, "'Police Don't Live Here. They Don't Really Care!': A New Idea in Community-Oriented Policing," *Law and Order*, August 1992, pp. 45, 54. For more on Elgin's program, see Charles A. Gruber, "Elgin Designs and Builds a Community Policing Facility," *Police Chief*, August 1996, pp. 16–24; Sheila Schmitt, "ROPE: The Resident Officer Program of Elgin," *Law and Order*, May 1995, pp. 52, 56–58; and, "Resident Police Officers Go Beyond the Call of Duty," *Community Policing Exchange*, July/August 1997, p. 6.

---

money-down mortgages to buy houses in neighborhoods that have high crime rates or deterioration. The mortgages include renovation costs, so officers and their families can live in newly rehabilitated homes they otherwise might not have been able to afford. At the same time, the officers are a physical presence to deter crime. By 1992, seven police officers owned homes in high crime and deteriorating neighborhoods as a result of the program, and in 1995 the number grew to eleven.[35] Since the program's inception, Columbia has added take-home patrol cars for participating officers and feedback from residents showed that the vehicles were definitely noticed. Police Chief Charles Austin reported in 1995 that there had been a decline in both major and minor crimes and that the program had helped bridge the communications gap between the police and the community.[36]

In 1997, New York City became one of the latest cities in the United States to adopt a resident officer program. A limited number of two-bedroom apartments in

New York City's public housing developments have been provided for up to sixty-three police officers and their families at an unbelievably low (for New York City) cost of $347 per month. In exchange for the reduced rent, the officers reside in the apartments and provide five hours a month of community service in addition to their normal police work. The new program leapfrogs police officers over an estimated 200,000 families now on the waiting list for public housing.[37]

In 1997, President Clinton came onto the resident officer bandwagon when he announced a plan to give 50 percent discounts to 2,000 police officers to buy federally foreclosed homes in 500 low-income neighborhoods nationwide. Participants must agree to live in the homes for at least three years. This program, called "Officer Next Door," is part of a wide-ranging "Urban Homestead Initiative" designed to reduce crime and make low-income neighborhoods more attractive to homeowners. As of August 1997, five cities had agreed to participate in the program: Cleveland; Miami; Kansas City, Missouri; Los Angeles; and Springfield, Massachusetts. A total of twenty-four cities are eventually expected to participate in the program.[38]

Other communities adopting resident officer programs include Alexandria, Virginia; Bloomington and Springfield, Illinois; Jackson, Michigan; and Waterloo, Iowa. Officials in these cities say that resident officers provide a high-profile presence that helps to prevent crime.

Unfortunately, a resident officer program did not get off to such a good start in Denver, Colorado. The first Denver police officer to move into a high-crime area under the program was burglarized. Thieves took the officer's computer, compact disks, and ski parka.[39]

The Federal Government and Community Policing

In the 1992 presidential race, Bill Clinton championed the concept of community oriented policing and promised to add 100,000 more police officers to the nation's streets. Since the election, the federal government has made tremendous contributions to the state of community policing strategies throughout the nation. This section will discuss the 1994 Crime Bill, the Department of Justice's Office of Community Oriented Policing Services, and the Community Policing Consortium.

President Bill Clinton signing the 1994 Crime Bill.

The Crime Bill

After much political debate, the Violent Crime Control and Law Enforcement Act (**The Crime Bill**) was signed into law by President Clinton in 1994. The provisions of this bill authorized the expenditure of nearly $8 billion over six years for grants to law enforcement agencies to reduce crime.

Office of Community Oriented Policing Services (COPS)

As the research and evaluation arm of the Department of Justice, the National Institute of Justice (NIJ) has mounted a broad agenda to study changes in policing. In the wake of the passage of the Crime Bill, Attorney General Reno established the **Office of Community Oriented Policing Services (COPS)**.[40] The COPS office was established to administer the grant money provided by the Crime Bill and to promote community oriented policing. In its first two years of existence the office

> ### PATROLLING THE NET
>
> **How to Really Learn about Community Policing: Click on with COPS**
>
> The Community Policing Consortium (Office of Community Oriented Policing Services [COPS]) has established its own web site, loaded with community policing success stories, contact information, and upcoming events.
>
> Anyone interested can visit their web site at: http://www.communitypolicing.org.
>
> At their homepage, click onto anything and everything that interests you about community policing. They have it all.
>
> The Community Policing Consortium comprises five of the leading policing organizations in the United States: the International Association of Chiefs of Police (IACP), the National Organization of Black Law Enforcement Executives (NOBLE), the National Sheriffs' Association (NSA), the Police Executive Research Forum (PERF), and the Police Foundation. The consortium was established under the auspices of the 1994 Crime Bill and is funded by the U.S. Department of Justice, Office of Community Oriented Policing Services (COPS). It issues a bimonthly publication, *Community Policing Exchange,* which is mailed without charge to law enforcement professionals, community organization representatives, municipal and civic leaders, and government officials.

awarded over 100 grants, totaling $23.9 million, to research and evaluate community oriented policing. These grants included a national evaluation of community policing, evaluations of specific policing strategies, locally initiated police-researcher partnerships, and other research and evaluation initiatives.[41]

The mission statement (reflecting its values and goals) of the COPS office reads:

> We . . . dedicate ourselves, through partnerships with communities, policing agencies and other public and private organizations, to significantly improve the quality of life in neighborhoods and communities . . . by putting into practice the concepts of community policing in order to reduce levels of disorder, violence, and crime through the application of proven, effective programs and strategies.[42]

As of 1997, about 80,000 of the 100,000 additional officers promised by President Clinton and endorsed by the 1994 Crime Bill were on our nation's police departments. An additional $45 million was allocated in 1998 to fund recruitment grants and law enforcement scholarships programs, including the Police Corps.[43]

The method used by the COPS office to distribute federal grants to law enforcement agencies to hire additional officers is known as the Universal Hiring Program (UHP). This program allows agencies to apply for federal funds for up to 75 percent of the total cost of hiring a new police officer for a maximum of three years. The additional funding to receive these grants must be provided by the state or local government.[44]

Another program administered by the COPS office is the COPS MORE (Making Officer Redeployment Effective) program, which offers funds to departments to acquire new technologies that will enhance their operations, to pay for overtime, and to hire civilians for administrative support, thus allowing officers to spend more time on the street. COPS also funds programs to combat domestic violence, youth gangs, and firearms sales and possession. Another grant program is the "Problem Solving Partnership," which awards funds to deal with larcenies, alcohol-related problems, vandalism, graffiti, and prostitution.

COPS also supports the Regional Community Policing Institutes (RCPIs), which consist of partnerships across a variety of police agencies, community groups, and organizations to create a delivery system for training police officers in community oriented policing.

Another program financed by COPS is the Police Corps. This program, which was allocated $20 million for fiscal year 1997, allows participants to receive a college education by providing up to $7,500 per academic year, with a per-student maximum of $30,000. Upon graduation with the baccalaureate degree, the student is obligated to serve four years with a police agency. Yet another program sponsored by COPS is "Troops to Cops," in which former military personnel separating from active service, with some training and background in law enforcement, are trained as Community Oriented Policing officers.

Showing its commitment to community policing and partnerships with the community, NIJ officials wrote in 1997:

> Policing is undergoing a broad and dramatic transformation. The strategic shift toward community-oriented policing and problem-solving strategies has changed the ways in which police departments organize themselves, the strategies which departments employ to combat crime and disorder, and the types of partnerships formed in order to enhance effectiveness.[45]

Also in 1997, the director of COPS said, "Community policing is taking hold in communities of all sizes across the country. In just two years . . . COPS has benefited nearly 9,000 agencies . . . to supplement the sworn forces on our streets. Nationally, we are seeing crime rates drop and many law enforcement leaders credit the implementation of community policing as a major factor in this encouraging trend.[46]

Community Policing Consortium

The **Community Policing Consortium** comprises five of the leading policing associations in the United States: the International Association of Chiefs of Police (IACP), the National Organization of Black Law Enforcement Executives (NOBLE), the National Sheriffs' Association (NSA), the Police Executive Research Forum (PERF), and the Police Foundation. The consortium, funded by COPS, issues a bimonthly publication, *Community Policing Exchange,* dedicated to reporting the newest developments in community policing partnerships.

Its statement of purpose reads, "*Community Policing Exchange* strives to assist law enforcement practitioners in bridging the distance between communities, facilitating the exchange of information, and giving voice to all involved in the implementation of community policing."[47]

The Community Policing Consortium also publishes *Sheriff Times* and the *Community Policing Information Access Guide.*

★ Some Accomplishments of Community Policing

As reports of overall crime rate decreases hit the presses in the mid- and late-1990s, some police officials associated this decrease to closer relationships with their communities through community policing, as well as the addition of new community policing officers.[48] Some examples follow:

- Fort Worth, Texas, police attribute a 7 percent decrease in overall crime and a 50 percent drop in homicides to a closer relationship between the department and the community: "There's an unended line of communication between the police department and the citizens. . . . [They are] more aware about crime prevention efforts—what they can do to harden targets, get involved and keep an eye out for their neighbors."[49] Fort Worth police say that constituents are treated as equal players in the fight against crime and cites the city's successful Citizens on Patrol program, a recent auxiliary police innovation. Program participants are issued police radios and patrol neighborhoods in specially designated vehicles. Police report that this program has had a major impact on property crimes, such as larceny and burglary. Also, residents have approved a special sales tax that will provide the police department with an additional $25 million a year, which is earmarked for equipment and personnel.

- Wichita, Kansas, police also attribute an 11 percent decease in crime to community policing. "It's a whole different mindset toward problem-solving and that in itself can have a dramatic impact on how we serve the community."[50]

- Los Angeles police attribute a 4 percent crime decline to police-community participation, "There truly is a significant partnership with the community, with a lot more emphasis on problem-solving than there has been in the past. We'd like to believe that's at the root of these reductions."[51]

- Responding to the third decrease in crime in as many years, police officials in Baton Rouge, Louisiana, gave much of the credit to the community. "Community organizations and civic groups have come out of the woodwork in the last few years. All of that has made a difference."[52]

- Denver, Colorado, police officials, noting a 13 percent decrease in crime, said, "When the neighborhood takes stock in their community and they're serious they don't want crime, then you start to see crime go down."[53]

- Police officials in Austin, Texas, also credit increased citizen involvement with the community for a 23 percent drop in crime. Residents and police also reclaimed a city park that had become a haven for drug deals. The police chief reported that she had many people coming up to her and shaking her hand to thank her for giving them back their park.

- New Orleans police reported that a community policing plan had helped cut the murder rate by 18 percent. In three public housing developments, where police deployed community oriented police teams, homicide dropped by 83 percent.[54]

Although many attribute crime reduction to community policing strategies, many do not. Some believe that these new philosophies are merely rhetoric. Many others attribute the drastic decrease in crime rates in the mid- and late-1990s to more aggressive, strategic, and legalistic law enforcement, similar to that practiced in New York City and other metropolitan areas, as discussed in chapter 1.

★ Not All Agree with Community Policing

Not all community policing efforts have been successful. A study of community constables in England found that the constables actually spent very little of their time in direct contact with citizens, despite role expectations that emphasized community contact.[55] Research on the effectiveness of community-oriented policing has yielded mixed results. Foot patrol seems to make citizens feel safer, but it may not have much of an effect on the actual amount of crime.[56]

Many experts are not overly enthusiastic over the idea of community policing. Many argue over the definition of community. Jack Greene and Steve Mastrofski argue that the most significant problem in community policing is to define what is meant by "community." They found that in most community policing projects, the concept of community is defined in terms of "administrative areas" traditionally used by police departments to allocate patrols, instead of in terms of "ecological areas" defined by common norms, shared values, and interpersonal bonds. Greene and Mastrofski find this to be a very significant problem, because a major goal of community policing is to activate a community's norms and other methods of social control. If the police are using administrative areas instead of ecological areas, the authors say, they lose what they should be trying to get.[57]

Robert Sheehan and Gary W. Cordner tell us how some police may define community differently: "For the working police officer, the community generates police activity (law violations and calls for service) and provides the setting within which police work must be performed. For the police executive, the community represents a source of both support and complaints and most importantly, is the final arbiter of the quality of police services and the effectiveness of the police department."[58]

Additionally, many feel that community policing can actually have a negative effect on certain people. An analysis of a victim callback program established by the Houston Police Department found that the program, which was originally designed to help victims, had a generally negative effect on some minority groups (Asian-Americans and Hispanic-Americans), whose members may have been suspicious of the department's intentions.[59]

Also, an audit of the Houston Police Department by a consulting firm criticized the department's neighborhood-oriented policing (NOP) approach. It concluded that although "well-conceived," NOP faced a number of difficulties and had not produced any comprehensive improvements in police services. The report acknowledged that NOP has the potential to enhance the quality of police services without adding costs, but that the Houston program did not have tangible effects on citizens' security and quality of life. The report said that the program, which had been implemented at the ex-

---

All in the Line of Duty

Their Bikes Got Them There

While on bicycle patrol, Officers William Campbell and Pete Rangel of the Gilbert, Arizona, Police Department detected an odor of smoke. Checking the area, they traced the source of the smoke to a fire at a nearby residence. The officers entered the home, located the source of the fire, and proceeded to evacuate the occupants, one adult and three children, who were unaware of the emergency. As the officers led the occupants to safety, an explosion sent flames twenty feet into the air. After calling for backup patrol units and the fire department, Officers Campbell and Rangel then alerted and evacuated the occupants of surrounding residences. Due to the officers' decisive actions and teamwork, no one was injured during the evacuation, despite two large explosions. Fire department officials later credited the officers' actions with helping to prevent the fire from spreading to other residences.

Source: Adapted from *FBI Law Enforcement Bulletin*, July 1997, p. 33.

pense of more proactive law enforcement functions, such as arresting criminals, had resulted in mediocre performance in response time to emergency calls for service.[60]

According to Schobel, Evans, and Daly, the empirical evidence for community policing's effectiveness in solving the crime problem is both limited and contradictory.[61] Other researchers admit there are a number of documented successes of community policing programs, but there is also an indication that community policing may serve to displace crime. Indeed, several studies indicate there has been an increase in crime in the areas surrounding the community policing impact area.[62]

The debate continues to rage regarding community policing, even among officials of the same agency. Take, for example, the following statements by current and former members of the Baltimore County Police Department.

Kevin Novak, department spokesperson:

> You put 10 people in a room you'll get 20 different definitions. Each one is torn between at least two. . . . There are some areas where it's really not completely applicable. . . . Some things, like the widespread armed-robbery problem we had earlier this year are best handled through traditional enforcement-using informants, conducting aggressive patrol and enforcement strategies—and that's what we did.[63]

Captain James Johnson, patrol commander of a high-crime Baltimore precinct:

> [The effectiveness of community policing] really depends on how you define community policing. That's part of the problem. Academics and practitioners can't agree, and there's no agreement among police leaders in America today over what it really is. . . . Part of the problem for the line officer is that there's this nebulous terminology . . . and this makes it very clouded and obscure.[64]

Neil Behan, former police chief who led the department when it adopted the community-based policing philosophy in 1982, disagrees with the others and says community policing has had a concrete definition from the beginning:

> Community policing is a partnership with the community to improve the quality of life. What the Captain does not understand is that community policing never rejected traditional policing. It is an enhancement of traditional policing—sometimes in a different direction—but it never abandoned traditional policing.[65]

Present Baltimore chief, Terrence B. Sheridan, who has questioned the wisdom of some current practices involving community policing, has abandoned some of its policies in favor of more "enforcement-directed" policing.

As this text went into production, a dramatic issue has added to the debate over community oriented policing strategies. In September 1997 it was reported that the first cycle of U.S. Justice Department grants, begun in 1994 and mentioned earlier in this chapter, were coming to a close. Its conclusion would require agencies throughout the nation to fund all of the new officers added since the 1994 Crime Bill without the help of the federal government, which had been funding 75 percent of the cost. It has been reported that local officials may be tempted to scrap community policing programs or shift officers around in order to avoid retaining COPS hires.[66]

As an example of problems now being faced by departments, consider the example of Toledo, Ohio. The city was originally awarded $10 million to add 125 new officers to its police department, but refused some of the money and hired fewer officers. According to its police chief,

> All of a sudden, they [the federal government] gave us 75 officers in one crack, for a total award of $5.6 million. The cost for one officer in Toledo, with benefits, is $150,000. The city has to match $75,000, and that $5.5 million bill has come out of the general fund. There's no way we can fund that.[67]

Toledo is not alone. According to the chief of the South Pasadena, California, Police Department, "Every police chief I've talked to is worried about how to keep the officers hired with Federal money once the grant runs out."[68]

The debate continues.

Chapter Summary

The face of policing has changed dramatically. Community policing and problem-solving policing have been practiced for over one decade, and some say it has been tremendously popular and successful. Others have disagreed. The debate continues, and that is good for policing.

This chapter discussed three corporate strategies for modern policing, including strategic policing, community policing, and problem-solving policing. It discussed the underlying philosophy and genesis of community policing and problem-solving policing and then discussed how these strategies are designed to work.

The chapter then focused on numerous ways of implementing community oriented policing and focused on one particular strategy, the Resident Officer Program.

The chapter also discussed the federal government and its current role in community policing, including the 1994 Crime Bill, the Office of Community Oriented Policing Services, and the Community Policing Consortium. It discussed some empirical and anecdotal evidence of the benefits of COPS, but also showed how some scholars and practitioners do not agree with community policing strategies.

Despite many recent innovations in police departments throughout the United States, many problems still remain. There is much evidence that not all police officers are ready to accept new images of police work. Some researchers have warned that the police subculture is so committed to the traditional ways of policing that efforts to change it can demoralize an entire department, making the department ineffective in doing its basic tasks.[69] Some researchers of the police subculture warn that police departments will not become effective until the values of the average police officer match the formal values espoused by today's innovative police administrators.[70] It is hoped that our exploration of these issues will continue to add to the debate.

Learning Check

1. Define community policing and problem-solving policing and give three actual examples of each.
2. Discuss the importance of the research of scholars James Q. Wilson and George Kelling to the concept of community policing.
3. Discuss the contributions of Herman Goldstein to the concept of problem-solving policing.
4. Define a resident officer program and give three actual examples.
5. Name three of the programs administered and supported by the Office of Community Oriented Policing Services (COPS) of the U.S. Department of Justice and discuss them.

Review Exercise

After you receive your degree in criminal justice, you are hired by the Littletown Police Department as an assistant and consultant to the police chief. Littletown has no major crime problem but residents of the town's only public housing development are constantly complaining about youths who loiter in and around their buildings, causing noise and disorder problems, such as littering and fighting.

The chief tells you that she is thinking about ways to improve her department. She says she read an article once about Broken Windows, but does not remember it. Based on your reading of this chapter, what would you tell the police chief?

Web Exercise

Patrol over to the National Institute of Justice's web site and look for information on community policing or problem-solving policing in your community or a community nearby.

Key Concepts

corporate strategies for policing
community policing
problem-solving policing
James Q. Wilson and George Kelling
Herman Goldstein
broken windows model
resident officer programs
The Crime Bill
Office of Community Oriented Policing Services (COPS)
Community Policing Consortium

Notes

1. George Kelling, *Police and Communities: The Quiet Revolution, Perspectives on Policing,* no. 1 (Washington, D.C.: National Institute of Justice, 1988).
2. The twelve monographs in the *Perspectives on Policing* series were published in 1988 and 1989 by the National Institute of Justice, Washington, D.C.
3. Mark H. Moore and Robert C. Trojanowicz, *Corporate Strategies for Policing, Perspectives on Policing,* no. 6 (Washington, D.C.: National Institute of Justice, 1988).
4. Albert J. Reiss, Jr., "Shaping and Serving the Community: The Role of the Police Chief Executive," in *Police Leadership in America: Crisis and Opportunity,* ed. William A. Geller (New York: Praeger, 1985), p. 63.
5. James Q. Wilson and George Kelling, "'Broken Windows': The Police and Neighborhood Safety," *Atlantic Monthly,* March 1982, pp. 29–38.
6. Wilson and Kelling, "Broken Windows."
7. Wesley G. Skogan, *Disorder and Decline: Crime and the Spiral of Decay in American Neighborhoods* (New York: Free Press, 1990), pp. 21–50.
8. Robert C. Trojanowicz, "Building Support for Community Policing: An Effective Strategy," *FBI Law Enforcement Bulletin,* May 1992, pp. 7–12.

9. Jerome Skolnick and David Bayley, *Community Policing: Issues and Practices Around the World* (Washington, D.C.: National Institute of Justice, 1988).
10. Jeremy Travis, "What Difference Do the Police Make? Research Can Offer Some Answers," *Community Policing Exchange,* May/June 1997, p. 8.
11. Herman Goldstein, "Toward Community-Oriented Policing: Potential, Basic Requirements, and Threshold Questions," *Crime and Delinquency* 33 (1987): 6–30, at 27–28.
12. Malcolm K. Sparrow, Mark H. Moore, and David M. Kennedy, *Beyond 911: A New Era for Policing* (New York: Basic Books, 1990), p. 129.
13. James Ahern, *Police in Trouble* (New York: Hawthorn Books, 1992), pp. 83–85.
14. Mary Ann Wycoff et al., *Citizen Contact Patrol: Executive Summary* (Washington, D.C.: Police Foundation, 1985).
15. Michael J. Farrell, "The Development of the Community Patrol Officer Program: Community-Oriented Policing in the City of New York," in *Community Policing: Rhetoric or Reality?* ed. Jack R. Greene and Stephen D. Mastrofski (New York: Praeger, 1988), pp. 73–88.
16. David L. Carter, *Community Policing and DARE: A Practitioner's Perspective* (Washington, D.C.: National Institute of Justice, 1995), p. 2.
17. Joseph E. Braun, "Progress Through Partnerships," *Community Links,* January 1997.
18. Charles H. Wiegand, "Combining Tactical and Community Policing Considerations," *Law and Order,* May 1997, pp. 70–71, p. 70.
19. Anthony V. Bouza, *The Police Mystique: An Insider's Look at Cops, Crime, and the Criminal Justice System* (New York: Plenum Press, 1990), pp. 236–237. Note: *Law Enforcement News* has an extensive interview with Professor Herman Goldstein in its 14 February 1997 issue, "A LEN Interview with Professor Herman Goldstein, the 'Father' of Problem-Oriented Policing," pp. 8–11.
20. John E. Eck and William Spelman, "Who Ya Gonna Call? The Police as Problem Busters," *Crime and Delinquency* 33 (1987): 53.
21. Sparrow, Moore, and Kennedy, *Beyond 911,* pp. 16–17.
22. John E. Eck et al., *Problem Solving: Problem-Oriented Policing in Newport News* (Washington, D.C.: Police Executive Research Forum, 1987), pp. 100–101.
23. Sparrow, Moore, and Kennedy, *Beyond 911,* p. 129. See figure 10.1 for an example of one such new technique.
24. Harvey Rachlin, "Creative Community Policing Programs," *Law and Order,* April 1997, pp. 24–34, p. 24.
25. Charles A. Gruber, "Elgin Designs and Builds a Community Policing Facility," *Police Chief,* August 1996, pp. 16–24.
26. "A Place to Call Home: Resident Officer Programs Get a Federal Shot in the Arm," *Law Enforcement News,* July/August 1997, p. 17.
27. "A Place to Call Home."
28. Richard Glasser and Kevin P. Morison, "Examining Chicago's Alternative Policing Strategy," *Community Policing Exchange,* May/June 1997, pp. 1, 8.
29. Chris Krettler, "Small-Town Police Plan and Assess," *Community Policing Exchange,* May/June 1997, p. 2.
30. Krettler, "Small-Town Police Plan and Assess."
31. Sheila Schmitt, "ROPE: The Resident Officer Program of Elgin: If You Can't Beat 'Em, Join 'Em," *Law and Order,* May 1995, pp. 52, 56–57.
32. Schmitt, "ROPE: The Resident Officer Program of Elgin."
33. "A Place to Call Home." For more on Elgin, Illinois's resident officer program, see "Resident Police Officers Go Beyond the Call of Duty," *Community Policing Exchange,* July/August 1997, p. 6.
34. "The State of the Union: From Alabama to Wyoming, State-by-State Highlights of the Year in Policing," *Law Enforcement News,* 31 December 1995–15 January 1996, p. 13.
35. Walter Oleksy, "'Police Don't Live Here. They Don't Really Care?'": A New Idea in Community-Oriented Policing," *Law and Order,* August 1992, p. 45. See also Sheila Schmitt, "Columbia's Police Loan Program Houses Twice as Many Officers," *Law and Order,* May 1995, p. 59.
36. Schmitt, "Columbia's Police Loan Program Houses Twice as Many Officers."
37. Tom Topousis, "Cops Get in on the Ground Floor: New Deal Gives Them Rent Break in Projects," *New York Post,* 14 May 1997, p. 20. See also "A Place to Call Home."
38. "A Place to Call Home."
39. "The State of the Union," p. 10.
40. U.S.C. 3796dd-4, 3793.
41. National Institute of Justice, *Solicitation: Policing Research and Evaluation: Fiscal Year 1997* (Washington, D.C.: National Institute of Justice, 1997), p. 1; Willard M. Oliver, "The COPS Office: The Office of Community Oriented Policing Services," *Law and Order,* April 1997, pp. 45–49.
42. Oliver, "The COPS Office," p. 48.
43. "What Price Justice? For FY'98, the Tab Could Top out at $19.3B," *Law Enforcement News,* 28 February 1997, pp. 1, 6.
44. Oliver, "The COPS Office," p. 48.
45. National Institute of Justice, *Solicitation: Policing Research and Evaluation.*
46. "Progress Through Partnerships," *Community Links,* vol. 1, no. 1, January 1997, p. 1.
47. "Progress Through Partnerships." Those interested in contacting the Community Policing Consortium may do so

at: The Community Policing Consortium, 1726 M St. N.W., Suite 801, Washington, D.C. 20036. Publications: 1-202-530-0639 or toll free: 1-800-833-3085; fax: 1-202-833-9295. You may get on their mailing list and receive future issues or may submit newsworthy articles or features for publication to them. The consortium may also be reached on the Internet at [b@://www.communitypolicing.org].

48. "As Crime Rates Continue to Dip, Police Credit Community Efforts—and Their Own," *Law Enforcement News*, 15 September 1996, pp. 1, 14.
49. "As Crime Rates Continue to Dip," p. 1.
50. "As Crime Rates Continue to Dip," p. 14.
51. "As Crime Rates Continue to Dip," p. 14.
52. "Going Down for the Third Time: UCR Shows Another Decrease in Part 1 Crime in '94," *Law Enforcement News*, 15 June 1995, pp. 1, 6.
53. "Going Down for the Third Time," p. 6.
54. Jacob R. Clark, "New Orleans Chief Touts Lofty Gains in Ambitious Plan to Reform Department," *Law Enforcement News*, 30 November 1995, p. 1.
55. David Brown and Susan Iles, "Community Constable: A Study of a Policing Initiative," *NIJ International Summaries* (Washington, D.C.: National Institute of Justice, 1986).
56. Police Foundation, *The Newark Foot Patrol Experiment* (Washington, D.C.: Police Foundation, 1981).
57. Jack Greene and Steve Mastrofski, *Community Policing: Rhetoric or Reality?* (New York: Praeger, 1988).
58. Robert Sheehan and Gary W. Cordner, *Introduction to Police Administration* (Cincinnati: Anderson, 1989), p. 90.
59. Wesley Skogan and Mary Ann Wycoff, "Some Unexpected Effects of a Police Service for Victims," *Crime and Delinquency* 33 (1987): 490–501.
60. "Audit Rips Houston's Policing Style as a Good Idea That Falls Short of the Mark," *Law Enforcement News*, 30 September 1991, p. 1.
61. Gary B. Schobel, Thomas A. Evans, and John L. Daly, "Community Policing: Does It Reduce Crime, or Just Displace It?," *Police Chief*, August 1997, pp. 64–71.
62. Lisa M. Riechers and Roy R. Roberg, "Community Policing: A Critical Review of Underlying Assumptions," *Journal of Police Science and Administration*, June 1990, p. 110.
63. "C-OP Lives on in Baltimore Co.: Police Brass Say They're Not Abandoning the Concept," *Law Enforcement News*, 15 December 1996, p. 1.
64. "C-OP Lives on in Baltimore Co."
65. "C-OP Lives on in Baltimore Co."
66. Jacob R. Clark, "Time to Pay the Piper: COPS Funded Officers, Departments Near Day of Fiscal Reckoning," *Law Enforcement News*, 30 September 1997, pp. 1, 14.
67. Clark, "Time to Pay the Piper," p. 1.
68. Clark, "Time to Pay the Piper," p. 14.
69. Malcolm K. Sparrow, *Implementing Community Policing*, Perspectives on Policing, (Washington, D.C.: National Institute of Justice, 1988).
70. Robert Wasserman and Mark H. Moore, *Values in Policing*, Perspectives on Policing, (Washington, D.C.: National Institute of Justice, 1988).

11

Police and the Law

Chapter Outline

Crime in the United States
  How Do We Measure Crime?
  How Much Crime Occurs in the United States?
  Arrests in the United States
The Police and the U.S. Constitution
  Bill of Rights and the Fourteenth Amendment
  Role of the Supreme Court in Regulating the Police
  The Exclusionary Rule
  Impact of the Exclusionary Rule on the Police
The Police and Arrest
  Probable Cause
  Reasonable and Deadly Force in Making Arrests
  Stopping Vehicles

The Police and Search and Seizure
  The Warrant Requirement and the Search Warrant
  Exceptions to the Warrant Requirement
The Police and Custodial Interrogation
  The Path to Miranda
  The Miranda Ruling
  The Erosion of Miranda
  1990s and Miranda
  Miranda in Retrospect
The Police and Identification Procedures
  Lineups, Showups, and Photo Arrays
  Other Identification Procedures

Chapter Goals

■ To acquaint you with the amount and type of crime in the United States, as well as the number and type of arrests made by the police.

■ To apprise you of the role of the Bill of Rights and the U.S. Supreme Court in regulating the actions of the police.

■ To explain the role of the police in making arrests, searching people and places, and stopping automobiles.

■ To make you aware, through the exploration of case law, of the changing philosophy of the U.S. Supreme Court in areas regarding search and seizure, custodial interrogation, and identification procedures.

■ To make you aware, through the exploration of case law, of current standard police procedures in search and seizure, custodial interrogation, and identification procedures.

Introduction

When people think about the police, they generally think about the power of the police to arrest someone, about the power of the police to issue a summons for driving violations, or about some other enforcement activity. People think of the police in terms of the law. As this text has shown, the police do much more than enforce the law. Although the police role is not limited to law enforcement, that is definitely a major part of the police role.

This chapter will discuss the amount and types of crime in the United States, along with the amount and types of arrests made by the police. It will also discuss the U.S. Constitution and the Bill of Rights, focusing on the relationship between the police and the Bill of Rights as interpreted by the U.S. Supreme Court over the years. It will explore significant areas of police power, including the power to arrest people, to stop people and inquire as to their conduct, to search people and places and seize property, and to question people about their participation in a crime. Landmark Supreme Court cases will be used to show how the police have altered their procedures to comply with the provisions of the U.S. Constitution. The chapter provides the fact pattern behind some of the cases. A fact pattern is the events in a criminal case that led to the arrest, as well as the facts of the investigation and arrest. The fact pattern is considered by the courts in adjudicating a case. Reading these fact patterns will help you see that law is not abstract principles but rather the result of personal and dynamic events.

This chapter is perhaps the most important one in this text. The role of the police is a very special one in our society. The police enforce the law. When enforcing the law, they sometimes have to arrest people. By arresting people, the police take away what Americans value most highly—their freedom and their liberty. The police must know the law and must apply it correctly.

Crime in the United States

Crime is part of life in the United States. We read about crime in our newspapers, and often details of the crimes are the lead stories on our television news broadcasts. The following sections will discuss how we measure crime in the United States, how much crime occurs, and how many arrests are made.

How Do We Measure Crime?

Two major methods are used to measure crime in the United States. They are (1) the Uniform Crime Reports and (2) the National Crime Victimization Survey. As of 1998, both the Uniform Crime Reports and the National Crime Victimization Survey have been thoroughly studied and reviewed and significant changes and improvements are expected to be implemented during the next several years.

Uniform Crime Reports The **Uniform Crime Reports (UCR)** is collected and published by the FBI based on reports of crimes made to the police across the United States. The FBI publishes a yearly report entitled *Crime in the United States* based on all reports made to the police for the year and forwarded to the FBI. The Uniform Crime Reports has four major sections, the Crime Index, Crime Index Offenses Cleared, Persons Arrested, and Law Enforcement Personnel.

The FBI's Crime Index consists of data regarding the major **Index crimes** (murder and nonnegligent manslaughter, forcible rape, robbery, aggravated assault, burglary, larceny-theft, and motor vehicle theft). The Crime Index section of the yearly Uniform Crime Reports generally comprises over 200 pages of tables and graphs re-

---

All in the Line of Duty

The Vest Saved His Life: Wear Yours!

On May 17, 1973, Detroit, Michigan, Police Officer Ron Jagielski and several other officers were working on a plainclothes assignment involving narcotics trafficking. Jagielski was poised to raid a residence to effect a narcotics seizure when a shot pierced the front door and hit him in the chest. Subsequently found embedded in his ballistic vest, just below the heart area, was a .38-calibre special round. Had it not been for the protective vest, Jagielski would surely have suffered a fatal injury.

Note: Officer Jagielski was the first recipient of the International Association of Chiefs of Police (IACP) and the DuPont Corporation's "Survivors' Club," which recognizes officers who have survived potentially fatal or disabling injuries through the use of personal body armor. Since 1973, over 2,000 officers have been cited.

Source: Adapted from Joseph G. Estey, "2,000 Survivor's Club Hits: In the Past 10 Years, 2,000 Officers Have 'Dressed for Survival,'" *Police Chief*, May 1997, p. 18.

garding the Index crimes. Included on these pages are five-year analyses of each of the crimes using numerous variables, such as the relationship between perpetrator and victim, weapons used, age, race, and gender; crime trends; and crime rates for all offenses reported to the police for the previous year for each of the reporting cities, towns, universities/colleges, and suburban and rural counties.

The Crime Index Offenses Cleared section lists the clearance rates (rates of crimes solved by arrest) for the Index crimes according to certain variables, such as population group and geographic region of the country.

The section on Persons Arrested lists all arrests in the United States for the Index crimes and other crimes according to certain variables. These include geographic area, age, race, and gender.

The Law Enforcement Personnel section lists the number of all uniformed and civilian law enforcement employees for each reporting town, city, and county.

Prior to 1972, the Uniform Crime Reports was the only nationwide measure of crime in the United States. Scholars, however, became skeptical of the crime report data in the Uniform Crime Reports, because it was based solely on reports made to the police and did not recognize the fact that many crimes are not reported to the police. To get a truer account of crime, the National Crime Victimization Survey was started.

National Crime Victimization Survey The National Crime Victimization Survey is prepared by the National Institute of Justice (NIJ), the research arm of the U.S. Department of Justice. The National Crime Victimization Survey, as the name implies, is a survey of a random sample of U.S. households, asking them if a crime was committed against anyone in the household during the prior six months. It also asks them certain questions about the incident. Data from the National Crime Victimization Survey is published by the NIJ yearly as *Criminal Victimization in the United States*. The NIJ also issues periodic reports regarding trends in particular crimes.

How Much Crime Occurs in the United States?

Crime information for the latest year available for each of the Index crimes is shown in Table 11.1. The data in the Uniform Crime Reports are easy to read. For example, when we look at the figures for murder we see that there were 21,597 murders, which amounts to 8.2 murders for every 100,000 Americans.

Table 11.1 Uniform Crime Reports Data

Index Crime	Amount	Per 100,000 Inhabitants
Murder	21,597	8.2
Forcible rape	97,464	37.1
Robbery	580,545	220.9
Aggravated assault	1,099,179	418.3
Burglary	2,594,995	987.6
Larceny	8,000,631	3,044.9
Motor vehicle theft	1,472,732	560.5

Source: Adapted from Kathleen Maguire and Ann L. Pastore, eds., *Sourcebook of Criminal Justice Statistics—1996* (Washington, D.C.: U.S. Department of Justice, Bureau of Justice Statistics, U.S. Government Printing Office, 1997), Table 3.109, p. 316

The other crime measure, the National Crime Victimization Survey, reports the crime data shown in Table 11.2. Notice that the number of incidents for each crime are quite different in the two reports. The UCR data only include incidents actually reported to the police, whereas the National Crime Victimization Survey data are based on results of interviews with people, many of whom did not report their criminal victimization to the police. Note that the figures for motor vehicle theft (auto larceny) are closest in both reports. This is because most people in the United States are covered by automobile insurance and thus report an automobile theft to the police in order to make a claim with their insurance company.

Table 11.2 National Crime Victimization Survey Data

Crime	Number of Victimizations	Rates Per 100,000 Persons
Rape	167,550	0.8
Robbery	1,298,750	6.1
Aggravated assault	2,478,150	11.6
Simple assault	6,650,970	31.1
Household burglary	5,482,720	54.4
Theft	23,765,790	235.8
Auto larcenies	1,763,690	17.5

Source: Adapted from Kathleen Maguire and Ann L. Pastore, eds., *Sourcebook of Criminal Justice Statistics—1996* (Washington, D.C.: U.S. Department of Justice, Bureau of Justice Statistics, U.S. Government Printing Office, 1997), Table 3.1, p. 208.

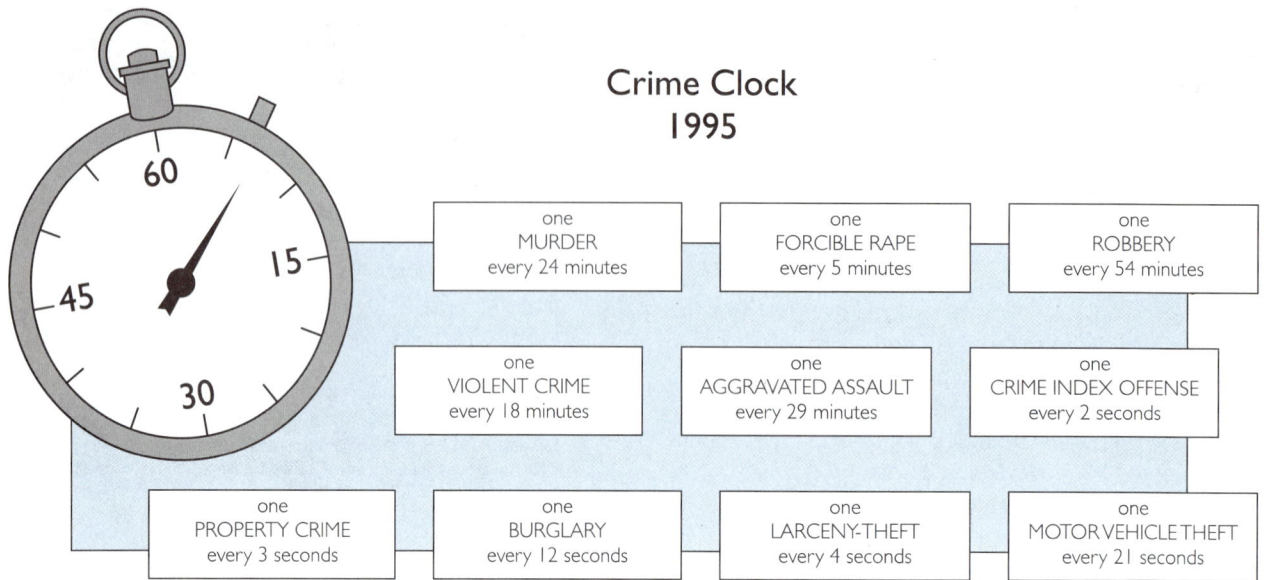

Figure 11.1
The crime clock is designed to convey the annual reported crime experience by showing the relative frequency of the Index Offenses. This mode of display should not be taken to imply a regularity in the commission of the Part I Offenses; rather, it represents the annual ratio of Part I Offenses to fixed time intervals.
Source: Adapted from *Crime in the United States: Uniform Crime Reports, 1996* (Washington, D.C.: Dept. of Justice, Federal Bureau of Investigation, 1997).

Arrests in the United States

Recently, the U.S. police have made about 15 million arrests a year for all criminal infractions except traffic violations. Of these 15 million arrests, less than 3 million were for the major Index crimes. Of the 15 million, 796,000 were for serious violent crime, including murder and nonnegligent manslaughter, forcible rape, robbery, and aggravated or felonious assault; approximately 2 million of the arrests were for property crimes, including burglary, larceny, and motor vehicle theft.

The remaining 12 million arrests were for various other offenses. The major categories of these arrests and their approximate totals follow: misdemeanor assaults, 1.3 million; drug abuse violations, 1.5 million; driving under the influence, 1.4 million; and liquor-related disorderly conduct, vagrancy, and loitering, 2.2 million.[1]

★ The Police and the U.S. Constitution

The United States is a nation governed by law. The primary law regulating life in the United States is the U.S. Constitution, including its many amendments. The following sections will discuss the first ten amendments to the Constitution (the Bill of Rights), the Fourteenth Amendment, the role of the U.S. Supreme Court in regulating the police, and the exclusionary rule and its impact on the police.

It must be remembered that the U.S. Constitution is a continuing, dynamic document constantly being reviewed by the United States Supreme Court. This chapter discusses hundreds of Supreme Court decisions, "landmark cases," which have affected the police and the entire criminal justice system, as well as our society. As this judicial review process of the Court is constantly reinterpreting the Constitution and constantly changing the rules that govern police behavior, all officers must constantly review their own organization's rules and directives with the realization that the law is always changing.

Bill of Rights and the Fourteenth Amendment

The U.S. criminal justice system is based on the Bill of Rights, the first ten amendments to the U.S. Constitution. Five of the first ten amendments specifically address freedoms or rights that people possess when involved with the criminal justice system. These free-

Amendment I (1791)
Congress shall make no law respecting an establishment of religion, or prohibiting the free exercise thereof; or abridging the freedom of speech, or of the press; or the right of the people peaceably to assemble, and to petition the Government for a redress of grievances.

Amendment IV (1791)
The right of the people to be secure in their persons, houses, papers, and effects against unreasonable searches and seizures, shall not be violated, and no Warrants shall issue, but upon probable cause, supported by Oath or affirmation, and particularly describing the place to be searched, and the persons or things to be seized.

Amendment V (1791)
No person shall be held to answer for a capital, or otherwise infamous crime, unless on a presentment or indictment of a Grand Jury, except in cases arising in the land or naval forces, or in the Militia, when in actual service in time of War or public danger; nor shall person be subject for the same offense to be twice put in jeopardy of life or limb; nor shall be compelled in any criminal case to be a witness against himself, nor be deprived of life, liberty, or property, without due process of law; nor shall private property be taken for public use, without just compensation.

Amendment VI (1791)
In all criminal prosecutions, the accused shall enjoy the right to a speedy and public trial, by an impartial jury of the State and district wherein the crime shall have been committed, which district shall have been previously ascertained by law, and to be informed of the nature and cause of the accusation; to be confronted with the witnesses against him; to have compulsory process for obtaining witnesses in his favor, and to have the assistance of Counsel for his defense.

Amendment VIII (1791)
Excessive bail shall not be required, nor excessive fines imposed, nor cruel and unusual punishments inflicted.

Figure 11.2
U.S. Constitution: Amendments Governing the U.S. Criminal Justice System

doms and rights apply to all U.S. citizens. See figure 11.2 for the amendments that specifically affect the U.S. criminal justice system.

To understand the U.S. system of criminal justice, we must go back to the birth of the United States. The early colonists came to escape persecution by the English king and to seek freedom. The colonists, however, continued to be persecuted and to be denied freedom. They rebelled, wrote the Declaration of Independence, fought for independence from England, and were able to defeat the British troops. As newly freed people, the former colonists wrote the U.S. Constitution to govern themselves. They then wrote the first ten amendments to the Constitution, which form the basis of our criminal justice system—the rights and freedoms we possess that can be used against government tyranny.

The Fourteenth Amendment also has an effect on the U.S. criminal justice system. The Supreme Court,

PATROLLING THE NET

The Communications Decency Act (1996)

The Communications Decency Act was passed in 1996 as a last-minute amendment to another bill, The Telecommunications Act of 1996. It was adopted without hearings and amid substantial doubts about its constitutionality. For that reason, its sponsors agreed to add a provision guaranteeing quick Supreme Court review after a hearing by a single three-judge court, a shortcut through the normal appellate process.

Violations of the Communications Decency Act, which never went into effect because of a stay issued by the lower court, carried penalties of two years in prison and a $250,000 fine. The law made it a crime to use a computer to transmit indecent material to someone under eighteen years old or to display such material in a manner available to a person under eighteen.

Source: Adapted from Linda Greenhouse, "Court, 9–0, Upholds State Laws Prohibiting Assisted Suicide; Protects Speech on Internet: Decency Act Fails," *New York Times,* 27 June, 1997, p. A-1, 20.

over the years, has extended the Bill of Rights to the states through the due process clause of the Fourteenth Amendment. The due process clause is that section of the Fourteenth Amendment that insures all citizens of the United States against any state's depriving them of life, liberty, or property except through the proper legal processes guaranteed by the U.S. Constitution. This section has been the vehicle through which much of the Bill of Rights has been interpreted to apply to state courts as well as federal courts.

Role of the Supreme Court in Regulating the Police

The U.S. Supreme Court, through its policy of judicial review, has made a significant impact on the way the police do their job. As early as 1914, in *Weeks v. United States,* the Court influenced the police by regulating how they should conduct their searches and seizures.[2]

In 1936, in *Brown v. Mississippi,* the Court began to affect the police by ruling certain methods of police interrogation unconstitutional.[3]

Most Supreme Court cases regarding criminal justice try to strike a balance between the rights of the individual and the rights of society. But what do we mean by the rights of the individual and the rights of society? A simple example, which could have occurred today in your classroom, might explain it. You and your fellow students want a safe classroom. You do not want a student walking into class with an illegal gun that could be used to shoot you (rights of society). However, which of you would like the police to be at the classroom door each morning searching you for illegal guns without just cause (rights of the individual)?

The Supreme Court has the difficult task of bringing balance between these two often-conflicting goals. There is an inherent inconsistency between protecting the rights of the individual and the rights of society. To

PATROLLING THE NET

U.S. Supreme Court Rules: Anything Goes on the Net: 1st Amendment Applies

On June 26, 1997, the U.S. Supreme Court, in *Reno v. American Civil Liberties Union,* No. 96-511, in a sweeping endorsement of free speech on the Internet, declared unconstitutional a federal law making it a crime to send or display indecent material online in a way available to minors.

The 7–2 decision was the Court's first effort to extend the principles of the First Amendment into cyberspace. The Court's decision, written by Justice John Paul Stevens, struck down the 1996 Communications Decency Act, ruling that the Internet is entitled to the highest level of First Amendment protection, similar to the protection the Court gives to books and newspapers. The Court has continuously held that more limited First Amendment rights applied to speech on broadcast and cable television, where the Court has tolerated a wide array of government regulation. The Court's action upheld a 1996 decision by a three-judge Federal District Court in Philadelphia that had struck down the Decency Law in 1996 shortly after its passage.

This decision makes it unlikely that any government-imposed restriction on Internet content would be upheld as long as the material has some intrinsic constitutional value. The Court held that the indecent material at issue in the case was not precisely defined by the 1996 law but was merely referred to in one section of the statute as "patently offensive" descriptions or images of "sexual or excretory activities."

Excerpt from Justice Stevens's decision:

> It is true that we have repeatedly recognized the governmental interest in protecting children from harmful materials. But that interest does not justify an unnecessarily broad suppression of speech addressed to adults. As we have explained, the government may not reduce the adult population to only what is fit for children.
>
> [In a previous case], we remarked that the speech restriction at issue there amounted to 'burning the house to roast the pig.' The [law] casting a far darker shadow over free speech, threatens to torch a large segment of the Internet community.
>
> As a matter of constitutional tradition, in the absence of evidence to the contrary, we presume that governmental regulation of the content of speech is more likely to interfere with the free exchange of ideas than to encourage it.

Source: Adapted from *Reno v. American Civil Liberties Union,* No. 96-511; Linda Greenhouse, "Court, 9–0, Upholds State Laws Prohibiting Assisted Suicide; Protects Speech on Internet: Decency Act Fails," *New York Times,* 27 June, 1997, p. A-1, 20; Steven Levy with Karen Breslau, "On the Net, Anything Goes," *Newsweek,* 7 July 1997, pp. 28–30; "U.S. v. the Internet: In a cyber showdown, the Decency Act Reaches the Supreme Court," *Newsweek,* 31 March 1997, pp. 77–79.

PATROLLING THE NET

Research Courts and Court Cases on the Net

Do you want to look up some U.S. Supreme Court cases and other legal information on the Net? Try some of these sites.

Supreme Court Decisions
http://www.law.cornell.edu/supct/supct.table.html

Supreme Court Justices
http://www.law.cornell.edu/supct/justices/fullcourt.html

U.S. Federal Courts Homepage
http://www.uscourts.gov

National Center for State Courts
http://www.ncsc.dni.us

Courts on the Internet
http://www.legalonline.com/courts.htm

---

have unlimited individual rights risks the chance of limiting the rights of society to be safe from crime. To have unlimited rights of society to be safe from crime risks giving up individual rights. It falls upon the Supreme Court to balance these two precious rights.

In police matters, the Supreme Court hears cases, on appeal, from people who have been the subject of police actions, including arrest, search and seizure, and custodial interrogation. The justices then decide whether or not the police action violated the person's constitutional rights. In most cases, they do this by interpreting one of the amendments to the Constitution. Supreme Court decisions can bring about changes in police procedures. Certain significant cases, such as *Mapp v. Ohio* and *Miranda v. Arizona,* are known as landmark cases.[4] The major method used by the Supreme Court to ensure that the police do not violate people's constitutional rights is the use of the exclusionary rule.

The Exclusionary Rule

The **exclusionary rule** is not a part of the U.S. Constitution. It is an interpretation of the Fourteenth Amendment by the Supreme Court that holds that evidence seized in violation of the U.S. Constitution cannot be used in court against a defendant. Such evidence is suppressed (not allowed to be used in court).

The exclusionary rule evolved in U.S. law through a series of Supreme Court cases. Since at least 1914, the Supreme Court has been concerned with the use of illegal means by the police to seize evidence in violation of the Constitution, and then their using that evidence to convict a defendant in court. Because the Bill of Rights, when written, only applied to agents of the federal government—not those of local governments—the Court first applied the exclusionary rule only to federal courts and federal law enforcement officers. The Court continually warned state courts and law enforcement agencies that they must amend their procedures in order to comply with the U.S. Constitution or risk the exclusionary rule's being imposed on them as well. By 1961, the Supreme Court, noting that states had not amended their procedures to conform to the Constitution, applied the exclusionary rule to state courts and law enforcement agencies, as well as federal ones. The following four landmark cases show how the exclusionary rule developed in this country.

Weeks v. United States (1914)   *Weeks v. United States* (1914) was the first case in which the exclusionary rule was used.[5] It involved federal law enforcement personnel entering an arrested person's home and seizing evidence without a warrant. The evidence was used against him in court, and he was convicted based on it.

On appeal, the Supreme Court overturned the man's conviction and established the exclusionary rule. Expressing the opinion of the Court, Justice William R. Day wrote the following:

> If letters and private documents can thus be seized and held and used in evidence against a citizen accused of an offense, the protection of the Fourth Amendment, declaring his right to be secure against such searches and seizures, is of no value, and so far as those thus placed are concerned, might as well be stricken from the Constitution. The efforts of the courts and their officials to bring the guilty to punishment, praiseworthy as they are, are not to be aided by the sacrifice of these great principles established by years of endeavor and suffering which have resulted in their embodiment in the fundamental law of the land.

YOU ARE THERE!

The Exclusionary Rule: Judge Kennedy-Powell's Ruling on the Admissibility of Evidence in the O.J. Simpson Case

This decision concerns the court's determination whether the warrantless entry into the property of O.J. Simpson and the recovery of certain important items of physical evidence (blood stains and a bloody glove that matched a bloody glove found at the murder scene) in the morning of Monday, June 13, 1994, was justified in the light of exigent (emergency) circumstances.

Judge Kathleen Kennedy-Powell:

The detectives testified that they were concerned about those children [the Simpson children had been taken to a Los Angeles police station after their mother's dead body was found] and wanted to make arrangements with regard to those children. They get to the gate and here, again, it seems to me they really do extraordinary things to try to make contact with the persons inside. I mean the testimony was that they rang that bell for some 15 minutes to try to rouse somebody from within the house. They could hear that phone ringing from out at the gate. There's no response. But what do they see? And this, apparently, also is uncontroverted in light of the testimony that was presented. There's a light on upstairs; there's a light on downstairs. There's several vehicles in the driveway, a suggestion that there are persons inside.

They see what they believe to be blood on the door handle or near the door handle of this white Bronco. A white Bronco that is parked on a public street where the officers have a right to be, and the court sees no problem with the observing or recovery of the blood samples from the door of the Bronco.

So, seeing what they believe to be blood and having seen droplets of blood leading away from the location, the officers even now are doing more to get in touch with the people inside by calling the Westec Security, who apparently dispatches at least one, if not two, vehicles to the location and eventually gives the police the telephone number. What they get at that point is an answering machine.

Defense lawyers in this case did an excellent job on cross-examination. But, when one looks at the result of that cross-examination, basically there were really no holes put in any of those detectives' testimonies that they felt that they were acting in an emergency situation at the time. This would be a very easy decision for me if, in fact, these officers went in there like storm troopers, fanning out over the property, examining every leaf, every car, every closet, every nook and cranny of this location, but the testimony as elicited by the officers and as supported by the witness that testified on behalf of the defense, show that this was not what happened.

What the testimony was, is that the officers went in search of persons on the property. They went into the guest quarters of Mr. Kaelin, woke him up.

We have to judge the officers' conduct and the exigency if there was one, not based upon what all of us know today, but based upon what the officers knew at the time. And the information that they had been provided by Westec Security was that there was a live-in maid at the location. Additionally, Westec Security advised them that they had not been informed that there was going to be a vacation and absence of the residents from that location.

We know now, obviously, that there was no dying person or injured person on the property at the Simpson estate at that time. We know that all the persons who were supposed to be there were accounted for. Mr. Simpson was in Chicago, Mr. Kaelin was in his quarters, Ms. Arnelle Simpson had been out and returned about 1 o'clock in the morning. And GiGi, the maid, was on her night off. But the officers didn't know that at the time.

And we know from Mr. Kaelin's testimony that there was a loud, jarring, banging on the wall of his guest quarters, one that scared him, that he didn't know the origin of, that he had mentioned to several other persons but had never really investigated himself. So the officers have that information from Mr. Kaelin and Detective Fuhrman walks down that path.

He doesn't go anywhere else on the property. Officers make no attempt to go upstairs; they don't start opening cupboards, lifting up carpets, opening vehicles. He goes down that path to the area approximately adjacent to the air-conditioner where that noise was seen and the picture jarred from the wall and finds a glove. A glove that appears to be the apparent mate to the glove found at the crime scene.

Contrary to the suggestions in the defense argument that a ruling allowing the officers' conduct—finding that it was reasonable and that there were exigent circumstances—would mean the end of the Fourth Amendment and the Constitution and anarchy, I disagree.

The court finds that they [the detectives] were, in fact, acting for a benevolent purpose in light of the brutal attack and that they reasonably believed that a further delay could have resulted in the unnecessary loss of life. And, therefore, the court denies the defense motion to suppress and will allow the introduction into evidence of the glove that was recovered and of the spattered blood spots that were located on the driveway once the sun came up, as well as the bloodstains from the Bronco, which was in plain view on the public street.

Source: Preliminary hearing in *People v. Orenthal James Simpson*, July 8, 1994.

YOU ARE THERE!

Weeks v. United States (1914)

Freemont Weeks was arrested at his place of business and charged with using the U.S. mail to conduct an illegal lottery. The police then searched Weeks's house and turned over articles and papers to a U.S. marshal. The marshal, then, together with the police, searched Weeks's room and confiscated other documents and letters. All the searches were conducted without a warrant.

Weeks was convicted based on the evidence seized from his home. On appeal to the U.S. Supreme Court, his conviction was overturned, and the exclusionary rule was established.

Source: Based on *Weeks v. United States*, 232 U.S. 383 (1914).

The exclusionary rule provided that any evidence seized in violation of the Fourth Amendment could not be used against a defendant in a criminal case. The exclusionary rule, as enunciated in the Weeks case, applied only to evidence seized in an unconstitutional search and seizure by a federal agent and used in a federal court. It did not apply to state courts.

The exclusionary rule gave rise to another form of police misconduct that has been called the silver platter doctrine. Under the silver platter doctrine, federal prosecutors were allowed to use evidence obtained by state police officers seized through unreasonable searches and seizures, provided that the evidence was obtained without federal participation and was turned over to federal officers.

Wolf v. Colorado (1949) Another case that involved the exclusionary rule was *Wolf v. Colorado*[6] in 1949. Mr. Wolf was suspected of being an illegal abortionist. A deputy sheriff seized his appointment book without a warrant and interrogated people whose names appeared in the book. Based on the evidence from these patients, Wolf was arrested, charged with committing illegal abortions, and convicted in court.

On appeal, the Supreme Court issued what could be seen as a rather strange decision. It ruled that although the Fourth Amendment did bar the admissibility of illegally seized evidence, it would not impose federal standards (the exclusionary rule) on state courts. The Court directed that the states create stronger state rules that would prevent illegally obtained evidence from being admitted into state courts. At the time of the Wolf decision, thirty-one states had rejected the exclusionary rule, and the Court had accepted this, respecting states' rights. By 1961, when *Mapp v. Ohio* reached the Supreme Court, many states had accepted the exclusionary rule.

Justice Felix Frankfurter, speaking for the Court, wrote, "We hold, therefore, that in a prosecution in a State Court for a State crime the Fourteenth Amendment does not forbid the admission of evidence obtained by an unreasonable search and seizure."

Rochin v. California (1952) In *Rochin v. California*, another landmark case in the development of the exclusionary rule, the police entered Mr. Rochin's home without a warrant and, upon seeing him place what they believed to be narcotics into his mouth, forcefully attempted to extract the narcotics from him.[7] Failing this, they brought Rochin to a hospital, where his stomach was pumped. The stomach pumping produced two capsules as evidence of illegal drugs. Rochin was convicted in court and sentenced to sixty days' imprisonment. The chief evidence against him was the two capsules.

The Supreme Court overturned Rochin's conviction, considering the forcible seizure of evidence as a viola-

YOU ARE THERE!

Rochin v. California (1952)

On July 1, 1949, based on information received that Mr. Rochin was selling narcotics, three Los Angeles County deputy sheriffs entered Rochin's house without a warrant and forced open the door to his apartment within the house. When the police entered Rochin's bedroom, they saw two capsules on his bedside table and asked him what they were. Rochin picked up the capsules and swallowed them. A struggle ensued between Rochin and the police, and the police attempted to open Rochin's mouth to get to the capsules. Failing to do this, they handcuffed him and forcibly took him to a hospital. At the hospital, under the direction of one of the police officers, a doctor forced an emetic solution through a tube into Rochin's stomach against his will. The stomach pumping caused Rochin to vomit. In the vomited matter were found two capsules, which proved to be morphine.

Source: Based on *Rochin v. California*, 342 U.S. 165 (1952).

tion of the Fourteenth Amendment's due process clause. Speaking for the Court, Justice Felix Frankfurter wrote,

> This is conduct that shocks the conscience. Illegally breaking into the privacy of Rochin, the struggle to open his mouth and remove what was there, the forcible extraction of his stomach's contents—this course of proceedings by agents of government to obtain evidence is bound to offend even hardened sensibilities. They are methods too close to the rack and screw to permit of constitutional differentiation.

In the Rochin case, the Court did not make the exclusionary rule applicable in all state cases, but only in those cases of extremely serious police misconduct—misconduct that, in Justice Frankfurter's words, shocks the conscience. The Court again urged the states to enact laws prohibiting the use of illegally seized evidence in state courts and threatened that if the states did not enact those laws, the Court might impose the exclusionary rule upon the states.

***Mapp v. Ohio* (1961)** *Mapp v. Ohio* was the vehicle the Supreme Court used for applying the exclusionary rule to state courts.[8] The case involved the warrantless entry of police into a woman's home to search for a man in connection with a bombing. While in her home, the police searched it and found "obscene materials," for which she was arrested and ultimately convicted in court.

Speaking for the Supreme Court, Justice Tom C. Clark wrote the following:

> The ignoble shortcut to conviction left open to the State tends to destroy the entire system of constitutional restraints on which the liberties of the people rest. Having once recognized that the right to privacy embodied in the Fourth Amendment is enforceable against the States, and that the right to be secure against rude invasions of privacy

YOU ARE THERE!

Mapp v. Ohio (1961)

On May 23, 1957, three Cleveland police officers went to the home of Dollree ("Dolly") Mapp to search for a man named Virgil Ogletree, who was wanted in connection with a bombing at the home of Donald King. (Donald King was the well-known boxing promoter who promoted former world heavyweight champion Mike Tyson, among other fighters.) The police knocked at the door and demanded entry. Mapp telephoned her lawyer and, on his advice, refused to allow the police to enter without a warrant.

Three hours later, the police again arrived with additional officers. The police then forced their way into the house. At this point, Mapp's lawyer arrived but was not allowed to see his client or to enter the house. As the police were rushing up the stairs to Mapp's second-floor apartment, Mapp was halfway down the stairs, rushing the police and demanding to see the warrant. In response to Mapp's demand, one of the officers held up a piece of paper purported to be a warrant. Mapp grabbed the piece of paper and stuffed it down the front of her clothing. A struggle ensued, during which the officers retrieved the piece of paper and then handcuffed Mapp because she was acting "belligerent." The officers then forcibly took her to her bedroom, where they searched a dresser, a chest of drawers, a closet, and some suitcases. They also looked through a photo album and some of Mapp's personal papers. The police also searched the living room, dining area, kitchen, and Mapp's daughter's bedroom. They then went to the basement and searched it and a trunk located there. During the search, the police found an unspecified amount of pornographic literature.

Mapp was charged with possession of "lewd and lascivious books, pictures and photographs" and subsequently convicted in court for possessing obscene materials. The warrant was never produced in court.

On appeal, the Supreme Court reversed Mapp's conviction based on the police's violation of the Fourth Amendment. It then extended the exclusionary rule to all state courts and law enforcement personnel.

Source: Based on *Mapp v. Ohio,* 367 U.S. 643 (1961).

Note: Do you know what happened to Dollree Mapp after this case?

In 1970, Dollree Mapp was arrested by New York City police for the possession of drugs. Suspecting that Mapp was dealing in stolen property, the police obtained a search warrant. While executing it, they found 50,000 envelopes of heroin and stolen property valued at over $100,000. Mapp was convicted and sentenced to a term of twenty years to life. On New Year's Eve in 1980, the New York governor commuted her sentence.

Source: Adapted from James A. Inciardi, *Criminal Justice,* 3d ed. (Orlando, Fla.: Harcourt Brace Jovanovich, 1990), p. 280.

by state officers is, therefore constitutional in origin, we can no longer permit that right to remain an empty promise. Because it is enforceable in the same manner and to like effect as other basic rights secured by the Due Process Clause, we can no longer permit it to be revocable at the whim of the police officer who, in the name of law enforcement itself, chooses to suspend its enjoyment. Our decision, founded on reason and truth, gives to the individual no more than that which the Constitution guarantees him, to the police officer no less than that to which honest law enforcement is entitled, and to the courts, the judicial integrity so necessary in the true administration of justice.

Impact of the Exclusionary Rule on the Police

Many police officers and citizens feel that the exclusionary rule is unfair—that it is procriminal and antipolice. They feel that the rule allows hardened criminals the chance to escape justice and be released "on a technicality." Since the Mapp and Miranda decisions, many have claimed that the Supreme Court has "handcuffed" the police and that the police no longer have the tools to fight crime. (The Miranda case will be discussed later in the chapter.) Academic studies of the effect of the exclusionary rule on crime have not confirmed these fears.

A study done in California revealed that the exclusionary rule is overwhelmingly used with drug offenses, not violent crimes such as murder, rape, robbery, and assault. Of all the cases studied in which the exclusionary rule was involved, only 0.1 percent were murder cases, 0.3 percent were rapes, 2.1 percent were robberies, and 3.2 percent were assaults; 71.5 percent involved drug cases. Furthermore, the study found that the exclusionary rule was responsible for evidence being suppressed in only 0.8 percent of all criminal cases and only 4.8 percent of all felonies.[9] Another study—a review of 7,500 felony cases in nine counties in three states—found that only forty-six cases (0.6 percent) were dismissed because of the exclusionary rule.[10]

The remainder of this chapter will deal with constitutional limitations on the police in the areas of arrest, search and seizure, custodial interrogation, and identification procedures.

All in the Line of Duty

His Life Was the 2,000th Saved by a Vest: Wear Yours!

On January 3, 1997, Deputy Sheriff Henry Huff, a member of the Walton County, Georgia, Sheriff's Office, was shot at point-blank range during a traffic stop by a 9mm-wielding sixteen-year-old. Because Huff's squad car was equipped with a surveillance camera, the entire incident was recorded on videotape.

Despite being shot twice in the chest, Huff was spared serious injury by his bullet-resistant vest, and has since returned to duty. According to his supervisor,

> We are thankful this shooting ended the way it did. If he had not been wearing his body armor, he wouldn't be talking to us now. Deputy Huff wears a guardian angel pin on his uniform shirt, and I believe that angel was looking out for him today.

Note: Deputy Huff was the 2,000th recipient of the International Association of Chiefs of Police (IACP) and the DuPont Corporation's "Survivors' Club," which recognizes officers who have survived potentially fatal or disabling injuries through the use of personal body armor. The award has been given since 1973.

Source: Adapted from Joseph G. Estey, "2,000 Survivor's Club Hits: In the Past 10 Years, 2,000 Officers Have 'Dressed for Survival'," *Police Chief,* May 1997, p. 18.

The Police and Arrest

The police authority to arrest is restricted by the Fifth Amendment, which forbids depriving citizens of life, liberty, or property without due processes of law. An arrest is also controlled by the Fourth Amendment's restrictions on searches and seizures, because an arrest is the ultimate seizure—the seizure of one's body. A state's criminal procedure law defines an arrest and directs who can make an arrest, for what offenses, and when. Most states define an arrest as "the taking of a person into custody, in the manner authorized by law for the purpose of presenting that person before a magistrate to answer for the commission of a crime."[11]

Arrests can be made with or without a warrant (a writ, or formal written order, issued by a judicial officer that directs a law enforcement officer to perform a specified act and affords the officer protection from damage if he or she acts according to the order). In general, police officers can arrest a person (1) for any crime committed in the officers' presence, (2) for a felony not committed in the officers' presence if they have probable cause to believe that a felony has occurred and that the person they have arrested committed the felony, or (3) under the authority of an arrest warrant. As an example of the first circumstance, an officer can arrest a man whom he or she observes committing a robbery with a gun. An arrest can also be made in the following scenario: An officer is called to a scene where there is a dead body and is told by witnesses that a woman in a black leather jacket was engaged in an altercation with the deceased and took out a gun and shot him. The officer searches the area around the crime scene and finds a woman in a black jacket; she is hiding under a staircase. Upon searching the woman, the officer finds a gun. In the event the officer does not find the woman after the crime, but witnesses positively identify her, the officer can respond to court and obtain an arrest warrant for the woman and a search warrant to search her house for the gun.

Probable Cause

Most of the arrests made by the average police officer do not involve a warrant, because most crimes an officer becomes aware of on the street necessitate immediate action and do not allow the officer the time necessary to go to court to obtain a warrant. Most of the arrests made by the police are based on the probable cause standard.

Probable cause can be defined as evidence that may lead a reasonable person to believe that a crime has been committed and that a certain person committed it. Probable cause is less than beyond a reasonable doubt, which is the standard used by a court to convict a person of a crime. Probable cause is more than reasonable suspicion. **Reasonable suspicion** is a standard of proof that would lead a reasonable person (a police officer) to believe a certain condition or fact (that a crime is, will be, or has occurred) exists. This is the standard necessary for police officers to conduct stop and frisks.

The evidence needed to establish probable cause must be established prior to arrest. For example, if an officer sees a man, walking down a block, adjust his jacket to the extent that a gun can be seen protruding from his waistband, the officer has reasonable suspicion to stop and question the man. If the possession of the gun is illegal, the officer has probable cause to make an arrest. Because the arrest is legal, the search that produced the gun is legal; therefore, the gun can be entered into evidence. In contrast, if an officer stops all people walking down the street and searches them without sufficient justification, any arrest for possession of a gun would be illegal, and the gun would be suppressed in court.

> ### YOU ARE THERE! »
>
> #### A Police Officer's Power to Arrest
>
> The Tennessee Code, Section 40.803, reads as follows:
>
> Grounds for arrest by officer without warrant—An officer may, without a warrant, arrest a person:
>
> 1. For a public offense committed or a breach of the peace threatened in his presence.
> 2. When the person has committed a felony, though not in his presence.
> 3. When a felony has in fact been committed, and he has reasonable cause for believing the person arrested to have committed it.
> 4. On a charge made, upon reasonable cause, of the commission of a felony by the person arrested.

In 1959, *Henry v. United States* set the precedent that an arrest must be made on firmer grounds than mere suspicion, and that the Fourth Amendment applies to searches and arrests.[12] The Supreme Court, in *Brinegar v. United States* (1949), ruled that relaxations of the fundamental requirements of probable cause, as it relates to the power of arrest, would leave law-abiding citizens at the mercy of police officers' whims.[13] *Draper v. United States* (1959) held that the identification of a suspect by a reliable informant may constitute probable cause for an arrest, where the information given is sufficiently accurate to lead the officers directly to the suspect.[14]

In 1991, in *County of Riverside v. McLoughlin,* the Court ruled that a person arrested without a warrant must generally be provided with a judicial determination of probable cause within forty-eight hours after arrest, including intervening weekends and holidays, meaning that weekends and holidays could not be excluded from the forty-eight hour rule.[15]

Reasonable and Deadly Force in Making Arrests

The amount of force an officer can use when making an arrest is called **reasonable force**. Reasonable force is that amount of force necessary to overcome resistance by the person being arrested by the police. For example, if a person is punching the officer in an effort to avoid the arrest, the officer may use similar force in an attempt to subdue the person and control him or her.

As a perpetrator's force escalates, an officer may escalate his or her use of force.

The best way to define reasonable force may be to define unreasonable force. Punching, kicking, or otherwise using force against a person who is not resisting and who is willingly submitting to an arrest would be the unreasonable use of force. Continuing to strike at a person after he or she is subdued, handcuffed, and under the officer's physical control would be an unreasonable use of force. The videotape of the Rodney King incident would appear to be an excellent example of unreasonable force, even though the jury apparently saw it differently. King does not appear to be resisting, yet the officers continue to hit him with their batons.

The use of deadly force (force sufficient to cause a person's death) has long been a controversial topic in policing. Chapter 15 covers it in depth. However, for the purposes of this chapter, it should be stated that the use of deadly force by the police is generally permitted (1) when an officer's life or another's life is at peril from the person against whom the deadly physical force is directed, (2) where the officer has probable cause to believe the suspect has committed a crime involving serious physical harm to another, or (3) in other serious felony cases.

Stopping Vehicles

"It was a routine traffic stop," many officers used to testify in court regarding summonses and arrests for drivers of automobiles. The routine traffic stop came to an end, however, in 1979, with the case of *Delaware v. Prouse*.[16] In this case, the Supreme Court ruled that the police cannot make capricious car stops and that "random spot checks" of motorists are a violation of a citizen's Fourth Amendment rights.

The Court, however, stated that police may still stop automobiles based on reasonable suspicion that (1) a crime was being committed or (2) a traffic violation occurred. The Court also said that the police can establish roadblocks as long as (1) all citizens are subject to the stop or (2) a pattern is set such as every third car is stopped.

Can a police officer legally order a driver or a passenger out of the vehicle after he or she has stopped it? Yes, ruled the Supreme Court in two cases. In *Mimms v. Pennsylvania* (1977), the Court ruled that the Fourth Amendment allows a law enforcement officer who has made a lawful routine stop of a vehicle for a traffic offense to order the driver to exit the vehicle without requiring any additional factual justification. In this case, the defendant was stopped for driving with an expired license plate. The officer then ordered the defendant to exit the vehicle. The officer later testified that he routinely ordered all drivers to exit vehicles following routine traffic stops out of a concern for his safety. When Mimms stepped out of the vehicle, the officer noticed a bulge in his jacket, prompting the officer to conduct a limited search for weapons and leading to the discovery of a handgun.[17]

In *Maryland v. Wilson* (1997), a Maryland state trooper pulled over a vehicle for speeding. The trooper, out of concern for his safety, directed the defendant, Wilson, a passenger in the vehicle, to step out of the vehicle. As the man exited the car, the trooper observed a bag of cocaine fall to the ground.[18] For a thorough discussion of Mimms and Wilson, see Lisa A. Regini, "Extending the Mimms Rule to Include Passengers," *FBI Law Enforcement Bulletin,* June 1997, pp. 27–32.

In both cases, the Court recognized the inherently dangerous nature of the traffic stop. In fact, in *Maryland v. Wilson,* the Court cited statistics showing that in 1994, the year in which this incident occurred, 5,762

> ## YOU ARE THERE!
>
> ### *Delaware v. Prouse* (1979)
>
> On November 30, 1976, at about 7:30 P.M., a New Castle County, Delaware, police officer stopped an automobile owned by William Prouse. Another man was driving Prouse's car, and Prouse was an occupant. As the officer approached the vehicle, he smelled the odor of marijuana. He then observed marijuana on the floor of the automobile. Prouse was arrested and later went on trial. At the trial, the officer testified that his stop of Prouse's car was "routine." He stated that he saw the car, and because he was not answering any other calls, he decided to stop the car. He further testified that he saw no traffic violations or vehicle equipment violations.
>
> The trial court ruled that the stop and detention had been capricious and was a violation of Prouse's Fourth Amendment rights. The state of Delaware appealed the case to the Supreme Court, which affirmed the opinion of the trial court. The Supreme Court ruled that random spot checks of automobiles are a violation of citizens' Fourth Amendment rights.
>
> Source: Based on *Delaware v. Prouse,* 440 U.S. 648 (1979).

officers were assaulted and 11 killed during traffic pursuits and stops.[19]

The Police and Search and Seizure

Search and seizure is the search for and taking of persons and property as evidence of crime by law enforcement officers. Searches and seizures are the means used by the police to obtain evidence that can be used by the courts to prove a defendant's guilt. Police searches are governed by the Fourth Amendment, which prohibits all unreasonable searches and seizures and requires that all warrants be based on probable cause and that they particularly describe the place to be searched and the persons or things to be seized. For the legal definitions of terms pertinent to searches and seizures, see Figure 11.3.

The Warrant Requirement and the Search Warrant

In the United States, the general rule regarding search and seizure is that law enforcement officers obtain a search warrant prior to any search and seizure. (However, there are many exceptions.) A search warrant is an order from a court, issued by a judge, authorizing and directing the police to search a particular place for certain property described in the warrant and directing the police to bring that property to court. Generally, to get a search warrant, a police officer prepares a typed affidavit applying for the warrant and then personally appears before a judge. The judge reads the application; questions the officer, if necessary; and signs the warrant if in agreement with the officer that there is probable cause that certain property that may be evidence of a crime, proceeds from a crime, or contraband (material that is illegal to possess, such as illegal drugs or illegal weapons) is present at a certain place.

Generally, a warrant can be executed only during daylight hours and within a certain time period. However, there are many exceptions. Officers executing a warrant generally must announce their presence before entering. At times, judges may add a no knock provision to the warrant, which allows the officers to enter without announcing their presence.[20]

Most searches by police officers are not made with warrants, because they are made on the street, where there is no time for an officer to proceed to court to obtain a warrant. Most searches are made in accordance with one of the exceptions to the search warrant requirement—situations involving **exigent circumstances** (emergency situations). Exceptions to the warrant requirement will be discussed at length in the next section.

The cases in which arrest warrants are generally used are lengthy investigations in which immediate action is not required. Also, warrants are often used in organized crime investigations.

One of the major uses of warrants is after an informant provides information to the police that certain people are engaged in continuous illegal acts, such as drug dealing. For example, a man tells the police that a certain person is a drug dealer and sells the drugs from her house. The police get as much information as they can from the informant and then dispatch a team of plainclothes officers to make undercover observations of the house. The officers do not see actual drug dealing, because it is going on inside the house, but they see certain actions that go along with the drug trade, such as cars stopping at the house and people entering the house for a short time and then leaving and driving away. Based on these observations, the police can then go to court and request that a judge issue a search warrant. If a search warrant is issued, the police can enter and search the house.

The Supreme Court has had several standards by which to determine what evidence would constitute probable cause for a judge to issue a warrant. The first standard was a two-part (two-pronged) test that mandated that the police show (1) why they believed the informant and (2) the circumstances that showed that the informant had personal knowledge of the crime. This standard was articulated in two major Supreme Court cases, *Aguilar v. Texas* (1964) and *Spinelli v. United States* (1969).[21] Obviously, there were problems with this standard. To show why the police believed the informant and how the informant obtained the information, the police would have to identify the informant or show how the informant was trustworthy in the past, or both. The identifying of the informant and the description of past tips could put the informant in danger.

In *Illinois v. Gates,* the Supreme Court in 1983 reversed the Aguilar-Spinelli two-pronged test.[22] The Court replaced it with the totality of circumstances test, which holds that an informant could be considered reliable if he or she gives the police sufficient facts to indicate that a crime is being committed and if the police verify these facts.

affidavit A statement in writing subscribed by a signature of a person that was affixed under oath before a notary public, a magistrate, or a commissioner of deeds.

arrest The initial taking into custody of a person by law enforcement authorities to answer for a criminal offense or violation of a code or ordinance.

crime Any act that the government has declared to be contrary to the public good, that is declared by statute to be a crime, and that is prosecuted in a criminal proceeding. In some jurisdictions, crimes only include felonies and/or misdemeanors.

evidence All matter of proof offered in a trial to prove or disprove an issue of fact.

exclusionary rule A judicially contrived procedure that prevents evidence unconstitutionally obtained by law enforcement officers from being introduced into evidence at a criminal trial and that is not to be considered by the triers of the facts of the case in arriving at a verdict.

felony A crime for which a person may be imprisoned for at least a year and a day.

frisk The patting down of the outer clothing of a person who is suspected of carrying a concealed weapon.

informant A person who supplies information to a law enforcement officer referring to the commission of a crime or to some set of facts requiring the attention of the law enforcement agency.

misdemeanor A class of criminal deviance that is usually punished by a maximum of $1,000 fine and/or up to one year in a county or city jail. A misdemeanor is less serious than a felony. Different jurisdictions classify misdemeanors and sanctions for violation thereof differently.

plain view A phrase that is applied to items of evidence that a law enforcement officer sees without having violated a person's constitutional rights and that the officer came upon inadvertently while performing normal duties.

probable cause The reasoning process that a reasonable person uses to conclude that (1) there is a good reason to make an arrest and (2) there is good reason to suspect that a person has contraband or evidence of crime in his or her possession.

search warrant A court order directing a law enforcement officer to search for, and return to the court, particular items of personal property to be used for the prosecution of a person for violation of a statute.

stop and frisk The act of an officer stopping a suspected person and patting that person's outer clothing to search for a concealed weapon. The officer must have reason to believe that the suspect is armed and dangerous.

suppression of evidence What occurs when evidence is unconstitutionally obtained by law enforcement authorities and the defendant makes a motion to suppress this evidence. After a hearing before a judge, the judge will indicate that the motion is granted. This means that the prosecutor is not permitted to use the unconstitutionally obtained evidence in the trial of this defendant. Often, the prosecutor is unable to proceed with the case without this evidence.

Figure 11.3
Legal Definitions Relative to Arrest and Search and Seizure

Exceptions to the Warrant Requirement

Many exigent circumstances arise in which the police cannot be expected to travel to court to obtain a search warrant. The evidence might be destroyed by a suspect, the suspect might get away, or the officer might be injured. The following are the major exceptions to the search warrant requirement and the rules established by the Supreme Court that govern these exceptions.

Incident to Lawful Arrest In *Chimel v. California* (1969), the U.S. Supreme Court established guidelines regarding searches at the time of arrest.[23] In this case, the Court ruled that incident to (at the time of) an arrest, the police may search the defendant and only that area immediately surrounding the defendant for the purpose of preventing injury to the officer and the destruction of evidence. This has become known as the "arm's reach doctrine."

On September 13, 1965, three police officers from the Santa Ana (California) Police Department arrived at Ted Chimel's house with a warrant to arrest him for the burglary of a coin shop. The police showed Chimel the arrest warrant and asked him if they could look around. Chimel objected, but the officers told him they could search the house on the basis of the lawful arrest. The officers then searched the entire three-bedroom house for forty-five minutes. They seized numerous items, including some coins. The coins were admitted into evidence, and Chimel was convicted at trial of burglary.

Upon appeal, the U.S. Supreme Court ruled that the warrantless search of Chimel's home was a violation of his constitutional rights. The Court thus established the "arm's reach doctrine."

YOU ARE THERE!

Illinois v. Gates (1983)

The Bloomingdale (Illinois) Police Department received by mail the following anonymous handwritten letter:

> This letter is to inform you that you have a couple in your town who strictly make their living on selling drugs. They are Sue and Lance Gates, they live on Greenway, off Bloomingdale Rd. in the condominiums. Most of their buys are done in Florida. Sue his wife drives their car to Florida, where she leaves it to be loaded up with drugs, then Lance flys down and drives it back. Sue flys [sic] back after she drops the car off in Florida. May 3 she is driving down there again and Lance will be flying down in a few days to drive it back. At the time Lance drives the car back he has the trunk loaded with over $100,000.00 in drugs. Presently they have over $100,000.00 worth of drugs in their basement.
>
> They brag about the fact they never have to work, and make their entire living on pushers. I guarantee if you watch them carefully you will make a big catch. They are friends with some big drugs dealers who visit their house often.
>
> "Lance & Susan Gates"
> "Greenway"
> "in Condominiums"

Obviously, the Aguilar-Spinelli two-pronged test could not apply to this case. The writer was anonymous; the police could not produce the writer and prove his or her reliability.

Based on this letter, however, the police performed the following investigatory actions:

1. They verified the Gates's address.
2. They obtained information from a confidential informant about Lance Gates.
3. They obtained information from an O'Hare Airport police officer that "L. Gates" had made a reservation on Eastern Airlines to West Palm Beach, Florida, departing Chicago on May 5 at 4:15 p.m.
4. They arranged for the Drug Enforcement Administration to conduct a surveillance of the May 5 Eastern Airlines flight.

The surveillance resulted in the information that Lance Gates arrived in West Palm Beach and went to a Holiday Inn room registered to one Susan Gates, as well as other information verifying the information in the letter. A judge issued a search warrant for the Gates's apartment and automobile. Using the warrant, the police seized approximately 350 pounds of marijuana, weapons, and other contraband.

The Gateses were arrested and indicted for violation of state drug laws. The evidence, however, was suppressed in a pretrial motion, as the judge ruled that the affidavit submitted in support of the application for the warrant was inadequate under the Aguilar-Spinelli standard. Upon appeal, the U.S. Supreme Court replaced the Aguilar-Spinelli standard with the totality of circumstances standard.

Source: Based on *Illinois v. Gates*, 462 U.S. 213 (1983).

In 1990, in *Maryland v. Buie*, the Court, considering officers' safety, extended the authority of the police to search locations in a house where a potentially dangerous person could hide, while an arrest warrant is being served.[24]

Field Interrogations (Stop and Frisk) In 1968, the Supreme Court established the standard for allowing police officers to perform a **stop and frisk** (pat down) of a suspect in *Terry v. Ohio*.[25] A stop and frisk is the detaining of a person by a law enforcement officer for the purpose of investigation, accompanied by a superficial examination by the officer of the person's body surface or clothing to discover weapons, contraband, or other objects relating to criminal activity. In *Terry v. Ohio*, the Court ruled that a police officer could stop a person in a public place to make reasonable inquiries as to the person's conduct. It ruled that when the following five conditions exist, a police officer is justified in patting down, or frisking, a suspect:

1. Where a police officer observes unusual conduct which leads him reasonably to conclude in light of his experience that criminal activity may be afoot . . .
2. . . . and that the person with whom he is dealing may be armed and dangerous . . .
3. . . . where in the course of investigating this behavior he identifies himself as a policeman . . .
4. . . . and makes reasonable inquiry . . .

5. ... and where nothing in the initial stages of the encounter serves to dispel his reasonable fear for his own or other's safety ... he is entitled to conduct a carefully limited search of the outer clothing of such persons in an attempt to discover weapons which might be used to assault him. Such search is a reasonable search under the Fourth Amendment and any weapons seized may properly be introduced in evidence against the person from whom they were taken.[26]

In 1993, in *Minnesota v. Dickerson,* the Court placed new limits on an officer's ability to seize evidence discovered during a pat down search conducted for protective reasons when the search itself was based merely upon suspicion and failed to immediately reveal the presence of a weapon. In this case, Timothy Dickerson was stopped by Minneapolis police after they noticed him acting suspiciously while leaving a building known for cocaine trafficking. The officers decided to investigate and ordered Dickerson to submit to a pat down search. The officer testified that he felt no weapon but did feel a small lump in Dickerson's jacket pocket, which he believed to be a lump of crack cocaine upon examining it with his fingers. Dickerson was arrested and convicted of drug possession. Upon appeal, the U.S. Supreme Court ruled that the search was illegal, saying, "While Terry entitled [the officer] to place his hands on respondent's jacket and to feel the lump in the pocket, his continued exploration of the pocket after he concluded that it contained no weapon was unrelated to the sole justification for the search under Terry."[27]

Hot Pursuit Another circumstance in which a warrant is not needed is hot pursuit, or close pursuit. If the police are chasing a person whom they have probable cause to arrest and the person enters a building, the police do not need to stop the pursuit and go to court to obtain a warrant to continue the chase. To do so would be self-defeating.

Consent Searches A police officer can also search without a warrant if consent is given by a person having authority to give such consent. Consent searches have some limitations. The request cannot be phrased as a command or a threat; it must be a genuine request for permission. An oral reply must be received by the police; a nod of the head is not consent. Also, the search must be limited to the area for which consent is given.

In *United States v. Matlock* (1974), the Court rule that a person sharing a room with another person could allow the police to search the room.[28]

In *Bumper v. North Carolina* (1968), the police searched a defendant's house by getting the permission of the defendant's grandmother, who also occupied the house.[29] To get the grandmother's permission, the police told her they had a lawful search warrant, which they actually did not have. The Court ruled that the search was in violation of the Fourth Amendment.

In 1990, in *Illinois v. Rodriguez,* the Court declared constitutional the actions of the police in entering the defendant's Chicago apartment with his former girlfriend's consent and key after she claimed he had seriously assaulted her. Upon entry, the police found the defendant, Rodriguez, and a quantity of cocaine and drug paraphernalia. Rodriguez's claim that his former girlfriend had no control over the apartment since she

---

YOU ARE THERE! »

Terry v. Ohio (1968)

Detective Martin McFadden, a veteran of the Cleveland Police Department's robbery squad, was on routine stakeout duty in a Cleveland downtown shopping district when he observed two men acting suspiciously on the street in the vicinity of Huron Road and Euclid Avenue. One of the suspects looked furtively into a store, walked on, returned to look at the same store, and then joined a companion. The companion, another male, then went to the store, looked in it, and then rejoined his companion. The two men continually repeated these actions and looked into the store numerous times. The two men then met with a third man.

McFadden suspected that the males were casing the store for a stickup and believed that they were armed. He approached the three men, identified himself as a police officer, and asked the men their names. The men mumbled something, whereupon McFadden patted them down (frisked them, or ran his hands over their outer clothing). His frisk and subsequent search revealed that one of the men, Terry, was in possession of a gun. Another frisk and subsequent search revealed that one of his companions, Richard Chilton, also had a gun.

Terry and Chilton were arrested for possession of a gun and were convicted. Upon appeal, the Supreme Court ruled that McFadden's actions were constitutional.

Source: Based on *Terry v. Ohio,* 392 U.S. 1 (1968).

> ## YOU ARE THERE!
>
> ### Florida v. Bostick (1991)
>
> Several years ago, the Broward County (Florida) Sheriff's Department, in an effort to find drugs, adopted a policy of routinely boarding buses at scheduled stops and asking passengers for permission to search their luggage. The officers referred to this duty as "working the buses." There was no claim that the police had probable cause to search anyone. In fact, the police admitted that they generally had no information at all about the passengers. The technique was so common that one officer testified that he searched more than 3,000 bags in a nine-month period.
>
> Terrence Bostick was a subject of officers' "working the buses" in Fort Lauderdale, Florida. He was arrested and charged with trafficking in cocaine. Bostick moved to suppress the cocaine on the grounds that it had been seized in violation of his Fourth Amendment rights. The trial court denied the motion. Bostick subsequently entered a plea of guilty but reserved the right to appeal the denial of the motion to suppress.
>
> Prior to the arrival of the Bostick case at the U.S. Supreme Court, the Florida Supreme Court held that a reasonable bus passenger accosted by police under these circumstances would not feel free to leave the bus and the officers. Accordingly, it held this form of police action to be the equivalent of seizing the passengers without probable cause. Even if the subject ultimately consented to being searched, that consent did not legitimize the unlawful police action. Any items seized pursuant to such a search were to be suppressed.
>
> The U.S. Supreme Court reversed the Florida court and ruled that "the mere fact that Bostick did not feel free to leave the bus does not mean that the police seized him." The Court held that the search was legal.
>
> Source: Based on Florida v. Bostick, 111 S.Ct. 2382 (1991).

had moved out at least a month earlier did not sway the Court.[30]

In 1991, in *Florida v. Bostick*, the Supreme Court reinterpreted consent searches by ruling that police requests to a person to look into his or her luggage do not require that the officer have reasonable suspicion that the person is violating the law.[31]

Plain View Plain view evidence is unconcealed evidence inadvertently seen by an officer engaged in a lawful activity. If an officer is at a location legally doing police work and observes contraband or other plain view evidence, its seizure without a warrant is legal, according to the U.S. Supreme Court in *Harris v. United States* (1960).[32]

Abandoned Property In *Abel v. United States*, the U.S. Supreme Court in 1960 established a standard regarding police searches of abandoned property.[33] A hotel manager gave an FBI agent permission to search a hotel room that had been previously occupied by Abel. The agent found incriminating evidence in a wastepaper basket. Abel was arrested and convicted based on this evidence. On appeal to the U.S. Supreme Court, the Court ruled that once Abel vacated the room, the hotel had the right to give law enforcement agents the right to search it.

In *California v. Greenwood* (1988), the Supreme Court extended the abandoned property rule to include garbage left at the curb.[34] In this case, the police in Laguna Beach, California, received information from an informant in 1984 that Billy Greenwood was engaged in drug dealing from his house. They made observations of the house and found numerous cars stopping there at night. The drivers would leave their cars and enter the house for a short time and then leave. The police made arrangements with the local garbage collector to pick up Greenwood's trash, which he left in brown plastic bags in front of his house, and to take it to the station house. The police searched the garbage and found evidence indicating a drug business, including razor blades and straws with cocaine residue and discarded telephone bills with numerous calls to people who had police records for drug possession. Using this evidence, the police obtained a search warrant. When they executed the warrant, they found hashish and cocaine, and they arrested Greenwood.

The U.S. Supreme Court ruled that searches of a person's discarded garbage were not violations of the Fourth Amendment. Speaking for the Court, Justice Byron White stated, "It is common knowledge that garbage bags left on or at the side of a public street are readily accessible to animals, children, scavengers, snoops and other members of the public. Requiring police to seek warrants before searching such refuse would therefore be inappropriate."

In 1991, in *California v. Hodari, D.*, the Court ruled the police were proper in arresting a defendant who fled from the police and threw away evidence as he retreated. In this case, a group of youths in Oakland, California, fled when they saw the approach of two police officers. The officers retrieved a rock of crack cocaine thrown away by one of the youths.[35]

The Supreme Court ruled in *California v. Greenwood* that the police may search discarded garbage.

Inventory In *Colorado v. Bertine,* the Supreme Court in 1987 ruled that the police may enter a defendant's automobile, which they impounded for safekeeping and were going to return to the defendant after initial police and court processing, and inventory its contents without a warrant to ensure that all contents were accounted for.[36] In this case, Bertine had been arrested for driving while intoxicated. Upon making an inventory of his van's contents, the police found canisters of drugs. Bertine was additionally charged with violation of the drug laws. The Supreme Court ruled that the police action did not violate Bertine's constitutional rights.

YOU ARE THERE!

Does the Fourth Amendment Protect Your Garbage: *California v. Greenwood* (1988)

In 1984, the police in Laguna Beach, California, received information from an informant that Billy Greenwood was engaged in drug dealing from his house. They made observations of the house and found numerous cars stopping there at night. The drivers would leave their cars and enter the house for a short time and then leave. The police made arrangements with the local garbage collector to pick up Greenwood's trash, which he left in brown plastic bags in front of his house, and to take it to the station house. The police searched the garbage and found evidence indicating a drug business, including razor blades and straws with cocaine residue and discarded telephone bills with numerous calls to people who had police records for drug possession. Using this evidence, the police obtained a search warrant for Greenwood's house. When they executed the warrant, they found hashish and cocaine, and they arrested Greenwood.

Greenwood appealed his conviction, stating that the seizure of his garbage by the police without a warrant was a violation of his Fourth Amendment rights. Two California courts ruled that the search of Greenwood's garbage was a violation of the Fourth Amendment. Upon appeal, the U.S. Supreme Court ruled that searches of a person's discarded garbage were not violations of the Fourth Amendment. Speaking for the Court, Justice Byron White stated, "It is common knowledge that garbage bags left on or at the side of a public street are readily accessible to animals, children, scavengers, snoops and other members of the public. Requiring police to seek warrants before searching such refuse would therefore be inappropriate."

Source: Based on *California v. Greenwood,* 486 U.S. 35 (1988).

Open Fields In *Hester v. United States* (1924), the Supreme Court established an "open fields exception" to the warrant requirement.[37] The Court said that fields not immediately surrounding a home did not have the protection of the Fourth Amendment and that no warrant was required to enter them and search. Justice Oliver Wendell Holmes, speaking for the Court, wrote,

> The special protection accorded by the Fourth Amendment to the people in their "persons, houses, papers, and effects," is not extended to the open fields. The distinction between the latter and the house is as old as the common law.

In *Oliver v. United States,* the Supreme Court was asked in 1984 to reexamine its open fields exception under the following circumstances:

> Acting on reports that marihuana was being raised on the farm of petitioner Oliver, two narcotics agents of the Kentucky State Police went to the farm to investigate. Arriving at the farm they drove past petitioner's house to a locked gate with a "No Trespassing" sign. . . . The officers found a field of marihuana over a mile from petitioner's house.[38]

Speaking for the Court, and reaffirming the open fields exception, Justice Lewis F. Powell, Jr., wrote the following: "We conclude that the open fields doctrine, as enunciated in Hester is consistent with the plain language of the Fourth Amendment and its historical purpose."

Two additional cases in the 1980s expanded the power of the police to watch over citizens without a warrant. In 1986, in *California v. Ciraola,* the Court ruled on the actions of the police who had received a tip that marijuana was growing in the defendant Ciraola's backyard.[39] The backyard was surrounded by fences, one of which was ten-feet high. Police flew over the yard in a private plane at an altitude of one thousand feet in an effort to verify the tip. On the basis of their observations, the police were able to secure and execute a search warrant, which resulted in the seizure of marijuana. Ciraola was convicted on the drug charges, and on appeal the Court ruled that the police action was not unconstitutional.

In 1989, in *Florida v. Riley,* the police flew a helicopter four hundred feet over a greenhouse in which Riley and his associates were growing marijuana plants.[40] Based on their observations, the police arrested Riley on drug charges. On appeal, the Court ruled that the police did not need a search warrant to conduct such a low-altitude helicopter search of private property because the flight was within airspace legally available to helicopters under federal regulations.

The Automobile Exception Many students complain about the actions of police officers who search their automobiles. "Don't we have Fourth Amendment rights when we are in our cars?" they ask. "Yes," the professor answers, "but less than in your house."

The automobile exception to the search warrant requirement goes all the way back to 1925, in *Carroll v. United States.*[41] In this case, the Supreme Court ruled that distinctions should be made between searches of automobiles, persons, and homes, and that a warrantless search of a vehicle, which can be readily moved, is valid if the police have probable cause to believe that the car contains evidence they are seeking. This decision has become known as the **Carroll doctrine.**

In 1981, in *New York v. Belton,* the Supreme Court ruled that a search incident to a lawful arrest of the occupant of an automobile can extend to the entire passenger compartment of the automobile, including the glove compartment and luggage boxes or clothing found in them.[42] This extended the Chimel arms reach doctrine, but only in the case of automobiles.

In *United States v. Ross* (1982), the Supreme Court held that if probable cause exists to believe that an automobile contains criminal evidence, the police may make a warrantless search of the automobile.[43]

YOU ARE THERE!

Carroll v. United States (1925)

On September 29, 1921, during Prohibition, two federal agents were in an apartment in Grand Rapids when George Carroll and John Kiro entered. The agents arranged to buy a case of whiskey from them. Arrangements were made for the two men to deliver the whiskey the next day, but they never returned. A few days later, on October 6, 1921, the agents observed Carroll and Kiro driving an automobile on a highway. They pursued them but lost them. Two months later, on December 15, 1921, the agents again observed them on the same highway and were able to overtake them and stop them. The agents searched the car and found sixty-eight bottles of whiskey behind the seats. Carroll and Kiro were arrested for violation of the Prohibition laws. Upon appeal, the Supreme Court established the automobile exception to the Fourth Amendment.

Source: Based on *Carroll v. Untied States*, 267 U.S. 132 (1925).

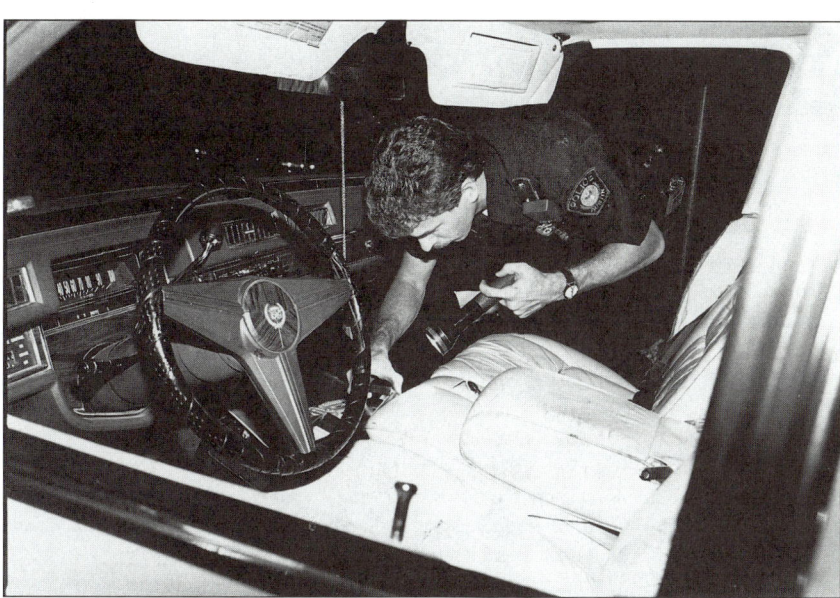

Searching of vehicles is one of the exceptions to the Warrant Requirement of the Fourth Amendment. This Austin, Texas officer is searching for drugs.

In 1991, the Supreme Court further extended police rights in vehicle searches. In *California v. Acevedo* and a similar case, *Florida v. Jimeno,* the Court ruled that the automobile exception not only covers vehicles but also permits warrantless searches of immobile packages that have been placed in cars.[44] In the Acevedo case, the police had observed the defendant leaving his house and carrying a brown paper bag the size of marijuana packages they had seen earlier. The defendant placed the bag in his car's trunk. As he drove away, the police stopped the car, opened the trunk, and seized and opened the bag.

Border Searches In *United States v. Martinez-Fuerte,* the Supreme Court ruled in 1976 that border patrol officers do not have to have probable cause or a warrant to stop cars for brief questioning at fixed checkpoints.[45]

Good Faith The Supreme Court established a "good faith" exception to the exclusionary rule in *United States v. Leon* (1984).[46] It waived the exclusionary rule in cases in which the police act in reasonable reliance and good faith on a search warrant that is later ruled faulty or found to be unsupported by probable cause.

Speaking for the Court, Justice Byron R. White stated the following: "In the absence of an allegation that the magistrate abandoned his detached and neutral role, suppression is appropriate only if the officers were dishonest or reckless in preparing their affidavit or could not have harbored an objectively reasonable belief in the existence of probable cause. . . ."

During the 1980s the Court continued its emphasis on "good faith" exceptions to the Fourth Amendment, in *Massachusetts v. Sheppard* (1984), *Illinois v. Krull* (1987), and *Maryland v. Garrison* (1987).[47]

In 1995, in *Arizona v. Evans,* the Court extended the "good faith" exemption by creating a "computer errors exception." In this case the police arrested Evans for a traffic violation. A routine computer check reported an outstanding arrest warrant for Evans and he was arrested and a search of his vehicle revealed possession of a controlled substance. Later, it was determined that the arrest warrant should have been removed from the computer a few weeks earlier. However, the Court reasoned that officers could not be held responsible for a clerical error made by a court worker and did, in fact, act in good faith.[48]

Searches by Private Persons In *Burdeau v. McDowell* (1921), the Supreme Court ruled that the Bill of Rights applies only to the actions of government agents; it does not apply to private security employees or private citizens not acting on behalf of, or with, official law enforcement agencies.[49] The fact that private security personnel are not bound by the tenets of the Constitution and cannot obtain warrants, however, does not mean that they can indiscriminately violate the rights of offenders. If they do, they can be sued at civil law and suffer severe financial damages.

YOU ARE THERE!

United States v. Leon (1984)

In August 1981, Officer Cyril Rombach, an experienced and well-trained narcotics investigator, prepared an application for a search warrant to search the homes and automobiles of several suspects in a drug investigation. In September 1981, a search warrant was issued by a state superior judge. The officer executed the search warrant and found large quantities of drugs at three residences and in two automobiles listed on the warrant. Rombach arrested several people, including Alberto Leon, for drug violations.

The defendants were indicted by a grand jury and charged with conspiracy to possess and distribute cocaine. The defendants filed motions to suppress the evidence, and the district court granted the motions to suppress in part. It concluded that the affidavit was insufficient to establish probable cause. The court recognized that Rombach had acted in good faith, but it rejected the government's suggestion that the Fourth Amendment exclusionary rule should not apply where evidence is seized in reasonable good faith reliance on a search warrant.

Upon appeal, the Supreme Court overruled the district court and established the "good faith doctrine." It ruled that evidence obtained in good faith, where the officers reasonably believed they had sufficient probable cause to get a warrant, is admissible in court. The Court said that the exclusionary rule should be applied only in cases in which the police purposely, recklessly, or negligently violate the law.

Source: Based on *United States v. Leon*, 468 U.S. 897 (1984).

The Police and Custodial Interrogation

The police have many crimes to investigate and often not enough resources to accomplish their mission. Also, in many cases, there is not enough physical evidence or eyewitnesses to assist the police in their investigation. Thus, police often seek to gain a confession from a defendant—particularly in murder cases—to gain a conviction. The history of methods used by the police to obtain confessions from suspects has been sordid; it includes beatings and tortures by the police, which came to be known as the third degree.

The Path to Miranda

From 1936 until 1966, the Supreme Court attempted to make the police stop this misconduct and comply with the Fifth Amendment. The following landmark cases show the development of rules regarding custodial interrogation (the questioning of a person in police custody—and thus not free to leave—regarding his or her participation in a crime) during those three decades, culminating in the famous Miranda case. See figure 11.4 for a summary. Figure 11.5 provides legal definitions for terms related to interrogations.

End of the Third Degree In *Brown v. Mississippi* (1936), the Supreme Court finally put an end to the al-

1936	*Brown v. Mississippi*
1957	The McNabb-Mallory Rule
1964	*Escobedo v. Illinois*
1966	*Miranda v. Arizona*
1966	The Miranda Rules

Figure 11.4
The Path to Miranda

admission A voluntary statement that is contrary to a person's position on trial. An admission falls short of a confession, which is a direct acknowledgment of guilt.
confession A direct acknowledgment of guilt.
custodial interrogation The confinement of a person by law enforcement agents or officers. The person is not free to leave and is questioned about a crime.
exculpatory Tending to prove that a person was not the perpetrator of a criminal offense.
incriminate To involve either oneself or another as responsible for criminal conduct.
inculpatory Tending to involve oneself or another as being responsible for criminal conduct; incriminating.
interrogation The questioning of a person to ascertain facts.

Figure 11.4
Legal Definitions Relating to Interrogations

Dempsey's Law

Law Is History—Know Your Facts

Professor Dempsey, I know we have to know the law, but I don't understand why we have to know the specific cases. Like *Mapp v. Ohio*—that was in 1961; that's ancient history! Why don't you just tell us that the police can't make an unreasonable search of a dude's house? And *Terry v. Ohio*—that was over twenty years ago. Why do we have to know the fact pattern, as you call it? Can't we just know that cops can make stops and frisks under certain circumstances?

Those are good questions. There are several reasons why I insist that you know the fact patterns of cases, not just specific principles of law, to which you seem to be referring.

First, I want you to know that the law is not mere theory or the application of reason to problems. U.S. law is as much history as it is reason and logic. As you know, I frequently paraphrase Justice Oliver Wendell Holmes in class by saying that there is more law in a page of history than in a volume of logic. This means that the law is dynamic. It changes over time, and it changes because it is responsive to the thoughts, feelings, and needs of society.

Second, I want you to know that the law—specifically, case law—is based on real experiences of real people. (Case law is the body of law that results from court interpretations of statutory law—law written by the legislative or executive branch of the government—or from court decisions where rules have not been fully codified or have been found to be vague or in error.) In this class, you often hear the names Dollree Mapp, Danny Escobedo, Ernesto Miranda, and even Donald or Don King, Mike Tyson's former boxing promoter. Sure, they were people who were often on the "other side of the law," but as Justice Felix Frankfurter once observed, "the safeguards of liberty have frequently been forged in controversies involving not very nice people" (Fred W. Friendly and Martha J. H. Elliot, *The Constitution: That Delicate Balance: Landmark Cases That Shaped the Constitution* [New York: McGraw-Hill, 1984], p. vii). Sure, Dollree Mapp was a small-time gambler and was hiding a man wanted by the police, Danny Escobedo was a murderer, and Ernesto Miranda was a rapist. But they influenced legal history, and they did it by exercising their rights under the U.S. Constitution—those very rights that also apply to all of us in this room.

Also, as you further your studies in criminal law, or if you enter law school, a text or a professor might refer to a "Terry stop" or say "as the Court ruled in Chimel" and assume that you know these concepts. And you should know these concepts.

---

most official pattern of brutality and violence used by the police to obtain confessions from suspects.[50] For an excellent description and history of the third degree, see Jerome H. Skolnick and James J. Fyfe, *Above the Law: Police and the Excessive Use of Force* (New York: Free Press, 1993). See also John S. Dempsey, *An Introduction to Public and Private Investigations* (Minneapolis/St. Paul: West, 1996), chapter 7. The case involved the coerced confessions, through beatings, of three men.

Speaking for the Court, Chief Justice Charles E. Hughes wrote the following:

> Because a State may dispense with a jury trial, it does not follow that it may substitute trial by ordeal. The rack and torture chamber may not be substituted for the witness stand. . . . It would be difficult to conceive of methods more revolting to the sense of justice than those taken to procure the confessions of these petitioners, and the use of the confessions thus obtained as the basis for conviction and sentence was a clear denial of due process.

The Supreme Court suppressed the confessions and emphasized that the use of confessions obtained through barbaric tactics deprived the defendants of their right to due process under the Fourteenth Amendment. The Court, in effect, said that coerced confessions were untrustworthy and unreliable.

YOU ARE THERE!

Brown v. Mississippi (1936)

On March 30, 1934, Raymond Steward was murdered. That night Deputy Sheriff Dial went to the home of Ellington, one of the African-American defendants, and requested him to accompany the police to the house of the deceased. A number of white men were gathered there, and they began to accuse Ellington of the crime. Upon his denial, they seized him and hung him up by a rope to the limb of a tree two times. When the men took Ellington down the second time, they tied him to a tree and whipped him. The trial record showed that signs of the rope on Ellington's neck were plainly visible during the trial. He was again picked up a day or two later and again severely beaten until he confessed.

The other two defendants, Ed Brown and Henry Shields, were also arrested and taken to jail. To obtain their confessions, the defendants were "made to strip and they were laid over chairs and their backs were cut to pieces with a leather strap with buckles on it and they were likewise made by the said deputy definitely to understand that the whipping would be continued unless and until they confessed, and not only confessed, but confessed to every matter of detail as demanded by those present."

The defendants made their confession on April 1, 1934. They were indicted on April 4, 1934, went on trial April 5, and were convicted and sentenced to death April 6. The deputy sheriff who administered over the beatings, Deputy Sheriff Dial, testified in court. Responding to an inquiry as to how severely a defendant was whipped, he stated, "Not too much for a negro; not as much as I would have done if it were left to me."

On appeal, the Supreme Court ruled that the actions against the three men were violations of their due process rights.

Source: Based on *Brown v. Mississippi*, 297 U.S. 278 (1936).

YOU ARE THERE!

Escobedo v. Illinois (1964)

On the evening of January 19, 1960, Danny Escobedo's brother-in-law, Manual, was shot to death. The next morning, the Chicago police arrested Escobedo and attempted to interrogate him. However, his attorney obtained a writ of habeas corpus requiring the police to free him.

On January 30, Benedict DiGerlando, who was then in police custody, told the police that Escobedo had fired the fatal shots at his brother-in-law. The police then rearrested Escobedo and brought him to police headquarters. Escobedo told the police he wanted to consult his lawyer. Shortly after the arrest, Escobedo's attorney arrived at headquarters and attempted to see him but was denied access to him. The police caused an encounter between Escobedo and DiGerlando at headquarters, during which Escobedo made admissions to the crime. Later, a statement was taken from Escobedo. He was never advised of his rights. He was convicted of the murder of Manual based on his statements.

The Supreme Court reversed Escobedo's conviction based on the fact that the police violated Escobedo's Sixth Amendment rights, which were obligatory on the states through the Fourteenth Amendment.

Source: Based on *Escobedo v. Illinois* 378 U.S. 478 (1964).

Note: do you know what happened to Escobedo after this case?

> Subsequent to his landmark Supreme Court case, Danny Escobedo was arrested for burglary and selling drugs and was sentenced to prison, from which he was paroled in 1975. In 1984, he was again sentenced to prison on sex crime charges involving a thirteen-year-old girl. While free on bond pending an appeal on that conviction, Escobedo was arrested in Chicago for attempted murder. He pleaded guilty.

Source: Adapted from James A. Inciardi, *Criminal Justice*, 3d ed. (Orlando, Fla.: Harcourt Brace Jovanovich, 1990), pp. 280–281.

Entry of Lawyers into the Station House In 1964, the Supreme Court ruled in *Escobedo v. Illinois* that the refusal by the police to honor a suspect's request to consult with his or her lawyer during the course of an interrogation constituted a denial of a person's Fifth Amendment right to counsel, which was made obligatory upon the states by the Fourteenth Amendment.[51] The decision rendered any incriminating statement elicited by the police during such an interrogation inadmissible in court. The Court ruled that once a suspect becomes the focus of a police interrogation and is taken into custody and requests the advice of a lawyer, the police must permit access to the lawyer.

The Miranda Ruling

The well-known case of *Miranda v. Arizona* (1966) was a culmination of many years of efforts by the Supreme Court to ensure the rights of individuals at police inter-

YOU ARE THERE!

Miranda v. Arizona (1966)

On March 2, 1963, in Phoenix, an eighteen-year-old woman was walking to a bus stop after work. She was accosted by a man who shoved her into his car and tied her hands and ankles. He then took her to the edge of the city, where he raped her. The rapist then drove the victim to a street near her home and let her out of the car. On March 13, the Phoenix police arrested a twenty-three-year-old, eighth-grade dropout named Ernesto Miranda and charged him with the crime. Miranda had a police record that began when he was fourteen years old, had been given an undesirable discharge by the army for being a window peeper, and had served time in federal prison for driving a stolen car across a state line.

Miranda was placed in a lineup at the station house and was positively identified by the victim. He was then taken to an interrogation room, where he was questioned by the police without being informed that he had a right to have an attorney present. Two hours later, police emerged from the interrogation room with a written confession signed by Miranda. At the top of the statement was a typed paragraph stating that the confession was made voluntarily, without threats or promises of immunity and "with full knowledge of my legal rights, understanding any statement I make may be used against me."

At trial, Miranda was found guilty of kidnapping and rape, and he was sentenced to twenty to thirty years' imprisonment. Upon appeal, the Supreme Court ruled that Miranda's confession was inadmissible.

Source: Based on *Miranda v. Arizona*, 384 U.S. 436 (1966).

Note: Do you want to know more about the Miranda case?

> The Miranda decision was a combination of cases involving four people: Ernesto Miranda; Michael Vignera, arrested in New York City for robbery; Carl Westover, arrested in Kansas City for robbery; and Roy Stewart, arrested in Los Angeles for robbery. What we now call the Miranda rules could have been called the Vignera rules, the Westover rules, or the Stewart rules.

Source: Based on *Miranda v. Arizona*, 348 U.S. 436 (1966).

Note: Do you want to know more about Miranda?

> In his new trial after the famous landmark decision, Ernesto Miranda was convicted for rape and kidnapping after his common-law wife, Twila Hoffman, testified that he had admitted to kidnapping and raping the victim. Miranda was sentenced to a twenty- to thirty-year prison term and was paroled in 1972. In 1974, he was arrested for the illegal possession of a gun and drugs. In 1976, at age thirty-four, Miranda was murdered in a Phoenix skid row bar during a quarrel over a card game.

Source: Adapted from James A. Inciardi, *Criminal Justice*, 3d ed. (Orlando, Fla.: Harcourt Brace Jovanovich, 1990), p. 281.

---

rogations.[52] In the Miranda case, the Supreme Court ruled that confessions are by their very nature inherently coercive and that custodial interrogation makes any statements obtained from defendants compelled and, thus, not voluntary. The Court felt that interrogations are against the Fifth Amendment, which guarantees that no one shall be compelled to be a witness against himself or herself in a criminal case, and that this guarantee is violated any time a person is taken into custody and interrogated.

The Court then established the well-known Miranda rules or Miranda warnings, which state that prior to any interrogation of a person in custody, the police must do the following:

1. Advise the suspect that he or she has the right to remain silent.
2. Advise the suspect that anything he or she says can and will be used in court against him or her.
3. Advise the suspect that he or she has the right to consult a lawyer and to have the lawyer present during questioning.
4. Advise the suspect that if he or she cannot afford an attorney, an attorney will be provided, free of charge, for him or her.

The Court further ruled that if prior to the interrogation or during the interrogation, the suspect in any way indicates a wish to remain silent or to have an attorney, the interrogation may no longer proceed.[53]

Ernesto Miranda (right) with his attorney in Phoenix, Arizona, in 1967.

The Erosion of Miranda

In the aftermath of the Miranda decision, there was tremendous confusion in the legal community over its exact meaning. A large number of cases were brought to the Supreme Court to challenge and question the decision. Eventually, the Supreme Court of the 1980s began to impose a series of exceptions to the Miranda decision. These decisions led the noted civil liberties lawyer and Harvard law professor Alan M. Dershowitz to write, "The Burger Court has chipped away at the exclusionary rule—carving out so many exceptions that it is falling of its own weight."[54] After explaining two cases, Dershowitz adds the following:

> Our twenty-five year experiment with the exclusionary rule may well be coming to an end. We have learned precious little from it, because the exclusionary rule was never really given a chance.[55]

Despite Dershowitz's thoughts, the Miranda rule still stands, and defendants in custody must still be advised of their constitutional rights prior to any interrogation. However, the Supreme Court is recognizing certain exceptions to the Miranda decision. A sample of post-Miranda cases that have led to the weakening of Miranda follow.

Harris v. New York (1971) In *Harris v. New York,* the Supreme Court in 1971 ruled that statements that are trustworthy, even though they have been obtained without giving a defendant his or her Miranda warnings, may be used to attack the credibility of a defendant who takes the witness stand.[56] In this case, the prosecutor accused Harris of lying on the stand and used statements taken by the police before the trial that were obtained without Miranda warnings.

Michigan v. Mosley (1975) In 1975, in *Michigan v. Mosley,* the Supreme Court ruled that a second interrogation, held after the suspect had initially refused to make a statement, was not a violation of the Miranda decision.[57]

Brewer v. Williams (1977) In *Brewer v. Williams,* decided in 1977, the Supreme Court seemed to extend the meaning of the word interrogation by interpreting comments made by a police detective as "subtle coercion."[58] This case was a pro-Miranda one, but it is presented here because of a second decision in the case, *Nix v. Williams* (1984), which can be seen as part of the erosion of Miranda.[59]

On Christmas Eve in 1968, ten-year-old Pamela Powers was present at a Des Moines YMCA with her parents to watch her brother participate in a wrestling match. Pamela told her parents that she wanted to use the bathroom, and she left. She was never again seen alive.

At about the time of Pamela's disappearance, a young boy saw a man, later identified as Robert Williams, walk out of the YMCA carrying a bundle wrapped in a blanket to his car. The boy told police that he thought he saw two legs under the blanket. Williams was a resident of the YMCA, a religious fanatic, and an escaped mental patient. On Christmas Day, William's car was found abandoned near Davenport, Iowa, 160 miles from Des Moines. On the day after Christmas, Williams walked into the Davenport Police Station and surrendered to the police. The Davenport police notified the Des Moines police, who arranged to come to Davenport to pick up Williams.

Detective Leaming arrived at the Davenport Police Station to pick up Williams. He was told by Williams's lawyer, Henry McKnight, that he did not want Williams to be the subject of any interrogation during the trip from Davenport to Des Moines. Leaming agreed to the lawyer's request.

In the car on the way back to Des Moines, Leaming, knowing that Williams was a religious fanatic, addressed him as "Reverend" and made what has become known as the "Christian Burial Speech":

> I want to give you something to think about while we're travelling down the road. . . . Number one, I want you to observe the weather conditions. It's raining, it's sleeting, it's freezing, driving is very treacherous, visibility is poor, it's going to be dark early this evening. They are predicting several inches of snow for tonight, and I feel that you yourself are the only person that knows where this little girl's body is, that you yourself have only been there once, and if you get a snow on top of it you yourself may be unable to find it. And, since we will be going right past the area on the way into Des Moines, I feel that we could stop and locate the body, that the parents of this little girl should be entitled to a Christian burial for the little girl who was snatched away from them on Christmas Eve and murdered.[60]

After this speech, Williams directed the police to Pamela Powers's dead body. Williams was convicted of her murder.

On appeal to the Supreme Court, the Court voted 5 to 4 that Leaming's "Christian Burial Speech" constituted custodial interrogation and that the evidence, Pamela's body, was illegally obtained and therefore not admissible in court.

The state of Iowa continued to appeal this decision. In 1984, the Supreme Court, in *Nix v. Williams,* promulgated the "inevitability of discovery rule," saying in effect that Pamela Powers's body would have been discovered inevitably, so it should be allowed to be used as evidence in the trial.

Rhode Island v. Innis (1980) The Supreme Court, in *Rhode Island v. Innis* (1980), clarified its definition of what is meant by interrogation.[61] The Court ruled that the "definition of interrogation can extend only to words or actions on the part of police officers that they should have known were reasonably likely to elicit an incriminating response."

In this case, a man told the police where he had left a shotgun he used in a shooting after the police had made remarks about the possibility of a handicapped child's finding the gun, as a home for handicapped children was nearby.

New York v. Quarles (1984) In *New York v. Quarles* (1984), the Supreme Court created a "public safety" exception to the Miranda rule.[62] In this case, a police officer, after arresting and handcuffing a man wanted in connection with a crime, and after feeling an empty shoulder holster on the man's body, asked him where the gun was without informing the man of his Miranda rights. The gun was suppressed as evidence, because the officer's question was not preceded by the Miranda warnings.

The Supreme Court, however, overruled the state court and said the officer's failure to read the Miranda warnings was justified in the interest of public safety. The Court wrote the following:

> We conclude that the need for answers to questions in a situation posing a threat to the public safety outweighs the need for the prophylactic rule protecting the Fifth Amendment's privilege against self incrimination. We decline to place officers such as Officer Kraft in the untenable position of having to consider, often in a matter of seconds, whether it best serves society for them to ask the necessary questions without the Miranda warnings and render whatever probative evidence they uncover inadmissible, or for them to give the warnings in order to preserve the admissibility of evidence they might uncover but possibly damage or destroy their ability to obtain that evidence and neutralize the volatile situation confronting them.

Moran v. Burbine (1986) In the *Moran v. Burbine* murder case, the Supreme Court ruled that the police failure to inform a suspect undergoing custodial interrogation of his or her attorney's attempts to reach him or her does not constitute a violation of the Miranda rule.[63] The Court reasoned that events that are not known by a defendant have no bearing on his or her capacity to waive knowingly his or her rights.

YOU ARE THERE!

New York v. Quarles (1984)

At 12:30 A.M., officers Frank Kraft and Sal Scarring were on routine patrol in Queens, New York, when a young woman approached them and told them that she had been raped by an African-American male, approximately 6 feet tall, who was wearing a black jacket with the name "Big Ben" printed in yellow letters on the back. She then told the officers that the man had just entered an A&P supermarket located nearby and that he had a gun. The officers put the woman into the police car and drove to the A&P.

Officer Kraft entered the store while his partner radioed for backup. Kraft observed the suspect, Quarles, approaching a checkout counter. Upon seeing the officer, Quarles turned and ran toward the rear of the store. Kraft took out his revolver and chased Quarles. When Quarles turned the corner at the end of an aisle, Kraft lost sight of him for several seconds. Upon regaining sight of Quarles, Kraft apprehended him and ordered him to stop and put his hands over his head. Kraft then frisked Quarles and discovered that he was wearing an empty shoulder holster. After handcuffing him, Kraft asked him where the gun was. Quarles nodded in the direction of some empty cartons and said, "The gun is over there." Kraft then retrieved a loaded .38-caliber revolver from one of the cartons, formally arrested Quarles, and read him his Miranda warnings.

At trial, the judge suppressed Quarles's statement ("The gun is over there") and suppressed the gun because Kraft had not given Quarles his Miranda warnings before asking where the gun was.

On appeal from the prosecutor to the U.S. Supreme Court, the Court reversed the New York ruling and created a "public safety" exception to the requirement that police give a suspect his or her Miranda warnings before interrogation.

Source: Based on *New York v. Quarles*, 104 S.Ct. 2626 (1984).

1990s and Miranda

During the first half of the 1990s, the U.S. Supreme Court made several important decisions regarding police interrogation and the Miranda rule.

In *Illinois v. Perkins*, in 1990, the Court continued in what many call the erosion of Miranda.[64] In this case, police placed an informant and an undercover officer in a cell block with Lloyd Perkins, a suspected murderer incarcerated on an unrelated charge of aggravated assault. While planning a prison break, the undercover officer asked Perkins whether he had ever "done" [murdered] anyone. In response, Perkins described at length the details of a murder-for-hire he had committed.

When Perkins was subsequently charged with the murder, he argued to have the statements he made in prison suppressed because no Miranda warnings had been given prior to his conversation with the informant and undercover police officer.

Rejecting Perkin's argument, the court recognized that there are limitations to the rules announced in Miranda. The Court expressly declined to accept the notion that the Miranda warnings are required whenever a suspect is in custody in a technical sense and converses with someone who happens to be a government agent. Rather, the Court concluded that not every custodial interrogation created the psychologically compelling atmosphere that Miranda was designed to protect against. When the compulsion is lacking, the Court found, so is the need for Miranda warnings.

Perkins bragged about his role in the murder in an effort to impress those he believed to be his fellow inmates. Miranda was not designed to protect individuals from themselves.

Also, in 1990, in *Pennsylvania v. Muniz*, the Court ruled that the police use of the defendant's slurred and drunken responses to booking questions (he was arrested for driving under the influence of alcohol) as evidence in his trial was not a violation of Miranda rights even though he was never given his Miranda warnings.[65]

In *Arizona v. Fulminante* (1991), the Supreme Court further weakened the Miranda decision by ruling that a coerced confession might be a harmless trial error.[66] In this case, the Court overruled years of precedent to hold that if other evidence introduced at trial is strong enough, the use of a coerced confession could be considered harmless and a conviction upheld. In other words, a coercive confession, by itself, is not sufficient to have a conviction overruled.

In 1991, in *Minnick v. Mississippi*, the Court clarified the mechanics of Miranda by ruling that once a suspect

Speaking for the Court, Justice Sandra Day O'Connor commented on the actions of the police in lying to the lawyer, Munson: "hold only that, on these facts, the challenged conduct falls short of the kind of misbehavior that so shocks the sensibilities of civilized society as to warrant a federal intrusion into the criminal processes of the States."

YOU ARE THERE!

Moran v. Burbine (1986)

On March 3, 1977, Mary Jo Hickey was found unconscious in a factory parking lot in Providence, Rhode Island. Suffering from injuries to her skull, which were apparently inflicted by a metal pipe found at the scene, she was rushed to a nearby hospital. Three weeks later she died from her wounds.

Several months after her death, the Cranston, Rhode Island, police arrested Brian Burbine and two others for a burglary. Shortly before the arrest, Detective Ferranti of the Cranston Police Department learned from a confidential informant that the man responsible for Hickey's death lived at a certain address and was also known by the nickname "Butch." Upon discovering that the burglary suspect, Burbine, lived at that address and used the nickname "Butch," Ferranti advised Burbine of his constitutional rights. Burbine refused to speak to the detective. Ferranti spoke to Burbine's two associates and received more incriminating information. Ferranti then called the Providence police, who sent three detectives to Cranston to interrogate Burbine.

That evening, Burbine's sister called the Providence public defender's office to obtain legal assistance for her brother. A lawyer from the Providence public defender's office, Allegra Munson, called the Cranston Detective Division. The conversation went as follows:

> A male voice responded with the word 'Detectives.' Ms. Munson identified herself and asked if Brian Burbine was being held; the person responded affirmatively. Ms. Munson explained to the person that Burbine was represented by attorney and she would act as Burbine's legal counsel in the event that the police intended to place him in a lineup or question him. The unidentified person told Ms. Munson that the police would not be questioning Burbine or putting him in a lineup and that they were through with him for the night. Ms. Munson was not informed that the Providence Police were at the Cranston police station or that Burbine was a suspect in Mary's murder.

Less than an hour after Munson's call, Burbine was brought to an interrogation room and questioned about Mary Jo Hickey's murder. He was informed of his Miranda rights on three separate occasions, and he signed three written forms acknowledging that he understood his right to the presence of an attorney and indicating that he did not want an attorney called or appointed for him. Burbine signed three written statements fully admitting to the murder. Based on his written statements, Burbine was convicted of murder. Upon appeal, the Rhode Island Court of Appeals reversed the conviction.

The U.S. Supreme Court reversed the decision of the court of appeals and ruled that Burbine's constitutional rights were not violated.

Source: Based on *Moran v. Burbine*, 475 U.S. 412 (1986).

---

in custody requests counsel in response to his or her Miranda warnings, law enforcement officers may no longer attempt to reinterrogate the suspect unless the suspect's attorney is present or the suspect initiates the contact with the law enforcement agents.[67]

Also, in 1991, the Court ruled in *McNeil v. Wisconsin* that an in-custody suspect who requests counsel at a judicial proceeding, such as an arraignment or initial appearance, is only invoking the Sixth Amendment right to counsel as to the charged offense and is not invoking his or her Miranda Fifth Amendment right to have an attorney present during the custodial interrogation.[68] Thus, officers may later approach that in-custody suspect for interrogation regarding uncharged crimes.

In *Davis v. United States,* 1994, in what may be an extremely significant case in the erosion of Miranda, the Court ruled that a suspect must make an unequivocal request for a lawyer in order to effectively assert his Miranda right to counsel. An equivocal or ambiguous request for counsel is not sufficient to force police to stop questioning the suspect and provide an attorney.[69]

In Davis, Naval Investigative Service (NIS) agents investigating a murder obtained both oral and written Miranda waivers from the defendant. After being interviewed for approximately ninety minutes, the defendant said: "Maybe I should talk to a lawyer." After asking some clarifying questions, the NIS agents continued to interrogate him. The Court ruled that the defendant's statement was not sufficiently unequivocal to constitute an assertion of his Miranda right to counsel. Moreover, the Davis Court emphasized that if a suspect makes an equivocal request for a lawyer, it is not necessary for the police to ask clarifying questions in an attempt to decipher the suspect's intentions.[70]

Miranda in Retrospect

What has been the result of the Miranda ruling on the administration of justice? Much empirical and anecdotal evidence supports the position that the clearest examples of the cost of the Miranda ruling are the statements that are suppressed due to a violation of Miranda.[71]

In a comprehensive analysis of numerous studies that analyzed the deterrent effect of Miranda warnings, Professor Paul G. Cassell discovered that compliance with Miranda has had a severe impact on the effectiveness of law enforcement. Professor Cassell's research revealed that approximately 79,000 property crimes, 42,000 drug cases, 6,500 robbery cases, 1,400 forcible rape cases, and 880 murder and non-negligent homicide cases went unprosecuted in 1993 alone due to suspects being deterred from making a statement after being given their Miranda warnings.[72]

Professor Cassell also discovered indirect costs of Miranda due to cases plea bargained to lesser charges. A review of a 1994 study indicated that 30.6 percent of suspects successfully questioned led to the charged offense, whereas only 15.4 percent of suspects who invoked their Miranda rights pled to the charged offense. In addition, he discovered that Miranda has a more significant effect on the most serious offenses. For example, one study cited by Professor Cassell revealed that, while the overall confession rate dropped 16.9 percent after the Miranda ruling, the confession rate dropped 27.3 percent in homicide cases and dropped 25.7 percent in robbery cases.[73]

It must be noted however, that Professor Cassell's study is only one of many studies regarding the effect of Miranda on law enforcement. Many other experts report that Miranda has not had a severe impact on law enforcement. Additionally, most criminal investigations and prosecutions do not involve the use of confessions.

★ The Police and Identification Procedures

Often law enforcement officers apprehend suspects based on descriptions given by victims of crimes. To ensure that the apprehended person is actually the perpetrator of the crime, the police must obtain assistance from the victim or employ other identification procedures. The following sections will discuss procedures used by the police to identify suspects properly as the actual perpetrators of crimes.

Lineups, Showups, and Photo Arrays

Lineups, showups, and photo arrays are important parts of the police investigation process, as are procedures requiring suspects to give samples of their voice, blood, and handwriting to be used in identification comparison procedures. Could these procedures be construed as violating a defendant's freedom against self-incrimination as provided by the Fifth Amendment to the U.S. Constitution?

A lineup is the placing of a suspect with a group of other people of similar physical characteristics (such as race, age, hair color, hair type, height, and weight) so that a witness or victim of a crime can have the opportunity to identify the perpetrator of the crime. Lineups are usually used after an arrest.

A showup involves bringing a suspect back to the scene of the crime or another place (for example, a hospital where an injured victim is) where the suspect can be seen and possibly identified by a victim or witness of a crime. The showup must be conducted as soon as possible after the crime, and with no suggestion that the person is a suspect. A showup is usually used after an arrest.

A photo array is similar to a lineup, except that photos of the suspect (who is not in custody) and others are shown to a witness or victim of a crime. Photo arrays are used prior to arrest. The following cases detail the decisions of the Supreme Court in lineup, showup, and photo array cases.

United States v. Wade (1967) In *United States v. Wade,* the Supreme Court in 1967 made two very important decisions regarding lineups.[74] It ruled that a person can be made to stand in a lineup and can be made to perform certain actions that were performed by the perpetrator during the crime, such as saying certain words or walking in a certain fashion. The Court also ruled that once a person is indicted, he or she has a right to have an attorney present at the lineup.

Kirby v. Illinois (1972) In 1972, in *Kirby v. Illinois,* the Supreme Court ruled that the right to counsel at lineups applies only after the initiation of formal judicial criminal proceedings, such as an indictment, information, or arraignment (that is, when a person formally enters the court system).⁷⁵ An information is a formal charging document drafted by a prosecutor and presented to a judge. An indictment is a formal charging document returned by a grand jury based on evidence presented to it by a prosecutor. The indictment is then presented to a judge. Indictments generally refer to felonies. An arraignment is a hearing before a court having jurisdiction in a criminal case, in which the identity of the defendant is established, the defendant is informed of the charge or charges and of his or her rights, and the defendant is required to enter a plea. In *Kirby v. Illinois,* the Court reasoned that because a lineup may free an innocent person, and the required presence of an attorney might delay the lineup, it is preferable to have the lineup as soon as possible, even without an attorney.

Thus, in a postarrest, preindictment lineup, there is no right to have an attorney present. Many police departments, however, will permit an attorney to be present at a lineup and make reasonable suggestions, as long as there is no significant delay of the lineup.

Stoval v. Denno (1967) In *Stoval v. Denno* (1967), the Supreme Court ruled that showups are constitutional and do not require the presence of an attorney.⁷⁶ The Court addressed the issue as follows:

> The practice of showing suspects singly to persons for purpose of identification, and not a part of a lineup, has been unduly condemned.... However, a claimed violation of due process of law in the conduct of a confrontation depends on the totality of the circumstances surrounding it and the record in the present case reveals that the showing of Stoval to Mrs. Behrendt in an immediate hospital confrontation was imperative.

Subsequent to *Stoval v. Denno,* a federal appellate court established a set of guidelines phrased in the form of questions that could decide the constitutionality of a showup. A careful review of the questions reveals that the court clearly prefers lineups to showups but will permit showups if certain conditions are met:

1. Was the defendant the only individual who could possibly be identified as the guilty party by the complaining witness, or were there others near him or her at the time of the showup so as to negate the assertion that he or she was shown alone to the witness?
2. Where did the showup take place?
3. Were there any compelling reasons for a prompt showup so as to deprive the police of the opportunity of securing other similar individuals for the purpose of holding a lineup?
4. Was the witness aware of any observation by another or any other evidence indicating the guilt of the suspect at the time of the showup?
5. Were any tangible objects related to the offense placed before the witness that would encourage identification?
6. Was the witness identification based on only part of the suspect's total personality?
7. Was the identification a product of mutual reinforcement of opinion among witnesses simultaneously viewing the defendant?
8. Was the emotional state of the witness such as to preclude identification?⁷⁷

YOU ARE THERE!

United States v. Wade (1967)

On September 21, 1964, a man with a piece of tape on each side of his face forced a cashier and a bank official to put money into a pillowcase. The robber then left the bank and drove away with an accomplice, who was waiting outside in a car.

In March 1965, six months after the robbery, an indictment was returned against Mr. Wade and an accomplice for the robbery. Wade was arrested April 2, 1965. Two weeks later, an FBI agent put Wade into a lineup to be observed by two bank employees. Wade had a lawyer, but the lawyer was not notified of the lineup. Each person in the lineup had strips of tape on his face, similar to those worn by the robber, and each was told to say words that had been spoken at the robbery. Both bank employees identified Wade as the robber. Wade was convicted based on the identification by the witnesses.

Upon appeal, the Supreme Court ruled that placing someone in a lineup and forcing that person to speak or perform other acts at the lineup did not violate the Fifth Amendment privilege against self-incrimination. The Court held, however, that because Wade had been indicted and was represented by counsel, the lawyer should have been allowed to be at the lineup. The Court's reversal of the conviction was based on Wade's Fifth Amendment right not to incriminate himself.

Source: Based on *United States v. Wade*, 388 U.S. 218 (1967).

United States v. Ash (1973) In *United States v. Ash* (1973), the Supreme Court ruled that the police could show victims or witnesses photographic displays containing a suspect's photograph (photo arrays) without the requirement that the suspect's lawyer be present.[78]

Other Identification Procedures

Does the Fifth Amendment's prohibition against self-incrimination involve all procedures used by the police to secure evidence from a defendant? We know that any type of testimony is governed by the Fifth Amendment. However, in most cases coming before it, the Supreme Court declared that procedures that are not testimonial are not under the purview of the Fifth Amendment. (Testimonial refers to oral or written communication by a suspect, as opposed to the taking of blood or exemplars as indicated in this section.) A sample of such cases follows.

Schmerber v. California (1966) In 1966, in *Schmerber v. California,* the Supreme Court ruled that the forced extraction of blood by a doctor from a man who was arrested for driving while intoxicated was not a violation of that man's constitutional rights.[79]

Winston v. Lee (1985) In *Winston v. Lee,* the Supreme Court in 1984 clarified its position on medical provisions regarding prisoners.[80] When the Court decided the Schmerber case, it warned, "That we today hold that the Constitution does not forbid the States' minor intrusions into an individual's body under stringently limited conditions in no way indicates that it permits more substantial intrusions, or intrusions under other conditions."[81] The Rudolph Lee case provided the test of how far the police can go in attempting to retrieve evidence from a suspect's body.

Lee, a suspect in a robbery, was shot by the victim. The police endeavored to have a bullet removed from Lee's body in order to use it for a ballistics examination.

Justice William J. Brennan, speaking for the Court, wrote the following: "We conclude that the procedure sought here is an example of the 'more substantial intrusion' cautioned against in Schmerber, and hold that to permit the procedure would violate respondent's right to be secure in his person guaranteed by the Fourth Amendment."[82]

United States v. Dionisio (1973) In *United States v. Dionisio,* the Supreme Court in 1973 ruled that a suspect must provide voice exemplars (samples of his or her voice) that can be compared with the voice spoken at the time of the crime.[83]

United States v. Mara (1973) In 1973, in *United States v. Mara,* the Supreme Court ruled that it was not a violation of one's constitutional rights for the police to require a suspect to provide a handwriting exemplar (a sample of his or her handwriting) for comparison with handwriting involved in the crime.[84]

> ## YOU ARE THERE! »
>
> ### Winston v. Lee (1985)
>
> On July 18, 1982, Ralph E. Warkinson was shot in a robbery attempt at his place of business. Warkinson fired at the shooter and believed he hit him in the side. The police brought Warkinson to a local hospital emergency room. Twenty minutes later, the police responded to a reported shooting and found Rudolph Lee suffering from a gunshot wound to the left chest area. Lee said he had been shot during a robbery attempt by two men. When Lee was taken to the hospital (the one to which Warkinson had been taken), Warkinson identified Lee as the man who had shot him. After a police interrogation, Lee was arrested for the shooting.
>
> In an effort to obtain ballistics evidence, the police attempted to have Lee undergo a surgical procedure, under a general anesthetic, for the removal of the bullet lodged in his chest. Lee appealed to the courts, which ruled in his favor and against the operation. The Commonwealth of Virginia appealed the case to the U.S. Supreme Court. The Court ruled that such a surgical procedure, without Lee's permission, would be a violation of his Fourth Amendment rights.
>
> Source: Based on *Winston v. Lee,* 470 U.S. 753 (1985).

Chapter Summary

This chapter explored numerous issues regarding the police and the law. It discussed how we measure crime, including the Uniform Crime Reports and the National Crime Victimization Survey. It looked at how many arrests the U.S. police make and for what crimes people are arrested. It discussed the role that the Bill of Rights and the U.S. Supreme Court play in regulating the police. The chapter also discussed the exclusionary rule, its development through case law, and its effect on the police.

The text explored four major areas of police power: arrest, search and seizure, custodial interrogation, and identification procedures. Numerous Supreme Court cases have defined police power in each area. An examination of specific cases illustrates the development of principles of law that govern our police and the changes in constitutional interpretations of the Bill of Rights over several decades. Law plays a special role in our society. The police must know that law and conform to it.

Learning Check

1. Explain how crime is measured in the United States. Determine how much crime occurs in the United States. Tell how many arrests are made in the United States and what the majority of the arrests are for.
2. Explain how the Bill of Rights and the actions of the U.S. Supreme Court regulate the police.
3. List several of the exceptions to the warrant requirement in search and seizure cases, and cite and discuss several U.S. Supreme Court cases to illustrate the exceptions.
4. Describe the development of the requirement to be advised of one's constitutional rights prior to police interrogation when in police custody. Cite and discuss several U.S. Supreme Court cases to show the changes in police interrogation procedures over time.
5. Explain the differences between lineups, showups, and photo arrays. Give an example of how each one can be legally used.

Review Exercise

Your younger brother, a high school sophomore, brags to his Future Government Leaders Club that you know everything there is to know about the U.S. Supreme Court. The club's faculty advisor calls you and asks you to participate in a debate at a future club meeting. The subject to be debated follows: "The Supreme Court of the 1980s and 1990s has swung too far to the right by overemphasizing the rights of society and underemphasizing individual rights." The advisor gives you a choice as to which side you wish to take and tells you to be prepared to quote as many cases as possible in the areas of search and seizure and custodial interrogation in order to defend your stand. Prepare yourself for the debate.

Web Exercise

Patrol over to the FBI homepage and obtain the latest (as current as possible to the date you are using this textbook) statistics on the Index crimes and arrests in the United States. Then patrol over to the NIJ homepage and obtain latest statistics for the NCVS.

Key Concepts

Uniform Crime Reports (UCR)
Index crime
Weeks v. United States
exclusionary rule
Mapp v. Ohio
probable cause
reasonable suspicion
reasonable force
exigent circumstances
Chimel v. California
stop and frisk
Terry v. Ohio
Carroll doctrine
Davis v. United States

Notes

1. Kathleen Maguire and Ann L. Pastore, eds., *Sourcebook of Criminal Justice Statistics—1996* (Washington, D.C.: U.S. Department of Justice, Bureau of Justice Statistics, U.S. Government Printing Office, 1997), Table 4.1, p. 368; and U.S. Department of Justice, Federal Bureau of Investigation, *Crime in the United States, 1996* (Washington, D.C., 1997), p. 208.
2. *Weeks v. United States,* 232 U.S. 383 (1914).
3. *Brown v. Mississippi,* 297 U.S. 278 (1936).
4. *Mapp v. Ohio,* 367 U.S. 643; and *Miranda v. Arizona,* 384 U.S. 436 (1966).
5. *Weeks v. United States.*
6. *Wolf v. Colorado,* 338 U.S. 25 (1949).
7. *Rochin v. California,* 342 U.S. 165 (1952).
8. *Mapp v. Ohio.*
9. National Institute of Justice, *The Effects of the Exclusionary Rule: A Study of California* (Washington, D.C.: National Institute of Justice, 1982), p. 12.
10. Peter Nardulli, "The Societal Cost of the Exclusionary Rule: An Empirical Assessment," *ABF Research Journal* (1983) pp. 585–609.
11. Wayne W. Bennett and Karen M. Hess, *Criminal Investigation,* 3d ed. (St. Paul: West, 1991), p. 258.
12. *Henry v. United States,* 361 U.S. 98 (1959).
13. *Brinegar v. United States,* 338 U.S. 160 (1949).
14. *Draper v. United States,* 358 U.S. 307 (1959).
15. *County of Riverside v. McLoughlin,* 111 S.Ct. 1661 (1991).
16. *Delaware v. Prouse,* 440 U.S. 648 (1979).
17. *Mimms v. Pennsylvania,* 434 U.S. 106 (1977).

18. *Maryland v. Wilson,* 117 S.Ct. 882 (1997).
19. *Maryland v. Wilson,* citing Federal Bureau of Investigation, *Uniform Crime Reports: Law Enforcement Officers Killed and Assaulted* (Washington, D.C.: Federal Bureau of Investigation, 1994).
20. *Wilson v. Arkansas,* 115 S.Ct. 1914 (1995). For a complete discussion of Fourth Amendment standards on search warrants, see Michael J. Bulzomi, "Knock and Announce: A Fourth Amendment Standard," *FBI Law Enforcement Bulletin,* May 1997, pp. 27–32.
21. *Aguilar v. Texas,* 378 U.S. 108 (1964); and *Spinelli v. United States,* 393 U.S. 410 (1969).
22. *Illinois v. Gates,* 462 U.S. 213 (1983).
23. *Chimel v. California,* 395 U.S. 213 (1983).
24. *Maryland v. Buie,* 110 S.Ct. 1093 (1990).
25. *Terry v. Ohio,* 392 U.S. 1 (1968).
26. *Terry v. Ohio.*
27. *Minnesota v. Dickerson,* 113 S.Ct. 2130 (1993).
28. *United States v. Matlock,* 415 U.S. 164 (1974).
29. *Bumper v. North Carolina,* 391 U.S. 543 (1968).
30. *Illinois v. Rodriquez,* 110 S.Ct. 2793 (1990).
31. *Florida v. Bostick,* 111 S.Ct. 2382 (1991).
32. *Harris v. United States,* 390 U.S. 234 (1968).
33. *Abel v. United States,* 362 U.S. 217 (1960).
34. *California v. Greenwood,* 486 U.S. 35 (1988).
35. *California v. Hodari, D.,* 111 S.Ct. 1547 (1991).
36. *Colorado v. Bertine,* 479 U.S. 367 (1987).
37. *Hester v. United States,* 265 U.S. 57 (1924).
38. *Oliver v. United States,* 466 U.S. 170 (1984).
39. *California v. Ciraola,* 476 U.S. 207 (1986).
40. *Florida v. Riley,* 488 U.S. 445 (1989).
41. *Carroll v. United States,* 267 U.S. 132 (1925).
42. *New York v. Belton,* 453 U.S. 454 (1981).
43. *United States v. Ross,* 456 U.S. 454 (1981).
44. *California v. Acevedo,* 111 S.Ct. 1982 (1991); and *Florida v. Jimeno,* 111 S.Ct. 1801 (1991).
45. *United States v. Martinez-Fuerte,* 428 U.S. 543 (1976).
46. *United States v. Leon,* 468 U.S. 897 (1984).
47. *Massachusetts v. Sheppard,* 104 S.Ct. 3424 (1984); *Illinois v. Krull,* 107 S.Ct. 1160 (1987); and *Maryland v. Garrison,* 107 S.Ct. 1013 (1987).
48. *Arizona v. Isaac Evans,* No. 93-1660 (1995).
49. *Burdeau v. McDowell,* 256 U.S. 465 (1921).
50. *Brown v. Mississippi.*
51. *Escobedo v. Illinois,* 378 U.S. 478 (1964).
52. *Miranda v. Arizona.*
53. Bennett and Hess, *Criminal Investigation,* p. 234.
54. Alan M. Dershowitz, "A Requiem for the Exclusionary Rule," in *Taking Liberties: A Decade of Hard Cases, Bad Laws and Bum Raps* (Chicago: Contemporary Books, 1988), p. 10.
55. Dershowitz, "Requiem for the Exclusionary Rule," p. 12.
56. *Harris v. New York,* 401 U.S. 222 (1971).
57. *Michigan v. Mosley,* 423 U.S. 96 (1975).
58. *Brewer v. Williams,* 430 U.S. 387 (1977).
59. *Nix v. Williams,* 467 U.S. 431 (1984).
60. *Brewer v. Williams.*
61. *Rhode Island v. Innis,* 446 U.S. 291 (1980).
62. *New York v. Quarles,* 104 S.Ct. 1246 (1991).
63. *Moran v. Burbine,* 475 U.S. 412 (1986).
64. *Illinois v. Perkins,* 110 U.S. 2394 (1991).
65. *Pennsylvania v. Muniz,* 496 U.S. 582 (1990).
66. *Arizona v. Fulminante,* 111 S.Ct. 1246 (1991).
67. *Minnick v. Mississippi,* 111 S.Ct. 486 (1991).
68. *McNeil v. Wisconsin,* 111 S.Ct. 2204 (1991).
69. *Davis v. United States,* 114 S.Ct. 2350 (1994).
70. For a complete discussion of Davis and Miranda, see Edward M. Hendrie, "Beyond Miranda," *FBI Law Enforcement Bulletin,* March 1997, pp. 25–32.
71. Hendrie, "Beyond Miranda."
72. Paul G. Cassell, "Miranda's Social Costs: An Empirical Reassessment," *Northwestern Law Journal* 387 (1996), as cited in Hendrie, "Beyond Miranda," p. 31.
73. For other studies regarding the Miranda warning and its effect on the criminal justice system, see Michael Wald et al., "Interrogations in New Haven: The Impact of Miranda," *Yale Law Journal* 76 (1967): 1519; Walter Lippman, "*Miranda v. Arizona*—Twenty Years Later," *Criminal Justice Journal* 9 (1987): 241; Stephen J. Scholhofer, "Reconsidering Miranda," *University of Chicago Law Review* 54 (1987): 435–461; Paul Cassell, "How Many Criminals Has Miranda Set Free?" *Wall Street Journal,* 1 March 1995, p. A-12.
74. *United States v. Wade,* 388 U.S. 218 (1967).
75. *Kirby v. Illinois,* 406 U.S. 682 (1972).
76. *Stoval v. Denno,* 388 U.S. 293 (1967).
77. *United States v. O'Connor,* 282 F.Supp. 963 (D.D.C. 1968).
78. *United States v. Ash,* 413 U.S. 300 (1973).
79. *Schmerber v. California,* 384 U.S. 757 (1966).
80. *Winston v. Lee,* 470 U.S. 753 (1985).
81. *Schmerber v. California.*
82. *Winston v. Lee.*
83. *United States v. Dionisio,* 410 U.S. 1 (1973).
84. *United States v. Mara,* 410 U.S. 19 (1973).

12
Police Ethics and Police Deviance

Chapter Outline

Ethics and the Police
The Dilemma of Law Versus Order
Review of the Police
Police Corruption
  Corruption Makes Good Books and Films
  Examples of Police Corruption
  Types and Forms of Corruption
  Effects of Police Corruption
  Reasons for Police Corruption
  Responses to Police Corruption
Other Police Misconduct
  Drug Abuse and Trafficking
  Drinking and Alcohol Abuse
  Cooping
  Police Deception
  Abuse of Authority
Police Brutality
  Tradition of Police Brutality
  Examples of Police Brutality
  Is Brutality Really the Problem?
  Police Department Responses to Police Brutality
  Citizen Oversight

Chapter Goals

■ To acquaint you with the various definitions, the types, and the extent of police corruption.

■ To explore various reasons for police corruption.

■ To acquaint you with forms of police misconduct other than police corruption, including misuse of alcohol and illegal drugs, cooping, and police deception.

■ To discuss the definition, types, and extent of police brutality.

■ To explore various responses to police brutality, including citizen complaint review boards.

287

Introduction

I recall being asked by a student once why there are so many studies of deviance by police officers, when other occupational groups rarely study deviance in their ranks. My answer was simple: "We give loaded guns and almost unlimited power to the men and women we appoint as police officers. We don't do that for most other occupations."

Police officers in the United States are given tremendous authority and wide latitude in using that authority. In addition, to the average citizen, the police are the most visible symbol of not only the U.S. criminal justice system, but also the U.S. government.

Many police officers complain that the press overdoes coverage of corrupt or brutal police officers. The 1991 Rodney King tape (the home videotape of the beating of African-American motorist Rodney King by four white Los Angeles police officers) was broadcast over every television network in the United States for weeks. The 1997 Abner Louima case (in which a New York City police officer allegedly inserted a stick into the rectum of a prisoner and then put the feces- and blood-covered stick into the prisoner's mouth) was worldwide news and will probably continue to be so for years. Police officers always ask, "Why do they [the media] try to make us all look bad? It was only a few cops, not all cops." Officers also complain about the media attention given to the allegations of racism, brutality, and abuse of authority of Detective Mark Fuhrman in the worldwide television coverage and commentary in the O.J. Simpson murder trial. "Hey, he's only one cop; we're not like that."

We must remember that the media operate under the following philosophy: If a dog bites a person, that is not news. Dogs bite people every day of the week. But if a person bites a dog, that's news. The news is that which is different and not normal. Police officers across the United States do hundreds of thousands of good acts a day. They arrest lawbreakers, find lost children and senile people, walk the elderly across the street, bring the sick and injured to the hospital, deliver babies, stop fights and arguments, and counsel the confused. That is their job, and they do it well, but that is not news. But when the very people we trust to uphold our law—to serve as the model of what our law is and what it stands for—violate that law, that is news. That is the person biting the dog. It is healthy that police misconduct is news. Imagine if this misconduct were so common that it did not qualify as news.

It must be remembered, before reading this chapter, that the vast majority of the over 800,000 men and women in our nation's law enforcement agencies are extremely ethical. Unfortunately, a few are not. Therefore, this chapter must exist. However, it is, indeed, about the person biting the dog, not the dog biting the person.

This chapter will discuss ethics; police deviance, including police corruption and other misconduct such as drug and alcohol abuse, cooping, police deception and abuse of authority; and police brutality.

Ethics and the Police

What is ethics? James N. Gilbert in his article "Investigative Ethics" tells us that ethics can be defined as the practical, normative study of the rightness and wrongness of human conduct. He says that all human conduct can be viewed in the context of basic and applied ethical considerations. Basic ethics are the rather broad moral principles that govern all conduct, while applied ethics focuses these broad principles upon specific applications. For example, a basic ethical tenet assumes that lying is wrong. Applied ethics would examine and govern under what conditions such a wrong would indeed take place.[1]

Gilbert concludes:

> The ethical dilemmas which face our police will not disappear as the world becomes more sophisticated and technological. On the contrary, such developments only widen the gap between professional behavior and possible unethical actions. As judicial guidelines become more complex, criminal operation more skilled, the temptation towards unethical conduct increases. Accordingly, education and training which addresses the poignant issue of ethical decision making will truly aid the investigator [and police officer].[2]

There has been a growing interest in ethics in the academic and law enforcement literature over the past few decades, including textbooks, studies, journal articles, and media articles.[3]

The Greek philosopher Aristotle in his classic *Nicomachean Ethics* stated that "every art and every inquiry and similarly every action and choice is thought to aim at some good."[4] Is Aristotle's "good" what we mean as ethics? This author thinks so. Could Aristotle's definition of good or ethics be the same as our modern saying "do the right thing?" Yes! If one is ethical, he or she does the right thing. If one does the right thing, he or she is ethical. Remember, the vast majority of the over 800,000 men and women in our police departments and other law enforcement agencies are ethical. They do the right thing hundreds of times a day. Unfortunately, some are not ethical. Some do the wrong thing.

How do we measure police ethical standards? What standards have been established to determine how police officers should act? Joycelyn Pollock, in her excellent book, *Ethics in Crime and Justice: Dilemmas and Decisions,* identified some of these standards:

- Organizational value systems or codes of ethics designed to educate and guide the behavior of those who work within the organization.
- An oath of office, which can be considered a shorthand version of the value system or code of ethics.
- The Law Enforcement Code of Ethics as promulgated by the International Association of Chiefs of Police (IACP). (See Appendix B of this text for the Law Enforcement Code of Ethics and the Police Code of Conduct.)[5]

Other standards governing police ethics are the U.S. Constitution and the Bill of Rights, case law as determined by appellate courts and the U.S. Supreme Court, and federal and state criminal laws and codes of criminal procedure.

Although these standards appear on the surface to set a perfect example for police officers and mandate exemplary performance by them, how widely accepted and followed are they by individual officers and departments? As Pollack explains, the police subculture, as discussed in chapter 6 of this text, often works against these official ethical precepts,

> It is apparent that the formal code of ethics or the organizational value system is quite different from subculture values. Violations of formal ethical standards such as the use of force, acceptance of preferential or discriminatory treatment, use of illegal investigation tactics, and differential enforcement of laws are all supported by the subculture. The police subculture has an ethical code of its own.[6]

Perhaps it is the police subculture, or perhaps it is just the individual actions of officers or groups of officers that create police deviance. Whatever the reason, deviance certainly occurs in policing. However, remember, as most officers know and apparently the public knows, most of our nation's police officers are highly ethical.

Evidence exists that the U.S. public believes to a great extent that our police are good, and ethical, and

All in the Line of Duty

The Only NYPD Police Officer Murdered in the Line of Duty Outside the United States

Giuseppe Petrosino, a boy from Salerno, Italy, emigrated to the United States and became a citizen. Eventually, he earned a position with the New York City Police Department (NYPD) as a patrolman. He quickly rose through the ranks and became the NYPD's first Italian-American detective.

As a lieutenant, Petrosino waged a valiant battle against the Black Hand, a loosely knit criminal organization of Italian immigrants who extorted money by terrorizing their fellow immigrants. Petrosino founded the Bomb Squad, the first unit of its kind in the United States, to counter the Black Hand's use of explosives to carry out its extortion threats.

From 1905 to 1909, Petrosino and the "Italian Branch" of the NYPD, an elite corps of Italian-American undercover cops, arrested thousands of members of the Black Hand, deported 500 and reduced crime against Italian-Americans by half. In 1909, Petrosino was dispatched to Palermo, Italy, to gather additional intelligence about Black Hand members. While there as a home-grown hero, the lieutenant was murdered by the Black Hand. His funeral was attended by over 200,000 people, and his vast funeral procession lasted five and a half hours. He was the first NYPD officer killed in the line of duty outside of the United States, and still the only one.

Source: Adapted from *Spring 3100* (New York: New York City Police Department, 1995).

do the right thing. In a 1995 poll asking respondents to rate the honesty and ethical standards of various occupations, the police came in with an 88 percent positive rating, with 41 percent of the public rating them very high and high and 44 percent rating them average. Only 14 percent of respondents gave them a low or very low rating. Ranking lower than police officers in honesty and ethical standards were bankers, journalists, building contractors, local officeholders, TV reporters, commentators, newspaper reporters, business executives, stockbrokers, lawyers, real estate agents, state officeholders, labor union leaders, U.S. Senators, insurance salespeople, advertising practitioners, Congress members, and car salespeople.[7]

★ The Dilemma of Law Versus Order

Police corruption and police brutality have always been part of policing. The names, places, and times change, but corruption and brutality remain.

There has always been an inherent conflict in the role of the police in maintaining law and order in U.S. society. Jerome Skolnick calls this conflict the "dilemma of law versus order," referring to police efforts at maintaining law and order, but doing so under the restraints of the law.[8] It would be very easy to maintain law and order by ensuring that our cops were bigger, meaner, and tougher than our criminals, and by letting the cops merely beat up all the criminals to ensure a safe society. Of course, we cannot do that. We must have our police comply with the same law they are paid to enforce. As Howard Abadinsky says, "Whatever goals and objectives we assign the police, we insist that they be achieved in conformity to law, and this is no small task."[9]

Elmer Johnson points out that "police observance of individual rights is essential to making democracy a reality in a mass society but achievement of this ideal is made particularly difficult by demands that the police also be efficient in protecting the community against criminals and the disorder attending social unrest."[10]

★ Review of the Police

Possibly because of the dilemma of law versus order, the police are constantly under review by government agencies, including federal, state, and local agencies; the courts; academics; the media; and the general public. Numerous national commissions have looked into the operations of the police. Among the most noteworthy were the National Commission on Law Observance and Enforcement, more popularly known as the Wickersham Commission (1931); the President's Commission on Law Enforcement and Administration of Justice (1967); the National Advisory Commission on Civil Disorders (1968); the National Advisory Commission on Criminal Justice Standards and Goals (1973); and the Commission on Accreditation for Law Enforcement Agencies (1982).[11]

> ### YOU ARE THERE! »
>
> **National Commissions Overseeing the Police**
>
> | | |
> |---|---|
> | 1931 | National Commission on Law Observance and Enforcement |
> | 1967 | President's Commission on Law Enforcement and Administration of Justice |
> | 1968 | National Advisory Commission on Civil Disorders |
> | 1973 | National Advisory Commission on Criminal Justice Standards and Goals |
> | 1982 | Commission on Accreditation for Law Enforcement Agencies |

In addition to the national commissions, numerous state and local commissions, panels, and hearings have looked into the behavior and operations of the police. The most notable was the Knapp Commission to Investigate Allegations of Police Corruption in New York City (known as the **Knapp Commission**).[12] The Knapp Commission was created in 1970 by New York City mayor John V. Lindsay in response to a series of articles in the *New York Times* detailing organized, widespread police corruption in New York City. It held public hearings, and its findings caused widespread changes in the policies and operations of the New York City Police Department. The police are also under constant review by the U.S. judicial system through the process of judicial review, as was discussed in chapter 11. **Judicial review** is the process by which the actions of the police in such areas as arrests, search and seizure, and custodial interrogation are reviewed by the U.S. court system at various levels to ensure the constitutionality of those actions. Judicial review has resulted in such landmark Supreme Court cases as *Mapp v. Ohio* and *Miranda v. Arizona*, which were discussed in chapter 11. In addition, the police are reviewed daily by the media: newspapers, magazines, radio, and television. Finally, they are under constant review by citizens, many of whom do not hesitate to report what they consider to be deviant conduct to the media, to the police themselves, or to other legal authorities.

PATROLLING THE NET

Criminology Society Offers Mentoring on the Net

The American Society of Criminology (ASC) offers a mentoring service to student members of the organization who have questions about career choices, research and theoretical issues, and other issues regarding the discipline. The society has mentors of all ages, races, ethnicities, and nationalities and offers areas of specialization to members. The ASC e-mail Mentoring Program is available on the web, allowing students to be mentored by faculty, researchers, and administrators outside their own universities through the ASC homepage. All a student has to do to hunt for a likely mentor is to hit the e-mail address and he or she is hotlinked to the mentor right away. The ASC homepage is http://sun.soci.niu.edu/~ascmentr.

Source: Adapted from American Society of Criminology, "The ASC E-Mail Mentoring Program," *The Criminologist,* July/August 1997, p. 2.

Police Corruption

Police corruption has many definitions. Herman Goldstein defines it as "acts involving the misuse of authority by a police officer in a manner designed to produce personal gain for himself or others."[13]

Frederick A. Elliston and Michael Feldberg define corruption as "the acceptance of money or the equivalent of money by a public official for doing something he or she is under a duty to do anyway, that he or she is under a duty not to do, or to exercise legitimate discretion for improper reasons."[14] Richard J. Lundman defines police corruption as follows: "when officers accept money, goods, or services for actions they are sworn to do anyway. It also exists when police officers accept money, goods, or services for ignoring actions they are sworn to invoke legal procedures against."[15]

Although these definitions differ, we can find enough commonalities to define corruption for our purposes as follows: A police officer is corrupt when he or she is acting under his or her official capacity and receives a benefit or something of value (other than his or her paycheck) for doing something or for refraining from doing something.

It is often difficult to distinguish among bribes, gratuities, and gifts. Is giving an officer a free cup of coffee or a sandwich an act of corruption? Michael Feldberg writes, "Sometimes, it is difficult to distinguish between genuine gifts (such as Christmas gifts), gratuities, bribes and corruption. At times, however, accepting any kind of gift is the beginning of the slippery slope syndrome where the path is paved for accepting other, larger gratuities in the future and eventually bribes."[16]

In the wake of the allegations of tremendous corruption in the New York City Police Department that led to the establishment of the Knapp Commission, reform police commissioner Patrick V. Murphy told his officers, "Except for your pay check there is no such thing as a clean buck."[17] Although some would dispute this, there is no question that Commissioner Murphy knew what he considered to be corruption, and that he was holding his officers accountable for it.

Corruption Makes Good Books and Films

Police corruption is a popular topic in literature and film. Does life imitate art, or does art imitate life? This external question is easily answered when we discuss police corruption: art imitates life.

As an example, the novel *Serpico,* by Peter Maas, and the movie starring Al Pacino were great successes.[18] *Serpico* tells the true tale of an honest NYPD plainclothes officer, **Frank Serpico**, who roams the police department and city government for a seemingly endless time in an attempt to report that there is corruption in his plainclothes division in the Bronx. Serpico tells his supervisors, his commanders, the chief of personnel, an assistant to the mayor, and the city's Department of Investigation his tale, and nothing is done; corruption remains rampant. Finally frustrated in his efforts, Serpico and a friend, Sergeant David Dirk, report their allegations to a reporter for the *New York Times.* This leads to

Frank Serpico testifying at the Knapp Commission hearings on police corruption in 1970.

the formation of the Knapp Commission and widespread changes in the NYPD's policies and procedures initiated by Commissioner Murphy, who was appointed soon after the allegations were made.

The novel *Prince of the City: The Story of a Cop Who Knew Too Much,* by Robert Daley, and the movie of the same name starring Treat Williams also were great successes.[19] *Prince of the City* tells the true story of a corrupt, experienced narcotics detective, Robert Leuci, assigned to the elite Special Investigations Unit of the New York City Police Department's Narcotics Division. Leuci was a corrupt cop who, to save his own skin, worked as a federal informer to obtain evidence to put his partners behind bars.

The book *Buddy Boys: When Good Cops Turn Bad,* by Mike McAlary, was a best seller.[20] *Buddy Boys* is also a true tale of thirteen corrupt police officers in Brooklyn's Seventy-seventh Precinct who stole drugs from drug dealers, sold drugs and guns, and committed other nefarious crimes.

Examples of Police Corruption

Despite all the attention police corruption has received in history and the efforts by police administrators to detect and eradicate it, there are still numerous recent examples of large-scale police corruption.

During the 1980s, seventy-five Miami police officers were arrested for serious acts of police corruption. Seven of these officers, who were dubbed the "Miami River Cops," were charged with high-level drug dealing. Three of them have also been charged with murder.[21]

In 1992, six New York City police officers, including Police Officer Michael Dowd, were arrested and charged with buying drugs in their inner-city precincts and selling them in the suburban communities in which they lived. This arrest led to allegations of murders committed by some of the officers, as well as charges that NYPD internal affairs investigators had known about the corrupt acts by these officers for years prior to the arrests and had taken no action. This resulted in the formation, by Mayor David Dinkins, of another Knapp-style commission to investigate corruption in the New York City Police Department.[22] This case supports the theory that a major corruption scandal surfaces every twenty years in the NYPD. The theory holds that after the scandal and the resultant investigatory commission, the department vigorously fights corruption and prevents large-scale, organized corruption from resurfacing. However, approximately twenty years later, it will resurface anyway.

In 1996, three Detroit police officers and one former officer were named in a federal indictment, which accused them of being key players in a Texas-to-Michigan cocaine-smuggling ring. Also, six current and former police officers from Ford Heights, Illinois, thirty miles south of Chicago, were indicted for taking bribes to look the other way as more than twenty drug dealers conducted a brisk, brazen business in the small, impoverished town.[23]

Also, in 1996, former New Orleans police officer Len Davis was sentenced to death for arranging the murder of a woman who had filed a brutality complaint against him. Davis was only one of several New Orleans officers charged in a 1994 FBI sting for transporting and guarding shipments of cocaine. Davis is not the only New Orleans officer on death row. A female officer, charged with the murder of a fellow officer during a robbery, has also been sentenced to death.[24]

Corruption is not limited to rank-and-file police officers. In 1992, Chief William L. Hart, Detroit's police chief since 1976, retired after a federal jury convicted him of stealing $2.6 million from police department funds.[25] In 1996, Newark, New Jersey, Police Director William Celester was forced out of office after being named in a wide-ranging indictment. He was charged with numerous counts of malfeasance, including mail and wire fraud, tax fraud, accepting illegal gratuities, making a false statement, and forging documents. In a plea bargain in July 1996, Celester pleaded guilty to using nearly $30,000 from a police account to pay for vacations, airline tickets, gifts for his girlfriends, and other personal expenses.[26]

Corruption and misconduct is by no means restricted to local police. Federal law enforcement agents have also succumbed to this temptation. In 1997, former FBI agent Earl Edwin Pitts was sentenced to twenty-seven years in prison for spying for the Soviet Union, and after that government fell, Russia. Pitts sold U.S. intelligence secrets for almost one-quarter million dollars from 1987 to 1992. Pitts is not the only FBI agent charged with selling out his country. Richard W. Miller was imprisoned for twenty years for similar acts in 1984.[27]

Also in 1997, Jerome R. Sullivan, a twenty-five-year veteran of the FBI, was indicted on charges of stealing more than $400,000, including at least $104,000 the FBI said was mob money he helped seize. Sullivan was the lead FBI agent in the arrest of Nicholas Corozzo, a leader in an organized crime family in South Florida, who was poised to take the place of imprisoned John Gotti as the family leader. Sullivan's lawyer reported that his client had alcohol and gambling problems that the FBI had been aware of but had not done enough to help him with.[28]

Several recent books have focused specifically on the issues of police deviance. For example, see Victor Kappeler, Richard Sluder, and Geoffrey Alpert, *Forces of Deviance, Understanding the Dark Side of Policing,* and Jerome H. Skolnick and James J. Fyfe, *Above the Law: Police and the Excessive Use of Force.*[29]

Types and Forms of Corruption

Corruption is not limited to the present day. Lawrence W. Sherman reports, "For as long as there have been police, there has been police corruption."[30] Herman Goldstein says, "Corruption is endemic to policing. The very nature of the police function is bound to subject officers to tempting offers."[31] Frank Schmalleger says, "Police deviance has been a problem in American society since the early days of policing. It is probably an ancient and natural tendency of human beings to attempt to placate or 'win over' those in positions of authority over them."[32]

Samuel Walker describes four general types of police corruption: taking gratuities, taking bribes, theft or burglary, and internal corruption.[33] Gratuities are small tips

YOU ARE THERE! »

The Twenty-Year Theory of Corruption in the NYPD

History has proved the theory that a major corruption scandal occurs in the New York City Police Department approximately every twenty years. These scandals have resulted in major investigations and public hearings. This theory was again proved with the Mollen Commission, which in September and October 1993 investigated charges of corruption in several NYPD precincts. This commission was brought about by the arrest of corrupt officer Michael Dowd and his associates, who stole drugs in their inner-city precincts and sold them in their suburban communities. The following time line lists the scandals:

1890s	The Lexow Commission and the Mazet Commission
1910s	The Curran Committee and the Becker/Rosenthal Scandals
1930s	The Seabury Hearings
1950s	The Harry Gross Investigation
1970s	The Knapp Commission
1990s	The Mollen Commission

or discounts on goods purchased. In many communities, taking gratuities is not considered corruption but merely the showing of good will to the police (with, of course, the hope that the police might perform their duties a little better for the person who shows them good will).

Police corruption also may involve taking bribes—the payment of money or other consideration to police officers with the intent to subvert the aims of the criminal justice system. According to Walker, bribes may take two forms: (1) the pad (formal, regular, periodic payments to the police to overlook continuing criminal enterprises) and (2) the score (a one-time payment to avoid arrest for illegal conduct).

Theft or burglary, the taking of money or property by the police while performing their duties, is another form of police corruption, according to Walker. The police have access to numerous premises, including warehouses and stores, while investigating burglaries. They also have access to homes while on official business. A corrupt police officer has plenty of opportunity to take property from others.

YOU ARE THERE!

The Knapp Commission Discovers Corruption

The Knapp Commission was created in 1970 by New York City mayor John V. Lindsay in response to allegations brought by New York City police officers Frank Serpico and David Dirk of widespread corruption in the New York City Police Department. These allegations were detailed in several articles in the *New York Times* and received national attention. The hearings conducted by the commission also received national attention in the media. The committee's final report was issued in 1972, and its findings were responsible for widespread changes in the policies and operations of the NYPD. The types of corruption in the NYPD discovered by the Knapp Commission through its hearings, investigations, and informants were so many and so varied that they could fill volumes.

The Knapp Commission discovered corruption in the following areas:

1. Gambling. Officers assigned to plainclothes (antigambling) units received regular monthly payments from the operators of illegal bookmaking, policy, and other gambling operations. The regular monthly payments were called the pad. Other payments that involved one-time-only payments were called scores.

2. Narcotics. Officers assigned to narcotics units extorted money and other bribes, including drugs, from drug addicts and dealers. The officers also conducted illegal wiretaps and used other unlawful investigatory techniques. Officers engaged in flaking people (claiming someone was in possession of narcotics when he or she was not—the drugs used for evidence were from the officer's own supply) and padding arrests (similar to flaking, but involving adding enough extra narcotics, or felony weight, to the defendant's total to raise the charge to a felony).

3. Prostitution. Officers involved in plainclothes units had maintained pads and received scores from houses of prostitution, prostitute bars, and prostitutes.

4. Construction. Uniformed officers received payoffs from contractors who violated city regulations or who did not possess proper licenses and permits.

5. Bars. Officers received payoffs from licensed and unlicensed bars to overlook crimes and violations.

6. Sabbath Law. Officers received payoffs from food store owners to allow the owners to violate the Sabbath Law, a former New York City law that required certain food stores—such as delicatessens, groceries, and bodegas—to close down on Sundays.

7. Parking and traffic. Officers received payoffs from motorists who wanted to avoid traffic summonses, as well as from business establishments to discourage officers from issuing summonses for illegal parking in front of their businesses.

8. Retrieving seized automobiles from the police. Officers at city automobile storage yards received payments from owners to retrieve their automobiles.

9. Intradepartmental payments. Certain officers received payments for doing paperwork for other officers and for temporary assignments, permanent assignments, and medical discharges.

10. Sale of information. Officers received payments for the sale of confidential police information to criminals and private investigation firms.

11. Gratuities. Officers received free meals, drinks, hotel rooms, merchandise, Christmas payments, and other gifts and tips for services rendered.

12. Miscellaneous. Officers received payments from fortune-tellers, loan sharks, automobile theft rings, hijackers, and peddlers. Officers stole money and property from dead bodies (DOAs) and their apartments. They burglarized stores and other premises.

The Knapp Commission's report distinguished between two types of corrupt officers: grass eaters and meat eaters. Grass eating, the most common form of police deviance, was described as illegitimate activity that occurs from time to time in the normal course of police work, such as taking small bribes or relatively minor services offered by citizens seeking to avoid arrest or to get special police services. Meat eating, in contrast, was a much more serious form of corruption involving the active seeking of illicit money-making opportunities. Meat eaters solicited bribes through threat or intimidation, whereas grass eaters made the simpler mistake of not refusing those that were offered.

Source: Adapted from Knapp Commission, *Report on Police Corruption* (New York: Braziller, 1973), pp. 1–5.

Dempsey's Law

Do Police Officers Have to Pay for Their Lunch?

Professor Dempsey, don't police officers have to pay for their lunches? The other day I saw an officer get a sandwich and a soda at the convenience store. He said thank you and left, but I never saw him give the cashier any money.

I get this question often. I generally respond that different departments around the country may have different standards regarding free or discounted meals for police officers. However, Dempsey's Law says that officers should pay for their meals, just as any other citizen should.

Yeah, Professor Dempsey, but once I saw an officer try to pay for a cup of coffee at the local diner, and the cashier wouldn't take the money. The officer looked really embarrassed. If that's corruption, should the officer have arrested the cashier for bribery?

No, the officer should not have arrested the cashier for bribery. That would be pretty stupid. However, there are ways to get around embarrassing situations like that. I used to always have several $1 bills in my wallet and have them ready in my hand at the register. If such a situation occurred, I would merely smile and say, "Thank you very much." Then I would leave the approximate cost of the meal on the counter. If the cashier continued to protest, I would return by my table and leave the money as a tip for the waiter. Hey, I made good money as an officer. I could afford the price of a meal.

Walker's final type of police corruption is internal corruption. Officers pay members of their departments for special assignments or promotions.

Thomas Barker and Julian Roebuck identified the following types of police corruption:

1. Acceptance of free or discounted meals and services.
2. Acceptance of kickbacks for referrals for services.
3. Opportunistic theft from helpless citizens or unsecured premises.
4. Shakedowns.
5. Protection of illegal activities.
6. Acceptance of money to fix cases.
7. Planned theft.[34]

Sherman discusses three general levels of police corruption.[35] The first is the "rotten apples and rotten pockets" theory of police corruption, which holds that only one officer or a very small group of officers in a department or precinct is corrupt. At first thought, this may not seem very serious. If only one officer or a handful of officers is corrupt, a department needs only to arrest the officer or group and use the arrest as an example to other officers of what might happen to them also, if they are corrupt. The dangerous part of this theory is that if police commanders believe that only a few officers are bad, they will not take the tough, proactive policies necessary to uncover and eradicate corruption in the entire precinct or department. New York City's Commissioner Patrick V. Murphy, in the wake of the Serpico allegations, faced a dilemma. He could accept the rotten apple theory, or he could admit that the entire barrel might be rotten. To his credit, and for the betterment of the NYPD, Murphy chose the latter and took the steps necessary to correct the situation.[36]

The second level of corruption that Sherman found might exist in a police department was pervasive, unorganized corruption, where a majority of the officers are corrupt but are not actively working with one another on an organized or planned basis.

Sherman's third level of corruption was pervasive, organized corruption, where almost all members of a department or precinct are working together in systematic and organized corruption. This type is essentially what the Knapp Commission discovered, particularly in the NYPD plainclothes units.[37]

Several stages of the moral decline of police officers have been identified. Sherman tells us about certain stages in an officer's moral career. The first stage involves the acceptance of minor gratuities, such as free meals. Peer pressure from other officers is extremely important at this stage. The second and third stages involve accepting gratuities to overlook regulatory offenses, such as accepting money to allow bars to remain open past regular closing hours, or accepting money from a motorist instead of giving him or her a summons. Peer pressure from other officers is also very important at this stage. The final stage involves changing from passively accepting gratuities to actively seeking bribes. As the corruption continues, it becomes more systematic. It involves larger amounts of money and includes numerous types of crimes, ranging from gambling violations and prostitution to dealing in narcotics.[38]

Effects of Police Corruption

"Nothing undermines public confidence in the police and in the process of criminal justice more than the illegal acts of [police] officers," said the President's Commission on Law Enforcement and Administration of Justice.[39] David Burnham, a *New York Times* writer, offered an interesting analysis of the social costs of police corruption. Burnham identified what he calls four hidden social costs of police corruption:

- It represents a secret tax on businesses that have to pay off the police to avoid harassment.
- It undermines the enforcement of the law, allowing widespread illegal activity to flourish.
- It destroys the department itself, robbing the police officer of self-respect and respect for superior officers and the department as a whole. Effective discipline becomes impossible when corruption is systematic.
- Knowledge of the existence of corruption undermines the public's faith in the police and the entire criminal justice system.[40]

Reasons for Police Corruption

Numerous theories attempt to explain corruption in law enforcement agencies. Frank Schmalleger offers an interesting theory about the reason some police officers become corrupt by tying Edwin H. Sutherland's theory of differential association to police corruption.[41] Sutherland's theory of differential association holds that crime is basically "imitative"; we learn crime the same way we learn other behavior. We tend to imitate the behavior that surrounds us. Schmalleger asks us to consider a police officer's typical day—associating with and arresting petty thieves, issuing traffic citations and other summonses to citizens who try to talk their way out of the tickets, dealing with prostitutes who feel hassled by the cops, and arresting drug users who think what they are doing is not wrong. Schmalleger asks us to combine these everyday experiences with the relatively low pay officers receive and the sense that police work is not really valued to understand how officers might develop a jaded attitude toward the double standards of the civilization they are sworn to protect. Such a jaded attitude, Schmalleger says, may entice officers into corruption.[42]

When we consider the enormous authority given to our police officers, the tremendous discretion they are allowed to exercise, and the existence of the police personality and police cynicism (discussed in chapter 6), it is easy to see that police work is fertile ground for the growth of corruption. Add to this environment the constant contact police have with criminals and unsavory people, the moral dilemma they face when given the responsibility of enforcing unenforceable laws regarding services people actually want (illegal drugs, gambling, alcohol, and prostitution), and the enormous amount of money that can be made by corrupt officers. Based on all these factors, it is little wonder that corruption is pervasive in police departments.

The current drug problem in the United States, including the desirability of drugs and the tremendous profits available from their sale, seems to increase the risks of police corruption. The Wickersham Commission in 1931 warned that the presence of laws against alcohol (National Prohibition) had the potential for corruption by police and other officials.[43] Is today's illegal drug business as tempting to corruption-prone law enforcement officers as the alcohol trade was to officers during National Prohibition?

The style of policing employed by a department may be somewhat responsible for the degree of corruption in that department. James Q. Wilson analyzed corruption according to the different styles of policing he described in *Varieties of Police Behavior: The Management of Law and Order in Eight Communities.*[44] He says that the greatest degree of police corruption is found in departments characterized by the "watchman style," in which police are expected merely to maintain order, not to deal with the causes of crime or to make attempts to improve conditions that may lead to crime. Wilson says that low salaries and the expectation that police will have other jobs increase the probabilities that the police will be involved in corruption in watchman-style departments.

Corruption is found to a lesser degree, Wilson says, in departments characterized by the "legalistic style." These departments emphasize formal police training, recruiting from the middle class, offering greater promotional opportunities, and viewing law as a means to an end rather than an end in itself. In this departmental style, formal sanctions are used more frequently than informal ones; police give less attention to community service and order maintenance than to law enforcement.

Wilson says that corruption is not a serious problem in the third type of police department style, the "service style." In this management style, law enforcement and order maintenance functions are combined with an emphasis on good relationships between the police and the community. The command of the department is decentralized; police on patrol work out of specialized units. Higher education and promotional opportunities are emphasized, and police are expected to lead exemplary private lives.

Responses to Police Corruption

The most important step in eliminating or reducing police corruption is to admit that corruption exists. The need for candor, Herman Goldstein argues, is paramount. Police officials have traditionally attempted to ignore the problem and deny that it exists.[45]

Many police departments have established **internal affairs divisions (IADs or IAs)** as their major department resource to combat corruption. Internal affairs divisions or units are the police who police the police department. Internal affairs investigators are not very popular with other members of the department, because many officers see them as spies who only want to get them in trouble. Internal affairs units are also used to investigate allegations of police brutality by most departments.

Internal affairs divisions can attack corruption in two ways, reactively and proactively. In a reactive investigation, the investigator waits for a complaint of corruption from the public and then investigates that specific complaint using traditional investigative techniques. In a **proactive investigation** into police corruption, investigators provide opportunities for officers to commit illegal acts, such as leaving valuable property at a scene to see if officers follow normal procedures regarding found property. Proactive investigations are often called **integrity tests**.

An excellent example of an integrity test or a proactive investigation that nabbed a corrupt officer occurred

All in the Line of Duty

Just Like the Movies, But This Was Real

Officer Curtis Kakiki of the Glendale, California, Police Department responded to the report of a robbery at an area liquor store. When a vehicle matching the description of one used in the robbery passed his patrol car, Officer Kakiki pursued the vehicle. During the pursuit, one of the riders, a juvenile gang member, leaned out of the vehicle and fired several rounds at Kakiki's cruiser. After crashing their vehicle in Hollywood, the three suspects were apprehended by Officer Kakiki and other officers from the Glendale and Los Angeles Police Departments.

Source: Adapted from *FBI Law Enforcement Bulletin*, July 1994, p. 33.

in the 33rd Precinct in New York City's Washington Heights in June 1997. Acting on tips that a precinct officer was corrupt, internal affairs investigators set up a sting for the officer. Reporting that they had just raided an apartment in a drug case, investigators had the suspect officer assigned to guard the apartment. The raid, however, was bogus, a ruse to allow the investigators to set up video surveillance equipment in the apartment and leave behind $20,000 and fake drugs. Upon the officer's return to the station house at the end of his shift, he was caught carrying $6,000 in cash. The officer was arrested on charges of grand larceny and official misconduct.[46]

Police corruption can also be investigated by local district attorneys, state and federal prosecutors, and special investigative bodies, such as the Knapp Commission (New York City police corruption, 1970s), the Mollen Commission (New York City police corruption, 1990s), and the Christopher Commission (Los Angeles police brutality, 1991). In addition, the FBI has jurisdiction to investigate police corruption, and their investigations have had a major effect on several police departments, including the Philadelphia and the New Orleans departments.

As recently as 1998, a three-year investigation by the FBI and the Internal Revenue Service resulted in a seventy-four-page indictment and the arrest of nine current and former members of the West New York, New Jersey, Police Department and numerous others for widespread police corruption.[47]

Other Police Misconduct

Police corruption and police brutality are the most serious forms of police deviance. Police brutality will be discussed later in the chapter. Other types of police deviance also exist. Chief among them are illegal drug use and trafficking by officers, drinking and alcohol abuse, cooping, police deception, and abuse of authority.

Drug Abuse and Trafficking

The abuse of drugs has been a serious problem in U.S. society for many years. In the 1960s and 1970s, we saw the terror of the heroin epidemic, as well as the problems caused by psychedelic drugs and other drugs, especially in cities. The 1980s and 1990s brought the rock cocaine, or crack, crisis, as well as the reemergence of the heroin crisis.

The police are not immune to the problems that face the rest of society. They are also participants in, or victims of, the drug crisis. Given that illegal drug use is a problem among police officers, should police departments conduct drug testing? The use of drug testing, particularly **random drug testing** without cause, has become a major issue in the U.S. criminal justice system. Some argue that drug testing is a violation of one's constitutional rights. Many agree that an employer can insist that an employee not use drugs when he or she is working, but that because drugs remain in one's system many days after use, drug tests do not differentiate between on-duty and off-duty use.

In an article in the *FBI Law Enforcement Bulletin,* Jeffrey Higginbotham cited numerous reasons supporting urinalysis drug testing programs for law enforcement officers: (1) to maintain public safety, (2) to maintain public trust in the police, (3) to reduce the potential for the corruption of the police, (4) to allow the presentation of credible testimony by the police, (5) to boost morale in the workplace, (6) to avoid loss of productivity, and (7) to avoid civil liability.[48]

The U.S. Supreme Court, in **National Treasury Employees Union v. Von Raab** in 1989, ruled that the random testing of U.S. Customs personnel involved in drug interdiction and/or carrying firearms was constitutional.[49] Prior to this case, police departments had tremendous problems trying to get drug testing—primarily random drug testing—accepted by police unions. In many cases, the unions fought the departments to prohibit the drug testing of officers. This case made it much easier for local government agencies to engage in drug testing of their employees.

In one year, the New York City Police Department gave drug tests to 5,174 probationary officers. (These tests are capable of discovering controlled substances, including marijuana, in a person's system.) Only eighteen tested positive for drug use—an extremely low positive rate of 0.003 percent. The New Jersey State Police also tested 2,300 of its members, and only five showed evidence of drug use—again an amazingly low positive rate of 0.002 percent.[50]

The National Institute of Justice conducted a telephone survey of thirty-three large police departments regarding measures being taken to identify officers and civilian employees using drugs. The survey found that almost all departments had written procedures to test those employees reasonably suspected of drug abuse. Of the departments surveyed, 73 percent tested applicants, and 21 percent reported that they were actively considering testing all officers. Also, 21 percent said they might offer treatment to identified violators rather than dismiss them, depending upon their personal circumstances.[51]

The International Association of Chiefs of Police (IACP) has made available to police departments a model drug testing policy. The IACP policy suggests the following:

1. Testing all applicants and recruits for drug or narcotics use.
2. Testing current employees when performance difficulties or documentation indicates they may have a potential drug problem.
3. Testing current employees when they are involved in the use of excessive force or when they suffer or cause on-duty injury.
4. Routine testing of all employees assigned to special high-risk areas, such as narcotics and vice.[52]

Drinking and Alcohol Abuse

As chapter 6 discussed, police stress and police suicide are special problems in police departments. Alcohol is generally involved in both problems.

Numerous academic studies have confirmed that alcohol abuse is a major problem in policing. Jerome Skolnick, in "A Sketch of the Policeman's Working Personality," concluded that officers drink heavily and usually drink together to avoid public criticism.[53] Danielle Hitz found that mortality rates for alcohol-related cirrhosis of the liver among the police officers studied were significantly higher than the rates for the general population.[54] W. Kroes estimated that 25 percent of all police officers have a serious alcohol dependence, and R. C. Van Raalte reported that 67 percent of a sample of police officers admitted to drinking on duty.[55]

Obviously, drinking and guns do not mix well. Therefore, police departments must be eternally vigilant in preventing alcohol abuse by officers.

Cooping

Police officers refer to the practice of sleeping, resting, or avoiding work while on duty as cooping. The coop is where the cooping occurs.

Former officer Gene Radano, in *Walking the Beat,* gives a very good description of cooping: "A coop is a shelter where cops go to sit down, grab a smoke, escape the weather or to lie down. . . . Cops move in like the proverbial camel nosing his way into the tent, and soon squatter's rights prevail."[56]

If a police officer is so inclined, it is very easy to coop. Supervisors generally must cover a very large area and are not likely to observe a police radio car at rest in the back of a school yard, by a closed factory, or in another desolate location.

Police Deception

Another form of police misconduct is police deception, which includes perjury while testifying in court and attempts to circumvent rules regarding searches and seizures of evidence.

Anyone familiar with the works of the novelist and former Los Angeles Police Department sergeant Joseph Wambaugh, particularly his classic *The Blue Knight,* is aware of the possibility that police may perjure themselves on the witness stand to secure a conviction against a defendant. In *The Blue Knight,* Wambaugh's protagonist, Police Officer Bumper Morgan, illegally entered a man's hotel room to arrest him on a warrant and then fabricated probable cause well after the event to cover his actions. In a dramatic scene in the book, after Morgan falsely testifies in court, evidence is presented to show clearly that Morgan perjured himself on the stand. The judge severely rebukes him in her chambers.[57]

Skolnick states that police deception, if it occurs, usually occurs at three stages of the police detection process: investigation, interrogation, and testimony in court. "Particularly objectionable," says Skolnick, "is the idea that a police officer would not be truthful when testifying under oath in court. However, much evidence suggests that there are 'tolerable' levels of perjury among police officers when testifying in court."[58]

Columbia University law students analyzed the effect of the landmark U.S. Supreme Court case *Mapp v. Ohio* on police practices in the seizure of narcotics.[59] This case, which was covered in depth in chapter 11, severely restricted the power of the police to make certain searches of persons or premises. The students found that before *Mapp v. Ohio,* police officers typically testified that they found narcotics hidden on the defendants' persons. After the Mapp case, police officers testified that the narcotics they found were dropped on the ground by the defendants. This became known as dropsy (from "drop-see testimony"). Prior to the Mapp case, narcotics evidence obtained from suspects by police, even when illegally seized, was admissible in court. After Mapp, this was no longer so. Hence, the researchers said, police officers began to commit perjury to circumvent the illegal seizure of evidence rule and to ensure that their testimony and the evidence would be admissible against defendants charged with narcotics possession.[60]

The FBI was involved in numerous deceptive practices during the time J. Edgar Hoover was at its head. Tony G. Poveda, in *Lawlessness and Reform: The FBI in Transition,* details the illegal conduct engaged in by the FBI. This conduct included disrupting political groups, performing illegal burglaries, maintaining secret files, and attempting to deceive the public.[61]

Abuse of Authority

The tremendous power and discretion given to the police provide numerous opportunities for the police to abuse their power or authority. In describing police deviance, Thomas Barker and David L. Carter distinguish between occupational deviance and abuse of authority. Occupational deviance, they say, is motivated by the desire for personal benefit. Abuse of authority, in contrast, occurs most often to further the organizational goals of law enforcement, including arrest, issuing tickets, and the successful conviction of suspects.[62]

Alan N. Kornblum gives us a definition of corruption of authority: "that corruption that comes from the broad discretion police have in much of their work and the tension between efficiency standards versus the activities that must ensure due process."[63] Robert D. Pursley defines corruption of authority by saying it means that the police either employ, or might be tempted to employ, certain corrupt practices, such as the violation of a person's civil rights, in an effort to be more efficient.[64]

Many people were shocked at the alleged reports of abuse of power by Los Angeles police detective Mark Fuhrman in the widely covered O.J. Simpson murder case. In addition to his self-reported acts of brutality and racism, he seemed proud to admit to numerous acts of abuse of his police authority and the violation of citizens' human and constitutional rights. Many say that the verdict of not guilty in the Simpson case, in spite of overwhelming forensic evidence to the contrary, was in reality an act of jury nullification brought about by Fuhrman's alleged actions.

★ Police Brutality

Police brutality has been defined as "the excessive or unreasonable use of force in dealing with citizens, suspects, and offenders."[65] Police violence in this country and charges of police brutality are not new.

Tradition of Police Brutality

In a classic and frequently cited article on police brutality, Albert J. Reiss, Jr., began his discussion with a 1903 quotation by a former police commissioner of New York City:

> For 3 years, there has been through the courts and the streets a dreary procession of citizens with broken heads and bruised bodies against a few of whom was violence needed to effect an arrest. Many of them had done nothing to deserve an arrest. In a majority of such cases, no complaint was made. If the victim complains, his charge is generally dismissed. The police are practically above the law.[66]

Police Captain "Clubber" Williams coined the phrase "There is more law in the end of a policeman's nightstick than in a decision of the Supreme Court."[67] Another nineteenth-century police officer recalls being told by his sergeant, "There's more religion in the end of a nightstick, than in any sermon preached to the likes of them."[68]

In the 1920s, the Wickersham Commission detailed numerous instances of police brutality, including the use of the third degree to obtain confessions.[69] For a complete discussion of the police and the third degree, see Dempsey, *Introduction to Public and Private Investigations* and Skolnick and Fyfe, *Above the Law*. The general acceptance of police brutality in the past can be seen in

Demonstrators protesting the August 1997, New York City, Abner Louima brutality case.

the landmark 1936 U.S. Supreme Court case *Brown v. Mississippi*. In this case, the deputy sheriff who administered beatings to three defendants to force them to confess to a murder actually answered the judge's inquiry at trial as to how severely a defendant had been beaten by saying, "Not too much for a negro."[70]

Police violence became a major topic for public discussion in the 1940s, when rioting by citizens provoked serious police backlash and brutality against citizens. Former Supreme Court associate justice Thurgood Marshall, then a lawyer for the National Association for the Advancement of Colored People (NAACP), referred to the Detroit police as a "Gestapo" after a 1943 race riot left thirty-four people dead.[71]

Examples of Police Brutality

Charges of police brutality have not disappeared. They were common during the civil disorders of the 1960s

YOU ARE THERE!

The Tale of New York City Police Captain Alexander "Clubber" Williams

In *The Blue Parade,* Thomas Reppetto tells the tale of the infamous New York City police captain Alexander "Clubber" Williams, a corrupt and brutal police officer at the turn of the century. When Williams was transferred to the brutal, yet money-laden, precinct that covered the Midtown area of Manhattan, he declared, "All my life I've never had anything but chuck steak, now I'm going to get me some tenderloin." His statement gave this crime-ridden area the name "The Tenderloin," which it kept for years.

Other stories Reppetto relates about Williams give us a good sense of the man and the times:

> Williams, on his first day on the job, picked a fight with the two toughest thugs in the neighborhood, clubbed them unconscious, and pitched them through the plate glass window of a saloon, bringing forth six of their buddies, who met the same fate.
>
> Even as an administrator, Williams continued to prowl the streets, making free with his club. He was brought up on charges before the Board of Commissioners on 358 occasions and fined 224 times, but he was never dismissed. Within his domain he was the absolute king. As a demonstration to reporters one day, he hung his watch on a lamppost while a number of local denizens looked on. Men had been murdered for less valuable items but the watch was still there when Clubber and party returned from a walk around the block. On another occasion he consented to referee a Madison Square Garden prizefight in full uniform with his club in hand.
>
> In 1894, in testimony before a legislative committee, he would admit to a personal fortune of $300,000 and an estate in Cos Cob complete with a private steam yacht, again demonstrating that in America a poor immigrant could rise to great wealth.

In testimony to the Lexow Committee (a committee established in 1894 by the New York state legislature to investigate reports of police corruption in New York City), it was revealed that a woman who owned a chain of houses of prostitution paid Williams $30,000 annually for protection. Owners of smaller houses of prostitution said they had paid an initial fee of $500 apiece when they opened their businesses and a fee of $25 to $50 per location thereafter. More than 600 policy shops (places where people could place illegal [off-track] bets on horse races) paid Williams $15 a month each; pool rooms contributed as much as $300; and high-class gambling joints, even more. Williams once explained to investigators that he had made his fortune through speculating on real estate in Japan. Williams died a millionaire.

Source: Adapted from Thomas Reppetto, *The Blue Parade* (New York: Free Press, 1978), pp. 49–50, 55, 56; and Luc Sante, *Low Life: Lures and Snares of Old New York* (New York: Farrar, Straus & Giroux, 1991), pp. 247–248.

---

and 1970s. As recently as 1997 and 1991, people in the United States were stunned by the use of excessive force by police officers in the Abner Louima and Rodney King cases.[72]

Recent history shows us the current public reaction to the use of force by the police against minority citizens. The shootings of African-American men by police officers were the spark that set off three riots in Miami between 1980 and 1989. The last disturbance, which occurred from January 16 to January 18, 1989, was set off by the shooting of an unarmed African-American motorcyclist by a Hispanic-American police officer; eleven citizens were wounded and thirteen buildings burned to the ground.[73] The 1992 Los Angeles riots, perhaps the most severe civil disturbance in U.S. history, came on the heels of not-guilty verdicts in the trials of the four LAPD officers accused of assaulting Rodney King.

Police brutality seems as intractable in policing as corruption is. Consider just a few examples. In 1979, the U.S. Department of Justice filed an unprecedented civil rights suit charging Philadelphia's Mayor Frank Rizzo and the Philadelphia Police Department with pervasive and systematic police brutality, as well as violations of the 1964 Civil Rights Act, federal laws, and the U.S. Constitution. This was the first time the federal government had charged an entire police department with indiscriminate brutality rather than proceeding against specific officers. The government reported, "The conditions we're addressing seem institutionalized, and putting away individual officers doesn't solve the problem."[74] The suit also said that the Philadelphia Police Department followed "procedures which result in widespread, arbitrary, and unreasonable physical abuse or abuse which shocks the conscience."[75] The

Dempsey's Law

When It's Over, It's Over

Professor Dempsey, did you see that tape from Los Angeles [the 1991 Rodney King incident]?

Tony, I had no choice to avoid it. It must have been shown every hour on television.

Well, what did you think?

It was disgusting! I think it set police work and relationships with the community back decades, if not centuries!

Yeah, but my friend said that the guy might have been resisting, and the police should have continued to hit him until he stopped moving. When is police physical force considered excessive force?

Look, Tony, sometimes police work is a contact sport. Sometimes you have to roll around in the mud. But like any contact sport, when it's over, it's over. You don't hit your opponent after the bell or after the ref blows the play dead. Do you know what I mean?

Yeah.

Was it over?

Yeah, it was.

That was excessive force, Tony.

---

suit also accused the department of "inflicting disproportionate abuse on black persons and persons of Hispanic origin."[76]

In 1986, a ranking officer and officers from the 106th Precinct in New York City were convicted of torturing an accused drug dealer with an electronic stun gun. This caused an enormous shake-up in the command structure of the NYPD, including transfer of each supervisor assigned to the precinct.

In 1989, Don Jackson, an African-American police officer from a neighboring town, began a ride through the streets of Long Beach, California, secretly accompanied by an NBC camera crew. In less than three minutes, Jackson's car was pulled over. He was verbally abused by a Long Beach police officer, his head was pushed through a plate glass window, and then his head was pounded on the trunk of a police car.[77]

Why do cases of police brutality dominate the headlines for weeks at a time? Is police violence against citizens that pervasive? Or does police brutality receive so much attention because it is so repugnant to our concept of "order under law"?

Is Brutality Really the Problem?

Despite the high incidence of headlines about police brutality, evidence suggests that the verbal abuse of citizens by officers is a more serious problem. The President's Commission on Law Enforcement and Administration of Justice reported,

> The commission believes that physical abuse is not as serious a problem as it was in the past. . . . Most persons, including civil rights leaders, believe that verbal abuse and harassment, not excessive use of force is the major police community relations problem today.[78]

Albert J. Reiss, Jr., of Yale University, conducted a classic study of police abuse. For several weeks, thirty-six observers (college students with backgrounds in law, police administration, and social science) rode in patrol cars in high-crime areas of Boston, Chicago, and Washington, D.C. The observers recorded and reported the outcomes of 5,360 interactions between the police and citizens.[79]

Of the 5,360 encounters between police and citizens, Reiss found only twenty-seven cases in which the police were observed using force improperly. He found that police verbal abuse toward citizens was far more common than the use of excessive force. Police behavior was observed to be uncivil toward 13 percent of all citizens with whom the police interacted.

The study found that the most common complaints of citizens against police, in order of frequency, were as follows:

1. Use of profane and abusive language.
2. Use of commands to move on or get home.

3. Stopping and questioning people on the street or searching them and their cars.
4. Use of threats to use force if not obeyed.
5. Prodding with a nightstick or approaching with a pistol.
6. Actual use of physical force or violence itself.

Reiss found that in cases in which offenders were taken into custody, the factors leading to the unnecessary use of force by police were the citizens' social class and behavior (deferring to versus defying the authority of the police). About half of the cases of unnecessary force involved people's openly defying police authority. Reiss found that the police were more likely to use excessive force against suspects and citizens when the police considered it necessary to clarify who was in charge and when the police were harassing drunks, members of the gay community, and narcotics users.

Although three-fourths of the white police officers in the Reiss study were observed making prejudicial statements about African-American citizens, they did not actually treat African-Americans any more uncivilly than they treated whites. Furthermore, there was no evidence of racial discrimination against African-Americans in cases where the police unnecessarily assaulted citizens.

In more than half of the instances of excessive force, officers who were present but not party to the violence did not restrain or report their fellow officers.

Reiss emphasizes that what the citizens he studied found especially disturbing was the status degradation aspect of police behavior. They felt they had not been treated with the full rights and dignity due to citizens in a democratic society.

Paul Chevigny notes that police abuses often stem from the traditions of police work and from the expectations of the police when confronting citizens. The police expect deference to, or at least acceptance of, their authority. Behavior that is inconsistent with the officers' expectations—ranging from a show of disrespect to outright resistance—usually brings a strong physical reaction by officers.[80]

To make citizens aware of the police reaction to conduct challenging their authority (as discovered by Reiss and Chevigny), Peter Scharf and Arnold Binder suggested "a community education program informing citizens about police expectations and about typical police responses to citizen threats. . . . [so] that citizens might communicate with police officers to avoid violent confrontations."[81] Also, as communication is a two-way street, police need to consider the appropriateness of their expectations of deference from citizens.

In a research study, David Bayley and James Garofalo observed 350 eight-hour tours in three precincts in New York City. They discovered that incidents of violence between police officers and citizens are relatively rare, even in a large urban area such as New York City. Of 467 potentially violent incidents they encountered, only 78 resulted in some type of actual conflict. Of these, in only 42 encounters was force used by the police against citizens or by citizens against the police. The force used by police consisted almost exclusively of grabbing and restraining; firearms were never used.[82]

Findings similar to these emerged from the questioning of citizens in fifteen cities about police misconduct for the National Commission on Civil Disorders. Gerald D. Robin and Richard H. Anson say, "Police incivility (verbal disrespect) rather than police brutality (physical abuse) is the salient issue in the public's criticism of the police."[83]

Also, the 1997 National Criminal Victimization Survey conducted by the Bureau of Justice Statistics revealed that less than 1 percent of the persons who reported a contact with the police during the prior reporting period said the police had used or threatened to use physical force on them. If force was used, respondents said it was usually because they provoked the officers.[84]

Police Department Responses to Police Brutality

Police departments respond to the problem of excessive force by the police with a variety of solutions. Carl B. Klockars tells us that the leading proposed solutions to police brutality are improved training, better screening of applicants, citizen review, more aggressive internal affairs investigations, increased discipline, closer press scrutiny, community policing, clearer policy, tighter rules, and stronger leadership.[85]

Police departments have several responses to documented cases of police brutality. Sometimes they arrest, suspend, or terminate the officer. In the 1991 Rodney King incident and the 1997 Abner Louima case, the officers were arrested and immediately suspended. The officers in the 106th Precinct stun gun case were all arrested, suspended from duty without pay, and eventually convicted. After conviction, they were terminated from the department.

YOU ARE THERE!

LAPD Reform in the Wake of the Rodney King Incident

In July 1991, several months after the beating of Rodney King by four Los Angeles police officers, the ten-member Christopher Commission, established to investigate the LAPD, made the following recommendations:

First, LAPD officials "must send a much clearer and more effective message" that excessive force will not be tolerated and that officers and their supervisors "be evaluated to an important extent by how well they abide by and advance" the police department's policy on the use of force.

Second, the police chief must see "tangible ways, for example, through the use of the discipline system," to show officers that racism and bias based on ethnicity, gender, or sexual orientation will not be tolerated. Minority and female applicants must be given "full and equal opportunity to assume leadership positions" in the LAPD.

Third, the department should embrace a community policing model—a shift in philosophy that will require "a fundamental change in values."

Fourth, officers should be retested regularly to determine psychological and physical problems that could lead to loss of control of their behavior.

Fifth, officers and supervisors should be rotated through various divisions to "ensure that officers work in a wide range of police functions and varied patrol locations during their careers." Such a program will increase officers' experience and allow more diversified patrols to be deployed.

Sixth, "a major overhaul" of the disciplinary system is necessary. The police commission should oversee the disciplinary process and participate in the processing and punishment of the most serious cases and should be responsible for overseeing the complaint intake process. The Internal Affairs Division, rather than the division of the involved officer, should investigate all excessive force complaints. The commission should set guidelines for discipline and hold the chief of police responsible for following them.

Finally, the police chief should serve a five-year term, renewable for one additional five-year term at the discretion of the police commission. The police commission should have the authority to terminate the chief prior to the expiration of the term, but the final decision must be approved by the mayor and a two-thirds vote of the city council.

Source: Adapted from "Recipe for Reform of the LAPD," *Law Enforcement News*, July/August 1991, p. 12.

Samuel Walker reports that some police departments take more proactive action to prevent officer–citizen violence, such as instituting specialized training programs to reduce brutality and amending and adding detailed rules of engagement limiting force in police and citizen encounters. Walker points out, however, that these rules usually are a reaction to a crisis situation in the department rather than a systematic effort to improve police-citizen interactions.[86]

A good example of rules made in response to a crisis situation is the response to the 1984 Bumpers case in New York City. An emotionally disturbed person, Eleanor Bumpers, while being evicted from a city housing project, attempted to stab one of the officers and was subsequently killed by an Emergency Services officer using a shotgun. The shooting caused serious disturbances in the minority community in the Bronx. The officer who fired the weapon was subsequently arrested by the Bronx district attorney for criminally negligent homicide but was later found not guilty at trial. In the wake of the shooting and the demonstrations, Police Commissioner Benjamin Ward changed department procedures regarding the police response to emotionally disturbed persons calls. The new rules called for the elimination of shotguns being carried in these cases by members of the Emergency Services Division and also mandated that a captain must respond to all such cases as the primary decision maker.

Some say that improved hiring practices can cause a reduction of police brutality. The U.S. Commission on Civil Rights, after field investigations and public hearings in Philadelphia and Houston, emphasized the importance of hiring more members of racial minority groups and upgrading their positions in police departments. The commission cited the study of the National Minority Advisory Council on Criminal Justice: "Central to the problem of brutality is the underrepresentation of minorities as police officers. . . . It has been shown that the presence of minority police officers has a positive effect on police-community relations."[87]

Citizen Oversight

Another important innovation suggested to reduce police brutality is **citizen oversight**, the process by which citizens (nonpolice) appointed by government executives review allegations of brutality or abuse by police officers. Generally, these boards have no power to discipline offending officers but can make recommendations to police officials. Many local governments have created citizen complaint review boards (CCRBs) to investigate alleged cases of police brutality. Citizen complaint review boards existed in the 1950s and early 1960s but became most popular after the civil disturbances of the 1960s and 1970s, primarily in areas where minorities believed that police were discriminating against them. CCRBs were bitterly opposed by some members of the police, and most either lasted only a short time or were not very powerful.[88]

Wayne Kerstetter has identified three different types of citizen complaint review boards based on the extent of citizen involvement. First, the citizen review model agency is outside of and independent from the police department and has the authority to receive and investigate complaints and to recommend discipline. Second, the citizen input model agency employs nonsworn police personnel to receive and investigate complaints, but the power to recommend discipline remains with sworn police officials. Finally, the citizen monitor model agency is part of the police department, and the agency receives, investigates, and adjudicates complaints. However, an independent citizen board serves as a check or safeguard over the process.[89]

In the 1980s, thirty cities established new citizen oversight agencies. Staff members from these agencies formed their own professional organization, the International Association for Citizen Oversight of Law Enforcement (IACOLE). By 1990, the police departments in half of the fifty largest U.S. cities had some form of mechanism for citizen oversight of police conduct.[90]

Citizen complaint review boards created to hear complaints against police have not always been successful. The Civil Rights Commission found the following about CCRBs: "Their basic flaws were that they were advisory only, having no power to decide cases or impose punishment, and that they lacked sufficient staffs and resources." The commission recommended that although disciplinary action must remain with the police department, there must be some outside review to assist the complaining citizen who is unsatisfied with the police department's finding.[91]

Despite calls for citizen complaint review boards to investigate allegations of police misconduct, some communities are not entirely comfortable with these boards. In 1991, the residents of Miami, Florida, defeated a resolution that would have given subpoena powers to citizen review boards. One proponent of this resolution—an attorney for the currently inactive Overtown Independent Review Panel, which was established in the wake of the 1989 Miami riots—complained, "If we can't even get an officer to come in and say what happened, then you don't have a real investigation." The president of the Miami Fraternal Order of Police, however, stated that the granting of subpoena powers to citizen boards would have given rise to "perceptions that someone had to be the fall-guy, and needless to say, it was going to end up being a policeman."[92]

Terry Hensley, chief of staff inspections for the St. Petersburg (Florida) Police Department, reports that law enforcement is generally opposed to the idea of citizen review, whereas community and civil liberty organizations are generally in support of it. In his review of the current literature regarding citizen review, Hensley lists the following pros and cons of the process.

In favor of citizen review, Hensley cites the following:

- There is a lack of communication and trust between the law enforcement and minority group communities.
- The lack of trust between law enforcement and minorities is accentuated by the belief that law enforcement agencies fail to discipline their own employees who are guilty of misconduct.
- Citizen review would theoretically provide an independent evaluation of citizen complaints.
- Citizen review would ensure that justice is done and actual misconduct is punished.
- Citizen review would improve public trust in law enforcement.[93]

Against citizen review, Hensley writes the following:

- Citizen complaint review boards ignore other legal resources that citizens have for registering complaints (for example, state's attorneys' offices, the federal EOC, civil suits, FBI civil rights investigations, and so forth).
- Citizens cannot understand the operations of law enforcement agencies and the laws, ordinances, and procedures that law enforcement officers must enforce.

YOU ARE THERE!

The Controversy over the "Lindsay" CCRB

The story of the creation of the first civilian-dominated New York City Civilian Complaint Review Board shows the many problems involved in the creation of civilian oversight boards to hear complaints against the police. To fulfill a campaign pledge to change the police department's methods of handling citizen complaints, newly elected New York City mayor John V. Lindsay, in July 1966, created a new citizen complaint review board (CCRB) to replace the former CCRB, which had been staffed entirely by uniformed police officials. The newly created "Lindsay" CCRB consisted of seven members. Four of the members were salaried civilians who had no experience with the police. The other three were members of the department who held the civilian title of deputy police commissioner; two of them had never been police officers. Thus, the Lindsay CCRB was nonpolice dominated.

If the CCRB could not settle a dispute informally, a closed hearing was held by the board; the hearing would result in either the officer's being exonerated or a recommendation to the police commissioner that charges be brought against the officer at a departmental trial.

During its four months of operation, the Lindsay CCRB received 442 complaints, many of which originated from police officers' order maintenance role in domestic disturbances. The number of cases processed by the board in this period was more than twice the number previously reported annually to the department's internal review board. A bare majority of the complaints—51 percent—were from nonwhites, and the most common allegation was the use of unnecessary force. Of the 170 cases disposed of before the board's demise, 55 cases were settled through conciliation, 110 complaints were found not substantiated and were dismissed, and 5 cases were forwarded to the police commissioner for action.

From the outset, New York City police officers, the officers' union, the Patrolman's Benevolent Association (PBA), and the incumbent police commissioner were adamantly opposed to the CCRB and were determined to have it abolished. Accordingly, the PBA brought the CCRB issue to a head in a public referendum on November 8, 1966. In a blistering campaign against the CCRB that many say had racial overtones and exploited the public's fear of crime, the police urged people to vote for the board's elimination. In the referendum, just four months after the board began operating, the public voted to abolish the Lindsay CCRB by an overwhelming two-to-one margin.

- Citizen review boards have a destructive effect upon internal morale.
- Citizen review boards invite abdication of authority by supervisors and management.
- Citizen review boards weaken the ability of upper-level management to achieve conformity through discipline.
- Creating citizen review boards is tantamount to admitting that the police cannot police themselves.[94]

Despite their problems, however, many still favor CCRBs. As Albert J. Reiss, Jr., wrote, "Greater citizen involvement in police administration is one community response to police corruption and citizen review boards may have merit, despite the negative sentiments of some police chiefs."[95]

In a 1997 report, Samuel Walker and Eileen Luna were highly critical of police oversight in Albuquerque, New Mexico. They stated that the oversight mechanisms were ineffective and in some cases, actually served to aggravate tension between residents and the Albuquerque P.D.[96]

In 1997, in Tucson, Arizona, officials approved a plan that provided a double layer of oversight for their police department, with the establishment of a ten-member Citizen Police Advisory Review Board, as well as an independent auditor to monitor the investigation of complaints against officers.[97]

Chapter Summary

Police deviance, which has a long tradition in U.S. police departments, appears to be intractable. This chapter discussed the many forms of police deviance, including corruption, drug and alcohol abuse, cooping, police deception, abuse of authority, verbal abuse of citizens, and police brutality.

The chapter detailed examples of police corruption, types and forms of corruption, reasons for police corruption, and responses to police corruption. It also discussed the tradition of police brutality, gave some recent examples of police brutality and police abuse, and talked about responses to police brutality (including citizen oversight).

The extremely serious problems that this chapter discussed tarnish the image of police departments and all police officers. Stories of police deviance sell newspapers. When a police officer or a group of officers commits deviant acts, they occupy the front pages of newspapers for weeks.

The temptations leading to corrupt and brutal acts by police officers are tremendous. However, not all police officers commit deviant acts. In fact, a very minor percentage of police officers are brutal or corrupt. It would be nice if we could eliminate all police deviance. Unfortunately, however, we recruit our police from the human race, so we will always have some bad police officers along with the many excellent ones. Police departments must do all that is necessary to prevent police deviance. Also, honest police officers must bring to light the actions of the few deviant police officers in their midst to keep the profession as honest as possible. Policing can then become a better and easier profession.

Learning Check

1. Define police corruption. Identify some of the forms it takes.
2. Explain why some police officers become corrupt.
3. Discuss whether something about police work makes police corruption and other police deviance intractable.
4. Define police brutality. Identify some of the forms it takes.
5. Identify and discuss forms of police deviance other than corruption and brutality.

Review Exercise

Because of your experience in taking this course, you have been appointed assistant to the police commissioner of Anyburgh, USA. Anyburgh has had a ten-year tradition of numerous brutality and corruption complaints against its officers. The commissioner requests your advice regarding the effects of these allegations on the integrity and effectiveness of the department, as well as methods he can take to reduce them.

Web Exercise

Patrol the web and find a few police departments or police associations that report their "mission statement" on their web pages. Do they mention ethics? What do they say about ethics?

Key Concepts

Knapp Commission
judicial review
Frank Serpico
internal affairs division (IAD or IA)
proactive investigation
integrity test
random drug testing
National Treasury Employees Union v. Von Raab (1989)
citizen oversight

Notes

1. James N. Gilbert, "Investigative Ethics," in Michael J. Palmiotto, ed., *Critical Issues in Criminal Investigations,* 2nd ed. (Cincinnati, OH: Anderson, 1988), pp. 7–14. This article is also contained in its entirety in John S. Dempsey, *An Introduction to Public and Private Investigations* (Minneapolis/St. Paul: West, 1996), pp. 376–380.
2. Gilbert, "Investigative Ethics," p. 14.
3. See: Joycelyn M. Pollock, *Ethics in Crime and Justice: Dilemmas and Decisions,* 3rd ed. (Belmont, Calif.: West/Wadsworth, 1993); Victor Kappeler, Richard Sluder, and Geoffrey Alpert, *Forces of Deviance, Understanding the Dark Side of Policing* (Prospect Heights, Ill.: Waveland Press, 1994); Jerome H. Skolnick and James J. Fyfe, *Above the Law: Police and the Excessive Use of Force* (New York: Free Press, 1993); Thomas Barker and David L. Carter, *Police Deviance* (Cincinnati, Ohio: Anderson, 1986); S. Bok, *Lying: Moral Choice in Public and Private Life* (New York: Pantheon, 1978); Frederick A. Elliston and Michael Feldberg, eds., *Moral Issues in Police Work* (Totowa, N.J.: Rowman and Allanheld, 1985); W. Heffernan and T. Stroup, eds., *Police Ethics: Hard Choices in Law Enforcement* (New York: John Jay Press, 1985); and Carl B. Klockars, "The Dirty Harry Problem," *Annals of the American Association of Political and Social Science* 452 (November 1980), pp. 33–37.
4. Aristotle, *Nicomachean Ethics* 1094(a): 1–22.
5. Pollock, *Ethics in Crime and Justice,* pp. 140–141.
6. Pollock, *Ethics in Crime and Justice,* p. 149.
7. Kathleen Maguire and Ann L. Pastore, eds., *Sourcebook of Criminal Justice Statistics—1995* (Washington, D.C.: National Institute of Justice, 1996), Table 2.16, p. 138.
8. Jerome Skolnick, *Justice without Trial: Law Enforcement in a Democratic Society,* 2d ed. (New York: Wiley, 1975).
9. Howard Abadinski, *Crime and Justice: An Introduction* (Chicago: Nelson Hall, 1987), p. 169.
10. Elmer Johnson, "Police: An Analysis of Role Conflict," (Paper presented at a symposium on criminology, Indiana State University at Terre Haute, 24 July 1969), as cited in Abadinsky, *Crime and Justice,* p. 169.

11. National Commission on Law Observance and Enforcement, *Report on Police* (Washington, D.C.: U.S. Government Printing Office, 1931); President's Commission on Law Enforcement and Administration of Justice, *The Challenge of Crime in a Free Society* (Washington, D.C.: U.S. Government Printing Office, 1968); National Advisory Commission on Criminal Justice Standards and Goals, *Police* (Washington, D.C.: U.S. Government Printing Office, 1973); and Standards for Law Enforcement Agencies, 2d ed. (Fairfax, Va.: Commission on Accreditation for Law Enforcement Agencies, 1987).
12. Knapp Commission, *Report on Police Corruption* (New York: Braziller, 1973).
13. Herman Goldstein, *Police Corruption: A Perspective on Its Nature and Control* (Washington, D.C.: The Police Foundation, 1975), p. 3.
14. Elliston and Feldberg, eds., *Moral Issues in Police Work*.
15. Richard J. Lundman, "Police Misconduct," in *The Ambivalent Force: Perspectives on the Police*, 3d ed., ed. Abraham S. Blumberg and Elaine Niederhoffer (New York: Holt, Rinehart & Winston, 1985), p. 158.
16. Michael Feldberg, "Gratuities, Corruption and the Democratic Ethos of Policing: The Case of the Free Cup of Coffee," in *Moral Issues in Police Work*, ed. Elliston and Feldberg, p. 21.
17. Goldstein, *Police Corruption*, p. 29.
18. Peter Maas, *Serpico* (New York: Bantam Books, 1974).
19. Robert Daley, *Prince of the City: The Story of a Cop Who Knew Too Much* (Boston: Houghton Mifflin, 1978).
20. Mike McAlary, *Buddy Boys: When Good Cops Turn Bad* (New York: Putnam, 1987).
21. John Dorschner, "The Dark Side of Force," in *Critical Issues in Policing: Contemporary Readings*, ed. Roger G. Dunham and Geoffrey P. Alpert (Prospect Heights, Ill.: Waveland Press, 1989), pp. 250–270.
22. Selwyn Raab, "Ex-Rogue Officer Tells Panel of Police Graft in New York," *New York Times*, 28 September 1993, pp. A1, B3.
23. "On the Side of the Law? Not Necessarily," *Law Enforcement News*, 31 December 1996, p. 19.
24. "On the Side of the Law? "
25. "Hart Broken in Detroit: Embezzlement Conviction Topples Veteran Chief," *Law Enforcement News*, 15 May 1992, p. 6.
26. "On the Side of the Law?"
27. "FBI Agent Who Spied Is Sentenced to 27 Years," *New York Times*, 24 June 1997, p. A-14; Evan Thomas, "Inside the Mind of a Spy," *Newsweek*, 7 July 1997, p. 35.
28. "FBI Leader in Gambino Case Is Indicted," *New York Times*, 27 June 1997, p. B-3. Also see Selwyn Raab, "Arrest of an Agent Threatens to Taint a Major Mob Case," *New York Times*, 14 June 1997, pp. A-1, 26.
29. Kappeler, Sluder, and Alpert, *Forces of Deviance, Understanding the Dark Side of Policing,* and Skolnick and Fyfe, *Above the Law*.
30. Lawrence W. Sherman, ed., *Police Corruption: A Sociological Perspective* (Garden City, N.Y.: Doubleday, 1974), p. 1.
31. Herman Goldstein, *Policing a Free Society* (Cambridge, Mass.: Ballinger Publishing, 1977), p. 218.
32. Frank Schmalleger, *Criminal Justice Today: An Introductory Text for the Twenty-first Century* (Englewood Cliffs, N.J.: Prentice-Hall, 1991), p. 191.
33. Samuel Walker, *The Police in America: An Introduction*, 2d ed. (New York: McGraw-Hill, 1992), pp. 175–177.
34. Thomas Barker and Julian Roebuck, *An Empirical Typology of Police Corruption: A Study in Organizational Deviance* (Springfield, Ill.: Charles C. Thomas, 1973), pp. 26–27.
35. Sherman, *Police Corruption*, p. 7.
36. Patrick V. Murphy and Thomas Plate, *Commissioner: A View from the Top of American Law Enforcement* (New York: Simon and Schuster, 1977).
37. Sherman, *Police Corruption*.
38. Lawrence W. Sherman, "Becoming Bent: Moral Careers of Corrupt Policemen," in *Police Corruption*, ed. Lawrence W. Sherman, pp. 191–208.
39. President's Commission on Law Enforcement and Administration of Justice, *Task Force Report: The Police* (Washington, D.C.: U.S. Government Printing Office, 1967), p. 208.
40. David Burnham, "How Police Corruption Is Built into the System—And a Few Ideas for What to Do About It," in *Police Corruption*, ed. Lawrence W. Sherman, pp. 310–311.
41. Edwin H. Sutherland and Donald Cressey, *Principles of Criminology*, 8th ed. (Philadelphia: Lippincott, 1970).
42. Schmalleger, *Criminal Justice Today*, p. 193.
43. National Commission on Law Observance and Enforcement, *Report on Police*.
44. James Q. Wilson, *Varieties of Police Behavior: The Management of Law and Order in Eight Communities* (Cambridge, Mass.: Harvard University Press, 1968).
45. Goldstein, *Police Corruption*, pp. 6–8.
46. "Police Officer Accused of Stealing $6,000," *New York Times*, 28 June 1997, p. 24; Rocco Parascandola, "Wash. Hts. Sting Bags 'Rogue Cop'," *New York Post*, 28 June 1997, p. 9.
47. David M. Herszenhorn, "Police in West New York Arrested in Bribery Inquiry; 9 Current and Former Officers are Charged," *New York Times*, 14 January 1998, p. B-5.
48. Jeffrey Higginbotham, "Urinalysis Drug Testing Programs for Law Enforcement," *FBI Law Enforcement Bulletin*, October 1986.

49. *National Treasury Employees Union v. Von Raab,* 489 U.S. 656 (1989).
50. Ordway Burden, "Police and Drug Abuse: What's All the Hullabaloo?" *Crime Control Digest,* 15 June 1987.
51. *Employee Drug Testing Policies in Police Departments* (Washington, D.C.: National Institute of Justice, 1986).
52. *Employee Drug Testing Policies.*
53. Skolnick, *Justice without Trial,* pp. 42–49.
54. Danielle Hitz, "Drunken Sailors and Others: Drinking Problems in Specific Occupations," *Quarterly Journal of Studies on Alcohol* 34 (1973): 496–505.
55. W. Kroes, *Society's Victim, The Policeman: An Analysis of Job Stress in Policing* (Springfield, Ill.: Charles C. Thomas, 1976); and R. C. Van Raalte, "Alcohol as a Problem among Officers," *Police Chief* 44, pp. 38–40.
56. Gene Radano, *Walking the Beat: A New York Policeman Tells What It's Like on His Side of the Law* (Cleveland: World Publishing, 1968), p. 13.
57. Joseph Wambaugh, *The Blue Knight* (Boston: Little, Brown, 1973).
58. Jerome H. Skolnick, "Deception by Police," in *Moral Issues in Police Work,* ed. Elliston and Feldberg, pp. 76–77.
59. *Mapp v. Ohio,* 367 U.S. 643 (1961).
60. Skolnick, "Deception by Police," pp. 76–77.
61. Tony G. Poveda, *Lawlessness and Reform: The FBI in Transition* (Pacific Grove, Calif.: Brooks/Cole, 1990), especially chapters 4 and 5; see also, Tony G. Poveda, "The Effects of Scandal on Organizational Deviance: The Case of the FBI," *Justice Quarterly* 2 (1985): 237–258. Note: There are a myriad of books regarding the history of the FBI, some reflecting views differing from Poveda's.
62. Barker and Carter, *Police Deviance.*
63. Alan N. Kornblum, *The Moral Hazards* (Lexington, Mass: Lexington Books, 1976), p. 6.
64. Robert D. Pursley, *Introduction to Criminal Justice,* 5th ed. (New York: Macmillan, 1991), p. 236.
65. Gerald D. Robin and Richard H. Anson, *Introduction to the Criminal Justice System,* 4th ed. (New York: Harper & Row, 1988), p. 86.
66. Albert J. Reiss, Jr., "Police Brutality," *Transaction Magazine* 5 (1968), reprinted in Richard J. Lundman, ed., *Police Behavior: A Sociological Perspective* (New York: Oxford University Press, 1980), pp. 274–275.
67. Luc Sante, *Low Life: Lures and Snares of Old New York* (New York: Farrar, Straus & Giroux, 1991), p. 247.
68. Sante, *Low Life,* p. 243.
69. Joseph P. Senna and Larry J. Siegel, *Introduction to Criminal Justice,* 5th ed. (St. Paul: West, 1990), p. 265.
70. *Brown v. Mississippi,* 297 U.S. 278 (1936).
71. Samuel Walker, *Popular Justice* (New York: Oxford University Press, 1980), p. 197.
72. For an excellent analysis of the Rodney King incident and the history and tradition of police brutality, see Skolnick and Fyfe, *Above the Law.*
73. George Hackett et al., "All of Us Are in Trouble," *Newsweek,* 30 January 1989, pp. 36–37.
74. *U.S. News and World Report,* 27 August 1979, p. 27.
75. *U.S. News and World Report,* p. 27.
76. *Time,* 27 August 1979, p. 27.
77. Bill Girdner, "Charges of Racism by Calif. Police Is Latest in Long Line," *Boston Globe,* 19 January 1989, p. 3.
78. President's Commission on Law Enforcement and Administration of Justice, *Task Force Report: The Police,* pp. 181–182.
79. Albert J. Reiss, Jr., *The Police and the Public* (New Haven, Conn.: Yale University Press, 1972).
80. Paul Chevigny, *Police Power: Police Abuses in New York City* (New York: Pantheon, 1969).
81. Peter Scharf and Arnold Binder, *The Badge and the Bullet: Police Use of Deadly Force* (New York: Praeger, 1983), p. 135.
82. David Bayley and James Garofalo, "The Management of Violence by Police Patrol Officers," *Criminology* 27 (1989): 1–27.
83. Robin and Anson, *Introduction to the Criminal Justice System,* p. 86.
84. "Police Abuse Rare, Study Says," *New York Times,* 23 November 1997, p. 29.
85. Carl B. Klockars, "The Only Way to Make Any Real Progress in Controlling Excessive Force by Police," *Law Enforcement News,* 15 May 1992, p. 12.
86. Samuel Walker, "The Rule Revolution: Reflections on the Transformation of American Criminal Justice, 1950–1988" (Working Papers, series 3, Institute for Legal Studies, University of Wisconsin Law School, Madison, December 1988), reprinted in Senna and Siegel, *Introduction to Criminal Justice,* p. 267.
87. National Minority Advisory Council on Criminal Justice, *The Inequality of Justice: A Report on Crime and the Administration of Justice in the Minority Community* (Washington, D.C.: U.S. Government Printing Office, 1980), pp. 15–16.
88. Gerald W. Lynch and Edward Diamond, "Police Misconduct," in *Encyclopedia of Crime and Justice,* vol. 3, ed. Sanford H. Kadish (New York: Free Press, 1983), p. 1160.
89. Wayne Kerstetter, "Who Disciplines the Police? Who Should?" in *Police Leadership in America: Crisis and Opportunity,* ed. William A. Geller (New York: Praeger, 1985), pp. 160–161.
90. Samuel Walker and Vic Bumphus, *A National Survey of Civilian Oversight of the Police* (Omaha: University of Nebraska at Omaha, 1991).

91. U.S. Commission on Civil Rights, *Who Is Guarding the Guardians: A Report on Police Practices* (Washington, D.C.: U.S. Government Printing Office, 1981), p. 163.
92. "The Voters Speak: Miami Police Review Board Will Have to Make Do without Subpoena Powers," *Law Enforcement News*, 15 December 1991, p. 1.
93. Terry Hensley, "Civilian Reviews Boards: A Means to Police Accountability," *Police Chief,* September 1988, pp. 45–47.
94. Hensley, "Civilian Review Boards."
95. Albert J. Reiss, Jr., "Shaping and Servicing the Community: The Role of the Police Chief Executive," in *Police Leadership in America,* ed. William A. Geller, p. 61.
96. "Systems Failures: Albuquerque Police Oversight Mechanisms Blasted in Report," *Law Enforcement News*, 31 May 1997, pp. 1, 11.
97. "New Faces Look over Cops' Shoulders: Review Board, Auditor to Monitor Handling of Complaints against Tucson Cops," *Law Enforcement News,* 30 April 1997, p. 6.

13

Women and Minorities in Policing

Chapter Outline

Discrimination in Policing
 Discrimination against Women
 Discrimination against Racial and Ethnic Minorities
 Discrimination against Gay Officers
How Did Women and Minorities Achieve Equality?
 Civil Rights Act of 1964
 Equal Employment Opportunity Act of 1972
 Federal Courts and Job Discrimination
 Affirmative Action Programs
White Male Backlash

Can Women and Minorities Do the Job?
 Academic Studies of Female Officers
 Academic Studies of African-American Officers
Women and Minorities in Policing Today
 Female Representation Today
 African-American and Other Minority Representation Today
Problems Persist for Women and Minorities in Policing
 Problems for Women
 Problems for African-Americans and Other Minorities

Chapter Goals

■ To acquaint you with the history and problems of women and minorities in policing.

■ To show you how discrimination affected women and minorities in obtaining employment and promotions in policing.

■ To acquaint you with the provisions of the U.S. legal system that enabled women and minorities to overcome job discrimination.

■ To introduce you to the academic studies showing that women and African-Americans can perform police patrol duty as effectively as men.

■ To give you a sense of the problems women and minorities still face in law enforcement as we approach the twenty-first century.

Introduction

Female police officers on uniformed patrol duty are common today, as are officers who are African-American or members of other minority groups. In fact, all races and ethnic groups are represented in U.S. police departments. However, this was not always the case. Until quite recently, white males dominated the ranks.

African-Americans were traditionally excluded from U.S. police departments. As just one example among many, before 1948, African-Americans were not allowed to be members of the Atlanta Police Department.[1] A police historian notes that the underrepresentation of minorities in police departments has not been limited to southern cities. He found that every major municipal jurisdiction in the United States has a history of discriminating against minorities.[2]

Although the United States has had organized, paid police departments since the 1840s, the first female police officer was not appointed until 1905. By 1919, over sixty police departments employed female officers. However, they were given only clerical duties or duties dealing with juveniles or female prisoners. It was not until the late 1960s that women were permitted to perform the same patrol duties as men.[3]

This chapter will focus on the roles of women and minority groups in U.S. police departments. It will review their experience and the methods they used to secure the same job opportunities as white males. The chapter will also show the extent to which women and minorities have influenced today's police departments and explore the capabilities of women to perform what has traditionally been viewed as a male occupation. Finally, it will examine the status of women and minorities in U.S. law enforcement today.

Discrimination in Policing

The United States has a long history of job **discrimination** against women and minorities. Discrimination is the unequal treatment of persons in personnel decisions (hiring, promotion, and firing) on the basis of their race, religion, national origin, gender, or sexual orientation. Only in the past several decades have women and minorities been able to share the American dream of equal employment. Their treatment in police departments was not much different from their treatment in other jobs and in society in general. The federal government admitted this fact in 1974 in an affirmative action guidebook for employers: "American law guarantees all persons equal opportunity in employment. However, employment discrimination has existed in police departments for a long time. The main areas of discrimination are race/ethnic background and gender."[4]

In addition to discrimination against women and ethnic and racial minorities, police departments have had a history of discrimination in employment decisions against homosexuals. As we will see later in this chapter, much of this discrimination has disappeared.

Discrimination against Women

Women have faced an enormous uphill struggle to earn the right to wear the blue uniform and perform the same basic police duties that men have performed for years. Why were women excluded from performing regular police work?

Until the 1970s, it was presumed that women, because of their gender and typical size, were not capable of performing the same type of patrol duty as men. Additionally, other social forces discriminated against women. Gerald Carden points to several possible reasons why women were kept out of policing: men did not want to put up with the social inhibitions placed on them by the presence of women; they did not want to be overshadowed by, or to take orders from, women; and they did not want to be supported by females in the performance of potentially dangerous work.[5] Other possible reasons for discrimination against women certainly existed. One former police commissioner stated the following:

> In the case of women joining the police force, as in so many other cases, heated controversy exists. However, controversy doesn't always reveal the true sentiments of the combatants. For example, many cops' wives object to women in the ranks for the ostensible reason of safety. The truth probably lies in their apprehension that cops may fall in love with their partners and the introduction of sex into the equation is bound to prove intolerable. What was labeled safety might have been concealing well-founded reasons for jealousy.[6]

Prior to 1967, women constituted only a very small percentage of U.S. police officers. The early female officers were restricted to issuing parking tickets or performing routine clerical tasks. Additionally, in the early days of female policing, women were normally used in only three actual police-related jobs: vice, juvenile work, and guarding female prisoners.[7] Catherine Milton, writing in 1972, found that female officers were

YOU ARE THERE!

The History of Women in the NYPD

In 1924, the Bureau of Policewomen was established in the New York City Police Department with Mary Hamilton named as its director. (Female officers were called policewomen, and male officers were patrolmen.) In 1938, the first test for appointment to the rank of policewoman was given. In 1959, policewomen were first used on foot patrol in Midtown Manhattan.

The real rise of women into the NYPD rank structure, and the impetus for the eventual unification of policewoman and patrolman ranks into the rank of police officer, began in 1961. An NYPD policewoman, Felicia Shpritzer, filed a lawsuit to achieve the right to take a promotional exam to the rank of sergeant. The city had always maintained that policewomen were not part of the civil service career path from patrolman to captain. In April 1964, the city gave a promotional examination to the rank of sergeant, and because of Shpritzer's lawsuit, women were given the right to take a makeup examination for that rank on March 12, 1965. Shpritzer and another policewoman, Gertrude Schimmel, successfully passed the examination and became the first women in NYPD history to hold the rank of police sergeant. In December 1967, Shpritzer and Schimmel successfully passed the promotional examination to the rank of lieutenant. In December 1971, Schimmel became the first female police captain in New York City's history.

In June 1972, a pilot project was established in three New York City police precincts using policewomen on regular uniformed patrol, acting in the same capacity as patrolmen. In 1973, the title of all New York City policewomen was changed to police officers; the ranks of patrolman and policewoman were replaced with the unisex rank of police officer.

In 1973 and 1974, the female ranks in the NYPD began to swell. Nearly 20 percent of the incoming police academy classes were women, due to the creation of the first unisex police examination and the settlement of numerous court cases. The future for women in the NYPD was promising, and many of the women were preparing for promotional examinations. In 1975, however, the city of New York, immersed in a financial crisis, was forced to terminate nearly 5,000 police officers. Because of civil service rules, the officers were laid off in reverse seniority, and the jobs of the newest 5,000 officers were terminated. This group included a significant number of women and minorities. Within a few years, many of the laid-off officers were rehired. Some, however, including many women, elected not to return because they had found new careers or started families. It was not until 1980 that the city again hired new police officers. In December 1976, for the first time, a New York City police precinct—the First Precinct, which covers Lower Manhattan, including the Wall Street area—was commanded by a woman, Captain Victoria Renzullo.

The gains of women have not been without their losses. On February 12, 1980, Mary Bembry became the first female officer to be shot in the line of duty. A few years later, Irma Losado, a New York City Transit Police officer, became the first female officer in New York City to be killed in the line of duty; she was attempting to subdue a robbery suspect.

---

used mainly as secretaries and dispatchers, and they were rarely afforded equal status with men.[8]

In the late 1960s and early 1970s, the role of women in the U.S. police departments began to change. Samuel Walker states that one of the possible causes for this change could have been the suggestion by the President's Commission on Law Enforcement and Administration of Justice that the greater use of female officers could help solve the police personnel crisis discovered by the commission. Walker also attributes the change to the woman's rights movement and to the efforts by female officers themselves to gain the right to perform patrol duty in order to achieve equality with male officers.[9]

Even as late as the mid-1970s, however, Timothy Egan writes, women were often still allowed to work only with juvenile offenders. In many cities (Chicago for one), female officers could not ride in patrol cars after dark.[10]

For an excellent look at the history of women in U.S. police departments and their transition and evolution from quasi-social workers to fully qualified police officers, see former police captain, and now professor, Dorothy Moses Schultz's excellent 1995 book, *From Social Worker to Crime Fighter: Women in United States Municipal Policing*.[11]

Today, police departments are very diverse in terms of race, ethnicity, and gender, as this scene of police roll call training shows. This was not always the case.

Discrimination against Racial and Ethnic Minorities

Members of racial and ethnic minority groups, like women, have experienced entry-level discrimination in police jobs. This section will focus on the history of African-Americans in U.S. policing and then discuss the dawning of the awareness of discrimination against all minorities in U.S. police departments.

Discrimination against African-Americans The first African-American police officer was appointed to the Chicago Police Department in 1872. In 1886, another African-American man was appointed to the Washington, D.C., Police Department. By 1890, there were approximately 2,000 African-American police officers in the United States, mostly employed by large cities. By the turn of the century, African-Americans made up 2.7 percent of all watchmen, police officers, and fire fighters. The number of African-American officers then decreased over the years until the 1970s, when the number of African-Americans entering police work began to rise again with the move to abolish job discrimination. Kuykendall and Burns report that African-Americans have been hired by police departments since the 1940s because of political pressure from African-American communities' complaints about the behavior of white officers.[12]

Historically, African-American police officers experienced significant discrimination. Their work assignments were frequently restricted to patrolling African-American neighborhoods, and their chances of promotion to higher ranks were restricted. In some areas, they had limited arrest powers and were required to call white police officers to make an arrest. Additionally, they were subjected to prejudicial attitudes by many white officers. As late as the 1950s, some white officers refused to ride in a patrol car with African-American officers.[13]

In his classic study of African-American police officers in the New York City Police Department, *Black in Blue: A Study of the Negro Policeman,* Nicholas Alex discovered that African-Americans were excluded from the department's Detective Division. Alex also found that African-American officers were usually accepted by white officers as fellow police officers but were socially excluded from the white officers' off-duty activities.[14]

Alex's major finding was that African-American police officers had to suffer **double marginality**—the simultaneous expectation by white officers that African-American officers will give members of their own race better treatment and hostility from the African-American community that they are traitors to their race. Additionally, the African-American officers were subjected to racist behavior of white cops. Alex found that African-American officers, to deal with this pressure, adapted behaviors ranging from denying that African-American suspects should be treated differently from whites to treating African-American offenders more harshly to prove their lack of bias. Thus, African-American cops,

Alex found, not only suffered from the racism of their fellow officers but also were seen to be rougher on African-Americans in order to appease whites.[15]

In a repeat of his study in 1976, *New York Cops Talk Back,* Alex claimed to have found a more aggressive, self-assured African-American police officer. The officers he studied were less willing to accept any discriminatory practices by the police department.[16]

Stephen Leinen, in his book *Black Police, White Society,* found significant discrimination in the New York City Police Department until the 1960s. African-American police officers were only assigned to African-American neighborhoods and were not assigned to specialized, high-profile units. Leinen also noted that disciplinary actions against African-American officers were inequitable when compared with those against white officers.[17] He found, however, that institutional discrimination had largely disappeared in recent years. He attributes this to the legal, social, and political events of the civil rights era, along with the efforts of African-American police officer organizations, such as the NYPD's Guardians.[18]

National Commissions to Study Discrimination In the 1960s and early 1970s, the U.S. government recognized the problems caused by the lack of minorities in policing. Various national commissions were established to study, and make recommendations toward improving, the criminal justice system.

The National Advisory Commission on Civil Disorders stated that discriminatory police employment practices contributed to the riots of the middle and late 1960s. It found that in every city affected by the riots, the percentage of minority group officers was substantially lower than the percentage of minorities in the community. The commission noted that in Cleveland, minorities represented 34 percent of the population but only 7 percent of the sworn officers, and in Detroit, minorities represented 39 percent of the population but only 5 percent of the sworn officers. The commission also noted that although African-Americans made up at least 12 percent of the U.S. population, they represented less than 5 percent of police officers nationwide. The Commission also reported that minorities were seriously underrepresented in supervisory ranks in police departments.[19]

Another commission formed at this time, the President's Commission on Law Enforcement and Administration of Justice, commented on the low percentage of minorities in police departments: "If police departments, through their hiring or promotion policies indicate they have little interest in hiring minority group officers, the minority community is not likely to be sympathetic to the police."[20]

All in the Line of Duty

They Stopped Counting the Bodies at Ten and Backed Out

Deputy Robert Brunk, a six-year veteran of the San Diego Sheriff's Office, was on routine patrol when the call came over the radio. "Check the Welfare" of residents at 18241 Colina Norte in Rancho Santa Fe, California. Brunk had never been there before. Neither had Deputy Laura Gacek, a four-year veteran who backed up Brunk's call for another deputy. The residence was surrounded by a large fence and the massive, 9,000-square-foot house was barely visible from the road. They were in one of the richest enclaves of Southern California. The anonymous caller had told 911 there were multiple suicides in the house.

When the deputies got close to the front door, they didn't have to say anything to each other. The smell was enough. Every cop knows the smell of a DOA. But these deputies didn't come across one dead body; they stopped counting at ten and backed out of one the strangest crime scenes any officer had ever come across. They called for supervisors and investigators.

A haz-mat (hazardous materials) team arrived and Deputies Brunk and Gacek were whisked away to a hospital for a thorough precautionary evaluation. Their uniforms were taken and placed in biohazard bags. They were showered thoroughly and poked with needles and instruments.

The final body count reached thirty-nine, males and females. All were dressed in dark clothing and wearing new Nike sneakers, many were lying in bunk beds, several to a room. All but two were covered over the upper torso with purple shrouds. Subsequent investigation revealed that the deceased were members of a computer-related cult called Heaven's Gate. They died believing a spacecraft was waiting to take them to heaven.

At the start of their tours of duty, a couple of hours earlier, Deputies Brunk and Gacek never would have believed they would have a front-row seat at the largest mass suicide ever to occur in the United States.

Source: Adapted from various news media accounts, March/April 1997.

Another group, the **National Advisory Commission on Criminal Justice Standards and Goals,** realized the need to recruit more minorities into U.S. police departments. This presidential commission, which was formed to study the criminal justice system, issued standards to which police agencies should adhere in order to reduce job discrimination. Among these standards were ones on the employment of women and minority recruitment. The commission stated the following on the employment of women:

> Every police agency should immediately insure that there exists no agency policy that discourages qualified women from seeking employment as sworn or civilian personnel or prevents them from realizing their full employment.[21]

Minority recruiting was discussed as follows:

> Every police agency immediately should insure that it presents no artificial or arbitrary barriers (cultural or institutional) to discourage qualified individuals from seeking employment or from being employed as police officers. Every police agency should engage in positive efforts to employ ethnic minority group members. When a substantial ethnic minority population resides within the jurisdiction the police agency should take affirmative action to achieve a ratio of minority group employees in approximate proportion to the makeup of the population.[22]

Discrimination against Gay Officers

In addition to discrimination against women and racial and ethnic minorities, police departments have had a history of discriminating against job applicants because of their sexual orientation. Until the beginning of the focus on equal employment opportunity, many police departments discriminated against homosexuals in employment decisions, and the International Association of Chiefs of Police (IACP) maintained a policy of opposing the employment of gay officers.

In 1969, the IACP rescinded its policy of opposing the employment of gay officers. It has been estimated that currently 20 percent of the sworn officers in the San Francisco County Sheriff's Department and perhaps 10 percent of officers in the Los Angeles Police Department are gay men or lesbians.[23]

Many police administrators have decided not to make an issue of sexual orientation in the background investigation. Charles R. Swanson, Leonard Territo, and Robert W. Taylor believe that this decision may reflect an overall change in society's social and sexual mores, as well as a concern by police administrators that if they do not voluntarily take the lead, the federal courts may be called upon to intercede on the behalf of the gay community, as the courts have already done in the case of minorities and women.[24]

How Did Women and Minorities Achieve Equality?

Despite pronouncements by national commissions, women and minorities were forced to take their cases to the U.S. courts in an attempt to achieve equality with white men in U.S. police departments. The primary instrument governing employment equality, as well as all equality, in U.S. society is the **Fourteenth Amendment** to the U.S. Constitution. This amendment, passed in 1868, guarantees "equal protection of the law" to all citizens of the United States. It states the following:

> Section 1. All persons born or naturalized in the United States, and subject to the jurisdiction thereof, are citizens of the United States and of the State wherein they reside. No State shall make or enforce any law which shall abridge the privileges or immunities of citizens of the United States; nor shall any State deprive any person of life, liberty, or property, without due process of law; nor deny to any person within its jurisdiction the equal protection of the law.

More than the Fourteenth Amendment was needed, however, to end job discrimination in policing (or any government agency). The path to equality had as milestones not only the Fourteenth Amendment but also the Civil Rights Act of 1964, Title VII of the same law, the Equal Employment Opportunity Act of 1972 (EEOA), federal court cases on discrimination, and government-mandated affirmative action programs.

Civil Rights Act of 1964

Despite the existence of the Fourteenth Amendment, discrimination by U.S. government agencies continued. In an effort to ensure equality, the **Civil Rights Act of 1964** was passed by Congress and signed into law by President Lyndon B. Johnson in 1964.[25] **Title VII** of this law was designed to prohibit all job discrimination based on race, color, religion, sex, or national origin. It covered all employment practices, including hiring, promotion, compensation, dismissal, and all other terms or conditions of employment.

Equal Employment Opportunity Act of 1972

The **Equal Employment Opportunity Act of 1972** (EEOA) extended the 1964 Civil Rights Act and made its provisions, including Title VII, applicable to state and local governments.[26] The EEOA expanded the jurisdiction and strengthened the powers of the Federal Equal Employment Opportunity Commission (EEOC). It allowed employees of state and local governments to file employment discrimination suits with the EEOC, strengthened the commission's investigatory powers by allowing it to document allegations of discrimination better, and permitted the U.S. Department of Justice to sue state and local governments for violations of Title VII. The EEOA stated that all procedures regarding entry and promotion in agencies—including application forms, written tests, probation ratings, and physical ability tests—are subject to EEOC review, in order to determine whether there has been any unlawful act of discrimination.

Federal Courts and Job Discrimination

Job discrimination may take several forms. The most obvious, of course, is where there is a clear and explicit policy of discrimination—for example, separate job titles, recruitment efforts, standards, pay, and procedures for female or minority employees. The second, and probably most prevalent, form of job discrimination is **de facto discrimination**. De facto discrimination is discrimination that is the indirect result of policies or practices that are not intended to discriminate but do, in fact, discriminate.

Under EEOC guidelines, discrimination in testing occurs when there is a substantially different rate of selection in hiring, promotion, or another employment decision that works to the disadvantage of members of a particular race, sex, or ethnic group. Let us say that a substantially different rate of passing a particular examination occurs for different racial or ethnic minority groups or members of a certain gender, and that this works to the disadvantage of a particular group. For example, if a certain examination results in the vast majority of females failing that test and the vast majority of males passing it, it can be said that the particular examination had an **adverse impact** on females. Adverse impact can be seen as a form of de facto discrimination. In the 1970s and 1980s, women and minorities began to use Title VII and the courts (particularly the federal courts) to attempt to achieve equality.

Job-relatedness The first important job discrimination case was *Griggs v. Duke Power Company* in 1971, which declared that the practices of the Duke Power Company were unconstitutional because they required that all of its employees have a high school diploma and pass a standard intelligence test before being hired.[27] The court ruled that these requirements were discriminatory unless they could be shown to measure the attributes needed to perform a specific job. The decision in *Griggs v. Duke Power Company* established the concept that job requirements must be job related—they must be necessary for the performance of the job a person is applying for.

De facto discrimination or adverse impact was found to be most prevalent in employment standards and entrance examinations. These standards and tests discriminated against certain candidates, particularly women and minorities. To eliminate the discriminatory effect of recruitment and testing practices, the EEOC required that all tests and examinations be job related. To prove that a test or standard is job related, an agency must provide evidence that the test, examination, or standard measures qualifications and abilities that are actually necessary to perform the specific job for which an applicant is applying or being tested. In the words of the EEOC, to be job related, a test must be "predictive or significantly correlated with important elements of work behavior which comprise or are relevant to the job or jobs for which candidates are being evaluated."[28]

How did all these regulations apply to police departments? Candidates who formerly were denied acceptance into police departments because they could not meet certain standards (height and weight) or could not pass certain tests (strength) began to argue that these standards were not job related—that is, the standards did not measure skills and qualifications needed to perform police work.

The requirement that officers not be less than a certain height (height requirement) was probably the strongest example of discrimination against female candidates. With very few exceptions, police departments lost court cases involving the height requirement. In *Mieth v. Dollard* (1976), a lawsuit against the Alabama Department of Public Safety, the court ruled as follows: "Evidence failed to establish . . . that tall officers hold an advantage over smaller colleagues in effectuating arrests and administering emergency aid; furthermore, the contention that tall officers have a psychological advantage was not, as a measure of job performance sufficient constitutional justification for blanket exclusion of all individuals under the specified height."[29] In another court case regarding height, the court in *Vanguard Justice Society v. Hughes* (1979) noted that the Baltimore Police Department's height requirement of 5 feet, 7 inches was a prima facie case of sex discrimination, because it excluded 95 percent of the female population, in addition to 32 percent of the male population.[30] (Prima facie is from the Latin, "at first sight." It refers to a fact or evidence sufficient to establish a defense or a claim unless otherwise contradicted.)

Previous forms of physical ability testing were also challenged and found discriminatory by the courts. Newly designed tests, known as physical agility tests, were developed to reduce adverse impact. The newly developed physical agility tests required much less physical strength than the former tests and relied more on physical fitness. Some researchers who have studied the newly developed physical agility tests have found that some still had an adverse impact on females. One study discovered that females were four times more likely than males to fail physical agility testing for deputy sheriff positions.[31] Another study concluded that the new physical agility tests do not represent realistic job samples, because they relate to aspects of the job that are rarely performed.[32] In cases in which the courts decided that the new tests still discriminated against females, the police departments were ordered to create new ones.

The Job Analysis Today, as indicated in chapter 4, to ensure that entry and promotion examinations are job related, police departments perform a job analysis for each position. An acceptable job analysis, declared constitutional by the courts, includes identification of tasks officers generally perform. This identification is based on interviews of officers and supervisors; reviews by another panel of officers and supervisors; computer analyses of questionnaires to determine the frequency of tasks performed; and analyses of the knowledge, skills, and abilities needed to perform the tasks.[33]

The courts have issued numerous rulings regarding testing and the job analysis. In *Vulcan Society v. Civil Service Commission* (1973), the court rejected personnel tests because of the lack of a job analysis.[34] In *United States v. State of New York* (1979), the court rejected the New York State Police Department's entrance examination because it was validated using a faulty job analysis.[35] However, in the case of *Guardians Association of New York City Police Department v. Civil Service Commission of New York* (1980), which is considered a landmark ruling, the court actually accepted the job analysis of the New York City Department of Personnel and the New York City Police Department as being nondiscriminatory.[36] This ruling showed that police departments had begun to follow the mandates of the federal courts without being ordered to do so.

Affirmative Action Programs

The most controversial method of ending job discrimination is the concept of **affirmative action.** In 1965, in Executive Order 11246, President Johnson required all federal contractors and subcontractors to develop affirmative action programs. Subsequent orders have amended and expanded the original executive order. In essence, the concept of affirmative action means that employers must take active steps to ensure equal employment opportunity and to redress past discrimination. Affirmative action must be result oriented—it must focus on the result of employment practices. It is not enough for an agency merely to stop discriminating; the agency must take steps to correct past discrimination and give jobs to those it has discriminated against in the past.[37] Basically, affirmative action is designed to make up for, or to undo, past discrimination.

Affirmative action programs involve several major steps. First, the agency must study its personnel makeup and determine a proper level of minority and female representation. If it does not meet that level, the agency must establish goals, quotas, and time tables to correct female and minority representation. It must make every effort to advertise job openings and actively seek out and encourage female and minority applicants. All tests and screening procedures must be validated as being job related, and any potentially discriminatory procedures must be eliminated.

YOU ARE THERE! »

The Path to Equality—Court Cases

1971	*Griggs v. Duke Power Company*
1973	*Vulcan Society v. Civil Service Commission*
1976	*Mieth v. Dollard*
1979	*Vanguard Justice Society v. Hughes*
1979	*United States v. State of New York*
1980	*Guardians Association of New York City Police Department v. Civil Service Commission of New York*

YOU ARE THERE!

The Walls Come Tumbling Down

Throughout the years, numerous lawsuits involving affirmative action were filed by and on behalf of women and minorities. The judicial findings and consent decrees (agreements between parties before, and instead of, a final decision by a judge) did much to ease the way for women and minorities into U.S. police departments. A sampling of these cases follows.

A lawsuit filed against the San Francisco Police Department resulted in a federal court order establishing an experimental quota of sixty women as patrol officers. The department also revised the height and weight requirements that had barred women from patrol jobs. In response to a lawsuit filed by the Department of Justice, Maryland agreed to recruit more female state police officers. Similarly, the New Jersey State Police agreed to establish, within a year, hiring goals for women in both sworn and nonsworn positions.

A rejected female applicant filed suit against the California Highway Patrol, charging that its male-only standards unlawfully discriminated against women under Title VII of the Civil Rights Act. Following the results of a two-year feasibility study, a decision was made in the plaintiff's favor. As a result, the California Highway Patrol officially began accepting qualified women for state trooper positions, ending a forty-six-year tradition of using only men as traffic officers. With the threat of a lawsuit in the offing, the New York City Police Department ended its height requirements, unfroze its list of female applicants, and increased its female officers on patrol to 400 in a brief period of time.

The Los Angeles Police Department signed a consent decree with the Justice Department awarding $2 million in back pay to officers who were discriminated against, agreeing that 45 percent of all new recruits would be African-American or Hispanic-American, and agreeing that 20 percent of all new recruits would be women. A consent decree required that one-third of all promotions in the Miami Police Department be given to women and minorities.

Source: Adapted from *New York Times*, 14 September 1976, p. 8; *New York Times*, 8 October 1975, p. 45; Glen Craig, "California Highway Patrol Officers," *Police Chief*, January 1977, p. 60; Anthony V. Bouza, "Women in Policing," *FBI Law Enforcement Bulletin*, September 1975, pp. 4-7; *Criminal Justice Newsletter*, 8 December 1980, p. 6; and Dianne Townsey, "Black Women in American Policing: An Advancement Display," *Journal of Criminal Justice* 10 (1982): 455-468.

The major concept behind affirmative action, and possibly the most disturbing concept to many, is the establishment of **quotas**. Under a quota arrangement, a certain percentage of openings are reserved for particular groups. In 1974, for example, the Detroit Police Department adopted a policy of promoting one African-American officer to sergeant for each white officer promoted. Largely as a result of its policy, Detroit has one of the best records for minority employment in the United States.[38]

Robert Sheehan and Gary W. Cordner provide an excellent summation of the efforts of women and minorities to gain equal employment through the courts and affirmative action:

> Such decisions have thrown the police service into some turmoil and have angered many white male police officers, who charge reverse discrimination. . . . That police administrators have been forced to hire and promote minority group members rather than attempting to do this on their own, is, in our opinion, a sad reflection on the administrators' real commitment to justice. The personnel task has been complicated significantly by this turn of events.[39]

It should be noted that in the late 1990s the concept of affirmative action was under attack on numerous fronts, ranging from U.S. Supreme Court cases to state and local laws.

White Male Backlash

As more police jobs and promotions began to go to women and minorities, fewer male whites, obviously, received these jobs and promotions. White males were passed over on entrance and promotion examinations by females and minorities, some of whom had received lower test scores. This resulted in the turmoil and angry white males referred to by Sheehan and Cordner in the quotation cited earlier. Anger, resentment, and counter lawsuits followed.

Critics of affirmative action argue that selecting police officers based on their race or gender actually violates the 1964 Civil Rights Act and is discriminatory. Critics also argue that selecting officers who have scored lower on civil service tests lowers the personnel standards of a police department and will result in poorer performance by the department. Sociologists James Jacobs and Jay Cohen relate that white police officers view affirmative action hiring and promotion programs as a threat to their job security.[40]

In Chicago, white officers intervened on the side of the city when an African-American police officer organization filed suit to change promotion criteria.[41] In Detroit, the Detroit Police Officer's Association filed suit to prevent the police department from setting up a quota plan for hiring African-American police sergeants.[42]

In 1995, a sergeant with the Los Angeles County Sheriff's Department formed the Association of White Male Peace Officers to protect the rights of white male officers through zero discrimination in hiring, promotion, or assignment. The Sheriff's Department said it cannot prevent officers from joining the group but reported that it does not sanction the group or understand the reason for its formation.[43]

Also in 1995, eighteen white Dallas police officers filed a $1.8 million lawsuit alleging they were passed over for promotion to senior corporal in favor of minority officers who scored lower on a promotional exam. The lawsuit called for an order barring the city from imposing quotas to implement its affirmative action plan.[44]

The continued need for affirmative-action programs is under renewed challenge from critics who contend that they have achieved their original goals of ending discrimination against minorities and providing parity with white males. In April 1995, Maryland State Police agreed to provide approximately $250,000 in back pay to ninety-nine male white troopers who claimed they were unfairly passed over for promotions in 1989 and 1990.[45]

Can Women and Minorities Do the Job?

Much of the discrimination against women in police departments was based on a fear that they could not do police work effectively because of their gender and size. Much of the discrimination against minorities was based on a fear that they would not be accepted by nonminority citizens, if not just on outright racism. The academic studies and anecdotal evidence presented in this section show that women and minorities do indeed make effective police officers.

Academic Studies of Female Officers

In the 1970s, many police officials argued that female officers could not handle the tasks of patrol duty effectively. According to this traditional, macho perspective,

> ### YOU ARE THERE! »
>
> #### Female Officer Named Officer of the Year
>
> In 1990, *Parade* and the International Association of Chiefs of Police (IACP) for the first time chose a woman for its Police Officer of the Year award. Katherine P. Heller, a U.S. Park Police officer and thirty-year-old native of Pontomac, Maryland, joined the U.S. Park Police in 1988. Heller was presented with the award on October 9, 1990, at the IACP annual meeting in Tulsa, Oklahoma.
>
> Officer Heller was on foot patrol on February 22, 1990, with her partner, Scott Dahl, in Lafayette Park, directly across from the White House. A man, bleeding from the head, approached the officers and complained that a vagrant had just bashed him on the head with a brick. Dahl crossed the street to investigate, as Heller checked the wounded man's condition. Heller then observed Dahl grappling with the vagrant on the ground. Heller rushed to Dahl's aid, repeatedly hitting the attacker over the head with her nightstick. The man then backed away, but with Dahl's gun in his hand. As the officers looked for cover, the attacker stalked Dahl around a car and began to level the weapon at the officer. Dahl ducked for cover as Heller fired at the man, killing him.
>
> The 5-foot, 3-inch, 107-pound Heller has earned a reputation as an aggressive officer. In 1989, she ranked sixth out of 350 patrol officers on the force in making felony arrests.
>
> Source: Adapted from "*Parade* Hails Park Police Hero," *Law Enforcement News*, 15 October 1990, p. 6.

policing required physical strength and a tough, masculine attitude. Two important academic studies, however—one by the Police Foundation and the other by the Law Enforcement Assistance Administration (LEAA)—found that female officers were just as effective on patrol as comparable males.[46] The latter study was performed for the Law Enforcement Assistance Administration, the precursor of the National Institute of Justice.

The study performed for the Police Foundation, *Policewomen on Patrol: Final Report*, evaluated and compared the performance of female recruits during their first year on patrol in Washington, D.C., with that of a matched group of new male officers in the same department. This was the first time a police department had

Dempsey's Law

The Dirty Harriet or Jane Wayne Syndrome

Professor Dempsey, you know, if we had more female officers, we wouldn't have cases like Rodney King. Women wouldn't use excessive force like those macho males do.

Maybe you're right, but I don't think we should generalize by gender. Female officers can use excessive force, just as male officers can. As a matter of fact, Connie Fletcher, a journalism professor at Loyola University who interviewed 125 Chicago police officers for her book *What Cops Know*, says that female police officers are not immune from using excessive force. Fletcher identified a tendency by some rookie female officers to overreact as they try to live up to a tough image. She said the cops call this the Dirty Harriet or Jane Wayne Syndrome, just as some male cops are said to have the Dirty Harry or John Wayne Syndrome.

Fletcher says that most brutality cases involve rookie cops who want to impress older officers. I tend to agree with her. In my experience, the vast majority of citizen complaints regarding excessive force concerned officers with less than five years on the job.

Source: Some of the material in this box is based on Connie Fletcher, *What Cops Know: Cops Talk About What They Do, How They Do It, and What It Does to Them* (New York: Random House, 1991).

---

integrated a substantial number of female officers into the backbone of the department. This research project was designed to determine the following: (1) the ability of women to perform patrol work successfully, (2) their impact on the operations of a police department, and (3) their reception by the community. The study found that female officers exhibited extremely satisfactory work performance. The female officers were found to respond to similar types of calls as male officers, and their arrests were as likely as the male officers' arrests to result in convictions. Additionally, the report found that women were more likely than their male colleagues to receive support from the community, and they were less likely to be charged with improper conduct.[47]

The study for LEAA was titled *Women on Patrol: A Pilot Study of Police Performance in New York City*. The study involved the observation of 3,625 hours of female police officer patrol in New York City, and it included 2,400 police-citizen encounters. The report concluded that female officers were perceived by citizens as being more competent, pleasant, and respectful than male officers. This study found that women performed better when serving with other female officers, as well as that women, when serving with male partners, seemed to be intimidated by their partners and were less likely to be assertive and self-sufficient.[48]

Thus, the first two large-scale studies of female patrol officers dispelled the myth that they were not able

PATROLLING THE NET

LEN Hits Cyberspace!

Law Enforcement News (*LEN*), the twice-a-month newspaper that has been covering law enforcement news around the nation and world from its offices at John Jay College of Criminal Justice, in New York City, for over twenty-five years, hit cyberspace in February 1997. It opened its own homepage on the World Wide Web—Len Online—as part of its information outreach to the police profession. You can access the *LEN* home page at: http://www.lib.jjay.cuny.edu/len.

Source: Adapted from "Join Us in Cyberspace!," *Law Enforcement News*, 28 February 1997, p. 1.

Dempsey's Law

When You Really Get to Know Someone . . .

Professor Dempsey, there are many women in this class, and some want to be police officers. But I know a lot of guys who say women can't do police work because they're not strong enough. What do you think?

I get this question often. I generally respond to it with my own experience rather than the empirical evidence that says women can be very effective officers. When women were first entering my department in large numbers, many male officers complained about female officers. However, I never heard a male officer with a steady female partner complain at all about her.

Also, I never heard a female officer who had a steady male partner complain about him. I guess what that says to me is that when we get past things like gender—and even race, ethnic group, and age—we start to see the real people we are working with, and we start to respect them for themselves.

I generally conclude by saying that some women make excellent police officers and some make poor officers, just as some men make excellent officers and some make poor officers.

---

to do the job. Follow-up anecdotal evidence and empirical studies further bolstered the assertion that women make effective patrol officers. The findings of the Washington, D.C., and New York City studies were supported by anecdotal reports of experiences in the Boston, Miami, and Dayton police departments.[49]

In addition to the studies cited above, numerous other academic studies of job performance by female police officers were conducted, with similar results. James David studied the behavior of 2,293 police officers in Texas and Oklahoma and found that the arrest rates of male and female officers were almost identical, despite the stereotype that women make fewer arrests than men. David also found that women were more inclined to intervene than were their male counterparts when violations of the law occurred in their presence.[50]

A study of police perceptions of spouse abuse, by Robert Homant and Daniel Kennedy, concluded that female officers were more understanding of, and sympathetic to, the victims of spouse abuse than were male officers, and they were more likely than male officers to refer those victims to shelters.[51]

In an analysis of the existing research on female police officers, Merry Morash and Jack Greene found that the traditional male belief that female officers could not be effective on patrol was not supported by existing research. Morash and Greene concluded that evidence existed showing that women make highly successful police officers.[52]

Former New York City police detective Sean Grennan's study of patrol teams in New York City found no basic difference between the way males and females, working as a patrol team, reacted to violent confrontations. Grennan also found that female police officers, in most cases, were far more emotionally stable than their male counterparts. Female officers also lacked the need to project the macho image, which, Grennan believes, seems to be inherent in the personality of most of the male officers he studied. He found that the female officer, with her less aggressive personality, was more likely to calm a potentially violent situation and less likely to cause physical injury. She was also less likely to use a firearm and no more likely to suffer on-the-job injuries.[53]

One of the biggest obstacles to women's entering the ranks of police officer has been the contention that women lack the necessary physical strength to do the job. In a review of the existing literature on female police officers, Michael Charles found that women can train themselves to achieve a level of strength and fitness well within the normal demands of the police profession.[54]

The foregoing studies show that female officers can effectively do patrol work and are well received by the public. However, researchers Kenneth Kerber, Steven Andes, and Michelle Mittler noted that citizens they surveyed in Illinois stated that female police officers were well suited for some tasks, such as settling family disputes or dealing with a rape victim, but were inadequate for action-oriented activities, such as car stops or stopping fistfights.[55]

A former police commissioner points out the following:

> Women can be expected to bring negotiating and conflict resolving skills that may defuse many altercations. Women are different from men and will therefore succeed or fail in different situations than men. They tend to be less violent and less reliant on force including the use of the gun. In some cases, when authoritarian male types would try for physical domination a woman's approach may succeed. However, in cases requiring physical strength, they may fail. It must be remembered that no one called for eliminating men from the ranks over their occasional failures. Women have demonstrated, especially since the mid 1970s, that they can do the job.[56]

Clearly, although women have been assigned to patrol duties for only about two decades, evidence exists that they are very effective as patrol officers. The former belief that they lacked the size, strength, and temperament to do the job has given way to a realization that being a patrol officer requires more than size, strength, and a tough attitude.

Academic Studies of African-American Officers

Unlike the situation for women, there have been no studies regarding the ability of African-Americans to do police work. Anecdotal evidence, however, suggests that they perform as well as any other group. For example, in a 1984 study in the aftermath of the 1980 Miami riots, Bruce Berg, Edmond True, and Marc Gertz found that African-American police officers were far less detached and alienated from the local community than were white or Hispanic-American police officers.[57] Considering that the 1968 National Advisory Commission on Civil Disorders reported a significant problem of alienation between the police and the community, the addition of minority officers has to be considered a plus for policing.

Women and Minorities in Policing Today

As this chapter has shown, during the past three decades, U.S. police departments have attempted to reflect better the communities they serve. Police administrators have intensified the recruitment of women and mi-

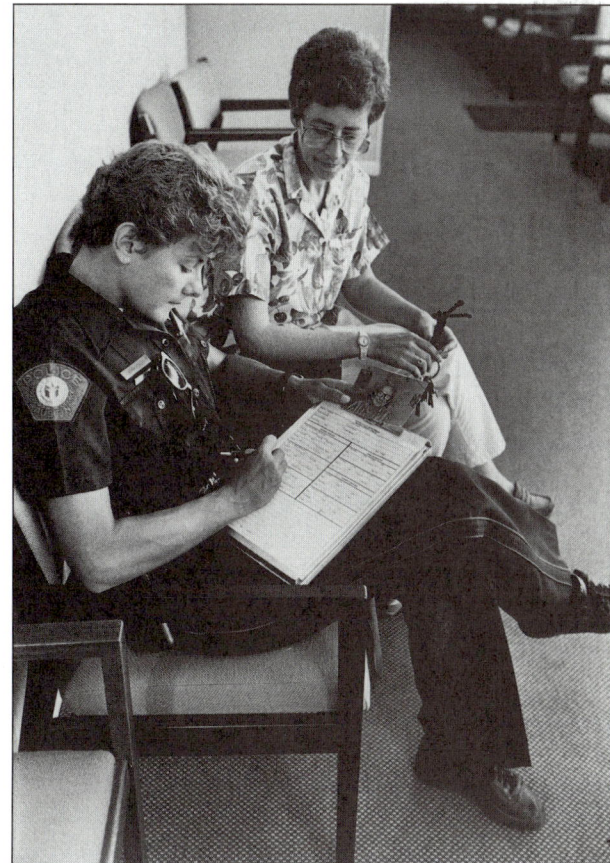

Women are involved in all aspects of policing. Here, a female officer takes a missing person report from a staff member at a nursing home.

norities to have more balanced police departments. They have altered their entry requirements and training curriculums—sometimes willingly, but more often under court mandate—to facilitate the hiring and training of women and minority officers. Today women and minorities serve in all aspects of police work and in all neighborhoods of all towns and cities across the United States.

As an example, as of 1996, minorities now make up 64 percent of the San Francisco Sheriff's Department, up from 45 percent in 1985, when the agency first began tracking efforts to bring diversity to the 649-deputy force. According to Sheriff Michael Hennessey, the diversity helps increase public esteem in the agency. Members of minority groups, he said, will be more trusting knowing that others of the same race, gender, or ethnicity are represented on the force. He also said that the improved racial and gender mix can also reduce the

> ### YOU ARE THERE! »
>
> **Woman Named Chief of Police in Houston**
>
> In January 1990, Houston Mayor Kathy Whitmire named Elizabeth M. Watson to replace Lee P. Brown as the city's police chief. Watson, a seventeen-year veteran, was the second woman to head a U.S. big city police department. "This is like the first woman in Congress, the first woman in the state legislature or the first woman CEO of a Fortune 500 Company," said Susan E. Martin of the Police Foundation.
>
> Source: Adapted from *Law Enforcement News*, 15/31 January 1991, p. 18.

Table 13.1 — Percentage of Women and Minorities in Policing, 1987 versus 1990 versus 1993

Year	% Women	% African-American	% Hispanic-American
Local Police			
1987	7.6	9.3	4.5
1990	8.1	10.5	5.2
1993	8.8	11.3	6.2
Deputy Sheriffs			
1987	12.6	8.3	4.3
1990	15.4	9.8	4.7
1993	14.5	10.0	5.8

Source: Based on Brian Reaves, *Local Police Departments, 1993* (Washington, D.C.: National Institute of Justice, 1996); and Brian Reaves, *Sheriffs' Departments, 1993* (Washington, D.C.: National Institute of Justice, 1996).

number of gender- or race-based complaints against officers from both within and without the department.[58]

On another positive note, the International Association of Women Police, a fraternal organization for women police officers, reported that in 1994 there were nearly 100 female chiefs of police throughout the nation.[59] Elizabeth Watson was the first woman to lead a police department in a city of over 1 million when she headed the Houston, Texas, Police Department from 1990 to 1992; upon leaving Houston, she became the first woman chief to head the Austin, Texas, Police Department.[60]

In 1996, Paula Meara became the first female chief in the history of the 500-officer Springfield, Massachusetts, Police Department. Meara is used to being first; she was the first Springfield female officer to have a college degree; the first to make sergeant, and then, the first to make lieutenant.[61] In 1997, Deborah K. Ness, who was the first of three women ever hired as patrol officers by the Minot, North Dakota, Police Department, became the first woman ever to be named police chief in North Dakota when she assumed command of the Bismarck Police Department.[62]

In 1995, Annette Sandberg, a female lieutenant with the Washington State Patrol, was appointed to lead the department as chief. It was the first time a woman had been named to lead a state police agency. At age 33, she was one of the youngest law enforcement executives in the nation. In her relatively short career, Sandberg gained a reputation as one of the State Patrol's rising stars. Her ability to nab drunk drivers earned her the King County Trooper of the Year award in 1988.[63]

The latest data available as this text went to print indicate that we have made significant progress in bringing more females and minorities into U.S. police departments. A 1996 National Institute of Justice report indicated that women accounted for 8.8 percent of all sworn or uniformed members in local police departments; African-Americans, 11.3 percent; Hispanic-Americans, 6.2 percent; and other minorities, 1.5 percent.[64] Another report indicates that among sheriff's offices, women now account for 14.5 percent, African-Americans, 10.0 percent; Hispanic-Americans, 5.8 percent; and other minorities, 1.1 percent.[65] Table 13.1 shows the percentages of local police and deputy sheriffs who were female, African-American, and Hispanic-American in 1993, 1990, and 1987.

Female Representation Today

To put these percentages into perspective, although the presence and status of women in law enforcement have risen, the percentage of female officers falls below 44.7 percent, the percentage of the labor force that women currently occupy. Women in policing appear to be lagging behind women in other traditionally male professions. In law, for example, women make up 21 percent of U.S. lawyers and judges. However, women in policing are doing well in comparison with other skilled blue-collar occupations. For example, women make up only 4 percent of mechanics and repairers and 2 percent of workers in the construction trades.[66]

Commenting on the increased female representation in U.S. police departments, Dean J. Champion notes that although female representation in policing is well below the proportional representation of women in the United States, "Few critics propose the creation of a 50–50 balance of males and females in law enforcement."[67] Larry K. Gaines, Mittie D. Southerland, and John E. Angell state that the use of female officers in all aspects of police work has increased in the past decade and that women are accepted as capable, competent police officers and managers by most people.[68]

How do female officers feel about their careers? In a study by Carole G. Garrison, Nancy Grant, and Kenneth McCormick, the researchers discovered that almost 87 percent of the female officers surveyed would recommend law enforcement as a career for other women. Nevertheless, 23 percent were considering a career change.[69]

African-American and Other Minority Representation Today

In the 1970s and 1980s, African-Americans were appointed as police commissioners or chiefs in some of the nation's biggest city police departments. Among them were William Hart, Detroit; Lee P. Brown, Atlanta, Houston, and New York City; and Benjamin Ward, New York City.

In the 1990s this trend continued with Willie Williams in Los Angeles in 1992. In 1997, Melvin H. Wearing was named police chief of New Haven, Connecticut, the first African-American to hold that post.[70] Also in 1997, Mel Carraway was the first African-American to be appointed to head the Indiana State Police.[71] However, many feel that African-Americans are still discriminated against in promotional assignments.[72]

Another traditional minority group in policing, Asian-Americans, received good news in 1996, as the San Francisco Police Department appointed Fred Lau to become the first Asian-American police chief in the department's history.[73]

Despite the increase in the number of minority group members in U.S. police departments, George F. Cole called the extensive campaigns to recruit more minority officers a failure. He says this may be the result of the following:

YOU ARE THERE! >>

New Commissioner's Number 1 Goal Is Hiring More African-Americans

Raymond N. Kelly, a twenty-nine-year veteran of the New York City Police Department, was appointed to the position of police commissioner on October 16, 1992, by New York City mayor David N. Dinkens. Kelly, in an interview, stated that the first and most vital item on his agenda was the recruitment of more African-American officers to the department. Kelly was responding to a recent study by Professor Samuel Walker of the University of Nebraska's Department of Criminal Justice that showed that New York City ranked last among the fifty largest cities in the country in the percentage of African-Americans in the police department. At the time of the study, African-Americans made up 11.5 percent of the uniformed personnel in the NYPD, whereas they made up 28.7 percent of New York City's population.

Kelly outlined a number of steps to achieve his goal, including the revision of testing and screening procedures and an "all-out" marketing campaign in African-American neighborhoods and among African-American groups, including the targeting of African-American churches and African-Americans in the military services.

Kelly said, "Without these actions, there will be increased tension between the communities and the police. Tension leads to hostilities and that will lead to more cries of racism in the department."

Several days later, Kelly announced that the police entrance examination scheduled for December 1992 would be delayed until May 1993 so that the police department could recruit more African-Americans to take the test.

1. Departments are not aggressive enough in their recruitment of minorities.
2. African-Americans have a negative view of law enforcement and hesitate to apply for the jobs.
3. Poor educational backgrounds leave minorities unable to pass police entrance examinations in the numbers desired.[74]

YOU ARE THERE! »

Chief Marched for Gay Rights in Portland

Portland (Oregon) police chief Tom Potter marched in a gay rights march with his daughter Katie, an admittedly gay police officer. Potter stated, "I believe the role of the police is not only to help people physically but to protect their rights—both constitutional rights and human rights. There are certain categories of citizens I do not believe enjoy all of the rights that other people do."

Stan Peters, president of the 800-member Portland Police Association (the police union), said, "It would be the same as if a police officer went to an anti-abortion rally in uniform. They would be ostracized if not disciplined severely by the chief for that act."

Source: Adapted from "Standing Up for Gay Rights in Portland," *Law Enforcement News*, July/August 1991, p. 7.

Progress is occurring in the representation of females and minorities in U.S. police departments, but progress comes slowly. It has been a slow, gradual process through the 1960s, 1970s, 1980s, and 1990s, and the progress has sometimes been accompanied by failures. Despite significant change, the U.S. Commission on Civil Rights reported:

> Serious under-utilization of minorities and women in local law enforcement agencies continues to hamper the ability of police departments to function effectively in and earn the respect of predominantly minority neighborhoods, thereby increasing the probability of tension and violence. . . . [P]olice departments remain largely white and male, particularly in the upper-level command positions.[75]

Problems Persist for Women and Minorities in Policing

Despite gains in actual numbers, women and minorities still encounter difficulties in being accepted in policing.[76]

Problems for Women

Gaines, Southerland, and Angell report that despite the gains women have made in policing during the last two decades, policing remains a male-dominated profession and females still face discrimination. They state, however, that today's discrimination is more subtle than in the past. They said that women have not really received equal opportunity in policing; they have just overcome the traditional barriers to entry into the profession.[77]

A series of studies conducted by researchers in the 1980s describe the problems women still face in today's workplace. Most of these problems involve acceptance and treatment by male officers. For example, Leslie Kay Lord found that male officers still harbor grave reservations about women's suitability to be competent police officers.[78] Daniel Bell reported that given the sometimes

California Highway Patrol officers recruiting at the Chinese New Year celebration in San Francisco.

hostile reception afforded them by their male peers and the general public, female police officers have been forced to perform their jobs under extreme pressure.[79] Bruce Berg and Kimberly Budnick concluded that women who prove themselves tough enough to gain respect as police officers are then labeled "lesbians" or "bitches" in order to neutralize their threat to male dominance, a process referred to as "defeminization."[80]

In a study of stress on the female officer, Judie Gaffin Wexler and Deana Dorman Logan quoted one female officer: "The academy said they didn't want women. We stuck together and said we were going to make it. One training officer said: 'This is my personal opinion. I don't think you should be in this job. You should go home and have babies.'"[81] Wexler and Logan concluded, "After six years of women on patrol, the men in the department still did not seem to accept them as officers. They were ignored, harassed, watched, gossiped about, and viewed as sexual objects. The hostility of the male co-workers has been so substantial that other stressors receded in comparison."[82]

Sally Gross reported that many women who enter police work are initially self-confident and idealistic about their roles and interactions with their male co-workers, but after eight weeks of training, many become disillusioned, experiencing sex role conflict, self-doubt, repressed anger, and confusion.[83] M. L. West wrote that in some instances, female recruits report sexual harassment by male officers.[84]

J. G. Wexler and V. Quinn reported that change in the area of promotion of women continues to come slowly, some male officers find it difficult to take orders from female supervisors, and some female officers may not seek promotion because they fear rejection from their male colleagues.[85]

M. Silbert wrote that female officers in the San Francisco Police Department exhibited signs of more burnout than male police officers, and they voiced more intention to leave policing.[86] A Canadian report says that the Royal Canadian Mounted Police experienced a higher rate of attrition among female officers than among male officers.[87]

Belinda Crawford Seagram and Cannie Stark-Adamec, of the University of Regina in Ontario, reported on a study of several Canadian police departments that revealed that female police officers resigned at a rate approximately three times greater than male officers. It is significant to know that 56 percent of the women resigning reported that they left their jobs because they wanted to raise their families or spend more time with them.[88]

Research in the 1990s also point to problems for women in police departments. One study found that female officers believed they had less opportunity for advancement on the job and less confidence in their performance on the job. They felt they were still struggling for acceptance and did not receive equal credit for their job performance.[89]

Other research indicates that only about one-third of male officers in recent surveys actually accept a woman on patrol, and that more than half do not think that women can handle the physical requirements of the job as well as men.[90]

Studies show that discrimination is still present in U.S. police departments, even after tremendous efforts to create a nondiscriminatory workplace. Susan Martin is "guardedly optimistic," however. She concludes, in "Female Officers on the Move? A Status Report on Women in Policing," that "as more women enter the occupation, move slowly into positions of authority and serve as role models and sponsors for other women there is reason for guarded optimism about the future of women in law enforcement, as well as a large number of questions waiting to be addressed."[91]

In 1995 and 1996, lawsuits involving gender discrimination in policing continue to indicate discrimination against women:

- In 1995, McHenry County, Illinois, settled a sex discrimination suit by agreeing to pay $440,000 and make dramatic changes in how the sheriff's department hires its patrol deputies. A Department of Justice investigation had found that not one woman had been hired as a patrol officer in seventeen years.[92]
- A former Los Angeles police officer was awarded $2.3 million after a jury agreed with her claim that she had been harassed by the department so ruthlessly when she joined its SWAT team that she could no longer work for either the unit or the agency.
- A federal jury in Pompano Beach, Florida, awarded a female sergeant over $100,000 after finding that the police chief had called her racial slurs.
- A former Southborough, Massachusetts, police dispatcher was awarded a $250,000 settlement in a sexual harassment claim.[93]

Despite the problems women still experience in police departments, they have shown that they will do all that is necessary to attain the job, and they have shown

> ### All in the Line of Duty
>
> **A Real Hero Dies in the Line of Duty**
>
> His name was Boris. No last name, only Boris; but everyone in the Bristol, Virginia, Police Department, called him Sergeant Boris. While tracking two shooting suspects, Boris caught up to them under a construction trailer. The two teenage suspects pumped four rounds into him. He emerged from under the trailer and died seconds later.
>
> More than 100 officers, 200 civilians, and 25 other police K-9s attended funeral services for the hero Belgian Malinois. The perpetrators were charged with the felony count of killing a police animal, among other charges.
>
> Boris's handler said of him:
>
> > He had an uncanny ability to go from a playful pup to serious police work at the snap of the fingers. He was unique that way. When I got the call, he was playing with my daughter. When we went to work, he changed 180 degrees from play to serious work. He was just a fantastic police dog.
>
> Source: Adapted from Steve Quinn, "Sgt. Boris Remembered as Hard-Working K-9," *Police*, February 1997, p. 26.

that they can do the job. Their future in policing will continue to be dynamic and interesting.

Problems for African-Americans and Other Minorities

Recent lawsuits reveal that discrimination against African-Americans and other minorities still exists in policing.

- In 1995, thirty African-American and Hispanic police officers in Suffolk County, New York, filed a discrimination suit with the U.S. Equal Employment Opportunity Commission. The suit alleged that little had been done to integrate the 2,575-member force since a 1986 consent decree promised to remove barriers to hiring and promotion.[94]
- In 1996, the Bureau of Alcohol, Tobacco, and Firearms agreed to pay $5.9 million in damages and legal fees to African-American agents who filed a lawsuit claiming they were assigned to lower-ranking jobs than whites and paid less. The ATF agreed to overhaul its hiring, recruiting, and promotion methods as part of the settlement.[95]

The following comments also point to problems experienced by African-American officers.

An African-American police officer from Washington, D.C., commenting on race relations between white and African-American officers, stated, "You may be their partner on the job, but the minute you're off duty, it's a different story. It's like you'll find a bunch of white cops hovering in the locker room snickering at something, then when you walk in they stop. Now what are you supposed to think?"[96]

An African-American sergeant in the Los Angeles Police Department said,

> We're asked to think of ourselves as being blue, not black. I had one fellow officer, who was white, tell me that if he calls blacks niggers it shouldn't offend me because I'm blue, not black. . . . It was destroying me as a black man. When I joined the force eight years ago I went along with the racial slurs in order to be accepted by the police fraternity. It began to turn me against my own people. I began to see fellow blacks as untrustworthy, as thieves and criminals. I began to shut myself off from my family and friends.[97]

The 1992 shooting of an African-American New York City Transit Authority police officer, Derwin Pannell, by fellow police officers is indicative of another problem faced by African-American officers, particularly those working in plainclothes assignments. Pannell and his partner, Kenneth Donnelly, both in plainclothes, were arresting a woman for fare evasion. Three other plainclothes officers observed Pannell with his gun pointed at the arrested woman and mistakenly believed they had come upon a robbery in progress. They fired shots at Pannell, hitting him three times.[98] One reporter investigating the case wrote the following: "The subsequent wounding of Officer Pannell confirmed the worst fear of these black and Hispanic officers that as they blend in with their surroundings, especially in high crime minority neighborhoods, they become an invisible presence camouflaged even to the brother and sister officers when it matters most."[99] An African-American undercover transit officer said, "Let's face it, when I'm down there, the white cops see me like I'm a mutt, I hear them. That's what they call the teenagers who wear their pants low and their caps backwards. When I'm in the hang-out pose looking for fare beaters, I dress that way. If I'm in a bad spot, if the going is bad and they don't recognize me, they'll think I'm a mutt too."[100]

Another shooting of an African-American police officer in a New York City subway points to the problems minority group police officers face. In 1994, Desmond Robinson, an undercover New York City Transit Authority police officer, was mistaken for a criminal and shot four times by an off-duty New York City police officer, Peter Del-Debbio. The incident was set in motion by the freak misfiring of a shotgun dropped by a suspect trying to escape the transit police and the pandemonium that followed on a Lexington Avenue subway platform.[101]

As these stories and quotations indicate, problems still persist for police officers who are members of minority groups.

Chapter Summary

This chapter discussed the history and extent of discrimination against women and racial and ethnic minorities in U.S. police departments. It explained how women and minorities used the Civil Rights Act of 1964, the Equal Employment Opportunity Act of 1972, the federal courts, and affirmative action programs to achieve job equality. The chapter also showed how this movement toward equality caused a white male backlash.

The chapter also discussed relevant academic studies and anecdotal evidence that women and minorities are effective in police work. It discussed the representation of women and minorities in policing today, as well the problems that persist for them.

Women and minorities have had a difficult time gaining admission into U.S. police departments. However, through their own efforts, and with the help of new laws and the federal courts, they have accomplished in a relatively short time gains that many would have thought impossible. Women and minorities have proved that they can perform the patrol officer's job as well as anyone else. In the future, most hope, discrimination in U.S. police departments will be completely eliminated.

Learning Check

1. Describe the role the federal government played in removing equal employment opportunity barriers to women and minorities in policing.
2. Discuss how police standards and testing procedures have changed in recent years to enable more women and minorities to enter policing.
3. Describe how affirmative action policies have affected white males in hiring and promotional policies.
4. Talk about how effective women are as patrol officers, as compared with their male counterparts.
5. Identify ways in which women and minorities still face problems in policing.

Review Exercise

You have been appointed personnel director of the city of Anywhere, USA. Anywhere, with a population of 60,000, has a police department of 120 officers. The department currently has no female officers, and it is expected to lose thirty officers through retirement this year.

The local chapter of the National Organization of Women (NOW) is claiming that Anywhere is discriminating against females in its police hiring process. Develop a comprehensive plan to increase female representation in the department. Consider ideas presented in this chapter and in chapter 4.

Web Exercise

Patrol the Net over to the National Institute of Justice's homepage. Click onto their statistical updates and obtain the latest (current to the date you are using this text) percentages of women and minorities in law enforcement. What percentage of local police departments are women? African-Americans? Hispanic-Americans? How about sheriffs' offices? State police departments? Federal agencies?

Key Concepts

discrimination
double marginality
National Advisory Commission on Criminal Justice Standards and Goals
Fourteenth Amendment
Civil Rights Act of 1964
Title VII
Equal Employment Opportunity Act of 1972 (EEOA)
de facto discrimination
adverse impact
Griggs v. Duke Power Company
affirmative action
quota

Notes

1. Jack Kuykendall and David E. Burns, "The Black Police Officer: An Historical Perspective," *Journal of Contemporary Criminal Justice* 1 (1980): 4–13.

2. Samuel Walker, "Employment of Black and Hispanic Police Offices," *Academy of Criminal Justice Sciences Today* 10 (1983): 1–5.
3. Samuel Walker, *A Critical History of Police Reform: The Emergence of Professionalism* (Lexington, Mass.: Lexington Books, 1977), pp. 84–94.
4. U.S. Department of Justice, *Civil Service System: Affirmative Action and Equal Employment: A Guidebook for Employers,* vol. 1 (Washington, D.C.: U.S. Department of Justice, 1974).
5. Gerald Carden, *Police Revitalization* (Lexington, Mass.: Lexington Books, 1977).
6. Anthony V. Bouza, *The Police Mystique: An Insider's Look at Cops, Crime, and the Criminal Justice System* (New York: Plenum Press, 1990), p. 142.
7. Chloe Owings, *Women Police* (Montclair, N.J.: Patterson Smith, 1969; originally published in 1925).
8. Catherine H. Milton, *Women in Policing* (Washington, D.C.: Police Foundation, 1972).
9. Samuel Walker, *The Police in America: An Introduction* (New York: McGraw-Hill, 1983), p. 24.
10. Timothy Egan, "New Faces, and New Roles, for the Police," in *Annual Editions: Criminal Justice 92/93,* ed. John J. Sullivan (Guilford, Conn.: Dushkin Publishing, 1992), p. 96; reprinted from *New York Times,* 25 April 1991, pp. A-1, B-10.
11. For an excellent look at the evolution of women as patrol officers, see educator and scholar Dorothy Moses Schultz's *From Social Worker to Crimefighter: Women in United States Municipal Policing* (New York: Praeger, 1995). Ms. Schultz is a former patrol captain with New York's Metro North Railroad Police and a professor at John Jay College of Criminal Justice in New York City. See the book review in *Law Enforcement News,* 15 September 1996, p. 13.
12. Kuykendall and Burns, "Black Police Officer."
13. Kuykendall and Burns, "Black Police Officer."
14. Nicholas Alex, *Black in Blue: A Study of the Negro Policeman* (New York: Appleton-Century-Crofts, 1969), pp. 87, 111.
15. Alex, *Black in Blue,* p. 87.
16. Nicholas Alex, *New York Cops Talk Back* (New York: Wiley, 1976).
17. Steven Leinen, *Black Police, White Society* (New York: New York University Press, 1984).
18. Leinen, *Black Police, White Society,* pp. 255–256.
19. National Advisory Commission on Civil Disorders, *Report* (Washington, D.C.: U.S. Government Printing Office, 1968), chap. 11.
20. National Advisory Commission on Civil Disorders, *Report,* p. 322.
21. National Advisory Commission on Criminal Justice Standards and Goals, *Police* (Washington, D.C.: U.S. Government Printing Office, 1973), p. 343.
22. National Advisory Commission on Criminal Justice Standards and Goals, *Police,* p. 329.
23. *Law Enforcement News,* October 1990, p. 1.
24. Charles R. Swanson, Leonard Territo, and Robert W. Taylor, *Police Administration: Structures, Processes, and Behavior,* 2d ed. (New York: Macmillan, 1988), p. 224.
25. 42 U.S.C.S. 2000 et seq.
26. Public Law No. 92-261.
27. *Griggs v. Duke Power Company,* 401 U.S. 424 (1971).
28. U.S. Equal Employment Opportunity Commission, *Affirmative Action and Equal Employment,* vol. 2 (Washington, D.C.: U.S. Government Printing Office, 1974), p. D-2.
29. *Mieth v. Dollard,* 418 F. Supp. 1169 (1976).
30. *Vanguard Justice Society v. Hughes,* 471 F. Supp. 670 (1979).
31. E. Hernandez, "Problems and Implications in Validating Physical Ability Test Criteria in Law Enforcement" (Paper presented at the annual meeting of the American Society of Criminology), as cited in Larry K. Gaines, Mittie D. Southerland, and John E. Angell, *Police Administration* (New York: McGraw-Hill, 1991), p. 274.
32. P. Maher, "Police Physical Ability Tests: Can They Ever Be Valid?" *Public Personnel Management Journal* 13: 73–183.
33. D. Thompson and T. Thompson, "Court Standards for Job Analysis in Test Validation," *Personnel Psychology* 35: 865–874.
34. *Vulcan Society v. Civil Service Commission,* 5 FEP 1229 (1973).
35. *United States v. State of New York,* 21 FEP 1986 (1979).
36. *Guardians Association of New York City Police Department v. Civil Service Commission of New York,* 23 FEP 909 (1980).
37. U.S. Equal Employment Opportunity Commission, *Affirmative Action and Equal Employment,* vol. 2, pp. D15–D25.
38. Lawrence W. Sherman, "Enforcement Workshop: Minority Quotas for Promotions," *Criminal Law Bulletin* 15 (January/February 1979): 79–84.
39. Robert Sheehan and Gary W. Cordner, *Introduction to Police Administration,* 2d ed. (Cincinnati: Anderson, 1989), p. 135.
40. James Jacobs and Jay Cohen, "The Impact of Racial Integration on the Police," *Journal of Police Science and Administration* 6 (1978): 182.
41. *Afro-American Patrolmen's League v. Duck,* 538 F.2d 328 (1976).
42. *Detroit Police Officers Association v. Young,* 46 U.S. Law Week 2463 (E.D. Mich. 1978). See also Sherman, "Enforcement Workshop," pp. 79–84.

43. "The State of the Union," *Law Enforcement News,* January 15, 1996, p. 10.
44. "The State of the Union," p. 18.
45. "Affirmative-Action Programs Looking a Little Black & Blue," *Law Enforcement News,* 30 April 1995, pp. 1, 7.
46. Peter B. Bloch and Deborah Anderson, *Policewomen on Patrol: Final Report* (Washington, D.C.: Police Foundation, 1974); and Joyce Sichel et al., *Women on Patrol: A Pilot Study of Police Performance in New York City* (Washington, D.C.: Department of Justice, 1978).
47. Sichel et al., *Women on Patrol,* foreword.
48. Sichel et al., *Women on Patrol,* foreword.
49. Anthony V. Bouza, "Women in Policing," *FBI Law Enforcement Bulletin,* September 1975, pp. 4–7.
50. James David, "Perspectives of Policewomen in Texas and Oklahoma," *Journal of Police Science and Administration* 12 (1984): 395–403.
51. Robert Homant and Daniel Kennedy, "Police Perceptions of Spouse Abuse: A Comparison of Male and Female Officers," *Journal of Criminal Justice* 13 (1985): 49–64.
52. Merry Morash and Jack Greene, "Evaluating Women on Patrol: A Critique of Contemporary Wisdom," *Evaluation Review* 10 (1986): 230–255.
53. Sean Grennan, "Findings of the Role of Officer Gender in Violent Encounters with Citizens," *Journal of Police Science and Administration* 15 (1988): 75–78.
54. Michael Charles, "Women in Policing: The Physical Aspects," *Journal of Police Science and Administration* 10 (1982): 194–205.
55. Kenneth Kerber, Steven Andes, and Michelle Mittler, "Citizen Attitudes Regarding the Competence of Female Police Officers," *Journal of Police Science and Administration* 5 (1977): 337–346.
56. Bouza, *Police Mystique.*
57. Bruce Berg, Edmond True, and Marc Gertz, "Police, Riots, and Alienation," *Journal of Police Science and Administration* 12 (1984): 186–190.
58. "Diversity Rules for Sheriff's Office: Minorities Are a Majority for San Francisco Agency," *Law Enforcement News,* 15 October 1996, p. 7.
59. Dorothy Moses Schultz, "California Dreaming Leading the Way to Gender-Free Police Management?" *Criminal Justice: The Americas,* June/July 1994, pp. 1, 8–10.
60. "For She's a Jolly Good Fellow Watson Leaves Austin PD for COPS Office Visiting Fellowship," *Law Enforcement News,* 14 February 1997, p. 4.
61. "Meara Image," *Law Enforcement News,* 31 December 1997, p. 16.
62. "First, Again," *Law Enforcement News,* 28 February 1997, p. 4.
63. "Straight to the Top," *Law Enforcement News,* 30 April 1995, p. 4.
64. Bureau of Justice Statistics, *Local Police Departments, 1993* (Washington, D.C.: National Institute of Justice, 1996), pp. 3–4, Table 6.
65. Bureau of Justice Statistics, *Sheriff's Departments, 1993* (Washington, D.C.: National Institute of Justice, 1996), p. 3, Table 5, and p. 4, Table 6.
66. Susan E. Martin, *Women on the Move? A Report on the Status of Women in Policing* (Washington, D.C.: Police Foundation, 1989), pp. 1–8.
67. Dean J. Champion, *Criminal Justice in the United States* (Columbus, Ohio: Merrill, 1989), pp. 150–151.
68. Gaines, Southerland, and Angel, *Police Administration,* p. 455.
69. Carole G. Garrison, Nancy Grant, and Kenneth McCormick, "Utilization of Police Women," *Police Chief,* September 1988, pp. 32–35.
70. "Father Figure," *Law Enforcement News,* 28 February 1997.
71. "New Tune for Indiana SP: Superintendent Hopes to Have Agency Humming Along," *Law Enforcement News,* 15 April 1997.
72. Peggy Sullivan, "Minorities in Policing," in *Critical Issues in Policing,* ed. Roger G. Dunham and Geoffrey P. Alpert (Prospect Heights, Ill.: Waveland Press, 1988), pp. 331–345.
73. "He Accepts," *Law Enforcement News,* 31 December, 1996, p. 14.
74. George F. Cole, *The American System of Criminal Justice,* 5th ed. (Pacific Grove, Calif.: Brooks/Cole, 1989), p. 281.
75. U.S. Commission on Civil Rights, *Who Is Guarding the Guardians?: A Report on Police Practices* (Washington, D.C.: U.S. Government Printing Office, October 1981), p. 2.
76. For an interesting and entertaining book on women and their history and experiences in law enforcement, see Connie Fletcher, *Breaking and Entering: Women Cops Break the Code of Silence to Tell Their Stories from the Inside* (New York: Simon & Schuster, 1995). Fletcher is also the author of two other books on law enforcement, *What Cops Know* and *Pure Cop.*
77. Gaines, Southerland, and Angel, *Police Administration,* p. 233.
78. Leslie Kay Lord, "A Comparison of Male and Female Peace Officers," *Journal of Police Science and Administration* 14 (1986): 83–97.
79. Daniel Bell, "Policewomen: Myths and Reality," *Journal of Police Science and Administration* 10 (1982): 112–120.
80. Bruce Berg and Kimberly Budnick, "Defeminization of Women in Law Enforcement: A New Twist in the Tradi-

tional Police Personality," *Journal of Police Science and Administration* 14 (1986): 314–319.
81. Judie Gaffin Wexler and Deana Dorman Logan, "Sources for Stress among Women Police Officers," *Journal of Police Science and Administration* 11 (1983): 46–53, 50.
82. Wexler and Logan, "Sources for Stress," p. 52.
83. Sally Gross, "Women Becoming Cops: Developmental Issues and Solutions," *Police Chief*, 51: 32–35.
84. M. L. West, "Sexual Harassment Complaints: A Growing Concern for Police Management," *Journal of California Law Enforcement* 20 (1984): 55–88.
85. J. G. Wexler and V. Quinn, "Considerations in the Training and Development of Women Sergeants," *Journal of Criminal Justice* 13 (1985): 98–105.
86. M. Silbert, "Job Stress and Burnout of New Police Officers," *Police Chief*, 49: 46–48.
87. R. Linden, *Women in Policing: A Review* (Report prepared for the Ministry of the Solicitor General of Canada, cat. no. 1984-92).
88. Belinda Crawford Seagram and Cannie Stark-Adamec, "Women in Canadian Urban Policing: Why Are They Leaving?" *Police Chief*, October 1992, pp. 120–128.
89. James Daum and Cindy Johns, "Police Work from a Woman's Perspective," *Police Chief* 61 (1994): 46–49.
90. Mary Brown, "The Plight of Female Police: A Survey of NW Patrolmen," *Police Chief* 61 (1994): 50–53.
91. Susan Martin, "Female Officers on the Move? A Status Report on Women in Policing," in *Critical Issues in Policing,* ed. Roger G. Dunham and Geoffrey P. Alpert (Prospect Heights, Ill.: Waveland Press, 1988), p. 328.
92. "Law Enforcement around the Nation," *Law Enforcement News,* 15 January 1996, p. 28.
93. "The High Cost of Discrimination," *Law Enforcement News,* 31 December 1996, p. 19.
94. "The State of the Union," p. 9.
95. "The High Cost of Discrimination."
96. Lena Williams, "Police Officers Tell of Strains of Living as a 'Black in Blue,'" *Annual Editions: Criminal Justice—90/91,* ed. John J. Sullivan (Guilford, Conn.: Dushkin Publishing, 1990), pp. 112–113.
97. Williams, "Police Officers Tell of Strains," pp. 112, 113.
98. Robert D. McFadden, "Darkness and Disorder in Subway: Questions Swirl in Police Shooting," *New York Times,* 20 November 1992, pp. A-1, B-2.
99. Craig Wolff, "Alone, Undercover, and Black: Hazards of Mistaken Identity," *New York Times,* 22 November 1992, pp. A-1, A-48.
100. Wolff, "Alone, Undercover, and Black," p. A-48.
101. Clifford Krauss, "Undercover Police Ride Wide Range of Emotion: Boredom and the Adrenaline Rush," *New York Times,* 29 August 1994, p. B-3.

14

Technology in Policing

Chapter Outline

Computers in Policing
  Computer-Aided Dispatch (CAD)
  Automated Databases
  Automated Crime Analysis
  Computer-Aided Investigation
  Computer-Assisted Instruction
  Administrative Uses of Computers
  Computer Networks/The Internet
Innovations in Fingerprinting
  Automated Fingerprint Identification Systems
  Other Fingerprinting Innovations
Less-Than-Lethal Weapons
  Chemical Irritant Sprays
  The TASER and Other Stun Devices
  Safety and Effectiveness of Less-Than-Lethal Weapons
Surveillance Technology
  Surveillance Vans
  Night Vision Devices

Advanced Photographic Techniques
  Mug Shot Imaging
  Age Progression Photographs
  Composite Sketches
Modern Forensic or Criminalistic Techniques
  The Modern Crime Lab
  Crime Lab Accreditation
  Some New Laboratory Criminalistic Techniques
DNA Profiling
  The Blooding
  The Castro Case
  The Frye Test
  The Debate Goes On
Videotaping
Robots
Fear of Technology by Civil Libertarians

Chapter Goals

■ To acquaint you with the latest technological advances in policing.

■ To show you how the computer is revolutionizing policing.

■ To acquaint you with the latest uses of computers in police operations, criminal investigations, and police management tasks.

■ To introduce you to the latest forensic techniques, including DNA profiling.

■ To alert you to the threat to civil liberties caused by rapidly advancing technology.

Introduction

Video cameras, videocassette recorders (VCRs), microcomputers, personal computers, cash machines, cellular telephones, satellites, and the Internet are all very familiar to the students reading this text. However, many might not be aware that little was known of this technology on the day they were born. The past few decades have seen advances in technology that most of us would never have foreseen. The computer chip has revolutionized society. The criminal justice system, and the police in particular have benefited greatly from this technological revolution. Also, the daily televised coverage of the O.J. Simpson double murder case and other cases have heightened public awareness of the police and forensic and scientific evidence to an extent that had never existed before.

This chapter will discuss technology in policing, including computers and their applications in record keeping, crime analysis, communications, personnel allocation, investigations, administration, and training. It will also discuss automated fingerprint identification systems, less-than-lethal weapons, and the surveillance and administrative improvements that are revolutionizing police operations and police investigations. AFIS, CATCH, HOLMES, TASER, and other acronyms that are becoming common in police work will be introduced. The chapter will also discuss the latest in forensics, including ultraviolet forensic imaging, age-progression photographs, and DNA profiling.

Computers in Policing

In 1964, St. Louis was the only city in the United States with a computer system for its police department. By 1968, ten states and fifty cities had computer-based criminal justice information systems. Today almost every metropolitan department with a population of more than 50,000 has some sort of computer support system.[1]

As Charles R. Swanson, Leonard Territo, and Robert W. Taylor tell us,

> Literally thousands of software packages are available that provide singularly or in combination a number of functions directly related to law enforcement. Records management, data analysis, graphics, telecommunications, and word processing are application programs that currently exist in the software market. Most of these software packages require little customizing or adapting for police usage.[2]

Some people may think that computerization has to be an expensive undertaking available only to a large police department, but this is far from the truth. In recent years, a small department of twenty officers, with an operating budget of less than $100,000 per year (not including salaries), could become computerized with a basic $2,500 computer system, including easily available database software management programs.[3] The following sections discuss the most commonly used applications of computers in police work.

Computer-Aided Dispatch (CAD)

Prior to the computer revolution, the police communications system was slow and cumbersome. A citizen would call the police with a seven-digit telephone number. A police telephone operator would take the information, write it on an index card, and put the card on a conveyor belt, where it would travel to the dispatcher's desk. The dispatcher would then manually search maps and records for the police car that covered the area from which the call originated and then call the car, giving the officer all the information from the index card. All records were kept manually.

The 911 emergency telephone number system was introduced by American Telephone and Telegraph (AT&T) in 1968. Today, almost all U.S. police departments in cities with a population over 250,000 operate a 911 system.[4]

Today **computer-aided dispatch (CAD)** allows almost immediate communication between the police dispatcher and police units in the field. Numerous CAD system software packages are available for purchase by police departments. With typical CAD systems, after a 911 operator takes a call from a citizen, the operator codes the information into the computer, and the information immediately flashes on the dispatcher's screen. The CAD system prioritizes the calls on the dispatcher's screen, putting more serious calls (such as crimes in progress and heart attacks) above less serious calls (such as past crimes and nonemergency requests for assistance). The system also verifies the caller's address and telephone number, as well as determining the most direct route to the location. It also searches a database for dangers near the location to which the officers are responding, calls to the same location within the last twenty-four hours, and any previous history of calls to that location. The CAD system also constantly main-

Dempsey's Law

No Computers for Me! Forget About It!

Professor Dempsey, one of the reasons I want to be a police officer is that I hate office work. I'd never want to work with computers, and computers have taken over offices. I'm going to be a cop and ride around in my police car and just deal with people, not machines.

Jason, let me read this quote to you from Rich Owens, a member of the Idaho State Police: "All of the various electronic tools that are at our disposal are finding their way into the patrol car. The toughest thing right now is finding room for the officer."

Source: Adapted from *Law Enforcement News*, 15/31 January 1991, p. 5.

---

tains the status of each patrol unit. In this way, the dispatcher knows which units are available and where all units are located. The system also determines which patrol unit is closest to the location needing police assistance.

Some CAD systems have automatic transponders within patrol units. These enable dispatch personnel to monitor visually all patrol vehicles via a computer monitor and to assign them in coordination with this computer-generated information.

Newer CAD systems, including **enhanced CAD** and enhanced 911 (**E-911**), use **mobile digital terminals (MDTs)** in each patrol unit. In systems using MDTs, voice communications are replaced by electronic transmissions that appear on an officer's MDT, a device put into a police vehicle that allows the electronic transmission of messages between the police dispatcher and the officer in the field. Officers receive messages via a computer screen and transmit messages via a keyboard. Enhanced CAD, or enhanced 911, systems are the latest, most sophisticated, state-of-the-art communications systems. Most involve MDT transmissions as well as the option of traditional voice transmissions, along with sophisticated databases.

MDT systems offer the following advantages over voice systems:

1. A direct interface between the patrol unit and local, county, state, and federal criminal justice information system computers, enabling an officer to query names, license plates, and driver's licenses with almost immediate response, and without interfering with radio communications or requesting the services of a dispatcher.
2. The elimination of many clerical duties.
3. The availability of more detailed information, including addresses displayed with the nearest cross streets and map coordinates (and in some cases, even floor plans).
4. Better coordination of all emergency agencies, because their movements can be monitored visually by both officers at the scene and dispatchers.
5. Automatic processing of incident information via a preformatted incident form, eliminating the need for the officer to drop off an incident report at the station house and the need for someone to type up a report.
6. A dramatic increase in response time as the entire dispatch process, from call to arrival, is fully automated.
7. The capability for the accumulation of large amounts of data regarding police incidents and personnel, which can be used in crime analysis and staff allocation planning to assign personnel when and where crime is highest or calls for assistance are heaviest.[5]

Jerome H. Skolnick and David H. Bayley state the following about the computer terminals in the Houston Police Department's patrol cars:

> The terminals increase enormously the amount of relevant information patrol officers have. For example, they can determine before they step out of their cars if the vehicle they have just signaled to a stop is stolen or if its owner, who may be the driver, is wanted in any connection. Officers cruising down the street often idly type in the license plate numbers of cars driving ahead or parked at sleazy motels . . . in the faint hope that something interesting will turn up, like hitting a jackpot in a slot machine.[6]

The Nassau County (New York) Police Department is among the many departments in the nation that have established an enhanced 911 (E-911) system. When a person calls 911 for assistance, vital information is immediately flashed on a screen in front of the operator. The screen gives the exact address of the telephone being used; the name of the telephone subscriber; whether it is a residence, business, or pay telephone; the police patrol post it is on; the nearest ambulance; and the closest fire department.[7] This system gives the police the ability to assist people at risk even if they cannot communicate because of illness, injury, or an inability to speak English. For example, if a sick or injured person initiates a call to 911 for assistance and then passes out or can no longer continue the conversation for some other reason, the police, having the information in the computer, are still able to respond with assistance.

A good example of the use of newly available communications systems is the experience of the Union/Essex Counties Auto Task Force. The New Jersey counties of Essex and Union experience the highest number of vehicle thefts in the nation. In an effort to suppress these thefts and to arrest auto thieves, twelve law enforcement agencies established the Union/Essex Counties Auto Theft Task Force. The task force officers are equipped with portable mobile data terminals (MDTs). In the first five months of the Task Force's existence they recovered 160 vehicles worth $1.5 million and arrested sixty adult auto theft suspects and 101 juvenile suspects. Auto thefts dropped significantly. Each MDT is linked directly to the NCIC and New Jersey's State Criminal Information Center. Each MDT has an

YOU ARE THERE! »

Translators on Call

The AT&T Language Line Services offer interpreters in some 140 foreign languages. If a call comes in that a police dispatcher cannot understand, the dispatcher can roll it over to the Language Line, and an interpreter will come on. The Monterey-based Language Line Services operations center can readily identify virtually any language presented to it and have an interpreter on the line immediately.

According to Major William Devine, commanding officer of the Providence (Rhode Island) Police Department Night Uniform Division, "When you have a victim whose language you don't understand, you just dial the number and you've got an operator who can get you an address, get you to the area, tell you what happened and what was taken. Then we can put the whole thing together."

Source: Adapted from Harvey Rachlin, "Meeting the Demands of Foreign Languages in Small and Medium-Sized Communities," *Law and Order*, September 1992, pp. 99–102.

YOU ARE THERE! »

How the LAPD Works the Phones

The Los Angeles Police Department's 911 system, which handles over 3 million calls a year, uses the Emergency Command Control Communications System (ECCCS). The main components of the ECCCS are the central dispatch center (CDC), the mobile digital terminal (MDT), and the hand-held remote out-of-vehicle emergency radio (ROVER).

The CDC is the nerve center of Los Angeles's 911 system and is located in City Hall East in Los Angeles. Citizens' calls for service are received at the CDC, and when appropriate, CDC operators issue dispatch orders based on the computer-displayed recommendation for field unit assignment.

The MDTs are mounted in LAPD vehicles. They receive and transmit dispatch and status information, including officer-initiated emergency messages and database inquiries. The MDT has a keyboard for entering data and a screen for displaying messages and data.

The ROVERs are used by field officers for voice communications throughout the city. ROVERs are used for high-priority communications and to back up the MDT communications. Using a ROVER, a field officer can talk to CDC operators and with other field officers. The ROVER has an emergency trigger that transmits an instant "officer needs help" message to the CDC, bypassing normal voice channels to obtain faster assistance.

The New York City Police Department's 911 system is the primary answering point for requests for police, fire, and emergency medical assistance. The system receives approximately 22,700 calls each day. The police dispatch almost 12,000 radio runs. In addition, 331 calls are forwarded to the fire department for dispatch, as are almost 1,900 calls for emergency medical service runs. New York City has implemented an E-911 system similar to the one operated by the LAPD. The project cost over $200 million.

Source: Personal correspondence with the vendor, System Development Corporation, 2500 Colorado Ave., Santa Monica, CA 90406; and personal communication with supervising communications technician Martin Stander of the NYPD Communications Division.

emergency "hot key" that, when pressed, summons all other vehicles with MDTs to back up an officer in distress.[8]

A 1997 report on the use of mobile data access to law enforcement databases reveals that officers with in-car data access technology make more than eight times as many inquiries on driving records, vehicle registrations, and wanted persons or property per eight-hour shift than do officers without in-car computers.[9]

The latest in communications technology is the cellular telephone, which can be used in an investigator's automobile or kept in a pocket. The cellular telephone allows an investigator to make calls without leaving an observation post to access a public phone.[10]

Automated Databases

As we approach the year 2000, computer technology is doing things that were previously unthinkable in policing. A simple example of how far we have come is a 1997 system in Mesa, Arizona. The Mesa Police Department's Cellular Digital Packet Data (CDPD) technology, an automated database, gives officers immediate access, via mobile computers, to critical information contained in the city's mainframe computer. The department's divisions using this system include homicide, pawn detail, auto theft, public information, gang control, and hostage negotiation.[11]

The availability of automated databases has revolutionized police work. An automated database is an enormous electronic filing cabinet that is capable of storing information and retrieving it in any desired format. The FBI created a major automated database, the National Crime Information Center (NCIC), in 1967. The NCIC collects and retrieves data about people wanted for crimes anywhere in the United States; stolen and lost property, including stolen automobiles, license plates, identifiable property, boats, and securities; and other criminal justice information. The NCIC also contains criminal history files and the status (prison, jail, probation, or parole) of criminals. The NCIC has over 6 million active records, which are completely automated by computers that process over 270,000 inquiries every twenty-four hours.[12] The NCIC provides virtually uninterrupted operation day or night, seven days a week. Although the NCIC is operated by the FBI, approximately 70 percent of its use is by local, state, and other federal agencies.[13]

NCIC is moving toward becoming NCIC-2000. With this system, a police officer will be able to identify fugitives and missing persons quickly using automated fingerprint identification system (AFIS) technology, which will be discussed later in this chapter. The officer will place a subject's finger on a fingerprint reader in a patrol car, and the reader will transmit the image to the NCIC computer at FBI Headquarters. Within minutes, the computer will forward a reply to the officer. A printer installed in patrol cars will allow officers to get copies of a suspect's photograph, fingerprint image, signature, and tattoos, along with artist's conceptions and composite drawings of unknown subjects. The printer

> **YOU ARE THERE!**
>
> ### Where Are Computers Taking Us?
>
> In the near future, an officer may pull his patrol vehicle in behind a violator and with a simple touch of a button instantly access all pertinent information available on that subject.
>
> As the scanner behind the vehicle's grill reads the bar coded license plate, the MDT (mobile digital terminal) will display complete registration information almost instantly. In addition, it will check NCIC (National Crime Information Center) and warn if there's a "want" involving the plate.
>
> With the touch of another button, the terminal will position the patrol unit's location from the satellite locator system and send a signal to the dispatcher that the subject vehicle has been stopped at that location. Accuracy will be within a few feet.
>
> After advising the driver that he is being cited for failing to stop at a stop sign and after returning to his vehicle, the officer will position the driver's license on a little screen on the MDT. Bar coded information on the license will be checked automatically and displayed with the vehicle information.
>
> If there are no red flags, simply touching another button (that has been precoded) will activate the miniprinter and produce the proper citation completely filled out. The offender is presented with his hard copy and is quickly on his way....
>
> If there was some reason to be suspicious of the operator of the vehicle, ... the subject could be asked to place a finger into the small box presented to him and touch the surface inside. By plugging the box into the computer console the fingerprint is quickly checked against the state's AFIS [Automated Fingerprint Identification System] file to confirm the driver's identity.
>
> Source: Adapted from Bill Clede, "Where Are Computers Taking Us?" *Law and Order,* November 1991, p. 40.

will also be able to receive images of stolen goods, including cars.[14]

The FBI also maintains the Violent Criminal Apprehension Program (VICAP) database, which contains information on unsolved murders. VICAP has been used increasingly to track down serial murderers.

In addition to these national databases, local law enforcement agencies maintain their own databases. For example, the Los Angeles Police Department uses a computer to maintain a database of over 60,000 gang members.[15]

Another system for storing and reading databases is the CD-ROM, which is capable of storing massive files of data. The advantages of CD-ROM technology is that it is inexpensive and has numerous law enforcement applications. New data can always be added to the disks; however, once entered the data cannot be edited and can be used in read-only format.[16]

Police departments and investigators can store numerous types of archived files onto CD-ROM, such as closed cases, mug shots, fingerprint cards, motor vehicle records, firearm registration information, wanted notices, court decisions, missing person photos and information, and known career criminal files, including photographs and fingerprints.

Automated Crime Analysis

Numerous software application programs aid the police in crime analysis. Crime analysis entails the collection and analysis of data regarding crime (when, where, who, what, how, and why) to discern criminal patterns and assist in the effective assignment of personnel to combat crime. The most basic use of crime analysis is to determine where and when crimes occur, in order to assign personnel to catch perpetrators in the act of committing the crime or to prevent them from committing it.

The latest in the use of automated crime analysis is the New York City Police Department's COMPSTAT program, which was discussed in chapter 1. COMPSTAT provides instant statistical updating of all reported crimes, arrests, and other police activities, such as summonses. This program and its movie screen-type visual displays provide the framework for the weekly crime analysis meetings at NYPD's headquarters in which precinct commanders must account for all increases in crime and must provide strategies to combat these crimes. The keynote of the NYPD re-engineering program of the mid-1990s and the envy of police departments throughout the world, COMPSTAT is a process that began to evolve in early 1994 when, after changes in the leadership of many of the NYPD's bureaus, disturbing information emerged. It appeared that the NYPD did not know most of its own current crime statistics, and there was a time lag of three to six months in its statistical reporting methods. Upon learning this, the department made a concerted effort to generate crime activity data on a weekly basis.[17]

Computer-Aided Investigation

Computer-aided investigation is revolutionizing the criminal investigation process. For example, the New York City Police Department's Detective Division has created an automated mug shot file called CATCH (Computer-Assisted Terminal Criminal Hunt). Using CATCH, detectives feed the description and modus operandi information of an unknown robbery perpetrator into the computer and then receive a computer printout that lists, in rank order, any potential suspects. The detectives can then obtain photographs of possible suspects and show them in photo arrays to victims for possible identification. A computer database, HITMAN, has been used by the Los Angeles Police Department since 1985 and operates in a manner similar to CATCH.[18]

HOLMES (an acronym for Home Office Large Major Enquiry System and a reference to the legendary fictional detective Sherlock Holmes) is a sophisticated

---

YOU ARE THERE! »

Modus Operandi

The term modus operandi (MO) comes from the Latin and can be translated as "method of operation." An MO includes a summary of the habits, techniques, and peculiarities of a person's behavior. The same criminal will generally use a similar MO when committing different crimes.

Some examples of MOs that can be fed into a computer to assist investigators in solving crimes follow:

- Robbery cases: Armed with a gun; states "Your money or your life."
- Murder cases: Commits sexual acts with the dead body, then dismembers it.
- Rape cases: Breaks into college dormitories between 3 and 5 A.M.

computer program developed for British police forces to aid them in managing complex investigations. (In Great Britain, an investigation is called an enquiry.) HOLMES is a complete case management system that can receive, process, organize, recognize, interrelate, and retrieve all aspects of information on a case. It also keeps track of progress, or the lack of it, in investigations. The system was created in response to the infamous Yorkshire Ripper case, in which thirteen women were killed between 1974 and 1981. When the perpetrator was finally apprehended in 1981, it was discovered that he had been detained and questioned by at least six different police forces in relation to the attacks. Because sharing of information on related cases was so cumbersome for the neighboring forces at that time, the connection was never made.[19]

Sergeant Glenn Moore, of the St. Petersburg (Florida) Police Department, traveled to England to study HOLMES and became the case manager in developing HOLMES for the St. Petersburg department. Moore points out that every person involved in an investigation can be up to date on its status in minutes: "All they have to do is ask HOLMES."[20]

Investigators in Washington State battle violent crime with the Homicide Investigation and Tracking System (HITS). HITS, an electronic investigation system, stores, collates, and analyzes characteristics of all murders and sexual offenses in Washington State. Investigators statewide can then retrieve information from the system on these violent crimes to help them solve related cases. The system relies on the voluntary submission of information by law enforcement agencies throughout the state. These agencies submit data on murders, attempted murders, missing persons (when foul play is suspected), unidentified dead persons believed to be murder victims, and predatory sex offenders.[21]

With the cooperation of all law enforcement agencies in the state, researchers have entered over 1,300 murder files into the HITS system. Based on the information provided by the detectives, HITS analysts can query the database for any combination of the victim's gender, race, lifestyle, method and cause of death, geographic location of the crime, the absence or presence of clothing on the body, concealment of the body and/or the dates of death and body discovery. In this way, analysts can identify other murder cases with common elements. Once the database is accessed, analysts can then supply detectives with the names of similarly murdered victims (if known), investigating agencies, case numbers, and the primary investigator's name and telephone number. Designing the query usually takes only few minutes, as does the data search.

A database connected to HITS stores information contained in over 145,000 records from the Washington State Department of Corrections. This file gives HITS immediate access to the identification of present and former inmates with murder and sexual assault convictions. Their physical descriptions can be checked against the physical descriptions of unidentified suspects in recent sexual assault investigations.

HITS has received more than 400 requests for investigative assistance in murder cases. The following example demonstrates how HITS assists law enforcement agencies in their investigation.

After a brutal rape, a detective made a request to the HITS unit for information about offenders having certain physical descriptions and MOs. The HITS staff provided the investigator with a list of known sexual offenders released from prison during the past five years and the areas to which they had been released. Along with this information, the HITS staff provided a collection of photographs to the detective, and the victim immediately identified one of the former offenders as her assailant.[22]

The Institute of Police Technology and Management in Florida has developed "SHERLOCK" (again, a reference to the legendary investigator Sherlock Holmes), a

> **YOU ARE THERE!**
>
> **His Personal Computer Solved the Crime**
>
> A burglar was identified and picked up just a few hours after committing a crime. Released from prison only two weeks before, he was identified by fingerprints recovered at the scene. The Danbury, Connecticut, police officer investigating the 8 P.M. burglary was back in his lab by 9:45 P.M. and identified the perpetrator by 10 P.M. Detectives spotted the burglar strolling on the avenue just forty-five minutes later.
>
> How did the investigating officer break the case? Using a software program called Felon/Find'r on his personal computer, he entered the classification of the listed latent print, and a list of suspects appeared on the screen. The suspect that he sought was among them.
>
> Source: Adapted from Bill Clede, "Computer Chatter, *Law and Order,* January 1994, p. 45.

major case/death investigation management system. This program is designed for the personal computer and can index and cross-reference people, places, things, and vehicles; automatically generate leads; create a "time clock" of victims or suspects; generate a status report on all phases of investigations; provide management controls of evidence and documents; and handle serial crimes.[23]

The Royal Canadian Mounted Police has created a new crime analysis computer program, the Major Crime Organizational System, which enables police to immediately compare similarities in homicides and sexual assaults. It uses guidelines from the Washington State Police Homicide Information Tracking System, the Iowa sex crimes section, and the FBI criminal profiling system. From those sources, investigators have compiled a list of 200 questions to be answered in each murder, sexual assault, and missing persons case.[24]

It must be stated that despite the influence of the computer in the investigative process it will never replace the investigator. The successful investigation of crimes and other police incidents will always primarily depend on the intelligence and hard work of investigators and police officers.

Computer-Assisted Instruction

Computers are valuable teaching tools in police departments. Computer-assisted instruction (CAI) is a learning process in which students interact one on one with a computer, which instructs them and quizzes them.[25]

The Nassau County (New York) Police Department is among the departments that have introduced the Firearms Training System (FATS), a computer-driven laser disk mechanism, to train police officers to make decisions in life-threatening situations. FATS assists both veteran officers and new recruits in making shoot/don't shoot decisions.[26]

Administrative Uses of Computers

Police departments use computers to perform many administrative functions. Management information systems and automated clerical processing systems free personnel to concentrate on serving the public. Software packages can assist police departments in jail and prisoner management. Automated patrol allocation is also possible.

Management Information Systems Police departments, like other U.S. businesses, use management information systems. Robert Sheehan and Gary W. Cordner define management information systems as "those systems that provide information needed for supervisory, allocation, strategic, tactical, policy and administrative decisions."[27] They list the following management information systems found in police departments: (1) personnel information systems, (2) warranty control information systems, (3) equipment inventory systems, (4) evidence and property control systems, (5) booking information systems, (6) detention information systems, (7) case-tracking systems, (8) financial information systems, and (9) fleet maintenance information systems.[28]

Computers are perfect vehicles for management information systems, especially in larger police departments. Their use eliminates the need to keep handwritten records and conduct manual searches. Many of the management information systems just listed are now computerized in most large, modern police departments. For example, in 1997, the Prince George's County, Maryland, Police Department joined a growing roster of law enforcement agencies nationwide that have instituted computer-aided early-warning systems to identify officers who are experiencing stress or other problems so that positive interventions can be made before the situation becomes career-threatening.[29]

Automated Clerical Processing Systems Policing involves a tremendous amount of paperwork, including arrest reports, incident and follow-up reports, and accident and injury reports. The computer simplifies the report-writing process. For example, the St. Petersburg (Florida) Police Department equips all its officers with portable computers, which has reduced the time necessary to write and duplicate reports.[30]

Jail and Prisoner Management Many software packages can assist in jail and prisoner management. This application of computers is useful for police departments and sheriff's offices that are responsible for the lodging of prisoners awaiting appearance in court. The most common software package is Jail Administration Management System (JAMS-II). JAMS-II performs booking, updating, record inquiry, daily logs and audit trails, medical accounting, classification/pretrial release, inmate cash accounting, and billing.[31] The federal prison system uses a computer system called SENTRY to keep track of all offenders in the system. SENTRY keeps data on sentence length, offense, address, classification, and custody, among other prisoner information. The com-

Technology in Policing 341

A Helena, Montana, police officer accesses the Criminal Justice Information Network via the new laptop computer in his police car.

puter automatically makes certain decisions, such as keeping inmates who are enemies from being lodged near each other.[32]

Patrol Allocation Design Patrol allocation is a very important responsibility for police administrators. Sheehan and Cordner summarize the major issues in patrol allocation as follows:

1. Determining the number of patrol units needed in each precinct, at each time of the day, and for each day of the week.
2. Designing patrol beats.
3. Developing policies to dispatch and redeploy patrol units.
4. Scheduling patrol personnel to match variations in the number of units on duty.[33]

Several computerized models are available for automated patrol allocation. The Patrol Car Allocation Model (PCAM) can be used on a microcomputer, whereas PATROL/PLAN must be operated on a large computer system. These software packages determine the number of patrol units needed by precinct, day of the week, and shift, based on predetermined objectives.[34]

Another computerized patrol deployment program, Police Patrol Scheduling System (PPSS), has led two experts to declare the following: "The advent of microcomputers and the PPSS approach to scheduling offers the newest way to bring the power of management science and mathematics into the analysis of patrol deployment. Resource allocation by tradition or speculation will no longer be acceptable now that the age of the computer is here."[35]

Computer Networks/The Internet

A computer network allows users from many different areas to communicate with one another and also to access the network's database. Computer networks are becoming common in policing.

The International Association of Chiefs of Police (IACP) has formed a nationwide computer network for the exchange of semiofficial and informal communications among police departments.[36]

The IACP network updates news and provides legislative information, special topic reports, calendars of events, department profiles, electronic mail, and a "Yellow Pages" of IACP.

As of 1997, a great many police departments, large and small, have created their own web sites and homepages on the Internet. Students using the web

PATROLLING THE NET

High Tech and the Internet Has Helped Police Departments

In August 1996, the *FBI Bulletin* polled police departments all over the nation regarding their use of the Internet. Some of their responses were printed in the January 1997 issue of the *Bulletin*.

All of the responding agencies reported they use their homepages to provide basic information about their departments to citizens. This information generally includes the agency's mission statement, a brief history of the department, and a message from the commanding officer. Departments also feature local fugitives (some even include a list of the FBI's Ten Most Wanted), crime prevention tips, and crime tip hotlines. Some agencies use the Internet to obtain product information or simply to contact other police agencies. The majority of responding agencies provide a list of state and local criminal statutes. Also, many of the agencies use their Internet sites to provide citizens with detailed information about criminal activity occurring in the community and to provide numerous community and law enforcement services.

Here are some specific representative responses and programs:

- The King County, Washington, Police Department worked with a local computer firm to develop a software application that enables the department to include electronic pin maps on its homepage. These maps display information on all arrests, residential burglaries, aggravated assaults, auto thefts, and other crimes occurring throughout the county.
- The Chicago, Illinois, Police Department developed an online form for residents to register their bicycles with the department.
- The Beaufort City, South Carolina, Police Department issues press releases to local media via the Internet, eliminating the scheduling problems caused by officers having to meet in person with different news organizations that need information. The department now posts all press releases on its web site, making them instantly available to media groups and the general public alike.
- In Davis, California, the police department's youth services division assisted in the development of an online coloring book that allows young students to color pictures via the Internet. When completed, the pictures—each of which reinforces a different safety message—can be printed or sent via e-mail to other computers.

In addition to creating homepages, several responding agencies have applied more interactive approaches to their web sites:

- The Wakefield, Massachusetts, Police Department established an interactive e-mail capability coupled with voice mailboxes routed to officers' work stations. This capability allows citizens—most notably crime victims and witnesses—to leave messages for individual officers.
- The Des Moines, Washington, Police Department hosts various e-mail conferences on its web site—including a popular "ask a cop" conference in which citizens get direct answers to law enforcement-related questions.
- The city of Tempe, Arizona, recently established several computerized information kiosks that draw information from the Internet server. This year, the police department's homepage will be included in this system, significantly broadening its potential audience.

Source: Adapted from "FaxBack Response: Previous Question: How Has the Internet Helped Your Agency?," *FBI Law Enforcement Bulletin*, January 1997, pp. 23–25.

---

exercises at the end of each of the chapters of this text know how easy, interesting, and enjoyable it is to surf or patrol police web sites.

Innovations in Fingerprinting

Fingerprints have been an essential tool of policing for years because they provide a positive means of identification (no two people can have the same fingerprints). They also can be definitive evidence in court and essential in obtaining confessions from suspects. There are two basic categories of fingerprints: inked prints and latent prints. Inked prints are the result of the process of rolling each finger onto a ten-print card (each finger is rolled onto a separate box on the card) using fingerprinting ink. Inked prints are kept on file at local police departments, state criminal justice information agencies, and the FBI. When a person is arrested, he or she is fingerprinted, and those inked prints are compared

**Figure 14.1
Positive Identification of a Fingerprint.**
Three men checked into a motel at 11:00 P.M. Shortly after midnight, when a new desk clerk came on duty, the men went to the office and committed an armed robbery. Police investigating the scene went to the room occupied by the three men and found the latent fingerprint on an ashtray. This print was later matched up to one of the suspects, whose fingerprints were on file with the police department.

Source: Adapted from Henry M. Wrobleski and Karen M. Hess, *Introduction to Law Enforcement and Criminal Justice,* 3d ed. (St. Paul: West, 1990), p. 288.

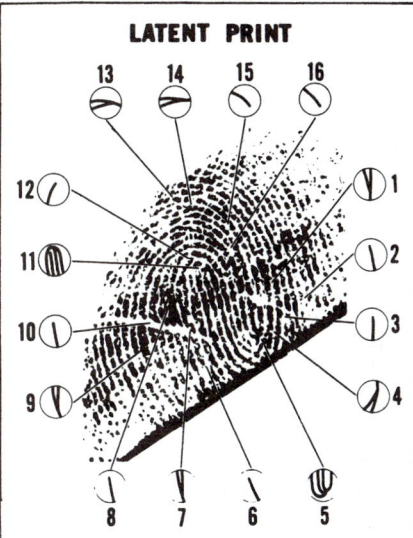
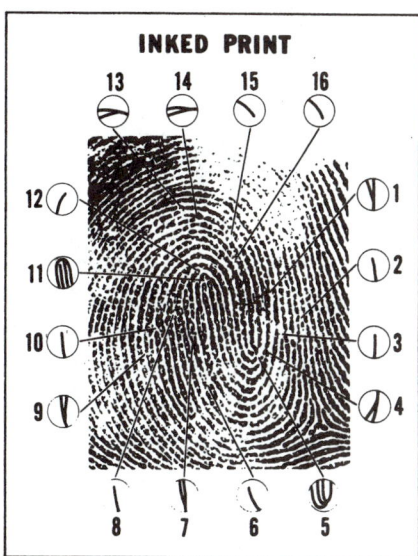

with fingerprints on file for positive identification. Latent prints are impressions left on evidence. These prints may be "lifted" and then compared with inked prints on file to establish the identity of the perpetrator (see figure 14.1). Formerly, this was a time-consuming process requiring a manual search of all prints on file.

Automated Fingerprint Identification Systems

By the 1980s, **automated fingerprint identification systems (AFISs)** began to be developed. Using AFIS, a print technician can enter unidentified latent fingerprints into a computer. The computer then automatically searches its files and presents a list of likely matches, which can be visually examined to find the perfect match. Additionally, using AFIS technology, a person's prints can be taken and stored into memory without the use of traditional inking and rolling techniques.[37]

The Los Angeles Police Department estimates that fingerprint comparisons that in the past would have taken as long as sixty years to complete can now be performed in one day using AFIS technology.[38] Washington, D.C., police report that computerized fingerprint systems enable them to make over one hundred identifications a month from latent fingerprints taken at crime scenes. Other departments reporting successful results using AFISs are those of San Jose, Houston, and Minneapolis.[39] In the State of Kansas alone, AFIS has regis-

> ## YOU ARE THERE! »
>
> ### The Will West Case
>
> The Will West case was instrumental in causing the demise of anthropometry as the primary means of criminal identification and replacing it with fingerprinting. Anthropometry was the use of body measurements to record the identity of arrested criminals. In 1903, a man by the name of Will West was committed to the U.S. Penitentiary at Leavenworth, Kansas. Upon arrival, he was measured using the Bertillon system and photographed. Will West denied having been in the penitentiary before. After taking his photo and measurements, the measuring clerk checked the penitentiary's records and found a previous file with nearly identical measurements and a photograph of a man who appeared to be the prisoner. However, Will West still denied that he had ever been in the prison. The record clerk, upon further examination, found that the file card belonged to inmate William West, who was already a prisoner in Leavenworth, having been committed to a life sentence on September 9, 1901, for murder. The Will West case led to the belief that anthropometry could lead to mistaken identifications and that another more positive method was necessary to ensure proper identification.
>
> Source: Adapted from Federal Bureau of Investigation, *Fingerprint Identification* (Washington, D.C.: Federal Bureau of Investigation, 1975), p. 7.

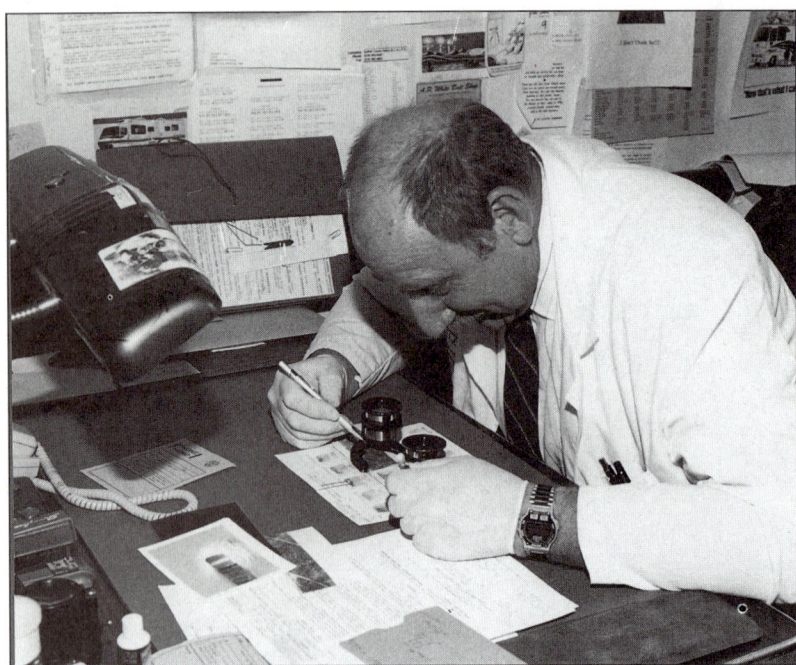

Although AFIS systems have computerized fingerprint identification, the fingerprint examiner still makes the final comparison between the latent fingerprint and a known print.

tered over 1,000 matches since 1990.[40] AFIS technology has solved cases that never could have been solved with normal fingerprinting techniques.[41]

The following are some more examples of the success of automated fingerprint identification systems:

- Since the Milwaukee, Wisconsin, Police Department implemented its AFIS, 232,000 ten-print cards have been entered into the system, with a 37 percent identification rate on unknown latent prints. A Milwaukee police official reports that many serious crimes in the area are now solved with "no suspect information at all—just a fingerprint."[42]

- The Royal Canadian Mounted Police (RCMP) operate a national AFIS system that takes prints from all Canadian law enforcement agencies and holds 2.6 million ten-print cards. A networking system has been in place since early 1990 that allows seven remote sites with compatible equipment to access the central site's system in Ottawa. At its central AFIS site alone, the RCMP made 1,700 latent hits in one year.[43]

Another example of the way in which AFIS technology can help in criminal investigations was its use by the Washoe County, Nevada, Sheriff's Office. When they arrested a person on charges of using stolen credit cards to obtain money from teller machines, an AFIS search identified the suspect as a repeat offender with a prior criminal record in Oregon. This identification led in turn to an FBI record check indicating that the suspect was wanted by the U.S. Secret Service, the State of North Carolina, and the District of Columbia for fraud and weapons violations. The suspect had also been arrested in seven states using multiple aliases.[44]

Until very recently, AFIS technology has been extraordinarily expensive and therefore procured only by the largest agencies. However, today's software-based systems allow any computer based on the UNIX operating system to interface with other systems.[45]

The FBI's new Integrated Automated Fingerprint Identification System (IAFIS) will revolutionize the FBI's ability to maintain a current and effective fingerprint identification operation. The key concept of IAFIS is the electronic (paperless) transmittal of fingerprint images to the FBI's Identification Division, eliminating fingerprint cards in every step of the process.[46]

AFIS technology is moving across the world. In 1997, the United Kingdom set up its National Automated Fingerprint Identification System (NAFIS), which provides fingerprint matching facilities for all police forces of England, Wales, Scotland, and Northern Ireland.[47]

YOU ARE THERE!

The Power of Fluorescent Print Detection: The Polly Klass Case

The power of fluorescent print detection was recently demonstrated in the Polly Klass kidnap/murder case in Petaluma, California. The young victim was abducted from her bedroom by an unknown intruder. Police used black powder methods to discover several prints, none of which matched the subsequently identified suspect.

In an effort to locate more evidence, the FBI's new Evidence Response Team (ERT) was called upon. ERTs are trained and equipped with the latest forensic technology. Agents from the San Francisco ERT processed the scene using an Omniprint 1000. After the victim's wooden bed frame was dusted with Redwop illumination at 450nm, a clear palm print was revealed.

A suspect was subsequently arrested, but he denied any knowledge of the crime. However, when learning of the palm-print evidence, he admitted to the crime and directed investigators to the location of the victim's body. The palm print was the only print that matched the suspect and could not have been found by traditional fingerprint techniques.

Unfortunately, solving the crime did not prevent the death of the victim. The FBI is building a computerized fingerprint database of all convicted sex offenders. It is hoped that rapid matching of any prints found at an abduction scene will lead to the apprehension of the suspect before the victim is physically harmed. Fluorescent print detection is clearly going to be a widely used tool in these efforts.

Source: Adapted from Mary C. Nolte, "The Role of the Photon in Modern Forensics," *Law and Order*, November 1994, pp. 51–54.

YOU ARE THERE!

Solve This Crime

A man meets a woman in a singles bar. She invites him to her apartment. He has a drink with her in the apartment and then shoots and kills her. The detectives investigating the case can find no one who saw the man and woman together, and they have no suspects. While processing the crime scene, they find the two glasses from which the man and woman were drinking. Using forensic techniques, they dust the glasses and come up with a partial latent print (an impression caused by the contact of the man's finger against the glass).

Comparing an unknown latent print or an unknown partial latent print to a known print was once an extremely difficult undertaking. There are millions of fingerprint files in police departments around the United States, as well as over 200 million print files within the FBI's fingerprint records. To match the unknown print to a known print—assuming that our murderer has been fingerprinted—a latent print examiner must search through countless numbers of fingerprints, hoping to find a match. This is similar to searching for the proverbial needle in the haystack.

Fortunately, automated fingerprint identification system (AFIS) technology is available today. Using it, investigators may be able to solve this case.

Other Fingerprinting Innovations

Although still in their infancy as a forensic tool, lasers can be used to lift fingerprints from surfaces that often defy traditional powder or chemical techniques, including glass, paper, cardboard, rubber, wood, plastic, leather, and even human skin.[48] Laser technology even allowed the FBI to detect a forty-year-old fingerprint of a Nazi war criminal on a postcard.[49]

In a recent article, Harold J. Grasman, Special Agent in charge of the Forensic Services Division of the U.S. Secret Service, cited numerous cases of the successful use of sophisticated fingerprint technology. He mentioned such high profile cases as the bombing of the World Trade Center in New York City and the killing of two CIA employees in Langley, Virginia.[50]

Keep in mind, however, that some say the value of fingerprint identification is questionable. Samuel Walker, for example, says, "Despite the great publicity they receive, fingerprints are rarely an important factor in solving crimes." Walker declares that a major part of the problem with fingerprints is obtaining for analysis a useful print from a crime scene.[51]

Less-Than-Lethal Weapons

Police departments throughout the United States are using technological devices to stop and disable armed, dangerous, and violent subjects without resorting to the use of firearms. The term **less-than-lethal weapons**, or nonlethal weapons, is used to identify innovative alternatives to traditional nonfirearm weapons (such as batons and flashlights) and tactics (such as martial arts techniques and other bodily force techniques, including tackles and choke holds). Nonlethal weapons can be seen as shooting-avoidance tools, because these weapons can control unarmed but resisting suspects early in a confrontation, before they have the opportunity to become armed and attack an officer. Also, these weapons can be used against a subject who is armed with less than a firearm—for example, a knife, club, or other instrument that can cause injury to officers. Among the most popular nonlethal weapons being used by the police are chemical irritant sprays and the TASER.

Chemical Irritant Sprays

Chemical irritant sprays are hand-held liquid products that contain the active ingredients of cayenne pepper or CS or CN tear gas. They can be sprayed into the face of a resisting suspect from a distance of up to fifteen feet in order to cause discomfort and temporary disorientation. Thus, officers gain the necessary time to subdue the subject safely.

For many years, the aerosol CN tear gas, originally introduced by Smith and Wesson under the name Chemical Mace, was regarded by law enforcement as the closest thing to a perfect nonlethal weapon. Today, however, police are experimenting with other types of aerosol sprays. Aerosol subject restraints (ASRs), for example, are different from CS or CN sprays in that they do not rely on pain. They cause a subject's eyes to close and double the subject over with uncontrollable coughing. They also cause a temporary loss of strength and coordination. ASRs cause no physical damage and require no area decontamination. Among popular ASRs are oleoresin capsicum (OC, the hot ingredient in chili peppers), Aerko (Punch), Def-Tee (Pepper Mace), Guardian Personal Security Products (Bodyguard), and Zarc (Cap-Stun).[52]

In March 1997, the NYPD announced that it was switching to a more powerful form of pepper spray. Pepper spray is an aerosol-propelled mist that is composed partly of cayenne pepper and causes people to gag, cough, close their eyes, and sometimes experience shortness of breath. It has been used by the NYPD since 1993, but recently police officials said it has not been strong enough. The department is now issuing larger cans of spray that can shoot nearly twice as far, fifteen feet rather than eight feet. The new spray is mixed with citrus fibers, which give it a foamy quality and help it stick to its target, causing a stronger reaction.[53] Chief of Department Louis R. Anemone said, "We're encouraging the use of pepper spray. We want the cops to use this rather than a nightstick or hand-to-hand combat or the butt of a gun or radio or firing a weapon. We think this is an effective less-than-lethal tool."[54]

Shortly after pepper spray was first widely used in the early 1990s to largely replace tear gas and Chemical Mace, several people who had been exposed to it died in police custody, raising fears about its safety. But after reviewing a national sample of such deaths, the National Institute of Justice in 1997 concluded that pepper spray did not cause any of these deaths.[55]

The TASER and Other Stun Devices

The TASER, an acronym for Thomas A. Swift's Electric Rifle, is a hand-held electronic stun gun that discharges a high-voltage, low-amperage, pulsating current via tiny wires and darts, which can be fired from up to fifteen feet away. When the darts strike the subject, the electric current causes a temporary incapacitation of the muscles. This gives the officers the necessary time to subdue the subject safely. The electricity can penetrate up to two inches of clothing. The TASER discharges only a few watts of power and is not harmful to cardiac patients with implanted pacemakers, nor can it be modified to produce a lethal charge.

The TASER has been used by the LAPD since 1980 and was used more than 600 times in one year alone. It has proved to be an effective tool in confrontations with violent people under the influence of phencyclidine (PCP). PCP, "Angel Dust," is an illegal drug that can cause users to exhibit bizarre behavior coupled with extreme violence. Such people are very hard to control, since they exhibit the phenomenon known as superhuman strength. Officers frequently refer to people under the influence of PCP as "dusters."[56]

Another increasingly popular less-than-lethal-weapon is the "beanbag" gun. The one-inch square canvas bag, filled with bird shot, has been used by SWAT teams for several years and more recently by regular patrol officers. The beanbag gun produces a velocity of 320 feet per second and gives an accuracy within a few inches from up to 30 feet away with nonlethal force.[57]

Safety and Effectiveness of Less-Than-Lethal Weapons

J. P. Morgan, chief of the Goldsboro (North Carolina) Police Department, points to a possible drawback of the

All in the Line of Duty

They Got Everyone Out before the Walls Came Tumbling Down

They were just seconds away from being entombed by tons of bricks and mortar when the outside walls of their Brooklyn, New York, apartment building began to collapse on them. With the help of five of New York City's Finest, however, everyone got out alive.

Officers from Brooklyn's 63rd Precinct raced to the collapsing five-story building on Flatbush Avenue at 3:30 a.m., August 6, 1997, in response to a 911-report of falling debris from the building. Officer Joseph Hanna guarded the entrance while dodging debris, while the other four rushed inside. The cops began banging on doors and shouting "Get out!" in the hallways.

Officers Louis Graziano and John Murano carried a ninety-three-year-old woman out of the building, while Officers Kevin Whalen and Jimmy Couroy rescued a man trapped on the third floor, which had already partially given way.

The city's Mayor Giuliani called the rescues a miracle and said that if the officers hadn't acted as they did all of the building's eighty-one residents would have been killed.

When the crisis was over, a sixty-year-old man studied the name tags under the shield of all of the officers at the scene. When he spotted Officer Whalen's, he grabbed the cop's hand and began shaking it vigorously.

"Thank you for pulling my friend out," the man said, nearly crying, "You saved him."

"No problem," the embarrassed officer replied.

Source: Adapted from "'Get Out!' Cops Lead 81 to Safety as B'klyn Building Collapses," *Daily News*, 7 August 1997, p. 1; Tara George, Michele McPhee, and Corky Siemaszko, "A Huge Crash—Then Silence," *Daily News*, 7 August 1997, pp. 6–7, 48.

---

less-than-lethal weapon: "Sometimes . . . it can give a false sense of security, as evidenced by an officer's response to the offer of a back-up. 'I don't need one, I got my OC' [oleoresin capsicum, a pepper spray]."[58]

Just how safe are less-than-lethal weapons? A study of 502 use-of-force incidents not involving the use of firearms attempted to discover the injury rate to officers and subjects from eight specific types of force used by the officers. The force was used to cause a suspect to fall to the ground so that the officers could safely subdue him or her. The types of force studied were (1) striking with a baton; (2) a karate kick; (3) a punch; (4) striking with a flashlight; (5) swarming techniques, or organized tackles by a group of officers; (6) miscellaneous bodily force, including pushing, shoving, and tackling; (7) chemical irritant sprays (CS and CN); and (8) the TASER.[59]

The most used types of force in the study were the baton, miscellaneous bodily force, and the TASER; the least used were chemical irritant sprays, flashlights, and punches. The TASER was used in 102 cases and chemical irritant sprays, in 21 cases. The TASER was about as effective as the other forms of nonlethal force in subduing a subject, and it resulted in fewer injuries to officers and subjects. The researcher concluded, "Expanded use of nonlethal weapons, along with the concurrent development of the next generation of such devices, will lead to fewer and less severe injuries to suspects and officers, reduced civil liability claims and payments, reduced personnel complaints, reduced disability time out of the field, reduced disability pension payments and an improved public image for law enforcement."[60]

The use of the TASER has been upheld in court. In *Michenfelder v. Sumner*, a federal court found the following: "Authorities believe the TASER is the preferred method for controlling prisoners because it is the 'least confrontational' when compared to the use of physical restraint, billy clubs, mace or beanbag guns. . . . When contrasted to alternative methods for physically controlling inmates, some of which can have serious after-effects, the TASER compared favorably."[61]

Surveillance Technology

Police agencies use surveillance for a variety of reasons. Surveillance might be used to provide cover for an undercover officer and an arrest team in a buy and bust narcotics operation or to gather intelligence or to establish probable cause for arrest. Today's advances in technology provide us with more surveillance devices than ever before.[62] Formerly, surveillance equipment consisted of a nearly broken down undercover van used to store the typical surveillance equipment: a camera and a pair of binoculars. Times have changed. Today's investigators have high-tech state-of-the-art listening, recording, and viewing devices, high-tech surveillance vans, night vision devices, and surveillance aircraft, among other innovations.

> ### YOU ARE THERE! »
>
> #### How Wisconsin Police Used Electronic Surveillance to Catch Their Man
>
> Jeff Rickaby, sheriff of Florence County (Wisc.), had a familiar problem. "We had a number of warrants on a man, some of them felonies. We knew where he lived, but we simply didn't have the manpower to sit on the location until he showed up. He'd slip in and out when we weren't around and it was driving us nuts."
>
> Then, Rickaby had an idea. He hung a sophisticated battery-powered, heat- and motion-sensitive surveillance system on a tree outside the man's house and waited. Within days, the alarm radioed an alert. Deputies responded to the location and the felon literally walked into their arms.
>
> "The guy was totally bewildered," Sheriff Rickaby said. "He had absolutely no idea how we'd caught him."
>
> Source: Adapted from Craig Peterson, "Electronic Surveillance and Holdup Camera Systems Aid Lawmen in Combating Crime," *Law and Order*, October 1993, p. 58.

Scientific breakthroughs in the areas of surveillance, mobile communications, and illicit drug detection are arming law enforcement agencies with increasingly sophisticated tools in their fight against illegal drug traffickers and other criminals.[63] This section will discuss the latest in surveillance and night vision devices.

Surveillance Vans

A vehicle specialist describes today's state-of-the-art surveillance van: "When talking about surveillance vehicles today, . . . we tend to think of a van whose interior looks slightly less complex than the bridge of Star Trek's USS Enterprise." He describes the ideal surveillance van as having the following equipment: power periscopes operated by a video game-like joystick; six cameras to cover 360 degrees of the van's exterior, plus a periscope-mounted observer's camera; videotape decks to record everything happening on the street; quick-change periscope camera mounts; portable toilets; video printers; motion detection cameras; night vision cameras; cellular telephones; AM/FM cassette entertainment systems; CB radios, police radios, and police scanners; and other personalized equipment.[64]

Night Vision Devices

Among the most sophisticated surveillance devices being used today are enhanced night vision gear, including monocular devices small enough to hold in one hand that can be adapted to a camera, video camera, or countersniper rifle. The latest in night vision technology includes infrared (IR) technology and thermal imaging (TI). This technology requires no light at all to see objects in total darkness.[65]

The following are some recent successes using sophisticated night vision equipment:

- The U.S. Border Patrol used night vision devices to find a carefully concealed tunnel used by an organized gang of alien smugglers by detecting the heat of the bodies moving in the tunnel.

- Suburbanites in a large northeastern city were suspected of growing their own marijuana under lamps in their basements. Using thermal cameras, police detected heat emissions from the suspected homes, obtaining enough evidence to get a "probable cause" search warrant.

- Recognizing a familiar MO, two detectives pinpointed one individual as the most likely suspect for a particularly brutal crime. When questioned, the suspect claimed he was at home at the time of the crime. The officers had brought an IR thermal imaging camera with them, which they used to scan the suspect's car. It was "warm," indicating it had been used quite recently. Faced with the evidence, the suspect eventually broke down and confessed.[66]

Advanced Photographic Techniques

Photography has always played a major role in policing. Innovations and advanced techniques have increased this role. This section will discuss mug shot imaging systems, age-progression photography, and composite sketching.

Mug Shot Imaging

Mug shot imaging is a system of digitizing a picture and storing its image on a computer so that it can be retrieved at a later time. The picture is taken with a video camera and is then transferred to a color video monitor, where it appears as an electronic image. When the image is filed, the operator enters identifying data, such as race, gender, date of birth, and the subject's case number. Using this system, victims of crimes can quickly view possible mug shots on a computer screen.[67]

The Orange County, Florida, Sheriff's Office is using a mug shot imaging system with a laser printer to produce wanted flyers for those sought on warrants. The pictures on these flyers are very clear, with excellent resolution. Major John J. Pavlis, of the sheriff's office, writes that this system could also be used for the following:

- Photos of missing children or other missing people, once digitized, could be sent to all locations that have imagery workstations. Quality pictures could then be sent quickly to officers in the field.
- Photos of all department employees could be digitized and kept in files for use in internal affairs investigations.
- Photos of wanted individuals, once digitized, could be sent to other agencies via a computer.[68]

A good example of mug shot imaging is the ALERT (Advanced Law Enforcement Response Technology) System. This system allows a photo of a subject to be transmitted from one police cruiser to others with the necessary equipment, giving officers an immediate view of a wanted suspect or a missing person.[69] In a demonstration in June 1997, digital photographs were transmitted between two specially equipped police cars—one parked in College Station, Texas, the other sitting in an Alexandria, Virginia, hotel parking lot. The Alexandria Police Department spokesperson said it took about twenty seconds.[70]

Age Progression Photographs

One of the newest innovations in investigative photography is the age progression photo. The ability to recognize a face may be thwarted by the changes that naturally occur to the face with age. To counter this problem, technology has emerged that can "age" an earlier photo of a person to show how he or she would look today, using sophisticated anatomical knowledge. Computers have enabled the National Center for Missing and Exploited Children to get thousands of these age-progressed pictures onto milk cartons and flyers.[71]

The FBI uses its own age-progression program for adult faces. The system allows artists to do such things as thin hair, add jowls, or increase wrinkles, while the computer maintains the basic facial proportions. The FBI's software for aging children's faces allows pictures of parents and older siblings to be fused into photos of missing children to obtain a more accurate image.[72]

Composite Sketches

Police have for many years sought the assistance of forensic artists in preparing composite sketches. The FBI began the use of composite sketching in 1920, and other agencies began their use even earlier. These portrait-style drawings generally require hours of interview, drawing, and revision. Today the FBI has converted its

> ## YOU ARE THERE! »
>
> ### Capture of John List Through Age-Progression Photos
>
> In 1987, the FBI's Newark, New Jersey, field office forwarded a request for forensic assistance to the Special Projects Section of the FBI Laboratory for age-enhanced photos of J. E. List, who had eluded detection since murdering his entire family seventeen years previously.
>
> The FBI produced age-enhanced photographs of List and forwarded them to the field office. The office then publicized an age-enhanced photograph in various national publications. A woman recognized her neighbor as List, who lived under the assumed name Robert P. Clark. She had seen List's age-enhanced photograph in a supermarket tabloid. The neighbor dared Clark's wife to confront her husband with the photo but the wife never did.
>
> Two years later, in 1989, the television show, "America's Most Wanted," featured a plaster bust, prepared by a forensic artist, that was based on the photograph of List. By this time List had moved to Midlothian, Virginia, a suburb of Richmond. Convinced that Clark was, in fact, John List, his former neighbor asked her son-in-law to call the FBI and provide investigators with List's new address. When agents confronted the man, he denied he was List. But fingerprints from a gun permit application filed a month before the slayings revealed the truth. List was arrested and returned to New Jersey, where he was convicted of murder and sentenced to life in prison.
>
> Source: Adapted from Gene O'Donnell, "Forensic Imaging Comes of Age," *FBI Law Enforcement Bulletin,* January 1994, pp. 5–10.

YOU ARE THERE! »

Finding Missing Children Through Age-Enhanced Photos

An investigator from Oakland, California, reached out across the United States and Canada with age-enhanced images of two missing brothers. After exhausting every lead, the investigator turned to the television program "Unsolved Mysteries."

On the evening of the broadcast, hundreds of calls poured in from the Albuquerque, New Mexico, area. Authorities located the children in a trailer on the outskirts of town, where they lived with their mother and her new husband—a known drug dealer. The boys were returned to their father, who had not seen them in several years. Although the aged images of the boys were very accurate, the relentless determination of the investigator and the assistance of the public ultimately solved the case.

Source: Adapted from Gene O'Donnell, "Forensic Imaging Comes of Age," *FBI Law Enforcement Bulletin*, January 1994, p. 9.

Evidence technician analyzes an article of clothing.

book of photographs, used for interviewing witnesses for composites, into handdrawn images using forensic imaging to use as a database on a computer that will automatically generate images similar to those that are handdrawn. Once the witness selects features from the catalog, the composite image appears on the computer screen in just a few minutes.[73]

Often, an artist is not even necessary. With practice, investigators can place the features on the screen and modify the image as the witness instructs. The system can be loaded into a laptop computer to further speed up the process by taking it directly to a crime scene. It can also be accessed via a modem hookup or put outline, with an artist in another city available to prepare the composite while a witness views and suggests changes.

Modern Forensic or Criminalistic Techniques

The use of scientific technology to solve crime is referred to as forensic science, or criminalistics. Today's crime laboratories contain numerous computerized devices and advanced scientific technology to help police investigate crime.

The controversy regarding the collection and analysis of physical evidence at the crime scenes in the O.J. Simpson double murder case clearly indicates the importance of forensics or criminalistics in today's investigations.

The terms **forensic science** and **criminalistics** are often used interchangeably. Forensic science, more specifically, is that part of science applied to answering legal questions. It is the examination, evaluation, and explanation of physical evidence in law. Fields in forensic science include pathology, toxicology, physical anthropology, odontology, psychiatry, questioned documents, ballistics, tool work comparison, and serology, among others. Criminalistics is actually one branch of forensic science, which deals with the collection and study of physical evidence related to crime.[74] In order to simplify the information in this chapter for the non-

YOU ARE THERE! »

The Use of Forensic Evidence

A nationwide study of prosecutor case files by the National Institute of Justice revealed that laboratory reports were used in about one-quarter to one-third of felony cases that had survived initial screening. The following were specific findings of the study:

- Drugs and fingerprints made up from 60 to 80 percent of the evidence described in the laboratory reports. This suggests that laboratories can expect to focus on evidence that is mandatory for prosecution of a case or can conclusively link the defendant with a crime.
- The next most frequently used types of forensic evidence are firearms, blood and bloodstains, and semen.
- Virtually all murder and drug prosecution files had laboratory reports.
- Forensic evidence is least often used in burglary, robbery, and attempted murder or aggravated battery cases.
- Laboratory directors generally agreed with prosecutors on what cases need priority. They cited forensic evidence as having its greatest impact in drug and homicide prosecutions, moderate importance in arson and burglaries, and minimal importance in aggravated batteries, robberies, and larcenies. Lab directors also believed their examinations have substantial impact in rape cases, but prosecutors are more tentative about the value of this evidence.
- Although we frequently read or hear about more esoteric forms of forensic evidence—e.g., hairs, fibers, glass, paint, soil, etc.—research shows they rarely appear in routine criminal cases. One reason, of course, is that prosecutors have less interest in evidence whose analysis may only partially or statistically link a defendant with a crime.

Source: Adapted from Joseph L. Peterson, *Use of Forensic Evidence by the Police and Courts* (Washington, D.C.: National Institute of Justice, 1987), p. 3.

YOU ARE THERE! »

Crime Laboratory Caseloads

A nationwide survey of crime laboratories by the National Institute of Justice revealed that only about a quarter of crime laboratory caseloads involve personal or property crimes. About two-thirds of the work is identification of drugs and narcotics and the determination of alcohol content of samples from suspected drunk drivers. In fact, forensic laboratories fight a continuing battle to manage their drug caseloads and still respond to other investigations. This reflects the fact that drug possession or sale and driving-while-intoxicated cases require a scientific analysis for prosecution.

Source: Adapted from Joseph L. Peterson, *Use of Forensic Evidence by the Police and Courts* (Washington, D.C.: National Institute of Justice, 1987), p. 3.

---

science student, the word criminalistics will be used interchangeably with forensic science.

Criminalistic evidence includes such clues as fingerprints, blood and blood stains, semen stains, drugs and alcohol, hairs and fibers, and firearms and toolmarks.[75]

Forensic technicians, forensic scientists, forensic chemists, or the more generic term, criminalists, generally specialize in one or more of the following areas: analysis of trace evidence, serology, drug chemistry, firearms/toolmarks, and questioned documents.

The purpose of forensic science or criminalistics is to take physical evidence from a crime or a crime scene and to use it to identify the person who committed the crime and exonerate others who may be under suspicion. For example, was the revolver found on a suspect the one that fired the bullet found in the body of a murder victim? If so, did the suspect fire it? Criminalistic evidence also can establish an element of the crime and reconstruct how the crime was committed.

In a study of criminalistic evidence and the criminal justice system, the NIJ discovered that the police are on average about three times more likely to clear (solve) cases when scientific evidence is gathered and analyzed; prosecutors are less likely to agree to enter into plea negotiations if criminalistic evidence strongly associates the defendant with the crime; and judges issue more severe sentences when criminalistic evidence is presented at trials.

This section will cover the modern crime lab, crime lab accreditation, and some new laboratory criminalistic techniques.

YOU ARE THERE!

How Criminalistics Evidence Led to a Serial Killer: The Wayne Williams Case

For twenty-two months in 1980 and 1981, the residents of Atlanta, Georgia, lived in growing fear and outrage as a serial killer methodically hunted their children. The body count reached thirty victims before the killer was apprehended. The victims ranged in age from seven to twenty-eight, and most were young males. Some were shot or strangled; others were stabbed, bludgeoned, or suffocated. All the victims were African-American. The deaths of so many black young people gave rise to a variety of theories and accusations, including belief in a plot by white supremacists to systematically kill all African-American children. Atlanta became a city under siege and inevitably attracted the attention of the entire country, including the resources of the federal government.

It appeared the murders would never stop until one night, as police staked out a bridge over the Chattahoochee River, they heard a car on the bridge come to a stop, followed by a distinct splash caused by something being dropped into the river. They pulled Wayne B. Williams, twenty-three, over for questioning and finally arrested him as a suspect in the child murder cases. Williams was found to be a bright young African-American man who lived with his retired parents and involved himself in photography. A media and police "groupie," Williams would often listen on his shortwave radio and respond to ambulance, fire, and police emergency calls. He would then sell his exclusive pictures to the local newspapers. At age eighteen, he was arrested for impersonating a police officer. He spent one year at Georgia State University but dropped out when he felt his "rising star" was moving too slowly.

Wayne's freelance work as a cameraman was never steady, and he began to focus his energies on music. As a self-employed talent scout, he eventually lured his victims into his control. He was known to distribute leaflets offering "private and free" interviews to African-Americans between the ages of eleven and twenty-one who sought a career in music. At his trial, Williams was depicted as a man who hated his own race and wanted to eliminate future generations. He was described as a homosexual, or a bisexual, who paid young boys to have sex with him. A boy, age fifteen, claimed he had been molested by Williams, and several witnesses testified they had seen him with some of the victims.

Williams denied guilt, and the prosecution had only elaborate forensic evidence on which to base their case against him. The forensic evidence suggested a distinct link between Williams and at least ten of the homicides and indicated a pattern surrounding the murders. The judge ruled the evidence admissible, and Williams was found guilty of murdering two of his older victims, Nathaniel Cater, twenty-seven, and Ray Payne, twenty-one. Due to the nature of the circumstantial evidence, the judge sentenced Williams to two consecutive life sentences. He was eventually named as being responsible for twenty-four of the Atlanta slayings.

Source: Adapted from Eric W. Hickey, *Serial Murderers and Their Victims* (Pacific Grove, California, 1991), p. 168.

The Modern Crime Lab

There are more than 300 crime laboratories in the United States, 80 percent of which are located within police agencies.[76] Most large police departments operate their own police laboratories. Smaller departments may contract out the use of large county crime labs, state police crime labs, or the FBI lab. Table 14.1 lists the major sections of a typical police crime laboratory, along with sophisticated forensic specialty sections.

Private (nongovernment) labs are becoming an important part of the U.S. legal system. Their analyses are often introduced into criminal and civil trials to present evidence or contradict evidence presented by a prosecutor that has been analyzed in a police lab.

Crime Lab Accreditation

Crime labs and criminalistic techniques received much negative attention in the O. J. Simpson case. Despite overwhelming forensic evidence, Simpson was acquitted of double-murder charges. Some called the verdict jury nullification and some say it came from a lack of belief and trust in crime lab technology. Crime lab accreditation is designed to ameliorate some of the problems in certification and standardization of labs (see Table 14.2).

Table 14.1 Police Forensic Laboratories

Major Section	Function
Ballistics	Examination of guns and bullets
Serology	Examination of blood, semen, and other body fluids
Criminalistics	Examination of hairs, fibers, paints, clothing, glass, and other trace evidence
Chemistry	Examination of drugs and alcohol
Document analysis	Comparison of handwriting

Specialty Sections	Function
Forensic toxicology	Analysis of poisons and other toxic substances in a person's body
Forensic pathology	Examination of dead bodies
Forensic physical anthropology	Examination of skeletal remains
Forensic odontology	Study of teeth formation

Source: Professor Paschal L. Ungarino, Suffolk Community College, New York.

Table 14.2 The O. J. Simpson Case and the Police Lab

Piece of Evidence	Section of Police Lab
Bloody glove	Serology
Hair from the blue watch cap	Criminalistics
Blood droplets	Serology
Shoeprint impressions	Criminalistics
O.J.'s apology letters to Nicole	Document analysis

As of 1997, only half of the crime labs in the United States were accredited by the American Society of Crime Lab Directors (ASCLD). Although labs in Australia, Hong Kong, Singapore, and New Zealand were accredited, the FBI's lab still was not. Labs seek accreditation and certification by the ASCLD as a way to ensure quality control. It is a check of the lab's policies, procedures, physical space, security, and housekeeping. The National Forensic Science Technology Center, a nonprofit spin-off of ASCLD, is available to assist unaccredited labs. The center's consultants do pre-accreditation inspections and help labs review and write policies and procedures. Certification of lab employees is conducted by the American Board of Criminalists (ABC). By ensuring that lab personnel are all held to the same standard, certification helps analysts fend off courtroom salvos about their experience, background, and training.[77]

Accreditation and certification is certainly needed in the nation's labs. According to Ron Urbanovsky, director of the Texas Department of Public Safety's statewide system of crime labs, "Part of the Simpson case fallout was that we've seen much longer and stiffer cross-examinations in court. Testimony that used to take two to three hours now takes eight to 12 hours, and it's grueling. We are asked to be perfect in a non-perfect world."[78]

Some New Laboratory Criminalistic Techniques

Some of the newest techniques employed at crime labs follow.

■ Neutron activation is a relatively new technique to test evidence at a crime scene. With neutron activation, a piece of evidence is bombarded with neutrons and made radioactive; then it is analyzed to determine its component elements.[79]

■ The scanning electron microscope is another relatively new device that can magnify material up to 100,000 times. It can uncover and identify extremely minute particles of trace evidence, such as gunpowder residue. Another device, the gas chromatograph-mass spectrometer, can separate and identify the components of extremely minute mixtures.[80]

■ Another new technique is automated handwriting technology. The U.S. Secret Service has developed a new computer tool, the Forensic Information System for Handwriting (FISH) that allows examiners to treat writing data with special mathematical programs and search them against previously entered writings. According to Richard A. Dusak, a document analyst for the U.S. Secret Service in Washington, D.C., "The Secret Service has been able to effect case solutions, consolidate investigative information and identify previously unknown individuals with the aid of the Forensic Information System for Handwriting."[81]

■ The use of ultraviolet or invisible light technology is in its early stages in forensics but has already been useful in solving some crimes. One application of ultraviolet light is the photographing of bite marks on human skin. Ultraviolet lighting provides more detail and contrast to an injured area than do standard lighting tech-

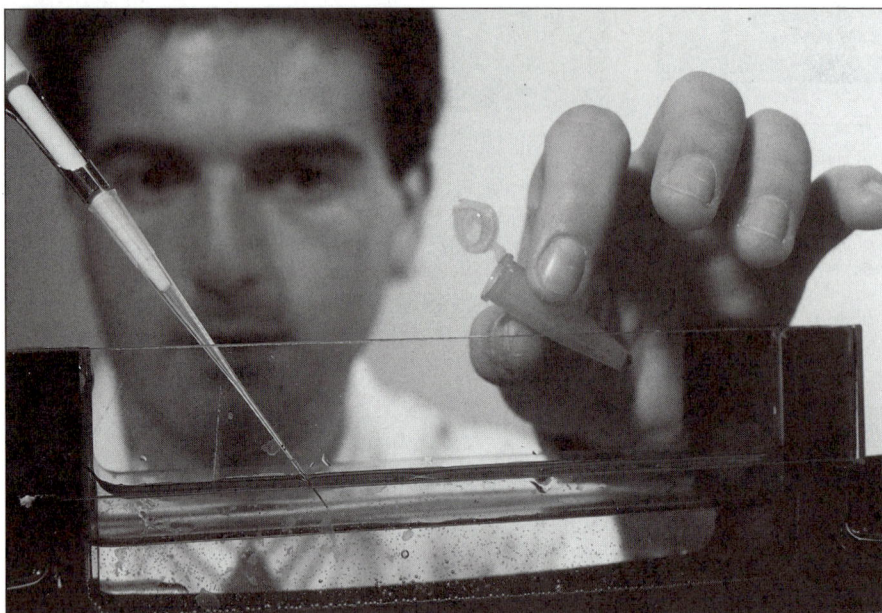

A lab technician processing DNA evidence.

niques. The resultant photographs show wounds in greater detail than would be possible with conventional photography. Ultraviolet lighting techniques have also been used to scan entire crime scenes after the areas have been searched by technicians and investigators. Additional evidence missed during the initial search—including footprints, fingerprints, and trace metal fragments—has been found. Medical and dental experts report that although the application of ultraviolet light is still a relatively new field, it promises to be an indispensable tool for law enforcement agencies in the investigation of crime scenes.[82]

- There have also been several innovative techniques revolutionizing the science of ballistics. In 1994, a computerized ballistics identification system that stores bullet "signatures" in a database was established to allow ballistics examiners to quickly determine whether a spent bullet is linked to a crime. The new technology is being hailed as a revolutionary advance in the painstaking, time-consuming science of ballistics.[83]

Also, another new computerized ballistics system, DRUGFIRE, has come on line. This system, which deals with the comparison of shell casings and bullets, is a national database giving firearms examiners the capability to link firearms and projectiles used in drive-by, serial, gang, and drug-related shootings across the nation.[84]

DNA Profiling

DNA profiling, also called genetic fingerprinting or DNA typing, holds much promise in helping the police solve crimes and ensuring that those guilty of crimes are convicted in court. **Deoxyribonucleic acid** (DNA) is the basic building code for all of the human body's chromosomes and is the same for each cell in an individual's body, including skin, organs, and all body fluids (such as blood and semen). The characteristics of certain segments of DNA vary from person to person and thus form a genetic "fingerprint" for each individual. Therefore, it is possible to analyze certain substances, such as blood, hair, semen, or body tissue, and compare them with a sample from a suspect.

DNA profiling, or **genetic fingerprinting**, is the examination of DNA samples from a body fluid (usually blood or semen) to determine whether they came from a particular subject. For example, semen on a rape victim's jeans can be positively or negatively compared with a suspect's semen. DNA profiling has been used in thousands of criminal investigations since 1987, yet some researchers believe it is being used prematurely. There is not yet complete acceptance of the new techniques by the scholarly scientific community.[85]

As a further example of the utility of DNA profiling, the U.S. Defense Department has established a repository of genetic information regarding the over 2 million

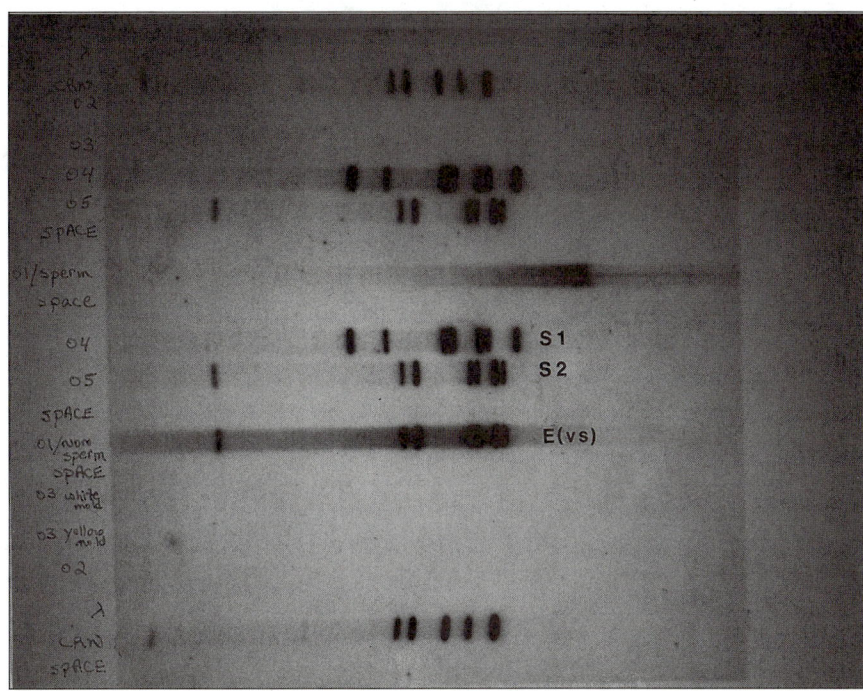

The results of DNA profiling or genetic fingerprinting are shown on the Autorad.

members of the U.S. Armed Forces as a way of identifying future casualties of war. DNA is collected and stored by the Armed Forces Institute of Pathology. Formerly, unidentified dead were identified, if possible, by fingerprints and medical records. However, DNA can now be used to identify people from body parts, like a single leg. The current plan calls for including only active personnel and destroying the specimens when people leave the military.[86]

The application of DNA technology for law enforcement is changing rapidly. A new procedure—PCR-STR (polymerase chain reaction-short tandem repeat)—has several distinct advantages for law enforcement over RFLP (restricted fragment length polymorphism), an earlier DNA procedure. PCR-STR requires only pin-size samples, rather than the dime-size samples needed for RFLP; it can analyze samples degraded or broken down by exposure to heat, light, or humidity; it requires only two days for laboratory analysis, compared to eight weeks for RFLP; and it can automate the entire DNA process, which will greatly reduce the possibility of human error.[87]

The latest in the rapidly marching DNA technology is the possibility now being developed in clinical research of a handheld computer that could be used at a crime scene for DNA testing. This device would give investigators instantaneous feedback on the number of suspects or victims at the crime scene based on the number of different DNA profiles developed.[88]

Another current DNA innovation is CODIS (Combined DNA Index System), a computerized forensic database that deals with the comparison of blood, semen, hair, and other human tissue. CODIS contains DNA profiles obtained from subjects convicted of homicide and sexual assault. Using this system, investigators are able to search evidence from their individual cases against CODIS' extensive national file of DNA genetic markers. In 1996, investigators in Florida recorded some seventy-two statewide matches in CODIS that have linked 113 different cases. These cases involved previously unsolved homicide and sexual assault crimes.[89]

The Blooding

DNA profiling was the subject of *The Blooding,* a novel by Joseph Wambaugh. In this book, which was based on a true story, two young girls are brutally beaten and murdered in the English county of Leicestershire, and the police have no clues to the identity of the killer. Eventually, a young man, whom Wambaugh calls only the "kitchen porter," confesses to the murder of the first girl and is also charged by the police with the second murder. Hoping to get physical evidence to corroborate the confession, the police ask Dr. Alec Jeffries, a young geneticist at nearby Leicestershire University who discovered genetic fingerprinting, to compare DNA samples found on the victims to the DNA of the defendant. After performing his testing, Jeffries tells the police that their suspect definitely did not commit the murders. He also tells them that one man—not their suspect—is responsible for the murder of both girls.

The police decide to embark on a campaign of "blooding" to find the killer. They "request" that all men within a certain age group who live, work, or have business in the area appear at the police station and submit to a venipuncture (the drawing of a vial of blood). The blood is then analyzed using Jeffries's technique. After over 4,500 men "voluntarily" gave a sample of their blood, the police still have no suspects.

Eventually it is discovered, over a few beers in a local pub, that a young man, Colin Pitchfork, had paid another young man, Ian Kelly, to appear and be "bloodied" for him. When the police approach Pitchfork, he willingly confesses to both murders. His blood samples are then tested, and the DNA tests reveal that he is indeed the murderer of both girls. It must be emphasized that the DNA analysis did not solve the case, although it did eliminate a suspect and it did confirm guilt. Even if DNA profiling is fully accepted by the scientific community, it will never replace regular detective work.

DNA profiling has gained popularity at an exponential rate since its introduction. It was initially hailed as foolproof and 99 percent positive. Most of the positive claims about DNA profiling were based on the testimony of interested parties, such as scientists from companies involved in DNA testing and prosecutors. Defense attorneys were often unable to combat DNA profiling evidence in court or to find experts to testify against it. Generally, defendants confronted with a DNA match pleaded guilty in a plea bargain—until the Castro case.[90]

The Castro Case

In 1987, twenty-three-year-old Vilma Ponce and her two-year-old daughter were stabbed to death in their apartment in the Bronx, New York. There were few leads until police arrested the building's superintendent, Joseph Castro, and found some dried blood in the grooves of his watch. When questioned, he said the blood was his own. Prosecutors sent the blood from the watch, samples of the victims' blood, and a sample of Castro's blood to a firm called Lifecodes for testing.

Lifecodes declared a match between the DNA from the blood on the watch and the DNA from Vilma Ponce's blood. Defense attorneys Barry Scheck and Peter Neufeld located experts who agreed to testify against the admission of the DNA typing evidence. For twelve weeks the evidence was argued before New York Supreme Court acting justice Gerald Sheindlin, who listened to experts from both sides. The experts for the defense were able to uncover such serious blunders committed by Lifecodes in its performance of the tests that the prosecution's expert witnesses recanted their position. In an unprecedented move, two expert witnesses for the defense and two for the prosecution issued a joint statement: "The DNA data in this case are not scientifically reliable enough to support the assertion that the samples . . . do or do not match. If these data were submitted to a peer-reviewed journal in support of a conclusion, they would not be accepted. Further experimentation would be required."[91] Ultimately, Justice Sheindlin ruled the evidence of the match inadmissible, and the case against Castro was dismissed.

The Frye Test

The major problem with DNA profiling is that it cannot pass the Frye test. The **Frye test** is based on the court case *Frye v. United States,* in which the court ruled that novel scientific evidence will not be accepted into evidence until it has gained general acceptance in the particular scientific discipline in which it belongs.[92] Although DNA profiling is accepted by some courts and rejected by others, its reliability will be in question until it has gained general acceptance by the scientific community. Some researchers suggest that at the present time, DNA profiling will find its best use as an investigative tool rather than as a courtroom measure to determine guilt or innocence.[93]

The Debate Goes On

A 1992 unanimous decision by the U.S. Court of Appeals for the Second Circuit, one of the most influential federal appeals courts, may change the rulings of courts nationwide on DNA evidence. The court approved the use of DNA evidence and affirmed the kidnapping conviction of Randolph Jakobetz, who had been sentenced to twenty-nine years in prison for raping a woman in Vermont and leaving her along a highway in the Bronx. Jakobetz was convicted when an FBI analysis of the DNA from semen recovered from the woman was matched to Jakobetz's DNA from a blood test.

Legal experts have said that this decision was the first clear-cut guidance from the federal appellate bench on the use of DNA fingerprinting. Previously, many courts would not allow DNA evidence to be used at a trial unless it was presented first at a pretrial hearing. Under the new ruling, courts could allow DNA evidence without such hearings and let the jury determine the worth of the evidence. In this case, the court seems to have overruled the Frye test by ruling that "scientific evidence was like any other and that it could be admitted if its 'probativeness, materiality and reliability' outweighed any tendency to mislead, prejudice and confuse the jury."[94]

The Jakobetz case was followed by two important U.S. Supreme Court cases, *Daubert v. Merrell Dow Pharmaceuticals, Inc.* (1993) and *General Electric Co. v. Joiner* (1997), which further undermined the restrictive Frye test by ruling that federal courts should generally allow admission of all relevant evidence. This ruling applied to all evidence in civil and criminal cases, including DNA evidence and other forensic science issues.[95]

Many states, including Arizona, California, Florida, Illinois, Iowa, Kansas, Louisiana, Michigan, Minnesota, Nevada, Oregon, South Dakota, Virginia, and Washington, have enacted laws authorizing the establishment of databases to store DNA identification records for law enforcement purposes.[96]

A twelve-member panel consisting of forensic, legal, and molecular biology experts, after a two-year study, has endorsed DNA profiling in the identification of suspects in criminal cases. The study, conducted under the auspices of the National Academy of Sciences, concluded that DNA fingerprinting or typing is a reliable method of identification for use as evidence in criminal trials, but it found problems with current methods of sampling, labeling, and general quality assurance. The panel of experts recommended that accreditation be required of forensic laboratories performing DNA typing. The panel's report, *DNA Technology in Forensic Science*, called for the creation of a national DNA profile data bank that would contain DNA samples and document information on the genetic makeup of felons convicted of violent crimes.[97]

DNA is helping those who claim they have wrongly been accused of crimes. In 1996, the U.S. Department of Justice published a study of twenty-eight cases in which suspects had been wrongfully convicted and imprisoned, but later exonerated by DNA evidence. On average, each spent seven years in prison for a crime he had not committed.[98]

> **YOU ARE THERE! »**
>
> ### How DNA Profiling Freed a Prisoner: The Leonard Callace Case
>
> On a January day in 1985, an eighteen-year-old woman was leaving a supermarket in a mall in Selden, New York. She told the police that a man with a full, bushy beard and a head of long, frizzy blond hair pulled her into a car and sexually assaulted her. The women went to the police, who took her blue-jeans because they had been stained with semen.
>
> The police had no leads until a year and a half later. Then, they said, they received an anonymous tip that a man named Leonard Callace had bragged in a barroom about the crime. He was arrested, placed in a lineup, and identified by the victim as the attacker from the parking lot eighteen months earlier. The case was not strong, so while Callace was in jail awaiting trial, he was offered a deal by the prosecution to plead guilty and serve only four more months. He turned it down, saying he was innocent and wished the jury to find him not guilty.
>
> During the trial, defense witnesses came up with pictures of Callace that they said had been taken just before the sex attack and showed he didn't have the long hair and scruffy beard described by the victim. But, the victim was certain he was the attacker. Her blue-jeans, with the semen stain, were introduced as evidence. The "A" blood type of the semen was the same as Callace's but also the same as about 80 million other people. No DNA testing was done as this technology was not yet available. The jury, in less than an hour, returned a verdict of guilty. The judge sentenced Callace to a twenty-five-year prison term.
>
> In 1990, Callace heard about DNA technology from a jailhouse lawyer and drew up his own legal papers asking that the DNA in the semen stain on the blue-jeans be tested and compared to his own. It wasn't until the summer of 1992 that Callace's request was granted. The blue-jeans were tested at Lifecodes Corporation in Stamford, Connecticut. The DNA testing revealed that the DNA in the semen on the victim's blue-jeans did not match Callace's DNA.
>
> In September, 1992, Leonard Callace walked out of prison a free man.
>
> Source: Various national news media reports, September 1992.

Unfortunately, as knowledge about DNA increases, confusion seems to get worse. In June 1997, a new study released by the Victoria Forensic Science Center in Victoria, Australia, suggests that people leave their own DNA on everything they touch, from pens, keys, coffee mugs, and the like, and that this genetic material can be traced back to them. This raises a cautionary note for investigators. Since people can pick up other people's DNA on their hands, there is always the possibility that a person could plant or accidentally leave somebody else's DNA at a crime scene.[99]

Videotaping

The use of hand-held compact videotaping equipment is an example of the growing use of technology as a policing tool. For many years, the police have also been using videotape in investigations, undercover operations, and recording the confessions of suspects.

Two recent innovative uses of videotaping have potential in police work. The Franklin County (Ohio) Sheriff's Office and the Columbus (Ohio) Police Department were the recipients of several video cameras donated by insurance companies and Mothers Against Drunk Drivers (MADD). The cameras are mounted to the dashboards of police cars. When an officer sees a vehicle that appears to be operated by an alcohol-impaired driver, the officer begins to record the suspect's driving and notes on tape the location and the circumstances raising suspicions of drunk driving. When the vehicle is stopped, the officer approaching the car wears an activated wireless microphone that is able to record conversations up to 500 feet from the camera. The videotape provides corroborating evidence to the officer's testimony.[100]

The other example of a promising application of videotaping involves departments equipping its patrol vehicles with video recorders. These cameras automatically record everything said or done within their range. The system was originally intended to aid in drug interdiction cases, in prosecuting alcohol-impaired drivers, and in accident investigations. However, the police discovered that the video cameras provided reliable, unbiased evidence in citizen complaint cases. In one case, a trooper was accused of being rude and using profanity during a traffic stop. The videotape proved that the charges were unfounded. In another case, a trooper was accused of shooting an unarmed motorist. The videotape revealed that the trooper had issued at least twenty-six warnings for the person to drop his gun before the officer fired. The videotape can also confirm wrongdoing by an officer. In one case in which a trooper was accused of raping a motorist he had stopped for a traffic violation, the videotape was admitted into evidence against him.[101]

There have been numerous cases of officers catching their own assault, and several, their own felonious death, on the patrol vehicle's video recorder. One, on January 3, 1997, involved Deputy Sheriff Henry Huff, a member of the Walton County, Georgia, Sheriff's Office, who was shot at point-blank range during a traffic stop by a 9mm-wielding sixteen-year-old. Since Huff's squad car was equipped with an automatic surveillance camera, the entire incident was recorded on videotape. Fortunately, despite being shot twice in the chest, Huff was spared serious injury by his bullet-resistant vest and has since returned to duty.[102]

Robots

Robots have been available to law enforcement since the early 1970s. However, because of their high cost, they were seldom purchased for law enforcement use. Since the mid-1980s, robots have become very popular in police departments for bomb disposal.

The bomb robots can be operated by an electric cable or by radio control. They can take X-rays, photographs of packages, search suspect locations, and place explosive devices into a transport vessel, thus keeping bomb personnel safely away from the immediate area. Robots can have closed-circuit video systems, audio systems, and spotlights. Some of the more sophisticated robots can climb stairs, cross ditches, and knock down doors.[103]

Fear of Technology by Civil Libertarians

Civil libertarians fear that technological developments, such as improved computer-based files and long-range electronic surveillance devices, will give the police more power to intrude into the private lives of citizens.[104] A Congressional report found reason to believe that DNA fingerprinting may work against a suspect's reasonable expectation of privacy.[105]

Even the magazine *Popular Mechanics* worries about the civil liberties issues of enhanced police technology:

Along with the advantages, however, has come new potential for abuse. For example, the same computer databases that make AFIS possible could also be used for random searches that might focus suspicion on people because they have stayed in a homeless shelter, or because they fall into certain categories based on age, race or other discriminatory criteria.[106]

The noted civil liberties lawyer Alan M. Dershowitz, of Harvard University Law School, in *Taking Liberties: A Decade of Hard Cases, Bad Laws, and Bum Raps,* comments on the 1986 U.S. Supreme Court case *California v. Ciraolo.*[107] In this case, the Court ruled that evidence obtained by the police's flying over and photographing a person's property was not a violation of the person's Fourth Amendment rights. Dershowitz says, "You can be sure that our Constitution's Founding Fathers would have been appalled at this breach of privacy. A person's home—whether it be a walled estate, a plantation, or small cottage—was regarded as his castle, free from the intruding eye of government, without a warrant based on probable cause."[108]

Chapter Summary

Tremendous improvements have been made in the police use of technology in the past few decades in the fields of computers, communications, criminal investigation, surveillance, and criminalistics. Computers have enabled the police to dispatch officers immediately to any calls for service. They have also aided the police in the investigation process by enabling officers to feed descriptions and MOs into the computer and to receive almost instantaneous printouts on possible suspects. Computers have enabled police to maintain better records more easily. The computer has also caused a revolution in the processing of fingerprints through automated fingerprint identification system (AFIS) terminals.

In recent years, the police have also used science to develop less-than-lethal weapons, such as TASERs and chemical irritant sprays, as an alternative to using deadly force. Other technology, including improved surveillance devices and improved forensic techniques (such as DNA profiling) is enhancing the ability of the police to solve crime.

As technology continues to improve, and if the police remain receptive to testing and accepting new technology, unheard-of methods of investigating crimes and processing evidence will seem commonplace tomorrow.

It must be remembered, however, that despite the advances that science brings to police work, the key to police work will always be people—the men and women we hire to serve and protect us.

Learning Check

1. Discuss the advantages of computer-aided dispatch (CAD) systems, including enhanced CAD.
2. List and discuss some of the major uses of the computer in police departments today.
3. Explain the latest advances in fingerprint processing.
4. Define DNA and talk about the accuracy of the results of genetic fingerprinting (DNA profiling).
5. Discuss some of the threats to civil liberties posed by the use of recent technology.

Review Exercise

You have been hired by the Typical City Police Department as a consultant to implement computerization in the department. The department now has no computerized systems at all. The commissioner tells you that he has a large but limited budget for the computerization of the department. He wants the following department functions to receive priority this year: (1) the 911 system, (2) crime analysis, and (3) the police laboratory. Based on your reading of this chapter, prepare a report to the commissioner specifying the equipment he or she should purchase using the budgeted funds.

Web Exercise

Patrol over to the National Institute of Justice's web site and find the latest reports on its grants and assistance to local police departments in the fields of computerization and technology.

Key Concepts

computer-aided dispatch (CAD)
enhanced CAD
enhanced 911 (E-911)
mobile digital terminal (MDT)
Automated Fingerprint Identification System (AFIS)
computer-aided investigation
less-than-lethal weapon
forensic science/criminalistics
deoxyribonucleic acid (DNA)
DNA profiling
Frye test
genetic fingerprinting

Notes

1. Mark Birchlet, "Computers in a Small Police Agency," *FBI Law Enforcement Bulletin* (1989): 7–9.
2. Charles R. Swanson, Leonard Territo, and Robert W. Taylor, *Police Administration: Structures, Processes and Behavior* (New York: Macmillan, 1988), p. 367.
3. Bruce Williams, "Small Agencies Can Afford to Computerize," *Law and Order,* December 1989, p. 45.
4. National Institute of Justice, *Local Police Departments, 1993* (Washington D.C.: National Institute of Justice, 1996), p. 18; and National Institute of Justice, *Sheriffs' Departments, 1993* (Washington, D.C.: National Institute of Justice, 1996), p. 20.
5. Swanson, Territo, and Taylor, *Police Administration,* pp. 381–383.
6. Jerome H. Skolnick and David H. Bayley, *The New Blue Line: Police Innovation in Six American Cities* (New York: Free Press, 1986), pp. 100–101.
7. Nassau County Police Department, *1990 Annual Report* (Mineola, N.Y.: Nassau County Police Department, 1991).
8. Andrew K. Ruotolo Jr., "MDTs Aid Auto Theft Task Force," *Police Chief,* September 1992, pp. 29–34.
9. Kenneth B. Marshall, "The Many Benefits of Mobile Data Access," *Law Enforcement News,* 30 June 1997, pp. 8, 10.
10. "Focus on Technology: Digital Telephony, Keeping Pace with Technology," *FBI Law Enforcement Bulletin,* August 1992, pp. 16–17.
11. "Cellular Digital Packet Data (CDPD) Technology Assists Plainclothes Officers," *Police Chief,* March 1997, pp. 14–15.
12. John Probert, "Police Telecommunications: The Influence of Computers on Law Enforcement," *Police Chief,* May 1986, p. 57.
13. William S. Sessions, "Recent Developments in FBI Computer Applications," *Police Chief,* September 1992, p. 8.
14. William S. Sessions, "Criminal Justice Information Services: Gearing Up for the Future," *FBI Bulletin,* February 1993, pp. 1–3. See also Terry L. Knowles, "Meeting the Challenges of the 21st Century," *Police Chief,* June 1997, pp. 39–43.
15. Preston Gralla, "Hollywood Confidential: PC Crime Fighters," *PC Computing,* January 1989, p. 188.
16. Bill Clede, "Storing Massive Records," *Law and Order,* January 1994, p. 45.
17. Howard Safir, Police Commissioner, City of New York, *The Compstat Process* (New York: New York City Police Department, no date); William J. Bratton, Police Commissioner, City of New York, "Great Expectations: How Higher Expectations for Police Departments Can Lead to a Decrease in Crime," Paper presented at the National Institute of Justice Research Institute's "Measuring What Matters" Conference, Washington, D.C., November 28, 1995; Rudolph W. Guiliani, Randy M. Mastro, and Donna Lynne, *Mayor's Management Report: The City of New York* (New York: City of New York, 1997); Peter C. Dodenhoff, "LEN Salutes Its 1996 People of the Year," *Law Enforcement News,* 15 January 1997, p. 4.
18. Gralla, "Hollywood Confidential."
19. Sharon Hollis Sutter, "Holmes . . . Still Aiding Complex Investigations," *Law and Order,* November 1991, pp. 50–52.
20. Sutter, "Holmes," p. 52.
21. Robert D. Keppel and Joseph G. Weis, "HITS: Catching Criminals in the Northwest," *FBI Law Enforcement Bulletin,* April 1993, pp. 14–19.
22. Keppel and Weis, "HITS: Catching Criminals in the Northwest," p. 18.
23. Lois Pilant, "Equipping a Forensics Lab," *Police Chief,* September 1992, pp. 37–47.
24. "International News: Crime Analysis Program," *Law and Order,* July 1992, p. 6.
25. Paul Palumbo, "Firearms Training: Computer-Assisted Target Analysis," *Police Chief,* May 1983, pp. 67–69; Paul Smith, "Inservice Training for Law Enforcement Personnel," *FBI Law Enforcement Bulletin* 53 (1988): 20–21; Barbara Gengler, "Computer-Based Training for Law Enforcement," *Police Chief,* November 1996, pp. 48–51; Gengler, " 'Hidden Treasure': A Case Study in CBT for Law Enforcement," *Police Chief,* November 1996, p. 50.
26. Nassau County Police Department, *1990 Annual Report.*
27. Robert Sheehan and Gary W. Cordner, *Introduction to Police Administration,* 2d ed. (Cincinnati: Anderson, 1989), p. 419.
28. Sheehan and Cordner, *Introduction to Police Administration,* p. 422.
29. "PG County Police Opt for Computer-Aided System to Red-Flag Stressed-Out Officers," *Law Enforcement News,* 30 June 1997, p. 5.
30. Brewer Stone, "The High-Tech Beat in St. Pete," *Police Chief* 55 (1988): 23–28.
31. Swanson, Territo, and Taylor, *Police Administration,* pp. 380–381.
32. Ronald J. Waldron, *The Criminal Justice System: An Introduction* (New York: Harper & Row, 1989), pp. 457–458.
33. Sheehan and Cordner, *Introduction to Police Administration,* p. 428.
34. Margaret J. Levine and J. Thomas McEwen, *Patrol Deployment* (Washington, D.C.: National Institute of Justice, 1985), p. 48.
35. Stephen J. Huxley and Philip E. Taylor, "Strategic Issues in Patrol Deployment: A Computer Analysis," *Police Chief,* February 1989, p. 59.

36. Bill Clede, "Police Computer Networks Competing," *Law and Order,* January 1992, p. 15.
37. U.S. Congress, Office of Technology Assessment, *Criminal Justice: New Technologies and the Constitution: A Special Report* (Washington, D.C.: U.S. Government Printing Office, 1988), p. 18.
38. Los Angeles Police Department, *Annual Report, 1985* (Los Angeles: Los Angeles Police Department, 1986).
39. William Stover, "Automated Fingerprint Identification—Regional Application of Technology," *FBI Law Enforcement Bulletin* 53 (1984): 1–4.
40. Knowles, "Meeting the Challenges of the 21st Century."
41. William Folsom, "Automated Fingerprint Identification Systems," *Law and Order,* July 1986, pp. 27–28; Judith Blair Schmitt, "Computerized ID Systems," *Police Chief,* February 1992, p. 35; "AFIS Users Compare Notes," *Police Chief,* January 1997, pp. 29–31, 48.
42. Schmitt, "Computerized ID Systems."
43. Schmitt, "Computerized ID Systems."
44. Schmitt, "Computerized ID Systems."
45. Tony Lesce, "Verafind AFIS System: Flexible and Software Based," *Law and Order,* December 1994, p. 53–54.
46. Selena P. Hutchinson, "How the FBI Is Working to Put the Finger on Crime (Faster & Better Than Ever)," *Law Enforcement News,* 15 June 1997, pp. 8, 11; Sessions, "Criminal Justice Information Services," p. 2.
47. David Kinchin, "NAFIS: New National Automated Fingerprint Identification System Connects Departments throughout England and Wales," *Law and Order,* June 1997, pp. 47–48. For innovative fingerprint technology in New Zealand, see Dominic Andrae, "New Zealand Fingerprint Technology," *Law and Order,* November 1993, pp. 37–38.
48. "High-Tech Crime Hunters," *Popular Mechanics,* December 1991, p. 30.
49. T. F. Wilson and P. L. Woodard, *Automated Fingerprint Identification Systems—Technology and Policy Issues* (Washington, D.C.: National Institute of Justice, 1987), p. 5.
50. Harold J. Grasman, "New Fingerprint Technology Boosts Odds in Fight against Terrorism," *Police Chief,* January 1997, pp. 23–28, p. 23. Note: The author is the special agent in charge of the Forensic Services Division of the U.S. Secret Service, in Washington, D.C.
51. Samuel Walker, *The Police in America: An Introduction,* 2d ed. (New York: McGraw-Hill, 1992), p. 155.
52. Bill Clede, "A Bouquet of Aerosol Sprays," *Law and Order,* September 1992, pp. 57–59.
53. Michael Cooper, "Hoping for Less Lethal Force, Police to Switch to Stronger Pepper Spray," *New York Times,* 27 March 1997, p. B-3. See also "NYPD Wants More Potent Pepper," *Law Enforcement News,* 30 April 1997, p. 7.
54. Cooper, "Hoping for Less Lethal Force."
55. "OC Is OK: Pepper Spray Gets a Qualified Thumbs-Up," *Law Enforcement News,* 30 April 1997, p. 7. See also Cooper, "Hoping for Less Lethal Force."
56. Grey Meyer, "Nonlethal Weapons vs. Conventional Police Tactics: Assessing Injuries and Liabilities," *Police Chief,* August 1992, p. 13. For more on the TASER, see Sherri Sweetman, *Report on the Attorney General's Conference on Less-Than-Lethal Weapons* (Washington, D.C.: U.S. Government Printing Office, 1987).
57. John Graham, "Officers Armed with Beanbags," *Law and Order,* June 1997, pp. 67–68, p. 68.
58. J. P. Morgan, "Oleoresin Capsicum Policy," *Police Chief,* August 1992, p. 26.
59. Meyer, "Nonlethal Weapons vs. Conventional Police Tactics," pp. 15–16.
60. Meyer, "Nonlethal Weapons vs. Conventional Police Tactics," p. 18.
61. *Michenfelder v. Sumner,* 860 F.2d 328 (9th Cir. 1988).
62. For a comprehensive article on advanced surveillance devices, see Lois Pilant, "Spotlight on . . . Achieving State-of-the-Art Surveillance," *Police Chief,* June 1993, pp. 25–34.
63. Albert E. Brandenstein, "Advanced Technologies Bolster Law Enforcement's Counterdrug Efforts, *Police Chief,* January 1997, pp. 32–34.
64. Tom Yates, "Surveillance Vans," *Law and Order,* December 1991, pp. 52, 56.
65. Bill Siuru, "Seeing in the Dark and Much More: Thermal Imaging," *Law and Order,* November 1993, pp. 18–20.
66. Siuru, "Seeing in the Dark and Much More;" and Tom Yates, "'Eyes' in the Night," *Law and Order,* November 1993, pp. 19–24.
67. John J. Pavlis, "Mug-Shot Imaging Systems," *FBI Law Enforcement Bulletin,* August 1992, pp. 20–22.
68. Pavlis, "Mug-Shot Imaging Systems," p. 22.
69. Darrel L. Sanders, "The Critical Role of Technology," *Police Chief,* July 1997, p. 6. Note: The author is chief of the Frankfort, Illinois, Police Department and president of the International Association of Chiefs of Police (IACP). See also Charles E. Samarra and G. Thomas Steele, "Technology on Patrol," *Police Chief,* November 1996, pp. 16–19.
70. "Picture This: Digital Photos Beam from Texas to Virginia via High-Tech Patrol Cars," *Law Enforcement News,* 15 June 1997, p. 1.
71. "High-Tech Crime Hunters," p. 31.
72. "High-Tech Crime Hunters." See also Gene O'Donnell, "Forensic Imaging Comes of Age," *FBI Law Enforcement Bulletin,* January 1994, pp. 5–10.
73. O'Donnell, "Forensic Imaging Comes of Age."
74. In this section I relied primarily on information found in: Marc H. Caplan and Joe Holt Anderson, *Forensic: When*

Science Bears Witness (Washington, D.C.: National Institute of Justice, 1984); F. Cunliffe and P. B. Piazza, *Criminalistics and Scientific Investigation* (Englewood Cliffs, N.J.: Prentice-Hall, 1980); Peter DeForest et al., *Forensic Science: An Introduction to Criminalistics* (New York: McGraw-Hill, 1983); Lois Pilant, "Equipping a Forensics Lab," *Police Chief,* September 1992, pp. 37–47; R. Saferstein, *Criminalistics: An Introduction to Forensic Science,* 3rd ed. (Englewood Cliffs, N.J.: Prentice-Hall, 1987); R. Saferstein, *Forensic Science Handbook* (Englewood Cliffs, N.J.: Prentice-Hall, 1988); Charles C. Wilber, *Ballistic Science for the Law Enforcement Officer* (Springfield, Ill.: Charles C. Thomas, 1977).

75. Joseph L. Peterson, *Use of Forensic Evidence by the Police and Courts* (Washington, D.C.: National Institute of Justice, 1987) p. 2.
76. Peterson, *Use of Forensic Evidence by the Police and Courts,* p. 5.
77. Lois Pilant, "Crime Laboratory Developments," *Police Chief,* June 1997, pp. 31–37.
78. Pilant, "Crime Laboratory Developments," p. 31.
79. Colleen Wade, "Forensic Science Information Resource System," *FBI Law Enforcement Bulletin* 57 (1988): 14–15.
80. Waldron, *Criminal Justice System,* p. 455.
81. Richard A. Dusak, "Automated Handwriting Technology a Boon to Police," *Police Chief,* January 1997, pp. 39–41.
82. Michael H. West and Robert E. Barsley, "Ultraviolet Forensic Imaging," *FBI Law Enforcement Bulletin,* May 1992, p. 14. See also J. Michael Aaron, "Reflective Ultraviolet Photography Sheds New Light on Pattern Injury," *Law and Order,* November 1991, p. 34.
83. "Hey Buddy, Got a Match?: New System Does for Bullets What AFIS Did for 'Prints," *Law Enforcement News,* 30 April 1994, p. 1.
84. Knowles, "Meeting the Challenges of the 21st Century."
85. Peter J. Neufeld and Neville Colman, "When Science Takes the Witness Stand," *Scientific American,* May 1990, p. 46.
86. Warren E. Leary, "Genetic Record to be Kept on Members of Military," *New York Times,* 12 January 1992, sec. 1, p. 15.
87. C. Thomas Caskey and Holly A. Hammond, *Automated DNA Typing: Method of the Future?* (Washington, D.C.: National Institute of Justice, 1997), p. 1.
88. Knowles, "Meeting the Challenges of the 21st Century."
89. Knowles, "Meeting the Challenges of the 21st Century."
90. Janet C. Hoeffel, "The Dark Side of DNA Profiling: Unreliable Scientific Evidence Meets the Criminal Defendant," *Stanford Law Review* 42 (1990): 465–538.
91. Hoeffel, "Dark Side of DNA Profiling."
92. *Frye v. United States,* 293 F. 1013 (D.C. Cir. 1923).
93. "DNA Fingerprinting ID Method May Streamline Investigations," *Current Reports, BNA Criminal Practice Manual* 1, no. 19 (1987).
94. Ronald Sullivan, "Appeals Court Eases Rules on Genetic Evidence," *New York Times,* 11 January 1992, p. 8.
95. "Supreme Court Clarifies Ruling on Admitting Scientific Evidence," *Criminal Justice Newsletter,* 1 December 1997, p. 1.
96. "Legislative Guidelines for DNA Databases," *FBI Law Enforcement Bulletin,* March 1992, p. 9. See also Charlotte Anne Smith, "One Department's DNA Laboratory," *Law and Order,* June 1997, pp. 45–46.
97. "DNA Typing Endorsed by National Academy of Sciences," *CJ Update,* Fall 1992, p. 1.
98. Edward Connors, *Convicted by Juries, Exonerated by Science: Case Studies in the Use of DNA Evidence to Establish Innocence after Trial* (Washington, D.C.: National Institute of Justice, 1996), p. 4.
99. "People Constantly Shed DNA, Study Finds," *New York Times,* 19 June 1997, p. B-11.
100. Michael Giacoppo, "The Expanding Role of Videotape in Court," *FBI Law Enforcement Bulletin,* November 1991, p. 3.
101. Giacoppo, "Expanding Role of Videotape."
102. Joseph G. Estey, "2,000 Survivors' Club Hits: In the Past 10 Years, 2,000 Officers Have 'Dressed For Survival'," *Police Chief,* May 1997, p. 19.
103. Lois Pilant, "Spotlight on . . . Equipping a Bomb Unit," *Police Chief,* October 1992, pp. 58–67.
104. U.S. Congress, Office of Technology Assessment, *Criminal Justice.*
105. U.S. Congress, Office of Technology Assessment, *Criminal Justice.*
106. "High-Tech Crime Hunters," p. 31.
107. *California v. Ciraolo,* 476 U.S. 207 (1986).
108. Alan M. Dershowitz, *Taking Liberties: A Decade of Hard Cases, Bad Laws, and Bum Raps* (Chicago: Contemporary Books, 1988), p. 209.

15

Specific Police Problems and Issues

Chapter Outline

Police and Danger
  Officers Killed in the Line of Duty
  Officers Assaulted in the Line of Duty
  Police and AIDS
Police Shootings: Use of Deadly Force
  Number of Citizens Shot by the Police
  Police Shooting Rates by City, Region, and State
  Do Police Discriminate with Their Trigger Fingers?
  Departure from the "Fleeing Felon" Rule
Police Automobile Pursuits
  Studies Involving Police Pursuits
  Establishment of Police Pursuit Policies

Police and Domestic Violence
  Traditional Police Response to Domestic Violence
  Minneapolis Domestic Violence Experiment
  Police Response to Domestic Violence Today
Police and Radical and Hate Groups
Police Civil and Criminal Liability
  State Liability
  Federal Liability
  Reasons for Suing Police Officers
  Effects of Lawsuits on Police Departments and Officers

Chapter Goals

■ To make you aware of dangers facing the police, including being killed and injured in the line of duty and dealing with contagious diseases, such as AIDS.

■ To acquaint you with the academic studies involving police shooting incidents, the "fleeing felon" rule, the landmark Supreme Court case *Tennessee v. Garner,* and current police policies regarding the use of deadly force.

■ To acquaint you with the problem of police high-speed automobile pursuits and current policies regarding them.

■ To introduce you to the problems of both spouses and the police in domestic abuse cases.

■ To acquaint you with some of the radical and hate groups operating in our nation today and the problems they present to the police and society.

■ To explore the issue of police civil and criminal liability.

Introduction

This chapter focuses on some specific issues that face police departments and the people who serve in them. This book has discussed numerous problems that are endemic to police work, such as corruption, brutality, cynicism, and racism. The police issues and problems discussed in this chapter are as serious as the ones discussed earlier.

One problem is danger. How often are police officers killed or injured in the line of duty? What are the specific threats to the police regarding personal safety? Closely connected to police officer safety is the issue of police shootings—the use of deadly force by the police. One question to be investigated is, when can a police officer legally shoot a criminal?

Another action by police that may lead to death and serious injuries to both officers themselves and the public is high-speed police pursuits. How fast should officers drive, and how long should they continue to pursue motorists who try to avoid being stopped?

The chapter will also discuss the special problems presented to the police by domestic violence, along with new procedures police are using in these cases. Radical and hate groups and the threats they pose to our society and the police are also discussed.

The chapter concludes with a discussion of what can happen if the police make mistakes in using force or in pursuing fleeing motorists, or even if the police do not make mistakes but an innocent citizen is killed or injured. The concept of civil liability can subject a police department, and even a police officer, to the payment of large sums for damages.

Police and Danger

No one would disagree with the statement that police work is dangerous. Unfortunately, its dangers are increasing, too. Each year many officers are injured or killed in the line of duty. Also, the chances of contracting life-threatening diseases, such as AIDS, are increasing as more of the general population is affected. This section, and the entire chapter, puts these dangers into perspective.

Officers Killed in the Line of Duty

The tragic assassination of twenty-two-year-old rookie New York City police officer Edward Byrne by vicious drug dealers in 1988 shocked the United States. This murder was particularly shocking because the drug dealers were attempting to send a message that they, not ordinary citizens, controlled our streets.

Officer Byrne was assigned to guard a man, Arjune, who was helping the police identify drug dealers in his Jamaican neighborhood. Three men shot Byrne to death as he was sitting alone in his police car at 3:25 A.M., guarding Arjune's house. The killers were acting under the orders of a drug kingpin who ordered the police assassination from his prison cell to teach law enforcement officers a lesson—to stop harassing his drug dealers. Officer Byrne was murdered not because he was Eddie Byrne but because he represented us—decent, law-abiding U.S. citizens.

How dangerous is police work? Are murders similar to that of Officer Byrne and the murders and deaths of other officers common in the United States?

Why Is Police Work Dangerous? Police officers perform necessary and often dangerous tasks. They deal constantly with what may be the most dangerous species on this planet—the human being—often in the most stressful and dangerous situations. They respond on a daily basis to people shooting at each other, stabbing each other, and beating each other. In a typical tour of duty, officers can deal with the full range of human emotions. Also, daily, they respond to calls where they may meet armed adversaries: "burglary in progress," "robbery in progress," "investigate screams for help," "investigate open door."

The dangerous conditions facing U.S. police officers are compounded by the irrationality produced by alcohol and drugs. The urban drug business of the 1980s and 1990s is characterized by an emphasis on tremendous inflows of cash and instant gratification. The proliferation of young, urban, uneducated, and unemployable males, armed with a plethora of weapons (including military-like automatic assault weapons), makes officers more and more fearful for their safety. As Barbara Raffel Price of the John Jay College of Criminal Justice says, "It would be foolish not to recognize that the violence associated with the drug business puts the police and citizens in greater jeopardy and that it makes the job of policing almost impossible."[1]

Specific Police Problems and Issues 365

Police officers salute the flag-draped casket of Sergeant Peter King, killed in the line of duty in Long Branch, New Jersey in 1997.

Table 15.1	Murders of Law Enforcement Officers, 1978 to 1995
Year	Number Murdered
1995	74
1994	76
1993	70
1992	63
1991	69
1990	66
1989	66
1988	78
1987	74
1986	66
1985	78
1984	72
1983	80
1982	92
1981	91
1980	104
1979	106
1978	93

Source: Adapted from Kathleen Maquire and Ann L. Pastore, eds., *Sourcebook of Criminal Justice Statistics—1996* (Washington, D.C.: U.S. Department of Justice, Bureau of Justice Statistics, U.S. Government Printing Office, 1997), Table 3.154, p. 354.

FBI Statistics on Police Murders Despite the dangers the police face, the FBI (which maintains records of all law enforcement officers murdered in the line of duty each year) reported that seventy-four law enforcement officers were feloniously slain in the line of duty during 1995. This figure was one of the lowest since the FBI started collecting such data in the 1960s.[2] See Table 15.1.

During 1995, seventy-four officers were feloniously murdered. In this year, which is the latest that we have full statistics for, the most officers were killed in arrest situations (21), investigating suspicious circumstances or persons (17), and in ambush (14). Other situations in which murders occurred included disturbance calls (8), enforcing traffic laws (9), handling the mentally deranged (1), and handling prisoners (4).[3] See Table 15.2.

The FBI reports that from 1980 to 1989, (the latest set of full-decade statistics available) a total of 801 law enforcement officers were feloniously slain in the line of duty in the U.S.[4]

Table 15.2	Circumstances of Law Enforcement Murders, 1995
Circumstances	Number
Disturbance call	8
Arrest situation	21
Enforcing traffic law	9
Ambush	14
Investigating suspicious circumstances or persons	17
Handling prisoners	4
Mentally deranged	1
Total	74

Source: Adapted from Kathleen Maquire and Ann L. Pastore, eds., *Sourcebook of Criminal Justice Statistics—1996* (Washington, D.C.: U.S. Department of Justice, Bureau of Justice Statistics, U.S. Government Printing Office, 1997), Table 3.154, p. 354.

All in the Line of Duty

Thank God the Officer Was Driving By

While off duty, Officer Michael R. Pruneau of the Crystal City, Missouri, Police Department was driving through town when he observed a small boy with his head hanging out of the window of a parked vehicle. The child's face appeared to be discolored as if he were being strangled by the window. As Officer Pruneau later determined, the child's 2-year-old brother had closed the window while the boy's head was outside the vehicle. Office Pruneau immediately pulled over, alerted the parents, and freed the child. He removed the boys from the vehicle, but could not locate a pulse. The officer initiated CPR to stimulate a heartbeat and administered rescue breathing until the child began to breathe on his own. Arriving paramedics transported the child to an area hospital. He was later flown to a children's hospital in St. Louis for further treatment. Officer Pruneau's quick response saved the child's life.

Source: Adapted from *FBI Law Enforcement Bulletin,* July 1996, p. 33.

Thirty percent fewer officers (801) were murdered in the 1980s than in the 1970s, when 1,143 officers were murdered (see Table 15.1). During 1980, the highest number of officers (104) were killed. Prior to 1990, the lowest number of officers killed (66) were in 1986 and 1989. The 1986 and 1989 numbers of reported murders were the lowest since records regarding felonious officer deaths have been kept.[5]

The FBI analyzed officer deaths in the 1980s in the following categories: victims, circumstances, types of assignments, weapons used against victims, body armor worn, regions, times of occurrence, and profiles of assailants.[6] Of the 801 murdered officers in the 1980s, 783 were male and 18, female. Seventy-seven were under twenty-five years of age; 515 were age twenty-five to forty, and 209 were over forty years old. Of the slain officers, 703 were white, 96 were African-American, and 2 were of other ethnic groups. The officers had an average seniority of nine years. Seven of every ten officers were in uniform when murdered.

As for circumstances of the murders, 324, or 40 percent of the officers, were slain while attempting to make an arrest. Of the rest, 132 were killed while responding to disturbance calls (bar fights, persons with guns, or family disturbances); 117 were investigating suspicious persons or circumstances; 107 were conducting traffic pursuits or stops; 71 were ambushed; 34 were handling, transporting, or maintaining custody of prisoners; and 12 were handling mentally deranged individuals. One officer was slain during a civil disorder.

What types of assignments were the murdered officers performing? Sixty-seven percent of all slain officers were patrol officers, 23 percent were detectives or officers on special assignment, and 10 percent were off duty but acting in an official capacity. Of the patrol officers, 78 percent were assigned to one-officer vehicles; 20 percent, to two-officer vehicles; and 2 percent, to foot patrol.

In regard to weapons, 92 percent of the officers (735) were killed by firearms. Of those murders, 70 percent were by handguns; 13 percent, by rifles; and 9 percent, by shotguns. Of the officers killed by firearms, 16 percent were killed by their own weapons. Nonfirearm killings included 33 officers intentionally struck with automobiles; 17 knifed; 7 beaten with blunt objects; and 5 beaten with hands, fists, and feet. Additionally, 2 were burned, 1 was drowned, and 1 was asphyxiated.

Of the 735 officers slain with firearms, 157 were wearing protective body armor. However, the bullets entered areas not covered by the vests, such as the head, below the vest, or between panels of the vests. Six officers were slain when bullets penetrated their protective vests.

Southern states accounted for 46 percent of the fatalities. Western states had 18 percent, midwestern states had 17 percent, northeastern states had 13 percent, and U.S. territories had 5 percent.

As for time of occurrence, 62 percent of the killings occurred between 6:00 P.M. and 6:00 A.M. The highest number of murders occurred between 8:00 p.m. and 10:00 P.M.

Who were the assailants? Ninety-eight percent of the murders have been cleared or solved, with 1,077 suspects identified. Of the suspects, 1,034 were male and 43, female. Fifty-six percent were white, 42 percent were African-American, and 2 percent were of other ethnic groups. Of the assailants, 62 percent were younger than thirty years of age. Seventy percent of the suspects had previous arrests, and 50 percent had previous convictions.

A 1997 report, *Death on Patrol: Felonious Killings of Police Officers,* by Lorie A. Fridell and Anthony Pate, of Florida State University, analyzed law enforcement murders over a twenty-one-year period. In their report, the researchers pointed to the following conclusions:[7]

- Thirty-four percent of the slain officers were dispatched to the incident that resulted in their deaths. Another one-third proactively initiated the contact as a result of observations. Twenty percent were on assignment at the time of their deaths, serving warrants, questioning witnesses, or conducting surveillance. In 6 percent, the police action was unanticipated as police walked in on crimes or had crimes walk in on them. In 8 percent of the incidents officers were ambushed by assailants.
- In 40 percent of the incidents, officers were killed at entry—the point at which the officer and assailant were first interacting.
- About one-half of the officers slain were patrolling in one-officer vehicles, most of them dispatched to the incidents that led to their deaths.
- The total number of police officers who were feloniously killed each year fell markedly between 1972 and 1986, but has remained generally stable since then. The researchers indicated that this could be due to a number of factors, including the wider use of protective vests, improved training, and higher levels of concern about the issue.
- The relatively high incidence of felonious killings among officers in state agencies (6 of the highest 10 rates, if one considers state, municipal, and county agencies) led the researchers to conclude that solo patrols without the possibility of quick backup (a common situation in state agencies) might be a contributing factor.

Accidental Police Deaths In addition to the 801 officers feloniously slain during the 1980s and the total of 1,217 slain feloniously from 1980 to 1995, 1,076 officers lost their lives in accidents while performing official duties from 1980 to 1995. Automobile accidents were the leading cause of accidental deaths (496). Other automobile-related accidental deaths of officers included officers' being struck by vehicles while engaging in traffic stops, performing road blocks, directing traffic, and assisting motorists. Other accidental deaths were the result of aircraft accidents, accidental shootings, motorcycle accidents, falls, and drowning.[8] Table 15.3 lists reasons for the accidental deaths of police officers from 1980 to 1995.

Table 15.3 Law Enforcement Officer Accidental Killings, 1980–1995

Type of Incident	Number
Automobile accidents	496
Motorcycle accidents	82
Aircraft accidents	137
Struck by vehicle	219
Accidental shooting	55
Accidental shooting in training	13
Self-inflicted accidental shooting	9
Other	65
Total	1,076

Source: Adapted from Kathleen Maquire and Ann L. Pastore, eds., *Sourcebook of Criminal Justice Statistics—1996* (Washington, D.C.: U.S. Department of Justice, Bureau of Justice Statistics, U.S. Government Printing Office, 1997), Table 3.16, p. 356.

Other Studies of Police Murders Other studies over the years give us information regarding the murder of police officers. William Geller and Michael S. Scott's study revealed that in 1971 police were feloniously killed at a rate of 38 per 100,000 officers, but this rate decreased steadily until it reached 12 per 100,000 officers in the 1990s.[9]

PATROLLING THE NET

National Law Enforcement Officers Memorial Fund on the Net

The National Law Enforcement Officers Memorial Fund has launched its own World Wide Web site: http://www.Inleomf.com.

This site offers browsers, photographs, and a history of the memorial to slain law enforcement officers, as well as facts, statistics, and the special features "Officer of the Month" and "Line of Duty," which pay tribute to active and slain officers. The web site also focuses on criminal acts in a "Crime of the Week" section.

Source: Adapted from "Virtual Tribute," *Law Enforcement News*, 15 April 1997, p. 16.

YOU ARE THERE!

Cancer from Police Radar?

Controversy has recently surrounded the cancer threat to police officers from radar. In 1991, three Connecticut officers, seven other officers, and the widow of a Wisconsin state trooper who died of cancer filed lawsuits claiming that their (or a spouse's) cancer was caused by the use of police radar. The Food and Drug Administration's Office of Science and Technology reported that no concrete evidence exists to verify that police radar guns cause cancer, but recommended that operators not place radar antennae within five inches of any part of their bodies.

Although the association between radar and cancer remains inconclusive, John M. Violanti, a professor of criminal justice at the Rochester Institute of Technology and a member of the Department of Social and Preventive Medicine, School of Medicine, University of New York at Buffalo, states that the present research certainly points to a possible link between radar and cancer. Violanti recommends that until researchers know more about the cause-and-effect relationship between cancer and radar, police departments should take precautionary steps to protect police officers from potential harm caused by radar units. Specifically, he recommends that radar units be mounted outside of police vehicles instead of being held by officers.

Source: Adapted from John M. Violanti, "Police Radar: A Cancer Risk?" *FBI Law Enforcement Bulletin*, October 1992, pp. 14–16.

David Constantin's study of three years of data from the FBI Uniform Crime Reports regarding the murder of police officers found that most of the incidents in which police were killed were initiated by the officers themselves taking some type of action.[10]

David Lester's study of the characteristics of cities that have high rates of police officer fatalities indicated that these cities were mainly located in the South. The cities had low population densities, high murder rates, and a high proportion of gun ownership.[11]

Research by William Geller has shown that off-duty police officers and plainclothes officers have high rates of shooting fatalities.[12] His explanation for these high rates was that off-duty officers, who are usually armed, are expected to take appropriate action when they encounter criminal situations. However, they suffer from the lack of normal tactical advantages, such as communication, cover, and backup. Additionally, Geller indicated that plainclothes officers may often be mistaken for perpetrators in criminal situations.

Police officers themselves comprehend the dangers in policing better than does the average citizen. In a study involving police officers and perceptions of danger, Frances T. Cullen found that police officers were aware of the difference between the possibility of danger and its actual occurrence in police work. When officers were asked whether they felt that "a lot of people" were hurt in the line of duty, 87 percent of the officers disagreed. At the same time, however, nearly 75 percent of the officers interviewed stated that they worked in a dangerous occupation.[13]

Explanations for Low Police Murder Rate What accounts for the relatively low murder rates of police officers despite the constant possibility of violence with which they are faced? There are several explanations.

People who would not think twice about shooting a fellow citizen might hesitate in shooting a police officer, knowing that society places a special value on the lives of those they depend on for maintaining law and order on the streets. They also know that the criminal justice system reacts in a harsher way to a "cop killer" than to an "ordinary killer."

Also contributing to the relatively low level of officer killings is the fact that professional criminals, including organized crime members and drug dealers, know that killing a police officer is "very bad for business." Such a killing will result in tremendous disruption of their business while the police hunt for, and prosecute, the killer.

Another reason for the relatively low number of killings of police officers is their awareness of the dangers they face every day and the resultant physical and mental precautions they take to deal with such dangers. The discussion of the police personality in chapter 6 characterized it as suspicious, loyal, and cynical. Most experts believe that the police personality is caused by the dangers of police work. Possibly the negative aspects of the police personality keep officers relatively safe.

Finally, current tactical training of police officers emphasizes cover and backup. Officers are taught not to blindly rush into dangerous situations. Also, police officers have increasingly become used to wearing bulletproof vests.

Officers Assaulted in the Line of Duty

Police officers have relatively low murder rates, but how often are officers injured by criminal assaults in the line of duty? A review of the most recent statistics reveal that almost 57,000 officers reported on-duty assaults during 1995. Firearms were used in over 15 percent of the assaults, knives or other cutting instruments in nearly 22 percent, other dangerous weapons in about 30 percent, and personal weapons in about 33 percent.[14]

Police and AIDS

In recent years, acquired immune deficiency syndrome (AIDS) has become a source of great concern to U.S. police officers, as well as to everyone else. AIDS, a deadly disease, is transmitted mainly through sexual contact and the exchange of body fluids. Although AIDS was formerly associated mainly with male homosexuals, intravenous drug users, and prostitutes, it is now known that anyone could be subject to infection by this disease. The toll of AIDS in the 1990s is staggering: 230,179 cases of AIDS have been reported in the United States, and over 150,000 people have died from AIDS in the United States alone. There are an estimated 10 to 12 million cases of HIV infection worldwide, and the projected number of people to be infected worldwide by the year 2000 has been set at 40 million.[15]

Police officers frequently come into contact with all types of people—including those having infectious diseases—and officers often have contact with blood and other body fluids. Therefore, officers are at special risk for catching such infectious diseases as AIDS. They must take precautionary measures during searches and other contacts with possible carriers of infectious diseases, as well as at crime scenes, where blood and other body fluids may be present.[16]

The New York City Police Department, in addition to myriad other departments, has prepared a special manual for its members that explained AIDS and established safety procedures for officers dealing with people and evidence possibly infected with the AIDS virus. The manual also stressed the care and dignity that should be shown to possible victims of the disease: "Police Officers have a professional responsibility to render assistance to those who are in need of our services. We cannot refuse to help. Persons with infectious diseases

---

Dempsey's Law

Where Is the Real Danger in Police Work?

Professor Dempsey, isn't police work dangerous? Isn't it easy to get killed or hurt as a police officer?

Empirical data suggests that police work is not the physically dangerous occupation that many say it is. However, the real danger in police work is not death and physical injury. It is the toll that police work takes on your personal and family life.

John, suppose you're an officer right now. You have just come off a busy 4 to 12; your nerve endings are electrified. Do you think you can go right home and go to sleep?

No.

You're newly married. You have a small apartment. Your wife is a schoolteacher, and she has to be up at 6:00 A.M. Can you go home and wake her up to talk to you while you relax?

No.

Can you go home and play music or watch television or a tape in your little apartment?

No, that would wake her up.

Can you expect her to meet you at a local restaurant or bar to have something to eat and drink with you?

No.

So, John, what do you do to relax to come down after the highs of the tour?

Probably go out to the bar with my friends from work.

Yeah, John, and guess who else is at the bar? Yeah, Cathy, over there. And she's there because she had a tough tour, too, and her husband has to be up at 5 A.M. to go to his highway job.

If you're not careful, John and Cathy, more than just friendship can occur at these meetings. Police work is dangerous. If you're not careful, it can be dangerous to your family life.

must be treated with the care and dignity we show all citizens."[17]

The FBI has published sixteen recommendations on how to collect and handle evidence that might be infected with the viruses, bacteria, and germs of infectious diseases.[18] The National Institute of Justice has also published recommendations on dealing with possibly infected evidence.[19]

Despite serious medical risks, police officers may not refuse to handle incidents involving persons infected with the AIDS virus or with other infectious diseases. Failing to perform certain duties—such as rendering first aid, assisting, or even arresting a person—would be a dereliction of duty, as well as discrimination against a class of people.[20]

Police Shootings: Use of Deadly Force

Historically, the shooting of a citizen by the police has been a major problem facing the police. Police shootings have had a serious negative impact on police community relations. Numerous incidents of civil unrest have followed police shootings of civilians. James Q. Wilson has stated, "No aspect of policing elicits more passionate concern or more divided opinions than the use of deadly force."[21]

Police shootings receive tremendous media attention. However, James J. Fyfe, a former New York City police lieutenant and one of the leading experts on the police use of deadly force in the United States, reported that the systematic examination of the use of deadly force has been largely neglected until a series of police shootings and other police problems precipitated the urban violence of the 1960s.[22]

Number of Citizens Shot by the Police

Although the FBI maintains sophisticated statistics regarding crimes reported to the police and arrests made by the police, it does not publish nationwide statistics on the use of deadly force by police shootings. Accordingly, there is some debate as to the number of citizens killed by the police.

Kenneth I. Matulia, in a study of data for the International Association of Chiefs of Police, estimated that approximately 260 people a year were killed by the police in the fifty-seven largest U.S. cities for a specified period of time.[23] Researchers using statistics from the National Center for Health Statistics report that annual statistics for "death by legal intervention of the police" reveal 200 to 400 police killings of citizens a year.[24]

Lawrence O'Donnell reports that police kill about 600 people every year; shoot and wound another 1,200; and fire at, but miss, another 1,800.[25] Fyfe estimates that roughly 1,000 people a year may be the victims of police homicide. He adds, however, that the number is speculative.[26]

Police Shooting Rates by City, Region, and State

Research has indicated a significant disparity in the number of police shootings in various U.S. cities and regions. Gerald Robin, for example, reports that the police in Akron, Ohio, were forty-five times more likely to kill a citizen than were police in Boston.[27] Matulia reported that during the years of his study, police in Jacksonville, Florida; New Orleans, Louisiana; Long Beach, California; and Houston, Texas, had the highest police homicide rates. Buffalo, New York; Honolulu, Hawaii; St. Paul, Minnesota; and Sacramento, California were among the large cities with the lowest police homicide rates. Matulia also reported that police homicide rates were highest in the South and lowest in the Northeast.[28]

Lawrence Sherman and Robert Langworthy, in a study of police shooting rates in forty-eight cities, found a strong association between the police use of force and the "gun density"—the proportion of suicides and murders committed with a gun. They also found that many people shot by the police were nonresidents of an area who were caught at or near the scenes of robberies or burglaries of commercial establishments.[29] Richard Kania and Wade Mackey found that fatal police shootings were closely related to an area's reported violent crime rates and criminal homicide rates.[30] Kania and Mackey also found that statewide rates of persons killed by the police ranged from a low of 2.97 per 100,000 population in New Hampshire to a high of 37.97 in Georgia.[31] David Jacobs and David Britt found that police shootings were most numerous in states with great disparities in economic opportunity.[32]

Do Police Discriminate with Their Trigger Fingers?

In addition to differences in the number of fatal police shootings in different cities, states, and regions, researchers have found a great deal of disparity between the shootings of white and African-American citizens by the police. In fact, Paul Takagi has stated that the police have "one trigger finger for whites and another for blacks."[33]

Numerous studies have been conducted to determine if there is, in fact, racial discrimination in the police use of deadly force. If one considers only total numbers, the overwhelming difference in the percentage of African-Americans shot over the percentage of whites shot could lead to the conclusion that discrimination does indeed exist.

A number of research studies report that a disproportionate number of police killings involve minority citizens—almost 80 percent in some of the cities studied.[34] William A. Geller estimates that the ratio of African-Americans to whites shot and killed by the police ranges from a high of 15 to 1 to a low of 3 to 1.[35]

In one of the first studies of police shootings, Robin found that Chicago police, over a ten-year period, shot and killed African-Americans at a rate of 16.1 per 100,000 citizens, compared with 2.1 whites per 100,000 citizens. Other cities had even greater disparities. In Boston, the police shot and killed African-Americans twenty-five times more often than they did whites.[36]

Fyfe's analysis of citizens shot and killed by the Memphis police over a five-year period found a pattern of extreme racial disparity, particularly with respect to unarmed citizens. Overall, twenty-six of the thirty-four people shot and killed in that period (85.7 percent) were African-American. In the category of nonassaultive and unarmed people, the Memphis police shot and killed thirteen African-Americans and only one white. Half of all the African-Americans shot and killed were nonassaultive and unarmed. The data suggest that the Memphis police were much more likely to shoot unarmed African-Americans than unarmed whites. Fyfe states that "blacks and Hispanics are everywhere overrepresented among those on the other side of police guns."[37]

There is another side, however, to the analysis of race and police shootings. Two studies indicate that people who engage in violent crime or who engage the police in violent confrontations are much more likely to be the victims of police shootings.

In one study, participation in violent crime was used as a relevant variable in police shootings, because generally, participation in crime places a person at risk of being confronted by the police and being shot by the police. The Chicago Law Enforcement Study Group examined shootings by Chicago police over a five-year period. The group first analyzed the rate at which whites, African-Americans, and Hispanic-Americans were shot and killed according to their number in the population and then the rate at which the same groups were shot and killed while participating in violent crimes. The data indicated that African-Americans were shot and killed six times as often as whites in terms of the total population, but the disparity disappeared when participation in violent crimes was a factor. Whites were shot and killed at a rate of 5.6 per 1,000 arrests for forcible felonies, compared with 4.5 African-Americans shot and killed per 1,000 arrests for the same category of crime.[38]

In the other study—Fyfe's pioneering Ph.D. dissertation, "Shots Fired," a study of New York City police shootings over a five-year period—Fyfe found that police officers are most likely to shoot suspects who are armed and with whom they become involved in violent confrontations. Fyfe found that if factors such as being armed with a weapon, being involved in a violent crime, and attacking an officer are considered, the racial differences in the police use of deadly force became nonsignificant.[39]

In a 1993 study, David Lester, pointing to the jurisdictional variation of police use of deadly force, reported that police officers kill more people in communities with high violence rates and during years in which the homicide rates were highest.[40]

Departure from the "Fleeing Felon" Rule

Before the great amount of attention given to police shootings in the wake of the civil disorders of the 1960s, most U.S. police departments operated under the common law **"fleeing felon" doctrine**, which held that law enforcement officers could, if necessary, use deadly force to apprehend any fleeing felony suspect. This doctrine evolved in the common law tradition of medieval England, when all felonies were capital offenses. Because there was very little official law enforcement in those days, and very few escaping felons were able to be apprehended, the law permitted that a person who had committed a felony could be killed while fleeing the scene.

The fleeing felon rule, like most of England's common law, came to the United States. Today, however, there is little need for the fleeing felon rule in the United States, because we have sufficient armed police and modern communications systems to aid in the

YOU ARE THERE!

U.S. Supreme Court Case of *Tennessee v. Garner*

The Garner case finally ended the fleeing felon rule. On October 3, 1974, at about 10:45 P.M., two Memphis police officers, Elton Hymon and Leslie Wright, responded to a prowler run (a report of "prowler inside"). Upon reaching the location, they were met by a neighbor, who told them she had heard someone breaking into the house next to hers. Officer Wright radioed for assistance as Officer Hymon went to the rear of the house. As the officer approached the backyard, he heard a door slamming, and he observed someone running across the backyard. The fleeing person stopped at a 6-foot-high chain-link fence at the end of the yard. The officer shone his flashlight and saw what appeared to be a seventeen- or eighteen-year-old youth about 5 feet 7 inches tall. The officer yelled, "Police! Halt!" However, the youth began to climb the fence.

If You Were Officer Hymon, What Would You Do?

The officer, thinking that the youth would escape, fired a shot at him, which struck him in the back of the head. The youth later died on the operating table. Ten dollars and a purse taken from the house were found on his body. The dead youth was later identified as Edward Garner, a fifteen-year-old eighth grader. At the trial, the officer admitted that he knew that Garner was unarmed and was trying to escape. The officer testified that he was acting under the provisions of Tennessee law that stated that an officer may use all the necessary means to effect an arrest if, after notice of the intention to arrest, the defendant either flees or forcibly resists.

The U.S. Supreme Court ruled 6 to 3 that the use of deadly force against apparently unarmed and nondangerous fleeing felons is an illegal seizure under the Fourth Amendment. The Court ended the common law fleeing felon rule by stating the following:

> The use of deadly force to prevent the escape of all felony suspects, whatever the circumstances, is constitutionally unreasonable. It is not better that all felony suspects die than they escape. Where the suspect poses no immediate threat to the officer and no threat to others, the harm resulting from failing to apprehend them does not justify the use of deadly force to do so. It is no doubt unfortunate when a suspect who is in sight escapes, but the fact that the police arrive a little late or are a little slower afoot does not always justify killing the suspect. A police officer may not seize an unarmed, nondangerous suspect by shooting him dead.

If you had been a member of the Court, would you have agreed with this ruling?

Source: Based on *Tennessee v. Garner*, 471 U.S. 1 (1985).

---

apprehension of fleeing felons. Also, the legality and morality of the fleeing felon rule comes into question because of the U.S. legal concept of presumption of innocence. Most U.S. states, however, maintained the fleeing felon rule well into the 1960s and 1970s. In 1984, the fleeing felon rule was declared unconstitutional by the U.S. Supreme Court in the landmark case *Tennessee v. Garner*.

Prior to the Garner case, and subsequent to the urban riots of the 1960s, many states replaced the fleeing felon rule with new state laws, internal rules of police departments, and court decisions. During the 1970s, many police departments developed an alternative to the fleeing felon doctrine, based in part on recommendations by the American Law Institute and the Police Foundation. This rule used the **"defense of life" standard**, which allowed police officers to use deadly force against people who were using deadly force against an officer or another person, as well as in certain violent felony situations.

The replacement of the common law fleeing felon rule by the defense of life standard changed the incidence of police shootings. O'Donnell found that police departments with effective deadly force rules showed sharp decreases not only in citizen deaths but also in officer deaths. In Kansas City, Missouri, for example, after the department adopted a rule that prohibited police from shooting juveniles except in self-defense, the number of youths under eighteen shot by the police dropped dramatically.[41]

Fyfe found that the number of police shootings dropped sharply following the New York City Police Department's adoption of a strict deadly force rule (defense of life standard). He also found that the average number of shots fired by New York City police officers was reduced by 30 percent. The greatest reduction oc-

YOU ARE THERE!

Alternatives to the Fleeing Felon Rule

In the 1970s, the American Law Institute proposed a Model Penal Code, which included new policies on the use of deadly force. Many states replaced their existing penal codes with this model code. Additionally, during the same time period, the Police Foundation proposed its own policies regarding the use of deadly force, which were adopted by many police departments.

Model Penal Code

The Model Penal Code, developed by the American Law Institute, permits the use of deadly force by police officers if an officer believes that (1) the felony for which the arrest is made involved the use, or the threatened use, of deadly force; or (2) there is a substantial risk that the suspect will cause death or serious bodily injury if not immediately apprehended; and (3) the force employed creates no substantial risk of injury to innocent people.

The Police Foundation Standard

After studying the deadly force policies of numerous police departments, including those of Birmingham, Detroit, Indianapolis, Kansas City (Missouri), Oakland, Portland, and Washington, D.C., the Police Foundation recommended that police departments develop rules governing the use of deadly force after consultation with citizens and police line officers. It recommended that officers be allowed to shoot to defend themselves and others, as well as to apprehend suspects in deadly or potentially deadly felonies.

The Police Foundation also recommended several internal police policies that could lead to an improved use of deadly force by the police. These policies included carefully screening recruits to eliminate both unstable and violence-prone officers, dismissing probationary officers who demonstrate instability or propensity to violence, and providing more meaningful training in the rules of deadly force.

The Police Foundation proposed the following deadly force rules that departments might adopt: Officers might use deadly force to defend themselves or others from what the officers reasonably perceive as an immediate threat of death or serious injury, when there is no apparent alternative. Officers also might use deadly force to apprehend an armed and dangerous subject when alternative means of apprehension would involve a substantial risk of death or serious injury, and when the safety of innocent bystanders would not be additionally jeopardized by the officers' actions.

Any of the following could make an armed subject dangerous enough to justify the use of deadly force: (1) the subject has recently shot, shot at, killed, or attempted to kill someone, or has done so more than once in the past; (2) the subject has recently committed a serious assault on a law enforcement officer acting in the line of duty; and (3) the subject has declared that he or she will kill, if necessary, to avoid arrest.

Source: Adapted from American Law Institute, *Model Penal Code*, section 307(2)(b); and Catherine H. Milton et al., *Police Use of Deadly Force* (Washington, D.C.: Police Foundation, 1977).

---

curred in fleeing felon situations. Fyfe found, moreover, that the number of police officers shot also dropped. Hence, Fyfe concluded, stricter deadly force rules appear to reduce not only citizen but also police fatalities and woundings.[42] He observed that "reductions in police shooting frequency and changes in police shooting patterns have followed implementation of restrictive administrative policies on deadly force and weapon use."[43]

The Sherman and Cohn survey of police shooting trends in the fifty largest U.S. cities found that the total number of people shot and killed by the police per year was cut in half between 1970 and 1984.[44]

In 1995, after tremendous negative publicity, and after detailed investigations into the actions of federal agents at the deadly siege of the Branch Davidian compound in Waco, Texas, and at the home of anti-government separatist Randy Weaver, in Ruby Ridge, Idaho, the federal government announced that it was refining the deadly force policy used by federal agents. The "imminent danger" standard, basically the same defense of life standard that law enforcement agencies have been following for years, restricts the use of deadly force to only those situations where the lives of agents or others are in imminent danger. The revised policy also permits deadly physical force against a prisoner attempting escape who was being held in or sentenced to a high-security prison. The new policy also forbids the firing of warning shots and shooting at moving vehicles in an attempt to disable such vehicles.[45]

Police Automobile Pursuits

The police practice of using high-powered police vehicles to chase speeding motorists has resulted in numerous accidents, injuries, and deaths to innocent civilians, police officers, and the pursued drivers. The practice had not been studied until recently. Geoffrey P. Alpert and Lorie A. Fridell, however, in their 1992 book *Police Vehicles and Firearms: Instruments of Deadly Force,* report that in the past few years, a "great deal of progress has been made in the research, policy development and training associated with pursuit driving."[46]

Geoffrey Alpert and Patrick R. Anderson characterize the police high-speed automobile pursuit as the most deadly force available to the police.[47] They define high-speed pursuits as "an active attempt by a law enforcement officer operating an emergency vehicle to apprehend alleged criminals in a moving motor vehicle, when the driver of the vehicle, in an attempt to avoid apprehension, significantly increases his or her speed or takes other evasive action."[48]

Alpert and Anderson point out several outcomes of such chases:

- The pursued driver stops the car and surrenders.
- The chased vehicle crashes into a structure, and the driver and occupants are apprehended, escape, are injured, or are killed.
- The chased vehicle crashes into another vehicle (with or without injuries to the driver and other occupants in the chased vehicle or another vehicle).
- The vehicle being chased strikes a pedestrian (with or without injuries or death).
- The police use some level of force to stop the pursued vehicle, including firearms, roadblocks, ramming, bumping, boxing, and so on.
- The police car crashes (with or without injuries to officers or civilians).[49]

Clearly, not all of these possible outcomes are acceptable for the police or innocent civilians. A debate has begun that questions whether the police should pursue fleeing vehicles, especially when such a pursuit could risk injuries to the police or innocent civilians. Certainly, no one wants officers or civilians injured. However, people on the other side in the debate say that if the police do not pursue fleeing drivers, they are sending a message to violators that they can get away with traffic violations by fleeing.

Studies Involving Police Pursuits

Studies have been conducted to determine what happens in a rapid pursuit. This information may help police administrators establish policies on rapid pursuits.

A review by the California Highway Patrol of nearly 700 pursuits on its highways over a six-month period revealed the following about the typical pursuit:

- It starts as a traffic violation.
- It occurs at night.
- It covers only a mile or so.
- It takes approximately two minutes to resolve.
- It involves at least two police cars.
- It ends when the pursued driver stops his or her vehicle.
- It results in the apprehension of more than three-fourths of the pursued drivers.
- It ends without an accident 70 percent of the time.[50]

The California Highway Patrol Study also revealed that drivers failed to stop for the following reasons, based on the judgment of the pursuing officer:

- To avoid DWI or drug arrest (19 percent).
- To avoid a summons for a traffic infraction (14 percent).
- Because the driver was driving a stolen vehicle (12 percent).
- To avoid an arrest for a law violation (11 percent).
- Because of unknown or miscellaneous reasons, such as the driver's being afraid of the police, disliking the police, or enjoying the excitement of the chase (44 percent).[51]

The California Highway study concluded that although there are risks in high-speed pursuits, the pursuits are worth the risks:

> Attempted apprehension of motorists in violation of what appear to be minor traffic infractions is necessary for the preservation of order on the highways of California.... One can imagine what would happen if the police suddenly banned pursuits. Undoubtedly, innocent people may be injured or killed because an officer chooses to pursue a suspect, but this risk is necessary to avoid the even greater loss that would occur if law enforcement agencies were not allowed to aggressively pursue violators.[52]

Geoffrey P. Alpert and Roger G. Dunham studied 952 pursuits in Dade County, Florida, by the area's two ma-

Table 15.4 Police High-Speed Pursuit Data, Minnesota

Pursuits conducted	823
Pursuits resulting in accidents	44%
Pursuits resulting in injuries	24%
Pursuits resulting in deaths	0.2%
Pursuits voluntarily terminated by the officer	21%
Percentage of pursuit violators stopped by police	51%
Cause of pursuit	
Traffic offense	76%
Suspicion of DWI offense	6%
Suspicion of a felony	16%

Source: Adapted from data presented in Geoffrey P. Alpert and Lorie A. Fridell, *Police Vehicles and Firearms: Instruments of Deadly Force* (Prospect Heights, Ill: Waveland Press, 1992), p. 108.

jor police departments, the Metro-Dade Police Department and the City of Miami Police Department. The researchers found that 38 percent of the pursuits resulted in an accident, 17 percent in injury, and 0.7 percent resulted in death. Of the 160 pursuits with injury, 30 involved injury to the police officer; 17, injury to an innocent bystander; and 113, injury to the fleeing driver, the passengers, or both. Alpert and Dunham also concluded that 54 percent of the pursuits were initiated for traffic offenses; 2 percent, for reckless driving or impaired driving; 33 percent, for serious criminal activity; and 11 percent, for BOLO ("be on the lookout") alarms.[53]

Alpert and Fridell also studied high-speed pursuit data in Minnesota. The results are shown in Table 15.4.

Despite differences in the studies and confusion over the statistics, the fact remains that there is a high probability of a traffic accident when police involve themselves in rapid pursuits (30 percent in the California study and 38 percent in the Alpert and Dunham studies). Therefore, this area of police work requires much further study.

Establishment of Police Pursuit Policies

Alpert and Fridell state the following: "Policies on pursuit driving can be reduced to a simple concept: When the risk created by the driving outweighs the need for immediate apprehension of the suspect, such risky driving must be terminated. It is not only acceptable to terminate pursuits in which the potential benefit is minimal, but it is wise, safe and in good judgment to terminate pursuits which incorporate high risks!"[54]

The number of accidents and injuries resulting from police high-speed pursuits has led many U.S. police departments to establish formal **police pursuit policies** (policies regulating the circumstances and conditions under which the police should pursue or chase motorists driving at high speeds in a dangerous manner). Some departments are even telling their officers to discontinue a pursuit under certain circumstances.

Fairly typical of new pursuit policies being established is that of the Louisiana State Police, which cautions its officers as follows:

> When the violator begins to seriously endanger the lives of innocent persons upon the highway, by passing on curves or in the face of oncoming traffic, the trooper should discontinue the pursuit except as follows:
> a) the violator is a felon who has committed a crime which endangered life; or
> b) the actions of the violator are such that the trooper reasonably believes that his continued freedom would seriously jeopardize the lives of others.[55]

In 1996, in Missoula County, Montana, a new policy regarding pursuits was issued in which sheriff's deputies are now able to terminate pursuits without "criticism, regardless of circumstances, if they feel the public interest is outweighed."[56]

Considering the widely televised beating of two unresisting Mexicans with nightsticks by Riverside County, California deputies, in April 1996, after a lengthy and chaotic chase, a proposal by Geoffrey Alpert, a professor of criminology at the University of South Carolina, seems to make a great deal of sense. Alpert, in a 1996 study of police pursuit policies, recommended that suspects be apprehended by officers other than those who led the chase. Alpert found that officers chasing suspects experience an adrenaline high that can lead to the use of excessive force once they've caught up with the fleeing suspects.[57]

In a 1997 report, Alpert, in another study of police pursuits, concluded that police pursuit driving remains a controversial and dangerous activity. For generations the conventional police wisdom was that effective law enforcement demanded that officers apprehend suspects, even at great social costs. The tragic accidents that have resulted from pursuits testify to their danger.[58]

Police and Domestic Violence

Domestic violence, including spousal abuse and lover abuse, is one of the most serious problems facing the police, as well as U.S. family life and society in general. A national survey has led researchers to estimate that during any one year, 1.7 million U.S. citizens face a spouse threatening them with a knife or gun. The study also estimated that well over 2 million U.S. citizens had experienced a severe beating at the hands of a spouse, and that 50 to 60 percent of all husbands assaulted their wives at least once during their marriage.[59]

A Police Foundation study concluded that the majority of domestic homicides were preceded by previous police calls to the residence.[60] FBI crime statistics indicate that 30 percent of female homicide victims were killed by their husbands or boyfriends, and 4 percent of male homicide victims were killed by wives or girlfriends. Nine of every ten female homicide victims were killed by males.[61]

A 1997 University of Michigan study found that violence between intimate couples of opposite gender may start very early. In a survey of 635 suburban, middle-class high school students, about 36 percent of girls and 37 percent of boys said they had experienced physical abuse from a date. Half of the girls—and just 4 percent of the boys—had said their worst abusive experience "hurt a lot." Among the other key findings were that 44 percent of the girls stayed with boys after moderate violence, including slapping, and 36 percent stayed after severe abuse, including choking and punching.[62]

Traditional Police Response to Domestic Violence

A reviewer of two books on family violence writes that "domestic violence has a long history in all cultures, but it is only during the last 20 years or so, and only in some advanced industrial nations that this type of human conflict has gotten the attention and reactions of the criminal justice system."[63]

The police, the courts, and society in general have traditionally adopted a hands-off policy toward domestic violence, treating it as a private affair that should be handled within the family. The police have generally not made arrests in domestic violence cases, even in those involving assaults with injuries that constitute a felony. Two assumptions prevailed: (1) that the arrest would make life worse for the victim, because the abuser might retaliate, and (2) that the victim would refuse to press charges.

Most police departments had no formal policies regarding domestic violence, and officers used many different techniques to deal with the problem when called to the scene. Among the techniques used were attempts to calm down both parties, mediating the conflict, and referring the participants to social service agencies for assistance in dealing with their problems. Often officers would escort abusive spouses out of the residence and advise them not to return until the next day or until things calmed down. Some officers would place abusive spouses in the police car and drive them to a location where it would take them an inordinate amount of time to find out where they were and to find their way home. Other officers just ignored domestic violence cases.

Two important lawsuits—brought forward by women's groups in New York City (*Bruno v. Codd*, 1978) and Oakland, California (*Scott v. Hart*, 1979)—began to change the police response in domestic violence cases. The suits charged that the police departments had denied women equal protection of the law by failing to arrest people who had committed assaults against them. As a result of the lawsuits, both departments formulated official written policies mandating arrests in cases of felonious spousal assault.[64]

Minneapolis Domestic Violence Experiment

Subsequent to these lawsuits, the Police Foundation conducted the **Minneapolis Domestic Violence Experiment** (1981 to 1982). This experiment was designed to examine the deterrent effect of various methods of dealing with domestic violence, including mandatory arrest. During this experiment, officers called to incidents of domestic violence were required to select at random one of a group of instructions to tell them how to deal with the incidents. The officers' forced choice required them to do one of the following: (1) arrest the offender, (2) mediate the dispute, or (3) escort the offender from the home. Repeat violence over the next six months was measured through follow-up interviews with victims and police department records of calls to the same address.[65]

The findings indicated that arrest prevented further domestic violence more effectively than did separation or mediation. Repeat violence occurred in 10 percent of the arrest cases, compared with 19 percent of the mediation incidents and 24 percent of the separation incidents. The actual sanction imposed by arrest involved

Police officers take photographs of domestic violence victims to use as evidence in court proceedings.

little more than an evening in jail; only 3 of the 136 people arrested were ever convicted and sentenced.[66]

The Minneapolis experiment has been replicated in a number of other localities to determine whether the results would be the same. A study in Omaha revealed that arrest by itself did not appear to deter subsequent domestic conflict any more than did mediation or separating the spouses in the dispute.[67]

Police Response to Domestic Violence Today

Despite the lack of a clear consensus regarding the effectiveness of arrest in domestic violence cases, police departments nationwide began to establish new police guidelines for domestic violence cases. Recently, the percentage of big city police departments with a **proarrest policy** (the policy that an abusive spouse must be arrested if the assault is a felony, even if the victim refuses to prosecute) increased from 10 to 46 percent. Also, twenty-one states revised their laws affecting the police and domestic violence. Several states expanded the arrest power of police in domestic violence cases, giving officers the power to make arrests for misdemeanor assaults that did not occur in their presence, for violations of orders of protection, or both. Some states enacted laws mandating arrest in cases of felonious domestic assault.[68] Many police departments have followed the lead of the Seattle Police Department, which has listed a number of factors (for example, gunshot wounds, broken bones, and intentionally inflicted burns) that should always be considered to involve a felony and thus should always involve an arrest.[69]

Mandatory arrests for domestic violence, however, are still controversial. Eve Buzawa argues that a mandatory arrest policy may deter female victims from calling the police in the first place; many victims simply want the police to help with the immediate crisis but do not necessarily want an arrest.[70] Also, some women feel that arresting an abusive spouse might make him angrier and cause him to commit further violence against the woman.

Many localities, including Washington, D.C., and Detroit, are forming special police task forces to deal with enforcing domestic violence laws. The Detroit Police Department, in 1996, deployed a fifty-member homicide-reduction task force charged with investigating every domestic homicide reported to police.[71]

A 1996 law, The Domestic Violence Offender Gun Ban, was passed by Congress. This law prohibits anyone with misdemeanor domestic violence convictions from possessing a firearm. (Persons with felony convictions are already prohibited from possessing a firearm.) Upon passage, the law began to rock law enforcement, sparked lawsuits, forced police agencies to conduct background checks of officers to ensure compliance with the law, and in some cases, cost officers their jobs. The law, police organizations say, threaten law enforce-

YOU ARE THERE!

The April LaSalata Story

The April LaSalata case tells a chilling tale of domestic violence in the United States and illustrates how the failure to deal with this violence can have deadly consequences.

In the fall of 1987, the marriage of April and Anthony LaSalata, high school sweethearts, was officially terminated by divorce. On February 26, 1988, April was stabbed three times by Anthony. "She came in dead," recalls Dr. Alexander Melman, the surgeon at Southside Hospital in Bay Shore, New York, who saved LaSalata by sewing her back together on the night of February 26. "She had no blood pressure, she had wounds to the lungs and the diaphragm and part of her liver was sticking out. The son of a bitch turned the blade, an old trick to create more injuries. It reminded me of a wartime injury."

Then, on January 3, 1989, as LaSalata reached the concrete steps in front of her door, her former husband came out from behind some shrubs. He aimed his sawed-off rifle at her chest and fired. Then he stood over her body and shot her twice in the head.

Why was Anthony LaSalata free on January 3, 1989, to do this? Was it because we in the United States do not pay enough attention to domestic violence? Or was it because there is no room left in our prisons?

Source: Adapted from Richard C. Firstman, "Hunted: The Last Year of April LaSalata," *Newsday*, 28 January 1990, pp. 10–15, 20–23.

In 1997, the New York City Police Department was forced to investigate at least 125 officers who may have been affected by the law. Many officers, nationwide, faced loss of their jobs due to the bill. In May 1997, it was reported:

> Thousands of law enforcement officers could be forced to turn in their guns—and holster their careers—under the law, which bars anyone with a misdemeanor domestic-violence conviction from owning or carrying a firearm. A handful of officers have been let go already, and more are expected to be fired as departments continue reviewing old records to determine whether officers have domestic-violence convictions in their past.[73]

A recent New York City case points to the problem of domestic abusers who are police officers. In June 1996, a twenty-five-year-old woman, Jo-Ann Cote, was gunned down by her NYPD officer-boyfriend, who then shot and killed himself. The couple had broken up the previous Christmas. In 1997, it was disclosed that the victim had appealed for help on numerous occasions, by calling the police to her home, going to her boyfriend's police command, and even calling his commanding officer. A police sergeant faces dismissal for refusal to take proper police action in this case.[74]

Police and Radical and Hate Groups

Radical and hate groups have long presented a serious problem to the police. Throughout a major part of our history, the Ku Klux Klan terrorized and killed thousands of citizens. In the 1960s and 1970s, radical hate groups, such as the Black Panthers and the Black Liberation Army, raged urban warfare against the police,

ment careers by penalizing people convicted of spousal abuse without taking into account that they may have successfully dealt with their domestic problems.[72]

PATROLLING THE NET

Help From the Net for Victims of Domestic Violence

The following are some sites from the World Wide Web that offer help for victims of Domestic Violence:

Violence Against Women Office, U.S. Department of Justice Domestic Violence Information Center
  http://www.usdoj.gov/vawo
FMF-Domestic Violence Information Center
  http://www.feminist.org/other/dv/dvhome.html
Safety Net Domestic Violence Resources
  http://www.cybergrrl.com/dv.html
Men Against Domestic Violence
  http://www.silcom.com/~paladin/madv

Source: Daniel J. Kurland and Christina Polsenberg, *Internet Guide for Criminal Justice* (Belmont, Calif.: Wadsworth, 1997), p. 71.

maiming and killing scores of police officers. Also, in that period of our history, militant student and antiwar groups caused tremendous problems for the police. Historically, in our nation, radical groups have been involved in assassinations, bombings, terrorism, and other crimes and acts of violence to protest the policies of the United States and to attempt to impose their distorted views on all members of our society.

Foreign terrorism has long threatened the lives and safety of U.S. citizens; however, in the 1990s, a new brand of home-grown terrorism has shocked America. These antigovernment groups are known by a myriad of names, including militias, Patriots, and white supremacists.

The convicted bomber in the worst case of mass murder and domestic terrorism in U.S. history, Timothy McVeigh, who was sentenced to death in 1997 for the bombing of the Alfred P. Murrah Federal Building in Oklahoma City on April 19, 1995, was alleged to have had links to white supremacists and Patriot groups. The bombing killed 168 people.[75]

Domestic terrorism was also probably responsible for the bombing in Centennial Olympic Park at the Atlanta Olympics Games on July 27, 1996, in which one women was killed and 111 other people were injured. It was reported in the media that the FBI originally suspected security guard Richard A. Jewell of complicity in the bombing, but later the FBI indicated that there was no evidence that he had any criminal part in it. On June 9, 1997, an FBI task force linked the Olympic bombing to the January 16, 1997, bombing at the Sandy Springs Professional Building (housing the Atlanta Northside Family Planning Services clinic—an abortion clinic) and the February 2, 1997, bombing at an Atlanta lesbian nightclub. The FBI claimed that letters mailed to the press by a militant religious cell known as the "Army of God" connected this group to the bombings.[76]

One type of the radical or hate group particularly worries the police. A 1997 report, entitled *Two Years After: The Patriot Movement Since Oklahoma City,* indicated that at least 858 so-called Patriot groups, including 380 armed militias, were active in the United States in 1996. This number represents a 6 percent increase over the number of such groups identified in 1994 and 1995 by the Klanwatch Project, an arm of the Montgomery, Alabama-based Southern Poverty Law Center, which monitors extremist groups around the nation.[77]

The Klanwatch Project created its Militia Task Force in 1994, a year before the existence of the Patriot movement exploded into the national consciousness following

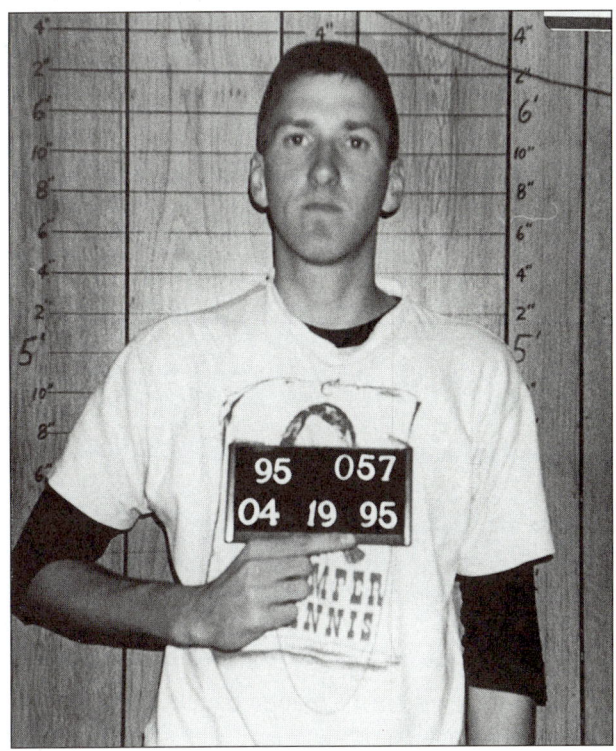

Police booking photo of Timothy McVeigh, convicted of the bombing of the Alfred P. Murrah Federal Building in Oklahoma City, on April 19, 1995. Note the date in the photo: McVeigh was arrested a short time after the bombing by an Oklahoma State Trooper for a traffic violation and possession of a weapon. Several days later, he was charged with the bombing.

ing the attack on the Oklahoma City Federal building. Six months before the blast on April 19, 1995, Klanwatch warned the U.S. Attorney General, "The mixture of armed groups and those who hate is a recipe for disaster." In 1996, U.S. law enforcement authorities arrested numerous Patriot and militia members for illegal activities they committed to further their cause. Over one-third of the crimes involved explosives.[78]

Klanwatch has warned that militia groups may also launch a biochemical terrorist attack on the United States and have reported that the extremist groups have sophisticated intelligence-gathering operations for collecting information on public and private targets. Evidence has been compiled that many of the groups are increasingly influenced by racist ideology.

In 1997, in response to fears regarding major terrorist threats to the nation, the federal government began a $42-million effort to conduct training exercises for po-

Suspicious fires have destroyed numerous houses of worship throughout the United States.

lice agencies to prepare them in responding to chemical or biological attacks.[79]

FBI Special Agents James E. Duffy and Alan C. Brantley give us this profile of the typical militia member:

> Most militia organization members are white males who range in age from the early 20s to the mid-50s. The majority of militia members appear to be attracted to the movement because of gun control issues. . . . Militia members generally maintain strong Christian beliefs and justify their actions by claiming to be ardent defenders of the Constitution.[80]

Aggressive enforcement by federal and local law enforcement resulted in the following major cases against militia members around the nation in 1996 and 1997:

- Three members of the Phineas Priesthood, a white supremacist group, were charged in Spokane, Washington, with bank robbery and conspiracy. They twice robbed a Spokane bank and planted three pipe bombs set to go off during the heists to divert authorities.
- In West Virginia, four separate federal trials began against the Mountaineer Militia, accused of planning to bomb the FBI's new fingerprint facility in Clarksburg, West Virginia. The group's leader, Floyd Ray Looker, and one other man were indicted in 1996 on weapons, explosives, and terrorism charges.
- In Georgia, a government informant testified that two leaders of the Militia-at-Large for the Republic of Georgia had hoped to amass a stockpile of weapons at the Summer Olympics of 1996.
- Militia leader John Pittner and seven others were arrested in Washington State on weapons and explosives charges. Informants testified in the trial that the militia members discussed blowing up radio towers and railroad tunnels.
- William Michael Gleason, a member of the United States Militia at Large in Michigan, was allegedly murdered by two fellow members who suspected him of informing on them to another militia leader. One of the suspects is in jail; the other remains at large.
- In Ohio, Richard Guthrie pleaded guilty to charges of robbing eighteen banks to finance an underground group, the Aryan Republican Army. Guthrie agreed to testify against a fellow extremist, but hanged himself in jail nine days later.
- Ten of twelve members of the Viper Militia in Arizona pled guilty to weapons and explosives charges. The group was accused of plotting to blow up government buildings in Arizona.[81]

Many claim that the radical hate groups are motivated by what they consider to be oppressive federal government actions against groups like themselves. Two of these actions have received a great deal of criticism in the press and have caused the federal government to change many of their enforcement procedures.[82]

The fire at the culmination of the 51-day federal government siege of the Branch Davidian compound in Waco, Texas, took 80 lives.

The most widely publicized of these actions—a fifty-one-day siege of the Branch Davidian compound in Waco, Texas—ended on April 19, 1993, when eighty members of the Branch Davidian sect died after a fire and a shootout with police and federal agents. David Koresh, leader of the group, died of a gunshot wound to the head sometime during the blaze.

The other controversial action occurred in 1992, when U.S. Marshals tried to arrest white separatist Randall C. Weaver on firearms charges. During the resulting siege in Ruby Ridge, Idaho, Weaver's unarmed wife, Vicki, and his son, Sammy, age 14 (as well as U.S. Marshal William Degan) were killed. In 1995, the U.S. Government, without admitting guilt in the case, agreed to pay $3.1 million to Weaver and his three surviving children.[83]

Regarding Ruby Ridge, one news source stated, "Like Waco, Ruby Ridge long ago entered the political mythology of the paranoid ultraright. Like Waco, it attests to the emergence of a reckless mentality that sullies the image of the FBI and plays straight into the hands of those who like to demagogue the federal government."[84]

Two recent situations that could have ended like Ruby Ridge and Waco fortunately had different conclusions.

In Fort Davis, Texas, in April 1997, Richard L. McLaren, head of the Republic of Texas, a separatist group who believed that Texas was never legally annexed into the United States, held off local police and Texas authorities for eight days. The siege ended peacefully as the separatists surrendered.[85]

For eighty-one days, from March 25, 1996, to June 13, 1996, twenty-one members of the Montana Freemen, a radical right-wing group, and some of their families held local police and federal investigators at bay in a tense standoff. The siege ended peacefully when the Freemen surrendered.[86]

Police Civil and Criminal Liability

Police officers may be held legally liable—that is arrested, sued, and prosecuted for their conduct. This concept of police legal liability comes in many different forms. **Police civil liability** means that a police officer may be sued in civil court for improper behavior, using such civil law concepts as negligence and torts. Civil liability is a relatively new approach to correcting improper actions by the police through lawsuits and the resultant monetary judgments. Officers may also be sued under the provisions of a state civil rights law for violation of a person's civil rights.

Rolando V. del Carmen has identified several major sources of police legal liability. Under state law, police are subject to (1) civil liabilities, including state tort laws and state civil rights laws; (2) criminal liabilities, including state penal code provisions applicable only to public officials and general state penal law provisions; and (3) administrative liabilities. Under federal law, police are subject to (1) civil liabilities, including three sections of Title 42 of the U.S. Code; (2) criminal liabilities, including three sections of Title 18 of the U.S. Code; and (3) administrative liabilities.[87]

State Liability

Police may be sued in state civil courts for torts. A tort is a private wrong, as opposed to a crime that is considered a public wrong. Torts can be classified as intentional torts or negligence torts.

As for criminal liability, many states have provisions in their penal codes that make certain actions by police officers or other public servants a crime. Police officers, like everyone else, are also subject to being charged with violations of the state penal law, such as murder, assault, or larceny.

Police officers are also subject to administrative liability: They are liable to the rules and regulations established by their department to govern the conduct of its officers. Officers charged with violations of a department's internal rules and regulations may be subject to discipline in the form of fines, demotions, and even dismissal from the department.

Federal Liability

In recent years, an increasing number of lawsuits against police officers have been brought to federal courts on civil rights grounds. These federal suits are known as 1983 suits, because they are based on Section 1983 of Title 42 of the U.S. Code (Civil Action for Deprivation of Civil Rights):

> Every person who, under color of any statute, ordinance, regulation, custom, or usage, of any State or Territory, subjects or causes to be subjected, any citizen of the United States or other persons within the jurisdiction thereof to the deprivation of any rights, privileges or immunities secured by the Constitution and laws, shall be liable to the party injured in an action at law, suit in equity, or other proper proceeding for redress.

This law was passed in 1871 by Congress to ensure the civil rights of individuals. It requires due process of law before any person can be deprived of life, liberty, or property and provides redress for the denial of these constitutional rights by officials acting under color of state law (under the authority of their power as public officials).[88]

Section 1983 of Title 42 of the U.S. Code was originally know as Section 1 of the Ku Klux Klan Act of April 20, 1871, enacted by Congress as a means of enforcing the Fourteenth Amendment guarantee of rights to the newly freed slaves. This law originally was given a narrow interpretation by the courts and was seldom used. Between 1871 and 1920, only twenty-one cases were decided under Section 1983.[89] Police officers who violate a person's civil rights by unlawfully searching or detaining a person can be sued under this law. It can also be used in abuse-of-force cases.

Two other sections of Title 42 of the U.S. Code also apply to police officers. Section 1985 (Conspiracy to Interfere with Civil Rights) can be used against two or more officers who conspire to deprive a person of the equal protection of the law. Section 1981 (Equal Rights under the Law) can also be used against officers.

In addition to being sued by a plaintiff civilly for violation of a person's civil rights, a police officer can face criminal charges by the government, using Title 18 of the U.S. Code, Section 242 (Criminal Liability for Deprivation of Civil Rights), and in conspiracy cases, Title 18 of the U.S. Code, Section 241 (Criminal Liability for Conspiracy to Deprive a Person of Rights). Title 18 of the U.S. Code, Section 245 (Federally Protected Activities), may be used against officers who interfere with certain activities such as voting, serving as a juror in a federal court, and other federally regulated activities.

Federal law enforcement officers are also subject to administrative liability—to the rules and regulations of their agencies—just as state officers are subject to the rules and regulations of their departments. The violation of these regulations may lead to such disciplinary action as fines, demotions, or dismissal.

Reasons for Suing Police Officers

Charles R. Swanson, Leonard Territo, and Robert W. Taylor report that the most common source of lawsuits against the police involve assault, battery, false imprisonment, and malicious prosecution.[90] Del Carmen found that a survey of police chiefs from the twenty largest U.S. cities and dozens of other municipalities with populations over 100,000 revealed that most of the chiefs, their officers, and their departments have been sued. The areas in which most suits were brought, in order of frequency, were as follows: (1) use of force; (2) auto pursuits; (3) arrests and searches; (4) employee drug tests; (5) hiring and promotion; (6) discrimination based on race, sex or age; (7) insurance or risk management; (8) record keeping and privacy; and (9) jail management.[91]

In *Civil Liabilities in American Policing: A Text for Law Enforcement Personnel,* del Carmen includes chapters on the following types of liabilities affecting law enforcement personnel: liability for nondeadly and deadly use of force; liability for false arrest and false imprisonment; liability for searches and seizures; liability for negligence, specific instances of negligence in police work; liability for jail management; liabilities of police supervisors for what their subordinates do; and liabilities of police supervisors for what they do to their subordinates.[92]

The following are some examples of civil lawsuits against the police. In *Biscoe v. Arlington,* Alvin Biscoe, an innocent bystander who was waiting to cross the street, was struck by a police car that had gone out of control while involved in a high-speed automobile pursuit. The accident caused Biscoe to lose both legs. Biscoe was awarded $5 million by the court.[93]

Kaplan v. Lloyd's Insurance Company was another lawsuit involving an accident that resulted from a high-speed police chase. The officer driving the police car, who drove 75 miles per hour in a 40-mile-per-hour zone, was found to be negligent and was held liable for damages.[94]

The city of Boston agreed to pay $500,000 to the parents of a teenager who was shot to death by a police officer, even though the youth was in a stolen car involved in a high-speed chase with the police.[95]

In *Prior v. Woods,* a Detroit police officer mistakenly shot and killed a man, David Prior, in front of his home, because the officer suspected Prior of being a burglar. A $5.7 million judgment was imposed against the Detroit Police Department.[96]

In 1996, Drewey and Mona Scarberry were awarded $950,000 by the city of Tacoma, Washington, as the result of a car crash that left Drewey Scarberry partially paralyzed. The couple's car was broadsided by a carload of gang members being pursued by the police.[97]

Effects of Lawsuits on Police Departments and Officers

The use of civil lawsuits against the police has been increasing at a rapid rate and is having a dramatic effect on the treasuries of some counties and cities. Advocates of police civil damage lawsuits see these lawsuits as a vehicle for stimulating police reform. They assume that the dollar cost of police misconduct will force other city officials to intervene and force improvements in the police department. However, Edward J. Littlejohn's study of police misconduct litigation in Detroit suggested that this assumption is incorrect. Littlejohn found that even when damage awards increased substantially, there was no feedback from other agencies of city government. He found that one agency of government argued the case in court and another paid the bill when the case was lost. The damage awards did not create pressure for changes in police operations.[98]

A Yale Law School study of 149 police misconduct suits filed in Connecticut found that the suits had little apparent effect on the police. The plaintiffs rarely won, mainly because juries tend to be sympathetic to the police. Furthermore, even when the plaintiffs did win, neither the departments nor the individual officers directly bore the financial cost of losing.[99]

So many suits have been filed against the police that the U.S. Supreme Court, in *Canton v. Harris,* made it more difficult for victims to sue for damages. The Court ruled that to be liable, police departments must be de-

All in the Line of Duty

Despite Being Shot, He Helped His Brother Officer and Also Caught the Perp

During a multiagency drug investigation, Investigator Vincent E. Jeter of the Rock Hill, South Carolina, Police Department and an officer from a police department in a neighboring city approached a group of suspects who had just sold crack cocaine to an undercover agent. When they identified themselves as police officers, the suspects fled on foot. At this time, another suspect approached the officers from behind and fired several shots at close range. One of the rounds lodged in Investigator Jeter's thigh; a second round struck the other officer in the back of the neck, exiting through his face. Although wounded, Jeter pursued two of the escaping suspects and was able to apprehend and handcuff one of them. He then returned with the suspect to the scene of the shooting to render assistance to the fallen officer, radioing for medical assistance and backup police units. When they arrived, he refused treatment until the other officer was attended to and transported to the hospital. Investigator Jeter subsequently was treated for his wounds and returned to duty after several weeks of recuperation. The assailant was apprehended a short time after the shooting.

Source: Adapted from *FBI Law Enforcement Bulletin,* January 1996, p. 33.

liberately indifferent to the needs of the people with whom police come in contact.[100] Joseph J. Senna and Larry J. Siegel said that despite this tightening of liability standards, "the threat of large civil penalties may prove to be the most effective deterrent yet to the police use of excessive force."[101]

To many, however, the $4.3 million dollar lawsuit awarded to convicted subway mugger Bernard McCummings, in a 1993 U.S. Supreme Court decision in a civil suit, appears ludicrous. McCummings was shot twice in the back in 1984 by a New York City Transit Authority officer as he attempted to flee a subway platform after beating and robbing a seventy-one-year-old man. At the time of the crime, McCummings had just gotten out of prison for robbery. McCumming's mugging victim, Jerome Sandusky, decried the ruling, saying, "It's justice turned upside down . . . and it sends a terrible message . . . that crime does pay."[102]

Chapter Summary

Although police work can be dangerous, not many officers are murdered in the line of duty. Additionally, the number of murdered officers has decreased in recent years.

Police shooting policies have changed significantly in recent years in response to changes in state laws, police philosophy, and court cases, including the landmark U.S. Supreme Court case of *Tennessee v. Garner*. Additionally, police have begun to address the problem of rapid automobile pursuits, with many departments severely restricting them. Perhaps these changes will reduce the incidents of police civil liability, also discussed in this chapter.

The chapter also discussed the damage to U.S. society from domestic violence, along with efforts by the police to address this problem. Radical and hate groups and the threats that they pose to our police and our society were also covered.

Finally, the chapter discussed how police officers can be held legally liable for their conduct. They can be arrested under their state's criminal law and sued under civil law.

Learning Check

1. Discuss how dangerous it is to be a police officer in the United States. Talk about whether this danger has changed at all during the past several years.
2. Explain the fleeing felon rule and why it existed.
3. Discuss some recent changes in police shooting policies and how they have affected officers' safety.
4. Explain why many police departments have started to introduce limited pursuit policies.
5. Discuss the seriousness of the domestic violence problem in our society.

Review Exercise

Last year you passed your local police department's entrance examination. During this year you have passed the department's physical agility, psychological, and medical examinations, as well as its background investigation. This morning you received a letter in the mail from the police department. It told you that you have been accepted for appointment and advised you to report to City Hall next Monday to be sworn in as a probationary police officer.

You have never told your parents about your plans to become a police officer. You are sure they will object, because they consider police work to be extremely dangerous. Now you must tell your mother, an accountant, and your father, a high school English teacher, that you plan to become a police officer. You are sure they are going to be very upset about your decision and very concerned about your future safety. Plan what you will tell your parents about the degree of danger in police work.

Web Exercise

Patrol the web and find some sites that discuss radical and hate group philosophies and operations. Hint: Often information about such groups can be accessed through police officer-oriented homepages.

Key Concepts

"fleeing felon" doctrine
Tennessee v. Garner
"defense of life" standard
police pursuit policy
Minneapolis Domestic Violence Experiment
proarrest policy
radical and hate groups
police civil liability

Notes

1. Barbara Raffel Price, as quoted in Karen Polk, "New York Police: Caught in the Middle and Losing Faith," *Boston Globe,* 28 December 1988, p. 3.
2. Kathleen Maquire and Ann L. Pastore, eds., *Sourcebook of Criminal Justice Statistics—1996* (Washington, D.C.: U.S.

Department of Justice, Bureau of Justice Statistics, U.S. Government Printing Office, 1997), Table 3.154, p. 354.

3. Maguire and Pastore, *Sourcebook—1996*, Table 3.154, p. 354.
4. Victoria L. Major, "Law Enforcement Officers Killed 1980–1989," *FBI Law Enforcement Bulletin,* May 1991, pp. 2–5.
5. Major, "Law Enforcement Officers Killed 1980–1989."
6. Major, "Law Enforcement Officers Killed 1980–1989."
7. "One-Officer State Police Cars Raise the Risks to Cops' Lives," *Law Enforcement News,* 14 February 1997, pp. 1, 14.
8. Maquire and Pastore, *Sourcebook—1996*, Table 3.16, p. 356. Table 15.3 lists reasons for the accidental deaths of police officers from 1980 to 1995.
9. William Geller and Michael S. Scott, *Deadly Force: What We Know* (Washington, D.C.: Police Executive Research Forum, 1992), pp. 549–550.
10. David Constantin, "Homicides of American Law Enforcement Officers, 1978-1980," *Justice Quarterly* 1 (1984): 113–128.
11. David Lester, "The Murder of Police Officers in American Cities," *Criminal Justice and Behavior,* January 1984, pp. 101–113.
12. William Geller, "Deadly Force: What We Know," *Journal of Police Science and Administration* 10 (1982): 151–177.
13. Frances T. Cullen et al., "Paradox in Policing: A Note on Perceptions of Danger," *Journal of Police Science and Administration* 11 (1983): 457–462.
14. Maquire and Pastore, *Sourcebook—1996*, Table 3.163, p. 359.
15. See Theodore M. Hammett, Harold W. Jaffee, and Bruce A. Johnson, *The Cause, Transmission, and Incidence of AIDS* (Washington, D.C.: National Institute of Justice, 1988); Don Des Jarlais and Dana E. Hunt, *AIDS and Intravenous Drug Use* (Washington, D.C.: National Institute of Justice, 1988). Statistics cited are from the Centers for Disease Control, World Health Organization AIDS Resource Network, as reported in *New York Times,* 16 August 1992, p. A-10.
16. Theodore M. Hammett and Walter Bond, *Risks of Infection with the AIDS Virus through Exposures to Blood* (Washington, D.C.: National Institute of Justice, 1987).
17. New York City Police Department, *AIDS and Our Workplace* (New York: New York City Police Department, 1987).
18. Federal Bureau of Investigation, "Collecting and Handling Evidence Infected with Human Disease-causing Organisms," *FBI Law Enforcement Bulletin,* July 1987.
19. Theodore M. Hammett, *Precautionary Measures and Protective Equipment: Developing a Reasonable Response* (Washington, D.C.: National Institute of Justice, 1988).
20. Theodore M. Hammett, *AIDS and the Law Enforcement Officer: Concerns and Policy Responses* (Washington, D.C.: National Institute of Justice, 1987).
21. James Q. Wilson, "Police Use of Deadly Force," *FBI Law Enforcement Bulletin,* August 1980, p. 16.
22. James J. Fyfe, "Police Use of Deadly Force: Research and Reform," *Justice Quarterly* 5 (1988): 164–205.
23. Kenneth J. Matulia, *A Balance of Forces,* 2d ed. (Gaithersburg, Md.: International Association of Chiefs of Police, 1985).
24. Sid Harring et al., "The Management of Police Killings," *Crime and Social Justice* (1977): 34–43; and Richard R. E. Kania and Wade C. Mackey, "Police Violence as a Function of Community Characteristics," *Criminology* 15 (1977): 27–48.
25. Lawrence O'Donnell, *Deadly Force* (New York: William Morrow, 1983), p. 14.
26. Fyfe, "Police Use of Deadly Force," p. 177.
27. Gerald Robin, "Justifiable Homicide by Police," *Journal of Criminal Law, Criminology, and Police Science,* May/June 1963, pp. 225–231.
28. Matulia, *Balance of Forces.*
29. Lawrence Sherman and Robert Langworthy, "Measuring Homicide by Police Officers," *Journal of Criminal Law and Criminology* (70): 546–560.
30. Kania and Mackey, "Police Violence."
31. Kania and Mackey, "Police Violence."
32. David Jacobs and David Britt, "Inequality and Police Use of Deadly Force: An Empirical Assessment of a Conflict Hypothesis," *Social Problems,* January 1979, pp. 403–412.
33. Paul Takagi, "A Garrison State in a 'Democratic' Society," *Crime and Social Justice* 5 (1974): 34–43.
34. Mark Blumberg, "Race and Police Shootings: An Analysis in Two Cities," in *Contemporary Issues in Law Enforcement,* ed. James Fyfe (Beverly Hills, Calif.: Sage Publications, 1981), pp. 152–166; and Catherine Milton et al., *Police Use of Deadly Force* (Washington, D.C.: Police Foundation, 1977).
35. Geller, "Deadly Force: What We Know," pp. 151–177.
36. Robin, "Justifiable Homicide by Police."
37. James J. Fyfe, "Reducing the Use of Deadly Force: The New York Experience," in National Institute of Justice, *Police Use of Deadly Force* (Washington, D.C.: National Institute of Justice, 1978), p. 29.
38. William A. Geller and Kevin J. Karales, *Split-Second Decisions* (Chicago: Chicago Law Enforcement Study Group, 1981), p. 119.
39. James Fyfe, "Shots Fired" (Ph.D. diss., State University of New York, Albany, 1978).

40. David Lester, "Predicting the Rate of Justifiable Homicide by Police Officers," *Police Studies* 16 (1993): p. 43; see also Kania and Mackey, "Police Violence."
41. O'Donnell, *Deadly Force,* p. 14. See also Abraham Tennenbaum, "The Influence of the Garner Decision on Police Use of Deadly Force," *Journal of Law and Criminology* 85 (1994).
42. James J. Fyfe, "Administrative Interventions on Police Shooting Discretion: An Empirical Analysis," *Journal of Criminal Justice* 7 (1979): 309–323; and James J. Fyfe, cited in O'Donnell, *Deadly Force.*
43. Fyfe, "Police Use of Deadly Force," p. 181.
44. Lawrence W. Sherman and Ellen G. Cohn, *Citizens Killed by Big-City Police, 1970–1984* (Washington, D.C.: Crime Control Institute, 1986).
45. *Law Enforcement News,* 15 November 1995, p. 1. See also John S. Dempsey, *West Home Page,* April 1996.
46. Geoffrey P. Alpert and Lorie A. Fridell, *Police Vehicles and Firearms: Instruments of Deadly Force* (Prospect Heights, Ill.: Waveland Press, 1992), pp. 105–106.
47. Geoffrey Alpert and Patrick R. Anderson, "The Most Deadly Force: Police Pursuits," *Justice Quarterly* 3 (1986): 1–14.
48. Alpert and Anderson, "Most Deadly Force," p. 5.
49. Alpert and Anderson, "Most Deadly Force," p. 3.
50. California Highway Patrol, *Pursuit Study* (Sacramento Calif.: California Highway Patrol, 1993).
51. California Highway Patrol, *Pursuit Study,* p. 72.
52. California Highway Patrol, *Pursuit Study,* p. 21.
53. Geoffrey P. Alpert and Roger G. Dunham, *Police Pursuit Driving: Controlled Responses to Emergency Situations* (Westport, Conn.: Greenwood Press, 1990); Geoffrey P. Alpert, "Questioning Police Pursuit in Urban Areas," *Journal of Police Science and Administration* (1987): 298–306; and Geoffrey P. Alpert and Roger G. Dunham, "Research on Police Pursuits: Applications for Law Enforcement," *American Journal of Police* 7 (1988): 123–131. For a discussion of these three studies, see Alpert and Fridell, *Police Vehicles and Firearms,* pp. 105–106.
54. Alpert and Fridell, *Police Vehicles and Firearms,* p. 115.
55. Gorden E. Misner, "High Speed Pursuits: Police Perspectives," *Criminal Justice: The Americas,* December/January 1990, p. 17.
56. "Life, Liberty and Pursuits," *Law Enforcement News,* 31 December 1996, p. 26.
57. "Life, Liberty and Pursuits."
58. Geoffrey P. Alpert, *Police Pursuit: Policies and Training* (Washington, D.C.: National Institute of Justice, 1997).
59. Murray A. Straus, Richard J. Gelles, and Suzanne Steinmetz, *Behind Closed Doors: Violence in the American Family* (Garden City, N.Y.: Anchor Press, 1980), pp. 25–26, 32–36, 49.
60. Police Foundation, *Domestic Violence and the Police: Studies in Detroit and Kansas City* (Washington, D.C.: Police Foundation, 1977).
61. Federal Bureau of Investigation, *Uniform Crime Reports, 1990: Crime in the United States,* pp. 11–13.
62. "Where New York's Anti-crime Miracle Ends: Crime-Reduction Strategies Aren't Having as Much Impact on Domestic Homicide," *Law Enforcement News,* 30 April 1997, p. 7.
63. T. S. Duncan, "Changing Perception of Domestic Violence," *Law Enforcement News,* 31 October 1991, p. 13. The two books reviewed are Michael Steinman, ed., *Woman Battering: Policy Responses* (Cincinnati: Anderson, 1991); and Douglas J. Besharov, ed., *Family Violence: Research and Public Policy Issues* (Washington, D.C.: University Press of America, 1990).
64. Nancy Loving, *Responding to Spouse Abuse and Wife Beating: A Guide for Police* (Washington, D.C.: Police Executive Research Forum, 1980).
65. Lawrence W. Sherman and Richard A. Berk, *The Minneapolis Domestic Violence Experiment* (Washington, D.C.: Police Foundation, 1984).
66. Sherman and Berk, *Minneapolis Domestic Violence Experiment.*
67. Franklyn W. Dunford, David Huizinga, and Delbert S. Elliott, "The Role of Arrest in Domestic Violence Cases," *Criminology* 28 (1990): 204.
68. Ellen G. Cohn and Lawrence W. Sherman, *Police Policy on Domestic Violence, 1986: A National Survey* (Washington, D.C.: Crime Control Institute, 1987).
69. National Institute of Justice, *Confronting Domestic Violence: A Guide for Criminal Justice Agencies* (Washington, D.C.: National Institute of Justice, 1986), p. 34.
70. Eve Buzawa, "Police Officer Response to Domestic Violence Legislation in Michigan," *Journal of Police Science and Administration* 10 (1982): 415–424.
71. "On the Other Side of the Law? Not Necessarily," *Law Enforcement News,* 31 December 1996, p. 19.
72. Jacob R. Clark, "Police Careers May Take a Beating from Fed Domestic-Violence Law," *Law Enforcement News,* 14 February 1997, pp. 1, 14. See also "Battle Lines Form on Law Disarming Some Cops," *Law Enforcement News,* 15 March 1997, p. 7.
73. "Battle Lines Form on Law Disarming Some Cops."
74. Murray Weiss and Cathy Burke, "A Grieving Mother's Crusade: Wants NYPD to Fight Cop Domestic Abuse," *New York Post,* 29 July 1997, p. 14.
75. Jo Thomas, "Army Buddy Says McVeigh Saw Victims as Part of 'Evil Empire,'" *New York Times,* 13 May 1997, pp. A-1, 14; Michael Fleeman, "Prosecutor Says McVeigh Wanted Blood," *Tampa Tribune,* 25 April 1997, pp. 1, 9; "Families Break into Tears as Victims' Names Recited,"

Tampa Tribune, 25 April 1997, p. 9; Jo Thomas, "McVeigh Guilty on All Counts in the Oklahoma City Bombing," *New York Times,* 3 June 1997, pp. A-1, 18; Rick Bragg, "Survivors Respond: Still Haunted, Families See Justice in Shape of a Killer's Grave, *New York Times,* 3 June 1997, pp. A-1, 19; James Collins, "The Weight of Evidence," *Time,* 28 April 1997, pp. 37–43.

76. Kevin Sack, "U.S. Says FBI Erred in Using Deception in Olympic Bomb Inquiry," *New York Times,* 9 April 1997, p. A-47; Sack, "Officials Link Atlanta Bombings and Ask for Help," *New York Times,* 10 June 1997, pp. A-1, D-24.

77. "In Okla. City Bombing's Wake, Militias Still Seen Posing Public-Safety Threat," *Law Enforcement News,* 15 April 1997, p. 5.

78. "In Okla. City Bombing's Wake."

79. "Coming to Your Town: Bio-Chem Terror Training," *Law Enforcement News,* 15 May 1997, p. 8.

80. James E. Duffy and Alan C. Brantley, "Militias: Initiating Contact," *FBI Law Enforcement Bulletin,* July 1997, pp. 22–26, p. 23.

81. "Policing Keeps an Eye on the Radical Right," *Law Enforcement News,* 31 December 1996, p. 8; "FBI Turns up the Heat on Domestic Terror," *Law Enforcement News,* 30 April 1997, p. 9; "Agents Tell of Militia Life from Within," *New York Times,* 6 June 1997, p. A-22.

82. Duffy and Brantley, "Militias: Initiating Contact."

83. "Ruby Ridge," *Newsweek,* 28 August 1995, pp. 25–33.

84. "Ruby Ridge," p. 25.

85. Sam Howe Verhovek, "Hostages Taken in Standoff with Militant Texas Group," *New York Times,* 28 April 1997, p. A-10; Verhovek, "Texas Standoff Continues," *New York Times,* 30 April 1997, p. A-16; Verhovek, "One Texas Secessionist Who Fled into Mountains Is Killed," *New York Times,* 6 May 1997, p. A-16; Matthew Cooper, "Shutting Down a Siege," *Newsweek,* 12 May 1997, p. 46; "Group Frees 2 Hostages but Siege Continues," *New York Times,* 29 April 1997, pp. A-1, D-23; Michael Wines, "Swap to Free 2 Hostages Was Right, Experts Say," *New York Times,* 29 April 1997, p. D-23.

86. James Brooke, "For Radical Freemen, All the Courts Are Stages," *New York Times,* 26 March 1997, p. A-18.

87. Rolando V. del Carmen, *Civil Liabilities in American Policing: A Text for Law Enforcement Personnel* (Englewood Cliffs, N.J.: Prentice-Hall, 1991), pp. 7–14.

88. Frank Schmallenger, *Criminal Justice Today: An Introductory Text for the Twenty-first Century* (Englewood Cliffs, N.J.: Prentice-Hall, 1991), p. 205.

89. del Carmen, *Civil Liabilities in American Policing,* p. 29.

90. Charles R. Swanson, Leonard Territo, and Robert W. Taylor, *Police Administration: Structures, Processes, and Behavior,* 2d ed. (New York: Macmillan, 1988).

91. del Carmen, *Civil Liabilities in American Policing,* pp. 2–3.

92. del Carmen, *Civil Liabilities in American Policing.*

93. *Biscoe v. Arlington* (1984) 80-0766, *National Law Journal,* 13 May 1985.

94. *Kaplan v. Lloyd's Insurance Co.,* 479 So.2d 961 (La.App. 1985).

95. Sean Murphy, "City Made $500,000 Settlement in Shooting," *Boston Globe,* 6 December 1988, p. 1.

96. *Prior v. Woods* (1981), *National Law Journal,* 2 November 1981.

97. "Life, Liberty and Pursuits."

98. Edward J. Littlejohn, "Civil Liability and the Police Officer: The Need for New Deterrents to Police Misconduct," *University of Detroit Journal of Urban Law* 58 (1981): 365–431.

99. "Project: Suing the Police in Federal Court," *Yale Law Journal* 88 (1979): 781–824.

100. *Canton v. Harris,* 86-1088, 44 Crl. 3157 (1989).

101. Joseph J. Senna and Larry J. Siegel, *Introduction to Criminal Justice,* 5th ed. (St. Paul: West, 1990), p. 273.

102. "Mugger Shot by Cop to Keep $4.3 Million," *USA Today,* 30 November 1993, p. 1-A.

Sources of Employment Information in Law Enforcement

Where do you find information about available jobs in policing or criminal justice in general? Many sources are available, including media advertising. Many police departments today are recruiting through radio, television, and newspaper advertising.

Civil service publications are another source. Many large cities have civil service weekly or monthly newspapers on sale in local stores. These newspapers carry information regarding openings in civil service jobs, and some even carry advertisements for courses to help you prepare for civil service exams.

Many cities have an office in their city hall or other government buildings that contain up-to-date job information on civil service jobs. You can also easily obtain information about the next police entrance examination or other information about the police by visiting or calling the local police station or headquarters.

Many police departments, in an effort to recruit college-educated men and women, participate in college job fairs. Additionally, many high school career days include representatives from local police departments or other criminal justice agencies.

Another source of information on jobs in policing is national publications. Later in this appendix you will find subscriber information for several publications that list police jobs and other criminal justice jobs in the United States.

Word-of-mouth advertising by family members and friends is probably the most common way people receive information about jobs in policing and criminal justice. A recent study found that over 64 percent of new recruits surveyed received information on available positions in police departments from police officers, friends, or relatives. Only a small percentage of the recruits learned of job openings through the more traditional newspaper employment ads. At the college at which I teach, most students taking civil service tests or securing jobs in criminal justice agencies or private law enforcement received the information regarding those opportunities from professors who announced local opportunities in class.

Today, one of the best and easiest ways to obtain information on jobs in law enforcement is through the Internet. Access to a computer and a modem and a few minutes of time can give one access to a myriad of job opportunities. Many police departments have their own web page on the World Wide Web and include job information among other information provided to the public. A feature of this text, Patrolling the Net, contains information about the role of the Internet in finding jobs in law enforcement.

Finally, many colleges and universities provide intern programs, in which students work for a local government agency for a semester while earning college credit. These programs are valuable for two major reasons: (1) students see firsthand what working in a particular agency is like and thus are better equipped to make well-informed decisions regarding future career plans, and (2) students may obtain information about job opportunities that may not be available to the general public.

How to Call for Information

When calling a particular police department in which you are interested, it is best to ask for the personnel department if it is a large agency. For smaller agencies, you may get the best information from the person answering the call. Some agencies may refer you to the city's or county's civil service commission or personnel agency for information.

How to Write for Information

When writing for information on employment, a basic business letter is most appropriate. A sample letter follows:

```
465 West Fulton St.
Anycity, NY 11754
January 12, 1998

The Honorable Raymond Kelly
Commissioner
New York City Police Department
1 Police Plaza
New York, NY 10003

Dear Commissioner Kelly:

I am an 18-year-old college student who is
interested in employment as a New York
City police officer. Would you kindly send
me information telling me how I may apply
for this position? Thank you very much.

Very truly yours:

John Q. Citizen
```

Some National Publications

The following publications provide current listings of job opportunities in the field of law enforcement.

National Directory of Law Enforcement Administrators: Correctional Institutions and Related Agencies

This directory has been published annually since 1964 by the National Police Chiefs and Sheriffs Information Bureau, Stevens Point, Wisconsin. It contains names, addresses, telephone numbers, and fax numbers of agency heads to contact about job information for the following types of agencies for each of the fifty states:

1. Municipal law enforcement.
2. County law enforcement.
3. Prosecutors.
4. Campus law enforcement.
5. State police—highway patrols.
6. State criminal investigation units.
7. State correctional agencies.
8. General state agencies.
9. Airport and harbor police.
10. Federal (U.S.) agencies.
11. Military agencies.
12. General national agencies.
13. International agencies.
14. Canadian law enforcement.

The 1997–98 edition costs $53. The mailing address follows:

National Police Chiefs and Sheriffs Information Bureau
P.O. Box 365
Stevens Point, WI 54461
Telephone: (715) 345-2772

Note: You might want to talk to the head of your school's criminal justice department and see if he or she could order this directory through the college library for use by all students.

Seeking Employment in Law Enforcement, Private Security, and Related Fields

This book, written by J. Scott Harr and Karen M. Hess and published by West Publishing Company, is an excellent reference about seeking a job in law enforcement. It contains fourteen fact-filled chapters: "Employment Trends: The World of Work," "Careers in Law Enforcement and Private Security," "Other Options to Consider," "On Choosing a Career: Knowing the Job and

Knowing Yourself," "Physical Fitness and Testing," "Other Forms of Testing," "Beneficial Attributes of the Successful Candidate," "The Resume: Selling Yourself on Paper," "On Not Getting the Job: Preparing for Rejection," "The Application Process: Finding and Applying for Jobs," "Presenting Yourself as the One to Hire," "The Interview: A Closer Look,""At Last! You've Got the Job!," and "The Future Revisited."

It also has thirty pages of appendixes that you can readily use in the job-searching process, including resume work sheets, sample résumés, sample cover letter and follow-up letter, job information sources, sample application forms, and Equal Employment Opportunity (EEO) guidelines.

You can order a copy of this book from the publisher or ask your bookstore to order it for you.

National Employment Listing Service (NELS)

This small booklet is published monthly by the Criminal Justice Center of Sam Houston State University in Huntsville, Texas. It advertises job opportunities nationwide in (1) academics and research, (2) community service and corrections, (3) institutional corrections, and (4) law enforcement and security.

The publication includes recent news from the U.S. Department of Justice regarding crime in the United States and other criminal justice system information, advertisements for law enforcement seminars and training sessions, a monthly calendar of events for criminal justice conferences and symposiums, and a list of publications available from the Criminal Justice Center of Sam Houston State University.

Subscription fees are $17.50 for six months or $30.00 per year. The mailing address follows:

National Employment Listing Service
Criminal Justice Center
Sam Houston State University
Huntsville, Texas 77341-2296
Telephone: (409) 294-1692
Fax: (409) 294-1653

Police Chief

This magazine is published monthly by the International Association of Chiefs of Police (IACP), Arlington, Virginia. It contains information about job openings for police chief and upper management positions nationwide. The magazine also includes articles regarding police, information on new products affecting the police, information about IACP educational courses, and information on police conferences in the United States and abroad.

Subscription fees are $25 per year. The mailing address follows:

Police Chief
1110 N. Glebe Rd., Suite 200
Arlington, VA 62201
Telephone: (703) 243-6500

Law Enforcement News

This newspaper is published monthly by the John Jay College of Criminal Justice, City University of New York. It contains job offers in police departments nationwide, articles regarding the police, "Around The Nation," a coast-to-coast roundup of police news; and information workshops and conferences.

Subscription fees are $18 a year. The mailing address follows:

Law Enforcement News (LEN)
899 Tenth Ave.
New York, NY 10019
Telephone: (212) 237-8442

A Networking Guide to Recruitment, Selection, and Probationary Training of Police Officers in Major Police Departments of the United States of America

This book, written by Peter and Deirdre Strawbridge and published by the John Jay College Press, contains extensive data on scores of major city and county police departments. It is organized in an easy-to-use format. The book provides agency and community profiles and examines working conditions, race and gender of officers, the use of various testing methodologies in the selection process, the length and nature of the training process, and the length and conditions of probation and field training.

The price is $9. The mailing address follows:

John Jay College of Criminal Justice
Office of Graduate Studies
899 Tenth Ave.
New York, NY 10019

B

The "Law Enforcement Code of Ethics" and "The Police Code of Conduct"

Law Enforcement Code of Ethics

As a law enforcement officer, my fundamental duty is to service the community; to safeguard lives and property; to protect the innocent against deception, the weak against oppression or intimidation and the peaceful against violence or disorder; and to respect the constitutional rights of all to liberty, equality and justice.

I will keep my private life unsullied as an example to all and will behave in a manner that does not bring discredit to me or to my agency. I will maintain courageous calm in the face of danger, scorn or ridicule; develop self-restraint; and be constantly mindful of the welfare of others. Honest in thought and deed both in my personal and official life, I will be exemplary in obeying the law and the regulations of my department. Whatever I see or hear of a confidential nature or that is confided to me in my official capacity will be kept ever secret unless revelation is necessary in the performance of my duty.

I will never act officiously or permit personal feelings, prejudices, political beliefs, aspirations, animosities or friendships to influence my decisions. With no compromise for crime and with relentless prosecution of criminals, I will enforce the law courteously and appropriately without fear or favor, malice or ill will, never employing unnecessary force or violence and never accepting gratuities.

I recognize the badge of my office as a symbol of public faith, and I accept it as a public trust to be held so long as I am true to the ethics of police service. I will never engage in acts of corruption or bribery, nor will I condone such acts by other police officers. I will cooperate with all legally authorized agencies and their representatives in the pursuit of justice.

I know that I alone am responsible for my own standard of professional performance and will take every reasonable opportunity to enhance and improve my level of knowledge and competence.

I will constantly strive to achieve these objectives and ideals, dedicating myself before God to my chosen profession . . . law enforcement.

Police Code of Conduct

All law enforcement officers must be fully aware of the ethical responsibilities of their position and must strive constantly to live up to the highest possible standards of professional policing.

The International Association of Chiefs of Police believes it important that police officers have clear advice and counsel available to assist them in performing their duties consistent with these standards, and has adopted the following ethical mandates as guidelines to meet these ends.

Primary Responsibilities of a Police Officer

A police officer acts as an official representative of government who is required and trusted to work with the law. The officer's powers and duties are conferred by statute. The fundamental duties of a police officer include serving the community, safeguarding lives and property, protecting the innocent, keeping the peace and ensuring the rights of all to liberty, equality and justice.

Performance of the Duties of a Police Officer

A police officer shall perform all duties impartially, without favor or affection or ill will and without regard to status, sex, race, religion, political belief or aspiration. All citizens will be treated equally with courtesy, consideration, and dignity.

Officers will never allow personal feelings, animosities or friendships to influence official conduct. Laws will be enforced appropriately and courteously and, in carrying out their responsibilities, officers will strive to obtain maximum cooperation from the public. They will conduct themselves in appearance and deportment in such a manner as to inspire confidence and respect for the position of public trust they hold.

Discretion

A police officer will use responsibly the discretion vested in his position and exercise it within the law. The principle of reasonableness will guide the officer's determinations, and the officer will consider all surrounding circumstances in determining whether any legal action shall be taken.

Consistent and wise use of discretion, based on professional policing competence, will do much to preserve good relationships and retain the confidence of the public. There can be difficulty in choosing between conflicting courses of action. It is important to remember that a timely word of advice rather than arrest—which may be correct in appropriate circumstances—can be a more effective means of achieving a desired end.

Use of Force

A police officer will never employ unnecessary force or violence and will use only such force in the discharge of duty as is reasonable in all circumstances.

The use of force should be used only with the greatest restraint and only after discussion, negotiation and persuasion have been found to be inappropriate or ineffective. While the use of force is occasionally unavoidable, every police officer will refrain from unnecessary infliction of pain or suffering and will never engage in cruel, degrading or inhuman treatment of any person.

Confidentiality

Whatever a police officer sees, hears or learns of that is of a confidential nature will be kept secret unless the performance of duty or legal provision requires otherwise.

Members of the public have a right to security and privacy, and information obtained about them must not be improperly divulged.

Integrity

A police officer will not engage in acts of corruption or bribery, nor will an officer condone such acts by other police officers.

The public demands that the integrity of police officers be above reproach. Police officers must, therefore, avoid any conduct that might compromise integrity and thus undercut the public confidence in a law enforcement agency. Officers will refuse to accept any gifts, presents, subscriptions, favors, gratuities or promises that could be interpreted as seeming to cause the officer to refrain from performing official responsibilities honestly and within the law. Police officers must not receive private or special advantage from their official status. Respect from the public cannot be bought; it can only be earned and cultivated.

Cooperation with Other Police Officers and Agencies

Police officers will cooperate with all legally authorized agencies and their representatives in the pursuit of justice.

An officer or agency may be one among many organizations that may provide law enforcement services to a jurisdiction. It is imperative that a police officer assist colleagues fully and completely with respect and consideration at all times.

Personal–Professional Capabilities

Police officers will be responsible for their own standard of professional performance and will take every reasonable opportunity to enhance and improve their level of knowledge and competence.

Through study and experience, a police officer can acquire the high level of knowledge and competence that is essential for the efficient and effective performance of duty. The acquisition of knowledge is a never-ending process of personal and professional development that should be pursued constantly.

Private Life

Police officers will behave in a manner that does not bring discredit to their agencies or themselves.

A police officer's character and conduct while off duty must always be exemplary, thus maintaining a position of respect in the community in which he or she lives and serves. The officer's personal behavior must be beyond reproach.

Source: Reprinted from *Police Chief*, January 1992, pp. 15–17. Copyright held by the International Association of Chiefs of Police, 515 N. Washington Street, Alexandria, VA 22314, USA. Further reproduction without express written permission from IACP is strictly prohibited.

C

The National Law Enforcement Officers Memorial, Washington, D.C.

In 1991, President George Bush concluded a two-day "National Salute to Law Enforcement" by dedicating the National Law Enforcement Officers Memorial in Washington, D.C. The memorial consists of the "Pathway of Remembrance"—two marble walls listing the names of officers who gave their lives in the service of law enforcement throughout U.S. history. The list includes law enforcement officers from all the states, as well as U.S. territories and federal agencies.

The memorial is the culmination of a seven-year effort to establish a tribute to fallen police officers. More than 1 million Americans, including 250 corporations, donated money to the memorial project, which was financed entirely through private contributions. Craig W. Floyd, the project's organizer and chairman of the Memorial Fund, declared, "This monument is truly a gift of appreciation from a caring nation."[1]

The names of 12,561 officers killed in the line of duty were initially inscribed in the wall. The earliest recorded law enforcement death occurred in 1794, when a U.S. marshal, Robert Forsyth, was killed while serving an arrest warrant in Augusta, Georgia. California is the state with the most line-of-duty deaths, with 1,094, whereas Vermont has the fewest, with 11. There are 59 female officers listed on the memorial, as well as 711 federal officers. The memorial can hold a total of 29,233 names.

The 1991 dedication ceremony began with a procession in which 10,000 law enforcement personnel, police supporters, and survivors of deceased officers representing the fifty states, U.S. territories, and federal agencies marched from the Capitol to the memorial site. Following the procession, over 160 individuals took part in a twenty-four-hour "Roll Call of the Fallen Officer," where the names of the 12,561 fallen officers were read nonstop at the memorial site.

Speaking at the dedication, President Bush stated the following:

> We gather here today to dedicate this memorial to uniformed heroes . . . who enforce the law and keep us secure here at home. For too long, America's lawmen and women have been the forgotten heroes—forgotten until there is trouble. . . . Today we remember these heroes and heroines.
> . . . They devoted themselves to the timeless values that society shares. They valued the law. They valued peace. . . . They valued human life—so much that they were prepared to give their lives to protect it. They gave much and asked little. They deserve our remembrance. Here in America's capital, for as long as these walls stand, they will be remembered, not for the way they died, but for how they lived.[2]

On May 15, 1997, in a wreath-laying ceremony, President Bill Clinton, with flags flying at half staff, honored the 116 officers killed during the latest year: "Our safety was their purpose and passion. And, while we can never repay them for their ultimate sacrifice, we can and we must honor their memory not only in words but in actions."[3]

Commenting on recent gun-control legislation that he believes is responsible for fewer police officer deaths in very recent years, Clinton said, "It has now become a winning cause, and it is our job—those of us who remain—to make sure that we press on and on and on until such tragedies are a stunning exception not a numbing statistic."[4]

At the time of the president's speech 13,500 names were already on the wall. An additional 253 names were added in 1997.

Let us hope and pray that fewer names will be added as time goes on.

Notes

1. Andrew DiRosa, "Law Enforcement Officers Memorial Dedicated," *FBI Law Enforcement Bulletin,* May 1992, p. 6.
2. DiRosa, "Law Enforcement Officers Memorial Dedicated," p. 6.
3. International Narcotic Enforcement Officers Association, "National Police Week, May 12–15," *International Drug Report,* June 1997, p. 1.
4. International Narcotic Enforcement Officers Association, "National Police Week, May 12–15."

D
Police-Related Associations and Organizations

Academy of Criminal Justice Sciences (ACJS)
Northern Kentucky University
403 Nunn Hall
Highland Heights, Ky. 41099-5998
(606) 572-5634
fax (606) 572-6665

Air Force Security Police Association
818 Willow Creek Circle
San Marcos, Texas 78666-5060
(800) 782-7653 ext. 267
fax (512) 396-7328

Airborne Law Enforcement Association, Inc.
P.O. Box 82982
Tampa, Fla. 33682
(813) 961-3144
fax (813) 960-5307

American Academy of Forensic Sciences
P.O. Box 669
410 North 21st Street
Colorado Springs, Colo. 80901-0669
(719) 636-1100
fax (719) 636-1993

American Board of Forensic Odontology
c/o Dr. L. Thomas Johnson, secretary
Suite B252, Bay Shore Mall
5900 North Port Washington Road
Glendale, Wis. 53217
(414) 332-8008

American College of Forensic Examiners
2750 E. Sunshine St.
Springfield, Mo. 65804
(800) 423-9737
fax (417) 881-4702

American Federation of Police
3801 Biscayne Blvd.
Miami, Fla. 33137
(305) 573-0070
fax (305) 573-9819

American Police Hall of Fame
3801 Biscayne Blvd.
Miami, Fla. 33137
(305) 573-0070
fax (305) 573-9819

American Polygraph Association
P.O. Box 8037
Chattanooga, Tenn. 37414-0037
(423) 892-3992 or (800) 272-8037
fax (423) 894-5435

American Society of Criminology
1314 Kinnear Road
Columbus, Ohio 43212
(614) 292-9207
fax (614) 292-6767

American Society for Industrial Security
1677 North Fort Myer Drive, Suite 1200
Arlington, Va. 22209-3198
(703) 522-5800
fax (703) 243-4954

Appendix D

American Society of Law Enforcement Trainers (ASLET)
102 Dock Road
Box 361
Lewes, Del. 19958-0361
(302) 645-4080
fax (302) 645-4084

Association of American Railroad Police
50 F Street N.W.
Washington, D.C. 20001
(202) 639-2384

Association of Certified Fraud Examiners
716 West Avenue
Austin, Texas 78701
(800) 245-3321
fax (512) 478-9297

Association of Firearm and Toolmark Examiners
7857 Esterel Drive
La Jolla, Calif. 92037
(619) 453-0847

Association of Public Safety Communications Officials International, Inc. (APCO)
2040 S. Ridgewood Avenue
South Daytona, Fla. 32119-8437
(800) 949-2726
fax (904) 322-2501

Blacks in Law Enforcement Inc.
256 E. McLemore Avenue
Memphis, Tenn. 38106-2833
(901) 774-1118
fax (901) 774-1139

Commission on Accreditation for Law Enforcement Agencies, Inc.
10306 Eaton Pl., Suite 320
Fairfax, Va. 22030-2201
(800) 368-3757
fax (703) 591-2206

Concerns of Police Survivors, Inc.
P.O. Box 3199
South Highway 5
Camdenton, Mo. 65020
(573) 346-4911
fax (573) 346-1414

Council of International Investigators (CII)
27999 Clemmons Road
Cleveland, Ohio 44145
(216) 892-1000
fax (216) 892-9439

D.A.R.E.—America
P.O. Box 2090
Los Angeles, Calif. 90051
(310) 215-0575
fax (310) 215-0180

Do the Right Thing, Inc. (Miami, Fla. Police Dept.)
400 N.W. 2nd Avenue, Rm. 412
Miami, Fla. 33128
(305) 579-3344
fax (305) 579-6634

Evidence Photographers International Council
600 Main Street
Honesdale, Pa. 18431
(717) 253-5450
fax (717) 253-5011

Federal Bureau of Investigation Agents Association
P.O. Box 250
New Rochelle, N.Y. 10801
(914) 235-7580
fax (914) 235-8235

Federal Law Enforcement Officers Association
P.O. Box 508
East Northport, N.Y. 11731-0472
(516) 368-6117
fax (516) 368-6429

Gang Resistance, Education and Training (G.R.E.A.T.)
AFT Branch
P.O. Box 50418
Washington, D.C. 20091
(800) 726-7070

National Association of Field Training Officers (NAFTO)
P.O. Box 815
Niwot, Colo. 80544-0815
(303) 442-0482
fax (303) 546-6791

National Association of Police Organizations (NAPO)
750 First Street N.E., Suite 920
Washington, D.C. 20002-4241
(202) 842-4420
fax (202) 842-4396

National Association of Town Watch
7 Wynnewood Road, Suite 215
P.O. Box 303
Wynnewood, Pa. 19096
(610) 649-7055
fax (610) 649-5456

National Association of Veteran Police Officers
P.O. Box 684068
Austin, Texas 78703
(512) 476-1042
fax (512) 479-1376

National Center for Women in Policing
8105 West Third Street
Los Angeles, Calif. 90048
(213) 651-2532
fax (213) 653-2689

National Crime Prevention Council
1700 K Street N.W. 2nd floor
Washington, D.C. 20006
(202) 466-6272
fax (202) 296-1356

National Criminal Justice Reference Service
P.O. Box 6000
Rockville, Md. 20850
(800) 851-3420

National Fraternal Order of Police
1410 Donelson Pike, #A17
Nashville, Tenn. 37217
(615) 399-0900
fax (615) 399-0400

Institute of Police Technology and Management
University of N. Florida
4567 Saint Johns Bluff Road South
Jacksonville, Fla. 32224-2645
(904) 620-4786
fax (904) 620-2453

International Association of Arson Investigators
300 S. Broadway, Suite 100
St. Louis, Mo. 63102-2808
(314) 621-1966
fax (314) 621-5125

International Association of Auto Theft Investigators (IAATI)
P.O. Box 1176
Hwy. 351 North
Cross City, Fla. 32628-1176
(352) 498-3446
fax (352) 498-0021

International Association of Campus Law Enforcement Administrators
638 Prospect Avenue
Hartford, Conn. 06105
(860) 586-7517
fax (860) 586-7550

International Association of Chiefs of Police (IACP)
515 N. Washington Street
Alexandria, Va. 22314
(800) THE-IACP
fax (703) 836-4543

International Association of Financial Crimes Investigators
1620 Grant Avenue
Novato, Calif. 94945
(415) 897-8800
fax (415) 898-0798

International Association of Law Enforcement Firearms Instructors (IALEFI)
390 Union Avenue
Laconia, N.H. 03246
(603) 524-8787
fax (603) 524-8856

International Association of Law Enforcement Planners
1000 Connecticut Avenue N.W., Suite 9
Washington, D.C. 20036
(202) 857-8485

International Association of Marine Investigators
9 Sherwood Drive
Westford, Mass. 01886
(508) 392-9292

International Association of Women Police
5413 W. Sunnyside Avenue
Chicago, Ill. 60630
(312) 736-3405

International Conference of Police Chaplains
P.O. Box 5590
Destin, Fla. 32540
(904) 654-9736
fax (904) 654-9742

International Critical Incident Stress Foundation, Inc.
4785 Dorsey Hall Dr., Suite 102
Ellicott City, Md. 21042
(410) 730-4311
fax (410) 730-4313

International Foundation for Protection Officers
4200 Meridian, Suite 200
Bellingham, Wash. 98226
(360) 733-1571
fax (360) 671-4329

International Law Enforcement and Emergency Services
Video Association (LEVA)
P.O. Box 126167
Benbrook, Texas 76126
(817) 249-4002
fax (817) 249-4002

International Narcotic Enforcement Officers Association, Inc.
112 State Street, Suite 1200
Albany, N.Y. 12207
(518) 463-6232
fax (518) 432-3378

International Police Association—U.S.Section
P.O. Box 651
Auburn, Calif. 95604
(916) 885-4711
fax (916) 885-8228

International Police Mountain Bike Association
190 W. Ostend Street, Suite 120
Baltimore, Md. 21230-3755
(410) 539-3399
fax (410) 539-3496

International Union of Police Associations
1421 Prince Street, Suite 330
Alexandria, Va. 22314
(703) 549-7473
fax (703) 683-9048

Law Enforcement Alliance of America
7700 Leesburg Pike, #421
Falls Church, Va. 22043
(703) 847-2677 or (800) 766-8578
fax (703) 556-6485

Narcotic Enforcement Officers Association
29 North Plains Highway
Suite 10, Phoenix Park
Wallingford, Conn. 06492
(203) 269-8940
fax (203) 284-9103

National Association of Chiefs of Police
3801 Biscayne Blvd.
Miami, Fla. 33137
(305) 573-0070 or (202) 293-9088
fax (305) 573-9819

National Insurance Crime Bureau
10330 S. Roberts Road
Palos Hills, Ill. 60465
(708) 430-2430
fax (708) 430-2446

National Law Enforcement Council
888 16th Street N.W., Suite 700
Washington, D.C. 20036
(202) 835-8020
fax (202) 331-4291

National Law Enforcement Officers Memorial Fund, Inc.
605 E Street N.W.
Washington, D.C. 20004
(202) 737-3400
fax (202) 737-3405

National Law Enforcement Research Center
P.O. Box 70966
Sunnyvale, Calif. 94086
(408) 245-2037
fax (415) 960-0559

National Organization of Black Law Enforcement Executives
4609 Pinecrest Office Park Drive, Suite F
Alexandria, Va. 22312-1442
(703) 658-1529
fax (703) 658-9479

National Police Officers Association of America
7811 Old Tree Run
Louisville, Ky. 40222
(502) 425-9215
fax (502) 326-3705

National Reserve Law Officers Association
P.O. Box 6505
San Antonio, Texas 78209
(210) 820-0478
fax (210) 804-2463

National Sheriff's Association
1450 Duke Street
Alexandria. Va. 22314
(703) 836-7827
fax (703) 683-6541

National Tactical Officers Association (NTOA)
P.O. Box 529
Doylestown, Pa. 18901
(800) 279-9127
fax (215) 230-7552

National Troopers Coalition
112 State Street, 12th floor
Albany, NY 12207
(518) 462-7448
fax (518) 462-0790

National United Law Enforcement Officers Association, Inc.
256 E. McLemore Avenue
Memphis, Tenn. 38106-2833
(901) 774-1118
fax (901) 774-1139

Naval Criminal Investigative Services
Headquarters Washington Navy Yard
Bldg. 111
901 M. Street S.E.
Washington, D.C. 20388-5000
(202) 433-6790

Nevada Gang Investigators Association
5150 Mae Anne Ave., #213-116
Reno, Nev. 89523
(702) 328-6311

Park Law Enforcement Association
2775 South Quincey Street
Arlington, Va. 22206
(703) 820-4940

Peace Officers Research Association of California
1911 F Street
Sacramento, Calif. 95814
(916) 441-0660
fax (916) 325-0769

Police Executive Research Forum (PERF)
1120 Connecticut Avenue N.W., Suite 930
Washington, D.C. 20036
(202) 466-7820
fax (202) 466-7826

Police Foundation
1001 22nd Street
Washington, D.C. 20037
(202) 833-1460

Police Marksman Association
6000 E. Shirley Lane
Montgomery, Ala. 36117
(334) 271-2010
fax (334) 279-9267

Police Supervisors Group
P.O. Box 416
Hayes, Va. 23072
(804) 642-2343
fax (804) 642-2343

Police Writers Club
P.O. Box 416
Hayes, Va. 23072
(804) 642-2343
fax (804) 642-2343

Reserve Peace Officers of America, Inc.
101 N. Fairfield Drive
Dover, Del. 19901
(800) 706-1133, ext. 4809

United Federation of Police Officers
540 N. State Road
Briarcliff Manor, N.Y. 10510
(914) 941-4103
fax (914) 941-4472

United Federation of Security Officers
540 N. State Road
Briarcliff Manor, N.Y. 10510
(914) 941-4103
fax (914) 941-4472

United States Police Canine Association, Inc.
8480 Cooper Way E.
Inver Grove Heights, Minn. 55706
(800) 332-3758

Western States Vice Investigators Association
Attn: Kevin Jones
P.O. Box 66145
Houston, Texas 77266-6145
(713) 247-5774
fax (713) 247-8789

Adapted from *Police Magazine*, August 1997, pp. 86–90.

Bibliography

Abadinski, Howard. *Crime and Justice: An Introduction.* Chicago: Nelson-Hall, 1987.

Ahern, James. *Police in Trouble.* New York: Hawthorn Books, 1972.

Albanese, Jay S., and Robert D. Pursley. *Crime in America: Some Existing and Emerging Issues.* Englewood Cliffs, N.J.: Regents/Prentice-Hall, 1993.

Alex, Nicholas. *Black in Blue: A Study of the Negro Policeman.* New York: Appleton-Century-Crofts, 1969.

———. *New York Cops Talk Back.* New York: Wiley, 1976.

Alpert, Geoffrey P., and Roger G. Dunham. *Police Pursuit Driving: Controlling Responses to Emergency Situations.* Westport, Conn.: Greenwood Press, 1990.

———. *Policing Urban America.* 2d ed. Prospect Heights, Ill.: Waveland Press, 1992.

Alpert, Geoffrey P., and Lorie A. Fridell. *Police Vehicles and Firearms: Instruments of Deadly Force.* Prospect Heights, Ill.: Waveland Press, 1992.

American Bar Association. *Standards Relating to Urban Police Function.* New York: Institute of Judicial Administration, 1974.

Aristotle. *Nicomachean Ethics.*

Asbury, Herbert. *The Gangs of New York.* New York: Capricorn, 1970. Original edition, 1927.

Ayres, Richard M., and George S. Flanagan. *Preventing Law Enforcement Stress: The Organization's Role.* Washington, D.C.: National Sheriff's Association, 1990.

Ayto, John. *Dictionary of Word Origins.* New York: Arcade, 1990.

Bailey, F. Lee, Roger E. Zuckerman, and Kenneth R. Pierce. *The Employee Polygraph Protection Act: A Manual for Polygraph Examiners and Employers.* Severna Park, MD: American Polygraph Association, 1989.

Bailey, William G., ed. *The Encyclopedia of Police Science.* New York: Garland, 1989.

Baker, Mark. *Cops: Their Lives in Their Own Words.* New York: Simon & Schuster, 1985.

Barker, Thomas, and David L. Carter. *Police Deviance.* Cincinnati: Anderson, 1986.

Barker, Thomas, and Julian Roebuck. *An Empirical Typology of Police Corruption: A Study in Organizational Deviance.* Springfield, Ill.: Charles C. Thomas, 1973.

Bayley, David H. *Forces of Order: Police Behavior in Japan and the United States.* Berkeley: University of California Press, 1976.

———. *Patterns of Policing: A Comparative International Analysis,* New Brunswick, N.J.: Rutgers University Press, 1985.

Bayley, David, and Harold Mendelsohn. *Minorities and the Police.* New York: Free Press, 1969.

Becker, Harold K., and Jack E. Whitehouse. *Police of America: A Personal View: Introduction and Commentary.* Springfield, Ill.: Charles C. Thomas, 1980.

Bennett, R., ed. *Police at Work: Policy Issues and Analysis.* Beverly Hills, Calif.: Sage Publications, 1983.

Bennett, Wayne W., and Karen M. Hess. *Criminal Investigation.* St. Paul: West, 1991, 1994.

Benyon, J., L. Turnbull, A. Willis, R. Woodward, and A. Beck. *Police Co-operation in Europe: An Investigation.* Leicester, U.K.: Centre for the Study of Public Orders, University of Leicester, 1993, reprinted 1995.

Berman, Jay Stuart. *Police Administration and Progressive Reform: Theodore Roosevelt as Police Commissioner of New York.* New York: Greenwood Press, 1987.

Besharov, Douglas J., ed. *Family Violence: Research and Public Policy Issues.* Washington, D.C.: University Press of America, 1990.

Bittner, Egon. *The Function of Police in Modern Society.* Cambridge, Mass.: Oelgeschlager, 1980.

Black, Donald. *The Manners and Customs of the Police.* New York: Academic Press, 1980.

Bloch, Peter B., and Deborah Anderson, *Policewomen on Patrol: Final Report.* Washington, D.C.: Police Foundation, 1974.

Blumberg, Abraham S., and Elaine Niederhoffer, eds. *The Ambivalent Force: Perspectives on the Police.* New York: Holt, Rinehart & Winston, 1985.

Bok, S. *Lying: Moral Choice in Public and Private Life.* New York: Pantheon, 1978.

Bopp, William J., and Donald O. Schultz. *A Short History of American Law Enforcement.* Springfield, Ill.: Charles C. Thomas, 1977.

Bouza, Anthony V. *The Police Mystique: An Insider's Look at Cops, Crime, and the Criminal Justice System.* New York: Plenum Press, 1990.

Boydstun, J. E. *San Diego Field Interrogation: Final Report.* Washington, D.C.: Police Foundation, 1975.

Bridenbaugh, Carl. *Cities in Revolt: Urban Life in America, 1743–1776.* New York: Knopf, 1965.

———. *Cities in the Wilderness: Urban Life in America, 1625–1742.* New York: Capricorn, 1964.

Broderick, John J. *Police in a Time of Change.* 2d ed. Prospect Heights, Ill.: Waveland Press, 1987.

Brown, Michael. *Working the Street.* New York: Russell Sage Foundation, 1981.

Brown, Sam, and Gini Graham Scott. *Private Eyes: The Role of the Private Investigator in American Marriage, Business, and Industry.* New York: Citadel Press, 1991.

Burgess, Ann Wolbert. *Sexual Assault of Children and Adolescents.* Lexington, Mass.: D.C. Heath, 1978.

Cahn, Michael F., and James M. Tien. *An Alternative Approach in Police Response: The Wilmington Management of Demand Program.* Cambridge, Mass.: Public Systems Evaluation, 1981.

Carden, Gerald. *Police Revitalization.* Lexington, Mass.: Lexington Books, 1977.

Carter, David L., Allen D. Sapp, and Darrel W. Stephens. *The State of Police Education: Policy Direction for the 21st Century.* Washington, D.C.: Police Executive Research Forum, 1989.

Chaiken, J. M., M. W. Lawless, and K. A. Stenson. *The Impact of Police Activity on Crime: Robberies in the New York City Subway System.* New York: Rand Institute, 1974.

Champion, Dean J. *Criminal Justice in the United States.* Columbus, Ohio: Merrill, 1989.

Chapman, Samuel G. *Police Patrol Readings.* 2d ed. Springfield, Ill.: Charles C. Thomas, 1970.

Chapman, S. G., and T. E. St. Johnston. *The Police Heritage in England and America.* East Lansing: Michigan State University, 1962.

Chevigny, Paul. *Police Power: Police Abuses in New York City.* New York: Pantheon, 1969.

Coffey, Alan. *Law Enforcement: A Human Relations Approach.* Englewood Cliffs, N.J.: Prentice-Hall, 1990.

Cohen, Bernard, and Jan M. Chaiken. *Police Background Characteristics and Performance.* Lexington, Mass.: Lexington Books, 1973.

Cohn, Alvin, ed. *The Future of Policing.* Beverly Hills, Calif.: Sage Publications, 1978.

Cohn, Alvin W., and Emilio C. Viano. *Police Community Relations: Images, Roles, Realities.* Philadelphia: Lippincott, 1976.

Cohn, Ellen G., and Lawrence W. Sherman. *Police Policy on Domestic Violence, 1986: A National Survey.* Washington, D.C.: Crime Control Institute, 1987.

Cole, George F. *The American System of Criminal Justice.* 6th ed. Pacific Grove, Calif.: Brooks/Cole, 1992.

Cooper, Jerry M. "Federal Military Intervention in Domestic Disorder," in *The United States Military under the Constitution, 1989–1978,* ed. Richland H. Koh, New York: New York University, 1991.

Cunliffe, F., and P. B. Piazza. *Criminalistics and Scientific Investigation.* Englewood Cliffs, N.J.: Prentice-Hall, 1980.

Cox Commission. *Crisis at Columbia: Report of the Fact-Finding Commission Appointed to Investigate the Disturbances at Columbia University in April and May 1968.* New York: Vintage, 1968.

Cox, Steven M., and Jack D. Fitzgerald. *Police in Community Relations: Critical Issues.* 2d ed. Dubuque, Iowa: William C. Brown, 1992.

Critchley, T. A. *A History of Police in England and Wales.* 2d ed. rev. Montclair, N.J.: Patterson Smith, 1972.

Culbertson, R., and M. Tezak, eds. *Order under Law.* Prospect Heights, Ill.: Waveland Press, 1981.

Cunningham, William C., John J. Strauchs, and Clifford W. Van Meter. *The Hallcrest Report: Private Security and Police in America.* Portland, Oreg.: Chancellor Press, 1985.

———. *The Hallcrest Report II: Private Security Trends, 1970–2000.* Boston: Butterworth-Heinemann, 1990.

Daley, Robert. *Prince of the City: The Story of a Cop Who Knew Too Much.* Boston: Houghton Mifflin, 1978.

Davis, Kenneth Culp. *Police Discretion.* St. Paul: West, 1975.

DeForest, Peter. *Forensic Science: An Introduction to Criminalistics.* New York: McGraw-Hill, 1983.

del Carmen, Rolando V. *Civil Liabilities in American Policing: A Text for Law Enforcement Personnel.* Englewood Cliffs, N.J.: Prentice-Hall, 1991.

Dempsey, John S. *An Introduction to Public and Private Investigations.* Minneapolis/St.Paul: West, 1996.

———. *Criminal Justice Update.* Minneapolis/St.Paul: West, 1996.

Dershowitz, Alan M. *Taking Liberties: A Decade of Hard Cases, Bad Laws, and Bum Raps.* Chicago: Contemporary Books, 1988.

Dunham, Roger G., and Geoffrey P. Alpert. *Critical Issues in Policing,* 3rd ed. Prospect Heights, Ill.: Waveland Press, 1997.

Eck, John E. *Managing Case Assignments: The Burglary Investigation Decision Model Replication.* Washington, D.C.: Police Executive Research Forum, 1979.

Eck, John E., et al. *Problem Solving: Problem-Oriented Policing in Newport News.* Washington, D.C.: Police Executive Research Forum, 1987.

Eisenberg, Terry, et al. *Police Personnel Practices in State and Local Governments.* Washington, D.C.: Police Foundation, 1973.

Elliston, Frederick A., and Michael Feldberg, eds. *Moral Issues in Police Work.* Totowa, N.J.: Rowman and Allanheld, 1985.

Emsley, Clive. *Policing and Its Context, 1750–1870.* New York: Schocken, 1984.

Faller, Kathleen Coulborn. *Child Sexual Abuse: An Interdisciplinary Manual for the Diagnosis, Case Management and Treatment.* New York: Columbia University Press, 1988.

Farmer, Michael T., ed. *Differential Police Response Strategies.* Washington, D.C.: Police Executive Research Forum, 1981.

Fay, John J. *The Police Dictionary and Encyclopedia.* Springfield, Ill.: Charles C. Thomas, 1988.

Figgie International. *The Figgie Report, Part 4: Reducing Crime in America—Successful Community Efforts.* Willowby, Ohio: Figgie International, 1983.

Fletcher, Connie. *Breaking and Entering: Women Cops Break the Code of Silence to Tell Their Stories from the Inside.* New York: Simon & Schuster, 1995.

Fogelson, Robert M. *Big City Police.* Cambridge, Mass.: Harvard University Press, 1977.

Friendly, Fred W., and Martha J. H. Elliot. *The Constitution: That Delicate Balance: Landmark Cases That Shaped the Constitution.* New York: McGraw-Hill, 1984.

Fyfe, James J. "Shots Fired." Ph.D. diss., State University of New York, Albany, 1978.

———. *Contemporary Issues in Law Enforcement.* Beverly Hills, Calif: Sage, 1981.

Fyfe, James J., Jack R. Greene, William F. Walsh, O. W. Wilson, and Roy Clinton McLaren. *Police Administration.* 5th ed. New York: McGraw-Hill, 1997.

Gaines, Larry K., Mittie T. Southerland, and John E. Angell. *Police Administration.* New York: McGraw-Hill, 1991.

Gallati, Robert J. *Introduction to Law Enforcement and Criminal Justice.* Springfield, Ill.: Charles E. Thomas, 1969.

Gardiner, John A. *Traffic and the Police: Variations in Law Enforcement Policy.* Cambridge, Mass.: Harvard University Press, 1969.

Geffner, Edwin S. *The Internist's Compendium of Patient Information.* New York: McGraw-Hill, 1987.

Geller, William A., ed. *Police Leadership in America.* New York: Praeger, 1985.

Geller, William A., and Kevin J. Karales. *Split-Second Decisions.* Chicago: Chicago Law Enforcement Study Group, 1981.

Geller, William, and Michael S. Scott. *Deadly Force: What We Know.* Washington, D.C.: Police Executive Research Forum, 1992.

Gellerman, S. W. *Motivation and Productivity.* New York: American Management Association, 1963.

Gerber, S., ed. *Chemistry and Crime.* Washington, D.C.: American Chemical Society, 1983.

Germann, A. C., Frank D. Day, and Robert R. J. Gallati. *Introduction to Law Enforcement and Criminal Justice.* Springfield, Ill.: Charles C. Thomas, 1969.

Goldstein, Herman. *Police Corruption: A Perspective on Its Nature and Control.* Washington, D.C.: Police Foundation, 1975.

———. *Policing a Free Society.* Cambridge, Mass.: Ballinger Press, 1977.

———. *Problem-Oriented Policing.* New York: McGraw-Hill, 1990.

Gottfredson, Michael R., and Don M. Gottfredson. *Decision Making in Criminal Justice: Toward the Rational Exercise of Discretion.* Cambridge, Mass.: Ballinger Press, 1980.

Graves, G., et al. *Developing a Street Patrol: A Guide for Neighborhood Crime Prevention Groups.* Boston: Neighborhood Crime Prevention Council, Justice Resource Institute, 1985.

Greene, Jack, and S. Mastrofski. *Community Policing: Rhetoric or Reality?* New York: Praeger, 1988.

Greenwood, Peter W., and Joan Petersilia. *The Criminal Investigation Process: Summary and Policy Implications.* Santa Monica, Calif.: Rand Corporation, 1975.

Grimshaw, Allen D. *Racial Violence in the United States.* Chicago: Aldine, 1969.

Harris, Richard. *The Police Academy: An Inside View.* New York: Wiley, 1973.

Heaphy, John, ed. *Police Practices: The General Administrative Survey.* Washington, D.C.: Police Foundation, 1978.

Heffernan, W., and T. Stroup, eds. *Police Ethics: Hard Choices in Law Enforcement.* New York: John Jay Press, 1985.

Horan, James D., and Howard Swiggett. *The Detective Dynasty That Made History.* New York: Crown, 1967.

———. *The Pinkerton Story.* New York: Putnam, 1951.

Hungerford, Edward. *Wells Fargo: Advancing the American Frontier.* New York: Bonanza, 1949.

Hunt, W. E. *History of England.* New York: Harper & Brothers, 1938.

Inciardi, James A. *Criminal Justice.* 3d ed. Orlando, Fla.: Harcourt Brace Jovanovich, 1990.

International Association of Chiefs of Police. *A Survey of the Police Department of Youngstown, Ohio.* Washington, D.C.: International Association of Chiefs of Police, 1964.

———. *Operational Issues in the Small Law Enforcement Agency.* Arlington, Virginia: International Association of Chiefs of Police, 1990.

———. *Training Catalog: IACP Educational Programs.* Alexandria, Virginia: International Association of Chiefs of Police, published yearly.

———. *A Report by the Indian Country Section of the International Association of Chiefs of Police.* Alexandria, Virginia: International Association of Chiefs of Police, 1994.

Jacob, Herbert. *Urban Justice.* Boston: Little, Brown, 1973.

Johnson, David R. *American Law Enforcement: A History.* St. Louis: Forum Press, 1981.

Kadish, Sanford H. *Encyclopedia of Crime and Justice.* New York: Free Press, 1983.

Kappeler, Victor, Richard Sluder, and Geoffrey Alpert. *Forces of Deviance, Understanding the Dark Side of Policing.* Prospect Heights, Ill.: Waveland Press, 1994.

Kelling, George L. *The Kansas City Preventive Patrol Experiment: A Summary Report.* Washington, D.C.: Police Foundation, 1974.

Kenney, Dennis Jay, ed. *Police and Policing: Contemporary Issues.* New York: Praeger, 1989.

Kirkham, George L., and Laurin A. Wollan, Jr. *Introduction to Law Enforcement.* New York: Harper & Row, 1980.

Klein, Irving J. *Constitutional Law for Criminal Justice Professionals.* Miami, Fla.: Coral Gables, 1986, 1993.

Klockars, Carl B., ed. *Thinking about Police: Contemporary Readings.* New York: McGraw-Hill, 1983.

Klockars, Carl B., and Stephen D. Mastrofski, eds. *Thinking about Police: Contemporary Readings.* 2d ed. New York: McGraw-Hill, 1991.

Kluger, Richard. *Simple Justice.* New York: Vintage, 1977.

Knapp Commission. *Report on Police Corruption.* New York: Braziller, 1973.

Kornblum, Alan N. *The Moral Hazards.* Lexington, Mass.: Lexington Books, 1976.

Kroes, W. *Society's Victim, The Policeman: An Analysis of Job Stress in Policing.* Springfield, Ill.: Charles C. Thomas, 1976.

Kurian, George Thomas. *World Encyclopedia of Police Forces and Penal Systems.* New York: Facts on File, 1989.

Kurland, Daniel J., and Christina Polsenberg. *Internet Guide for Criminal Justice.* Belmont, Calif: Wadsworth, 1997.

Lake, Carolyn. *Undercover for Wells Fargo.* Boston: Houghton Mifflin, 1969.

Lane, Roger. *Policing the City.* New York: Atheneum, 1975.

——— . *Policing the City: Boston 1822–1885.* Cambridge, Mass.: Harvard University Press, 1967.

Leinen, Steven. *Black Police, White Society.* New York: New York University Press, 1984.

Loving, Nancy. *Responding to Spouse Abuse and Wife Beating: A Guide for Police.* Washington, D.C.: Police Executive Research Forum, 1980.

Lundman, Richard. *Police and Policing.* New York: Holt, Rinehart & Winston, 1980.

——— . *Police Behavior: A Sociological Perspective.* New York: Oxford University Press, 1980.

McAdam, Doug. *Freedom Summer.* New York: Oxford University Press, 1988.

McAlary, Mike. *Buddy Boys: When Good Cops Turn Bad.* New York: Putnam, 1987.

Martin, Susan E. *Women on the Move? A Report on the Status of Women in Policing.* Washington, D.C.: Police Foundation, 1989.

Mass, Peter. *Serpico.* New York: Bantam Books, 1974.

Matulia, Kenneth J. *A Balance of Forces.* 2d ed. Gaithersburg, Md.: International Association of Chiefs of Police, 1985.

Miller, Wilbur R. *Cops and Bobbies: Police Authority in New York and London, 1830–1870.* Chicago: University of Chicago Press, 1977.

Milton, Catherine H. *Women in Policing.* Washington, D.C.: Police Foundation, 1972.

Milton, Catherine H., et al. *Police Use of Deadly Force.* Washington, D.C.: Police Foundation, 1977.

Monkkonen, Eric. *Police in Urban America: 1860–1920.* Cambridge, Mass.: Harvard University Press, 1981.

Morgan, Edward P. *The 60's Experience: Hard Lessons about Modern America.* Philadelphia: Temple University Press, 1991.

Muir, W. K., Jr. *Police: Streetcorner Politicians.* Chicago: University of Chicago Press, 1977.

Murphy, Patrick V., and Thomas Plate. *Commissioner: A View from the Top of American Law Enforcement.* New York: Simon & Schuster, 1977.

Nash, Jay Robert. *Encyclopedia of World Crime.* Wilmette, Ill.: Crime Books, 1990.

National Police Chiefs and Sheriffs Information Bureau. *National Directory of Law Enforcement Administrators.* Stevens Point, Wisc.: National Police Chiefs and Sheriffs Information Bureau, published yearly.

Niederhoffer, Arthur. *Behind the Shield: The Police in Urban Society.* Garden City, N.Y.: Anchor Books, 1967.

O'Donnell, Kenneth. *Deadly Force.* New York: William Morrow, 1983.

Owings, Chloe. *Women Police.* Montclair, N.J.: Patterson Smith, 1969. Original edition, 1925.

Palmiotto, Michael J., ed. *Critical Issues in Criminal Justice.* Cincinnati, Ohio: Anderson, 1988.

Pike, Owen. *A History of Crime in England.* London: Smith, Elder, 1873–1876.

Pinkerton, Allan. *The Expressman and the Detective.* New York: Arno Press, 1976.

Pinkerton Investigation Division. *Investigations Department Training Manual.* Encino, Calif: Pinkerton's Security and Investigations Services, 1990.

——— . *Pinkerton Reference Guide to Investigation Services.* Encino, Calif.: Pinkerton Security and Investigation Services, 1995.

Police Executive Research Forum. *Survey of Police Operational and Administrative Practice, 1981.* Washington, D.C.: Police Executive Research Forum, 1982.

Police Foundation. *Domestic Violence and the Police: Studies in Detroit and Kansas City.* Washington, D.C.: Police Foundation, 1977.

——— . *Experiments in Police Improvement: A Progress Report.* Washington, D.C.: Police Foundation, 1972.

——— . *The Newark Foot Patrol Experiment.* Washington: D.C.: Police Foundation, 1991.

Pollock, Joycelyn M. *Ethics in Crime and Justice: Dilemmas and Decisions,* 3rd ed. Belmont, Calif: West/Wadsworth, 1998.

Poveda, Tony. *Lawlessness and Reform: The FBI in Transition.* Pacific Grove, Calif.: Brooks/Cole, 1990.

Prassel, Frank R. *The Western Peace Officer: A Legacy of Law and Order.* Norman, Okla.: University of Oklahoma Press, 1972.

Press, S. J. *Some Effects of an Increase in Police Manpower in the 20th Precinct of New York.* New York: Rand Institute, 1971.

Pringle, Patrick. *Highwaymen.* New York: Roy, 1963.

——— . *Hue and Cry: The Story of Henry and John Fielding and Their Bow Street Runners.* New York: Morrow, 1965.

——— . *The Thief Takers.* London: Museum Press, 1958.

Punch, Maurice. *Control of the Police Organization.* Cambridge, Mass.: MIT Press, 1983.

Pursley, Robert D. *Introduction to Criminal Justice.* 5th ed. New York: Macmillan, 1991.

Radano, Gene. *Walking the Beat: A New York Policeman Tells What It's Like on His Side of the Law.* Cleveland: World Publishing, 1968.

Radelet, Louis A. *The Police and the Community.* Encino, Calif.: Glencoe, 1980.

Reid, Sue Titus. *Criminal Justice.* New York: Macmillan, 1993.

Reiss, Albert J. *The Police and the Public.* New Haven, Conn.: Yale University Press, 1971.

Reiss, Albert J., and Michael Tonry, eds. *Crime and Justice.* Chicago: University of Chicago Press, 1986.

Reith, Charles. *The Blind Eye of History: A Study of the Origins of the Present Police Era.* London: Faber, 1912.

Reppetto, Thomas. *The Blue Parade.* New York: Free Press, 1978.

Reuter, Peter, et al. *Drug Use and Drug Programs in the Washington Metropolitan Area.* Santa Monica, Calif.: Rand Corporation, 1988.

Richardson, James F. *The New York Police: Colonial Times to 1901.* New York: Oxford University Press, 1976.

——— . *Urban Police in the United States.* Port Washington, N.Y.: Kennikat Press, 1974.

Rieck, Albert. *Justice and Police in England.* London: Butterworth, 1936.

Robin, Gerald D., and Richard H. Anson. *Introduction to the American Criminal Justice System.* 4th ed. New York: Harper & Row, 1988.

Roe, Allan, and Norma Roe. *Police Selection: A Technical Summary of Validity Studies.* Ogden, Utah: Diagnostic Specialists, 1982.

Ross, H. Lawrence. *Deterring the Drunk Driver: Legal Policy and Social Control.* Lexington, Mass.: D.C. Heath, 1982.

Rubenstein, Jonathan. *City Police.* New York: Ballentine Books, 1978.

Ruchelman, Leonard. *Who Rules the Police?* New York: New York University Press, 1973.

Rush, George E. *The Dictionary of Criminal Justice.* Guilford, Conn.: Dushkin Publishing, 1994.

Saferstein, R. *Criminalistics: An Introduction to Forensic Science.* Englewood Cliffs, N.J.: Prentice-Hall, 1987.

——— . *Forensic Science Handbook.* Englewood Cliffs, N.J.: Prentice-Hall, 1988.

Sante, Luc. *Low Life: Lures and Snares of Old New York.* New York: Farrar, Straus & Giroux, 1991.

Scharf, Peter, and Arnold Binder. *The Badge and the Bullet: Police Use of Deadly Force.* New York: Praeger, 1983.

Schmalleger, Frank. *Criminal Justice Today: An Introductory Text for the Twenty-First Century.* Englewood Cliffs, N.J.: Prentice-Hall, 1991, 1994, 1997.

Senna, Joseph J., and Larry J. Siegel. *Introduction to Criminal Justice.* St. Paul: West, 1993, 1996.

Shaffer, Ron, Kevin Klose, and Alfred E. Lewis. *Surprise! Surprise!* New York: Viking, 1979.

Sheehan, Robert, and Gary W. Cordner. *Introduction to Police Administration.* Cincinnati: Anderson, 1989, 1995.

Sherman, Lawrence W. *Repeat Calls to Police in Minneapolis.* Washington, D.C.: Crime Control Institute, 1987.

——— . *Scandal and Reform: Controlling Police Corruption.* Berkeley: University of California Press, 1978.

——— . ed. *Police Corruption: A Sociological Perspective.* Garden City, N.Y.: Doubleday, 1974.

Sherman, Lawrence W., and Richard A. Berk. *The Minneapolis Domestic Violence Experiment.* Washington, D.C.: Police Foundation, 1984.

Sherman, Lawrence W., and Ellen G. Cohn. *Citizens Killed by Big-City Police, 1970–1984.* Washington, D.C.: Crime Control Institute, 1986.

Sherman, Lawrence W., et al. *The Quality of Police Education.* San Francisco: Jossey-Bass, 1978.

Schultz, Dorothy Moses. *From Social Worker to Crimefighter: Women in United States Municipal Policing.* New York: Praeger, 1995.

Shusta, Robert M., Deena R. Levine, Philip P. Harris, and Herbert Z. Wong. *Multicultural Law Enforcement: Strategies for Peacekeeping in a Diverse Society.* Englewoods Cliffs, N.J.: Prentice-Hall, 1995.

Silberman, Charles. *Criminal Violence, Criminal Justice.* New York: Vintage Books, 1978.

Siringo, Charles A. *A Cowboy Detective: A True Story of Twenty-Two Years with a World-Famous Detective Agency.* Lincoln, Neb.: University of Nebraska Press, 1988.

Skogan, Wesley G. *Disorder and Decline: Crime and the Spiral of Decay in American Neighborhoods.* New York: Free Press, 1990.

Skolnick, Jerome H. *Justice without Trial: Law Enforcement in a Democratic Society.* New York: Wiley, 1975, 1995.

Skolnick, Jerome H., and David H. Bayley. *The New Blue Line: Police Innovation in Six American Cities.* New York: Free Press, 1986.

Skolnick, Jerome H., and James J. Fyfe. *Above the Law: Police and the Excessive Use of Force.* New York: Free Press, 1993.

Smith, Bruce. *Police Systems in the United States.* New York: Harper & Row, 1950.

——— . *Rural Crime Control.* New York: Columbia University Institute of Public Administration, 1933.

Sparrow, Malcolm, Mark Moore, and David Kennedy. *Beyond 911: A New Era for Policing.* New York: Basic Books, 1990.

Spelman, W., and D. K. Brown. *Calling the Police: Citizen Reporting of Serious Crime.* Washington, D.C.: Police Executive Research Forum, 1981.

Staufenberger, Richard A. *Progress in Policing: Essays on Change.* Cambridge, Mass.: Ballinger Press, 1980.

Steffens, Lincoln. *The Autobiography of Lincoln Steffens.* New York: Harcourt Brace Jovanovich, 1958. Original edition, 1931.

——— . *The Shame of the Cities.* New York: Hill and Wang, 1957. Original edition, 1902.

Steinman, Michael, ed. *Woman Battering: Policy Responses.* Cincinnati: Anderson, 1991.

Straus, Murray A., Richard J. Gelles, and Suzanne Steinmetz. *Behind Closed Doors: Violence in the American Family.* Garden City, N.Y.: Anchor Press, 1980.

Sutherland, Edwin H., and Donald Cressey. *Principles of Criminology.* 8th ed. Philadelphia: Lippincott, 1970.

Swank, C., and J. Conser, eds. *The Police Personnel System.* New York: Wiley, 1983.

Swanson, Charles R., Leonard Territo, and Robert W. Taylor. *Police Administration: Structures, Processes, and Behavior.* 2d ed. New York: Macmillan, 1988.

Territo, Leonard, Charles R. Swanson, and N. C. Chamelin. *The Police Personnel Selection Process.* Indianapolis: Bobbs-Merrill, 1977.

Terry, W. Clinton. *Policing Society: An Occupational View.* New York: Wiley, 1985.

Theoharis, Althan, and John Stuart Cox. *The Boss.* Philadelphia: Temple University Press, 1988.

Thibault, Edward A., Lawrence M. Lynch, and R. Bruce McBride. *Proactive Police Management.* Englewood Cliffs, N.J.: Prentice-Hall, 1985, 1991.

Tien, James M., James W. Simon, and Richard C. Larson, *An Alternative Approach in Police Patrol: The Wilmington Split-Force Experiment.* Cambridge, Mass.: Public Systems Evaluation, 1977.

Tobias, John J. *Crime and Police in England, 1700–1900.* New York: St. Martin's Press, 1979.

Tonry, Michael, and Morris, N. *Crime and Justice: A Review of Research.* Chicago: University of Chicago Press, 1990.

Trojanowicz, Robert C., and Dennis W. Banas. *The Impact of Foot Patrol on Black and White Perceptions of Policing.* East Lansing, Mich.: National Neighborhood Foot Patrol Center, School of Criminal Justice, Michigan State University, 1988.

———. *Perceptions of Safety: A Comparison of Foot Patrol versus Motor Patrol Officers.* East Lansing, Mich.: National Neighborhood Foot Patrol Center, School of Criminal Justice, Michigan State University, 1985.

Trojanowicz, Robert C., and Bonnie Bucqueroux. *Community Policing: A Contemporary Perspective.* Cincinnati: Anderson, 1990.

Trojanowicz, Robert C., and H. A. Harden. *The Status of Contemporary Community Policing Programs.* East Lansing, Mich.: National Neighborhood Foot Patrol Center, School of Criminal Justice, Michigan State University, 1984.

Viorst, Milton. *Fire in the Streets: America in the 1960's.* New York: Simon & Schuster, 1970.

Wackenhut Investigations Division. *Integrity Testing and Other Shopping Services.* Coral Gables, Fla.: The Wackenhut Corporation, 1995.

———. *Investigative Services.* Coral Gables: Fla.: The Wackenhut Corporation, 1995.

Waldron, Ronald J. *The Criminal Justice System: An Introduction.* 4th ed., New York: Harper & Row, 1989.

Walker, Samuel. *A Critical History of Police Reform: The Emergence of Professionalism.* Lexington, Mass.: Lexington Books, 1977.

———. *The Police in America: An Introduction.* New York: McGraw-Hill, 1992, 1995.

———. *Popular Justice: History of American Criminal Justice.* New York: Oxford University Press, 1980.

———. *Sense and Nonsense about Crime.* Monterey, Calif.: Brooks/Cole, 1985.

Walker, Samuel, and Vic Bumphus. *A National Survey of Civilian Oversight of the Police.* Omaha, Nebr.: University of Nebraska at Omaha, 1991.

Wambaugh, Joseph. *The Blue Knight.* Boston: Little, Brown, 1973.

Webb, Walter Prescott. *The Texas Rangers: A Century of Frontier Defense.* Boston: Houghton Mifflin, 1935.

Weiner, Norman. *The Role of Police in Urban Society: Conflict and Consequences.* Indianapolis: Bobbs-Merrill, 1976.

Westly, William. *Violence and the Police: A Sociological Study of Law, Custom, and Morality.* Cambridge, Mass.: MIT Press, 1970.

Whited, Charles. *The Decoy Man.* New York: Playboy Press, 1973.

Wilber, Charles C. *Ballistic Science for the Law Enforcement Officer.* Springfield, Ill.: Charles C. Thomas, 1977.

Willbanks, William. *The Myth of a Racist Criminal Justice System.* Monterey, Calif.: Brooks/Cole, 1987.

Williams, Juan. *Eyes on the Prize: America's Civil Rights Years, 1954–1965.* New York: Penguin, 1983.

Wilson, James Q. *Thinking about Crime.* New York: Basic Books, 1983.

———. *Varieties of Police Behavior: The Management of Law and Order in Eight Communities.* Cambridge, Mass.: Harvard University Press, 1968.

Wilson, O. W. *Police Administration.* New York: McGraw-Hill, 1950.

Wilson, O. W., and Roy Clinton McLaren. *Police Administration.* 4th ed. New York: McGraw-Hill, 1977.

Wycoff, Mary Ann, et al. *Citizen Contact Patrol: Executive Summary.* Washington, D.C.: Police Foundation, 1985.

Yuille, John C., ed. *Police Selection and Training: The Role of Psychology.* Dordrecht, The Netherlands: Martinus Nijhoff Publishers, 1986.

Government Publications

ABT Associates. *New York City Anti-Crime Patrol: Exemplary Project Validation Report.* Washington, D.C.: U.S. Government Printing Office, 1974.

Baker, B. T. *Law Enforcement within Indian Country: An Introduction.* Artesia, N.M.: Federal Law Enforcement Training Center, 1993.

Bittner, Egon. *The Functions of the Police in Modern Society.* Washington, D.C.: U.S. Government Printing Office, 1970.

Bureau of Indian Affairs, Division of Law Enforcement. *Indian Law Enforcement History.* Washington, D.C.: U.S. Government Printing Office, 1975.

Brown, Lee P. *Community Policing: A Practical Guide for Police Officials.* Perspectives on Policing, no. 12. Washington, D.C.: U.S. Government Printing Office, 1989.

U.S. Department of Justice, Bureau of Justice Statistics. *Crime and the Nation's Households.* Washington, D.C.: U.S. Government Printing Office, published annually.

———. *Criminal Victimization in the United States.* Washington, D.C.: National Institute of Justice, published annually.

———. *Report to the Nation on Crime and Justice.* 2d ed. Washington, D.C.: U.S. Government Printing Office, 1991.

———. *Sourcebook of Criminal Justice Statistics.* Washington, D.C.: U.S. Government Printing Office, published annually.

———. *Special Report: Reporting Crimes to the Police.* Washington, D.C.: U.S. Government Printing Office, 1985.

California Highway Patrol. *Pursuit Study.* Sacramento, California Highway Patrol, 1983.

Calvert, Geoffrey N. *Portable Police Pensions—Improving Inter-Agency Transfers.* Washington, D.C.: U.S. Government Printing Office, 1971.

Caplan, Marc H., and Joe Holt Anderson. *Forensic: When Science Bears Witness.* Washington, D.C.: National Institute of Justice, 1984.

Campbell, Michael S. *Field Training for Police Officers: State of the Art.* Washington, D.C.: U.S. Government Printing Office, 1986.

Caskey, C. Thomas, and Holly A. Hammond. *Automated DNA Typing: Method of the Future?* Washington, D.C.: National Institute of Justice, 1997.

Cawley, Donald F., et al. *Managing Criminal Investigations: Manual.* Washington, D.C.: U.S. Government Printing Office, 1977.

Chaiken, M., ed. *Street Level Drug Enforcement: Examining the Issues.* Washington, D.C.: National Institute of Justice, 1988.

Chaiken, Marcia, and Jan Chaiken. *Priority Prosecutors of High Rate Dangerous Offenders.* Washington, D.C.: National Institute of Justice, 1991.

Cohen, Bernard, and Jan Chaiken. *Investigators Who Perform Well.* Washington, D.C.: National Institute of Justice, 1987.

Commission on Accreditation for Law Enforcement Agencies. *Standards for Law Enforcement Agencies.* Fairfax, Va.: Commission on Accreditation for Law Enforcement Agencies, 1987.

Connors, Edward. *Convicted by Juries, Exonerated by Science: Case Studies in the Use of DNA Evidence to Establish Innocence After Trial.* Washington, D.C.: National Institute of Justice, 1996.

Cox Commission. *Crisis at Columbia: Report of the Fact-Finding Commission Appointed to Investigate the Disturbances at Columbia University in April and May 1968.* New York: Vintage, 1968.

Cunningham, William C., John J. Strauchs, and Clifford W. Van Meter. *Private Security: Patterns and Trends.* Washington, D.C.: U.S. Government Printing Office, 1991.

Cunningham, William C., and Todd H. Taylor. *The Growth of Private Security.* Washington, D.C.: U.S. Government Printing Office, 1984.

DeJong, William. *Project DARE: Teaching Kids to Say "No" to Drugs and Alcohol.* Washington, D.C.: National Institute of Justice, 1986.

Federal Bureau of Investigation. *FBI Law Enforcement Bulletin.* Washington, D.C.: Federal Bureau of Investigation, published monthly.

——— . *Law Enforcement Officers Killed and Assaulted.* Washington, D.C.: U.S. Government Printing Office, published annually.

——— . *Uniform Crime Reports: Crime in the United States.* Washington, D.C.: U.S. Government Printing Office, published annually.

Finn, Peter E. *Block Watches Help Crime Victims in Philadelphia.* Washington, D.C.: National Institute of Justice, 1986.

Finn, Peter E., and Beverly N. W. Lee. *Establishing and Expanding Victim–Witness Assistance Programs.* Washington, D.C.: U.S. Government Printing Office, 1988.

Finn, Peter E., and Monique Sullivan. *Police Response to Special Populations: Handling the Mentally Ill, Public Inebriate, and the Homeless.* Washington, D.C.: National Institute of Justice, 1988.

Foti, Charles C., Jr. *The Effect of Drug Testing in New Orleans.* Washington, D.C.: National Institute of Justice, 1993.

Freedman, Kenneth R., and Terry Estrada-Mullaney. *Using Dolls to Interview Child Victims: Legal Concerns and Interview Procedures.* Washington, D.C.: National Institute of Justice, 1988.

Garofalo, James, and Maureen McLeod. *Improving the Use and Effectiveness of Neighborhood Watch Programs.* Washington, D.C.: National Institute of Justice, 1988.

Geller, William. *Crime File: Deadly Force.* Washington, D.C.: National Institute of Justice, 1985.

Greenberg, Ilene, and Robert Wasserman. *Managing Criminal Investigations.* Washington, D.C.: U.S. Government Printing Office, 1979.

Griesinger, George W., et al. *Civil Service Systems: Their Impact on Police Administration.* Washington, D.C.: U.S. Government Printing Office, 1979.

Guiliani, Rudolph W., Randy M. Mastro, and Donna Lynn. *Mayor's Management Report: The City of New York.* New York: City of New York, 1997.

Halper, Andrew, and Richard Ku. *New York City Police Department Street Crime Unit.* Washington, D.C.: U.S. Government Printing Office, n.d.

Hammett., Theodore M. *AIDS and the Law Enforcement Officer: Concerns and Policy Responses.* Washington, D.C.: U.S. Government Printing Office, 1987.

——— . *Precautionary Measures and Protective Equipment: Developing a Reasonable Response: National Institute of Justice AIDS Bulletin.* Washington, D.C.: National Institute Of Justice, 1988.

Hammett, Theodore M., and Walter Bond. *Risks of Infection with the AIDS Virus through Exposures to Blood: National Institute of Justice AIDS Bulletin.* Washington, D.C.: National Institute of Justice,1987.

Hammett, Theodore M., Harold W. Jaffe, and Bruce A. Johnson. *The Cause, Transmission and Incidence of AIDS: National Institute of Justice AIDS Bulletin.* Washington, D.C.: National Institute of Justice, 1987.

Hartman, Francis X., ed. *Debating the Evolution of American Policing. Perspectives on Policing, no. 5.* Washington, D.C.: U.S. Government Printing Office, 1988.

Hayeslip, David W. *Local-Level Drug Enforcement: New Strategies.* Washington, D.C.: National Institute of Justice, 1989.

Houston Police Department. *Annual Report.* Houston: Houston Police Department, published annually.

International City Management Association. *Municipal Yearbook.* Washington, D.C.: International City Management Association, published annually.

Kakalik, James F., and Sorrel Wildhorn. *Private Police in the United States.* Washington, D.C.: National Institute of Justice, 1971.

Kansas City Police Department. *Response Time Analysis: Executive Summary.* Washington, D.C.: U.S. Government Printing Office, 1978.

Kelling, George L. *Foot Patrol.* Washington, D.C.: National Institute of Justice, 1987.

——— . *Police and Communities: The Quiet Revolution. Perspectives on Policing, no. 1.* Washington, D.C.: U.S. Government Printing Office, 1988.

———. *What Works? Research and the Police.* Washington, D.C.: National Institute of Justice, n.d.

Kelling, George L., and Mark H. Moore. *The Evolving Strategy of Policing. Perspectives on Policing, no. 4.* Washington, D.C.: U.S. Government Printing Office, 1988.

Kelling, George L., and James K. Stewart. *Neighborhoods and Police: The Maintenance of Civil Authority. Perspectives on Policing, no. 10.* Washington, D.C.: U.S. Government Printing Office, 1989.

Kelling, George L., Robert Wasserman, and Hubert Williams. *Police Accountability and Community Policing. Perspectives on Policing, no. 7.* Washington, D.C.: U.S. Government Printing Office, 1988.

Klockars, Carl B., Jack R. Greene, and S. Wissmann. *An Evaluation of Resource Allocation in the Wilmington Police Department.* Wilmington, Del.: Office of the Director of Public Safety, 1988.

Levine, Margaret J., and J. Thomas McEwen. *Patrol Deployment.* Washington, D.C.: National Institute of Justice, 1985.

Los Angeles Police Department. *Annual Report.* Los Angeles: Los Angeles Police Department, published annually.

McEwen, J. Thomas, Edward F. Connors III, and Marcia J. Cohen. *Evaluation of the Differential Police Responses Field Test.* Washington, D.C.: U.S. Government Printing Office, 1986.

McEwen, J. Thomas, Barbara Manili, and Edward Connors. *Employee Drug Testing Policies in Police Departments.* Washington, D.C.: National Institute of Justice, 1986.

Manili, Barbara, and Edward Connors. *Police Chiefs and Sheriffs Rank Their Criminal Justice Needs.* Washington, D.C.: National Institute of Justice, 1988.

Maguire, Kathleen, and Ann L. Pastore, eds. *Sourcebook of Criminal Justice Statistics.* Washington, D.C.: U.S. Department of Justice, Bureau of Justice Statistics, U.S. Government Printing Office, published annually.

Moore, Mark H., and Mark A. R. Kleiman. *The Police and Drugs. Perspectives on Policing, no. 11.* Washington, D.C.: U.S. Government Printing Office, 1989.

Moore, Mark H., and Robert C. Trojanowitz. *Corporate Strategies for Policing. Perspectives on Policing, no. 6.* Washington, D.C.: U.S. Government Printing Office, 1988.

———. *Policing and the Fear of Crime. Perspectives on Policing, no. 3.* Washington, D.C.: U.S. Government Printing Office, 1988.

Moore, Mark H., Robert C. Trojanowicz, and George L. Kelling. *Crime and Policing. Perspectives on Policing, no. 2.* Washington, D.C.: U.S. Government Printing Office, 1988.

Nassau County Police Department. *Annual Report.* New York: Nassau County Police Department, published annually.

National Advisory Commission on Civil Disorders. *Report.* Washington, D.C.: U.S. Government Printing Office, 1968.

National Advisory Commission on Criminal Justice Standards and Goals. *Police.* Washington, D.C.: U.S. Government Printing Office, 1973.

National Commission on Law Observance and Enforcement. *Lawlessness in Law Enforcement.* Washington, D.C.: U.S. Government Printing Office, 1931.

———. *Report on Police.* Washington, D.C.: U.S. Government Printing Office, 1931.

National Institute of Justice. *Community Policing in Seattle: A Modal Partnership between Citizens and Police.* Washington, D.C.: National Institute of Justice, 1992.

———. *The DARE Program: A Review of Prevalence, User Satisfaction, and Effectiveness.* Washington, D.C.: National Institute of Justice, 1994.

———. *The Effects of the Exclusionary Rule: A Study of California.* Washington, D.C.: National Institute of Justice, 1982.

———. *Employee Drug Testing Policies in Police Departments: Research in Brief.* Washington, D.C.: National Institute of Justice, 1986.

———. *Research Plan.* Washington, D.C.: National Institute of Justice, issued yearly.

———. *Toward the Paperless Police Department: The Use of Laptop Computers.* Washington, D.C.: National Institute of Justice, 1993.

———. *Confronting Domestic Violence: A Guide for Criminal Justice Agencies.* Washington, D.C.: National Institute of Justice, 1986.

National Institute of Law Enforcement and Criminal Justice. *Controlling Police Corruption: The Effects of Reform Policies, Summary Report.* Washington, D.C.: U.S. Department of Justice, 1978.

———. *Employing Civilians for Police Work.* Washington, D.C.: U.S. Government Printing Office, 1975.

National Minority Advisory Council on Criminal Justice. *The Inequality of Justice: A Report on Crime and the Administration of Justice in the Minority Community.* Washington, D.C.: U.S. Government Printing Office, 1980.

New York City Police Department. *AIDS and Our Workplace.* New York: New York City Police Department, 1987.

———. *Annual Report.* New York: New York City Police Department, published annually.

———. *Problem-Solving Strategies for Community Policing: A Practical Guide.* New York: New York City Police Department.

Peterson, Joseph L. *Use of Forensic Evidence by the Police and Courts.* Washington, D.C.: National Institute of Justice, 1987.

Police Department of Kansas City. *1966 Survey of Municipal Police Departments.* Kansas City: Police Department of Kansas City, 1966.

President's Commission on Crime in the District of Columbia. *A Report on the President's Commission on Crime in the District of Columbia.* Washington, D.C.: U.S. Government Printing Office, 1966.

President's Commission on Law Enforcement and Administration of Justice. *The Challenge of Crime in a Free Society.* Washington, D.C.: U.S. Government Printing Office, 1967.

———. *Task Force Report: The Police.* Washington, D.C.: U.S. Government Printing Office, 1967.

———. *Task Force Report: Science and Technology.* Washington, D.C.: U.S. Government Printing Office, 1967.

Reaves, Brian. *Profile of State and Local Law Enforcement Agencies, 1992.* Washington, D.C.: National Institute of Justice, 1993.

——— . *Sheriffs' Departments: 1990*. Washington, D.C.: National Institute of Justice, 1992.

——— . *Local Police Departments—1993*. Washington, D.C.: National Institute of Justice, 1996.

——— . *Sheriffs' Departments: 1993*. Washington, D.C.: National Institute of Justice, 1996.

Reiss, Albert. *Private Employment of Public Police*. Washington, D.C.: National Institute of Justice, 1988.

Rosenbaum, Dennis P., Arthur J. Lurigio, and Paul J. Lavrakas. *Crime Stoppers: A National Evaluation*. Washington, D.C.: National Institute of Justice, 1986.

Rubin, Paula. *The Americans with Disabilities Act and Criminal Justice: Hiring New Employees*. Washington, D.C.: National Institute of Justice, 1994.

Safir, Howard. *The Compstat Process*. New York: New York City Police Department, n.d.

Schack, Stephen, Theodore H. Schell, and William G. Gay. *Specialized Patrol: Improving Patrol Productivity*. Washington, D.C.: U.S. Government Printing Office, 1977.

Scott, Eric J. *Calls for Service: Citizen Demand and Initial Police Response*. Washington, D.C.: U.S. Government Printing Office, 1981.

Sherman, Lawrence, James Shaw, and Dennis Rogan. *The Kansas City Gun Experiment*. Washington, D.C.: National Institute of Justice, 1994.

Shubin, Lester D. *Research, Testing Upgrade Criminal Justice Technology*. Washington, D.C.: National Institute of Justice, 1988.

Sichel, Joyce, et al. *Women on Patrol: A Pilot Study of Police Performance in New York City*. Washington, D.C.: Department of Justice, 1978.

Skolnick, Jerome, and D. Bayley. *Community Policing: Issues and Practices around the World*. Washington, D.C.: National Institute of Justice, 1988.

Sparrow, Malcolm K. *Implementing Community Policing. Perspectives on Policing, no. 9*. Washington, D.C.: U.S. Government Printing Office, 1988.

——— . *Information Systems and the Development of Policing. Perspectives on Policing, no. 16*. Washington, D.C.: U.S. Government Printing Office, 1993.

Spelman, William, and John E. Eck. *Newport News Tests Problem-Oriented Policing*. Washington, D.C.: National Institute of Justice, 1987.

Stillman, Frances A. *Line of Duty Deaths: Survivor and Departmental Responses*. Washington, D.C.: National Institute of Justice, 1987.

Sullivan, George J. *Directed Patrol*. Kansas City, Mo.: Kansas City Police Department, Operations Resource Unit, 1976.

Sweetman, Sherri. *Report on the Attorney General's Conference on Less-than-Lethal Weapons*. Washington, D.C.: National Institute of Justice, 1987.

Tien, J., J. Simon, and R. Larson. *An Alternative Approach in Police Patrol: The Wilmington Split Force Experiment*. Washington, D.C.: U.S. Government Printing Office, 1978.

Uchida, Craig D., Brian Forst, and Sampson O. Annan. *Controlling Street-Level Drug Trafficking: Evidence from Oakland and Birmingham*. Washington, D.C.: National Institute of Justice, 1992.

U.S. Bureau of Census. *1990 Census of Population*. Washington, D.C.: U.S. Bureau of Census, 1991.

U.S. Commission on Civil Rights. *Who Is Guarding the Guardians? A Report on Police Practices*. Washington, D.C.: U.S. Government Printing Office, 1981.

U.S. Congress, Office of Technology Assessment. *Criminal Justice: New Technologies and the Constitution: A Special Report*. Washington, D.C.: U.S. Government Printing Office, 1988.

U.S. Department of Justice. *Civil Service Systems: Affirmative Action and Equal Employment: A Guidebook for Employers*. Washington, D.C.: U.S. Government Printing Office, 1974.

——— . *Justice Expenditure and Employment*. Washington, D.C.: U.S. Government Printing Office, published annually.

——— . *Police Departments in Large Cities, 1987*. Washington, D.C.: U.S. Government Printing Office, 1989.

——— . *Police Use of Deadly Force*. Washington, D.C.: U.S. Government Printing Office, 1978.

U.S. Department of Justice, Bureau of Justice Statistics. *Crime and the Nation's Households*. Washington, D.C.: U.S. Government Printing Office, published annually.

——— . *Criminal Victimization in the Untied States*. Washington, D.C.: National Institute of Justice, published annually.

——— . *Report to the Nation on Crime and Justice*. 2d ed. Washington, D.C.: U.S. Government Printing Office, 1991.

——— . *Sourcebook of Criminal Justice Statistics*. Washington, D.C.: U.S. Government Printing Office, published annually.

——— . *Special Report: Reporting Crimes to the Police*. Washington, D.C.: U.S. Government Printing Office, 1985.

Wasserman, Robert, and Mark H. Moore. *Values in Policing. Perspectives on Policing, no. 8*. Washington, D.C.: U.S. Government Printing Office, 1988.

Whitaker, Catherine. *Crime Prevention Measures*. Washington, D.C.: Bureau of Justice Statistics, 1986.

Wilson, James Q., and Barbara Boland. *The Effect of Police on Crime*. Washington, D.C.: U.S. Government Printing Office, 1979.

Wilson, T. F., and P. L. Woodard. *Automated Fingerprint Identification Systems—Technology and Policy Issues*. Washington, D.C.: U.S. Department of Justice, 1987.

Academic and Professional Journals

ABF Research Journal
American Behavioral Scientist
American Demographics
American Journal of Police
American Journal of Sociology
American Sociological Review
Annals of the American Association of Political and Social Science
CJ, The Americas

Community Policing Exchange
Crime Control Digest
Crime and Social Justice
Criminal Justice and Behavior
Criminal Justice Journal
Criminal Justice Newsletter
Criminal Law Bulletin
Criminology
Detroit Journal of Urban Law
Educator
Evaluation Review
FBI Law Enforcement Bulletin
Futurist
Journal of Applied Behavior Analysis
Journal of the American Optometric Association
Journal of California Law Enforcement
Journal of Contemporary Criminal Justice
Journal of Criminal Law, Criminology, and Police Science
Journal of Law and Criminology
Journal of Police Science and Administration
Journal of Research in Crime and Delinquency
Journal of Social Issues
Justice Quarterly
Law and Society Review
National Institute of Justice Journal
National Law Journal
New York Law Enforcement Journal
Northwestern Law Journal
Police Journal
Police Studies
Public Administration Review
Public Personnel Management Journal
Quarterly Journal of Studies on Alcohol
Security Journal
Social Problems
Stanford Law Review
Texas Police Journal
Urban Life

University of Chicago Law Journal
Yale Law Journal

Newspapers and National Magazines

Boston Globe
Commercial Advisor
New York Times
Philadelphia Bulletin
Time
Newsweek
Law Enforcement News
USA Today
Newsday
New York Post
Tampa Tribune
U.S. News and World Report
Wall Street Journal

Trade Magazines

Law and Order
National Centurion
PC Computing
Police
Police Centurion
Police Chief
Popular Mechanics
Scientific America
Security
Security Management
The NarcOfficer

Index

AARP. *See* American Association of Retired Persons
Abel v. United States, 270
Abuse of authority, 299–300
ADA. *See* Americans with Disabilities Act
Administrative units, 75–77
Admission, 274
Advanced photographic techniques
　age progression photographs, 349, 350
　composite sketches, 349–350
　mug shot imaging, 348–349
Aerosol subject restraints, 346
Affidavit, 267
Affirmative action, 83, 84, 318–319
　white male backlash, 319–320
AFIS. *See* Automated fingerprint identification system
AFL. *See* American Federation of Labor
African-American community, 201–202
African-American police officers
　academic studies of, 323
　chiefs, 325
　current numbers, 324t., 325
　discrimination against, 314–315
　ongoing problems, 328–329
　representation on NYPD, 325
AFSCME. *See* American Federation of State, County, and Municipal Employees
Age progression photographs, 349, 350
Age requirements, 97–98
Aguilar-Spinelli standard, 268
Aguilar v. Texas, 266
AIDS, 369–370
Albuquerque, New Mexico Crime Stoppers, 218
Alcohol abuse, 298–299
ALERT (Advanced Law Enforcement Response Technology) System
　mug shot imaging, 349

Alfred the Great, 3
Alliance for a Safer L.A., 222
Alzheimer's disease, 207
American Association of Retired Persons, 205
American Federation of Labor, 68–69
American Federation of State, County, and Municipal Employees, 69
American Law Institute, 373
American Society for Industrial Security, 49
American Society of Crime Laboratory Directors, 79, 353
American Society of Criminology Internet mentoring service, 291
American Society of Law Enforcement Trainers, 101
Americans with Disabilities Act, 95
AmeriCorps, 222–224
　sample public safety programs, 223
Anatomically correct dolls, 216
Anthropometry, 343
Anti-child abduction programs, 211
Anti-war demonstrations, 19–21
Arizona Highway Patrol, 67
Arizona Rangers, 12
Arizona v. Evans, 273
Armed robbery incident (Los Angeles), 61
Armored trucks, 47f.
Arrest power, 62
Arrests
　authority, 263–264
　and deadly force, 265
　defined, 267
　number of in United States, 256
　and probable cause, 264
　and reasonable force, 264–265
　stopping vehicles, 265–266
Aryan Republican Army, 380
ASC. *See* American Society of Criminology

ASCLD. *See* American Society of Crime Laboratory Directors
Asian-American community, 203, 248
ASIS. *See* American Society for Industrial Security
ASLET. *See* American Society of Law Enforcement Trainers
Assassinations, 19, 43, 60–61
Assault. *See* Police and danger
Assistant chiefs, 64
Associations, 399–403
AT&T
　introduction of 911 systems, 334
　Language Line Services (translators), 336
ATF. *See* Bureau of Alcohol, Tobacco, and Firearms
Atherton, Shirley M., 196
Augustus, 2
Austin, Stephen, 12
Austin, Texas
　community policing, 247–248
　Police Department, 324
Automated fingerprint identification system, 337, 343–344, 345
Automated handwriting technology, 353
Automobile pursuits, 374–375, 375t.
Auxiliaries, 68
Auxiliary services, 77

Background investigation, 95–96
Badges, 8, 9
Ballistics, 354
Baltimore (Maryland) Police Department, 105
　kobans, 221
Baton Rouge, Louisiana community policing, 247
Beadles, 4
Beanbag guns, 346
Beats, 69–71

415

Beaufort City (South Carolina) Police Department web site, 342
Belding, Michigan reserve officers, 68
Berkeley, California, 15
Bicycle patrol, 75f., 248
Bill of Rights, 256–258, 289
Birmingham (Alabama) Police Department, killings by, 121
Black Hand, 289
Black Liberation Army, 378–379
Black Panthers, 378–379
The Blooding, 355–356
Bloomingdale (Illinois) Police Department evidence test case, 268
Blue Curtain, 130
Blue flu, 69
The Blue Knight, 299
Blue Wall of Silence, 128
Bobbies, 5, 6f.
Bonny, Regina, 12
Boris (police dog), 328
Boston Police Department, 35
    arming, 10
    founding, 8
    police strike, 13, 14, 69
    traffic tickets, 121
Boswell, James, 238
Boulder (Colorado) Police Department and JonBenet Ramsey case, 164f.
Bow Street Runners, 5
Branch Davidians, 381
Brasco, Donnie, 186
Bratton, Lisa, 129
Bratton, William J., 24, 180
Brewer v. Williams, 278–279
Brinegar v. United States, 264
Brink's Company, 47
Broderick's operational styles, 117–118, 118f.
Broken windows model, 232, 232f.
Brown, Ed, 276
Brown, Lee P., 324, 325
Brown, Nicole, 25, 26
Brown v. Board of Education of Topeka, 17, 201
Brown v. Mississippi, 258, 274–275, 276, 300
Brubine, Brian, 281
Brunk, Robert, 315
Bruno v. Codd, 376
Buddy Boys, 292
Bulletproof vests, 254, 263
Bumpers, Eleanor, 304
Bumper v. North Carolina, 269
Burdeau v. McDowell, 273
Bureau of Alcohol, Tobacco, and Firearms, 42
Bureau of Diplomatic Security, 44
Bureau of Indian Affairs, 203
Bureau of Justice Assistance Clearinghouse, 39

Bush, George, 397
Businesses in cooperation with police, 222
Buster, Vernon, 12
Byrne, Edward, 364
Byrnes, Brian, 83

California Division of Law Enforcement, 38
California Highway Patrol, 38
    court-ordered acceptance of women, 319
    recruiting at Chinese New Year celebration, 326f.
California Personality Inventory, 93
California v. Acevedo, 273
California v. Ciraola, 272
California v. Greenwood, 270, 271, 271f.
California v. Hodari, D., 270
Callace, Leonard, 357
Campbell, Robert, 11
Campbell, William, 248
Campus disorders, 19–21, 22
Canton v. Harris, 383–384
Captains, 64
Carmichael, Stokely, 18
Car patrol, 159–161, 162
Carraway, Mel, 325
Carroll, George, 272
Carroll v. United States, 272
Cassidy, Butch, 13
Castro, Joseph, 356
CATCH (Computer-Assisted Terminal Criminal Hunt) mug shot file, 338
Celester, William, 292–293
Certified protection professionals, 49
Chain of command, 58, 59f.
Chemical irritant sprays, 346
Chemical Mace, 346
Chicago, Illinois, 19
    Chicago's Alternative Policing Strategy, 242
Chicago Eight (Seven), 19
Chicago Police Department
    and affirmative action, 320
    Public Transportation Section, 35
    web site, 342
Childbirth assistance, 38
Child pornography, 211
Children
    age progression photographs in locating missing children, 350
    and anatomically correct dolls, 216
    anti-child abduction programs, 211
    child pornography, 211
    and Internet, 212, 214
    victim assistance programs, 216
Chimel, Ted, 267
Chimel v. California, 267, 275
Christopher Commission, 297
Citizen complaint review boards, 305

Citizen marches, 219
Citizen oversight, 305–306
Citizen patrols, 218–219
Citizen police academies, 222
Citizen volunteer programs, 219–220
Civil and criminal liability, 381–382
    effects of lawsuits, 383–384
    federal level, 382
    reasons for lawsuits, 382–383
    state level, 382
Civil forfeiture, 42
Civilian personnel. *See* Nonsworn (civilian) personnel
Civilianization, 65–66
Civil liability enforcement teams, 184
Civil Rights Act of 1964, 316
Civil rights movement, 17–19
Civil service system, 60–61, 90
Clark, Tom C., 262–263
Cleveland Police Department
    officer selection screening, 90
    search and seizure test case, 269
Clinton, Bill, 218, 245, 245f., 246, 397–398
CN tear gas, 346
Code enforcement teams, 184
Cold Bath Fields riot, 6
Colorado Springs Police Department, 51
Colquhoun, Patrick, 5, 6
Columbia, South Carolina resident officer program, 243–244
Columbian Society, 69
Columbia University, 20, 21f.
Columbus (Ohio) Police Department, 358
Command
    chain of, 58, 59f.
    unity of, 59
Commission on Accreditation for Law Enforcement Agencies, 83, 290
Commissions, 290. *See also* Christopher Commission; Commission on Accreditation for Law Enforcement Agencies; Knapp Commission; Mollen Commission; National Advisory Commission on Civil Disorders; National Advisory Commission on Criminal Justice Standards and Goals; National Commission on Law Observance and Enforcement; President's Commission on Law Enforcement and Administration of Justice
Communications Decency Act, 257
Community crime prevention programs, 217
    citizen marches, 219
    citizen patrols, 218–219
    citizen police academies, 222

citizen volunteer programs, 219–220
Crime Stoppers, 218
Eyes and Ears program, 219
Guardian Angels, 218
home security surveys, 220
mass media campaigns, 221–222
National Night Out, 220–221
Nation of Islam Security Agency, 218
Neighborhood Watch, 217–218
Operation Identification, 220
police storefront stations, 221, 221f.
ride-along programs, 222
station tours, 222
Community policing, 52, 230–231, 237
and academic research, 233
Austin, Texas, 247–248
author's experience, 236
Baton Rouge, Louisiana, 247
benefits, 233–234
broken windows model, 232, 232f.
and civil unrest, 233
Community Policing Consortium, 247
Community Policing Officer (CPO), 235
COPS web site, 246
and crime rate, 233
critical attitudes needed, 235
Dallas, 241
defined, 231, 235, 249
Denver, 247
Detroit, 235
and disorder, 232–233
dissenters, 248–249
Elgin, Illinois, 240–242
Forth Worth, 247
and gangs, 233, 240
Houston, 237, 248–249
incorporation of problem-solving policing, 239
and individual violence, 233
and the Internet, 234
Kansas, 242
Los Angeles, 247
National Center for Community Policing, 233
New Orleans, 248
Office of Community Oriented Policing Services (COPS), 245–247
partnerships, 234
and police brutality, 233
and police community relations movement, 231–232
Prince George's County, Maryland, 241
resident officer programs, 242–245
Sagamore Hills, Ohio, 242
success stories, 247–248
synonyms for, 234
Toledo, Ohio, 249
training, 106

Wichita, Kansas, 247
Community Policing Consortium, 106, 247
web site, 246
Community Policing Officers, 235
Community relations, 196–197
African-American community, 201–202
anti-child abduction programs, 211
Asian-American community, 203, 248
and chiefs, 196
college intern programs, 212
cultural diversity training, 201, 202
deaf people, 216
defined, 197–198
disabled people, 216–217
Drug Abuse Resistance Education (DARE), 209–210
gay community, 203–204, 326
Hispanic-American community, 202–203, 248
homeless, 214–216
and human relations, 197
and individual officers, 197
and languages, 202–203
minority communities, 200–204
and multiculturalism, 200–201
Native Americans, 203
networking with mental health professionals, 215
new immigrants, 204
Officer Friendly programs, 210
police athletic leagues, 212
police-business cooperation, 222
police community relations movement, 197–198
Police Explorer programs, 209, 210, 213
police rock bands, 210
police trading cards, 210–211, 222
and public opinion, 198–199, 199t.
and public relations, 197
robots, 211
school resource officers, 211
senior citizens' programs, 204–208
special populations, 204–217
student-ride-alongs, 211–212
TRIAD program, 205
victim assistance programs, 216
women, 203
young people's programs, 208–213, 208f., 209f.
Community relations unit, 75
Community service officers, 66–67
Community services unit, 75
Composite sketches, 349–350
Compstat, 24–25
COMPSTAT software, 338
Computer-aided dispatch, 334–337
Computer-aided investigation, 338–340

Computers, 334, 335. *See also* Internet, National Crime Information Center
administrative uses, 340–341
automated clerical processing systems, 340
automated crime analysis, 338
automated databases, 337–338
automated fingerprint identification system, 337, 343–344, 345
COMPSTAT software, 338
computer-aided dispatch, 334–337
computer-aided investigation, 338–340
computer-assisted instruction, 340
future applications, 337
IACP network, 341
jail and prisoner management, 340–341
management information systems, 340
mobile digital terminals (MDTs), 335–337
and modus operandi, 338
networks, 341–342
patrol allocation design, 341
Confession, 274
Confidentiality, 394
Constables
America, 8
colonial America, 7
England, 3, 4
Coolidge, Calvin, 14, 16, 69
Cooperation, 394
Cooping, 299
Cop Net & Police Resource List, 34
COPS. *See* Office of Community Oriented Policing Services
Cops, derivation of term, 8
Coral Gables (Florida) Police Department, 139
Corporals, 63
Corporate spying, 48
Corruption
art imitating life, 291–292
bribes, 293
defined, 291
and drugs, 296
effects of, 296
forms of, 293–295
gratuities, 293
and integrity tests, 297
internal, 295
and internal affairs divisions, 297
levels of, 295
reasons for, 296–297
recent examples, 292–293
stages of personal moral decline, 295–296
theft, 293
Cote, Jo-Ann, 378
County of Riverside v. McLoughlin, 264

Couroy, Jimmy, 347
CPI. *See* California Personality Inventory
CPOs. *See* Community Policing Officers
Cranston (Rhode Island) Police Department interrogation test case, 281
Crime
　defined, 267
　Index crimes, 254–255, 256f.
　measurement, 254–255
　　National Crime Victimization Survey, 255, 255t.
　　Uniform Crime Reports, 254–255, 255t.
　United States, 254–256
Crime Bill (1994), 245, 246
Crime clock, 256f.
Crime laboratories, 79, 352. *See also* Forensic science
　accreditation, 352–353
Crime prevention unit, 75
Crime rate, 24, 172, 180, 233
Crime Stoppers, 218
Criminal investigations unit, 75
Criminalistics. *See* Forensic science
Criminalists, 79
Criminal record restrictions, 100
Crown Point (Indiana) Police Department, 222
Crystal City (Missouri) Police Department, 366
CSOs. *See* Community service officers
Cultural diversity. *See* Multiculturalism
Custodial interrogation, 274. See *also* Interrogations
Customs Service, 42
Cyber cop, 65
CyberAngels, 220
Cyber Patrol, 212
Cynicism, 133

Dahl, Scott, 320
Dahmer, Jeffrey, 120
Daley, Richard J., 19
Daley, Robert, 292
Dallas County (Texas) Sheriff's Department community policing, 241
Dallas Police Deparment
　and affirmative action, 320
　and sexual orientation, 101
　traffic tickets, 121
　web site, 60
Danger. *See* Police and danger
DARE. *See* Drug Abuse Resistance Education
Databases, 337–338
　CATCH, 338
　HITMAN, 338
　HITS (Homicide Investigation and Tracking System), 339
　and modus operandi, 338

Daubert v. Merrell Dow Pharmaceuticals, Inc., 357
Davis, Forrest, 38
Davis, Len, 292
Davis (California) Police Department web site, 342
Davis v. United States, 281–282
Day, William R., 259
Dayton (Ohio) Police Department antidrug rock and roll band, 210
DEA. *See* Drug Enforcement Administration
Deadly force, 265. *See also* Police shootings
Deaf people, 216
Dean, Kimberly, 187
Deaths. *See* Police and danger
Deception, 299
Decoy operations, 182–183, 182f.
Degan, William, 381
Delaware v. Prouse, 265
Del-Debbio, Peter, 329
Delegation of responsibility and authority, 59
Denver, Colorado
　community policing, 247
　resident officer program, 245
Deputies, 63
Des Moines (Washington) Police Department web site, 342
Detectives, 63, 163f.
　activities, 163–164
　centralized vs. decentralized organization, 163–164
　mystique, 164–165
　retroactive investigation of past crimes, 153–154, 175–178
Detroit Police Department
　and affirmative action, 320
　bulletproof vest incident, 254
　corruption, 292
　Mini-Station Program, 235
　selection procedures, 92
　STRESS (Stop the Robberies, Enjoy Safe Streets), 183
DiGerlando, Benedict, 276
Dinkins, David, 292, 325
Dirk, David, 291
Dirty Harriet Syndrome, 321
Dirty Harry Problem, 133–134, 134f., 135
Disabled people, 216–217
Discipline, 60
Discretion, 119–121, 394
　case study, 120
　controlling, 123
　defined, 119
　exercising, 121
　factors influencing, 121–123
　and gender, 123
　and race, 122–123

　reasons for, 121
Division of labor, 58, 59f.
DNA profiling, 354–355
　Castro case, 356
　in establishing innocence, 357
　and Frye test, 356
　PCR-STR procedure, 355
　rulings on, 356–358
　and Wambaugh's *The Blooding,* 355–356
Dolan, Joseph, 177
Domestic violence, 376
　LaSalata case, 378
　Minneapolis experiment, 376–377
　new police approach, 377–378, 377f.
　by police officers, 377–378
　traditional police response, 376
　web sites, 378
Domestic Violence Offender Gun Ban, 377–378
Dowd, Michael, 292
Downers Grove, Illinois home security surveys, 220
Draper v. United States, 264
Drug Abuse Resistance Education, 209–210
Drug culture
　and dangers to police, 364
　and Internet, 189
Drug Enforcement Administration, 41
DRUGFIRE computerized ballistics system, 354
Drug investigations, 188, 189–190
Drugs
　antidrug rock and roll band, 210
　and officers, 298
　and police corruption, 296
Drug use, 100
Du Page County (Illinois) Sheriff's Office
　selection procedures, 92
DuPont Corporation, 254, 263
Durk, David, 22

Earp, Wyatt, 11
East Dallas, Texas ministations, 221
East St. Louis, Missouri, 222
Eastwood, Clint, 133, 134f.
Education requirements, 98–100
Elder abuse, 206
Elgin, Illinois
　community policing, 240–242
　resident officer programs, 241, 243, 244
Elizabeth, New Jersey
　ministations, 221
Emerald Society, 69
Emergency Command Control Communications System, 336
Emergency Response Teams, 53

Emergency service units, 166, 166f., 167f., 177
Employment information. *See* Job information
England. *See also* Great Britain
   early police, 3–6
   Marine Police, 2, 5
Entrapment, 190–191
Equal employment opportunity, 83–84
Equal Employment Opportunity Act of 1972, 317
Escobedo, Danny, 275, 276
Escobedo v. Illinois, 17, 276
Essex County (New Jersey) Sheriff's Department, 54
Ethics
   defined, 288–289
   IACP mandates, 393–395
   Law Enforcement Code of Ethics, 393
   and police subculture, 289
   standards for police, 289
Evidence, 267
Exclusionary rule, 259–263
   defined, 267
   in O.J. Simpson case, 260
Exculpatory (defined), 274
Eyes and Ears program, 219

Failla, Paul, 84
Families and private life, 138–139, 369, 395
Farell, Loren, 61, 66
Fargo, William G., 13, 47
Fast-food restaurants, 183
FATS. *See* Firearms Training System
FBI. *See* Federal Bureau of Investigation
Federal Bureau of Investigation, 16, 25, 32, 39–41, 104
   corruption, 293
   Crime Laboratory, 40
   Evidence Response Team, 345
   Identification Division, 40
   Integrated Automated Fingerprint Identification System, 344
   National Crime Information Center, 16, 40
   Operation Road Spill, 186
   recommendations on handling infected evidence, 370
   statistics on police murders, 365–368, 365t.
   Uniform Crime Reports, 40–41, 254–255
   Violent Crimes and Major Offenders Program, 40
   Violent Criminal Apprehension Program, 338
   web site, 34
Federal Judiciary Act of 1789, 11–12

Federal Law Enforcement Training Center, 104
Federal Trade Commission, 44
Federal Witness Security Program, 41
Felon/Find'r software, 339
Felony (defined), 267
Fielding, Henry, 4–5, 6
Field interrogations, 178, 179–180, 268–269
Field training, 104
Fingerprinting, 342–343
   automated fingerprint identification system, 337, 343–344, 345
   Felon/Find'r software, 339
   fluorescent detection, 345
   laser technology, 345
   positive identification process, 342–343, 343f., 344f.
   replacement of anthropometry, 343
Firearms training, 104–105
Firearms Training System, 340
First Amendment and Internet, 258
FIs. *See* Field interrogations
FISH. *See* Forensic Information System for Handwriting
Fish and Wildlife Service, 43
FLETC. *See* Federal Law Enforcement Training Center
Fletcher, Connie, 321
Florence County (Wisconsin) Sheriff's Department use of electronic surveillance technology, 348
Florida Department of Law Enforcement, 99
Florida Highway Patrol, qualifications for, 90
Florida v. Bostick, 270
Florida v. Jimeno, 273
Florida v. Riley, 272
Fogelson, Robert M., 10
Food and Drug Administration, 44
Foot patrol, 23, 159–162
FOP. *See* Fraternal Order of Police
Force, 394. *See also* Deadly force; Police shootings; Reasonable force
Forensic Information System for Handwriting, 353
Forensic science, 350–351, 350f.
   automated handwriting technology, 353
   ballistics, 354
   case loads of crime labs, 351
   crime lab accreditation, 352–353
   crime labs, 352
   criminalistics as branch of, 350
   defined, 350
   lab sections, 353t.
   neutron activation, 353
   new techniques, 353–354
   scanning electron microscope, 353

ultraviolet technology, 353–354
   uses of, 351
   and Wayne Williams case, 352
Fort Lauderdale (Florida) Police Department selection procedures, 89, 92
Forth Worth, Texas community policing, 247
Fosdick, Raymond Blaine, 16
Fourteenth Amendment, 257–258, 259, 316
France, early law enforcement in, 2–3
Frankfurter, Felix, 261, 262, 275
Franklin County (Ohio) Sheriff's Office, 358
Fraternal Order of Police, 69
Fraternal organizations, 69
Frisk (defined), 267
Frye test, 356
Frye v. United States, 356
Fuhrman, Mark, 260, 300

Gacek, Laura, 315
Gangs, 233, 240
Garfield, James, 60–61
Garner, Edward, 372
Gates, Daryl, 65
Gates, Lance, 268
Gates, Sue, 268
Gay community, 203–204, 326
Gay Officers Action League, 69, 204
Gay police officers, 101, 203–204
   discrimination against, 316
Gendarmerie Nationale, 3
General Electric Co. v. Joiner, 357
General Services Administration, 44
Gerontology, 205
Gilbert (Arizona) Police Department, 248
Gilroy (California) Police Department Gang Suppression Program, 240
Glatzle, Mary, 182f.
Gleason, William Michael, 380
Glendale (California) Police Department, officer under fire, 297
Golden State Peace Officers Association, 204
Goldman, Ronald, 25, 26
Goldsboro (North Carolina) Police Department
   firearms training, 105
   and less-than-lethal weapons, 346–347
Goldstein, Herman, 237
Golf cart patrol, 162
Gordon v. Warren Consolidated Board of Education, 188
Gotti, John, 41
Gravano, Salvatore (Sammy the Bull), 41

Graziano, Louis, 347
Great Britain
  HOLMES software, 338–339
  National Automated Fingerprint Identification System, 344
Greenwood, Billy, 271
Griggs v. Duke Power Company, 317
Gruber, Charles A., 241–242, 243
GSPOA. *See* Golden State Peace Officers Association
Guardian Angels, 218
  CyberAngels, 220
Guardians Association, 69, 86
Guardians Association of New York City Police Department v. Civil Service Commission of New York, 86
Gunning, Charles R., 231
Guthrie, Richard, 380

Hambley, Kathleen, 43
Handwriting technology, 353
Hanger, Charles J., 151
Hanna, Joseph, 347
Harding, Warren G., 16
Harrisburg (Pennsylvania) Bureau of Police, 121
Harris v. New York, 278
Harris v. United States, 270
Hart, William L., 292, 325
Hate groups, 378–381
Havermeyer, William F., 8
Heaven's Gate incident, 315
Height and weight requirements, 96–97
Heller, Katherine P., 320
Henghold, David, 139
Henry, Paul, 43
Henry v. United States, 264
Herig, Jeffrey, 65
Hesston (Kansas) Police Department, 222
Hester v. United States, 272
Hickey, Mary Jo, 281
Hickock, James Butler (Wild Bill), 11
Highway patrol. *See also* State police
  Arizona, 67
  California, 38, 319, 326f.
  Florida, 90
  Oklahoma, 151
Hill, Henry, 41
Hill, Rod, 11
Hispanic-American community, 202–203, 248
HITMAN database, 338
HITS (Homicide Investigation and Tracking System), 339
Hogan, James, 238
Hogan's Alley programs, 104
Holmes, Oliver Wendell, 272, 275
HOLMES (Home Office Large Major Enquiry System) case management software, 338–339

Holmes Security, 47
Homeless, 214–216
Home security surveys, 220
Homestead Riots, 13
Honor, 128
Hoover, Herbert, 15
Hoover, J. Edgar, 13, 16–17, 299
Horry County, South Carolina, 221
Hot pursuit, 269
House fire incident (Nassau County, New York), 83
Houston (Texas) Police Department, 324
  community policing, 237, 248–249
Hudak, Ed, 139
Hue and cry, 3, 11
Huff, Henry, 263, 358
Huffman, Brian D., 44
Hughes, Charles E., 275
Humphries, Robert L., 131
Hunter, Matthew, 114
Huntington Beach (California) Police Department, 130
Hurricane Andrew, 139
Hymon, Elton, 372

IACOLE. *See* International Association for Citizen Oversight of Law Enforcement
IBPO. *See* International Brotherhood of Police Officers
ICPA. *See* International Conference of Police Associations
Identification procedures, 282
  lineups, 282–283
  other procedures, 284
  photo arrays, 282, 284
  showups, 282, 283
Illinois v. Gates, 266, 268
Illinois v. Krull, 273
Illinois v. Perkins, 280
Illinois v. Rodriguez, 269–270
Immigrants, 204
Immigration and Naturalization Service, 41
Incriminate (defined), 274
Inculpatory (defined), 274
Index crimes, 254–255
  crime clock, 254–255, 256f.
Indiana State Police
  qualifications, 91
Individuality, 128
Informant (defined), 267
Infrared surveillance devices, 348
INS. *See* Immigration and Naturalization Service
In-service training, 105
Inspectors, 64
Integrity, 394
Integrity shoppers, 51, 187
Integrity tests, 297

Internal affairs divisions, 297
Internal Revenue Service, 42
International Association for Citizen Oversight of Law Enforcement, 305
International Association of Chiefs of Police, 15, 49, 69, 106, 201, 203, 205, 254, 263, 316, 320
  computer network, 341
  ethical mandates, 393–395
  magazine, 391
  model drug testing policy, 298
  and sexual orientation, 101
  web site, 34
International Association of Women Police, 324
International Brotherhood of Police Officers, 69
International Conference of Police Associations, 69
International Union of Police Associations, 69
Internet, 7, 341–342
  American Society of Criminology mentoring service, 291
  and child pornography, 211
  and children, 212, 214
  Communications Decency Act, 257
  and community policing, 234
  COPS web site, 246
  CyberAngels, 220
  Cyber Patrol, 212
  Dallas Police Department home page, 60
  departmental web sites, 342
  domestic violence web sites, 378
  and drug culture, 189, 212
  equipment needed, 10
  and First Amendment, 258
  hits on local police home pages, 48
  and indecent acts, 119
  information on the Supreme Court, 259
  job information, 83, 85, 389
  Law Enforcement News web site, 321
  law enforcement sites, 34, 37
  learning how to use, 16
  Millerville University on-line police academy, 87
  National Law Enforcement Officers Memorial Fund web site, 367
  and pedophiles, 130
  pornography, 212, 214
  recruiting, 85
Intern programs, 83, 159, 212
INTERPOL, 45
Interrogations, 258, 274
  defined, 274
  field, 178, 179–180
  Miranda Rule, 276–277, 282
  Miranda Rule exceptions, 278–280
  Miranda Rule in the 1990s, 280–282

pre-Miranda restrictions, 274–276, 274f.
related terms, 274
Interstate Commerce Commission, 44
Investigations, 41, 42, 44, 50. *See also* Detectives; Federal Bureau of Investigation
  computer-aided, 338–340
  jobs for college students, 50
  SHERLOCK investigation software, 339–340
Investigators, 63. *See also* Detectives
Inwald Personality Inventory, 93
IPI. *See* Inwald Personality Inventory
IRS. *See* Internal Revenue Service
IUPA. *See* International Union of Police Associations

Jackson, Don, 302
Jackson State College, 21
Jacobson v. U.S., 190, 191
Jagielski, Ron, 254
Jail Administration Management System software, 340
Jakobetz, Randolph, 356–357
JAM-II. *See* Jail Administration Management System software
Jane Wayne Syndrome, 321
Jeter, Vincent E., 383
Job analysis, 86–87, 318
Job discrimination
  affirmative action programs, 318–319
  Civil Rights Act of 1964, 316
  de facto, 317
  Equal Employment Opportunity Act of 1972, 317
  and federal courts, 317–318
  and job analysis, 318
  significant court cases, 318
Job information, 82–83, 389–390
  calling or writing to a department, 390
  Internet, 83, 85, 389
  national publications, 390–391
Johnson, David R., 17
Johnson, Lyndon B., 318
Joint Council of Law Enforcement and Private Security Associations, 49
Judicial review, 290
Justice Statistics Clearinghouse, 39
Juvenile Justice Clearinghouse, 39
Juvenile services unit, 75

Kaczynski, Theodore, 39f.
Kaelin, Kato, 260
Kakiki, Curtis, 297
Kansas community policing programs, 242
Kansas City Police Department, 149–151

Kansas City Preventive Patrol Experiment, 23, 173
Kansas City Study, 148, 149–151, 149f., 150t.
Kefauver, Estes, 17
Kefauver Committee, 17
Kelling, George, 150
Kelly, Clarence, 149, 150
Kelly, Raymond N., 325
Kennedy, John F., 18, 19
Kennedy, Robert F., 19, 105
Kennedy-Powell, Kathleen, 260
King, Donald, 262, 275
King, John A., 9
King, Martin Luther, Jr., 18, 19, 21, 22
King, Rodney, 19, 25–27, 65, 288, 301, 302, 303, 304
King County (Washington) Police Department web site, 342
Kirby v. Illinois, 282–283
Kiro, John, 272
Klanwatch Project, 379
Klass, Polly, 345
Knapp Commission, 22–23, 290, 291, 292, 294, 297
Knowledge, skills, and abilities, 87
Kobans, 221
Kraft, Frank, 280
KSAs. *See* Knowledge, skills, and abilities
Ku Klux Klan, 43, 378

Laguna Beach (California) Police Department garbage-searching test case, 271
Lakewood (Colorado) Police Department volunteer programs, 219
Larson, Richard C., 150
LaSalata, Anthony, 378
LaSalata, April, 378
Lau, Fred, 325
Law and Order, 106
Law enforcement. *See also* Private security
  county, 35–36
  employment statistics, 46f.
  federal, 38–45
  industry in U.S., 32–34
  international, 45
  local, 34–37
  local control, 32
  metropolitan, 35
  nonpolicing jobs, 32
  rural and small town, 36–37
  spending statistics, 47f.
  state, 37–38
  task forces, 44–45
  U.S. employees, 33t.
Law Enforcement Assistance Administration, 23, 176
  study of women officers, 321

Law Enforcement Code of Ethics, 393
Law Enforcement Education Program, 98
Law Enforcement News, 391
  web site, 321
Law enforcement sites on the web, 34
Lawsuits against police
  effects of, 383–384
  reasons for, 382–383
Law vs. order, 290
LEAA. *See* Law Enforcement Assistance Administration
Lee, Rudolph, 284
LEEP. *See* Law Enforcement Education Program
LEN. *See Law Enforcement News*
Leon, Alberto, 274
Less-than-lethal weapons, 345–346
  aerosol subject restraints, 346
  beanbag guns, 346
  chemical irritant sprays, 346
  Chemical Mace, 346
  CN tear gas, 346
  pepper spray, 346
  safety and effectiveness of, 346–347
  stun devices, 346
  TASER guns, 346
Leuci, Robert, 292
Lictors, 2
Lieutenants, 64
Lifesaving efforts, 38, 44
Lincoln, Nebraska agility test, 95
Lincoln (Illinois) Police Department, 231
Lindsay, John, 23, 290, 306
Line functions, 74
Lineups, 282–283
List, John, 349
Little John, 4
Local control, 32
London Metropolitan Police, 3
Longbaugh, Harry. *See* Sundance Kid
Long Beach (California) Police Department
  cultural awareness course, 201
  racism and brutality incident, 302
Looker, Floyd Ray, 380
Los Angeles County Sheriff's Department, Association of White Male Peace Officers, 320
Los Angeles Police Department, 25, 26, 27, 151
  and armed robbery gun battle, 61, 66
  chief of police, 65
  community policing, 247
  court-ordered acceptance of women and minorities, 319
  Emergency Command Control Communications System, 336
  gang database, 338
  gay officers, 316

Los Angeles Police Department (cont'd)
  HITMAN database, 338
  O.J. Simpson case, 25, 26, 163f.
  reform following Rodney King incident, 304
  and sexual orientation, 101
  and Spanish language and culture, 202
Louima, Abner, 25, 300f., 301, 303
Louis IX, 2
Loyalty, 128

Maas, Peter, 291
MacConagy, Gene, 86
Mace, 346
Macon, Georgia resident officer program, 243
MADD. See Mothers Against Drunk Driving
Magistrates, 2, 4
Major Crime Organizational System, 340
Management training, 105
Managing Criminal Investigations, 176–178
Mapp, Dollree, 262, 275
Mapp v. Ohio, 17, 259, 262–263, 275, 290, 299
Maréchausée, 3
Marin County (California) Sheriff's Office selection procedures, 92
Marino, Louis, 160
Marshall, Thurgood, 300
Marshals
  colonial America, 7
  federal, 11–12, 18, 41
  frontier America, 11–12
Martin, Susan E., 324
Martinez, David, 177
Maryland State Police and affirmative action, 320
Maryland v. Buie, 268
Maryland v. Garrison, 273
Maryland v. Wilson, 265
Massachusetts v. Sheppard, 273
Mass media campaigns, 221–222
Master patrol officers, 63
Mayne, Richard, 6
McAlary, Mike, 292
McCummings, Bernard, 384
McDonald's, 183, 221
McFadden, Martin, 269
McGruff, 222
MCI. See Managing Criminal Investigations
McKinley, William, 43
McLaren, Richard L., 381
McLaren, Roy Clinton, 150–151, 155
McNamara, Joseph D., 150
McNeil v. Wisconsin, 281
McVeigh, Timothy J., 151, 379, 379f.

MDTs. See Mobile digital terminals
Meara, Paula, 324
Medical examination, 95
Medico, Nicole, 160
Mental health professionals, 215
Meredith, James, 18
Mesa (Arizona) Police Department selection procedures, 92
Methamphetamine, 36–37
Metro-Dade (Florida) Police Department, 51
Miami, Florida, 25
Miami Police Department
  corruption, 292
  STAR (Safeguarding Tourists Against Robberies), 182
Michigan Department of State Police sobriety checkpoints, 185
Michigan v. Mosley, 278
Mieth v. Dollard, 317
Military
  police, 43–44
  and policing functions, 2, 12
  quasi-military organizational model of police, 61
  U.S. Coast Guard, 44
Militia-at-Large for the Republic of Georgia, 380
Militia groups, 379–381, 380f., 381f.
Militias (colonial America), 7
Miller, Richard W., 293
Millerville University on-line police academy, 87
Milwaukee (Wisconsin) Police Department, 91
  automated fingerprint identification system, 344
  Jeffrey Dahmer case, 120
Mimms v. Pennsylvania, 265
Ministations, 221, 221f.
Minneapolis Domestic Violence Experiment, 376–377
Minnesota Multiphasic Personality Inventory, 93
Minnesota v. Dickerson, 269
Minnick v. Mississippi, 280–281
Minority communities, 200–204
  and police shootings, 370–371
Minority police officers
  academic studies of, 323
  court-ordered acceptance by LAPD, 319
  current numbers, 324t., 325–326
  discrimination against, 314–316
  forces for employment equality, 316–319
  ongoing problems, 328–329
  and white male backlash, 319–320
Minot (North Dakota) Police Department, 324
Miranda, Ernesto, 275, 278f.

Miranda Rule, 276–277, 282
  exceptions, 278–280
  in the 1990s, 280–282
  pre-Miranda restrictions, 274–276, 274f.
Miranda v. Arizona, 17, 259, 276–277, 290
Misconduct. See also Corruption; Ethics; Police brutality
  abuse of authority, 299–300
  alcohol abuse, 298–299
  cooping, 299
  deception, 299
  drug abuse and trafficking, 298
  perjury, 299
  verbal abuse, 302–303
Misdemeanor (defined), 267
Missouri police training requirements, 101
Mitchell, Alison, 160
MMPI. See Minnesota Multiphasic Personality Inventory
Mobile digital terminals, 335–337
Mollen Commission, 297
Molly Maguires, 13
Montana Freemen, 381
Moonlighting, 50–52
Moore, Glenn, 339
Moran v. Burbine, 279–280, 281
Morgan, J. P., 346–347
Mothers Against Drunk Driving, 184–185, 358
Motorcycles, 13
Mountaineer Militia, 380
Mug shot imaging, 348–349
Multiculturalism, 200–201
Murano, John, 347
Murphy, Patrick, 209, 295
Mutual pledge, 3

Nassau County (New York) Police Department
  burning building rescue, 83
  enhanced 911 system, 336
  and Firearms Training System (FATS), 340
National Advisory Commission on Civil Disorders, 22, 290, 315
National Advisory Commission on Criminal Justice Standards and Goals, 152, 176, 290, 316
National Center for Community Policing, 233
National Center for Rural Law Enforcement, 37
National Commission on Law Observance and Enforcement, 15, 98, 290
National Crime Information Center, 16, 40, 336, 337
  creation and description, 337–338

National Crime Prevention Council, 211
National Crime Victimization Survey, 39, 255, 255t., 303
National Criminal Justice Reference Service, 39
National Directory of Law Enforcement Administrators, Correctional Institutions and Related Agencies, 82, 390
National Employment Listing Service, 391
National Forensic Science Technology Center, 353
National Gallery of Art, 44
National Hot Rod Association, 211
National Institute of Justice, 33, 39, 49, 214, 245, 247
   recommendations on handling infected evidence, 370
National Law Enforcement Officers Memorial, 397–398
   Fund, 367
National Minority Advisory Council on Criminal Justice, 304
National Night Out, 220–221
National Organization of Black Law Enforcement Executives, 106
National Park Service, 43
National Police Chiefs and Sheriffs Information Bureau, 82
National police forces, 32, 38
National Rifle Association, 211
National Sheriffs' Association, 49, 106, 205
   web site, 34
National Treasury Employees Union v. Von Raab, 298
National Victims Resource Center, 39
Nation of Islam Security Agency, 218
Native Americans, 203
NCIC. *See* National Crime Information Center
NCJRS. *See National Criminal Justice Reference Service*
NCRLE. *See* National Center for Rural Law Enforcement
Neighborhood Watch, 52, 53, 53f., 217–218
NELS. *See* National Employment Listing Service
Ness, Deborah, 324
A Networking Guide to Recruitment, Selection, and Probationary Training of Police Officers in Major Police Departments of the United States of America, 391
Neufeld, Peter, 356
Neutron activation, 353
Newark (New Jersey) Police Department
   chief's corruption, 292–293

Newark Foot Patrol Experiment, 23
New Castle County, Delaware, 265
New Jersey regionalized police departments, 53–54
New Jersey State Police and court-ordered acceptance of women, 319
New Mexico Mounted Patrol, 12
New Orleans Police Department
   community policing, 248
   corruption, 292
Newport News (Virginia) Police Department
   problem-solving approach to prostitution and robbery, 238
   selection procedures, 92
New York City Police Department, 35, 160
   AIDS manual, 369–370
   Board of Police Commissioners, 13
   books based on corruption in, 291–292
   Bureau of Policewomen, 313
   CATCH mug shot file, 338
   Civilian Complaint Review Board, 306
   collapsing building incident, 347
   Community Patrol Officer Program, 237
   corruption, 22, 25
   court-ordered acceptance of women, 319
   deadly force policies, 123, 372–373
   and domestic violence among officers, 378
   early constables and night watch, 7
   education requirements, 98, 100
   Emergency Service Unit, 166, 177, 304
   first police department, 8
   fraternal organizations, 69
   Gay Officers Action League, 204
   goal of hiring more African-American officers, 325
   Homeless Outreach Program, 215
   job analysis, 86–87
   and Knapp Commission, 290, 291, 291, 294, 297
   Metropolitans vs. Municipals (19th century), 9
   New Immigrants Unit, 204
   911 system, 336
   officer murdered in Italy, 289
   Patrolman's Benevolent Association, 306
   and police suicide, 140
   psychological testing, 140–141
   public safety exception test case, 280
   resident officer program, 244–245
   Street Crime Unit (SCU), 183
   Tactical Patrol Force, 179
   Taxi-Truck Surveillance Unit, 183

   training, 102, 105
   undercover officer, 182f.
   zero-tolerance policies, 180
New York v. Belton, 272
New York v. Quarles, 279, 280
Niederhoffer, Arthur, 133
Night vision devices, 348
NIJ. *See* National Institute of Justice
911 calls and systems, 148, 151–153, 157
   and community policing, 236
   differential response, 174–175, 175t.
   enhanced (E-911), 335–336
   introduction of, 334
NOBLE. *See* National Organization of Black Law Enforcement Executives
Nonsworn (civilian) personnel, 61, 62, 65–66
Norfolk, Virginia, 222
North Carolina reserve officers, 67
Northern Virginia Criminal Justice Academy, 102
No-smoking policies, 100
NSA. *See* National Sheriffs' Association

Office of Community Oriented Policing Services, 245–246
   Making Officer Redeployment Effective (MORE) program, 246
   Regional Community Policing Institutes, 246
   Universal Hiring Program, 246
   web site, 246
Officer at Risk Examination, 140
Ogletree, Virgil, 262
Ohio regionalized police departments, 53–54
Oklahoma City bombing (1995), 11, 12, 23, 24f., 25, 151
Oklahoma Highway Patrol, 151
Oliver v. United States, 272
On-line police academy, 87
Operational styles, 117
   Broderick's, 117–118, 118f.
   enforcers, 117–118
   idealists, 118
   legalistic, 119
   optimists, 118
   realists, 118
   service, 119
   watchman, 118
   Wilson's, 118–119
Operational units, 74–75
Operation Identification, 220
Oral interview, 92
Orange County (Florida) Sheriff's Office mug shot imaging, 349
Organizations, 399–403
Organized crime unit, 75
Oswald, Lee Harvey, 19

Pacino, Al, 291
Padula v. Webster, 101
Pann, Doug, 131
Pannell, Derwin, 328
Parade magazine, 320
Parker, Robert Leroy. *See* Cassidy, Butch
Park rangers, 43
Patrol, 156f. *See also* Highway patrol
   academic studies, 155–159
   aggressive tactics, 178–181
   allocation software, 341
   alternative approaches, 172–175
   car, 159–161, 162
   directed, 172–174
   distribution of time, 158, 158t., 160
   field interrogations, 178, 179–180
   foot, 23, 159–162
   golf cart, 162
   Kansas City Preventive Patrol Experiment, 23, 173
   master patrol officers, 63
   officer activities, 154–155
   officers, 63
   random routine, 149–151, 149f.
   saturation, 181–182
   split force, 174
   traffic, 165
   unit, 75
Patrol Car Allocation Model software, 341
Patrol officers, 63
   distribution of time, 158, 158t., 160
PATROL/PLAN software, 341
PCAM. *See* Patrol Car Allocation Model software
PCR movement. *See* Police community relations movement
Pedophiles, 130
Peel, Robert, 3, 5–6, 5f., 114
Pendleton Act, 15, 60
Pennsylvania State Police
   exchange-of-fire incident, 114
   selection procedures, 92
Pennsylvania v. Muniz, 280
Pepper spray, 346
Perello, Martin, 61, 66
PERF.*See* Police Executive Research Forum
Perjury, 299
Perkins, Lloyd, 280
Peters, Stan, 326
Petrosino, Giuseppe, 289
Philadelphia Police Department
   brutality case, 301–302
   Cold Turkey operation, 181
   SWAT team, 165
Phineas Priesthood, 380
Phoenix (Arizona) Police Department
   school resource officers, 211
   Spanish language training, 202

Photo arrays (for identification), 282, 284
Photographic techniques
   age progression photographs, 349, 350
   composite sketches, 349–350
   mug shot imaging, 348–349
Physical agility test, 95
Physical requirements, 96–97
Pinellas Park (Florida) Police Department, 196, 198
Pinkerton, Allan, 13, 47
Pinkerton Agency, 13, 47, 188
Pistone, Joseph D., 186
Pittner, John, 380
Pitts, Earl Edwin, 293
Plain view (defined), 267
Police
   action while off duty, 121, 129
   and armed robbery incident in Los Angeles, 61
   authority to arrest, 263–266
   bank robbery incident, 131
   bizarre duties of, 76
   burning house incident, 196
   childbirth assistance, 38, 117f.
   civil and criminal liability, 381–384
   and conflict between individual's and society's rights, 115
   contemporary developments, 23–27
   corruption, 22–23, 25
   definition and derivation, 2
   early history, 2–3
   exchange of fire, 114
   and exclusionary rule, 259–263
   fraternal and professional organizations, 69
   Greece, 2
   and Hurricane Andrew, 139
   identification procedures, 282–284
   impact of economic recession, 53–54
   INTERPOL, 45
   job information, 82–83, 389–391
   lifesaving efforts, 38, 44
   and military, 2, 12
   national commissions overseeing, 290
   New Jersey, 53–54
   private, 13
   private employment of, 50–52
   regionalization of police departments, 53–54
   rescue of strangled child, 366
   research, 23, 69
   responding to house fires, 83, 248
   rock bands, 210
   Rome, 2
   and search and seizure, 266–274
   shooting incident, 383
   state, 12
   strikes, 69

   and Supreme Court, 258–259
   Tijuana River rescue, 86
   and Tim McVeigh capture, 151
   trading cards, 210–211, 222
   unconscious man incident, 198
   and U.S. Constitution, 256–263
   water rescue, 231
   wives, 22
Police and danger, 364. *See also* Domestic violence; Police shootings; Police stress; Police suicide
   accidental deaths, 367, 367t.
   AIDS, 369–370
   assault on officers, 368–369
   automobile pursuits, 374–375, 375t.
   exacerbation by drug culture, 364
   factors in danger, 364
   handling infected evidence, 370
   low police murder rate, 368
   officers killed, 364–368, 365f.
   possible connection between radar and cancer, 368
   radical and hate groups, 378–381
   statistics on police murders, 365–367, 365t.
Police athletic leagues, 212
Police auxiliaries, 68
Police brutality
   citizen oversight, 305–306
   and community policing, 233
   compared with other forms of abuse, 302
   defined, 300
   departmental responses to, 303–304
   reasons for attention to, 288
   recent examples, 300–302
   tradition of, 300
Police cars, 13–14, 14f.
Police Chief magazine, 391
Police chiefs, 64–65. *See also* International Association of Chiefs of Police; Police commissioners
   African-American, 325
   and community relations, 196
   women, 324
Police Code of Conduct, 393–395
Police commissioners, 64–65. *See also* Police chiefs
   and community relations, 196
Police-community partnerships, 52
Police community relations movement, 197–198, 231–232
Police Corps, 105–106, 246
Police culture, 128–129
Police department
   administrative units, 75–77
   area organization, 69–71
   assistant chief, 64
   auxiliaries, 68
   auxiliary services units, 77

beats, 69–71
bicycle patrol, 75f.
blue flu, 69
captain, 64
chain of command, 58, 59f.
chief of police (police commissioner), 64–65
and civil service system, 60–61
civilianization, 65–66
community relations unit, 75
community service officers, 66–67
community services unit, 75
corporal (master patrol officer), 63
crime prevention unit, 75
criminal investigations unit, 75
day tour, 73, 73f.
delegation of responsibility and authority, 59
detective (investigator), 63
discipline, 60
division of labor, 58, 59f.
duty chart, 71, 72t.
evening tour, 73
functional organization, 74–77, 74t., 78t.
inspector, 64
juvenile services unit, 75
lateral transfers, 68, 68t.
lieutenant, 64
line functions, 74
midnight tour, 73
nonsworn (civilian) personnel, 61, 62
operational units, 74–75
organized crime unit, 75
patrol unit, 75
personnel organization, 60–69
police officer, 63
posts, 69–71
precincts, 71
probationary period, 106
promotions, 64
quasi-military organizational model, 61
rank structure, 62–65, 63f., 64
reserve officers, 67–68
rules and regulations, 59–60
sectors, 70f., 71
sergeant, 63–64
span of control, 58–59
squad, 63–64
staff functions, 74
steady (fixed) tours, 73
and strikes, 69
sworn personnel, 61–62
three-tour system, 71–72, 72f.
time organization, 71–73
tour conditions, 73
traffic unit, 75
unions, 68–69
units, 74–77

unity of command, 59
vice unit, 75
zones, 71
Police dogs, 328
Police Executive Research Forum, 69, 106, 200
educational requirements study, 98
Police Explorer programs, 209, 210, 213
Police Foundation, 35, 106, 149, 197
deadly force standard, 373
study of women officers, 320–321
Police officers, 63. *See also* African-American police officers; Gay police officers; Minority police officers; Women police officers
Community Policing Officers (CPO), 235
desired characteristics, 88–90
distribution of time, 158, 158t., 160
performance of duties, 394
personal and professional development, 395
primary responsibilities, 394
probationary period, 106
Police Officer's Internet Directory, 34
Police operations (new approach), 172
aggressive patrol tactics, 179–181
alternative patrol approaches, 172–175
alternatives to retroactive investigation of past crimes, 175–178
civil liability and code enforcement teams, 184
decoy operations, 182–183, 182f.
differential response to calls for service, 174–175, 175t.
directed patrol, 172–174
drunk driver programs, 184–185
field interrogations, 178, 179–180
Managing Criminal Investigations (MCI), 176–178
proactive tactics, 178–185
Repeat Offender Programs, 178
saturation patrol, 181–182
split force patrol, 174
stakeout operations, 183
sting operations, 183–184, 187
undercover operations, 186–190
uniformed tactical operations, 178–182
Police operations (traditional approach), 148
academic studies of patrol, 155–159
car patrol, 159–161, 162
detectives, 163–165
distribution of time, 158, 158t., 160
evaluating effectiveness of police work, 148–149
foot patrol, 159–162
golf cart patrols, 162

Greene and Klockars study, 158, 159t.
Kansas City Study, 148, 149–151, 149f., 150t.
O. W. Wilson and Roy Clinton McLaren, 150–151, 155
patrol officer activities, 154–155
patrol operations, 154–162, 156f.
random routine patrol, 149–151, 149f.
rapid response to 911 calls, 148, 151–153, 157
retroactive investigation of past crimes by detectives, 153–154
special operations, 165–166, 167f.
traffic, 165
Police Patrol Scheduling System, 341
Police personality, 129–132
cynicism, 133
Dirty Harry Problem, 133–134, 134f., 135
Police role, 112, 116f., 117f.
ambiguity of, 114–116
breakdown of calls for service, 113t.
and conflict between individual's and society's rights, 115
crime fighting, 112
order maintenance, 112, 113–114, 113f.
Police shootings, 370
defense-of-life standard, 372–373
and discrimination, 370–371
fleeing felon doctrine, 371–373
Model Penal Code (American Law Institute), 373
numbers of, 370
Police Foundation standard, 373
regional variations in rate of, 370
Police storefront stations, 221, 221f.
Police stress, 135
causes, 136–137, 137t.
computer-aided stress early-warning systems, 340
departmental attempts to deal with, 139–140
effects of, 136t., 137–138, 138f.
effects on families, 138–139, 369
flight-or-fight response, 135
nature of, 135–136
stress defined, 135
testing for ability to handle, 140–141
Police suicide, 136, 140, 141–142
Police unions, 68–69
Policewoman's Endowment Society, 69
Policing
associations and organizations, 399–403
goals and objectives, 116–117
and politics, 9–10
Politia, 2
Polygraph examination, 93–94

Portland (Oregon) Police Department, 326
  and gays, 326
  killings by, 121
Posse comitatus, 11, 12
Posts, 69–71
Potter, Katie, 326
Potter, Tom, 326
Powell, Lewis F., Jr., 272
PPSS. *See* Police Patrol Scheduling System
Praefectus Urbi, 2
Praetorian Guard, 2
Precincts, 71
President's Commission on Campus Unrest, 22
President's Commission on Law Enforcement and Administration of Justice, 22, 68, 98, 103, 152, 290, 313, 315
Prince George's County (Maryland) Police Department
  computer-aided stress early-warning systems, 340
  Psychological Services Division, 140
Prince of the City, 292
Private life, 395
Private police, 13
Private security, 45–46. *See also* Pinkerton Agency; Wells, Fargo and Company
  categories, 46–47
  certified protection professional examination, 49
  and the Constitution, 48
  current problems, 48
  employment statistics, 46f.
  future need for, 49–50
  history of, 47
  information security, 48
  jobs for college students, 45, 51, 52
  licensing, 48
  personnel security, 48
  physical security, 47
  professionalization and training, 49
  shopping services, 187
  silent witness programs, 188
  spending statistics, 47f.
  store detectives, 188–189
  undercover operations, 186–189
Probable cause, 62, 264
  defined, 267
Probationary period, 106
Problem-solving policing, 237–239
  defined, 231
  merger with community policing, 239
  SARA technique, 239, 239f.
Professional organizations, 69
Prohibition, 13, 14–15
Prouse, William, 265

Pruneau, Michael R., 366
Psychological appraisal, 93
Public opinion and confidence, 198–199, 199t.
Pueblo County (Colorado) Sheriff's Office selection process, 87–88

Quasi-military organizational model, 61
Questors, 2

Radano, Gene, 299
Radar and possible cancer danger, 368
Radical and hate groups, 378–381
Radio, 13–14
Ramirez, Joe, 240
Ramsey, Jim, 11
Ramsey (JonBenet) case, 164f.
Random routine patrol, 149–151, 149f.
Rand Study of the Investigative Process, 153–154, 164, 176
Rangel, Pete, 248
Rank structure, 62–63, 63f., 64
  assistant chief, 64
  captain, 64
  chief of police (police commissioner), 64–65
  corporal (master patrol officer), 63
  deputy, 63
  detective (investigator), 63
  inspector, 64
  lieutenant, 64
  police officer, 63
  and promotions, 64
  sergeant, 63–64
  trooper, 63
Rapid response to 911 calls, 148, 151–153, 157
Reasonable force, 264–265
Reasonable suspicion, 264, 265
Recruitment process, 83–86, 84f.
Recruit training, 101–105, 103f., 105f.
Remote out-of-vehicle emergency radio, 336
Reno, John, 13
Reno, Nevada Homeless Evaluation Liaison Program, 216
Reno, Simeon, 13
Reno v. American Civil Liberties Union, 258
Repeat Offender Programs, 178
Republic of Texas, 381
Reserve officers, 67–68
Residency requirements, 100–101
Resident officer programs, 241, 242–245
  Columbia, South Carolina, 243–244
  Denver, Colorado, 245
  Elgin, Illinois, 241, 243, 244
  federal assistance, 245–247
  Macon, Georgia, 243
  New York City, 244–245

Rickaby, Jeffy, 348
Ride-along programs, 211–212, 222
Rights, inherent conflict between individual's and society's, 115
Riots, 6, 13, 20, 21–22, 179
  following Rodney King verdict, 19, 25–27, 27f., 151, 179
Rizzo, Frank, 301
Robin Hood, 4
Robinson, Desmond, 329
Robots, 211, 358
Rochin v. California, 261–262
Rock bands, 210
Rockford (Illinois) Police Department, 131
Rock Hill (South Carolina) Police Department, 383
Rodriquez, Matt, 208–209
Rokeach, Milton, 130
Rombach, Cyril, 274
Rome
  law enforcement officers, 2
  magistrates, 2
Roosevelt, Theodore, 13
ROPE. *See* Resident officer programs
ROPs. *See* Repeat Offender Programs
Routine traffic stops, 265–266
ROVER. *See* Remote out-of-vehicle emergency radio
Rowan, Charles, 6
Rowland, Daryl, 130
Roy, Mike, 36
Royal Canadian Mounted Police
  Major Crime Organizational System, 340
  national automated fingerprint identification system, 344
Ruby, Jack, 19
Ruby Ridge incident, 381
Rules and regulations, 59–60

SADD. *See* Students Against Drunk Driving
Sagamore Hills, Ohio community policing, 242
St. Martin Parish (Louisiana) Sheriff's Department Adopt a Senior program, 205
St. Petersburg (Florida) Police Department
  adoption of HOLMES software, 339
  use of portable computers, 340
Salava, Kathy, 198
Salem, Illinois reserve officers, 67–68
Sandberg, Annette, 324
San Diego Police Department, 100
  educational experience, 98
San Diego Sheriff's Office, Heaven's Gate incident, 315
Sandusky, Jerome, 384

San Francisco County Sheriff's Department and gay officers, 316
San Francisco Police Department
  court-ordered acceptance of women, 319
  and gay officers, 101, 203
San Jose (California) Police Department, 150
Santa Ana (California) Police Department, warrantless search incident, 267
Sante, Luc, 9
Saturation patrol, 181–182
Scanning electron microscope, 353
Scarring, Sal, 280
Scheck, Barry, 356
Schmerber v. California, 284
Schofield, Tracey, 198
Schomrin Society, 69
School resource officers, 211
Scott v. Hart, 376
Seales, Bobby, 19
Search and seizure
  abandoned property (including garbage), 270
  automobile exception, 272–273, 273f.
  border searches, 273
  consent searches, 269–270
  exceptions to warrant requirement, 267–273
  field interrogations, 268–269
  good faith exception, 273, 274
  and hot pursuit, 269
  incident to lawful arrest, 267–268
  inventory, 271
  open fields exception, 272
  in plain view, 270
  by private persons, 273
  related terms, 267
  search warrants, 266
  warrant requirement, 266
Search procedure, 103f.
Search warrants, 266
  defined, 267
  exceptions to warrant requirement, 267–273
Seattle Police Department, 51
Secret Service, 42–43
  Forensic Information System for Handwriting, 353
Sectors, 70f., 71
Securities and Exchange Commission, 44
Seeking Employment in Law Enforcement, Private Security, and Related Fields, 390–391
Selection process, 87–88
  advice on interviewing, 94
  age requirements, 97–98
  background investigation, 95–96
  and criminal record restrictions, 100
  desired officer characteristics, 88–90
  education requirements, 98–100
  Florida Highway Patrol, 90
  Fort Lauderdale, Florida, 89
  guidelines, 90–91
  height and weight requirements, 96–97
  Indiana State Police, 91
  medical examination, 95
  multiple testing, 90
  and no-smoking policies, 100
  oral interview, 92
  physical agility test, 95
  physical requirements, 96–97
  polygraph examination, 93–94
  and prior drug use, 100
  psychological appraisal, 93, 140–141
  Pueblo County (Colorado) Sheriff's Office, 87–88
  residency requirements, 100–101
  in selected police departments, 92
  sexual orientation, 101
  standards, 96–101
  vision requirements, 97
  written entrance examination, 91–92
Selma, North Carolina reserve officers, 68
Senior citizens' programs, 204–208
  and Alzheimer's disease, 207
  and American Association of Retired Persons, 205
  and elder abuse, 206
  and gerontology, 205
  TRIAD program, 205
SENTRY software, 340–341
Sergeants, 63–64
Sergott, Ed, 86
Serpico, 291–292
Serpico, Frank, 22, 291–292, 292f.
Sexual orientation, 101
Shearer, Robert, 121
Sheindlin, Gerald, 356
Shelton, Brad, 131
Sheppard, Jack, 4
Sheriffs
  colonial America, 6–7
  contemporary, 35–36
  deputies, 63
  England, 3, 36
  frontier America, 11, 36
SHERLOCK investigation software, 339–340
Shields, Henry, 276
Shire-reeves. *See* Sheriffs
Shopping services, 187
Showups, 282, 283
Shrinkage, 188
Silent witness programs, 188
Simpson, O.J., 25, 26, 352, 353t.
  exclusionary rule in Simpson case, 260
Sinthasomphone, Konerak, 120
Sketches, 349–350
Smith, Bruce, 16
Sobriety checkpoints, 185
Society of Competitor Intelligence Professions, 48
Software
  automated crime analysis, 338
  computer-aided investigation, 338–340
  patrol allocation, 341
  prisoner management, 340–341
Sours, Kathy, 139
South Carolina reserve officer requirements, 67
South Pasadena (California) Police Department, 249
Span of control, 58–59
Spartanburg County (South Carolina) Sheriff's Office selection procedures, 92
Specialized training, 105
Special operations
  emergency service units, 166, 166f., 167f.
  SWAT teams, 165–166
Special weapons and tactics teams. *See* SWAT teams
Spinelli v. United States, 266
Springfield (Massachusetts) Police Department, 324
Squad, 63–64
Staff functions, 74
Staggs, Jim, 12
Stakeout operations, 183
State police, 12, 37–38. *See* also Highway patrol
  centralized model, 38
  decentralized model, 38
  Indiana, 91
  Maryland, 320
  Michigan, 185
  New Jersey, 53–54
  Pennsylvania, 92, 114
  trooper, 63
Statute of Winchester, 3
Steinmann, Rick, 32
Stevens, John Paul, 258
Steward, Raymond, 276
Sting operations, 183–184, 187
Stonecipher, Eric, 9
Stop and frisk, 267, 268–269
Store detectives, 52, 188–189
Stoval v. Denno, 283
Strategic policing, 231
Stress. *See* Police stress
Strikes, 69
Student Non-Violent Coordinating Committee, 18

Student ride-alongs, 211–212
Students
  jobs in investigating, 50
  jobs in private security, 45, 51, 52
Students Against Drunk Driving, 184–185
Stun devices, 346
Suffolk County, New York, 84, 90
Suicide by cop, 136, 137f. *See also* Police suicide
Sullivan, Jerome R., 293
Sundance Kid, 13
Suppression of evidence, 267
Supreme Court. *See* U.S. Supreme Court
Surveillance technology, 347–348
  night vision devices, 348
  vans, 348
SWAT teams, 53, 165–166
Sworn personnel, 61–62

"Take a Bite Out of Crime" program, 221–222
Tampa Bay, Florida
  police program for seniors, 205
Target hardening, 53
TASER guns, 346
Task forces, 44–45
Taylor Law, 69
Tear gas, 346
Technology, 334
  advanced photographic techniques, 348–350
  and civil libertarians, 358–359
  computers, 334–342
  DNA profiling, 354–358
  fingerprinting innovations, 342–345
  less-than-lethal weapons, 345–347
  modern forensic techniques, 350–354
  robots, 358
  surveillance, 347–348
  videotaping, 358
Tempe (Arizona) Police Department information kiosks, 342
Tennessee v. Garner, 372
Terry, Joe, 32
Terry v. Ohio, 268, 269, 275
Texas Rangers, 12
Thermal imaging surveillance devices, 348
Thief-takers, 4, 5
Tijuana River rescue, 86
Tippett, J. D., 19
Todd v. Navarro, 101
Toledo, Ohio community policing, 249
Tonuzi, Hanna, 160
Tours
  day, 73, 73f.
  duty chart, 71, 72t.
  evening, 73
  midnight, 73
  steady (fixed), 73
  three-tour system, 71–72
Trading cards, 210–211, 222
Traffic patrol, 165
Traffic stops, 265–266
Traffic unit, 75
Training process, 101
  community policing training, 106
  field training, 104
  firearms training, 104–105
  in-service training, 105
  management training, 105
  Police Corps, 105–106
  and probationary period, 106
  recruit training, 101–105, 103f., 105f.
  sample programs, 106
  selected departments, 102
  specialized training, 105
  variations in requirements, 101–104
TRIAD program, 205
Troopers, 63
Trutt, John, Jr., 83
Tulsa (Oklahoma) Police Department, 67
Turpin, Dick, 4

UCR. *See* Uniform Crime Reports
Ultraviolet technology, 353–354
Undercover operations, 186
  drug investigations, 188, 189–190
  and entrapment, 190–191
  federal, 186
  by police, 186
  by private security, 186–189
  shopping services, 187
  silent witness programs, 188
  store detectives, 188–189
Uniform Crime Reports, 40–41, 254–255, 255t.
Uniformed tactical operations, 178–179
  aggressive patrol tactics, 179–181
  saturation patrol, 181–182
Uniforms, 8
Union/Essex Counties (New Jersey) Auto Task Force, 336–337
Unions, 68–69
United States
  colonial law enforcement, 6–7
  eighteenth- and nineteenth-century police, 7–13, 114
  first police departments, 8, 9
  frontier policing, 11–13
  law enforcement industry, 32–34, 33t.
  politics in policing, 9–10
  twentieth-century policing, 13–27
U.S. Bureau of Land Management, 203
U.S. Coast Guard, 44
U.S. Commission on Civil Rights, 139, 304, 305
U.S. Constitution, 256, 289. *See also* U.S. Supreme Court
  amendments governing criminal justice system, 257f.
  Bill of Rights, 256–258
  Fourteenth Amendment, 257–258, 259, 316
  and private security, 48
U.S. Department of Agriculture, 44
U.S. Department of Defense, 43–44
U.S. Department of Health and Human Services, 44
U.S. Department of Justice, 39–41, 245
  Office of Community Oriented Policing Services, 106
  web site, 34
U.S. Department of Labor, 44
U.S. Department of State
  Bureau of Diplomatic Security, 44
U.S. Department of the Interior, 43
U.S. Department of Transportation, 44
U.S. Marshals, 11–12, 18, 41
United States Militia at Large, 380
U.S. Park Police, 320
U.S. Postal Service, 44
U.S. Supreme Court, 17, 44. *See also* U.S. Constitution
  exclusionary rule, 259–263
  on First Amendment and Internet, 258
  Miranda ruling, 276–280
  reasons for knowing cases, 275
  related web sites, 259
  role in regulating police, 258–259
  and search warrants, 266
U.S. Treasury Department, 41–43
United States v. Ash, 284
United States v. Dionisio, 284
United States v. Leon, 273, 274
United States v. Mara, 284
United States v. Martinez-Fuerte, 273
United States v. Matlock, 269
United States v. Ross, 272
United States v. Wade, 282, 283
Units, 74–77
Unity of command, 59
Urban riots, 21

Vanguard Justice Society v. Hughes, 318
VCMOP. *See* Violent Crimes and Major Offenders Program
Verbal abuse (by police), 302–303
VICAP. *See* Violent Criminal Apprehension Program
Vice unit, 75
Victim assistance programs, 216
Videotaping, 358
Vietnam War, 19
Vigilantism, 7, 11
Vigiles, 2
Violanti, John M., 142

Violent Crimes and Major Offenders Program, 40
Violent Criminal Apprehension Program, 338
Viper Militia, 380
Virginia Beach, Virginia Crime Stoppers, 218
Vision requirements, 97
Vollmer, August, 13, 15, 101

Wackenhut Security Corporation, 47, 187–188
Wakefield (Massachusetts) Police Department web site, 342
Walinsky, Adam, 105
Walker, Samuel, 10
Walton County (Georgia) Sheriff's Office, 263, 358
Wambaugh, Joseph, 299, 355–356
Ward, Benjamin, 325
Warkinson, Ralph E., 284
Washington, D.C., Hispanic Police Association, 203
Washington, D.C., Police Department Operation Clean Sweep, 181
Washington State Patrol, 324
Washoe County (Nevada) Sheriff's Office use of automated fingerprint identification system, 344
Watch and ward, 3
Watson, Elizabeth, 324
Wearing, Melvin H., 325
Weaver, Randall C., 381
Webster, William H., 27
Wechsler Adult Intelligence ScaleDRevised, 93
Weeks, Fremont, 261
Weeks v. United States, 258, 259–261
Wells, Fargo and Company, 13, 47
Wells, Henry, 13, 47
West, Will, 343
Whalen, Kevin, 347
White, Byron, 271, 273
Whitmire, Kathy, 324
Wichita, Kansas, 15
  community policing, 247
Wickersham Commission. *See* National Commission on Law Observance and Enforcement
Wickersham Commission Report, 13, 15
William J. Burns International Detective Agency, 47
Williams, "Clubber," 300
Williams, Kathy, 139
Williams, Treat, 292
Williams, Wayne, 352
Williams, Willie, 65, 325
Wilson, James Q., 17
Wilson, O. W., 13, 15–16, 150–151, 155
Wilson's operational styles, 118–119
Winnebago County (Illinois) Sheriff's Office, 131
Winston v. Lee, 284
WISCDR. *See* Wechsler Adult Intelligence ScaleDRevised
Wisconsin, University of, 20
Witness Protection Program. *See* Federal Witness Security Program
Wolf v. Colorado, 261
Women and police community relations, 203
Women police officers, 323f.
  academic studies of, 320–323
  court-ordered acceptance by police departments, 319
  current numbers, 323–325, 324t.
  Dirty Harriet Syndrome, 321
  discrimination against, 312–313
  forces for employment equality, 316–319
  International Association of Women Police, 324
  New York City Police Department, 313
  ongoing problems, 326–328
  partners' assessments, 322
  and white male backlash, 319–320
  woman named officer of the year, 320
  women chiefs, 324
Wood, Fernando, 9
World Trade Center, 23, 25
World Wide Web. *See* Internet
Wright, Leslie, 372
Written entrance examination, 91–92

Zinermon v. Burch, 214
Zones, 71

Photo Credits

Chapter 1 p. 5, The Image Works; p. 6, Corbis-Bettmann; p. 14, Courtesy of Jack Dempsey; p. 21, Barton Silverman/*The New York Times*; p. 24, Charles Porter IV/Sygma; p. 27, Paul Sakuma/AP/Wide World Photos.

Chapter 2 p. 39, Reuters/Rick Wilking/Archive; p. 42, Courtesy of Jack Dempsey; p. 47, Kent Reno/Jeroboam; p. 53, Michael Weisbrot/Stock Boston.

Chapter 3 p. 63, Courtesy of Jack Dempsey; p. 73, Rudi Von Briel/Photo Edit; p. 75, Robert Brenner/Photo Edit.

Chapter 4 p. 84, p. 103, p. 105, Courtesy of Jack Dempsey.

Chapter 5 p. 113, AP/Wide World; p. 116, Marilyn Yee/*The New York Times*; p. 117, Steve Berman/*The New York Times*.

Chapter 6 p. 134, Photofest; p. 137, Copyright *New York Post*; p. 138, Jim Mahoney/The Image Works.

Chapter 7 p. 156 (top left), Johnny Crawford/The Image Works; (top middle), Larry Mulvehill/The Image Works; (top right), Spencer Grant/Photo Edit; (bottom), Tony Freeman/Photo Edit; pp. 163, 164, AP/Wide World; pp. 166, 167; Courtesy of Jack Dempsey.

Chapter 8 p. 179, Bill Gentile/Sipa Press; p. 182, UPI/Corbis-Bettmann; p. 185, Nancy Pierce/*The New York Times*.

Chapter 9 p. 197, Stephen Agricola/Stock Boston; p. 204, Mike Parker; p. 208, Brooks Kraft/Sygma; p. 209, Courtesy of Jack Dempsey; p. 221, Adele Woodyard.

Chapter 10 p. 232, UPI/Corbis-Bettmann; p. 237, Leslie O'Shaughnessy; p. 243, Courtesy of Lt. Paul McCurtain, City of Elgin (Illinois) Police Department, p. 245, Reuters/Mike Thieler/Archive Photos.

Chapter 11 p. 271, Courtesy of Jack Dempsey; p. 273, Daemmrich/Stock Boston; p. 278, UPI/Corbis-Bettmann.

Chapter 12 p. 292, UPI/Corbis-Bettmann; p. 300, Tony Savino/Sipa Press.

Chapter 13 p. 314, Michael Newman/Photo Edit; p. 323, Daemmrich/The Image Works; p. 326, Hal Rubin.

Chapter 14 p. 341, AP/Wide World; p. 344, Courtesy of Jack Dempsey; p. 350, N.R.Rowan/Stock Boston; p. 354, Richard Nowitz/Photo Researchers; p. 355, Larry Mulvehill/Photo Researchers.

Chapter 15 p. 365, AP/Wide World; p. 377, Ted Soqui/Sygma; p. 379, Gary Caskey/Sipa Press; p. 380, Nell Redmond/AP/Wide World; p. 381, Ron Heflin/AP/Wide World.